Not Just a Passing Phase

Social Work Knowledge
Frederic G. Reamer, Series Editor

Social work has a unique history, purpose, perspective, and method. The primary purpose of this series is to articulate these distinct qualities and to define and explore the ideas, concepts, and skills that together constitute social work's intellectual foundations and boundaries and its emerging issues and concerns.

To accomplish this goal, the series will publish a cohesive collection of books that address both the core knowledge of the profession and its newly emerging topics. The core is defined by the evolving consensus, as primarily reflected in the Council on Social Work Education's Curriculum Policy Statement, concerning what courses accredited social work education programs must include in their curricula. The series will be characterized by an emphasis on the widely embraced ecological perspective; attention to issues concerning direct and indirect practice; and emphasis on cultural diversity and multiculturalism, social justice, oppression, populations at risk, and social work values and ethics. The series will have a dual focus on practice traditions and emerging issues and concepts.

David G. Gil, *Confronting Injustice and Opression: Concepts and Strategies for Social Workers*

Frederic G. Reamer, *Social Work Research and Evaluation Skills*

Not Just a Passing Phase

Social Work with Gay, Lesbian, and Bisexual People

GEORGE ALAN APPLEBY
Southern Connecticut State University

AND

JEANE W. ANASTAS
Smith College

COLUMBIA UNIVERSITY PRESS
New York

Columbia University Press
Publishers Since 1893
New York   Chichester, West Sussex
Copyright © 1998 by George Alan Appleby and Jeane W. Anastas

Library of Congress Cataloging-in-Publication Data
Appleby, George A.
   Not just a passing phase : social work with gay, lesbian, and
   bisexual people / George Alan Appleby and Jeane W. Anastas.
      p.   cm.
   Includes bibliographical references and index.
   ISBN 0–231–10322–0 (cloth : alk. paper).—ISBN 0–231–10323–9
   (pbk. : alk. paper)
   1. Social work with gays—United States. 2. Social work with
   lesbians—United States. 3. Social work with lesbians—United
   States.   I. Anastas, Jeane W.   II. Title.
   HV1449.A66   1998
   362.8—dc21
                                                         97–37962

Casebound editions of Columbia University Press books are printed on
permanent and durable acid-free paper.
Printed in the United States of America
c 10 9 8 7 6 5 4 3 2 1
p 10 9 8 7 6 5 4 3 2 1

Contents

Preface

> The only freedom which deserves the name is that of pursuing our own good
> in our own way, so long as we do not attempt to deprive others of theirs,
> or impede their efforts to obtain it.
> —John Stuart Mill

The social work profession, like the larger society, is in conflict over nondiscrimination issues as they affect lesbian, gay, and bisexual people (Parr & Jones 1996; Van Soest 1996). Some of the controversy stems from a lack of knowledge about sexual orientation. Some of it, as in other areas like reproductive rights, reflects differences of opinion among professionals. These controversies are coming to the forefront in the social work profession because of the social changes resulting from the gay liberation movement and the increasing visibility of gay, lesbian, and bisexual people in the United States. In the mid-1990s, the major professional associations in social work—the National Association of Social Workers (NASW) and the Council of Social Work Education (CSWE)—significantly strengthened their policies related to gay, lesbian, and bisexual people. For these reasons, students and professional social workers in all practice settings are being called upon to know more about and develop better skills for working with gay, lesbian, and bisexual people, their families, and their communities.

While every form of prejudice and discrimination is different (Young-Breuhl 1996), oppression is now understood to influence all aspects of gay, lesbian, and bisexual life. However, efforts on behalf of human rights for all lesbian, gay, and bisexual people are often misunderstood. What gay, lesbian, and bisexual people seek is not new or special rights but, rather, the extension of existing rights guaranteed to all American citizens by the Constitution and identified by the Declaration of Independence as the purpose, not the gift, of government. Ending discrimination does no more than dismantle the social and legal props by which one group of citizens unfairly enjoys a superior status over another group of citizens. Lesbians and gay men are fighting for the right to secure the conditions under which they may lead ordinary, civilized lives (Nava & Dawidoff 1994).

> The majority culture's attachment to its stereotypes of gay men and women constitutes the single greatest impediment to gay and lesbian civil rights. The anti-gay lobby exploits these stereotypes and plays on the fear and distaste they call forth to justify the prejudices that support punitive laws and discriminatory practices against gay Americans. They could not use the stereotypes if they were not already in people's minds and in the culture's folkways. . . . [Gay men and lesbians] recognize how stereotypes, misconceptions, and libels stand in the way of the recognition and protection of these equal rights. . . . The challenge of democracy is that in order to claim one's rights, it may be necessary to fight for them.   (Nava & Dawidoff 1994:29–31)

This text is designed to prepare social workers and other health and human services professionals to better assess the concerns, problems, and issues presented by gay, lesbian, and bisexual clients and their families. It offers both a *value base* and a *knowledge base* for social work practice. While gay, lesbian, and bisexual people may have the same needs for assistance as their nongay counterparts, their sexual orientation may have an impact on the perception of the problem, how the problem is sustained in the social environment, and the resources available to help resolve the problem. The book is therefore designed to aid in intervention at a variety of levels—the individual, the interpersonal, the organizational, and the social and institutional.

We began working together as coauthors addressing gay and lesbian issues some years ago. When Armando Morales and Brad Sheafor decided to add a chapter on gays and lesbians to the "Special Populations" section of their foundational text on social work practice, *Social Work: A Profession of Many Faces* (see Appleby & Anastas 1992), they approached one of us (Appleby), who in turn enlisted the other (Anastas) for the project. Our greatest struggle with that chapter (revised in 1997 for the eighth edition: Appleby & Anastas 1997) was to condense the large and ever-growing body of knowledge about the diversity of gay, lesbian, and bisexual people usefully—that is, in a way that can inform social work practice. There is simply too much relevant information available for just one chapter to contain.

On the basis of the chapter we had written, we then did some workshops together at professional conferences. One of these was attended by an editor (then with Columbia University Press) who suggested we do a book. The new curriculum policy statement implemented by the Council on Social Work Education (CSWE) in 1992 required that social work programs include content on gay and lesbian people. As professional social work educators, we were acutely aware of the limited (though growing) body of literature available to meet the educational need, especially material developed specifically from a social work perspective. By the time we were ready to begin work on a book, John Michel was the editor at Columbia University Press who helped us secure a contract with Columbia for this project; since then, he has encouraged and supported us in the work patiently, skillfully, and unfailingly, for which we thank him most sincerely.

As we have worked on this book over the last three years, despite much new literature that has appeared, we have become even more convinced of the need for a book like this one. We have tried to be as comprehensive and coherent in our summary of what is and is not known about social work practice with lesbian, gay, and bisexual people as possible. In selecting the content to include, we have used social work authors and sources wherever possible, but we have drawn on sound social science research from related disciplines when needed as well. We have included only a limited amount of popular literature in order to remain true to what is a significant although still limited research base. Since social and cultural context is so important in shaping lesbian, gay, and bisexual lives, the focus has been limited to gay, lesbian, and bisexual people in the United States, the context in which we live and work. As when we wrote the chapter referred to earlier, in writing this book we have found the social work perspective on knowledge and on practice to be well suited to the development of a comprehensive and compassionate understanding of gay, lesbian, and bisexual people and their struggles to survive and thrive in an often hostile social environment. It is this kind of understanding that helping professionals need in order to work effectively with gay, lesbian, and bisexual people and their families.

Organization of the Book

This book is organized into three major sections. Part 1 provides an overview of what being gay, lesbian, or bisexual is. Sexual orientation illustrates well the usefulness of social work's *biopsychosocial* perspective on human behavior. Chapter 1 defines and describes *heterosexism* and *homophobia* and the concept of *heterosexual privilege*. Just as race in America cannot be understood without understanding racism, and gender cannot be understood without understanding sexism, so sexual orientation cannot be understood without knowing about the pervasive negative attitudes about it that form the context for gay, lesbian, and bisexual lives. *Oppression* and *power* are key concepts, and *stigma* and *stigma management* are also covered. The chapter also locates the perspective of the book as a whole in the *ecological model* that informs so much of social work thinking and practice today. This model is well suited to sexual orientation issues because it encompasses and directs intervention to a variety of levels—the individual, the interpersonal (couple, family, and group), the institutional and organizational, and/or the social structural, including policy issues.

The second chapter provides an overview of contemporary scholarship on sexual orientation itself—its definition, its origins, and the variations in its expression. It compares genetic and social explanations of sexual orientation. How sexual orientation is defined and measured has everything to do with how many people are thought to be lesbian, gay, or bisexual, which is explained as well. The chapter also describes the process by which a person comes to identify him/herself as lesbian, gay, or bisexual—the process often termed *coming out*. It also discusses the various identity management strategies that gay, lesbian, and bisexual people use in living in a heterosexist and homophobic society.

Chapter 3 discusses the gay and lesbian *community* that has been developed in some parts of the United States as one adaptation that gay, lesbian, and bisexual people make to the oppression they face. Limited attention is directed to the adaptation of rural and ethnically isolated populations because of the meager literature. Specific attention is given *culture*, as well as to *race* and *social class*, as these influence individual adaptation, and how various levels of *acculturation* and identity conflict impact on involvement in the broader lesbian and gay community. Introduced are several important concepts: *biculturalism*; *multi-* or *polycultural identity*; and *psychological* and *social identity development*. It also includes attention to the specialized social service organizations that have developed to address the unmet needs of lesbian, gay, and bisexual people.

Part 2 covers a variety of life transitions as conceptualized by the ecological model of social work practice. These may be a source of specific stressors in lesbian, gay, and bisexual lives and are organized around *individual and family life cycle* stages. Some, such as childhood and adolescence or midlife and old age, are determined by chronology; others, such as entering into *sexual and romantic relationships* or *parenting* or the *world of work*, are not. What these transitions do have in common, however, is that they often require new adaptations at the individual, interpersonal, and social levels. They may also be points at which formal health, mental health, and social service organizations are encountered for reasons related or unrelated to a person's sexual orientation. Whatever the reason that services are sought or used, sexual orientation and the oppression that may limit the available options for gay, lesbian, and bisexual people and their families must be taken into account. Each chapter in this section ends with a summary of the implications of its content for social work practice at the level of the *individual*, the *interpersonal*, the *organizational* and *institutional*, and for *social policy* and *social change*.

Chapter 4, by guest author Gerald Mallon, covers lesbian, gay, and bisexual children and adolescents. As the age at which young people become sexually active in any form has gone down, the challenges of dealing with a lesbian, gay, or bisexual *identity* have become explicit for people at younger ages as well. Because of the unique needs of adolescents for peer and social approval, for example, *stress* can result. In addition, while members of other oppressed groups usually share their *stigmatized identity* with their parents who can help them learn how to cope and adapt, gay, lesbian, and bisexual teens usually do not; in fact, they may be rejected by their families. This chapter reviews what is known about children and adolescents who are gay, lesbian, or bisexual and suggests ways in which social work should be responding.

Entering into a sexual or intimate relationship is a normal life transition that presents special challenges to lesbian, gay, and bisexual people. Information about same-gender sexual behavior is presented in chapter 5 in the context of the sharply contrasting ideas that shape views of sexuality in general and same-gender sex in particular. In addition, the process of *dating* and/or *becoming a couple* may in fact expose the gay, lesbian, or bisexual person to stress and risk, both in public and in private. However, despite powerful *myths* that suggest that lesbian and gay relationships are not successful, many gay, lesbian, and bisexual people in fact do manage to form and sustain satisfying, long-term intimate relationships, which must be seen as a developmental achievement whatever the specific nature of the relationship. The current controversy about *same-sex marriage* is also covered.

Even without the legal benefits of marriage, *parenting* is an increasingly viable option or fact of lesbian and gay life. Many more gay and lesbian people are or want to become parents than is commonly believed. In recent years, more gay and lesbian people are choosing to become parents through donor insemination, surrogacy arrangements, or adoption. The very existence of these families throws into question just how the idea of "family" should be defined. Chapter 6 reviews the various ways in which gay and lesbian people become parents (including attention to the role of the *co-parent*) and how each of the ways in which they become parents places them in a very different relationship to the state as represented by the legal and child welfare systems. Research on children reared by an openly gay or lesbian parent is reviewed, showing that the outcomes for them are at least equal to that for comparable children reared by heterosexuals. Finally, given the complicated ecology of families with children and the heterosexism and homophobia that these particular families face, issues of *boundary maintenance* within and around the family are also covered.

Because *work* and economic self-sufficiency are major concerns of adulthood, chapter 7 covers *workplace issues* and challenges. Most gay, lesbian, and bisexual people work for a living, but unfortunately homophobia and heterosexism can be major influences in the workplace. The effects can range from harassment at work to overt discrimination in hiring and/or promotion to social marginalization on the job. Ways to address and combat heterosexism and homophobia in the workplace are presented. The chapter concludes with a special section on the situation of lesbian, gay, and bisexual people within the social work profession itself; because of prejudices encountered on the job, *identity management* remains a major issue for gay, lesbian, and bisexual professionals within our own field.

Chapter 8, by guest authors Nancy Humphreys and Jean Quam, covers midlife and old age. The life situations of older people reflect the cumulative effects of the adaptive successes and challenges that they have faced throughout the life course up to that point. Despite powerful myths to the contrary, evidence from studies of senior gays and lesbians suggests that, in some ways, they may be better prepared than average for the challenges of old age. Nevertheless, their ability to cope is still hampered by various structural obstacles that they face due to their sexual orientation, and the practice implications of these issues are emphasized.

Finally, part 3 addresses certain special issues and challenges to adaptation that gay and lesbian people commonly face, such as mental health and substance abuse, covered in chapter 9. Because of their specific history of oppression in psychiatry (which is briefly reviewed), gay, lesbian, or bisexual people who may need mental health services, even for reasons totally unrelated to their sexual orientation, often encounter barriers to receiving effective and affirming help. In fact, the mental health and substance abuse fields are moving from a view of a gay, lesbian, or bisexual orientation as dysfunction to one of difference. The limited material available on the incidence and prevalence of mental health and substance abuse problems among lesbians and gays is reviewed. While bias in mental health treatment is, sad to say, still much too common, principles to guide the *affirmative treatment* of lesbian, gay, and bisexual people with mental health and substance abuse problems are presented.

Unfortunately, violence and the threat of violence are major stressors in lesbian, gay, and bisexual lives. Chapter 10 defines violence broadly, relating it to the full spectrum of oppression based on sexual orientation. Lesbians and gay men are frequently the targets for humiliating and sometimes dangerous verbal and physical assaults (*gay-bashing*). Initially, such violent crimes were considered to be merely pathological by criminal justice and mental health professionals; however, the consensus now is that such acts are bias or hate crimes that reflect the socially condoned or sanctioned attitudes of a violent culture that opposes gender-norm violations or other behaviors viewed as unacceptable in a heterosexist society. Gay- and lesbian-bashing is analyzed from two different perspectives—*cultural heterosexism* and *psychological heterosexism*—with the intention of helping the social worker to consider both micro and macro interventions. In addition, the newly recognized problem of lesbian and gay *domestic violence* within some relationships is a community secret that needs airing and social work attention.

While some content on AIDS and the HIV epidemic is integrated into several chapters, the pandemic has had and continues to have such a major effect on the gay and lesbian communities that a separate chapter (chapter 11) was needed. The psychological, political, economic, and social impact of HIV disease has been widespread but is most noticeable in those places (mainly urban areas) where gay and lesbian community organization is at its most mature. The trauma of this death-saturated culture has caused such damage in the social fabric of gay men's lives that, as Rofes (1996) states, it amounts to "a civil war of the psyche" (230).

The book concludes with a final chapter that ties together all the previously presented *theory for practice* with the practice concepts introduced in chapter 1. In addition, it summarizes these various issues and practice implications in terms of the several domains of social work concern as defined by the Council on Social Work Education: *social work practice, human behavior and the social environment, social welfare policy and services, field education*, and *research*. This summary will be useful both for social work educators in course and curriculum planning and for students and graduates in evaluating the education they have received in relation to knowledge about and practice with gay, lesbian, and bisexual people. It thus serves not just as a summary but as a blueprint for action in knowledge development and knowledge dissemination for the field. The boxed quotes found throughout the text were chosen because they captured the theme of the chapter. Each observation is from a nationally and often an internationally known social work scholar, activist, or leader, all of whom are lesbian or gay.

Finally, we have included two appendix sections with additional resources.

Appendix 1 lists printed, e-mail, and Web site resources for further information on various lesbian, gay, and bisexual issues. Appendix 2 includes a variety
of experiential exercises for classroom and workshop use. The exercises are
focused on developing greater self-awareness in dealing with gay, lesbian, and
bisexual people and issues.

Limits of Content

A note on the inclusion of *bisexuality* in this book: in keeping with current
trends in the field, we have attempted to take into consideration the concerns
of bisexual people. This topic has not been without controversy. For example,
are bisexual people really oppressed in the same way gay and lesbian people
are? Is there really such an "identity" as bisexual (see chapter 2)? However,
because the labels *gay* and *lesbian* are themselves being questioned, we decided to include bisexuality. Also, it is our belief that, to the extent that a bisexual person is identified as or participates in same-gender relationships and
activities like a gay or lesbian person does, discrimination and oppression may
follow. Moreover, bisexual people may not find the same access to support
from organized gay and lesbian communities as gay- and lesbian-identified
people do. However, current knowledge about a bisexual orientation is even
more limited than that on gay and lesbian people, which has hindered the content on bisexuality throughout this volume. Nevertheless, through the use of
notes we try to clarify these difficulties in discussing bisexuality as we encountered them.

   On the other hand, we have not attempted to encompass the concerns of
transgendered people. This decision was made mainly due to lack of available
research. Our focus, then, is on those people who define their sexual orientation as involving significant sexual and intimate same-gender relationships.
However, we do recognize that there may well be some political and scholarly purpose in linking gay, lesbian, and transgender issues. We also acknowledge our profession's need to know more about transgendered people, even
though we have not been able to meet that need in this work.

Last, but not least, some well-deserved acknowledgments: I (Appleby) want to
thank my students who have patiently listened and critiqued my ideas for their
relevance to social work practice. My colleagues on the NASW National Committee on Lesbian, Gay, and Bisexual Issues have helped me to refine the logic
of my points. My colleagues at Southern Connecticut State University, Julia
Hamilton and Edgar Colon, without even knowing it, were major sources of
support and feedback as we tackled another project, a text on practice with

culturally diverse and oppressed minorities. There have been many lesbian and gay scholars who touched my life and have been a tremendous motivation for this project; some of these are Gary Lloyd, Manuel Fimbres, Hilda Hildago, Ron Federico, Travis Peterson, and Bernice Goodman. Most of all, I thank my partner, Paul Kuehn, for his concern, support, patience, and his ability to keep me focused while I became computer literate.

I (Anastas) also have a number of people I especially want to thank for their contribution to this work. Smith School for Social Work colleagues James Drisko and Joyce Everett read and made useful comments on portions of the work in draft. A dear friend, Mary Quigley, also read draft chapters and commented most helpfully on them. Workshop participants have also provided very valuable feedback on ideas that inform the book. Karen A. Bell and Starr Wood, along with the reference librarians at Nielson Library, Smith College, provided invaluable help in locating and documenting literature for us. Several anonymous readers selected by Columbia University Press have been critical in the very best sense of the word, offering praise and encouragement as well as pointed and useful suggestions for improvement. I have also learned a great deal from my graduate students over the years, especially those whose own research addresses gay and/or lesbian issues. Based on their studies (and others), I know that the future of knowledge and practice in social work related to gay, lesbian, and bisexual people will be brighter than in the past. Most of all, I thank my life partner, Jan Gibeau, for her comments and suggestions; I am grateful for the love, support, and forbearance she has shown during my labors on this project.

Not Just a Passing Phase

Part 1

Context, Definitions, and Community
An Overview

Homophobia and Heterosexism

Understanding the Context of Gay, Lesbian,

and Bisexual Lives

Issues and problems in living affecting gay, lesbian, and bisexual people often arise from the homophobia and heterosexism that form the context of their lives. An ecological approach to social work is presented to frame the knowledge, values, and skills that are necessary for effective practice with gay, lesbian, and bisexual people, their families, and their communities. Understanding how heterosexism and homophobia, power and oppression, and stigma and stigma management affect gay, lesbian, and bisexual people is essential for social work assessment, intervention, and knowledge-building.

Lesbian, gay, and bisexual people have demonstrated profound social, psychological, and political resiliency throughout an almost universal history of violence and oppression. However, in the course of the life cycle, some gay, lesbian, and bisexual people will find need for mental health or social services. This text is designed to prepare social workers and other health and human services professionals to better assess the concerns, problems, and issues presented by gay, lesbian, and bisexual clients and then to more effectively intervene with the widest array of interpersonal and social change methods appropriate to the presenting problem. Since social workers comprise the largest professional discipline in the mental health and social service systems, they must be well prepared to deal effectively with these needs.

It has been well documented that lesbians and gay men experience oppression at the behest of religion, culture, and civil and criminal legal codes (Berube 1990; Chauncey 1994; D'Emilio 1983; Katz 1976, 1995). As targets of institutionalized discrimination, they continue to be at risk of stigmatization and violence. Therefore, it is understandable that gay and lesbian clients appear in the full range of social work agencies and programs. While most have the same needs as their nongay counterparts, the differences are significant in that sexual orientation may have an impact on the perception of the problem, how the problem is sustained in the social environment, and the availability of formal and informal resources to help resolve the problem.

The primary goal of this book is to present information to students and professionals designed to improve the delivery of health, mental health, and human services to gay, lesbian, and bisexual people, their families, and their communities. The objectives are practice-oriented and quite specific: to increase skills in *biopsychosocial* assessment and the effectiveness of psychosocial interventions. Ultimately, this is an effort to help social workers minimize the influences of heterosexism and homophobia in their practice and, over time, in the environments in which their clients function. Because this volume is designed to supplement the rich literature related to generalist and specialized practice and to our expanding knowledge of human diversity in general, the authors will not attempt to introduce, elaborate, or summarize the general foundation knowledge, values, and skills commonly associated with social work practice. Rather, the emphasis is on the knowledge, values, and skills needed for practice with this population—gay, lesbian, and bisexual people— specifically.

Social workers are uniquely situated to serve lesbians, bisexuals, and gay men. Social work emphasizes the dual focus on the individual and his/her social environment. Social work interventions are directed at the interaction between people and society. This work at the interface involves helping individuals understand and cope with their environments as well as advocating for social change aimed at improving opportunities and the quality of people's lives.

This text focuses on typical problems and treatments for psychological and life task issues but does not discuss major psychiatric problems. The problems selected for discussion exclude those involving gross social dysfunction or serious psychopathology requiring intensive psychiatric intervention. The issues covered include internalized homophobia and guilt and shame; lack of integrated positive gay identity; family conflict; relationship difficulties; substance abuse; violence; AIDS; aging; and the impact of heterosexism and "homohatred" on the access to health and social services, the development of community, and the recognition of social, political, and legal rights. The interventions included are designed to maximize human potential, improve psychological and interpersonal functioning, and develop a positive self/sexual identity as well as to promote group consciousness and development, community and institution building, and institutional change to sustain supportive and nurturing social environments for all gay, lesbian, and bisexual people.

Theory for Practice

The groundwork for this proposed change-oriented practice with gay, lesbian, and bisexual people is laid by distinguishing among three kinds of theory: a theory of practice, a theory for practice, and a theory of caring. Robert Vinter (1967:245) describes a *theory of practice* as consisting of "a body of principles, more or less systematically developed and anchored in scientific knowledge, that seeks to guide and direct practitioner action." These principles are "directed not at understanding reality, but at achieving control over it" (432). A theory of practice could be formulated by observing social workers as they go about their work with lesbian, gay, and bisexual clients and then codifying what they are doing. From these observations it should be possible to specify what social workers do and what results they get. A theory constructed from observations may describe present practice, but it has a limited ability to improve it or to bring about change. In addition, psychosocial interventions specifically designed for lesbian and gay clients have had too short a history for systematic observation. Contemporary theories of practice, especially the *ecological model* (Compton & Galaway 1989; Germain 1991; Hepworth & Larsen 1993; Meyer 1993), supported by a diversity framework and the strengths and empowerment perspectives (Saleebey 1997; Solomon 1982), appear to be effective in addressing the needs of this population. This is the theory of practice advanced in this text.

A *theory for practice* is a system of ideas or statements that explain social work practice. It provides for the development of practice models and principles out of which actual practice might evolve. Rather than being based in the norms and roles of the profession, it is more likely to be indebted to the social, behavioral, and biological sciences. A proposed theory for practice could be developed from the ideas and content in this book, but only after it is bolstered with the clinical and empirical research of practitioners. Longres (1995:3) suggests that "a theory for practice is a prerequisite for the development of a practice theory. . . . It can be understood as a system of statements intended to explain human behavior and make it comprehensible, toward the ultimate purpose of learning how to control human behavior."The discussions that follow are structured to make the life experiences of gay men and lesbians comprehensible to the social work practitioner. The authors seek to contribute to practice theory by synthesizing a body of theory related to lesbian, bisexual, and gay people from a social systems perspective.

The purpose or function served by social workers is to help people out of their predicaments. In the process of doing this, it is hoped, a better society will result. Behind these vague general statements lie many contradictions and complexities. Does practice help the client by helping her adjust and cope with the realities and demands of the larger society? Does practice help the client by championing her cause and insisting that society accommodate her needs? These questions form the core of an age-old dilemma within the profession: whether the function of social work is social control or social change. In practice it is not always easy to distinguish between these philosophies. Longres (1981:55–56) suggests that in reality most practice is oriented somewhere in between: "it follows what might be called a liberal philosophy, accepting a certain degree of conformity while working for a certain degree of within-system change."

Longres (1981) further notes that social workers by tradition operate on the basis of a theory of caring. While theories of practice and for practice strive to be empirical and therefore free of values, a theory of caring is value-dominated. Practitioners adopt the value that it is good to show care, and they support their practice with political and ideological values concerning the best ways to show care. While this is both necessary and good, practice cannot be based solely on values. However, a value stance that discrimination and prejudice directed against any group are damaging to the social, emotional, and economic well-being of the affected group and of society as a whole leads to a commitment to advancing policies and practices that will improve the status and well-being of all lesbian, gay, and bisexual people (NASW 1997b). In this book we develop a perspective on practice with gay, lesbian, and bisexual people which combines a theory for practice with a theory for caring—that is, with a particular set of underlying values. As we present theories of human behavior, we will evaluate them from a social work value perspective of concern for human dignity and social justice.

Value Base for Practice

The value base for practice with gay, lesbian, and bisexual people is a theory of caring based on values of justice, independence, and freedom, the importance of community life, client self-determination, and social change. Justice must be accessible to all on an equal basis; it must be impartially applied. Social conditions must be just. People want to feel a sense of self-worth and have a real ability to make decisions that affect their own lives. Independence and freedom are needed to experiment, reflect, and change. People generally want to create their own communities, to have a chance to experience support and a feeling of belonging, to have greater power over their lives, and to find ways of resolving problems. On the other hand, when people are isolated they may become victims of exploitation and alienation and feel powerless, vulnerable, and unimportant. People want a chance to affect their own future, to make choices. A sense of accomplishment comes from engaging in action, not from being acted on. Products of change are all around us, and it is these that feed our sense of optimism (Appleby & Anastas 1992).

Social work has a long tradition of concern and advocacy for various minorities and oppressed groups. The National Association of Social Workers (NASW) reaffirmed in 1993 and again in 1996 its landmark 1977 social policy statement addressing the profession's concern for the political and psychosocial status of gay men and lesbians (NASW 1977, 1997b). In its most recent social policy statement on "Lesbian, Gay, and Bisexual Issues," the profession clearly recognizes that homosexuality and gay, bisexual, and lesbian cultures have existed throughout history, a history characterized by persistent social condemnation and discrimination (NASW 1997b). It is the position of NASW that gay, lesbian, and bisexual people be afforded the same respect and rights as heterosexuals and that discrimination and prejudice directed against any group be viewed as damaging to the social, emotional, and economic well-being of the marginalized group as well as to society as a whole. A series of "action steps" were prescribed related to (1) requiring gay, bisexual, and lesbian content in professional and continuing education; (2) developing political strategies related to national, state, and local antidiscrimination laws and policies addressing civil rights, inheritance, insurance, property rights, immigration, employment, housing, professional credentialing, licensing, public accommodation, child custody, foster parenting and adoption, the right to marry, and domestic partnership; (3) designing programs to increase public awareness related to hate crimes and antigay violence, and to increase the general understanding of the richness and diversity of gay, lesbian, and bisexual communities; and (4) encouraging the expansion of comprehensive psychological and social services and social supports for lesbian, bisexual, and gay people and their families.

In 1996 NASW updated its *Code of Ethics* (NASW 1996), clarifying its ban on discrimination based on sexual orientation and encouraging its approximately 200,000 members to act to expand access, choices, and opportunities for oppressed people and groups. In addition to this social action commitment, the new *Code* specifically states:

> Social workers should obtain education about and seek to understand the nature of social diversity and oppression with respect to race, ethnicity, national origin, color, sex, sexual orientation, age, marital status, political belief, religion, and mental or physical disability. . . . Social workers should not practice, condone, facilitate, or collaborate with any form of discrimination on the basis of race. ethnicity, national origin, color, sex, sexual orientation, age, marital status, political belief, religion, or mental or physical disability.   (NASW 1996:9, 23)

The Council on Social Work Education (CSWE) in 1992 revised its Accreditation Standards, requiring approximately three hundred BSW (Bachelor of Social Work) and one hundred MSW (Master of Social Work) programs to include course content related to lesbian and gay service needs and practice concerns into their core curriculum. This mandate is an expression of the profession's commitment to social and economic justice and its respect for human diversity. Although the mandate seems clear, there is controversy about the commitment itself and the implementation of the mandate (Parr & Jones 1996; Van Soest 1996), and the curricular and academic resources to fulfill this commitment are not yet in place (Mackelprang, Ray, & Hernandez-Peck 1996).

Putting theory and values effectively into practice, in addition, is easier said than done. While much of the social science knowledge base is relevant to practice with gay, lesbian, and bisexual people, translating this knowledge into constructive action in the complex situations that clients present is a challenge, as the following case example illustrates.

> A social worker employed as a case manager for an AIDS service organization has developed a relationship with an underage female prostitute who is currently "squatting" with several young male hustlers. The worker's initial involvement with this client centers around a referral to a health clinic because of a vaginal infection and the need for safe-sex and clean needle use education. Eventually the worker would like to help her to explore other life options and different survival strategies because of the dangers of AIDS, drug abuse, and violence associated with street life. Getting her back into school with supportive friends, counselors, and teachers, and possible reunification with her parents (if there is a goodness of fit with this environment because they

might be able to supply the necessary emotional and financial support at this crucial point in her development) seem like appropriate goals. To accomplish all this, the worker would need to reconnect the client with the network of friends and family she left behind, and to set up a range of social and health services designed for these types of problems in individual development and family functioning.

When broaching the need to secure a "temporary" safe home with the client, the social worker discovered that the client had done poorly in school, had been disowned by her family, and subsequently was asked to leave the foster home she had lived in for the past year. The client was surviving by selling her body and by moving in with some "friendly guys" for companionship and protection. This underground arrangement also made it possible for her to avoid the child welfare agency and the possibility of placement in another foster or group home.

The worker, in time, learned that her client identified herself as a lesbian, who, like her gay "roommates," had been kicked out of her home and then had run away from her foster parents because of their violent reaction to her gayness. The child welfare agency had warned her not to tell her foster family that she was a lesbian and had recommended she begin dating boys, claiming that eventually she would grow out of the phase. When she refused to follow this advice, she was harassed by her foster brothers and some of the kids at school. She ran away when her foster mother and her child welfare worker recommended that she be placed in a psychiatric facility for youth.

The worker's initial reaction was confusion, revulsion, and, to some degree, a sense of helplessness. How would she begin to understand what had happened to her client? How would she begin to understand her own reaction? What should she do? She already had a theory of caring, the values of the profession. She needed both a theory for practice and a theory of practice. Those theories that help us to understand the context of practice with lesbian, bisexual, and gay people also form the foundation of a theory for practice.

Homophobia and Heterosexism: The Context of Practice

Despite the gay rights movement and some supportive legislation, homosexuality is largely hidden in American society and, when publicly recognized, it is often condemned or stigmatized. While American attitudes toward homosexuality have gradually changed in the latter decades of the twentieth century, we are still a society that condemns homosexuality. In 1973, 73 percent of the general population thought homosexuality was wrong. This percentage dropped to 61 percent in 1996 (Bagley 1996). However, according to a 1996 *Newsweek* poll, nearly 84 percent of Americans support equal employment rights for gay men and lesbians. The Human Rights Campaign found that, in 1994, 70 percent of the voting population did not realize that antigay job discrimination is still widespread and predominantly legal (Goldberg 1996). Although these statistics may be viewed as contradictory, while Americans strongly disapprove of gay men and lesbians, their sense of fairness is violated by discrimination in the workplace. Over the decades of the 1970s, 1980s, and 1990s, scholars have sought to explain this phenomenon of widespread disapproval of homosexuality and a slowly developing tolerance in some areas of life.

Homophobia and *heterosexism* are interrelated social forces that serve as the context of the psychosocial development of gay men and lesbians. These forces not only create major environmental pressures which impact on individual development and the potential for forming a healthy gay identity but also act on the ability to cope and to adapt to the social and psychological stressors associated with a stigmatized social status. These forces can become barriers to healthy adaptation, to managing life tasks and transitions, and to mastering the interpersonal processes necessary for optimal social functioning. They also affect the service systems that people turn to in times of crisis and need. Thus the first task is to understand these concepts and then to identify their manifestations in the lives of gay and lesbian people, which can include the experiences of stigma, guilt, and shame.

OPPRESSION AND POWER

A primary construction in Western cultural thought is the belief that the superior should control the inferior. Western religious and philosophical thought is the ideological basis of all forms of oppression in the United States. Interactions based on differential power can be characterized by dominance-subordination or inequality and can be affected by a variety of statuses and roles assigned by society.

Pellegrini (1992) in her study of gender inequality points out that *oppression*, a key concept that ties sexism and homophobia together, is all about *power*: the power to enforce a particular worldview; the power to deny equal access to housing, employment opportunities, and health care; the power alternately to define and/or to efface difference; the power to maim, physically, mentally, and emotionally; and, most importantly, the power to set the very terms of power. Homophobia and heterosexism together form a system of institution-alized domination. Being oppressed means the absence of choices. Power thus defines the initial point of contact between the oppressed and the oppressor.

Pharr (1988) broadens the analysis of the oppression of lesbian, gay, and bi-sexual people by pointing out that homophobia is a weapon of sexism. She sug-gests that the following are elements of all oppression: the imposition of nor-mative behavior supported by institutional and economic power; disincentives for nonconformity, including the threat and use of violence for those who do not conform; social definition as "other"; invisibility of the "outsiders"; distor-tion and stereotyping; blaming the victim; internalized oppression; and the iso-lation or assimilation with tokenism of the "outsider." Most gay and lesbian scholars who view power and oppression from a social psychological or socio-political framework reference each of these elements of oppression (DeCecco & Shively 1984; D'Emilio 1983; Herek & Berrill 1992; Humphries 1972).

Power exists on various levels: individual, interpersonal, institutional, and societal. Heller (1985), Wrong (1980), and Pinderhughes (1989) all de-fine power as the capacity to produce desired effects on others; perceived mastery over self and others; the capacity to influence the forces that affect one's life. Adding sexual orientation to Pinderhughes's analysis of power shows its relevance:

> Power is a stance that undergirds certain of our societal values: status, per-fection, possession, achievement, competition, independence, and so forth. These values, though contrasting sharply with other American values such as justice, equality, and the right of all citizens to pursue happiness, have formed the backdrop for the ethic of the melting pot, which itself embodies the notion of power. In its emphasis on the values and life-styles of persons from a specific class, racial group, and [sexual orientation], i.e., the White, hetero-sexual middle class, the melting pot has devalued and ignored people of color, the poor, and [lesbian, gay, and bisexual people].
>
> (Pinderhughes 1989:112)

While oppression based on race, ethnicity, class, gender, age, or sexual orien-tation is each unique (Young-Bruehl 1996), gay men and lesbians share life experiences with other oppressed people in that power or the lack thereof is central to their social functioning.

The converse of power, powerlessness, is the inability to exert such influ-ence. Powerlessness is painful, and people defend against feeling powerless by doing whatever is necessary to bring them a sense of power. The stereotypic, overly aggressive, cynical verbal behavior with humorous overtones of some gay men and lesbians (often referred to as *camp* or *camping*) is an example of trying to redefine the interaction between people with unequal power. It both mocks and rejects the norms of the more powerful and serves to render them "outsiders."

Basch (1975:513) states that "the feeling of controlling one's destiny to some reasonable extent is the essential psychological component of all aspects of life." A sense of power is critical to one's mental health. Power is manifest in the individual's sense of mastery or competence. Coping with submission to power is the earliest formative experience, be it in the family, in the group, or in the adaptation to social roles. John Hodge (1975) stresses that the family in our society, both traditionally and legally, reflects the dualist values of hierarchy and coercive authoritarian control which are exemplified in the parent-child and husband-wife relationships. As hooks (1984:36) notes:

> It is in this form of the family where most children first learn the meaning and practice of hierarchical, authoritarian rule. Here is where they learn to accept group oppression against themselves as non-adults, and where they learn to accept male supremacy and the group oppression of women. Here is where they learn that it is the male's role to work in the community and control the economic life of the family and to mete out the physical and financial punishments and rewards, and the female's role to provide the emotional warmth associated with motherhood while under the economic rule of the male. Here is where the relationship of superordination subordination, of superior-inferior, or master-slave is first learned and accepted as "natural."

Power and privilege relationships are thus played out within a complex web of gender-role expectation, performance, and violation. The dynamics of sexism provide valuable insights into heterosexism and homophobia.

In her text *Feminist Theory: From the Margin to the Center*, bell hooks (1984) notes that unlike other forms of oppression, most people witness and/or experience the practice of sexist domination (a primary oppression) in family settings. We tend to witness and/or experience racism or classism as we encounter the larger society, the world outside the home. Heterosexism and homophobia, however, like sexism, are often first experienced within the home.

Homophobia and Heterosexism Defined

In *Society and the Healthy Homosexual* (1972), George Weinberg first presented the concept of *homophobia* as society's fear, dislike, or hatred of gays, lesbians, and bisexuals, an attitude which often resulted in acts of discrimination. Homophobia, like all forms of oppression, is used to impose and reinforce control and mastery over others. Weinberg's use of "phobia" deliberately suggested that homophobia is irrational, fear-driven, and, at least for some people, a defensive maneuver to ward off something both feared and desired. Before Weinberg's astute observation, negative attitudes toward homosexuality were not usually seen as a cause of concern. Naming this negative attitude has been an extremely important step in defining it as a social problem. However, Weinberg's definition does not make distinctions among the various kinds and levels of negative feeling, understanding, or action toward gay, lesbian, and bisexual people.

Since Weinberg's book, the concept of homophobia has been studied and debated by numerous scholars (see Neisen 1990 and Young-Bruehl 1996). Herek (1992b), a prolific student of homophobia, offers a necessary refinement of the earliest concept. He suggests that the focus be shifted to an analysis of societal behaviors and the impact this has on attitudes and beliefs. Homophobia is now understood to be a result of *heterosexism*, "an ideological system that denies, denigrates, and stigmatizes any nonheterosexual form of behavior, identity, relationship, or community" (1992:89). Herek further notes that—like racism, sexism, and other ideologies of oppression—heterosexism is manifested both in societal customs and institutions and in individual attitudes and acts. In institutions such as religion and the legal system, it constitutes *cultural heterosexism*; as manifested in individual attitudes, perceptions of reality, and behaviors, it constitutes *psychological heterosexism*. These definitions of heterosexism also capture much of the meaning commonly associated with the term *homophobia*.

Indeed, according to Blumenfeld (1992:283), *homophobia* is "the fear and hatred of those who love and sexually desire those of the same sex." Homophobia, which has its roots in sexism, is manifest in the fear and hatred that encourages damaging heterosexist acts. Heterosexism is discrimination by neglect, omission, and/or distortion, whereas often its more active partner, homophobia, is discrimination and hurtful behavior by intent and design (Blumenfeld & Raymond 1993). Homophobia and heterosexism, like other forms of oppression, are used to impose and reinforce control and mastery over others by a system of rewards and punishments at both systemic and interpersonal levels. This text uses both terms—heterosexism and homophobia—in just this way: to indicate both passive and active forms of antihomosexual prejudice.

The following examples from Elze (1992) show both passive and active ways in which homosexuality is discouraged.

Before I got into junior high, my friends and I would always be touching each other, hugging each other, and holding hands. That's what little girls do. When we got into junior high, that changed, you never saw much of that. No one ever did that in public anymore. No one touched each other. Everyone stopped hugging each other. We wouldn't brush each other's hair. We'd never hold hands. . . .[104]

I was in a rehab for adolescents. The health teacher asked us what we'd do if we found out our best friend was gay. There had been a movie on TV about it. Well, the kids in the rehab said things like they'd beat on the person. Then the teacher asked what we'd do if one of the kids in the rehab was gay. People's answers were really scary. "I'd beat on him." "I'd kick him out." One guy said he'd kill the person. A gay resident left after that. He was just coming out about his sexuality and got really freaked out [108].   (Elze 1992)

The terms *homosexual* and *homophobia* are viewed by many contemporary scholars as overly medicalized and, as a result, as failing to capture the political and social psychological interactive nature of these concepts. Homophobia is not really a phobia in the true psychiatric sense of the term. The phobic and defensive connotation discourages recognition that attitudes toward homosexuality can serve other nonpsychological functions, such as expressing certain cultural or religious values. New terms such as *homo-ignorance, homonegativity*, or *homohatred* are more inclusive and neutral and are also used at times in this text. However, heterosexism and homophobia are used as well, in part because they are the most widely known and well-researched ways of conceptualizing antigay and anti-lesbian prejudices.

The reader is cautioned, however, that while many of these terms may be used interchangeably, each implies a different level of cognitive and affective involvement. *Homo-ignorance* suggests a minimal level of discriminatory or prejudicial behavior and results often from a lack of knowledge or from the uncritical acceptance of cultural stereotypes or myths (such as the assumption that a gay man will only choose noncompetitive and nurturing jobs because of his supposed identification with female gender roles). The homo-ignorant individual, for example, may find it hard to believe that there are gay construction workers, athletes, lawyers, or ruthless businessmen. Prejudice of this kind suggests that increased and more accurate knowledge can reduce negative attitudes. *Homonegativity* implies moderately discriminatory attitudes and behavior resulting from nominally held beliefs that stigmatize gay, lesbian, and bisexual people. A homonegative individual may vote against extending the right of same-sex marriage because of a conservative religious conviction seemingly divorced from any appreciation for the civil rights implications and the privileges associated with the institution of marriage. *Homohatred* is the most active form of discrimination and prejudice, stemming from strongly held religious beliefs and heterosexist convictions which allow for no other religious or cultural possibilities. Homohatred is demonstrated by an individual who joins a local Family Values Council and becomes passionately involved in a political campaign to block the Board of Education's adoption of an inclusive diversity curriculum because it includes mention of gay and lesbian parenting. It is also illustrated by those who commit acts of violence against lesbian, gay, and bisexual individuals (see chapter 10).

Homophobia used in its broadest sense has many levels, starting with the personal—that is, the personal belief system that gay people deserve to be pitied or hated because they are unable to control their so-called perverted desires—and the interpersonal, wherein there is a transformation of the personal belief system into active bias or prejudice. This transformation, in turn, affects relationships. Another aspect of homophobia occurs at the institutional level. Here discrimination is systematic on the part of governments, businesses, and religious, educational, and professional organizations by promulgating laws, codes, or policies that invite or enforce discrimination. Cultural homophobia (sometimes referred to as *collective* or *societal homophobia*) refers to the social norms or codes of behavior that, although not expressly written into law or policy, nonetheless work within a society to legitimize oppression. This level of homophobia results in attempts either to exclude images of lesbians and gays from the media or from history or to represent these groups entirely in negative stereotypical terms.

In their exploration of gay and lesbian identity development in the context of homophobia, Appleby and Anastas (1992) note that cultural homophobia is manifested in a conspiracy to silence this minority by redefining the reality of gay and lesbian people as well as by denying the existence of their unique culture, their popular strength, and their efforts to define or label themselves. The dominant fear of overvisibility of gays and lesbians results in the creation of defined public spaces and negative symbolism or stereotyping. These elements are compatible with Pharr's (1988) conceptualization of oppression, as previously discussed.

THE ROOTS OF HOMOPHOBIA AND HETEROSEXISM

A thorough discussion of the etiology of homophobia and heterosexism includes consideration of several divergent explanations. A sociological and anthropological understanding might highlight the power of patriarchy in defining and maintaining gender roles and male privilege (Andersen 1983) and the process of socialization, as well as the nature and role of the family (Lynn 1966). The social control function of psychiatry and the medicalization of social life might also be considered (Altman 1971, 1982; Bayer 1987, 1989; Szasz 1970). Herek's concept of cultural heterosexism (1993b:90–91) calls attention to the "alternation between invisibility and condemnation [stigma] . . . readily apparent in four major societal institutions: religion, the law, psychiatry/psychology, and mass media." Psychological insight might be gained with a review of more recent psychoanalytic thought (Bayer 1987; Cabaj & Stein 1995; Drescher, in press; Isay 1989; Lewes 1988) or by examining the legacy of Leviticus and the Judeo-Christian tradition (Boswell 1980; Comstock 1991; McNeill 1993; Rapp 1991). While some attention will be given to each of these as a possible explanation of homophobia, this is an extensive literature, much of which is beyond the purview of this chapter.

Sociological explanations suggest that the current heterosexist social order is largely understandable in terms of gender-assigned roles based on a system of male privilege. These assigned roles convey differential power and privilege to heterosexual white males so long as they conform to the expected

> Living in a society in which legal and religious systems condemn same-sex orientation has consequences for even the most liberated individuals. Gay men and lesbians are reminded regularly that they are different and unwanted; unwanted for military service, as physicians, as teachers of small children or for job promotion.   —Gary A. Lloyd (1992:93)

patterns and ideologies. The result is a highly developed and systematic subordination of women to white men through the creation of particular rules and prohibitions according to one's gender. McIntosh (1988) views these hierarchies in our society as interlocking and notes that the white male privilege inherent in these hierarchies is simultaneously both denied and protected. It is a real system of *unearned advantage and conferred dominance* of white heterosexual males experienced daily by women, people of color, and gay, lesbian, and bisexual people.

Author bell hooks (1984) suggests that sexist oppression is the primary contradiction, the basis of all other oppressions, including racism, classism, and homophobia. She argues that sexism is of primary importance because it is the practice of domination most people experience, whether their role be that of a discriminator or discriminated against, exploiter or exploited. It is also a practice of domination and subordination that most people are socialized to accept before they even know that other forms of group oppression exist. This does not mean that eradicating sexist oppression would eliminate other forms of oppression. However, since all forms of oppression are linked in our society because they are supported by similar institutional and social structures, one system cannot be eradicated while the others remain intact. Racism, sexism, and heterosexism are all systems of unearned advantage and conferred dominance, but they should not be seen as the same. Moreover, it is difficult to disentangle aspects of unearned advantage which rest more on social class, economic class, race, religion, sex, and ethnic identity than on other factors. However, challenging heterosexist oppression is nevertheless a crucial step in the struggle to eliminate all forms of oppression.

In our society, sexist oppression perverts and distorts the positive function of family. Family exists as a space wherein we are socialized from birth to accept and support forms of oppression. In his discussion of the cultural basis of domination, John Hodge emphasizes the role of the family: "The traditional Western family, with its authoritarian male rule and its authoritarian adult rule, is the major training ground which initially conditions us to accept group oppression as the natural order" (quoted in hooks 1984:36). Power struggles, coercive authoritarian rule, and even brutal assertion of domination may shape family life for many so that it is often the setting of intense suffering and pain. According to Hodge (1975), the domination usually present within the family—of children by adults, and female by male—are forms of group oppression which are easily translated into the "rightful" group oppression of other people as defined by race (racism), by nationality (colonialism), by religion or by other means (i.e., sexual orientation [homophobia and heterosexism]). Thus politically, the white supremacist, patriarchal state relies on the family to indoctrinate its members with values supportive of hierarchical control and coercive authority. However, it is still important to affirm the primacy of family life because family ties are the only sustained support system for so many exploited and oppressed people. Practice designed to rid family life of its abusive dimension created by sexist and/or heterosexist oppression, yet without devaluing the positive aspects of family life, should be a goal of interpersonal or clinical social work intervention.

Herek (1990) argues that ideologies related to sexuality and gender hold this system of hierarchical roles together. The ideology of gender, a system of beliefs, values, and customs concerning "masculinity" and "femininity," is the context in which the individual defines his or her gender identity.

For a little girl there are now dolls to play with and take care of, pretty clothes to try on, shiny black patent-leather shoes, and as a special reward she may help mommy with house work and stir the batter in the big white bowl. No one ever really tells her to be "domestic" or "esthetic" or "maternal" but she's learning. A little boy, meanwhile, is learning other things. Balls and bats have miraculously appeared to play with, realistic toy pistols, and trains, blocks, and marbles. The shoes he finds in his closet are sturdy enough to take a lot of wear, and just right for running. One day there is an old tire hanging by a rope from a tree in the back yard, just right for swinging. No one ever tells him to be "active" or "aggressive" or "competitive" but somehow, he's learning.   (Blumenfeld 1992:23)

This gender ideology is a socially constructed and learned process wherein many meanings are attached to the self as male or female. Heterosexuality is equated with "normal" masculinity and "normal" femininity, whereas homosexuality is equated with violating norms of gender (Herek 1992b:89–104). Acceptable sexual roles and desires are gender- and sexually prescribed, while role violations are stigmatized as deviant, abnormal, inherently sick, or dangerous. This can be seen in extremist and violent reactions to gay men who violate gender-role expectations or who reject by default their "God-given" male privilege (see chapter 10). Confusion is sometimes increased with the gender-role nonconformity of growing numbers of straight (i.e., heterosexual) men and women as well as with the greater visibility of norm-violating lesbians, gay men, and bisexuals. This dynamic contains the ingredients for the violence experienced by more and more lesbians and gay men. Even in the absence of violence, these attitudes and prescriptive beliefs affect lesbians and gay men who must process this hostility in developing their own identities, fashion their own responses to gender roles, and navigate in a world of blatant and presumed heterosexuality and invisible homosexuality.

Gender-role conformity and nonconformity must also be evaluated within the context of different cultural expectations. What constitutes appropriate male or female role behavior is not always the same within or across cultures. Cultural cues may be sufficiently different so as to result in a misinterpretation of behaviors, especially those related to gender-role performance. These cues may be misinterpreted and labeled as deviant (i.e., lesbian/gay), as when diverse and culturally defined gender roles of "macho" men, "androgynous" men and women, "passive" men, and/or "assertive" women come in contact with dominant stereotypes (see chapter 3).

Since the nineteenth century, people have been defined in terms of what they do sexually, giving rise to social classifications based on sexual behavior, preference, and relationships (D'Emilio 1983). This happened as the focus of sexuality shifted from reproduction to intimacy and personal happiness, and from family and community to the individual (D'Emilio & Freedman 1988). In explaining the hegemonic status of procreative sexuality, Marcuse (1962: 32–33) argues that the demands of the Freudian "performance principle" required that sexuality be limited to genital function directed at the opposite sex. Only in that way could the body be desexualized and made available for work. Heterosexuality alone could guarantee the reproduction of labor so necessary for the conquest of nature. He went on to explain that sexuality unfettered by the performance principle was potentially seductive. Society's fear is represented in the existence of powerful taboos against perversion, the reliance on criminal law to repress such behavior, and the disgust experienced by those who encounter them. Threatened by their own unconscious wishes, men and women have had to protect themselves by punishing those who dared to satisfy the desires they could not themselves acknowledge. Gay-bashing and the sanctions against gay men, lesbians, and bisexuals are understandable as a manifestation of this social dynamic—that is, as the perceived violation of prescribed roles. Social categories were developed to describe those who transgressed the boundaries of existing marital and reproductive roles.

Rubin (1984:280–81) observes that acceptable sexuality should be heterosexual, marital, monogamous, reproductive, and noncommercial. It should be coupled, relational, within the same generation, and occur at home. It should not involve pornography, fetish objects, sex toys, or roles other than male and female. Gay and lesbian sexuality violates many of these rules.

In any discussion of homophobia or heterosexism, the interrelatedness of power, gender-role socialization, family, and religion must be recognized. Religion is a system of beliefs, values, and customs that forms the basis for group members' shared perception of social reality. It involves a worldview that is shared by its members, and includes valuing patriarchy—male privilege—with its system of roles, relationships, and approved behaviors. One major function of religion is to support the social order. While the family teaches us the preferred gender roles along with the expected behaviors, religion teaches us to value these roles as good, necessary, appropriate, and legitimate. These religious and cultural lessons are well learned and serve as the foundation for much of homophobia:

> Our oppression comes from people that oppress us in the name of Jesus, and that to me is so alien to what Jesus is all about that I just won't let them do that.
>
> (Bill Crews, Mayor of Melborne, Iowa, to the Associated Press,
> March 21, 1994)

Fanaticism, disguised as religious devotion, seems to be spreading among Christians, Jews, and Muslims. It is typical of the religious fanatics that the "orders" they get from God are always, essentially, one order: Thou shall kill. The god of all fanatics sounds more like the devil.

(Amos Oz, *Newsweek*, November 20, 1995)

A sizable portion of the American public is admittedly, proudly, and some-times militantly antihomosexual, despite antidiscrimination legislation and the visibility of lesbians and gay men as a growing political, economic, and cultural influence. The hatred for gay men and lesbians develops out of fear and self-righteousness. Religion has taught that gay people are inherently evil, and true believers are ever alert for the sins of their neighbors. Comstock (1991) identifies eight possible references to the disapproval of homosexuality in Judeo-Christian scripture: Genesis 19; Leviticus 18:22, 20:13; Romans 1:18–32; 1 Corinthians 6:9; 1 Timothy 1:10; and Revelations 21:8, 22:15. Biblical scholars are far from agreeing on which refer definitely to homosex-uality, but consensus is that the two verses in Leviticus alone clearly indicate and prohibit homosexual relations, explicitly condemning male homosexual-ity and prescribing death for those practicing it. Specifically, because of the Judeo-Christian roots of the legal system and social policy in the United States, it is these references that have influenced and continue to buttress social policy and legal practice concerning lesbians and gay men. This rela-tionship between religion and law is seen as a major dimension of Herek's notion of cultural heterosexism.

These biblical references suggest that those who consider themselves to be "truly religious" (the so-called biblical literalists) not only feel justified in hat-ing and denigrating homosexuals but are almost required to do so as an act of piety. Their self-righteousness justifies their attitudes and actions while insu-lating them from other points of view (Pierce 1990). These teachings, how-ever, also have a significant impact on gay, lesbian, and bisexual people them-selves: "Coping may be particularly difficult for people of color, from cultures that totally reject homosexuality, or from fundamentalist or doctrinaire reli-gious backgrounds that find scriptural reasons to define homosexuality as intrinsically sinful or evil" (Lloyd 1992:93).

Since most contemporary Christians do not believe in biblical inerrancy but interpret Scriptures within a historical, cultural, and linguistic context, antigay and lesbian laws literally based on these biblical references is irra-tional. This religion-based hatred of homosexuality is ironic, in light of the finding that the words *homosexual*, *homosexuality*, and *sodomite* do not exist in classic Greek or Hebrew, nor do they appear in the Bible until 1946 (Maniaci

& Rzeznik 1993). These are words not recorded before that time; neither are they words that would have had cultural meaning in that period of Hebrew and Greek history. Even without this relatively recent revelation, theologians and Biblical scholars such as Boswell (1980) have pointed to the contradictions in the text as well as to the selective attention given to homosexual behavior but not other behaviors equally vilified. He observed that "if prohibition which restrain a disliked minority are upheld in their most literal sense as absolutely inviolable while comparable precepts affecting the majority are relaxed or reinterpreted, one must suspect something other than religious belief as the motivating cause of the oppression" (7).

There are other social institutions that share responsibility for societal homophobia and heterosexism, including medicine, psychology, and psychiatry. These professions continue to contribute an aura of "scientific" legitimacy to the view that homosexuals are both mentally and physically deviant (DeCecco 1988). The twentieth century heralded the medicalization of broader domains of social life. Physicians often acted as if it were in their competence to advise in all aspects of social life. Psychiatry more specifically sought to assume responsibility for the control of a range of behaviors previously considered immoral: criminality, violence, alcohol and drug use, juvenile delinquency, sexual deviance. In attempting to provide an understanding of aberrant behavior, psychiatry assumed from the faltering religious tradition the function of protector of the social order, "substituting the concept of illness for that of sin" (Bayer 1987:10). In assuming that heterosexuality represented a medical norm to which they were obliged to help homosexuals conform, they unconsciously enforced the cultural hegemony of heterosexuality. While more psychiatrists today are apt to see mental illness as a social construction and that the profession reflects the values and demands of society, many are unconvinced of the naturalness of homosexuality. A survey of clinical psychologists found that more than one in five practicing therapists still treat homosexuality as a mental illness, despite the fact that it is no longer classified as such; in addition, 45 percent of those surveyed did not consider such behavior unethical (Douglas, Kalman, & Kalman 1985). Thus the religious and professional validation of antihomosexual prejudice reinforces the widespread view of homosexuals as undesirable and deviant persons in general society, and by extension within the family as well. These complementary sources of antigay condemnation mean that authorities to whom the individual or the family may turn for information about homosexuality are as likely as not simply to reinforce the family's misconceptions rather than encourage critical reflection on them (Strommen 1990).

HETEROSEXUAL PRIVILEGE

So far, the emphasis has been on negative attitudes toward gay, lesbian, and bisexual people. However, understanding homophobia and heterosexism also requires an appreciation of the systematic ways in which heterosexuality is supported. Blumenfeld (1992) offers an accessible synthesis of contemporary thinking related to homophobia and heterosexism which is consistent with the previous discussion of the ideologies of gender and sexuality. He conceptualized heterosexism as a system of advantages bestowed on heterosexuals. It is the institutional response to homophobia that assumes that all people are or should be heterosexual and therefore excludes the needs, concerns, and life experience of those who are not. This is *heterosexual privilege*: the daily ways that make married or straight persons comfortable or powerful, providing supports, asset, approvals, and regard to those who live or expect to live in heterosexual pairs.

> The reader is asked to image the assumptions that most people might make when learning that she is living with her husband. Your children do not have to answer questions about why you live with your partner (your husband). You have no difficulty finding neighborhoods where people approve of your household. Your children are given texts and classes which implicitly support your kind of family unit, and do not turn them against your choice of domestic partners. You can travel alone or with your husband without expecting embarrassment or hostility in those who deal with you. Most people you meet will see your marital arrangements as an asset to your life or as a favorable comment on your likability, your competence, or your mental health. You can talk about the social events of a weekend without fearing most listeners' reactions. You will feel welcomed and "normal" in the usual walks of public life, institutional and social.   (McIntosh 1988:16)

The fact that you live under the same roof with someone of the opposite sex triggers all kinds of societal assumptions about your worth, politics, life, and values. It also triggers a host of unearned advantages and conferred dominance or power (McIntosh 1988:16–17). This heterosexual privilege supported by the ideologies of gender and sexuality is the core of cultural heterosexism. It is like the air we breathe; it is so ubiquitous that it is hardly noticeable, especially to those who have it. However, those who do not participate in this privilege pay the price.

Stigma and Stigma Management

Oppression, heterosexism, and homophobia are social processes that are experienced personally as stigma, stress, guilt, and shame. It is stigma that significantly influences identity development. It is stigma that results in internalized homophobia that every lesbian, gay, and bisexual person must learn to manage in the process of developing a healthy identity. It is the social, economic, political, and psychological consequences of *stigma* that the social worker may be called upon to help reduce, extricate, or relieve. The concept of stigma comes out of sociological theory. This theory may be especially useful for social work practice because it unambiguously distinguishes between homosexual behaviors and feelings themselves and stigma as a particular reaction to them.

Erving Goffman (1963) talks about the nature of self-presentation and the role of stigma in interpersonal relations. People with stigmas are thought to be not quite human. The standards the stigmatized person incorporates from the wider society equip him or her to be acutely aware of what others see as his or her failing, inevitably causing him or her to agree that he or she does indeed fall short of what he or she really ought to be. Shame is one common consequence of a stigmatized person's failure to meet a specific set of standards, rules, and goals. Another is what I. Meyer (1995) terms "minority stress," or the conflict that arises with the social environment when the person does not fit the dominant values (39).

Stigma represents for Goffman (1963) a spoiled identity, the idea that somehow one is imperfect in regard to the standards of the society in which one lives. It is a "mark or characteristic that distinguishes a person as being deviant, flawed, limited, spoiled or generally undesirable. The deviating characteristics of the person are sufficient reason for the occurrence of the stigma" (Lewis 1992:194). Stigma relates the self to others' views and, although the feelings of being stigmatized may occur in the absence of other people, the feelings associated with it come about through the stigmatized person's interactions with other people, or through his anticipation of interaction with other people. Thus stigmatization is an interpersonal process. Stigmas represent a violation of what is considered normal. The very idea of stigma implies that social value and worth reside not in the spoiled individual but in the societal value system as reflected in its standards, rules, and goals. Thus a stigmatized person has an expectation of rejection and a vigilance about prejudice (Meyer 1995; Bhugra 1988).

As a result of continued exposure to prejudice and stigmatization, lesbians and gays become members of a minority group, a segment of the population that suffers unjustified negative acts by the rest of society. These acts may range from mild discrimination to scapegoating. Allport (1958) defines prejudice as a negative attitude based on error and overgeneralization. Prejudice can be acted out at three levels: antilocution (verbal attacks), discrimination, and violence.

Antilocution—verbal attacks against the group—entails the use of demeaning terms that serve as a foundation for discrimination and violence. Antilocution themes impute supposed danger from the (homosexual) group, such as the destruction of the family, the spreading of AIDS, the molestation of children, and even the endangerment of "moral order" or "civilization." Each of these myths, while untrue, carries profound power in society even in the face of compelling empirical evidence that they are untrue. Fears held by members of the dominant group are expressed and legitimized in antilocution (see chapter 10). Because they are stigmatized, lesbians and gays also experience prejudice in the form of discrimination. Discrimination limits the social roles, social identities, and in-group memberships available to the individual. The stigma assigned to homosexuality may result in discrediting all other social identities (e.g., one cannot be a Christian and a homosexual; one should not be granted full citizenship, as in the ban on military service). Denial of some in-group memberships is often more tragic, especially when it involves the most basic group, the family. The personal cost of the stigma may be seen as so great that many lesbians and gay men will conceal their homosexual identity to avoid it. Finally, violence against gay men and lesbians occurs as well; this phenomenon is discussed at length in chapter 10.

While there are important differences between the development of a gay, lesbian, or bisexual identity and the development of a racial or ethnic identity, there are also many similarities. Comparable stages in identity development have been found (see chapter 2). The primary task for each involves the transformation of a negative, stigmatized identity into a positive, affirming one. However, a racial or ethnic identity is an ascribed status that is recognized and acknowledged from birth, while sexual identity is an achieved status that is generally not adopted until adolescence or adulthood (Garnets & Kimmel 1993). Another way in which the groups differ is that persons of color, for the most part, are taught strategies by their families to manage their stigmatized identity. The families of gay men and lesbians cannot teach skills they don't have; on the contrary, these parents are often the initiators of gay and lesbian stigma.

EFFECTS OF STIGMATIZATION

People who have been stigmatized respond in a great variety of ways. Allport (1958) terms these "traits due to victimization" or "persecution-produced traits." Some of these traits can be quite constructive and creative while other can be rather unpleasant or destructive.

> Every form of ego defense may be found among member of every persecuted group. Some will handle their minority-group membership easily, with surprisingly little evidence in their personalities that this membership is of any concern to them. Others will show a mixture of desirable and undesirable compensations. Some will be so rebellious that they will develop many ugly defenses.   (Allport 1958:140)

Allport (1958) enumerates the varieties of negative responses to stigmatization including (1) obsessive concern resulting in feelings of deep anxiety, suspicion, and insecurity; (2) denial (from both oneself and others) of actual membership in the minority group; (3) social withdrawal and passivity; (4) clowning, being the "court jester" in an effort to be accepted by the dominant group; (5) slyness and cunning—oftentimes for mere survival; (6) identification with the dominant group, a sign of self-hate; (7) aggression against and directing blame to one's own group; (8) redirecting prejudice and discrimination against other minorities; (9) excessive neuroticism; (10) internalizing and acting out the negative social definitions and stereotypes, creating a self-fulfilling prophecy; and (11) excessive striving for status to compensate for the feelings of inferiority. Blumenfeld and Raymond (1993) emphasize that many of the more undesirable of these characteristics often are attributed to the minority as intrinsic but are in reality defenses and responses to discrimination. Unfortunately, when these responses occur, they often lead to reinforcement of negative stereotypes and beliefs.

The negative effects of stigmatization on gay, lesbian, and bisexual people have been known for some time, especially the connection between stigmatization and psychosocial dysfunction (Meyer 1995). Stigmatized individuals have been characterized as having disrupted emotional, cognitive, and behavioral response systems, likely to be caused in part by their feelings of shame and in part by their efforts to cope with prejudice. The stigma felt by the individual is profound, resulting in emotions as diverse as anger, sadness, humiliation, shame, and embarrassment. Lewis (1992) draws a major distinction between shame and guilt or regret. With shame the entire self is "no good," as captured in the expression "I am a bad person." Goffman's definition of stigma as a spoiled identity makes clear that a stigma constitutes a global attribution about the self as no good. In this case, a spoiled identity reflects a whole self made bad by homosexuality. The adjustment difficulties associated with stigma follow from the idea that the stigma defines the individual. The very act of stigmatization is shame-inducing. It is not surprising to find in the discussion of stigma associated feelings of low self-esteem, depression, and acting-out behaviors: "Stigmas speak to the idea of difference and how difference shames us and those we know" (1963:207).

Christopher Bagley (1996), a professor of social work at the University of Calgary, in his study of 750 youth (eighteen to twenty-seven years old) found a profoundly negative response to stigmatization in the fact that young gay and bisexual males are nearly fourteen times more at risk of suicide than their heterosexual contemporaries. This rate is far greater than the conventional wisdom that gay youth are at three times greater risk of suicide than their straight counterparts. Among all young men, gay and straight, those who are celibate are far more likely to try to harm or kill themselves than those who are sexually active: of those in Bagley's group who actually attempted suicide, sexually active heterosexuals comprised 2.8 percent, sexually active homosexuals 9.4 percent, celibate heterosexuals 17.7 percent, and celibate homosexuals 46.1 percent. (Readers may follow this study on the Internet at *http://www.virtualcity.com/youthsuicide*.) Dr. Joyce Hunter, on the social work faculty of Hunter College and one of America's leading experts on gay and lesbian youth and youth suicide, suggests that while gays and lesbians seem to be coming out at younger ages, that phenomenon does not necessarily suggest that they are under less pressure from internal and external homophobia and heterosexism than before: "The younger you come out, the more likely you are to attempt suicide because you don't have the coping skills" (Harvey Milk Institute 1997).

The negative impact of stigma is quite broad: it not only affects those who are stigmatized, but those who are associated with the person also are spoiled. Goffman called this phenomenon "courtesy stigma." Thus stigmas are contagious; they impact on members of the family, friends, and even those who help stigmatized persons, such as social workers and other mental health professionals. For example, the parents of someone with a stigma are themselves stigmatized and may suffer a similar fate as their stigmatized lesbian daughter or gay son. We see the impact of stigmatization when parents are informed that their child is gay: First they express shock and disbelief that their child is imperfect, lacking in "moral strength or mental health." Second, they experience anger and rage. Third, sadness replaces the anger. Finally, the parents enter the coping stage—that is, they learn to cope with their shame and embarrassment over having such a child. The shame at having such a child can last a lifetime and can lead to many family difficulties, including a high rate of marital discord and divorce as each parent seeks to blame the other for the stigmatized child. It can become the family secret, it can be tolerated, or it can be mourned as a loss. However, some parents may resist the negative social construction of their child's homosexuality and accept it in the fullest sense. Some become active in support groups or advocacy organizations, such as Parents and Friends of Lesbians and Gays (P-FLAG). This may be the most positive adjustment for the parents.

It is important to remember, however, that "stigmatized individuals are not merely passive victims but are frequently able actively to protect and buffer their self-esteem from prejudice and discrimination" (Crocker & Major 1989:624). Blumenfeld and Raymond (1988) note some positive outcomes of stigmatization for gay and lesbian people: (1) strengthening of ties with fellow minority-group members, which de Monteflores (1986) calls "ghettoization"; (2) sympathy with and support for other minorities; (3) enhanced striving and assertiveness; and (4) challenging the status quo so as to bring about progressive social change, which de Monteflores (1986) calls "confrontation." In fact, members of stigmatized groups often have much higher levels of self-esteem than might be predicted based on the prejudice and discrimination that they face (Crocker & Major 1989). There are several self-protective strategies that have been described which help increase self-esteem, such as identifying the prejudice directed against them for what it is and explaining experiences of rejection and perceived differences between themselves and others in the nonstigmatized group on that basis. Members of the stigmatized group may also reframe their own characteristics as positive and selectively devalue those of the dominant culture—what de Monteflores (1986) terms "specialization," that is, making oneself special as a consequence of the stigma. These strategies all tend to strengthen bonds among members of the stigmatized group (Crocker & Major 1989).

Concealment, or "passing," is one possible way to cope with stigma. A gay, lesbian, or bisexual person who does not fit the stereotype can "pass," that is, can allow or encourage others to believe that he or she is heterosexual, while those who meet the stereotyped expectations become visible. An individual may come to recognize his or her homosexual orientation without realistic models of what this means. The reaction may be "I'm the only person in the world like this"; or "I'm not like them, thank God." Parents and other family members and friends are also likely to avoid or deny disclosure when their loved one does not fit the stereotype. Passing also implies what de Monteflores (1986) calls "assimilation," or learning the ways of the dominant group. Thus a lesbian or gay person may have in-depth knowledge of both the dominant culture and the culture of the stigmatized subgroup, leading some to suggest that gay and lesbian people may be considered bicultural (Lukes & Land 1990).

Herek and Berrill (1992) in their study of gay and lesbian adolescents note that the rewards for appearing heterosexual are so great that those who can pass will as an effective stigma-avoiding strategy. However, the process of consciously hiding sexual orientation requires lying and often omitting some personal information. This strategy of deception distorts almost all relationships and creates an increasing sense of isolation. A major aspect of passing or concealment is the ever-present need to self-monitor (Martin & Hetrick 1988; Morrow 1993). Gay youth are reared in heterosexual families, peer groups, and educational institutions. Thus gay youth grow up learning the same stereotypes and negative judgments as their straight peers, threatening the sense of self. Because "passing" is so pervasive, gay youth are deprived of positive role models or the preparation for dealing with an openly gay, lesbian, or bisexual identity. Sustaining self-esteem and a sense of identity becomes problematic at best. However, many gay, lesbian, and bisexual people who feel compelled to hide their identities, their sexuality, and all facets of their individuality pay a heavy price.

Hammersmith (1989) also suggests there is a range of responses to stigmatization among lesbians and gays. These include stereotypic interpretations of behavior; social rejection, distancing, and discrimination; "passing" and altered self-concept; development of special subcultures; and "secondary deviation." The gay or lesbian, his or her parents, and the spouses and children of homosexual people are all confronted daily with this stereotyping and social rejection. The images of homosexuality are all negative: the "sinner," the "drag queen," the "child molester," the "diesel dyke." By the time one reaches adulthood, the association (not necessarily conscious) between homosexuality and the stereotype is formed. These dehumanizing stereotypes are perpetuated by the peer group, the mass media, and cultural tradition. The individual may feel pressure to establish distance from homosexuality. Few people, then, are socially and emotionally prepared to deal with this issues when it arises.

Rejection is another consequence of stigma, which produces distancing between those with the stigma and those without. Disclosure may become a critical issue in the family. The homosexual child may lose the sense of authenticity characteristic of family relationships if he or she keeps the secret, or face rejection if he or she seeks understanding and emotional support by disclosing the homosexuality. Potential alienation from the family is one way that the homosexual minority is different from other minority groups, who generally can count on support within the family in the face of stress from the outside world. This same dynamic will be true with friends and work colleagues. This process of deception may hinder the development of nonerotic friendships between members of the same sex. Closeness can be misunderstood. Maintenance of a facade becomes all-pervasive. Fears of ostracism, humiliation, and even violence deter the young homosexual from seeking to develop sympathetic others among peers. Secrecy brings about a different sort of distancing, such as the gay person who appears outwardly popular and well-liked by the group yet feels alienated and isolated.

The development of a subculture, a separate space that allows a sense of community and naturalness, is another possible response to stigma. The subculture may provide an opportunity to develop a special kinship with fellow victims of stigma. The stronger the disapproval by the majority culture, the more attractive a subculture as a source of stress reduction and mutual support will be. This strategy will be considered further in chapter 3.

The final means of coping with stigma identified by Hammersmith is that of the self-fulfilling prophecy or secondary deviance. This means that features of the stereotype may be embraced in protest or defiance or for lack of support for more normative styles of life. "Camp," "leather," and "bull dyke" are styles reflecting theatrical and humorous responses to society's arbitrary distinctions between masculine and feminine cultures and to specific stereotypes of gay and lesbian people. This poking fun at gender roles and stereotypes by flouting them is often seen by nongays as confirmation of their worst fears. In de Monteflores' (1986) terms, this strategy combines elements of confrontation and specialization.

INTERNALIZED HOMOPHOBIA

Gay men and lesbians must contend with psychological assault associated with stigma throughout life. Lesbians, gay men, and bisexuals have all grown up in a world where same-gender activity has often been considered morally repulsive and psychologically damaging. Lesbians and gay men have been taught to hate themselves—that is, to internalize homophobia or homonegativity. To "internalize" these negative attitudes means to take these negative attitudes into the self as conscious and/or unconscious beliefs. *Internalized homophobia* is defined here as a set of negative attitudes and affects toward homosexuality in other persons and toward homosexual features in oneself. These features include same-gender sexual and affectional feelings; same-gender sexual behavior; same-gender intimate relationships; and self-labeling as lesbian, gay, homosexual, or queer.

Internalized homophobia is a core construct in understanding gay and lesbian affirmative psychology and often in developing a focus for clinical intervention. First, the internalization of homophobia is a normative developmental event experienced to some degree by almost all gay men and lesbians in a heterosexist society. Second, it is a significant cause of psychosocial stress and pain. Third, reduction of internalized homophobia can be considered a successful outcome of ameliorative or preventive mental health intervention. "Similarly, conversion therapies that increase internalized homophobia can be viewed as psychologically damaging to gay persons" (Shidlo 1992:176).

Studies suggest that between 33 percent and 25 percent of lesbians and gay men (and possibly a larger proportion of black gay men) may have negative attitudes or feelings about their homosexuality at some point in their lives (Shidlo 1994). For example, in a study concerning attitudes of homosexuals about gay men, participants agreed that gay men are promiscuous, not effeminate, incapable of forming stable relationships, and should not be employed in schools. Cass (1979), Troiden (1979), and Sophie (1986), among others, suggest that successful lesbian and gay identity development, or coming out, involves a process of neutralizing internalized homophobia (see chapter 2).

The internalization of these negative attitudes often starts with an awareness of being different at an early point, at adolescence or even earlier. These negative feelings about sexual orientation may be overgeneralized to encompass the entire self. No one is totally protected from internalizing these negative attitudes, neither straights nor gays. Symptoms may range from a tendency toward self-doubt in the face of prejudice to unmistakable, overt self-hatred (Gonsiorek 1993a). Responses may include total denial of one's sexual orientation, contempt for the more open and "obvious" members of the community, distrust of other gay people, projection of prejudice onto others, sometimes marrying someone of the other sex to gain social approval, increased fear, and withdrawal from friends and relatives. Some even attempt to change their sexuality by entering into reparative or conversion therapy (see chapter 9). The high rates of suicide and substance abuse among lesbians and gays are thought to be indications of this self-hate (Bradford & Ryan 1988; Shernoff & Scott 1988). Shidlo (1994) summarized the observations of many other writers who suggest that internalized homophobia is related to distrust and loneliness, difficulties in intimate and affectional relationships, under- and overachievement, impaired sexual functioning, unsafe sex, domestic violence, avoidance in coping with AIDS, alcoholism, substance abuse, eating disorders, fragmentation, and borderline-like features and suicide.

Malyon (1982a), viewing internalized homophobia from a psychodynamic perspective, hypothesized that internalized homophobia not only causes depression but also influences identity formation, self-esteem, the elaboration of defenses, patterns of cognition, psychological integrity, object relations, and superego functioning. He views the pathogenic effects of internalized homophobia as a (usually temporary) suppression of homosexual feelings, an elaboration of a heterosexual persona, and an interruption of the process of identity formation. Mallon (1982a) proposed that negative attitudes are incorporated into one's self-image, causing a fragmentation of sexual and affectional facets of the self that interferes with the developmental process.

In summary, human beings cannot escape the influence of social position and social expectations on their individual development and self-perception. Bradford and Ryan (1988:4) note that "those who are discriminated against or who expect to face discrimination if their 'condition' were to become known are different from those who do not occupy stigmatized or 'deviant' social positions. The connection between living on the margins of society and the impact of this upon daily life and an adequate sense of psychosocial security" is yet to be fully documented. However, we do know that lesbians and gay men always live with this tension. Reflecting on her experience with racism, bell hooks notes that

> to be in the margin is to be part of the whole but outside the main body. . . . Living as we did—on the edge—we developed a particular way of seeing reality. We looked both from the outside in and from the inside out. We focused our attention on the center as well as on the margin. We understood both. . . . Our survival depended on an ongoing public awareness of the separation between margin and center and an ongoing private acknowledgment that we were a necessary, vital part of that whole. . . . This sense of wholeness, impressed upon our consciousness by the structure of our daily lives, provided us an oppositional world view—a mode of seeing unknown to most of our oppressors, that sustained us, aided us in our struggle to transcend poverty and despair, strengthen our sense of self and our solidarity.   (hooks 1984:preface)

Lesbian, gay, and bisexual people experience the margin and the center as a skill of bicultural competence—the ability to navigate successfully between two worlds—as do other minorities. To accomplish this, social supports are necessary. Discrimination often results in being barred from participation in community institutions that sustain other members of society. Lesbians and gay men must either create their own social systems or live in relative isolation from sympathetic others. Since lack of adequate social connection can have a significant impact on health, it is reasonable to assume that gay, lesbian, and bisexual people are often vulnerable to a type of stress not normally experienced by straights. These psychological vulnerabilities are, to a significant extent, the result of psychological heterosexism—that is, to the psychological effects of these stigmatization processes rather than to anything inherent in a lesbian, gay, or bisexual identity itself.

Attitudes Toward Lesbian, Gay, and Bisexual People

Although lesbian, gay, and bisexual stigmatization is widespread in the general population, there is great variability among individuals in their attitudes toward lesbian, gay, and bisexual people. As with racism, sexism, and other prejudices that are supported by the culture at large, the fact that heterosexism and homophobia are institutionalized in a variety of ways does not mean that every person in the society shares in those attitudes to the same degree. It is important to know what can make a difference in individual attitudes toward lesbian, gay, and bisexual people in order to create positive change.

There are several factors that have been consistently shown to make a difference on average in how people feel about gay and lesbian people.[1] People who say they personally know a gay or lesbian person are consistently less likely to oppose gay rights than those who do not (Nava & Dawidoff 1994; Herek 1995). Conversely, those who hold strong and/or traditional religious beliefs, traditional beliefs about gender roles, and/or who live in regions of the country where such beliefs are common are more likely on average to have negative attitudes toward gays and lesbians. In addition, those who are older and who have less education are also likely to be more negative in their views. On average, heterosexual women are less likely to express negative attitudes toward gay and lesbian people, especially gay men, than heterosexual men do (Herek 1995). Some of these factors, like having prior, pleasant contact with a person from the oppressed group, have been found to hold true for racism and other prejudices as well.

PROFESSIONALS' ATTITUDES

Health and mental health professionals, including social workers, are not immune from the negative attitudes toward gay, lesbian, and bisexual people that other Americans share. But their attitudes are especially significant in that these are the professionals who have responsibility for assisting gay, lesbian, and bisexual clients to cope with the personal and social consequences of homophobia, to work through the shame and guilt imposed by a homophobic and heterosexist society, to develop a positive lesbian or gay identity, and to help with the management of stigma and stress. Nonjudgmental attitudes are necessary to support social change and to end individual and organizational prejudice.

Mental health professionals must accept the fact that we, as individuals and as professionals, have been very much a part of the problem. In the past we have promoted the deviance labeling that the heterosexual majority uses to support oppressive laws, customs, and social actions.

(Woodman & Lenna 1980:24)

Gay men and lesbians have not always been well served by the health, mental health, and social services professions.

The homophobia of health and mental health professionals has been well documented (DeCrescenzo 1984; Moses & Hawkins 1982). In these studies homophobia was most prevalent among social workers. Because homophobia and heterosexism are social forces that permeate all aspects of social life, social service agencies and social work professionals are not immune to them. The belief that sexual minorities could change their orientation if they really wanted to is still a prevalent notion within our society. Other misconceptions that force lesbian, gay, and bisexual people to remain "in the closet" are that gays should not be teachers, should not have custody of their children, should be excluded from the military, are child molesters, and have a "choice" to act on their "preference." These misconceptions, shared by both the lay and professional public, make it difficult for lesbian and gay clients to seek help. As with all minorities, peer and practitioner validation are crucial to healthy identity development. Although attitudes about homosexuality in the helping professions as a whole have been changing for the better since the 1970s, both workers and clients may unfortunately still be affected by the residue of outmoded psychological theory that until recently viewed homosexuality as pathology (see chapter 9). For example, the history of gay and lesbian forced psychiatric hospitalization, imprisonment, socially sanctioned violence and discrimination is not a solid foundation for institutional trust but rather more rightly serves as a basis for cynicism and healthy paranoia. The elimination of homosexuality from the nosology of the APA's revised (1994) *Diagnostic and Statistical Manual of Mental Disorders* (DSM III-R) did not eliminate homophobic attitudes. As Forstein (1988) and Dulaney and Kelly (1982) note, this elimination has not changed the personal opinion of the majority of the professional mental health community. Unfortunately, the most recent studies continue to suggest that negative attitudes toward homosexuality and homosexual clients persist among some social workers and social work students (Berkman & Zinberg 1997; Eliason 1995; R. R. Greene 1994; Harris, Nightengale, & Owen 1995). Prejudice toward lesbian, gay, and bisexual social workers has also resulted in discriminatory personnel practices in health and social service agencies, which leads to unnecessary stress (see chapter 7).

A survey of counseling students regarding attitudes toward minority clients found average to high homophobia despite positive attitudes toward racial and ethnic minorities. Students with more experience with sexual minorities, however, demonstrated lower levels of homophobia (McDermott, Tyndall, & Lichtenberg 1989). Social workers' and other helping professionals' feelings, attitudes, and level of comfort with gay or lesbian orientation must be examined; they require self-exploration over time.

Unfortunately, the AIDS epidemic has had a negative effect on attitudes. Douglas, Kalman, and Kalman's (1985) study of homophobia among 91 physicians and 261 nurses found that 31 percent of the respondents admitted they have felt more negative about homosexuality since the emergence of AIDS (Eliason & Raheim 1996). Wallach (1989) reports similar findings among physicians and nurses in a major New York teaching hospital, with 9 percent of the respondents agreeing that AIDS is God's punishment to homosexuals and 6 percent agreeing that patients who choose homosexuality deserve to get AIDS. Dupras, Levy, and Samson (1989) found that negative attitudes about AIDS were better predicted by homophobia than by other measures.

In a comparative study of MSW students and age-matched lesbians living in urban Connecticut, progress is seen. While lesbians scored lower on the Index of Homophobia than did MSW students, both groups on average were not homophobic (Thompson 1991). In a study of undergraduate and graduate social work students, Appleby (1996) found graduate students to be significantly less homophobic than undergraduates. In addition, negative attitudes changed over time with greater exposure to affirmative lesbian and gay content in courses.

The Committee on Lesbian and Gay Concerns of the American Psychological Association conducted an extensive study of biased practice with lesbians and gay men (American Psychological Association 1991). They found that 58.2 percent of therapists reported personally knowing about incidents of professional bias against gay and lesbian clients. Examples of bias were reported in three broad therapeutic areas. "First, examples of bias in strategies of assessment and intervention included a therapist who attributes a client's problem to his/her sexual orientation without evidence that this attribution is accurate, a therapist's failure to recognize that a client's psychological symptoms or distress can be influenced by the client's own negative ideas about homosexuality, and a therapist who seeks to change the sexual orientation of a client when not requested to do so (10–14). A second set of examples of bias included therapists who viewed gay identity solely in terms of sexual behavior or who interpreted a client's identity as a "phase" that will be temporary. Third, they reported examples of bias in expertise and training where the therapist taught inaccurate information or expressed antigay attitudes to colleagues or students. These observations of biased psychotherapeutic practice serve as additional evidence of what Herek refers to as cultural heterosexism. Without a significant effort to expand affirming mental health services, the emotional needs of gays and lesbians will not be adequately met in formal health and mental health service systems, leading many to rely instead on self-help efforts (Appleby & Anastas 1992; Berger & Kelly 1986).

Psychoanalytic thinking has historically informed the practice of clinical social work and can be seen today as a continuing influence. Drescher (in press), an analyst, in his exceptionally thorough review of homosexuality and psychoanalytic thinking suggests that history "reinforces the impression that psychoanalytic theories cannot be divorced from the political, cultural, and personal context in which they are formulated" (13–14). He notes that, while the present psychoanalytic position is one of tolerance, this can be reversed as society becomes less tolerant. Nicolosi's (1991) *Reparative Therapy of Male Homosexuality* is offered by Drescher as an example of how contemporary religious intolerance of homosexuality can fuse psychoanalytic theories that pathologize homosexuality with pastoral counseling for homosexuals. The power to marginalize is an ever-present possibility in the act of labeling, assessing, or diagnosing.

Social stereotypes of lesbian, gay, and bisexual people lie at the heart of why homosexuality is a psychological issue of such significance to both gay, lesbian, and bisexual individuals and their families. Because the social stereotypes of homosexuality are so negative and so false, gay, lesbian, and bisexual people must reject them in order to establish a self-affirmed, psychologically adaptive identity (Weinberg & Williams 1974). Their families may experience similar processes and may also need help in resisting these negative social constructions. They must reject their own stereotypes and develop new values about homosexuality that do not stigmatize their gay, lesbian, or bisexual relative. Most lesbians and gay men and their families will work out these issues on their own with the support of friends and families of choice (Berzon 1992). However, there is a significant minority who need the assistance of a professional helping person to address the pain and hurt arising from these complex processes. In addition, like all people, they may need help for reasons totally unrelated to their sexual orientation but may fear getting it because they are uncertain about how they will be viewed. Because many gay men and lesbians remember or learn through oral tradition the vigor with which they have been pathologized by those who offered help, the social worker may find developing an effective working relationship with these clients a challenge. However, whatever the sexual orientation of the social worker, gay, lesbian, and bisexual people respond well to and will benefit from knowledgeable and affirmative practice. The social worker needs a framework for understanding and a framework for doing, a theory for practice and a theory of practice.

Implications for Practice

Most interpersonal practice with lesbians, gays, and bisexuals does not come to the attention of the social worker identified as such. The "friend" or "roommate" who brought the heart attack victim to the hospital and seeks to visit him or her in the intensive care unit; the parent of the first-grader with a visual impairment who meets with the school social worker to discuss the child's adjustment to school; the middle-aged woman attending a support group for those caring for elderly parents with Alzheimer's disease; the adolescent referred to the mental health center because he or she is feeling depressed or suicidal—any of these may be a client who is lesbian, gay, or bisexual.

Failure to consider that a client may be gay, lesbian, or bisexual (i.e., the presumption of heterosexuality) is the most common mistake made by workers in situations like the ones described above. Despite stereotypes, most lesbian, gay, and bisexual clients are not visually identifiable as such, and many may not identify themselves as gay or lesbian at first, especially when the problem for which they are seeking assistance may not have much to do with sexual orientation (Hall 1978). However, the social worker is unlikely to get a full enough picture of the client's situation in order to be helpful without keeping an open mind to the possibility of a gay, lesbian, or bisexual identity. Thus, effective practice with lesbians and gay men requires what Hall has termed a dual focus: "The practitioner must be able to see the ways in which the client's presenting problem is both affected by and separate from her sexual orientation" (1978:380). Damage to self-esteem resulting from oppression and stigmatization must always be considered, but at the same time the client probably occupies roles, works on developmental tasks, and experiences feelings in which being gay, lesbian, or bisexual is incidental.

In dealing with a situation where the sexual orientation of the client is unknown, having an attitude and using language that conveys an openness to either a heterosexual or a homosexual possibility are critically important. If a presumption of heterosexuality is made, as it usually is, or if it is assumed that the client's most important ties are only biological ones, it can be actively, if unwittingly, painful and alienating to the client seeking help. Exploring the situation with an open mind to whatever identity the client chooses to convey will be both more comfortable for the client and more fruitful for the worker who genuinely wishes to understand the client's reality.

FRAMEWORK FOR PRACTICE

Contemporary social work views human needs and problems as generated by the transactions between people and their environments. The goal of practice is to enhance and restore the psychosocial functioning of persons, or to change the oppressive or destructive social conditions that negatively affect the interaction between persons and their environments. The ecological model of practice (Compton & Galaway 1989; Germain 1991; Hepworth & Larsen 1993; Meyer 1993), the framework used in this text, consists of five interconnected domains or levels: (1) the historical, (2) the environmental-structural, (3) the cultural, (4) the familial, and (5) the individual. The lives and social conditions of lesbians, bisexuals, and gay men should be assessed in relation to each of these domains.

> Seeing only one "normal" pattern of [human functioning] ignores the cultural, social, and genetic factors that lead to multiple views of appropriate life goals and multiple resources and behavioral networks to achieve them. Therefore, human behavior must be understood as resulting from the interplay of equally important psychological, social, cultural, and biological factors.   —Ron Federico (1979:181)

The ecological model of practice recognizes that transactions between the individual and the environment are products of all these domains or levels and thus are complex and disruptive of the usual adaptive balance or goodness of fit, often resulting in stress. This approach to practice emphasizes the adaptive, evolutionary view of human beings in constant interchange with all elements of their environment (Compton & Galaway 1989; Germain 1991; Hepworth & Larsen 1993; Meyer 1993). Adaptation, a key concept in this framework, refers to the exchanges of information, energy, and matter between persons and environments. This is an active, dynamic, and often creative process wherein each element of the ecosystem shapes the other. The practitioner's task may be to assist directly or indirectly in the process of developing a positive gay identity, to manage the information around the stigmatized identity, and to advocate for more nurturing (nonhomophobic and nonheterosexist) environments. In this model, the worker's attention is directed to *people's problems of living*, and the importance of client strengths is readily apparent.

The *history* of positive and noxious factors in the experience of people sets the context for understanding any presenting problem. The history of group oppression and exploitation has been noted. It has taken form in religion, culture, law, and social sanction. American society, strongly influenced by interpretations of Judeo-Christian moral codes, is one of the most homophobic. While change is in fact taking place in each of these areas, not one of these social structures could be characterized as nurturing. At best, they are benign (Appleby & Anastas 1992).

Homophobia and heterosexism are probably the most relevant *environmental or structural issues* affecting lesbians and gays. This dynamic, compounded with sexism and racism, has generated barriers to the healthy development and well-being of lesbians and gays. In addition, popular images often suggest that gay and lesbian people are involved with a specific *subculture* or lifestyle. While styles, activities, and institutions designated as exclusively gay and/or lesbian do exist, in fact gay, lesbian, and bisexual people more often form an *invisible* minority, only some of whom choose to make themselves and their interests visible individually and collectively in the form of a subculture or community.

The *family* is the primary institution responsible for social adaptation. The practitioner focuses on the family to better understand the potential strengths and barriers to psychosocial functioning. Also, despite the many negative perceptions, millions of gays and lesbians are parents of minor children (see chapter 6), are involved in long-term, committed, coupled relationships (see chapter 5), and have positive relations with their family of orientation (birth) and family of choice (lover and friends). Thus while the concept of "family" has traditionally been seen as nearly irrelevant to them, families are just as important to lesbians and gays as to others (Laird & Green 1996).

The *individual domain* requires that we understand the unique experiences of lesbians, bisexuals, and gay people in relation to identity formation, adaptation, and development (see chapter 2), intrapersonal conflict, emotional support, and a wide array of psychosocial stressors throughout their life span. Lesbians and gay men seek psychotherapy more frequently than heterosexuals because of the many problems they face (see chapter 9). Some of these problems include but are not limited to the effects of increased rates of assault, feelings of regret, shame, and loss about being gay, relationship conflicts, discrimination, and alcoholism and other drug dependency. Studies designed to gauge client satisfaction with psychotherapy are frequently negative (Rudolph 1989b).

Practitioners must also be reminded that internalized homophobia, a core construct in identity development, impedes the ability to cope and adapt and to change one's environment. High internalized homophobia appears significantly associated with overall psychological distress and other measures of adjustment, lower self-esteem, lower social support and satisfaction with support, less gay support relative to nongay supports, less overlap between gay and nongay networks, greater loneliness, and high-risk sexual behavior (Shidlo 1994). Because of the strong relationship between internalized homophobia and a variety of psychopathological conditions, clinicians should routinely include assessment and treatment of internalized homophobia when working with lesbian and gay people (Gonsiorek 1982b; Malyon 1982a; Stein & Cohen 1984b). Placing individual needs, problems, or difficulties into a broader social fabric of oppression, power, heterosexism, homophobia, stigma, and stress management is necessary if we as social work practitioners are to gain a better understanding of the life space of gay, lesbian, and bisexual clients (Levi 1993).

The ecological model of practice also deals with the *processes* that give rise to stress and problems in living. Germain and Gitterman (1980) define stress as a psychosocial condition "generated by discrepancies between needs and capacities, on the one hand, and environmental qualities on the other. It arises in three interrelated areas of living; *life transitions, environmental pressures*, and *interpersonal processes*" (7; emphasis added). New responses are required by the changing demands associated with life transitions. All life transitions require cognitive, affective, and behavioral or relational shifts because of changes in the capacities, self-image, worldview, uses of environmental resources, and the development of new goals. All these shifts require the restructuring of one's life space. For example, the lesbian or gay client often experiences major shifts in confronting the life transitions of "coming out" (see chapter 2), pairing with a "life partner" (chapter 5), having children (chapter 6), or aging (chapter 8). Stress is likely to be especially great if the change is sudden and unexpected, whereas gradual change affords time for advance preparation.

Environments can be the source of stress depending on whether they support or interfere with life transitions. Opportunity structures may be closed to marginalized groups. The presence of well-organized hate groups such as the Society for the Advancement of Straight People or Family Values Councils, as well as state statutes that promote gay and lesbian discrimination, will cause stress in even the most well-adjusted individual. And organizations designed to meet adaptive needs, like health, mental health, and social service agencies, may themselves have stressful policies and procedures. Social networks, such as coworker and professional associations, may also be unresponsive, so that isolation or conflict results. Even physical settings may be unsuitable and lead to stress.

Interpersonal processes can also lead to adaptive challenges. Primary groups such as family and friends, in dealing with life transitions or unresponsive environments, may experience added stress because of relationship patterns within the group itself. Maladaptive processes such as inconsistent mutual expectations, exploitative relationships, and blocks in communication are sources of stress to the individual member and to the family or group itself (Germain 1991).

Interpersonal interventions should address client powerlessness by using strategies that enable clients to experience themselves as competent, valuable, and worthwhile both as individuals and as members of their gay and lesbian cultural group. The practitioner must use his/her professional power to facilitate a cognitive and behavioral shift in the client's sense of being trapped in a subordinate role, to counter the myths and stereotypes about homosexuality, to avoid the internalization or acting-out of stereotypes, to change negative cultural identity and the self-perception of being powerless and a victim, and to learn new strategies for not colluding in one's own victimization. Such strategies are often referred to as *stigma management*, a lifelong process of information management concerning sexual orientation and identity (Levi 1993). It is a process of carefully controlling what others know about one's sexuality. The practitioner may help the client learn to share his/her sexual identity or to conceal it, depending upon the particular situation. These strategies, according to Cain (1991b), actually involve complex interactional negotiations. Disclosure often entails careful planning and execution, and concealment requires close attention to many details of social presentation. Herdt and Boxer (1991) would argue, however, that the practice remedies discussed in this section represent an older and more traditional social service model, wherein pathology, stigma, contaminated self, and stigma management are core constructs and therefore are off the mark in terms of the needs of the lesbian, gay, and bisexual communities. They would advocate for a "queer" model that emphasizes building a "queer" community, positive "queer" identity, and radical social action. The practice interventions would include community development, community and public education, consciousness-raising and self-help groups, political mobilization, and coalition building with other oppressed groups, with the intent of transforming society. This controversy reflects an age-old macro versus micro practice debate or the "either/or" position of social transformation versus reform and remedial change. The profession historically has moved back and forth between these two positions. Many practitioners attempt to combine both approaches, leaving the philosophical and theoretical debate to social work faculty.

However, the perspective of this text suggests that the psychosocial forces previously discussed be reframed so as to inform social work practice that focuses on policy and community change. Practitioners must understand and direct their energies to environmental pressures (homophobia translated into discrimination, violence, prejudice, and the lack of civil rights protections) and into action that influences society's definition of and response to the social problems, needs, or concerns of the lesbian, gay, and bisexual community. Practitioners must be skilled in mobilizing the political and collective will so as to transform "personal troubles" into "public issues" (Mills 1959). Finally, practitioners should design and implement, with extensive input from lesbians, gay men, and bisexuals, effective laws, program policies, and community-based institutions and services. These should reflect the values of the profession and be based on sound knowledge about gay, lesbian, and bisexual people as presented in this text.

A Diversity Perspective

The task ahead is to better understand the life transitions, environmental pressures, and interpersonal processes that are unique to gay, lesbian, and bisexual people. While this general model of intervention moves us in that direction, it becomes more complicated in the specifics. If the practitioner were to draw upon normative theories of human functioning associated with the five levels of assessment noted above or the three processes in living just described when assisting a gay, lesbian, or bisexual client, the psychosocial assessment and the interventions made might well be wrong or even fail. The assumptions made by the clinician would not take into account the specific cultural context within which his/her gay, lesbian, or bisexual clients function, their strengths, their adaptations as a result of little-known community resources, or their effective coping strategies typical of most minorities.

This failure to recognize the lesbian or gay client's strengths would be partially due to the societal norm of cultural blindness, or the *melting pot* ethos. The yardstick used is that of the white, middle-class, heterosexual for understanding and delivering services (Pinderhughes 1989). Effective practitioners act on the social work commitment to respect human diversity by placing all clients in their own cultural context and then drawing upon a strengths perspective (Saleebey 1997) wherein it is assumed that all clients possess untapped reserves of mental, physical, and emotional resources than can be called upon to help them develop, grow, and overcome their problems. The social work literature related to feminist practice (Van Den Bergh & Cooper 1989) or work with people of color (DeVore & Schlesinger 1982; Pinderhughes 1989; and Solomon

1982) offers a clarity of perspective on assessment as well as a range of empowering interventions appropriate for the lesbian, bisexual, or gay client.

An ecological perspective that is supported by a diversity framework can help the worker to get beyond the ethnocentric, class-biased, heterosexist formulations of normative theories. The client's perception of his or her life problem or stress, as well as the worker's understanding of that perception, must be seen as complex and variable. Particular events or processes are not necessarily experienced by all people in the same way as either negative or positive. Other factors, such as social supports/networks (Maguire 1983; Waters 1994), hope (Snyder 1994), or a sense of coherence (Antonovsky 1987), may intervene in significant ways. Age, gender, sexual orientation, race, social class, spirituality/religion, ethnicity, abilities, lifestyle and culture, health status, experience, attitudes, vulnerability, and other personality features will affect whether an event, status, or process will be experienced as stressful or not. It is important to remember that there is often as much diversity within a particular group as between groups. Therefore, any client should be asked to differentiate his or her own individual experiences as a member of a particular diversity or reference group as a cautionary step against working from stereotypic assumptions (R. R. Greene 1994).

Just as there is an extensive literature related to ecological and empowerment models of social work practice, the recent attention given to cross-cultural or diversity practice has been impressive. There seems to be a consensus that, minimally, practitioners should start with an awareness of one's own culture; be open to cultural difference; be committed to a client-oriented, systematic learning style; use cultural awareness; and acknowledge the integrity of culture. Greene (1994) in her summary of this literature notes that it is impossible to gain intimate, comprehensive, detailed knowledge on all groups; thus it seems improbable that an overarching model will emerge. However, it is clear that for multicultural practice to be effective, the client (his/her experience and meaning) must be put at the center of the helping process. This involves an attitude of respect for the client's experiences and lifestyle, an appreciation of the client's right of self-determination, some knowledge about the culture of the client's group, skill in helping, and knowledge of human behavior. This text is designed to provide the social work practitioner with the knowledge about gay, lesbian, and bisexual people necessary to fulfill this goal.

Summary and Conclusions

Heterosexism and homophobia form the context of oppression in which gay, lesbian, and bisexual people live their lives. These prejudices affect all people—heterosexual and homosexual—including those who provide health, mental health, and social services. The ecological perspective on social work practice, with its emphasis on the life processes of adaptation and reciprocal interaction between people and their physical and social environments, supported by a diversity framework, seems well suited as a foundation for work with lesbian, gay, and bisexual people. Basic and applied research studies are needed to better understand the way gay, lesbian, and bisexual clients cope with life transitions and develop competent interpersonal processes, and how these influence or are influenced by the larger social and environmental forces. Effective interventions that focus on change in both the environment and the individual should be based on systematic practice research. However, there is already a substantial social science knowledge base addressing sexual orientation that can be applied successfully to social work with lesbian, gay, and bisexual people. The remainder of this book is devoted to presenting it in a way that emphasizes its application to practice in social work today.

2

Gay, Lesbian, and Bisexual Identities

Definitions and Dilemmas

What does it mean to be lesbian, gay, or bisexual? What causes a person to become lesbian, gay, or bisexual? How many lesbian, gay, or bisexual people are there in the United States? What does "coming out" mean? And how do race, culture, and ethnicity influence the development of a lesbian, gay, or bisexual identity? This chapter summarizes what is known about the answers to these important questions and the controversies that surround these issues today.

As the social sciences and the human services professions have begun to learn more about gay, lesbian, and bisexual people, it has become evident that there is tremendous variation in gay, lesbian, and bisexual lives as they are and have been lived in different social groups, cultures, geographical areas, and historical epochs. While this recognition of differences has led to increased tolerance and understanding, it has made defining and talking about sexual orientation more difficult and complex. This chapter will review the contemporary terms and concepts used in defining sexual orientation and its variations, highlighting the many controversies that surround how gay, lesbian, and bisexual identities are described and understood. While all these issues have important political ramifications, the emphasis here is on how these issues are understood in a professional context and how they inform assessment and intervention in social work practice today.

What Is Sexual Orientation?

A first-year college student, aged eighteen, seeks out a counselor at the student mental health service because of anxiety. While she has so far done well in her courses, she is finding it increasingly difficult to concentrate and is worried about passing her upcoming exams because she is finding it hard to study and to remember what she has read. She mentions being concerned that she sometimes feels sexually aroused by the sight of naked women. She dated men in high school but never in an intense or long-lasting relationship, and while she feels quite close to several female friends she has made in her dorm, she has not met any young man she has been interested in at college. She is lonely and confused and wants to know what her feelings about women mean.

A single medical technician in his twenties presents himself at a large city health center requesting a referral for counseling. He reports that, during his training, he had become close friends with a fellow student, a woman. After a long period of friendship, their relationship had become sexual and they had become engaged shortly before graduation. After graduation, however, she moved to another city because of an excellent job opportunity there. During this same period of study, the young man had also been mentored and seduced by a male instructor in the program. Although he had successfully broken off the sexual relationship with his mentor after only a brief period, he had remained in social contact with his former teacher, who urged him to acknowledge a gay identity. Meanwhile, he and his fiancée had not been able to commit to a wedding date or to adapt their personal plans so that they could live in the same city and resume a sexual relationship. He complains of loneliness, confusion about his sexual identity, and frustration in his efforts to develop a more satisfying intimate relationship with his fiancée.

A forty-five-year-old woman who has been married for twenty years seeks out a clinical social worker because she has become severely depressed. She has children aged eighteen, fifteen, and twelve to whom both she and her husband are very devoted. She identifies herself as a feminist and is rather unconventional in her dress, favoring extremely tailored and/or casual clothes. She has had two brief affairs with women, one many years ago when she was attending an all-female undergraduate college and another just a few years ago that grew out of a friendship made in a local feminist organization in which she was active. She complains that, while she loves her husband, they do not communicate well, although they continue to have sexual relations occasionally that are enjoyable to them both. However, she thinks she must confront the fact that she is "really" a lesbian because she has again become attracted to a woman.

Human behavior surrounding sexuality, intimacy, affection, and identity is complex, and this complexity has to be acknowledged when dealing with sexual orientation. Is a gay, lesbian, or bisexual orientation something that people are "born with" or something that is formed out of early developmental and/or later social and sexual experiences? Do people always have a single sexual orientation or identity throughout their lives or can it change? What is the difference between bisexuality and a multiple or changed sexual orientation or identity, or is there any? These complicated questions confront social workers and other helping professionals, and they confront their clients as well. How a person answers these questions for him/herself can have enormous consequences, as the case vignettes above illustrate. Social workers and other mental health professionals must understand the complex issues involved in defining sexual orientation in order to help the many clients they will see for whom questions about sexual orientation will arise, questions that may be troubling to them, as they were for the people described above. An informed professional understanding of these questions about the definitions and origins of sexual orientation are equally important for advocacy and policy.

Even the words that are used to describe gay, lesbian, and bisexual identity are complicated and hotly debated. For example, the term *sexual preference*, once considered "correct" for describing gay, lesbian, or bisexual phenomena, is now rejected by many because it seems to reduce a core identity or master status to a matter of taste, like whether one likes chocolate or vanilla ice cream. The term *sexual orientation*, which is the one used in this book, is now generally preferred because it seems to suggest something more fundamental to the person than just a casual choice among equally available alternatives. The other term used here, *sexual identity*. emphasizes self-labeling, although it has both social and psychological components. However, sexual orientation can be seen as more stable than sexual identity, which may change over a person's lifetime (Chung & Katayama 1996).

UNDERSTANDING SEXUAL ORIENTATION

Just as gay, lesbian, and bisexual people must negotiate their social and psychological identity development in the context of a homophobic and heterosexist society, social workers and other mental health professionals must develop their understanding of sexual orientation issues in a context that, until recently, viewed homosexuality as a pathology in and of itself. It was only in 1973 that the American Psychiatric Association (APA), which sets the prevailing terms in the United States for classifying psychopathology through its *Diagnostic and Statistical Manual*, now in its fourth edition (American Psychiatric Association 1994), removed homosexuality from its list of psychiatric disorders. Thus anyone living with such an identification or learning about mental health before that time had to deal with the prevailing psychiatric view that a homosexual sexual orientation was a mental illness. It is not surprising, therefore, that the remnants of that attitude are still commonly encountered in a professional context today—in professionals, in clients, in their families, and in the community.

The view of a gay, lesbian, or bisexual orientation as a form of psychopathology was gradually replaced by the idea that being lesbian or gay is a stable and fixed *positive* identity. The gay liberation movement became nationally visible after the Stonewall Rebellion of 1969, when gays and lesbians in New York City resisted a routine police raid on the Stonewall bar in Greenwich Village, touching off several days of street demonstrations. Assertion of an openly gay or lesbian identity began to have a formal political meaning connected to activism on behalf of gay rights. This movement for gay civil and human rights continues today, and being "out," or publicly self-identified, as gay or lesbian continues to be an important political statement as well as a personal one, especially in the urban areas that have openly gay, lesbian, and bisexual communities.

The controversy over the political strategy of "outing," or revealing someone else's previously undisclosed gay, lesbian, or bisexual orientation, has highlighted the great differences in how lesbian, gay, and bisexual people choose to manage their lives, especially when they do not live in those major metropolitan areas with visible gay and lesbian communities and/or when they fear that open identification of themselves as lesbian, gay, or bisexual may compromise their work or family lives (Garnets & Kimmel 1993). In addition, while some people assume a gay or lesbian self-identification relatively early in life and do not change in that identification over the life course, all the research studies done of human sexuality and sexual behavior, including the most recent at this writing (Laumann et al. 1994), demonstrate that many others have a more complicated identity over time or in the present and that what people actually do sexually is much more varied than a simple self-label of "gay" or "straight" implies. One of the consequences of this more realistic and complex understanding of sexuality and sexual orientation has been to focus attention on bisexuality as an identity rather than seeing it only as a "way station" to or from a "gay" or "straight" identity. For all these reasons, a sophisticated and up-to-date professional understanding of sexual orientation issues is essential for all social workers.

What is sexual orientation? As the term will be used in this book, *sexual orientation refers to a characteristic of an individual that describes the people he or she is drawn to for satisfying intimate affectional and sexual needs—people of the same gender, the opposite gender, or of both genders*. We use the terms *lesbian* and *gay* in preference to *homosexual* to refer to men and women who are not heterosexual, or "straight." In part, this is done because of the history of pathologizing attached to the term *homosexual*; but also, it is done because patterns of development and adaptation to a same-gender sexual orientation, like many other aspects of development, tend to differ somewhat between men and women. Nevertheless, we sometimes use the term *homosexual* to refer to both genders together, especially to refer to specifically sexual phenomena. Still, the term *homosexual* has been used in the past to refer only to males, so care must be taken in using the term not to render the experiences of women invisible (Garnets & Kimmel 1993). However, the terms *gay* and *lesbian* are often used to refer to men and women who not only engage in same-gender sexual and/ or affectional activities but who also adopt what is termed a homosexual "lifestyle" to some degree or other. Some object to this concept of "lifestyle," too, because it may seem to trivialize what is a life by suggesting that it has elements of "fashion" to it. In fact, this discussion touches on the controversy about whether or not there is a gay or lesbian culture in the true sense of the term and about whether or not open participation in that culture is necessarily desirable for lesbians, gays, and bisexuals (Lukes & Land 1990). This issue of culture will be discussed in greater depth in chapter 3.

The term *sexual identity*, which is increasingly emphasized in the literature, refers to *self-labeling as lesbian, gay, or bisexual* (Reiter 1989). Because sexual behavior and self-labeling are often not consistent with each other, some have differentiated the concepts by noting that "identity changes [while] orientation endures" (Reiter 1989:138). Although sexual identity is usually experienced as psychological, or internal, it is also influenced by interpersonal, social, and cultural experience (Cox & Gallois 1996). However, "sexual identity" is used by some authors to refer simply to sexual orientation, not necessarily to self-labeling (Burch 1993).

Garnets and Kimmel (1993) point out that there are three different levels of meaning for sexual orientation. The first is the political, which asserts that "sexual orientation has a particular meaning because one's social environment imposes that meaning" (55). This level of understanding of sexual orientation draws attention to the historical and social study of homosexuality and, in the context of present-day United States, to the history of gay and lesbian political activism in the latter half of this century. The second level is that of individual psychology, which is the one that most mental health professionals are familiar with. At this level, it is important to note that a gay, lesbian, or bisexual identity may have different psychological meanings to different individuals (Burch 1993). The third level posited by Garnets and Kimmel (1993) is "the interaction between the sociopolitical and the psychological viewpoints" (56), which is what makes the definition of sexual orientation or sexual identity, both in professional and social life, so complex. However, for social work, which is accustomed to dealing with the biopsychosocial interface, this concept of the interaction of the personal and the political is a framework that most are comfortable with.

Most of the efforts to define homosexuality and bisexuality in published research have used either self-identification or an assumption of sexual orientation based on the setting from which participants were recruited (Chung & Katayama 1996; Sell & Petrulio 1996). However, others have focused on the behavioral meaning of sexual orientation. Because Kinsey's research (Kinsey, Pomeroy, & Martin 1948; Kinsey et al. 1953) made such an impact and has been so widely read and quoted, it is important to understand it. Alfred Kinsey developed his famous scale to measure *degrees* of homosexuality because he did not believe that all people could be neatly divided into two groups, homosexual and heterosexual, a point of view that has been validated in his research and in all research on sexual behavior done since then. Kinsey in fact used a seven-point scale, from 0 through 6, to measure homosexuality; 0 indicated someone who reported only heterosexual experiences in his or her life, and 6 indicated someone who reported only homosexual experiences throughout his or her life. Although many people were indeed classified as 0 or 6 on this scale, which was based on retrospective accounts of self-reported sexual *behavior*, there were also many people who had ratings of 1, 2, 3, 4, and 5, reflecting specific *degrees* of variation in their sexual experiences. This idea of a degree of homosexuality has been retained in most subsequent research on sexual orientation and sexual behavior; in fact, in recognition of the observation that feelings, attractions, and behaviors often differ *within* individuals, this concept of degrees of homosexuality has been expanded to include sexual feelings, fantasies, and attractions (Laumann et al. 1994), affectional, emotional, and romantic or social attractions and preferences (Klein 1993; Shively and DeCecco 1993; Weinberg, Williams, & Pryor 1994), and past, present, and future (Klein 1993) as additional, independent dimensions useful in assessing sexual orientation.

While sexual orientation certainly involves sexuality, it is just as strongly related to affectional and social needs that are not only sexual. Gay, lesbian, or bisexual people who are not currently sexually active retain their basic sexual orientation, just as a heterosexual person does. In fact, viewing gay, lesbian, or bisexual people as overly sexualized or compulsively sexually active is one form that homophobia can take. Based on research findings and practice experience, we now know that *sexual orientation is not just about sex and sexuality; it is about sexuality, emotionality, and social functioning.* The development of a *sexual identity* represents *the integration of all these aspects of sexual orientation into a coherent whole, an authentic sense of self, with a self-label that is subjectively meaningful and manageable. Differences in sexual orientation are based on whether a person directs his or her sexual and intimate affectional feelings and behavior toward same-gender, opposite-gender, or both same- and opposite-gender others.* Thus, some bisexual people explain that their choice of love object is the result of finding specific personal qualities in the individuals they choose to intimately relate to and that the person's gender is less important than these qualities (Eliason 1996; Weinberg, Williams, & Pryor 1994). This conceptual definition suggests that sexual orientation should be assessed on multiple dimensions (Chung & Katayama 1996).

The definition of sexual orientation that we have so far given is primarily a psychological one; that is, it is mental, affective or emotional, and behavioral. It has nothing to do with appearance or identifiability because there is a tremendous range in how gay, lesbian, and bisexual people look as well as in how they present themselves, and thus in how identifiable they actually may be. In fact, the great majority of gay, lesbian, and bisexual people are *not* visible or identifiable as such. Nor is any visible gay, lesbian, or bisexual community or subculture readily available or necessarily attractive to all gay, lesbian, and bisexual people. In fact, the formerly pejorative term *queer* has recently been adopted by some gay, lesbian, and bisexual activists to indicate a specific identification with and participation in the visible gay, lesbian, and bisexual culture and political movement that flourishes in some large cities and to distinguish a cultural and/or political commitment from sexual orientation itself.

Sexual orientation and sexual identity also have to be distinguished from some other psychological concepts to which they are related but from which they are quite distinct. *Gender identity* or *core gender identity* refers to an individual's subjective sense of self as male or female. Gender identity is thought to be established quite early in development, in the second year of life, and to be extremely stable over the life course, even in cases of severe identity diffusion in other aspects of the self (Friedman 1988). Gay, lesbian, and bisexual people, like heterosexual people, are generally secure and stable in their gender identities; they know clearly that they are male or female and value the gender that they are. Thus gender dysphoria, or unhappiness about one's gender identity, is a different issue from sexual orientation or sexual identity.

> There is considerable confusion surrounding terms like gender identity, gender role, sexual object choice, and sexual orientation. . . . Most homosexuals, like most heterosexuals, have no doubt about their gender identity and are clear about being male or female. Gender role relates to learned behavior in accord with a particular culture's concepts of male and female behaviors. Homosexuals may or may not evidence opposite gender personality or behavior traits. Sexual object choice relates to choice of sexual partner. Identity as a homosexual requires accepting the implications of same-sex attraction, and sexual orientation involves acknowledging the significance of one's preference for sexual activity with the same sex.   —Diane Bernard (1992:25–26)

Most of the time, a person's gender identity is consistent with the appearance of their genitals and the gender others assume them to be based on how their bodies look. When this is not the case, a person is termed *transsexual*, that is, a person whose subjective or psychological sense of self as male or female does not match his or her body. Transsexual people may seek medical and surgical intervention in adulthood in order to alter their bodies to bring them closer in appearance and function to the gender they feel themselves innately to be. Thus, even if others might view (preoperative) transsexuals as being homosexual because the gender of the people they are attracted to is the same as the gender they are but don't wish to be, most transsexual people themselves don't see it that way: they consider themselves to be heterosexual because the gender of the people they are attracted to is the same as that of heterosexual people of the gender they feel themselves to be. For example, a (preoperative) transsexual male feels himself to be a female and thus is attracted to men and wants to be attractive to men in a way that is experienced as heterosexual by him. (However, it is interesting to note that most people, unless they knew otherwise, would probably *not* be able to identify a postoperative transsexual as even being a transsexual, so that the usual presumption of heterosexuality would remain intact.)

Gender role is another concept that is distinct from sexual orientation. Gender role refers to all the norms of behavior and appearance that are stereotypically attached to each gender, including both characteristics that are adopted by a person and characteristics that are ascribed to him or her by others based on gender. Pillard (1991) defines gender role as "a set of expectations (roles) about how men and women ought to behave in a given culture at a particular time in history" (35). While gay, lesbian, and bisexual people are generally secure in their core gender identity, they may or may not be traditional in gender role. To be attracted to someone of the same gender as opposed to someone of the opposite gender is in itself a violation of normative gender roles; our understanding of gender itself is predicated on what Adrienne Rich (1980) has termed "compulsory heterosexuality." Same-gender sexual behavior and desires thus may be seen as "atypical gender behavior" (Pillard 1991) or what Weinberg, Williams, and Pryor (1994) term a manifestation of an "open gender schema" (288). Thus having a gay, lesbian, or bisexual orientation is often, at least initially, subjectively experienced as a source of inadequacy and low self-esteem because it is a violation of normative gender-role behavior. In addition, some people who later define themselves as gay or lesbian report that as children they experienced themselves or were experienced by others as atypical for their gender in other ways, as not adequately masculine or feminine because, for example, they were not interested in the things that most other boys and girls were (Golden 1987). Epithets of being "tomboys" or "sissies" exemplify the negative affect associated with not fitting gender norms adequately. However, others do not recall experiencing themselves as different in gender-related behavior in any way until they were confronted with same-gender sexual fantasies or acts in adolescence or later in development. In fact, our understanding of gender-role behavior in heterosexuals based on paper-and-pencil tests suggests that people of either gender may be high on both masculine and feminine traits, a position termed "androgynous" (Bem 1983), and it may be that some gay and lesbian individuals are more androgynous than heterosexual individuals (Bailey et al. 1993). This androgyny, or "gender-role flexibility" (Bailey et al. 1993:42), may constitute a creative contribution made by lesbian, gay, and bisexual people to increasing the range of expression of human potential.

While same-gender sexual orientation violates gender norms in itself, there is great variation in how traditional or nontraditional in other aspects of gender-role and gender behavior gay, lesbian, and bisexual people are. The term *transgender* has been used in recent years to indicate those who are different in appearance and behavior from what is normative for their gender. For example, *cross-dressing*—that is, wearing clothes typically worn by the other gender, which is done by some heterosexuals as well as by some lesbians and gays—is considered a transgender phenomenon. Politically, it is suggested that gays, lesbians, bisexuals, transgender people, and transsexuals, despite the differences between and among them, share a similar oppression based on the violation of cultural gender-role and behavioral norms and thus share a common political interest in fighting this oppression.

To summarize, the idea of the "open gender schema" as described by Weinberg, Williams, and Pryor (1994) in their study of bisexuality is useful in differentiating among these different but related terms and concepts. Weinberg, Williams, and Pryor define an open gender schema as "a perspective that *disconnects gender and sexual preference*, making the direction of sexual desire (toward the same or opposite sex) *independent* of a person's own gender (whether a man or woman)" (288; emphasis in original). Lesbian and gay people generally regard their gender identities as fixed and stably male or female while they negotiate gender-role issues in ways that differ from the traditional because, at minimum, of an object choice that is atypical for their gender (that is, of being same-gender). For people who identify as bisexual, object choice is open and gender role is open to the degree at minimum that same-gender objects are selected. With this background understanding of what a homosexual or bisexual orientation is (and is not), what gay, lesbian, and bisexual people have in common can be defined as a fixed gender identity accompanied by a nontraditional gender-role stance that includes same-gender sexuality.

Influences on Sexual Orientation

If sexual orientation is complex, involving meanings at the social level, the psychological level, and the level of interaction between the two, then the influences on a gay, lesbian, or bisexual orientation must also be complex. Gender and sexuality, and hence sexual orientation, are currently understood by scholars in two profoundly different ways.[1] On one side of the contemporary debate are those who argue that such phenomena as gender, sexuality, and sexual orientation are "based in deep-seated biological or psychological influences" (Garnets & Kimmel 1993:10). Proponents of this view of sexual orientation tend to emphasize sexual behavior and point to the evidence of homosexual behavior in humans over time and across cultures to suggest that homosexuality is "innate" in at least some people (DeCecco & Elia 1993). The concept of a biological "fingerprint" (Garnets & Kimmel 1993:10) has given rise to considerable research into endocrinology, gender dimorphism in prenatal development, and brain anatomy as a way to explain what are for many stable and enduring differences in sexual orientation over the life course (Suppe 1994). It also corresponds to the subjective sense that many self-identified gay and lesbian people express of their sexual orientation as being innate, an expression of a "real" or core self and as something about which they do not feel they have a choice. As Phelan points out, the phrase "coming out" suggests "a revelation, an acknowledgement of a previously hidden truth . . . a process of discovery or admission rather than one of construction or choice" (1993:773). Other evidence cited for this point of view is the research that shows that "reparative or conversion therapies," or psychological treatments that aim to alter a person's sexual orientation from lesbian or gay to heterosexual, have an extremely poor success rate (Garnets & Kimmel 1993). This view of homosexuality is politically appealing to many activists in the gay rights movement because it suggests that gay, lesbian, and bisexual people need to be treated like others who have differences from the majority that they cannot change and thus are more like victims than like willful rebels or subversives. However, this point of view has been criticized for suggesting a kind of biological determinism that underemphasizes social, cultural, historical, and interpersonal influences on what are not just personal but interpersonal matters and for reducing the complexity of sexual orientation to sexuality (DeCecco & Elia 1993; DeCecco & Parker 1995; Young-Bruehl 1996).

In contrast, others argue "that sexual orientation is a creation of Western culture that can be traced back to the nineteenth century, when the terminology and supportive ideology of homosexuality as a pathology emerged" (Garnets & Kimmel 1993:10). These scholars use the same cross-cultural and historical data to argue that homosexual behavior has greatly different meanings in different cultural, historical, and social contexts. These meanings often do not include the idea of an identity as a different kind of person, which is what sexual orientation as a category or an identity implies. From this perspective, heterosexuality as an identity or "natural" characteristic to which homosexuality is contrasted is also problematic. This view emphasizes the historically, socially, and politically constructed nature of the linguistic and scientific categories that we use to analyze and understand all human behavior, including same-gender sexuality. This analysis of homosexuality is often traced back to the work of the French philosopher Michel Foucault (1978–1980), who argued that what had once been seen as "forbidden acts" committed by ordinary people came to be described as the products of "a singular nature," of a special and different kind of person who embodied "a kind of interior androgyny" (1:43). Previously, the concern had been with acts (e.g., sodomy), but the invention of sexual orientation categories suggested that these acts defined distinct types of people who then had to be "explained."

The concept of the "social script" (Garnets & Kimmel 1993) emphasizes "the particular meaning that individuals ascribe to their sexual feelings and activities, which will depend not only on the specific situation in which sexual conduct occurs but also on the significance of sexual orientation in a particular historical, social, and cultural context" (Richardson 1993:120). The social scripts available to a person who experiences same-gender sexuality are defined by and, in some social settings, may define a gay, lesbian, or bisexual culture. This perspective emphasizes the variability that often occurs in people's behavior and self-descriptions over the life course (Cox & Gallois 1996). It also points out how the emergence of a gay rights movement in this century has led to efforts to depathologize sexual orientation categories and to self-conscious attempts to convert them to a set of positive identities. However, this perspective has been criticized as de-emphasizing the physical basis of the sexual experience and the importance of individual choice and self-determination in the face of social and cultural influences (DeCecco & Elia 1993; DeCecco & Parker 1995).

Simply observing that social life has an influence on sexual behavior and orientation, however, is not enough to resolve the theoretical debate. In fact, the same phenomena or evidence can be interpreted in quite different ways from each perspective. To illustrate, Laumann et al. (1994) found that the percentages of people in their survey identifying themselves as lesbian, gay, or bisexual varied strikingly depending upon where people lived, whether in the twelve largest urban areas surveyed or elsewhere. However, they concede that this observed difference could be explained in two ways—by the migration of those who find themselves essentially to be lesbian, gay, or bisexual to those communities where there are known to be others like them already living or by the fact that those already in those environments have a greater opportunity to imagine and adopt such an identification because other gay, lesbian, and bisexual people can be seen and are accepted around them. Both common sense and the evidence from oral history suggest that multiple factors are operating. As a practical matter, this finding points out, in addition, that the social contacts and community support systems available to a gay, lesbian, or bisexual person in a rural or an urban environment are likely to be quite different (Herdt 1997).

The emergent view of sexual orientation—of gay, lesbian, and bisexual identity—in fact draws upon understandings contributed by scholars from both points of view to develop a picture of sexual orientation that emphasizes "the perspective that human lives are shaped by the interaction of both of these factors" (Williams 1987:137), that is, by biology and society. Conversely, no line of research to date—neither the biological nor the social/psychological—has adequately explained sexual orientation (DeCecco & Parker 1995; Suppe 1994). Figure 2.1, based in part on concepts discussed by Garnets and Kimmel (1993), gives a simplified picture of the multiple and interacting influences on the development of a lesbian, gay, or bisexual identity. The lines between concepts in the figure are two-directional and show that each factor is related to every other. This depiction suggests not just interactions but recursive and reciprocal relationships. For example, what a person does may influence his or her self-definition, which in turn may further influence what he or she does, and so on. In addition, this reciprocal influence is also simultaneously affected by what others think (and are thought to think), by biological endowment, and by the many social roles that the person is exposed to and participates in.

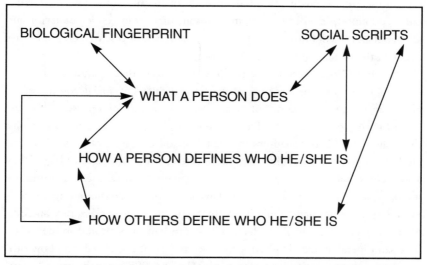

Figure 2.1 Influences on a gay, lesbian or bisexual orientation

This figure should also be seen as a model for thinking about all forms of sexual orientation, heterosexuality as well, a view that has replaced the idea that heterosexuality is simply "natural" and therefore needs no explanation. While a heterosexual orientation is much more common than a gay, lesbian, or bisexual one, heterosexual behavior and life is at least as complex and varied as homosexual behavior is. How heterosexuality is experienced and developmentally shaped must be understood as well.

The "biological fingerprint" and the "social script" both influence what a person does. In this case, "doing" is meant to refer to feeling—attraction, desire, romance, and intimacy—in addition to sexual acts. In particular, every study of sexual behavior has shown that many more people report experiencing same-gender sexual desire and participating in same-gender sexual behavior at some point in their lives than ever report a self-definition of being lesbian, gay, or bisexual. While *doing* influences self-defining or self-labeling, this relationship between doing and self-defining may not be simple or stable, and the relationship drawn between the two may be very different and may be explained very differently by different people (Cox & Gallois 1996).

Self-definitions and what a person does are influenced by and influence how others define the person as well. For example, the young boy whose pastimes are ridiculed as less than adequately manly may begin a process of questioning that in turn makes him more likely to doubt that he is heterosexual later in life. In fact, it is clear that ideas about social scripts have a strong influence on how others respond to gender-atypical behavior of any kind, including same-gender sexuality. When the process of coming out is described in detail (see below), it will be clear, in addition, that same-gender behavior and self-label and/or definition by others as lesbian, gay, or bisexual do not always occur in the order suggested in the figure.

One set of "social scripts" has to do with the ways that a gay, lesbian, or bisexual identity are (or are not) played out in different social communities. However, because sexual orientation is only one aspect of a person's life, the idea of multiple scripts also refers to the multiple roles that a person occupies throughout life. Later chapters in this book address some of these. They include life cycle stages: childhood, adolescence, adulthood, and old age. They also include roles such as intimate partner, parent, worker, and community member, some of which, like parent, have in the past been thought to be irrelevant to gay and lesbian people. They further include social class, race and ethnicity, and gender, which are factors that can have a profound influence on how same-gender sexual behavior may occur, how it is defined, and how others respond and react to it. For example, Herdt (1997) uses the term "sexual lifeways" to emphasize how culture shapes the meaning of same-gender sexual activity in different social and cultural contexts.

Referring back to figure 2.1, how one conceptualizes the relationships among the "biological fingerprint," "social scripts," and individual behavior depends on one's beliefs about the mind-body and biology-psychology interaction. This whole conceptual area is one of great current debate and controversy in a variety of fields. However, one clear example of the behavioral influence on biology, of what a person does (or can do) that influences the "biological fingerprint," occurs when the transsexual individual, whose everyday experience of his or her essential self contradicts a bodily reality that does not fit the psychological and social reality, elects to undergo medical (hormonal) and/or surgical treatment.

Critics of those who emphasize the role of the "biological fingerprint" in a gay, lesbian, and/or bisexual orientation point out that it tends to reduce people to their sexuality, thus minimizing other differences and dimensions of their identity such as race, ethnicity, class, age, and the like. Critics of those who emphasize the "social script," however, point out that an undue emphasis on social influences can in turn minimize the role of individual consciousness and intention as well as the bodily nature of the sexual experience (DeCecco & Elia 1993). What is clear, in any case, is that both biology and social life have a conjoint influence on an individual's behavior, even if the exact nature of the influence of each cannot be precisely explained. In addition, the "moral entitlements" that form at the basis for lesbian and gay rights do not depend on either view of the origins of sexual orientation (DeCecco & Parker 1995; Nava & Dawidoff 1994; Stein 1994).

Even those engaged in research on the possible genetic influence on sexual orientation do not discount other influences. Although there have been fewer studies of women than of men, reputable twin and sibling studies available of both men (Bailey & Pillard 1991; Hamer & Copeland 1994) and women (Bailey et al. 1993) suggest that there is some degree of genetic influence on sexual orientation, although the biological mechanisms that underlie it are thought to be different for men and women. Those committed to this line of research state that they want to "counter the prevalent belief that sexual orientation is largely the product of family interactions and the social environment" (Bailey et al. 1993:222), that is, that sexual orientation represents some form of developmental failure or problem. However, although they believe sexual orientation in both men and women to be "somewhat heritable, environment also must be of considerable importance" (Bailey et al. 1993:222). Thus a biopsychosocial model, such as that in figure 2.1, is widely accepted (see DeCecco & Parker 1995).

Finally, it is important to recognize that a view of sexual orientation as "innate" or "chosen" has major meaning for the individual and has implications in relation to the stigma that is attached to any aspect of difference (de Monteflores 1986). An identity that is "chosen" by implication can be changed;

one that is "innate" can only be denied. Discussing these implications as they affect class, race and ethnicity, and sexual orientation, de Monteflores observes:

> There is greater emphasis in current [practice] toward the internalization of responsibility, the rationale being that we can empower ourselves by recognizing that what we do to ourselves we can also undo. To the stigma of being the bearer of rejected traits of a society is added the secondary stigma of being seen as someone who does not choose to make himself, or herself, feel better, in essence, as a malingerer.
>
> I want to hypothesize that the illusion of absolute power over our intrapsychic lives, and to a large extent power over circumstance, is a class bias. Within a framework of opportunity, not to strive and make use of that opportunity is indeed a cause for shame. . . . For rejected groups, power, and the power to change, is not an internal psychological reality; power is rather an external fact, often at odds with our needs.
>
> To externalize all circumstance, on the other hand, and assume a lack of choice may render us even more powerless unless our assumed deficits are seen as potential sources of strength. This transformation of motive can be brought about by embracing and making a chronicle of our difference . . . [and by making] visible through anecdote and tale the workings of one's culture.
>
> (de Monteflores 1986:219–20)

Hence how people negotiate an identity of lesbian, gay, or bisexual reflects important power dynamics attached to the various ways sexual orientation is conceptualized. It also exemplifies how the psychological and the social are both involved in sexual orientation (DeCecco & Elia 1993).

The most important implication of figure 2.1 and all the scholarly debate about the origins and nature of sexual orientation is actually quite simple: there is currently no single "truth" that experts agree on about sexual orientation and its origins. This observation can be quite disconcerting to social workers and to their clients who seek such answers from them. However, there are some basic principles of practice with which social workers are quite familiar that can guide them in their assessments and interventions with clients who are struggling with issues of sexual orientation: to start where the client is in defining his or her sexual orientation and to explore the meanings the client ascribes to his or her past and present experiences. The goal is to help the client move toward a sense of coherence in identity in the context of his or her own particular life circumstances and in light of the other aspects of identity—race, ethnicity, class, gender, family, occupation, community— that are also meaningful to him or to her.

The Numbers Controversy

One of the questions most frequently asked is how many people are lesbian, gay, or bisexual in their sexual orientation. This question, while an obvious one, is a very difficult one to answer. Gay, lesbian, and bisexual people are not visually identifiable as such. Census data do not contain information about sexual orientation, and even when people are asked about their sexual behaviors and sexual orientation, it is assumed that at least some people do not report same-gender behavior or orientation because it is illegal and/or socially stigmatized in many settings and situations. Finally, it is hard to know on what basis to decide how many people are gay, lesbian, or bisexual: Should it be based on some aspect of what a person does or has done—the experience, past or present, of same-gender romantic or sexual feelings or same-gender sexual acts (and which ones?)? Or based on the label people choose for identifying themselves (Chung & Katayama 1996; Sell & Petrulio 1996)? These and other factors make questions about the numbers of people who are gay, lesbian, or bisexual extremely difficult to answer. Nevertheless, the question is an important one for political as well as for professional reasons.

The figure most often given is that approximately 10 percent of the American population is lesbian or gay. The most likely source for this common estimate is the pioneering research of Alfred Kinsey (Kinsey, Pomeroy, & Martin 1948; Kinsey et al. 1953). Laumann et al. (1994) and Gonsiorek and Weinrich (1991) discuss the various figures the Kinsey research generated in some depth; in fact, the Kinsey research, which showed that both male and female homosexual activity was much more common than had been thought at the time, produced many different estimates of the prevalence of homosexuality in men and in women, depending on how the question was asked. For example, the Kinsey estimates of how many said he or she will "probably have homosexual relations in the future" ranged from 6 percent to 12 percent for men and 2 percent to 4 percent for women while 10 to 17 percent of men and 3 to 5 percent of women reported that they had "had 5 or more partners or 21 or more orgasms from homosexual relations" (Gonsiorek & Weinrich 1991:4). However, since sexual orientation is defined in part by feelings and fantasies and not just by behavior, it is important to note that Kinsey's studies, like all studies done after it, showed that homosexual fantasies and desires are more common in both men and women than homosexual behavior is. The 10 percent figure most likely comes from a statement in the 1948 Kinsey study that "*10 percent* of the males are *more or less exclusively homosexual* . . . for at least three years between the ages of 16 and 55. This is one male in ten in the white male population" (quoted in Laumann et al. 1994; emphasis in the

1948 original). Note that in the original this estimate is limited to men—and to white men at that.

More recent studies of sexuality in general and homosexuality in particular have tried to use random sampling methods, which Kinsey did not, in order to obtain a more reliable estimate of the prevalence of homosexuality in the general population than a sample of volunteers would afford. For example, in a cross-cultural study of same-gender behavior among men in France, the United Kingdom, and the United States, 11.6 percent of American men reported same-gender sexual behavior since age fifteen and 6.3 percent reported same-gender behavior within the last five years preceding the study (Gonsiorek & Weinrich 1991:3–4). However, both random sampling and consistent definitions of sexual orientation have been difficult to achieve in research on gay, lesbian, and bisexual people (Chung & Katayama 1996; Sell & Petrulio 1996).

The Laumann et al. survey (1994) came up with a range of estimates that differed markedly based what "counts" as same-gender sexual orientation. Laumann et al. (1994), whose estimates of the incidence and prevalence of same-gender sexual behavior are seen as conservative by some, report that 8.6 percent of women and 10.1 percent of men report any adult same-gender sexuality, whether that be desire, behavior, or "identity," or self-definition as lesbian, gay, or bisexual. The figures were higher when adolescent experiences were included (before age eighteen) and lower when homosexuality was defined as activity with "a same-gender partner" and when the time period in question was limited to activity in the past five years or the past year. Binson et al. (1995) reported even higher rates of same-gender sex among men in more recent years in the largest U.S. cities. These are all ways in which the question about the incidence and prevalence of same-gender sexual orientation have been asked in different studies, making it difficult to compare estimates among them.

This question—what "counts" as homosexuality—is a key question in client assessment as well as in research, as illustrated by the vignettes at the beginning of the chapter, and in any advocacy or policy-making activity around gay, lesbian, and bisexual rights. It also has enormous implications for our theoretical understanding of individual human development and sexuality in general (Suppe 1994).

In the Laumann et al. (1994) study, when the question was asked as "Do you think of yourself as heterosexual, homosexual, bisexual or something else?" (Laumann et al. 1994:293), 2.8 percent of men and 1.4 percent of women "reported some level of homosexual (or bisexual) identity." Thus, as is common, far fewer people identified themselves to the researchers as lesbian, gay, or bisexual than had experienced same-gender feelings and behavior. However, no one in their study adopted the self-label of homosexual or bisexual without having experienced same-gender desire or behavior. Do note, too, that the gender-specific terms *lesbian* and *gay* were not used in the question, although they are the ones now most commonly used within the population.

Laumann et al. (1994:286) note that an either/or view of homosexuality was probably one influence on respondents in their survey:

> If respondents think that there are basically two types of people in the world, homosexuals and heterosexuals, they are likely to think about their own behavior in those terms. If those respondents see themselves as fundamentally heterosexual but have had on occasion homosexual feelings and experiences, they may simply not report such feelings or behaviors because they are not "real" or "truly indicative" of their underlying nature.

Similarly, many who have moved from some level of heterosexual experience to lesbian or gay experience define themselves as gay or lesbian, feeling that their earlier heterosexual experience did not express their "real" natures. Again, how clients and social workers think about homosexuality and whether or not it is an "either/or" phenomenon has a major impact on the assessments and interventions that social work practitioners make.

Another study of sexual behavior and orientation among men reported a much lower rate of homosexuality: 2.3 percent for any same-gender sexual activity and 1.1 percent for exclusively same-gender activity in the past ten years (Billy et al. 1993). Because of its focus on AIDS risk, this study, done in 1991, concentrated on sexual behavior in the previous ten years and specifically on those behaviors that can transmit the AIDS virus: vaginal intercourse, anal intercourse, and giving and receiving oral sex. In addition, respondents were asked whether their "sexual activity" in the last ten years had been "exclusively" or "mostly" heterosexual or homosexual. All the men interviewed in the survey were between twenty and forty years old, then considered the group at greatest risk for contracting HIV disease. For over half the men, therefore, adolescent sexual activity was by definition excluded, which is a time of life when same-gender sexual activity is most common among men. Thus, because these data do not include lifetime activity and because they exclude feelings and attractions, they cannot easily be compared with other data from more definitive studies. However, these low incidence rates were later widely publicized to suggest that there are fewer gay men in the United States than had previously been assumed. Nevertheless, even these limited data suggest that at least one in fifty men between the ages of twenty and forty has had same-gender sex in the past ten years, however they may define themselves.

Much of the debate about the "real" incidence and prevalence of same-gender sexuality, or "homosexuality," thus revolves around how homosexuality is or should be defined—that is, who qualifies as lesbian, gay, or bisexual. However, heterosexism and homophobia also influence the willingness of people to disclose their same-gender orientation. For example, Laumann et al. (1994) found that for men (although less so for women) the reports of same-gender sexual activity written down and given to the interviewers in sealed envelopes showed higher rates of such activity than those given as spoken answers to questions. The question about how people thought of themselves in relation to sexual orientation was one of those questions asked orally. Perhaps confidential written answers to the question about being homosexual or bisexual would have resulted in higher levels of disclosure as well. For these reasons, and because research in the field as a whole is quite limited, the controversy about how many gay, lesbian, and people there "really" are is likely to continue.

Bisexuality

So far, this discussion of terms and definitions has included gay, lesbian, and bisexual people together because all of them manifest some degree of same-gender romantic and sexual activity. However, it should be noted that bisexuality as an identity is often questioned among both gays and/or lesbians as well as among heterosexuals. Heterosexuals who are prejudiced against lesbians and gays often reject bisexuality because of its homosexual component. Gays and lesbians may reject people who claim a bisexual identity because they are able to benefit from heterosexual privilege based on their participation in heterosexual relationships (George 1993) or because they feel that bisexuality reflects an unwillingness to fully accept what is fundamentally a lesbian or gay identity.

As has already been shown in relation to same-gender sexuality in general, it is also essential to distinguish between bisexual behavior—that is, the fact that many people of both genders report having experienced both same-gender and opposite-gender attraction and behavior—and adopting a self-label of bisexuality (Blumstein & Schwartz 1993; Fox 1995; Klein 1993; Klein & Wolf 1985; Weinberg, Williams, & Pryor 1994). In the Laumann et al. study (1994), for example, among the 8.6 percent of women and 10.1 percent of men who reported having had any same-gender sexual partners since age eighteen, only 10.1 percent of women and 18.4 percent of men had never had an opposite-gender sexual partner. Thus opposite-gender sexual behavior, at least by history,[2] is very common among those who report any same-gender sexuality, even when same-gender activity that is confined to adolescence is eliminated. However, only about 0.5 percent of women and 0.8 percent of men in the Laumann et al. (1994) survey said that they thought of themselves as bisexual, and the ratio of those identifying as lesbian or gay as compared to those identifying as bisexual was about 2:1. All of these specific figures should be interpreted with some caution, however, because the authors of this study concede that the numbers of people reporting same-gender sexuality in adulthood in their study was so small that questions about variations among them could not be answered definitively. However, this general pattern of difference between self-identification as bisexual and variation in sexual history and behavior has been commonly observed.

Bisexuality has been studied even less than homosexuality (Sell & Petrulio 1996). The large-scale study by Weinberg, Williams, and Pryor (1994) investigated people who identified publicly as bisexual in San Francisco in depth in the 1980s. They reported that "the majority of bisexuals established heterosexuality first in their lives . . . [and that] homosexuality was something they later 'added on' " (7). However, many gays and lesbians, too, may establish or try to establish heterosexuality first and only come to adopt a gay or lesbian identity when these attempts fail or prove less than fulfilling.

Weinberg, Williams, and Pryor (1994) assessed sexuality by utilizing the Kinsey 0–6 scale with regard to three distinct categories—sexual feelings and desires, sexual behavior, and romantic feelings—and then rating each study participant separately from 0 to 6 on each dimension. Weinberg, Williams, and Pryor (1994) found that people using the self-label of bisexual were bisexual in different patterns that rarely reflected being in the middle of the 0–6 range in all three categories. For example, about a third of both the men and women they studied they termed "mid-types," that is, people whose reported sexual desires, behavior, and romantic feelings scored near (but rarely exactly at) the midpoint on all three levels. However, they also found substantial numbers of men and women in their sample of self-identified bisexuals who were either "heterosexual-leaning" or "homosexual-leaning" in all three aspects of sexual and romantic feelings measured. Finally, about 10 percent of the men and women were described as "varied," that is, of being substantially more homosexual or heterosexual in one or more aspects of their sexuality or romantic feelings than in others. The only difference found between the male and female bisexual people they studied was that the women scored significantly higher than the men in the degree of homosexuality in their romantic feelings. For some men and women, a bisexual identity is a long-term one while for others it represents a position of transition or one adopted until a long-term relationship with a same-gender or opposite-gender partner is established (Weinberg, Williams, & Pryor 1994).

Thus it appears that bisexuality is an extremely variable and complex phenomenon. Klein (1993), for example, distinguished between transitional bisexuality, historical bisexuality, sequential bisexuality, and concurrent bisexuality. Controversy about a biological basis of bisexuality also exists (VanWyk & Geist 1995). Given its complexity, it is not surprising that bisexuality is a self-label that is much less commonly adopted than a gay or lesbian identification. However, as sexual orientation in general is increasingly understood as a complex phenomenon, our ideas about bisexuality are becoming both more sophisticated and more accepting.

Coming Out

The process of assuming a self-definition as lesbian, gay, or bisexual is commonly referred to as "coming out." This aspect of lesbian and gay functioning and development has been by far the one most commonly studied. However, many of the same problems and complexities that have already been shown to affect how homosexuality is defined, understood, and counted also affect our understanding of the coming out process. In addition, the more coming out has been studied, the more it has been shown to be a variable rather than a stage-driven and unidirectional process. This section will give a brief overview of coming out issues; moreover, coming out issues as they are typically manifest at different life stages and over the life cycle as well as in different contexts are discussed further in part 2 and in various chapters throughout the book. The discussion here will focus on conceptual issues in and current debates about how the coming out process is viewed.

The term *coming out* originates in gay and lesbian culture. Gay or lesbian people who deliberately keep their same-gender sexual activities hidden from others as a method of stigma management are considered to be "in the closet." "Coming out," by contrast, refers to "coming out of the closet," that is, to a process in which a person decides not to continue keeping his or her activities or self-identification a secret any longer. Thus the term *coming out*, as used in the gay and lesbian community and in the gay liberation movement, has always implied some level of public declaration of one's homosexuality. However, it has also been colloquially observed that a person has first to decide internally—that is, to acknowledge to him/herself—that a label of homosexual—of gay, lesbian, or bisexual—fits and is legitimately applied before being able or willing to assume this label to others.

Heterosexism and homophobia along with fears of negative consequences from self-disclosure are what keep many people "closeted." Coming out, it has been argued, reduces the burdens of maintaining secrecy. In addition, by achieving successful adaptation to an openly lesbian, gay, or bisexual identity, it reduces heterosexism and homophobia, both as they affect heterosexual people and as they are internalized among gay, lesbian, and bisexual people. As Cain has described it, there has been a shift from "secrecy as normality" to "disclosure as normality" (Cain 1991a).

Given the roots of the term *coming out* in the community of people who have adopted a self-label of gay or lesbian, and, more recently, of bisexual, it is not surprising that the research that has given rise to the various stage theories of the coming out process has most often been conducted on samples of men and women who, in addition to participating in same-gender affectional and sexual behavior, adopt at least in some contexts the self-label of lesbian or gay (Chung & Katayama 1996; Sell & Petrulio 1996). Discussions of coming out, therefore, always embrace the issue of self-disclosure to some set of others of a gay, lesbian, or bisexual identity. This conceptualization draws from the sociological view of identity as "perceptions of self that are thought to represent the self definitively in specific social settings" (Troiden 1993:193).

Malyon (1982b), however, takes a more psychological perspective, emphasizing "psychological differentiation and identity consolidation" (Malyon 1993: 80) and intrapsychic "conflict resolution and self-actualization" (Malyon 1993: 81). From this perspective, an essential aspect of the coming out process involves confronting and reducing internalized homophobia (the negative feelings about and fears of homosexuality that gay, lesbian, and bisexual people themselves experience). Internalized homophobia can be manifested in overt and/or covert ways (Gonsiorek 1995; Malyon 1982b, 1993). Most importantly, these negative feelings about being lesbian, gay, or bisexual can be "overgeneralized to encompass the entire self" (Gonsiorek 1995:32). The coming out process therefore involves confronting these bad feelings about oneself and finding ways to feel better, whatever the identity management strategies adopted.

The first descriptions developed of the coming out process posited theories of stages that culminated in self-disclosure of a lesbian or gay self-identification that, once achieved and accepted and adopted for oneself, was assumed to be subsequently immutable (Cass 1979; Coleman 1982; Malyon 1982b; Troiden 1989). Implicit in these theories is the belief that the homophobia and heterosexism of others that is absorbed within the self from the cultural and social context constitute the major obstacle that people face in developing a comfortable identification and mode of life as a gay, lesbian, or bisexual person.

Also implicit in the concept of coming out is the idea that each person will seek to locate him/herself within a set of categories—gay, lesbian, bisexual, or straight—that are mutually exclusive even as it is acknowledged that different people define membership in these categories in different ways for themselves and/or for others (Brown 1995). For example, a person who acknowledges having had opposite-gender sexual relationships that were followed by same-gender ones (a very common pattern) may define him/herself as bisexual or as lesbian or gay.

While no two theories have described the stages of the coming out process in exactly the same way, several points on a continuum are generally common to them. One part of the process involves a period of confusion, questioning, and/or uncertainty when an assumed heterosexual identity is first called into question in the person's own awareness. At some point, there is also a choice within the self to assume a gay, lesbian, or bisexual self-identification. Coming out further involves risking disclosure and first describing or revealing oneself as lesbian, gay, or bisexual to some set of others as well as deciding which others to reveal that identity to. For example, one key issue in coming out concerns whether, when, and how to disclose a lesbian, gay, or bisexual identity to one's family of origin. The various models of coming out also describe something like what Troiden (1979) calls "commitment," or the development of increasing comfort with and a set of strategies for managing the gay, lesbian, or bisexual identity. Then there is the task of integrating a gay, lesbian, or bisexual identity into the total set of identifications and statuses, of self-descriptions, that are salient to the individual and to the important others in their lives.

Note that the parts of the coming out process outlined here are not linked to any life stages or specific ages as they were in the models as originally developed. While "coming out" may most often occur in adolescence and young adulthood, more recent research on homosexuality specifically and on adult development in general have both led to the understanding that this process can begin and may be revisited at any point in the life course.

It should be noted that all descriptions of the coming out process assume that a gay, lesbian, or bisexual identity is a socially stigmatized one, which has a powerful impact on all aspects of that process, both intrapsychic and interpersonal. All descriptions also assume, therefore, that some degree of emotional turmoil is likely to accompany the coming out process (Gonsiorek 1995). However, this distress is characterized as "the psychological experience of the homosexual individual in an oppressive environment—not psychopathology in a homosexual person" (Gonsiorek & Rudolph 1991:176).

It is important to recognize that same-gender affectional and sexual behavior has no specific place in this description of the coming out process. That is because it has been found that such behavior can coexist with a heterosexual identification, or it may first occur—whether in fantasy, affectional relationships, or sexual behavior with others—at any point in the coming out process. It may precede or follow the internal process of accepting a self-identification of lesbian, gay, or bisexual or the external process of asserting such an identification to others. In addition, it has been found that where sexual behavior enters into the process often differs for men and women, with same-gender sexual behavior more often preceding self-labeling in men and more often following it in women (de Monteflores & Schultz 1978; Gonsiorek 1995).

There are some interesting parallels between the stages of racial identity development as described for African-Americans by Cross (1991) and Tatum (1992) and the coming out process as described in the literature on gay and lesbian identity formation. This comparison is not made to suggest that racism and heterosexism and homophobia are the same in their nature or impact; rather it suggests that individuals who perceive themselves to be part of groups that are oppressed may have some similar reactions and may employ some similar coping strategies (Cox & Gallois 1996). The Cross (1991) theory of racial identity development begins with a "pre-encounter" stage when the individual absorbs the beliefs and values of the dominant culture and seeks to assimilate to it. The "encounter" stage occurs when some event or series of events forces the individual to confront his or her "outgroup" membership. It is common for the individual at this stage to become more aware of and sensitive to the oppression experienced and to respond to it with anger. The "immersion/emersion" phase involves rejecting the values of the dominant culture and immersing oneself in the subgroup and its culture. Finally, there is an "internalizing" phase in which the individual reaches a level of comfort with his or her identity as a member of an oppressed and stigmatized group, integrating that identity with other roles and characteristics and becoming comfortable with a chosen set of strategies for coping with ongoing oppression without becoming overwhelmed by it. This phase may also involve developing and expressing a conscious "commitment" to the cause of the group. However, the theory notes that "encounter" experiences (and other parts of the process) do reoccur, but each stage is then revisited from a different starting point—that is, with the benefit of prior experience in dealing with the painful feelings evoked (Tatum 1992).

Some differences in how gay, lesbian, and bisexual people choose to manage their sexual identities may have to do with what phase of a similar process they are in. Those who "cover" or "pass" in relation to their homosexuality may be in a "pre-encounter" phase. Such people may insist that their lesbian, gay, or bisexual identity is a personal, not a social, matter (Cox & Gallois 1996).

The initial pain that often accompanies the coming out process can be seen as a kind of "encounter" crisis, which can reoccur with additional experiences of oppression. Using new social comparison strategies or engaging in open protest and confrontation (Cox & Gallois 1996) illustrate parallels to the "immersion/emersion" phase. What Cox and Gallois (1996) call forms of "social creativity" seem to parallel the "internalizing" phase.

Given the variability in the process of gay, lesbian, or bisexual identity development, it is becoming more common to speak of "being out" (Harry 1993). The idea of "being out" underscores the fact that issues of identity and identity management are often revisited and renegotiated periodically, for example at periods of individual developmental change, life or situational transition, family life stage change, and/or community or social change. The concept of being out emphasizes the tensions between "personal desires to disclose and structural pressures to conceal" (Harry 1993:28). It also emphasizes the great variability in how lesbian, gay, and bisexual people actually manage the stigma associated with a gay, lesbian, or bisexual identity based on their assessments of the costs and benefits of disclosure in different situations.

Referring back to figure 2.1, the coming out process, then, is about self-definition and definition by others—about psychological and social identity. However, the coming out process is a powerful one because changes in how one defines oneself and how one is defined by others feed back to and further influence what one does in a recursive and self-reinforcing pattern. To negotiate the coming out process, then, is to suffer a series of losses in self-concept and previously stable and "taken-for-granted" patterns of interaction, relationships, and expectations for life in the future. This means that a social worker helping a gay, lesbian, or bisexual person through the coming out process will likely have to help acknowledge and grieve these losses (Thompson 1992). However, coming out is also a process of "coming into the self," of embracing previously disowned experiences, relationships, and possibilities that can be experienced quite joyfully. As de Monteflores describes it, "The process of coming out involves a transformation: *the transformation of a deficit into a strength*" (1993:223; emphasis in the original) through confrontation of difference and the development of strategies for living in the various communities and contexts in which gay, lesbian, and bisexual people find themselves.

> Rational outness [means] to be as open as possible, because it feels healthy to be honest, and as closed as necessary to protect against discrimination.
> —Joan Bradford and Caitlin Ryan (1977:77)

Cain (1991a) notes, however, that new norms of disclosure may reflect the position of the "predominantly white, middle class, urban and well-educated men" who have developed the emergent literature on gay, lesbian, and bisexual people in the social sciences (43). He observes that:

> Gays from other social and cultural backgrounds may not see themselves represented in the new psychological models. Cultural and social factors are important in shaping people's sense of identity, their sexuality, and how they manage personal information, but by stressing the importance of asserting one's sexuality and by viewing disclosure primarily in terms of identity development and individual adjustment, the new clinical views do not easily allow for consideration of how these social and cultural forces are experienced.
>
> (Cain 1991a:44)

However, although important cultural variations in patterns of disclosure exist, the general concept of coming out has been successfully applied in a variety of racial and ethnic groups in the United States (Gonsiorek 1995).

While the coming out process is described in terms of the gay, lesbian, or bisexual person him/herself, when family members learn about that identity they may go through a form of the coming out process themselves (Mallon 1998). There is often a family crisis surrounding the family member's disclosure, and, as individuals may do, the family may respond by urging the family member to "be discrete" and by keeping the secret themselves. However, over time, the family, like the individual, is likely to develop a more varied set of strategies for dealing with the fact of their family member's sexual orientation. At best, the knowledge of this aspect of the person's identity will be integrated into the family's prior feelings and perceptions of the person, and the family and the gay, lesbian, or bisexual individual together will arrive at ways of relating to each other that are comfortable for all.

The professional view of the coming out process, then, is quite different from and more complex than the political one within the activist lesbian, gay, and bisexual community. In the political context, the pressure is on every lesbian, gay, or bisexual person to "come out" in the sense of publicly identifying as lesbian, gay, or bisexual in all aspects of one's life. The professional view embraces an understanding of the greatly differing ways in which lesbian, gay, and bisexual people come to assume these identifications for themselves (Berger 1983; Nichols & Leiblum 1986; Reiter 1989; Rust 1993). It also emphasizes the variety of identity management strategies (Moses & Hawkins 1982) that gay, lesbian, and bisexual people and their families employ and that depend, in turn, on the social situations, responses, and "scripts" they encounter. Concretely, this means that there is no one "right" or "correct" way to adopt, negotiate, or manage a lesbian, gay, or bisexual orientation that all people should aspire to. It also means that the role of the professional helper must be to respect and affirm the choices people make for themselves (Reiter 1989). As de Monteflores has noted (1986), there can be power both in acknowledging the individual power to change and to exercise some control over one's own situation as well as in acknowledging the sources of oppression over which one has no control and then identifying and celebrating strategies of resistance to it. This understanding is especially important when the other sources of identity that are significant to people are taken into account. In addition, it reflects social work's central ethical commitment to supporting the self-determination of clients in all aspects of their lives.

Identity Complexity

> A sense of gay and lesbian identity is the gradual ability to integrate one's sexual and emotional orientation with what one can do, wants to do and is becoming with being a member of a given family, cultural, ethnic and class group, and with membership in the gay community. The affirmation of one's past and all one is with one's future hopes, as a complete, non-segmented person.   —Judith A. B. Lee (1992:11)

Sexual orientation is only one aspect of a person's identity. For example, one's racial, ethnic, and/or cultural identification is usually formed earlier in a person's development than when sexual orientation becomes an issue. Class and religious identifications also play a major role in a person's self-concept and life choices in general and specifically in relation to a gay, lesbian, or bisexual identity. Occupational and familial roles and identifications are important influences as well. How gender and gender roles intersect with sexual orientation has already been discussed. All of these other roles, identities, or "master statuses" (Cox & Gallois 1996; Laumann et al. 1994) interact with sexual orientation in complex ways. The research on how they affect the coming out process and the management of a lesbian, gay, or bisexual identity has been limited, especially so in relation to race and ethnicity.[3]

RACE, ETHNICITY, AND CULTURE

A nonwhite racial and/or nonmainstream cultural or ethnic identity is a devalued one, as is a gay, lesbian, or bisexual one. Gays, lesbians, and bisexuals of color are therefore commonly described as "doubly" or "multiply" oppressed or as "bicultural" or "polycultural" because they participate in differences that are negatively valued by mainstream society and its institutions and in those of their own ethnic/cultural/racial and sexual orientation groups (de Monteflores 1986; Espin 1987; Swigonski 1995b; Tremble, Schneider, & Appathurai 1989). These identifications, including that of class in particular (de Monteflores 1986), are not simply additive in their effects; rather they interact in complex gender- and culture-specific ways that can affect profoundly how a person negotiates being out (Cox & Gallois 1996; B. Greene 1994a; Tremble, Schneider, & Appathurai 1989). Culture will be discussed in greater detail in chapter 3.

The pervasive influence of social scripts on the various aspects of sexual orientation or identity—what one does, what one calls oneself, and how others define one—helps illuminate what the recent but limited research on homosexuality in different American racial and ethnic groups is making clear: that racism and ethnocentrism are additional problems that gay, lesbian, and bisexual people of color face. A gay, lesbian, or bisexual identity is negotiated in the context of the roles and relationships that a person maintains and wishes to maintain in the family and in the racial and ethnic community with which he or she identifies. In addition, the predominance of whites in the identifiable gay, lesbian, and bisexual community and the racism within it often make it a less useful resource to gays, lesbians, and bisexuals of color than it is to whites (B. Greene 1994a).

Because of the special importance of the family in immigrant and oppressed populations, for members of different racial and ethnic groups in the United States coming out to family members may be especially difficult. The fear of loss of a specific family role or of family regard may be very threatening to someone for whom the family of origin forms a haven from and a locus of resistance to oppression in the larger society. As in the African-American community, strong religious beliefs may be a barrier to acceptance (B. Greene 1994a). In some ethnic groups, including some Latin and Asian cultures, being indirect or not explicit about a gay, lesbian, or bisexual orientation may be more acceptable to the family and more culturally syntonic (B. Greene 1994a). For these reasons and others, then, coming out as a lesbian, gay, or bisexual person may be difficult for an individual to reconcile with maintenance of a strong ethnic, cultural, or nonwhite racial identity. Nevertheless, maintaining ties to one's racial or ethnic community as well as to one's family of origin is generally very important to the individual even when parts of that community may reject his or her sexual orientation (Garnets & Kimmel

1993; B. Greene 1994a; Tremble, Schneider, & Appathurai 1989). For example, one study of African-American lesbians has shown that more positive racial identity is associated with lower levels of internalized homophobia (Besses 1994).

Specific sexual behaviors and feelings have different meanings and salience in different ethnic, cultural, and racial groups; that is, they may be associated with different social scripts (Weinrich & Williams 1991). Therefore it should not be assumed that coming out within a "minority" family or social context will necessarily be more difficult than in the "majority" context, depending on the meaning that a gay, lesbian, or bisexual identity has in the specific ethnic or racial community in question. For men in some Latin cultures, for example, some forms of same-gender sexual behavior are considered quite normative and nonproblematic while others (specifically, assuming the "passive" position or sexual role) are quite stigmatized (B. Greene 1994a). Traditional beliefs among many Native Americans are accepting of gender-role nonconformity, but long exposure to Christianity may reduce that acceptance (B. Greene 1994a). If same-gender sexuality represents shame or deviance to a family, rejection is likely to follow a disclosure, but if it represents a vulnerability to a hostile world or being a "good person" like others the family has known, the family may be quite accepting (Tremble, Schneider, & Appathurai 1989).

As in all areas of social work practice, then, those who work with lesbian, gay, and bisexual people must be informed about the racial, ethnic, cultural, and language groups of the clients and communities they work with and about the specific views and practices related to homosexuality that are particular to those groups. Unfortunately, this information is often difficult to come by, and because the social science and professional knowledge bases are generally still inadequate in these areas, it may be necessary to turn to literature and to the gay-informed analysis and criticism of the literature of each ethnic, racial, or cultural group for guidance (Swigonski 1995a).

Summary and Conclusions

Social work practice with lesbian, gay, and bisexual people, their families, and their communities requires knowledge about how same-gender behavior and feelings have been viewed over time and in different cultural contexts. What research there has been shows same-gender sexual and affectional behavior and the adoption of a gay, lesbian, or bisexual identity to be very complex phenomena. This complexity suggests that the assessment of sexual orientation is a complicated matter, and people often bring their questions and conflicts about sexual orientation issues to the professional encounter, where social workers must deal with them.

Sensitivity to the variety of factors that influence sexual orientation and adaptation to a gay, lesbian, or bisexual life—including race, ethnicity, and culture—is essential. The principle of client self-determination is thus an important one for practice when issues of sexual orientation and identity arise. An appreciation for the diversity and creativity of gay, lesbian, and bisexual people in living with their sexual orientations must be coupled with an appreciation of the obstacles they face from the homophobia and heterosexism in American society, as outlined in chapter 1. Later, part 2 will deal with the particular issues that affect practice with lesbian, gay, and bisexual people at specific life stages and while engaged in specific life tasks. Chapter 3 focuses on the communities and cultures created by gay, lesbian, and bisexual people that form an important resource for them and that contribute to the vitality and diversity of social and cultural life in the United States today.

Culture, Community, and Diversity

Culture and community are important parts of the context of gay, lesbian, and bisexual identity development and social functioning. In addition to understanding the influence of the dominant culture on gay, lesbian, and bisexual people, it is important to recognize how the culture and communities created and sustained by gay and lesbian people over time operate to support them. A distinction is made between homosexual culture and gay culture as a historical reference point in the development of contemporary gay/lesbian culture and community. The impact of diversity based on ethnic/racial identity, rural or urban location, and marital status are also discussed in relation to interaction with and integration into the gay and lesbian community. Practice principles are presented that are useful for gays and lesbians from all cultures and communities.

The ecological model of social work practice, the orienting framework of this text, posits that stress is generated by discrepancies between the needs and capacities of people and the resources and qualities of their environments. Life transitions, environmental pressures, and interpersonal processes all require coping and adaptive skills. It is during these challenges that discrepancies—or person-and-environment problems—often become apparent. Chapters 1 and 2 described the influences of homophobia and heterosexism on gay, lesbian, and bisexual people in general and specifically on the development of a lesbian, gay, or bisexual identity. The discussion so far has been designed to underscore another ecological concept—the adaptive view of human functioning. No discussion of the adaptive capacities of gay, lesbian, and bisexual people would be complete without consideration of the cultures and communities that gay and lesbian people have created collectively and that form an important environmental resource for many gay, lesbian, and bisexual people today.

Thinking about social systems in regard to gay, lesbian, and bisexual people focuses our attention on homophobia and heterosexism as social arrangements that are so pervasive and so ingrained into the operations of the social institutions (family and community life) of the dominant culture in the United States, as well as in those cultures with which many past and recent immigrants identify, that people are unaware of the underlying assumptions that support and perpetuate oppression. Therefore, culture and community will be presented as sources for both potential environmental problems and environmental strengths within the person-in-environment context. This will help to clarify the diverse impact of social institutions on the individual's adaptive and coping capacities.

Lesbian, gay, and bisexual people confront the noxious influences of heterosexism and homophobia in all aspects of their social and personal lives, influences that originate in the social environment. These influences have the potential for significant damage to an individual's adaptive and coping capacities. The ecological approach or framework that guides most contemporary social work assessment and intervention assumes that "the state or condition of a system, at any one point in time, is a function of the interaction between it and the environment in which it operates; [and that] change and conflict are always evident in a system" (Longres 1995:17). This chapter also shows how the cultural and community systems created by gay, lesbian, and bisexual people in the United States have themselves changed over time and some of the diversity and tensions that exist within them.

Basic Concepts

The concept of system has been a mainstay in the social science literature for several decades, originating in sociology as functional theory. Two popular variants in the social work literature are the general systems model, introduced by Gordon Hearn (1969), and the ecological model introduced by Carel Germain and Alex Gitterman (Germain 1991; Germain & Gitterman 1980). These models have reinforced the need to see clients "not as isolated, self-contained entities, but rather as interdependent systems interacting in complex larger systems, as persons-in-situation, persons-in-environment" (DeHoyos & Jensen 1985:490).

Bronfenbrenner (1979) clarified the concept of systems by distinguishing between four levels based on size and function. *Microsystems* are settings in which individuals experience and create day-to-day reality; *mesosystems* are social arrangements or relationships between and among microsystems; and *exosystems* are settings or social arrangements that have power over individual lives but over which individuals possess little control. The fourth level of systems, *macrosystems*, constitutes the institutions and the ideology of a particular culture or subculture. *Culture* and *community* are examples of macrosystems.

Mesosystems and exosystems, the essential contexts for individual and family development, are set within macrosystems. Cultural arrangements are a very important influence on meso- and exosystems and thus on social work assessment. In addition, understanding communities as macrosystems will enhance our comprehension of the interactions between and among micro-, meso-, and exosystems. This understanding will help the worker to better assess the opportunities and barriers experienced by clients and to formulate more appropriate macro interventions.

A systems approach serves best as an orienting model or framework through which an analysis of human behavior can be made. Longres (1995) notes that "it tells us everything and yet it tells us nothing at all. For the systems approach to come to life in social work practice, a whole range of concepts and perspectives must be incorporated into it" (17). As human systems, individuals can only be understood within the context of their physical and social environments. The *physical environment* of a system is the geographically or spatially structured context in which it exits, and the *social environment* of the system is its location within a socially and historically determined context. The social environment consists of the personal and impersonal relations surrounding individuals and social systems. It includes the individual as a system and all the social systems—the other persons and the groups, families, organizations, communities, societies, and nations—with which the individual interacts and which directly or indirectly influence the individual's behavior and development. Each social system, the basic element in a social environment, is composed of individuals who share a common identity, who are held together by social norms and institutions, and who are organized in terms of roles and statuses. The competing forces of stability and conflict in social systems are always present in both primary and secondary groups (Longres 1995). Social workers are usually, although not always, concerned with social environments and social systems. While the physical environment should not be ignored by the worker, the emphasis in this chapter is on the social aspects of macrosystems.

A Case Illustration

Personal troubles, the focus of social work concern, often arise from public issues (Mills 1959), that is, from conditions in the social environment, not only in the more immediate environment of friends and families but in the larger environment of communities, organizations, cultures, and societies. For example, lesbian and gay children's self-confidence and sense of well-being are influenced by how much they are loved and how well they are treated by their parents, which in turn may depend on their parents' affirmation of or devaluation by the dominant society and culture, specifically in terms of the social roles they are able or allowed to achieve or that are ascribed to them. The troubles of lesbian and gay children and their parents, as is the case with members of a racial or ethnic minority, may be connected to the prejudice and discrimination operating in the larger society:

> Jeri, a sixteen-year-old African-American female, has been raised in a warm and supportive family of five with a mother and father who are both teachers and two older brothers who are in college. Her parents and extended family have always prepared her to deal with a racist world, and although troubled by people's insensitivity, she feels that she is able to cope with these constant assaults. She knows she does not fit society's negative and cruel stereotypes. She has always heard the message that she is bright, loving, and attractive, that she is a good daughter and a loyal friend and sister, and that she is a student with great potential for a challenging career.

> Recently Jeri has begun to accept the fact that her attraction to other girls is not just a passing phase. She has come to see herself as a lesbian. She wants to share this with her family but is confused and for the first time hesitant. She recalls the cruel "faggot" and "dyke" jokes that her brothers sometimes told at the dinner table and the fact that her parents always laughed. She remembers that her father once discussed one of his students, a gay Latino, whose parents he "felt sorry for." Her father eventually referred the student to a psychiatrist after the other students began to harass him. She also remembers overhearing a conversation in which her mother talked about her "sick" aunt who was one of "them" and who hated men and would have been "better off a

prostitute." She also recalled that the pastor in her church had given a sermon about "those people as abomination in the sight of God" who had "brought down the Lord's wrath with the AIDS plague which they deserved."

Jeri thought of herself as a "good kid" but wondered how she could also be so evil and disgusting. Her parents were clear about how they felt. Her teachers were probably like her parents. Her friends went to the same church. She had no one she trusted enough to talk with, and for the first time she began to feel uncertain that she was as bright, loving, attractive, good, loyal, and promising as people said she was.

While the same attitudes are often encountered by children in their families, whatever their racial or ethnic identities (see chapter 4), this case illustrates that people belong to more than one social system whose values may or may not be in conflict. Jeri is already vulnerable to social disapproval because of her race. Moreover, she worries that the family she feels sheltered by in dealing with racial issues may not shelter her when it comes to dealing with her sexual orientation in the wider world. Churches, schools, and other institutions are often not supportive either. The gay and lesbian community[1] may seem to be the only place to turn for affirmation and support of a lesbian, gay, or bisexual identity.

The Gay and Lesbian Community

A macrosystems focus will help us to understand the concept of creative adaptability as it occurs on a collective level. The term *subculture* is used often in relation to gay and lesbian social arrangements. This concept pertains to any group excluded from the dominant culture, either by self-definition or ostracism. However, this text will refer to "culture" rather than "subculture," as is consonant with a contemporary *multicultural* perspective on diversity.

Any outsider status allows for the development of a distinct culture based upon the very characteristics that separate the group from the mainstream. Over time, this culture creates and re-creates itself—politically and artistically—along with, as well as in reaction to, the prevailing cultural norms (Bronski 1984). Homosexuality and, by implication, homosexuals have been placed outside the prevailing social structures as defined by most theological, legal, and medical models. Lesbians and gay men, like other minorities, have had to create institutions, organizations, and rituals which serve as social, political, and psychological buffers to the hostility of the dominant culture. To best understand this adaptive response to negative environmental pressures, the ecological metaphor will be employed once again. Macrosystems analysis requires, however, that we consider three interrelated dimensions: (1) history, (2) environment-structure, and (3) culture.

HISTORY

Western history and thought is characterized by white, male, heterosexual control. This patriarchy is sustained through a complex network of gender, racial, and sexual arrangements. Erotophobia, the fear of sexuality, is thought to be the bulwark of support for these standards. As noted in chapter 1, patriarchy is supported to a large degree by sexual repression. Controlling sexuality legally, medically, and psychologically is a way for men, who are at the top of the power structure, to retain and strengthen their position. Because sexuality—and the gender arrangements and racial myths that develop in conjunction with it—is such a powerful urge, its control is necessary for establishing and reinforcing a hierarchical structure. Same-gender sexuality confronts both the gender and sexual aspects of this control. Because many lesbians and gays do not conform to strict gender assignments, they are perceived as a threat to normal sexuality. Bronski (1984:11) affirms that

> homosexual activity and passion directly challenges the heterosexual demand that all sexuality be reproductive. It exists in and of itself without any *raison d'être*, and as such is an affront to the heterosexuality and the sexual repression that remain controlling forces in our culture. This threat to the existing power structure is what makes homosexuality political. Much of gay culture and the gay sensibility, implicitly, rests upon this threat.

The ecological model directs our attention to both the positive and noxious factors in the historical experience of members of the population of interest. The history of minority group oppression and exploitation of gay and lesbian people has been noted. It has taken form in religion, culture, law, and social practices. American society, strongly influenced by selective interpretations of Judeo-Christian moral codes, is one of the most homophobic. While change is taking place in each of the primary institutions, not one of these social structures could be characterized as nurturing, or at the least benign.

There are numerous social histories of lesbian and gay communities (e.g., Berube 1990; Boswell 1980, 1995; Chauncey 1994; Cruikshank 1992; D'Emilio 1983; Faderman 1991; Fellows 1996; Fitzgerald 1986; Herdt 1992b; Katz 1976, 1995; Marcus 1992; Tripp 1975), and while these are interesting and informative, it is beyond the scope of this chapter to review them in detail. Each work chronicles the rich adaptive journeys of different gay or lesbian people (primarily urban, white, and middle class) forming supportive communities in cities and some rural areas at different points in this country's history. They provide evidence that there is no such thing as a monolithic gay and lesbian community or culture but rather many communities and cultures. These histories, however, will help the reader to understand the collective oppressive experiences which have resulted in generational and regional variation in social arrangements, attitudes, and politics. What will follow, however, is a brief overview of the cultural context in which contemporary (i.e., post-Stonewall, 1969) lesbian, gay, and bisexual communities have evolved in the United States.

In contrast to the accommodationist politics of the pre-Stonewall period, when deviance and psychopathology comprised the social construction of homosexuality, the post-Stonewall period emphasized a different view of reality. That is, society's negative attitudes about homosexuality were seen as the primary problems faced by gay men and lesbians. This was a significant paradigm shift. The contemporary position is "It is not me who is the problem, but it is you (society) who are my problem." This redefinition of the problem is similar to the shift in thinking seen in the earliest stages of the women's and black liberation movements. The slogan "out of the closets and into the streets" symbolized active resistance to harassment and marginalization and heralded a new phase in community building (Jay & Young 1977). "Coming out" became the strategy to assail prejudice and reduce stereotypes as well as to relieve personal isolation and alienation. The philosophy guiding the post-Stonewall gay liberation movement of the early 1970s was that invisibility maintained social oppression by reinforcing stereotypes and allowing myths to go unchallenged.

Krieger (1982) identifies another crucial feature of the period as the emergence of the lesbian-feminist movement, whose ideology had an important influence on many lesbian communities. The feminist movement challenged ideas about women's sexuality by critically analyzing the concept of gender. The development of lesbian communities was also spurred by the women's experience of sexism in gay male organizations. Women's communities appeared centering around a network of institutions such as coffeehouses, bookstores, women's health clinics, battered women's shelters, rape crisis centers, record companies, publishing corporations, and music festivals, often run by nonhierarchical collectives based on lesbian-feminist politics.

The simultaneous rise of a male-dominated gay liberation movement and the lesbian-feminist movement intensified differences between the groups.

Pearlman (1987) recalls that, for gay males, liberation meant freedom from harassment and the power to exercise sexual freedom, while for lesbian feminists it meant resisting patriarchal oppression and developing new forms of intimacy and community. Gay men moved to consolidate their political power through community organizations. This they did while experimenting with the conventional boundaries of sexuality and relationships. Lesbians assumed greater visibility and leadership in the women's movement (although not without controversy) and explored social organizations that were committed to social transformation.

Despite these differences, the growing sense of community was translated into the development of visible economic, social, and political institutions during the 1970s. Many lesbians and gay men migrated to a handful of large cities (New York, Boston, Philadelphia, Washington, D.C., Atlanta, Miami, Dallas, Chicago, Denver, Minneapolis, Phoenix, San Francisco, and Los Angeles) known to be more accepting of diversity (D'Augelli & Garnets 1995). This migration resonates with what Germain (1973) would refer to as an adaptive response to environmental pressures by either changing oneself, changing the environment, or migrating. Migrating appears to have been a common adaptation for may gay men and lesbians as they contemplated "coming out."

The antigay backlash of the last half of the 1970s initiated by the New Right served to mobilize various communities into political solidification. Three events—Anita Bryant's "Save our Children" campaign, the legislative attempt to ban lesbian and gay teachers in California, and the assassination of Harvey Milk, a gay member of the San Francisco Board of Supervisors—intensified community-building in face of a common enemy. Virulent new attacks from the religious right, such as those spearheaded by the Moral Majority, the Christian Coalition, and the Family Values Councils, activated greater collaboration between lesbians and gay men in organizing political groups and sponsoring massive public protests in the 1980s. These attacks forced many nonpolitical gays to join lesbian/gay groups and to strengthen their identification with the gay/lesbian community.

The AIDS epidemic was a major impetus to lesbian/gay community-building and will be discussed in greater detail in chapter 11. Intensified political organizing sought to obtain funding for research and critically needed services for those infected with HIV. AIDS service organizations developed rapidly in most urban areas, usually with the money raised by and energy provided by the lesbian/gay community. However, it was the lack of national political leadership, inadequate funding, and increased evidence of discrimination based on a combination of sexual orientation and HIV status which led to greater militancy. Groups such as the AIDS Coalition to Unleash Power (ACT-UP), Treatment Action Group (TAG), and Queer Nation rejected progressive politics in favor of civil disobedience and self-assertion (Kramer 1989; Shilts 1987). Others became active in less militant groups, such as the National Gay and Lesbian Task Force, the Human Rights Campaign, the Lambda Legal Defense and Education Fund, the National Lesbian and Gay Health Association, and/or various professional associations. As the epidemic spread through all strata of American life, eroding the persistent stereotypes held about gay and lesbian life, and as social circumstances put them in a position to do so (i.e., the loss of partners or friends, or because of active discrimination, including the challenging of rights of surviving partners), more people openly acknowledged their sexual orientation.

Today, the best-known lesbian/gay communities exist in geographically bounded neighborhoods in several large cities and are characterized by high visibility, many formal and informal institutions, and considerable political clout. The many community organizations and activities in these neighborhoods serve as cultural centers, gathering places, and forums for the expression of lesbian/gay culture. They foster a powerful psychological sense of community and facilitate socialization into the many different niches of urban lesbian/gay life (D'Augelli & Patterson 1995). By the mid-1990s almost every large and moderately sized city had at least some rudimentary lesbian and gay community (if nothing more than just a lesbian and/or gay bar in which to meet) and thus the means to share culture and to address other needs and concerns.

The important role of cultural symbols and rituals in the creation and maintenance of communities among lesbians and gay men should be noted. Coming out has been conceptualized as a rite of passage, and the ritual of telling one's coming out experiences to others forms our "tribal lore" (Zimmerman 1984:674). These stories help to develop a bond and affirm group identity. The symbols of shared oppression (e.g., the pink triangle of Nazi concentration camps), symbols of liberation (e.g., the lambda, the labyris, and the rainbow flag), and national events like the Gay and Lesbian Pride Day parades held throughout the country in the spring, the Gay Olympics, and National Coming Out Day in October also affirm a sense of group identity (D'Augelli & Garnets 1995).

An important recent development has been the visibility of bisexuality within lesbian and gay communities (Weise 1992). However, there are far fewer institutions and organizations concerned with bisexuality than with gay and lesbian issues. Although many lesbians and gay men have histories of heterosexual involvements of varying degrees, and despite the likelihood that responsiveness to both sexes is an inherent characteristic of people, women and men who self-identify as bisexual report feeling excluded by lesbian/gay communities as well as by mainstream society (Weinberg, Williams, & Pryor 1994). Bisexual people seem to be less restricted by gender in their sexual and affectional attractions than either gay men or lesbians. In addition, their sexual orientation may develop differently from those of lesbians or gay men (Bell, Weinberg, & Hammersmith 1981; Klein 1993; Weinberg, Williams, & Pryor 1994). A more radical analysis suggests that, with the increased presence of bisexuals in gay/lesbian communities, a more inclusive nonheterosexual community will emerge, perhaps under the rubric of "queer community." For most lesbians and gay men, the negative connotation of the term *queer* and the presumed radical political stance of "queer community" are major barriers in this paradigm shift. Different communities vary in how lesbians and gay men collectively interact and also in how bisexuality, ageism, classism, and racism are to be tackled. These are monumental problems that demand attention before considering a move to this newer, most inclusive notion of community.

During this period of contemporary history, some lesbian and gay social workers organized nationally and locally. After several decades of political struggle, the National Association of Social Workers (NASW) and the Council on Social Work Education (CSWE) now have gay, lesbian, and bisexual committees and caucuses that have been granted monitoring, education, and policy and program consultation roles in relation to practice and education standards, equity issues within the profession, and a social action and civil rights agenda for the profession directed to reducing discrimination against lesbian, gay, and bisexual people. After years of organizing, a majority of the state chapters of NASW have developed standing committees or lesbian and gay networks for the purpose of support for lesbian and gay workers, education for the general membership, and social action to end discrimination and to increase social justice. During this same period, almost every major academic or professional organization (e.g., the American Psychiatric Association, American Psychological Association, National Education Association, National Lesbian and Gay Health Association, National Nursing Association), as well as national bodies for accountants, architects, engineers, pharmacists, police, veterans, and university faculty in most disciplines have developed similar groups or caucuses. Many of these caucuses have begun formal dialogues with the intent of collaborating on issues of mutual concern (such as social workers and psychologists working together as advocates for lesbian and gay youth). The National Gay and Lesbian Task Force, the Human Rights Campaign, the Lambda Legal Defense and Education Fund, and the American

Civil Liberties Union are the principal national civil rights organizations addressing themselves to lesbian and gay civil rights issues such as nondiscrimination, domestic partnership, marriage, foster and adoptive parenting, antiviolence, and property and custody rights, both at the state and national levels. Given this history of community and organizational growth, the social, political, and economic visibility and influence of the lesbian, bisexual, and gay minority will continue to grow.

Environmental or Structural Factors

Ecological thinking directs our attention to certain elements of social systems that are fundamental to social environments. Social norms, or shared agreement, hold a system together, regulate it, and give it order and purpose. Norms are experienced by individuals as expectations, both of themselves and others, for proper behavior, and they are constantly being revised as individuals define them in their interactions. Some norms, known as social institutions, represent standardized, authorized ways of meeting people's needs and dealing with their problems. Other types of norms, known as institutional arrangements, reflect agreements that characterize all social institutions. They include symbols, cultures, and status divisions.

Longres (1995) points out that it is through roles that a person meets his or her environment. Individuals are tied to social systems through their roles and statuses—that is, the social positions they occupy.

> Roles can be defined from the point of view of others in the system (the prescribed role), the individual (the perceived role), or the behaviors of people in the roles (the enacted role). There are everyday roles in family, group, and work life, and master roles and statuses which connect individuals to the institutional structures of society. The basic transactions between the individual and the social environment are recruitment, socialization, interaction, innovation, and control.   (Longres 1995:45)

All of these transactions can be seen in the functioning of the lesbian, gay, and bisexual community.

Homophobia and heterosexism, as previously discussed in chapter 1, are the most relevant environmental or structural factors affecting lesbians, bisexuals, and gay men because they reflect the norms and social institutions of the dominant society and limit access to its master roles and statuses. Thus sexual orientation, along with class, race, and gender, is related to institutional barriers to equality in American culture.

Social science tells us that class, race, and gender matter because they structure interactions, opportunities, consciousness, ideology, and forms of resistance that characterize civic life. They shape the social location of different groups in contemporary society, their concepts of leadership, and their attitudes. They influence the process of social mobility and the opportunity structures experienced by different groups. Andersen (1996) writes that these are social structures that matter in structuring family experience and situating social policy and people's ideas of what must be done. *Race and ethnicity* are social structures, constructed through social interactions and manifested in the institutions of society, interpersonal interactions, and the minds and identities of those living in a racially based social order. *Class*, similarly, is a social structure that, like race, organizes material and ideological and interpersonal relations. *Gender* and *sexual orientation* are institutionalized in the fabric of society and shape, like race/ethnicity and class, material well-being, social identities, and group relationships. Race/ethnicity, class, gender, and sexual orientation structure power and privilege in society. The dominant culture (privileged, Eurocentric, white, heterosexual, middle class, male) thus sustains the belief that minorities, including lesbians, gays, and bisexuals, are sinful, criminal, deviant, pathological, and, at best, disadvantaged.

Social theory helps us to understand that various subgroups or minorities will position themselves to increase their access to power and privilege by adopting the ideology of the dominant group, thus perpetuating these same oppressive beliefs and social practices. In chapter 1 the powerful role of religion, specifically the Judeo-Christian tradition, was discussed as a cultural force in maintaining the system of power based on race, class, gender, and sexual orientation. The system of heterosexist privilege and contempt for gender nonconformity was presented as the context of identity formation for lesbians and gay men.

The impact of these environmental-structural factors is given a specific social form in the lives of homosexuals. Paul and Weinrich et al. (1982) identified three such forms: (1) social invisibility, (2) social diversity, and (3) social and personal differentiation. The great majority of homosexuals, including openly gay men and lesbians, are not easily identifiable and thus are invisible because of heterosexual presumption. There are as many kinds of gay, lesbian, and bisexual people as there are kinds of straights (Bell, Weinberg, & Hammersmith 1981). The ways in which people adapt to having a gay orientation vary according to the relative tolerance or hostility of the social environment, which is one source of diversity within the group. Social invisibility makes it possible for the general public to be ignorant of social diversity. The result has been the ability to create and perpetuate widely held inaccurate stereotypes.

Social and personal differentiation refers to the observation that human beings do not fit easily into psychosexual categories. Sexual orientation and social identity are not necessarily identical. In addition, class, race, gender, and, by extension, sexual orientation confer a variety of social identities, many of which conflict, and they also may result in participation in a variety of organizations and cultures outside the social norm. The competing forces of stability and conflict are thus at play as lesbians and gay men attempt to adapt to the norms and social institutions of the dominant culture and to create supportive organizational arrangements of their own.

> Institutionalized oppression of gay men and lesbians is as prevalent in America as racism and sexism, with the difference that many corrective steps have been incorporated in the laws to prevent blatant and law-supported discrimination on the basis of race and gender.
>
> —Hilda Hidalgo (1995:1)

The structural-environmental factors addressed here are not exhaustive. The profession's literature related to minority groups in general will be both informative and relevant to your understanding of lesbian and gay experiences. This literature, as noted previously, underscores how the "outsider" status of being marginalized by society allows for the development of a distinct culture that reflects the attitudes, moods, thoughts, and emotions of an oppressed group and provides an important source of positive group identity.

CULTURE

Culture is the way of life of a society and comprises institutions, language, artistic expression, and patterns of social and interpersonal relationships. It encompasses the values, knowledge, and material technology that people learn to see as appropriate and desirable. It prescribes ways of behaving, or norms of conduct, beliefs, values, and skills (Lukes & Land 1990). As such, culture establishes the parameters that guide and structure but may also limit thinking and behavior (Berger & Federico 1982). As a result, same-gender sexual behavior itself is understood very differently in different cultural contexts (Herdt 1997). In Western societies, many lesbians and gay men share varying degrees of a "gay" culture, and some share varying degrees of a "homosexual" culture. Some also share some or all aspects of an ethnic or racial culture while functioning in a dominant white, heterosexual culture. In addition, applying the concept of *biculturalism* to gay and lesbian adaptation points out that gay, lesbian, and bisexual people, like members of other oppressed groups, are generally called upon to develop competence in functioning in more than one cultural system—the dominant (heterosexual) and (subordinated) gay and lesbian one with all the potential for stress and conflict that this implies (Lukes & Land 1990).

Popular images often suggest that gay and lesbian people are involved with a specific "subculture" or "lifestyle." As a result, gays and lesbians may be thought to be readily identifiable by styles of dress or behavior, or to be invested only in activities or institutions designated as exclusively gay and/or lesbian. This is a stereotype which has become part of the system of shared myths surrounding those who are not heterosexual. However, lesbians, bisexuals, and gays are in fact an exceptionally diverse and largely invisible minority, only some of whom choose to make themselves and their interests visible individually and collectively in the gay and/or lesbian community. The reader is reminded of the richness of human diversity literature she has integrated in her training, as well as of the previous discussion of the *bi-* or *polycultural* quality of gay and lesbian socialization.

In examining the content of gay and lesbian culture, Creekmur and Doty (1995) note that "homosexual men and women have always had a close and complex relation to mass culture. Historians such as David Halperin, John D'Emilio, and Lillian Faderman have argued, in fact, that the identity that we designate *homosexual* arose in tandem with capitalist consumer culture" (1–2). Like all marginalized minorities, gay men and lesbians often found their cultural experience and participation constrained and proscribed by the dominant culture in which they were a generally ignored or oppressed part. Gays and lesbians have also related to culture differently, through an alternative or negotiated, subversive reception of the products and messages of popular culture—and, of course, by themselves producing popular literature, film, music, television, photography, and fashion within mainstream mass culture industries.

Altman (1993) and Herdt (1992b) note that it has become a preoccupation of the intelligentsia as to whether there is such a thing as a "gay culture" or a "gay sensibility." Social critics like Susan Sontag (1966) believe that Jews and gays are the outstanding creative minorities in contemporary urban culture. They are creative, in the truest sense, in that they are creators of sensibilities. These two minorities, according to Sontag, are seen as pioneers of modern sensibility: Jewish moral seriousness and gay aesthetics (attitude, sensitivity, or worldview) and irony (insight related to contradictions) (1966:146). It is more problematic whether there is a gay culture in the aesthetic sense that

Sontag means. Gay sensibility has been described as an erotic interest in one's sex; as an emphasis on sensuality, narcissism, and perhaps ambiguity; a sense of irony accompanied by parody, theatricality, and an emphasis on style; and also with a particular insight into emotions and human relations (Bronski 1984). Aesthetic sensibility is presented as a stress on style aimed at neutralizing moral indignation by promoting playfulness.

Much of gay sensibility also aims to gain some entry into and some acceptance by the mainstream culture. In the same way that other groups point to their particular achievements as a way of legitimizing themselves, so do gays and lesbians. The most common version of this process is the argument that gay men excel at innovation in and promotion of the arts or "high culture" (opera, "serious" writing, ballet) and popular culture (movies, musicals, designing and decorating). Sontag (1966) writes that "homosexuals have pinned their integration into society on promoting the aesthetic sense" (290). Appreciation and involvement with high culture is a means of attaining a certain degree of acceptance, of achieving upward mobility.

There are, however, few question as confusing as that of the existence of and nature of "gay culture." The literature of popular culture for the last thirty years has not always made a lucid distinction between gay culture as an aesthetic sense or as a sociological phenomenon. Clearly there is a gay culture in the sense of certain common aspects of social arrangements (lifestyle) found most among some urban gay males. However, it is less certain that this lifestyle is shared by lesbians or that gay and lesbian culture are the same or different. This lack of a common culture may be changing with the significant economic advancement of lesbians as they begin more business and professional careers and settle in suburbia. Popular media and market analysts in recent years suggest that if there is a commonality in gay and lesbian culture, it is a middle-class, consumer-oriented lifestyle focusing on relationships, family of choice, and community. Working-class white lesbians and gay men and minorities of color have not been studied sufficiently to ascertain whether or not they also share in a gay sensibility and common lifestyle.

This concept of a homosexual culture is viewed as controversial by some because intergenerational transmission of this culture and socialization into it does not ordinarily take place in the family of origin as it does in cultures as defined in other contexts (Lukes & Land 1990). In fact, gay and lesbian individuals are usually first socialized into majority, heterosexual culture. However, applying the concept of culture to gay and lesbian ways of life highlights the inclusiveness of a lesbian or gay identity, the shared experiences of gay and lesbian people over time and across societies, and the effect that the diversity of gays and lesbians have on other aspects of the culture, such as race, class, and gender.

Homosexual versus Gay Culture

Traditional gay culture—or what some would refer to as "homosexual" culture—largely associated with males (and some lesbians) with a pre-Stonewall worldview, is (and was) more generally concerned with survival. Contemporary lesbian and gay culture (post-Stonewall), referred to as "gay" culture here, is more concerned about self-affirmation and self-assertion. Altman (1993) further suggests that in both "homosexual" and "gay" cultures there "is a need to express a sense of community with other homosexuals and [to share] a view of the world based on the particular experience of being homosexual" (152); and as it is altered transactionally in a changing social context, gay culture changes. The traditional "homosexual" cultural preoccupation with sexuality and defensive survival skills are given less attention in contemporary "gay" culture. There is the realization that as a group lesbians and gay men possess not only rights but a unique heritage and a unique point of view.

Unlike traditional homosexual culture, the new culture publicly affirms rather than conceals identity. It confronts society with gay and lesbian sexuality and demands equal rights rather than seeking to win tolerance by neutralizing moral indignation. The new gay culture is concerned not just with affirming the rights and the legitimacy of being gay; its is also, and equally, concerned with working out ways of living as a lesbian or gay man in society. As Edmund White wrote, "Once one discovers one is gay one must choose everything, from how to walk, dress and talk to where to live, with whom and on what terms" (Altman 1982:155). Traditional homosexual culture accepted, at least on the surface, the basic norms of society and subverted them only through irony, fantasy, and ridicule. The new culture and lifestyle, like the old, confronts questions about sexuality, gender roles, and relationships, both sexual and nonsexual, but it does so much more openly; there is no longer a need for the evasions and irony of traditional "camp."

The use of "camp" is a form of self-defense, a particular way of dealing with oppression. *Camp*, perhaps gay culture's crucial contribution to modernism, is an attitude at once casual and severe, affectionate and ironic, and serves to deflate the pretensions of mainstream culture while elevating what that same culture devalues or represses, thus providing a strategy for rewriting and questioning the meanings and values of mainstream representations. Camp was also, for some time, an "insider's attitude and knowledge, a means not only of disturbing dominant cultural values but also of disseminating information about who (or what) was in, that is, 'in the life' (homosexual), in the know, au courant, avant-garde, or, to use a later term, hip" (Creekmur & Doty 1995:2). Perhaps one difference is that when one is socially invisible one has to be obscure in code meaning (irony), and when there is open discussion this is no longer necessary.

A 1997 performance of the Connecticut Gay Men's Chorus highlights these distinctions. The concert, held at the Shubert Theater in New Haven, a bastion of popular culture, was attended by almost equal numbers of gays and nongays of different generations. The first half of the performance showcased a popular female impersonator (drag queen) in the character of Judy Garland. The actor captured all the irony, fantasy, and ridicule of the individual's jour-ney through heartache and pain. This was quintessential homosexual culture. The second half focused on gay culture by presenting a newly commissioned work of songs and dance related to the "coming out" experiences of chorus members. Unlike the first half, these stories were proud statements about moving beyond the personal pain and confusion of being different. These sto-ries were shared as a collective experience, not as an isolated tragedy. Most importantly, the musical voice was that of hope and expectation for happiness and satisfaction with life.

While there is a tremendous degree of aesthetic production (in literature, theater, art, and music), a real sensibility (involving also professionals, educa-tors, and scholars), and a deep spirituality (through some clergy and devo-tional media) in the lesbian and gay community, these are the gifts of a few who share a way of coping with the marginalized experience of being a minor-ity, and not the point of view or experience of all gay and lesbian people (Altman 1982). He also observes that in relation to spirituality, "It is not sur-prising that in a country that has combined deep-seated and often violent homophobia with unrestrained commitment to materialist growth, that the ideas of spiritual commitment and oneness with nature should appeal to those homosexuals anxious to disassociate themselves from the dominant culture" (161). Thus social dissonance has been reframed as a form of creative adapt-ability for some lesbian and gay men. Generally, the dominant tone of gay cul-ture is upbeat, self-assured, and upwardly mobile. For many, because there are few of the economic demands associated with traditional marriage and fami-ly life, social and professional mobility is a reality. The social mobility of les-bians and gay men has been cited in the popular press as unparalleled by any other group in the population. However, these assertions are class-limited, stereotypical, and need further investigation.

The diversity within contemporary gay culture is important to note as well. For example, Jay and Young (1977) argue that there are innate differences between men and women that interact with social roles to produce quite different ways of perceiving the world between gay men and lesbians. Many authors have outlined differences between men and women that are apparent in gay identity development (e.g., de Monteflores & Schultz 1978; Faderman 1984; see also chapter 2, this volume). The flowering of culture has been particularly significant for lesbians, who did not previously enjoy the recognition of gay male "camp." Many lesbians identify themselves and are seen as being feminists rather than lesbians (Altman 1982). Thus the interrelationship between lesbian and "wimmin's" culture makes a specifically lesbian culture difficult to locate. What is common to the new gay culture of both men and women is that it involves the creation of values and institutions that help make sense of the experience of being homosexual in a hostile world (Jay 1995; Laird 1994).

The distinctions between "homosexual" and "gay" culture are important when attempting to assess the potential impact and possible use of the resources of a culture when working with clients of different ages and different classes. Some have observed that white working-class, rural gay men, and lesbians and gay men of color, seem to identify more with elements of the traditional "homosexual" culture than with contemporary "gay" culture. Since this observation is anecdotal, it must be treated with great caution. There are, of course, working-class gay and lesbian cultural practices, such as the organization of competing "houses" of male drag queens in the larger cities (Livingston 1991), and the "snapology" practiced among African-American and Latino urban gay men (Riggs 1995); but by and large, while homosexuality exists to a considerable extent across all class lines, self-conscious homosexuality—that is, not "closeted" and assertively "out"—may be much rarer outside an urban/suburban middle-class environment (Fellows 1996). The three exceptions are the communities of lesbian-separatists living in rural communes, the specialized categories of hustlers (mostly male but some female same-sex workers) and drag queens (female impersonators), and certain subgroups (as cited above) within some minorities of color. While class divisions and prejudices do of course exist among lesbians and gay men, as in any other group, there is more apparent mixing across class lines in the gay and lesbian communities. However, ethnic and class differences are important and will be given closer attention later in this chapter. The social worker, however, is advised to assess whether bi- or polycultural identification, if any, represents a support or a barrier in relation to the client's presenting problem.

Community Characteristics and Institutions

It is worth repeating that there is no singular entity called the gay and lesbian community. This, rather, is a cultural stereotype that assumes there is such a monolithic social organization, and, as such, it marginalizes gays and lesbians by refusing to recognize the scope of their presence, their cultural, racial, and class diversity, and the range of their identifications with other groups. However, there *are* identifiable gay and lesbian communities in the United States with their own distinct characteristics. Murray (1992) defines a gay community as "a concentration of interaction among those who identify themselves as gay into gay primary groups, concentration of space (of residence, but, more important, of community institutions) in specificated territory, learned (though not monolithic) norms, institutional completeness, collective action, and a sense of shared history" (113). Herrell (1992) defines lesbian and gay community as deriving "not from parents and peers during childhood, but from adult participation in a network of institutions and from shared responses to the pervasive denial of social personality itself" (248). These, then, are communities that evolve because of oppressive circumstances and often function to express and direct resistance to this oppression.

Four elements of community are stressed by McMillan and Chavis (1986), each of which is applicable to the lesbian and gay community:

1. Its constituents feel a sense of membership. They perceive boundaries to the community (who belongs and who does not), experience a sense of belonging and identification, invest themselves personally in the community (e.g., through the process of coming out), and share common symbols, myths, rituals, and holidays.
2. Members of the community mutually influence each other and are influenced by the community as a whole.
3. Membership in the community serves individual needs, both tangible (e.g., needs for information, mutual protection, recreation) and intangible (e.g., the need for coming together with others who share one's own values and goals).
4. Community members share an emotional connection, often on the basis of having a sense of shared history, spiritual bonds, and humor.

Community life is highly contextual, varying tremendously across settings. While urban existence has received the greatest research attention, lesbian and gay communities exist in suburban and rural areas as well. However, rural and small-town living can cause many difficulties because of the social, political, financial, and religious constraints within these communities. These often represent negative environmental pressures within nonnurturing meso- and exosystems. In addition, anonymity is more difficult to sustain in rural and small-town settings; thus risk of disclosure becomes more of a concern.

Keeping a secret takes a lot of energy and can put significant strain on one's coping ability and sense of well-being (microsystem). D'Augelli (1989) and Krieger (1982) observe that there are few legal protections against loss of employment and housing if there is a disclosure, especially in those states where there are no antidiscrimination laws. Due to the socially restrictive nature of nonurban areas, gay and lesbian communities are less visible and have far fewer formal organizations than would be found in an urban area. Thus in many rural areas, gay and lesbian communities take the form of small, densely connected informal networks which operate without drawing the attention of others. In some areas, a small gay and/or lesbian restaurant or bar provides a hub for these networks.

Whatever the setting, while some members of the gay community choose to remain closeted in an attempt to isolate themselves from the effects of oppression and stigma, others have committed themselves to action and self-realization. Many lesbians and gays recognized the community's potential political clout in the 1960s as they became aware of their size as a minority group and their significance as a voting bloc. This led to the enormous growth in the 1970s, 1980s, and 1990s of gay political organizations on local and national levels.

Unfortunately, widespread legal and social discrimination against lesbians and gays remains the current political reality. Only Wisconsin (1982), Massachusetts (1989), Hawaii (1990), New Jersey (1990), Connecticut (1991), Vermont (1991), California (1992), Minnesota (1992), Rhode Island (1995), Maine (1997), and New Hampshire (1997) have state laws protecting some lesbian and gay civil rights. Among the pro-gay rights bills pending in state legislatures at this writing are those in Illinois and Maryland. Approximately 150 cities and counties nationwide have passed local gay rights ordinances (Vaid 1995:8–9). One civil right is currently under attack. More and more states are pursuing legislation to prevent the recognition of lesbian or gay marriage after Congress passed the Defense of Marriage Act (DOMA) in 1996. The legal system in many states has criminalized certain acts of sexual expression. Legal rights are denied lesbians and gay men in relation to the prerogative to marry, the custody of their children, the opportunity to provide foster and adoptive care, the liberties of inheritance and decision making as a biological next of kin, employment rights, housing access to resources and services, immigration and naturalization protections, and the choice of military service. Many of the organizations and institutions within the gay and lesbian community have been established to fight this discrimination.

Aside from their goals for political and social change, many gay and lesbian people, as members of a stigmatized group, simply welcome and seek out places, occasions, and activities where they can enjoy the company of others who are clearly identified in that context as lesbian or gay as well. In some areas, especially in large cities, a gay and lesbian community or culture exists consisting of those gathering places such as restaurants, bars, coffeehouses, bookstores, community centers, churches, and synagogues. There are businesses seeking a gay and/or lesbian clientele (travel, insurance, liquor companies, real estate agencies, hotels, resorts and guest houses, accountants, repair and redecorating services, computer support services, printing and publishing, florists, photographers and pet care services). In the very largest cities there are annual Gay and Lesbian Business and Consumer Expos as well as Gay Pride Parades and festivals. There are also various organizations to cover social services, health care, political activities, arts and media, and much more—all dedicated to engaging and serving the lesbian and gay populations.

Because of the proliferation of organizations and services for the gay and lesbian community, a variety of institutions and mechanisms have developed to publicize and connect people with them. There is a gay and lesbian national hotline which can be reached on the Internet (e-mail at *glnh@msn.com* or on the Web at *http://www.excape.com/~irany/index.html*), and other resources can be found simply by using a search engine and such key words as GAY, LESBIAN, or BISEXUAL. In addition, many cities have a lesbian/gay telephone switchboard or information line for the purpose of identifying community resources, events, and activities. Some double as a crisis hot line and/or referral source for health, mental health, and legal services. Most bars and other businesses, such as bookstores, distribute regional newspapers and have a community bulletin board.

A cursory review of several typical community resource directories shows that they include political groups (ACT-UP, Gay and Lesbian Democrats, Bi-Nation, Queer Nation, AIDS Action Council, Lambda Law Students Association, Lesbian Avengers, Log Cabin Gay Republicans, Radical Faeries, Antiviolence League, and an array of other legal and civil rights groups) and professional groups (Gay and Lesbian Insurance Workers, Business Guild, Gay Mental Health Professionals, Network of Gay, Lesbian, and Bisexual Educators, Gay (Police) Officers Action League (GOAL), Gay and Lesbian Fire Fighters, Lambda Health Alliance, and Postal Employees Network). There are numerous support groups: for adolescents infected/affected by HIV/AIDS; for lesbians dealing with weight issues; for African-American men; Alcoholics Anonymous (AA), AL-ANON, and other twelve-step groups; groups for bisexuals, cancer patients, family and friends of persons newly diagnosed with HIV; for people of color, gay fathers, gay men, incest survivors, lesbians; for lesbians who are parenting, co-parenting, or wanting to parent; for married men, older lesbians, Parents and Friends of Lesbians and Gays (P-FLAG), spouses of lesbians and gays; for postoperative transsexuals; for youth and college students. There are social groups for nudists, lesbian and gay choruses, bikers, car enthusiasts, folk dancers, railway buffs, jugglers, classical music fans, theatergoers, gay Olympians, and leather men as well as for those interested in softball, golf, hiking, skiing, and other sports. Religious groups are listed for Christian Bible Study, Jews, Baptists, Catholics (Dignity), Unitarian Universalists, Ecumenical Catholics, Episcopalians (Integrity), Metropolitan Community Church (interdenominational), Congregational (United Church), Presbyterians, Methodists, witches covens, and New Age variants. The range and number of organizations that focus on some aspect of spirituality is impressive and reflective of how some gay men and lesbians cope with social dissonance. There is a growing literature chronicling the spiritual gatekeeper role that homosexuals have played historically and continue to assume in contemporary culture (Barzan 1995; Clark 1989, 1990; Evans 1978; Halifax 1979; McNaught 1988).

Access to such gay- or lesbian-identified institutions and organizations is often very important to individuals who have affirmed or who are exploring or consolidating a gay or lesbian identity. People who live in rural or small communities far removed from these centers of activity may thus feel disadvantaged in making connections with others like themselves, in developing ways to receive affirmation for significant parts of their lives, or in finding help or support in coping with homophobia. However, this isolation is starting to crumble with the globalization of culture because of the expansion of communications technology. There is a growing fiction and nonfiction literature available through a network of gay and lesbian bookstores, such as Lambda Rising in Washington, D.C., or A Different Light in New York City, as well as through national chains. These bookstores have catalog and Web site services which allow them to continue to be important sources of culture transmission and identity-building. National and state or regional newspapers, newsletters, and magazines such as the *Advocate* (California), *Gay People's Chronicle* (Ohio), *Washington Blade* (Washington, D.C.), *Gay Community News* (Boston), *Metroline* (Connecticut, Rhode Island, Massachusetts), *Out and About* and *Our Family Abroad* (travel), *POZ*, *Men's Style*, and *OUT*, to list a very small sample, are available through the mail; syndicated TV (Gay Entertainment Television and In-the-Life) and radio programs are transmitted widely; queer Web sites are on the Internet; and mail order catalogues covering an array of books, films, goods, and sex and dating services are beginning to narrow the distance between rural and urban areas.

> Though there are real and gender-specific differences between lesbians and gay men, our futures are inextricably tied together by the society-at-large that continues to perceive us as "other" or deviant. Our ability to respond to social perceptions and attempts at social control are also tied together, since collaboration and unity can only strengthen our response. Perhaps one clear, positive result of our shared tragedy, outrage and loss [AIDS] is the increased awareness of the need to build a strong and bonded lesbian and gay community. . . . We face many challenges. It is no small task to acknowledge and support our differences while not allowing them to separate us. . . . We will have to learn to balance our mutual, yet sometimes divergent, needs as communities. Others will encourage us to fight among ourselves for limited resources or with other health care and community-based agencies—pitting white against black; men against women; straight against gay. It is our job to find a way to work in coalitions, while trying to meet our various needs.
>
> —Judy Macks & Caitlin Ryan (1988:198–201)

Contact with the gay and/or lesbian culture, however, will quickly dispel any notion that gay and lesbian people are similar to each other in appearance or lifestyle beyond the sexual orientation that they share. Diversity within the identifiable lesbian and gay community is as great as among heterosexuals as a group. As in any other social group, these differences can be a source of tension, which may disappoint those looking to "the community" for an ideal way of life to emulate or for a conflict-free environment as they work on developing their own gay or lesbian identity or seek refuge from discrimination they face in the community at large. The relationship between the individual and the community can thus be a mutually enhancing or a conflicted one. Many lesbians and gays, however, draw essential support and affirmation from this culture and community.

Just as gay and lesbian people are often seen almost exclusively as sexualized beings because their minority status is defined by their sexual orientation, lesbian and gay organizations, institutions, and events are often seen as devoted only to sexual ends. In fact, the institutions within the gay and lesbian community provide essential social, informational, health, economic, and political resources for the population of gays and lesbians as a whole. While providing a safe place for dating and socializing is indeed a function of some parts of the community, homosexual organizations are no more inherently sexual than heterosexual ones. Most are devoted, as the list above illustrates, to other quality-of-life concerns, such as religion and spirituality, sports and recreation, or health and well-being.

In addition, many gay and lesbian people do not participate in the identifiable gay and lesbian community even when it is available to them. Their political, social, and recreational pursuits may not be related to their sexual orientation at all, and their social and emotional supports may come exclusively from friends and/or family. Sometimes this choice may stem from a wish to remain private or "closeted" in their sexual orientation out of fear; at other times it may result from a choice to give other dimensions of their lives and identity priority. Thus the degree of an individual's involvement with the gay or lesbian community is itself a dimension of diversity among lesbians and gays.

Cultural Diversity

America is a multicultural society, but it is also a society of multicultural individuals. To paraphrase the writer Ralph Ellison, Americans are all "cultural mulattos." Gay, bisexual, and lesbian status has different meanings in various cultures (Blackwood 1985; B. Greene 1994b). The experience more often than not does not parallel that of the white American lesbian or gay male. Shared sexual orientation does not guarantee that people have a great deal in common. Thus, there is a need for a bi- or polycultural understanding of sexual orientation that recognizes the multiplicity rather than the sameness, and that analyzes overlapping identities of gender, race/ethnicity, and sexual orientation (Appleby & Anastas 1992; Cohen 1991; B. Greene 1994b; Lukes & Land 1990).

Culture is an abstraction observable in communities comprised of people who interact with life partners, friends, families of origin and choice, and in social and task groups, institutions, and organizations. If the social worker has this understanding, then her psychosocial assessment of the client-in-environment will be based on the recognition of personal strengths and on the interpersonal and social resources of culture and community. However, social workers in the first half of this century, while thoughtful about the uniqueness of cultural patterns and the significant differences in relation to the dominant culture, seldom considered the negative dynamic this way of understanding cultural differences could set up. In practice, it had the impact of defining all that was outside the dominant culture as deviant or culturally disadvantaged. Therefore, social work interventions were often directed toward helping the client reach some normative standard as defined by the dominant culture. By contrast, contemporary social work scholars, many of whom were influenced by the Black Power and women's liberation movements, challenged this perspective as culture-bound and oppressive (de Anda 1984; Hartman 1993; Saleebey 1997).

There are several cultural concepts that are helpful when working with clients from any minority group. These include a dual perspective, sociocultural dissonance, and acculturation processes, and the concepts of bi- or polycultural identity. Practitioners have been enjoined to better understand a particular client's culture by adopting a *dual perspective*, that is, the practice of consciously and systematically perceiving and understanding simultaneously the values, attitudes, and behaviors of the minority client's cultural system as well as those of the larger systems (B. Greene 1994b). The dual perspective suggests the social worker recognizes that many clients are part of two systems: (1) the dominant or sustaining system, the source of power and economic resources, and (2) the nurturing system, the immediate social environment of the family and community (Chestang 1984). Practice will then often focus on the conflicts that can arise for the individual who must traverse two cultural systems, as is the case for lesbian, gay, and bisexual clients. For gay, lesbian, or bisexual people, however, the "family" may be differently defined, with the family of origin possibly in the oppressing, not the nurturing, group. For gays and lesbians of color, this tension around family may be especially acute (see the case illustration cited above).

Sociocultural dissonance may be manifest in the psychological difficulties of maintaining a positive self-image while having to integrate parts of the self identified with the majority and with the oppressed groups.

Acculturation, or the degree to which a person subscribes to the dominant or mainstream culture, may vary widely on a continuum from those most acculturated to those least acculturated. The extent of acculturation depends

---

Race and racism are key factors related to the adaptation and social adjustment of African American men regardless of their sexual orientation. African Americans live in a hostile environment which seriously impinges on their ability to form friendships and intimate relationships and to succeed economically. . . . The black community offers a nurturing environment, a respite from the daily reminder of racism. It facilitates the development of a positive sense of self and offers the possibility for healthy identity and personality. . . . Many African American gays experience the black community as a homophobic environment.

—Larry D. Icard (1996:32)

in part on such factors as the individual's degree of urbanization, the number of generations that have passed since the original family member came to the United States, the extent to which a person may prefer to preserve linguistic and cultural practices, or political beliefs about the mainstream culture (R. R. Greene 1994). The cultural ideal of the United States is assimilation, or the process of diverse racial and ethnic groups coming to share a common mainstream culture. Lesbian, gay, or bisexual clients may fall on any point along the continuum of acculturation, may or may not be assimilated in all aspects of their lives, and may or may not experience the anomie that results from cultural dissonance.

The concept of acculturation has been used to understand variations in same-gender behavior and sexual orientation identity in various racial and ethnic groups. For example, many Latino men and Latina women are native to the United States, but others come because of economic opportunity or to avoid persecution for their homosexuality in their countries of origin or to experience a more open gay/lesbian life (B. Greene 1994b). Sometimes they have immigrated in large numbers, such as the 10,000 to 20,000 migrants in the *Mariel* boat exodus from Cuba. "Acculturation appears to be related to sexual behavior in Latino men," according to Zamora-Hernández and Patterson (1996:80). Latino men in the United States report bisexual behavior more than any other ethnic or racial group, and this behavior is especially common in men born outside America who had lived here for ten or fewer years (Diaz et al. 1993). Latino males were more likely to be currently married than those of any other ethnic group (22 percent versus an average of 7 percent). These statistics further support the notion that homosexually active Latino men are less likely to identify as gay or homosexual, either to themselves or to others, as manifested in their relationship with women. These observations are important when analyzing the level of interaction with and integration into the broader gay and lesbian community.

The ideal of acculturation has recently been challenged because of the negative consequences for minorities in terms of loss of self and loss of social moorings. However, there are data that show that, at least in some recent immigrant groups, *bicultural* orientation is associated with better mental health (Chow, Wilkinson, & Zinn 1996; Lukes & Land 1990). Another helpful concept, that of *polyculturalism*, suggests that socialization is a multipronged process whereby an individual from an ethnic minority group is socialized into the values, perceptions, and normative behaviors of two (or more) cultural systems (Appleby & Anastas 1992; B. Greene 1994b; Lukes & Land 1990; Padilla 1980). This multicultural or tricultural reality may be the experience of a Latina lesbian, a black bisexual, or a differently abled gay white male functioning in the dominant culture. In social work practice, which is respectful of multicultural differences, behavioral norms do not need to be modeled on white mainstream standards but on the variations embedded in different historical and life experiences.

Hilda Hidalgo (1995), Gerald Sullivan and Laurence Wai-Teng Leong (1995), and John Longres (1996), as guest editors of special issues of the *Journal of Gay and Lesbian Social Services*, focus on gay men and lesbians of color. In so doing, they make an important contribution to the literature by increasing our understanding of the xenophobia, heterosexism, racism, and fear of HIV/AIDS that are part of the complex lives of lesbians and gay men of color (see below).

Homosexuality varies historically within cultures. Longres (1996) reminds us that in "European-American society, having sex with someone of the same sex regardless of what one may do in the sex act, constitutes sufficient behavior for a gay or bisexual identity. In Native American, Filipino, Latino, and African-American societies this does not appear to be the case. Sexual behavior rather than sexual object determines homosexual identity in these societies" (xx). While he may have overstated in the case for European-Americans, the point is well made and gives us pause to be much more thoughtful when assessing the lesbian or gay identities and behaviors of various ethnic minorities. Longres (1996) therefore speaks in terms of "homosexually active men of color" rather than in terms of identity. In addition, the common "ethnocentric mythology" about sexuality in general that is attached to a person's racial and ethnic group must also be considered when assessing the meaning that same-gender sex will have to a person of color (R. R. Greene 1994:393).

However, in spite of different constructions of homosexuality in various cultures, the gay rights movement, embodying the principle that gays and lesbians should be assured equal rights, is having a profound impact on all groups. The desire of various ethnic groups to participate in an open, gay community is an important reason for immigration.

RACIAL AND ETHNIC IDENTITY

Because social workers must continually assess client needs and strengths and evaluate the effectiveness of our service methods and service outcomes, improved understanding of ethnic differences and similarities is sorely needed. Donald Atkinson, George Morten, and Derald Wing Sue (1979) constructed a model of ethnic identity development that captures the complexity of the process.

TABLE 3.1   *Minority Identity Development Model*

Stages of Minority Development Model	Attitude Toward Self	Attitude Toward Others of the Same Minority	Attitude Toward Others of a Different Minority	Attitude Toward Dominant Group
Stage 1: Conformity	Self-depreciating	Group depreciating	Discriminatory	Group appreciating
Stage 2: Dissonance	Conflict between self-deprcciating and appreciating	Conflict between group appreciating and group depreciating	Conflict between dominant-held views of minority hierarchy and feelings of shared experience	Conflict between group appreciating and group depreciating
Stage 3: Resistance and immersion	Self-appreciating	Group appreciating	Conflict between feelings of empathy for other minority experiences and feelings of culturocentrism	Group depreciating
Stage 4: Introspection	Concern with basis of self-appreciation	Concern with nature of unequivocal appreciation	Concern with ethnocentric basis for judging others	Concern with the basis of group depreciation
Stage 5: Synergetic articulation and awareness	Self-appreciating	Group appreciating	Group appreciating	Selective appreciating

From D. R. Atkinson, G. Morten, and D. W. Sue, *Counseling American minorities* (Dubuque, Iowa: William C. Brown, 1979), 198. Copyright © 1979; reprinted by permission of The McGraw-Hill Companies.

The first stage, *conformity*, is characterized by a preference for dominant cultural values over one's own culture. The reference group is likely to be the dominant cultural group, and feelings of self-hatred, negative beliefs about one's own culture, and a positive attitude toward the dominant culture are likely to be strong. The second stage, or *dissonance*, is characterized by cultural confusion and conflict. Information and experiences begin to challenge accepted values and beliefs. Active questioning of the dominant-held values operates strongly. In stage three, *resistance and immersion*, an active rejection of the dominant society and culture and a complete endorsement of minority-held views become evident. A desire to combat oppression becomes the primary motivation of the person. There is an attempt to get in touch with one's history, culture, and traditions. Distrust and hatred of dominant society is strong. The reference group is one's own culture. Stage four, *introspection*, is characterized by conflict at the too narrow and rigid constraints of the previous stage. Notions of loyalty and responsibility to one's own group and notions of personal autonomy come into conflict. In stage five, *synergetic articulation and awareness*, individuals experience a sense of self-fulfillment with regard to cultural identity. Conflicts and discomfort experienced in the introspective stage have been resolved, allowing greater individual control and flexibility. Cultural values are examined and accepted or rejected on the basis of prior experience gained in earlier stages of identity development. The desire to eliminate all forms of oppression becomes an important motivation of the individual's behavior (Espin 1993:351). While this popular model appears to be a linear stage model, its use as an assessment tool is of value because it also recognizes the circular nature of the ethnic identity development process—that is, that the individual often returns to an earlier stage to rework a previously held position, value, or social practice.

In chapter 2 a model of gay and lesbian identity development was presented which contains similar stages and emotional components. Conflict, anger, confusion, self-doubt, alienation, separation, rejection, and then self-acceptance and pride are the feelings that can surround disclosure and eventually identity synthesis. It is at this point that sexual identity becomes merely one aspect of the self. Both models describe the internal process that must be undertaken by people who cope with stigmatized identities. As the individual adopts normative roles, she begins to experience the continuous assault of external factors constructing and stigmatizing homosexual identity.

CULTURAL FACTORS AND A GAY OR LESBIAN IDENTITY

Garnets and Kimmel (1993) identify several themes in the literature that are helpful to practitioners assessing the impact of family, culture, and ethnicity on lesbian and gay identity: (1) the importance of religion within the culture and the relevance of sexuality to central beliefs; (2) the significance of distinctions between male and female gender roles; (3) the nature and influence of the family structure; (4) the process of reconciling one's ethnicity, gender, and sexual orientation; and (5) the degree of interaction with and integration into the Anglo lesbian and gay community (331–37).

Religion

While all lesbians and gay men are usually socialized in environments that promote heterosexuality and condemn homosexuality, conservative Christianity has a significant cultural influence in the Latino and African-American communities. Latinos are a significant presence in the larger U.S. society and well represented in the gay and lesbian community (but are also, unfortunately, overrepresented in AIDS/HIV statistics). Latinos of Mexican origin make up almost 63 percent of the total, while Puerto Ricans (11 percent) and Cubans (5 percent) and people from nations of Central and South American (21 percent) comprise the rest. The Latinos may be white, black, Indian, Asian, or racially mixed and, like African-Americans and Asian-Americans, may have a strong sense of racial identity within the culture. This strong racial identity reflected in the family will have an impact on the coming out process.

Bonilla and Porter (1991) found that even though Latinos were less tolerant in terms of civil liberties, they were similar to European-Americans in their beliefs about whether homosexuality was acceptable on moral grounds, and in fact were more liberal on this issue than African-Americans. Morales (1995) notes that because of the centrality of Catholicism to Latino culture, homosexuality is viewed as a sin and thus is highly stigmatized and the source of shame and dishonor for the family. In Puerto Rican communities, the phrase *para pata mejor puta* (better to be a prostitute than a lesbian) is quite common (1995:98). *Fatalismo*, a fatalistic approach to life, may also be attributable to Catholic beliefs. *Fatalismo* often leads to the conviction that one has little control over one's life and to a reliance on saints, God, the Virgin Mary, and spirits (Morales 1992). However, the Catholic religion holds a less rigid and dogmatic position on the morality of homosexuality than do some black Protestant (Fundamentalist) churches.

Fundamentalist and Evangelical Protestantism, the core belief system of the African-American community, forcefully excludes the "abomination" of homosexuality from the Christian communion (Greene 1986; B. Greene 1994b). However, another source of the negative sanctions against gay men, bisexuals, and lesbians in the African-American community results from the view that homosexuality is a white phenomenon largely irrelevant to the interests of the black community. Specifically, gays and lesbians do not promote group survival through the propagation of the race (B. Greene 1994b; Icard 1986; Loiacano 1993).

The *berdache* tradition of gender nonconformity and the respected social and ceremonial status of homosexuality in Native American societies has been the subject of anthropological investigation and the object of intense missionary and governmental suppression (Tafoya & Wirth 1996). Traditionalists who practice the old ways, aboriginal religious ceremonies, and reject Christianity do not share the homophobia of the acculturated Native American (B. Greene 1994b; Katz 1976; Williams 1993). While it is difficult to generalize about all the different nations and cultures among Native Americans, some young Native Americans are blending traditional and progressive modern thinking by referring to gay, lesbian, and bisexual people as "Two Spirit" people (Tafoya & Wirth 1996).

The social science research literature seems silent in terms of Asian-Americans' religious beliefs and homosexuality, in part, perhaps, because of the diversity of nations, cultures, and religions represented among Asian-Americans. In their study of Korean-Americans, Sohng and Icard (1996) suggest that an analysis of social history, specifically Confucian religious practice and gender ideology, might offer some insights into other Asian-American homosexual practices and attitudes. Confucian doctrine stressed familial duty, moral asceticism, and moderation of feelings. Three features of Confucian gender ideology are particularly relevant for understanding same-sex relationships in modern society: (1) gender hierarchy, (2) gender-role specialization, and (3) gender segregation. "The roles and statuses of men and women [are] as an integral part of the overall social order which in turn is embedded in the *Um-yang* (Chinese *yin-yang*) view of the universe" (118). Gender hierarchy produces women who follow the "three obediences" (obedience to father, to husband when married, and to sons when widowed). In the Confucian framework, the male domain is public, outside, and frontstage, apart from the female role domain which is domestic, inside, and backstage. Gender-role segregation is so complete that men and women enjoy considerable autonomy in their own domains. However, a lesbian woman is considered to have brought shame both on herself and her mother because she is not adhering to these traditional duties (B. Greene 1994b).

Korea, like China and Japan, has maintained kinship as the fundamental social force to the present day. Family in Korea possesses a much wider significance than that possessed by the extended family of the West.

> Korean norms on kinship prevented, and still prevent, the emergence of a self-identified homosexual lifestyle independent of marriage. Koreans generally disparage homosexuality not for religious and ethical reasons, but because it disrupts the kinship tradition. . . . Confucianism has never approved of homosexuality, and yet, it does not condemn homosexuality as a sin or crime deserving of eternal damnation which is the case in the West.
>
> (Sohng & Icard 1996:121)

Although most contemporary Koreans conform to narrowly prescribed family-based sexuality, there is evidence of tolerance toward homosexuality. However, this acceptance is often very limited in scope (Sullivan & Leong 1995). The growth of the Asian-American community in the United States and, by implication, gays, lesbians, and bisexuals among them, warrant closer attention to their social adaptation in this society and their need for services (B. Greene 1994b).

Gender Roles
The gender-role expectations in both the Asian and Latino cultures are quite distinct. Women are expected to be passive, reliant, and deferential to men (B. Greene 1994b; Hidalgo 1984; Shon & Ja 1982). Men are to be forceful, assertive, and in control. *Machismo*, the term used to describe exaggerated masculine behavior in Latino cultures, may aggravate homophobic violence and social hostility because homosexuality is perceived as a threat to a *macho* identity (Morales & Bok 1992). *Maschista* homosexuality must be understood within the context of *machismo*, the Latin American system of gender roles and ideology which assigns men the tasks of providing for family members' economic security, physical safety, and protection of their good name. This system also requires men to be dominant, aggressive, and hypermasculine, whereas women are expected to be morally superior and submissive (Zamora-Hernández, & Patterson 1996).

   The Latino cultural emphasis on male privilege enables men to be sexual with other men and yet pass as heterosexual. It is the passive (*passivo*) but not the active (*activo*) men who are considered homosexual in some Latin American societies. *Activos* are largely indistinguishable from the rest of the male population and generally are not labeled as "gay" (Carrier 1985; Morales 1995). *Activos* tend to find their identity and status in the broader community: "Fear of isolation, rejection, violence and possible imprisonment has created a world in which only very effeminate homosexuals are identified as gay. Such men are expected to play the receptive, passive or 'woman's role' in anal and oral sex. Among Puerto Ricans, these men are called *locas* (crazies) or *loca vestida* or *draga* (drag queen)" (Morales 1995:94). Otherwise, men who have sex with men "have no consciousness about belonging to a sexual orientation which differs from heterosexuality"; neither do they identify as bisexuals (Schifter & Madrigal-Pana 1992:201).

Transitional bisexuals, also termed situationals (*bisexuales transicioanles*), are young, engaged men who believe that the women they are seriously involved with should remain virgins until they are wed. These men look for effeminate young men as substitutes for women. Once married, they may or may not continue their same-sex experiences (Carrier 1985). Transitional homosexual behavior also occurs in other cultures or in prisons or other closed institutions, where the more powerful and aggressive men use weaker men for sex as women but return to heterosexuality when the situation allows them to do so. Other male-dominated institutions such as all-male schools, the armed forces, and seminaries may also harbor this form of homosexuality.

Similarly, because of the rigidity of gender roles, only the openly "butch" type is recognized as lesbian. Coming out to oneself and others in the context of a sexist and heterosexist American society is compounded for Latinos by coming out in the context of a heterosexist and sexist Latin culture which is itself immersed in a racist society. In addition, openly asserting a lesbian (or gay) identity violates a cultural norm of being indirect about conflictual matters (B. Greene 1994b). A Latina is an ethnic minority who must be bicultural in American society and polycultural among her own people because she is a lesbian (Espin 1993).

While this discussion has focused on Latinos, many of these same social arrangements are also seen in the African-American and working-class, white, gay male communities. There is evidence that cultural socialization and limited development of a minority gay community in the United States may influence gay men who are members of racial and ethnic minority groups to be more variable in their sexual orientation than white gay men: "Many minority men may have extensive homosexual experience without affecting their heterosexual sexual orientation" (Peterson & Marin 1988:873).

Tafoya and Wirth (1996) note that Native American peoples used many words (*nadleeh, bote, winkte*) to describe cross-dressed men. These men assumed special roles within society and generally adopted the female role in sexual relations with "normal" men. There is some evidence that women, to a lesser degree, also adopted these cross-gender roles. The modern term, "Two Spirit people," recognizes the gender-role flexibility inherent in a gay, lesbian, or bisexual identity or way of life. Rodriguez (1996) chronicles a similar cultural arrangement among Filipinos who recognizes a man who acts like a woman as a *bakla*. The men who have sex with *bakla* consider themselves, and are seen by others, as heterosexual. Thus this separation between sexual object and sexual behavior appears to be fundamental in many cultures.

Family Support

The family, both nuclear and extended, and the community often serve as primary reference groups for their members, providing social networks and support. In addition, racism and the need to form group bonds against it make it essential for many gay men and lesbians of color to maintain their ties to their racial or ethnic communities and to their families of origin. The expectations of the family or the group may even supersede individual desires. Coming out to the family may be seen as jeopardizing both family relationships and ties with the ethnic community. It may be viewed as putting one's allegiance to one's own ethnic group to the test, that is, as a betrayal of one's own people, a disconnection with one's ethnic heritage, as reflecting badly on one's own culture or religion, or as representing assimilation into the Anglo world (Garnets & Kimmel 1993; B. Greene 1994b). As B. Greene (1994b) noted, "The quiet toleration observed in many ethnic minority families for a lesbian member is generally marked by denial and the need to view lesbian sexual orientations as something whose origins exist outside the culture" (413).

Conflicting cultural values may help to explain some of the reluctance of gay men and lesbians of color to identify themselves as openly gay or lesbian. For example, in Asian cultures being gay is frequently viewed as a rejection of the most important of roles for women and men, that of being a wife and mother and that of a father carrying on the family line through procreation, especially of sons. The family is valued as the primary social unit throughout a person's life, and the most important obligation is the continuation of the family through marriage and the bearing of children. If a son or daughter is gay, they are perceived as having rejected the importance of family and Asian culture, and their parents are perceived as having failed in their parental roles (Chan 1993, 1995; B. Greene 1994b). Therefore, it is understandable that there are low rates of disclosure to families among Asian, African-American, and Latino gay men and lesbians.

Managing Multiple Identities

The process of reconciling one's multiple identities involves managing the interacting impacts of racism, sexism, and heterosexism. Beverly Greene (1994b) characterizes this situation for lesbians of color as constituting "triple jeopardy" (390). Lesbians and gay men of color are confronted with conflicting value systems about their sexuality, and therefore must establish priorities among their commitments to their various communities. The aim is to synthesize their multiple identities. Too often this is not accomplished. Homosexually involved minorities face issues of loyalty and belonging to one group over another. These conflicts may inhibit one's ability to adapt and to maximize personal potentials. Ethnic minority homosexuals, who experience the isolation of belonging to a hidden community that lies at the intersection of ethnicity and sexual orientation, face bigotry and isolation in the wider gay community and prejudice in their ethnic communities. Like many white men, many Latino and African-American men will attempt to "pass" as heterosexual by engaging in anonymous sex; playing the active inserter role in anal or oral sex; having sex with men who act like women by adopting mannerisms and characteristics typically associated with females; limiting themselves to occasional physical (sexual) release with other men; and by combining these behaviors with heterosexual marriage. These are behaviors highly correlated with the transmission of sexually transmitted diseases (syphilis, gonorrhea, and herpes) and with HIV infection. In the United States, these men are often considered bisexuals even when they may not self-identify as such (Ryan, Longres & Roffman 1996). Similarly, African-American lesbians may be more likely to have continued involvements with men, to have children, and to maintain strong ties with their families of origin than their white counterparts (Greene 1994b).

Much of the literature related to lesbians and gay men of color emphasize the difficulties associated with managing the conflicting allegiances between those groups that represent the expression of intimacy and those that provide ethnic or racial foundation. If they overidentify with the dominant lesbian and gay community, they run the risk of losing support for their racial and ethnic identity. If they stay closeted in their ethnic group, they may lose the potential for sexual and emotional intimacy and the support of the broader gay and lesbian community. Many Latinos and Latinas in the United States are open about their sexuality and still maintain positions of leadership and authority, in spite of the fact that their cultures and communities view homosexuality with contempt. Many Latina lesbians, however, frequently seek other groups or networks to express their orientation. African-Americans in large urban areas are also carving out a lesbian and gay safe space while maintaining their racial identity. Roberts (1995), reflecting on the African-American experience, notes that gay men, bisexuals, and lesbians manage their lives by drawing upon previous coping strategies and resources, developing new supports and coping techniques, or by combining both approaches to enhance their repertoire of survival skills. Identity development is an ever-changing process, and individuals may base their involvement in any one identity or community on their changing needs for support, as well as on desires to share cultural factors.

Some of these needs are met better by other lesbians or gay men, some by other ethnic group members, some only by other ethnic group lesbian or gay American (Chan 1993).

Community Diversity

Unfortunately, gay men and lesbians of color experience racism within the larger gay and lesbian community (B. Greene 1994b; Tremble, Schneider, & Appathurai 1989). The reality of de facto racism conflicts with the popular ideology of the dominant lesbian and gay culture that acceptance and nondiscrimination prevail. For example, the dominant group norms in the Anglo lesbian community tend not to work well with the cultural style of lesbians of color. Latina lesbians report experiences of prejudice and discrimination that prevented them from feeling part of the community (Lockard 1985). Racism may take the form of being unacknowledged or unaccepted in the community or of experiencing the mixing of gender with sexual stereotypes. Icard (1986) suggests that lesbians and gay men of color do not get the same social supports, visible role models, and simultaneous acceptance for all aspects of their identities as do white gay men and lesbians. However, there is little systematic research available on gay men and lesbians of color and specifically on their community experiences and affiliations.

One study of 513 African-, Latino-, and European-American gay men by Ryan, Longres, and Roffman (1996) found an overall similarity across groups. No important differences were discovered with regard to sexual identity and behavior and social support. In all three groups, substantial proportions of the men were gay-identified, content with their sexuality, active in the gay community, and out to family and friends. "No ethnic differences were found in the percentages of networks that were male and gay, lesbian or bisexual. Similarly, social network members were equally likely to know about and accept the homosexual behavior of the respondent. . . . [However,] the social networks of African-American men lend modest empirical support to the observation that these men who have sex with men are hard-pressed to find acceptance that is uncompromised by homophobia and racism" (1996:20). However, the authors caution that as many within-group as between-group differences existed; therefore, social workers should not assume that all men of color are the same or that they are in all ways different from men of European descent. The results also suggest that "sexual identity can be as central to one's sense of self as ethnic identity. Those men of color who come to recognize their own homosexual interest or experience discrimination within their own communities are likely to seek a niche within the larger gay community. The results here suggest that many do find their niche and with it a greater sense of social acceptance" (1996:22).

The fact that Latino, African-American, and Asian-American men who are involved in gay communities tend to be highly acculturated (Carrier 1985) reflects more than opportunity to interact and to participate; it also indicates that acculturation influences the self-selection of homosexual men of color into gay environments. Similarly, lesbians of color appear to share a similar vision as Anglo lesbians, that is, a desire for personal wholeness, political visibility and social justice, and an appreciation that cultural structural change is necessary to accomplish these goals (Swigonski 1995). Thus there is some emerging evidence that as gay and lesbian communities grow, so does the diversity within them. As Ryan, Longres, and Roffman (1996) note, at least at times "sexual inclinations [are] serving as a bridge across ethnic boundaries" (17), even for European-Americans.

Lesbians and gay men of color over the last decade have formed groups and organizations specifically focused on their racial or ethnic group needs within the broader lesbian and gay community. These experiences provide a sense of community by creating new extended "families" that are more sensitive to their needs. These networks also help to unify efforts toward reducing oppression in each of the communities in which they interact (Moraga 1983).

Other Dimensions of Difference

Everyone has a race and an ethnicity; hence understanding how these identities affect the community and cultural involvements of gay, lesbian, and bisexual people is critical. However, there are a couple of other dimensions of difference among gay, lesbian, and bisexual people that have particular salience for understanding their community and cultural activities. These are their marital status and geographic location.

HETEROSEXUALLY MARRIED GAYS AND LESBIANS

The idea that an individual may be married and have feelings for persons of their same sex does not often occur to many people despite the fact that it does occur, especially in some of the racial and ethnic groups previously discussed. Cross-culturally, marriage and heterosexuality are seen as synonymous, just as homosexuality is associated with being unmarried; thus very little thought is ever given to this reality. Similarly, bisexuality is often ignored even though many single and married lesbians and gay men consider themselves bisexual and not lesbian or gay (MacDonald 1981). Heterosexually married people who have same-gender sex may in fact regard themselves as gay or lesbian, bisexual, or as heterosexual (Coleman 1985; Matteson 1985).

Lesbians and gay men have married for a variety of reasons. Many were not aware of their homosexuality at the time of their marriages. Many were aware of their same-sex attractions but were too fearful of societal pressure and social ostracism to act on them. Some married because of their need for acceptance and possibly their hope that the same-sex feelings would disappear after their marriage (Gochros 1989; Ross 1990). Others married because of a desire for a traditional family with children (Scott & Ortiz 1996). They married their husbands and wives because they loved them.

Another factor that has influenced gays and lesbians to marry has had to do with numerous negative stereotypes of a gay lifestyle that often did not portray homosexual relationships as loving, intimate, or long-lasting (Fox 1995; Matteson 1985). Some members of this group identify themselves as gay or lesbian, others as bisexual. Sometimes they attempt to renounce their same-gender attractions. Often they lead a double life, which can cause great stress for both the homosexual and the knowing nonhomosexual spouse. These same-sex feelings may be a source of guilt, shame, and self-hate. Secret feelings such as these may lead to emotional and/or sexual dysfunction in the marriage. While some married gays/lesbians or bisexuals seek support in the gay community by attending meetings of Gay Fathers or Lesbian Mothers organizations, most are fearful of disclosure and stay far away. On the other hand, some heterosexual marriages involving a gay or bisexual spouse endure (Coleman 1985; Matteson 1985). The social worker must be sensitive to the possibility that this may be seen as a functional adaptation for some because of cultural reasons or as a matter of thoughtful personal choice, while for others it may be the result of internalized homophobia that can be subject to change.

RURAL LESBIANS AND GAY MEN

Homosexuality is often seen as a purely urban experience, far removed from rural and small-town life. Gunther (1988) notes there are other misconceptions (e.g., that urban models of health and social services can successfully be adapted for rural lesbians and gay men, and that there is a strong, informal gay and lesbian support system operating in rural areas). While the needs of rural gays and lesbians are much the same as other gay/lesbian populations, there are unique barriers and limitations characteristic of these environments. Unfortunately, this diverse population has received little attention from the social sciences and the helping professions, limited voice in gay literature, and even less voice in the lesbian literature. Several oral histories and well-researched novels

(Bly 1982; Fellows 1996; Katz 1976; Reid 1973) have uncovered a commonality of experience of primarily gay men as they adapted to the limitations of rural life: rigid gender roles, social isolation, ethnic homogeneity and racism, suspicion of the unfamiliar, sexual prudishness, religious conservatism, and scant access to information. At the same time, these voices seem to speak with pleasure of their accomplishments in farm and home activities, their love for the rural life, and their appreciation of strong ties to family, church, and community. Many have migrated from farm communities to various urban areas for some of the same reasons that other ethnic and racial groups came to the United States. A few of those who remain in farm communities live quite openly in gay relationships or by themselves; others keep their sexual identity secret from their families and neighbors.

What we know is anecdotal, and thus generalization is impossible. Many of these stories come from the rural Midwest where German and Yankee ethnicity and conservative Protestantism and Republican politics are the norm. The gender ideology is traditional yet the physical isolation allows for personal freedom so long as there are few people around to impose the rigid gender roles. Silverstein (1981) notes that sex is not yet an idea whose time has come to the heartland. The churches teach generalized guilt concerning feelings of sexuality. The force of religion and the lack of alternatives in the heartland have unquestionably prevented many gay men from experiencing their homosexuality and in some cases prevented them from awareness of it until their later years (1981:324–25). Many of these stories point to the difficulty of being gay growing up on a farm, not so much because of homophobia but because of the absence of homosexuality in that culture. There were never any strong overtones about it being wrong, because it was never discussed.

Silverstein also noted that "repression of the homosexual identity appears more successful in the boondocks of America and in many of the small- to medium-sized cities of the South, the Southwest, and Midwest. . . . Men who have married without knowing they were gay live everywhere, but are probably less prevalent in the largest cities than elsewhere" (1981:322–23).

Fellows (1996) observes that media and communication technology has resulted in an increase, though slight, in the level of openness about being gay, and in the extent of involvement with local gay communities. While some of his informants assumed an activist orientation, most tended to be more conservative in their attitudes toward gay politics. This appears to be related to age. Disapproval of rocking the boat politically, of gay pride parades or other highly visible events, and of drag queens was widespread (1996:20–21).

Many of the men interviewed no longer live in rural communities or have gone back to them, but most of these men have responded to their feeling of being misfits by removing themselves from the farm to the city or suburbs. Since the late 1980s, AIDS has prompted an unprecedented reversal in the rural-to-urban migration, as many of the HIV-infected men have moved back to their parents' rural and small-town homes (Thompson 1994), revisiting and retesting family and community relationships, conflicts, and support. Unlike any other force, AIDS has pushed rural and other smaller communities to acknowledge that gay men's lives are connected intimately to their own. "Perhaps the devastation of HIV will provide an opening to greater understanding and acceptance of diversity of affectional and sexual identity" (Fellows 1996:315).

Unlike many of the gay men, many rural lesbians originated in an urban environment and left the cities to form communes. Rural lesbian communities offer women access to places that are safe and separate from male-dominated culture. Lord and Reid (1995) suggest that many women will continue to seek out "lesbianlands" or similar spaces to consolidate a sense of identity, to develop spiritually, and to sustain a quality lifestyle. Most of the lesbian communes of the 1980s have been dismantled. Only ten were cited among the 304 listings in the 1991 *Directory of Intentional Communities* (14). Lord and Reid (1995) also note that there has been a shift from radical separatist communities to more short-term communal events as a "time-out" place, a safe space to renew before returning to mainstream society. Some of the reasons for this decline: aging of those initially involved, a shift in political and cultural values, and exhaustion from the hard work required to run these communes. In summary, both gay men and lesbians have found rural life to be nurturing and healthy but also isolating and a hard existence, and as a result their numbers overall are small (Laumann et al. 1994).

Principles for Practice

It is not possible to present an exhaustive study of culture and community in one chapter. The rich diversity among lesbians, gays, and bisexuals is evidenced by the increased attention given in the popular media but also in the professional literature. The reader must explore this vast literature as she needs it. The *Journal of Gay and Lesbian Social Services*, *Journal of Gay and Lesbian Psychotherapy*, and the *Journal of Homosexuality* are devoted exclusively to lesbian, gay, and bisexual concerns and, increasingly, other professional journals are also giving more attention to these topics. Most of the human services professions, usually through their professional associations such as the National Committee on Lesbian, Gay, and Bisexual Issues of the NASW or the Commission on Gays and Lesbians of the CSWE, offer their membership bibliographies, information packets, workshops, and resource books and texts of varying quality and coverage. These are required reading for social workers who have lesbian, gay, or bisexual colleagues or clients or who work with clients' parents, families, or friends. These resources will help you to understand the client-specific micro-, meso-, exo-, and macrosystems and to develop a culturally sensitive biopsychosocial assessment and intervention plan whether the activity is directed at life transitions, environmental pressures, or interpersonal processes. These readings will also assist you in developing cultural competency, which is now required of all social work practitioners with the adoption of the new *Code of Ethics* (NASW 1996), specifically *cultural competency with respect to lesbian, gay, and bisexual people in all of their diversity.*

The first and most obvious practice implication of knowledge about gay and lesbian culture and community is that *assessing community and cultural resources, connections, and involvements must be part of any social work assessment.* These resources are not just relevant to gay, lesbian, and bisexual people themselves; they are often relevant to friends and family members as well (e.g., P-Flag). In addition, macrosystem interventions should be considered where and when they are appropriate to help in creating less oppressive and more nurturing social environments for lesbian, gay, and bisexual people. At a minimum, social workers must be knowledgeable about the cultural and community resources that their gay, lesbian, and bisexual clients might benefit from knowing about. Using the framework of biculturalism, Lukes and Land (1990) discuss practice with gay, lesbian and bisexual people:

> Social workers must recognize that practitioners' roles are multifaceted. These roles may include acting as [cultural] mediators, connecting the . . . client to services within the community or to other cultural translators and models who can provide corrective feedback; and helping the . . . client develop and implement analytical skills in problem-solving when values and norms from majority and minority groups collide.
>
> (Lukes and Land 1990:160)

While the cultures referred to are those of gays and lesbians and those of the heterosexual world, the same can be said of racial and ethnic cultures as well.

Being lesbian, gay, or bisexual in any racial and ethnic minority social environment can be quite different than for those who identify with the dominant racial and ethnic group. The worker, therefore, should take into account relevant ethnic social systems, such as values, religious and folk beliefs, and appropriate language and communication channels, when designing culturally appropriate services. If these factors are taken into account, there is greater likelihood that the lesbian, gay, or bisexual ethnic client will perceive the interventions as credible, appropriate, and relevant. The worker is cautioned about applying a mainstream American perspective to the situations of same-sex-active ethnic and racial minority men and women who are attempting to sort out issues of sexual identity. Equating homosexual behavior with identity, as has been stated before, is clearly an example of this kind of error (Zamora-Hernández & Patterson 1996). They suggest that it is

> important to assist the client in searching for his own understanding of his sexuality and the implications it will have for his relationships with family, ethnic community, and the gay community. . . . Practitioners should be careful not to underestimate the importance of discretion and the special risks of coming out in an [ethnic] context. Even those highly acculturated . . . may experience discomfort with [gay/lesbian] community norms . . . as well as prejudices against people of color. Recognizing the tensions between competing identities and communities may help clients clarify these issues and feel validated in both their ethnic and sexual identities.
>
> (Zamora-Hernández & Patterson 1996:86–87)

This would also be good advice when working with lesbians, gay men, or bisexuals from the dominant culture.

Icard (1996) offers an ecological assessment model that, while specifically designed for African-Americans, has some promise for other lesbian/gay ethnic groups. Its purpose is to identify the obstacles to healthy functioning and build on the client's strengths in order to facilitate social functioning. The model *focuses on psychosocial well-being by assessing the individual's ability to perform three fundamental developmental tasks: play, work, and love.* The individual's ability to carry out these developmental tasks is viewed as a function of resources and obstacles as mediated through his participation in reference groups. The value of the model as a tool for assessing the service needs of gays and lesbians lies in its emphasis on the interaction among personal characteristics (age, values, socioeconomic status, [ethnic] cultural values, institutional and individual racism) and reference groups (attitudes and characteristics of the [ethnic] gay/lesbian and [ethnic] gay/lesbian communities) as they relate to the individual' psychosocial functioning as a homosexual (Icard 1996: 25–49). This advice also resonates with appropriate practice approaches with mainstream gays and lesbians.

Sohng and Icard (1996) recommend the following general guidance when working with gay Korean immigrants. These strategies have been adapted for use with other ethnic groups:

Providing General Services

Help the client to understand the conflict between the desire for same-sex intimacy and the desire to remain connected to [ethnic] cultural traditions.

Help to sensitize [the ethnic community] to the needs of their gay and lesbian members.

Help to sensitize those who work in gay and lesbian services about the needs of gay [ethnic] immigrants.

Provide outreach through services in the gay community, the [ethnic] community, and the network of agencies in the wider community.

Inform gay [ethnic] immigrants of all the resources that are available through human services professionals and agencies.

Providing Direct Services

Develop a relationship of trust and friendship prior to initiating efforts to engage in problem-solving.

Understand [ethnic] values and attitudes on gender ideology, homosexuality, and male friendship patterns and try to offer help in a way that enables [ethnic] clients to remain identified with their community yet accepted as a gay man or lesbian.

Understand how [ethnic] normative expectations for men or women differ from American expectations.

(Sohng and Icard 1996:135–36)

Similarly, Tafoya and Wirth (1996) suggest that there is a range of skills involved in working effectively with Native American clients, including developing alliances with clients; gathering culturally relevant information; discussing culturally sensitive issues; and negotiating culturally appropriate interventions. Native American men and women in crisis from the stress of problems and disease often fall back on culturally defined modes of coping with difficulties. These traditional ways of coping with stress, frustration, and discrimination can be recognized as confrontation, accommodation ("yes is better than no"), retreat (avoidance/withdrawal), and empowerment through separatism and creativity (1996:51–67).

Closer study of these models will be especially helpful when working with culturally diverse gay, lesbian, and bisexual clients. While each of these models of practice is designed for a specific racial or ethnic, gay or lesbian population, their similarity to contemporary general models of strengths-oriented social work practice is striking. Each attempts to include relevant ethnic- and sexual orientation—related social systems (norms, institutions, roles) information into the assessment and intervention process.

Summary and Conclusions

This chapter has focused on culture and community as the context for gay, lesbian, and bisexual lives. Both the oppression of the dominant culture and its institutions and the resources of the gay and lesbian community and culture that has arisen in response to it must be acknowledged. As with other oppressed groups, there is controversy about the very idea of gay and lesbian culture, but the reality is that, at least in some parts of the United States, there is a vital and well-developed gay and lesbian community that is an important source of strength to its members. Even those who do not participate directly in it benefit from it and may feel supported simply by knowing it is there. However, it has also been noted that gay, lesbian, and bisexual people, like the rest of the U.S. population, are diverse with respect to race and ethnicity (and other factors). This diversity can affect even how sexual orientation itself is defined and understood. Thus it is important to attend to the multiple *communities* and *cultures* of clients as well as to the aspects of gender, religion, class, and geography of their social environments. Principles of practice now being articulated with respect to gay, lesbian, and bisexual people from minority racial and ethnic groups are thus shown to have relevance to working with all gay, lesbian, and bisexual people.

Part 2

৯৯

Life Transitions

4

Lesbian, Gay, and Bisexual Orientation in Childhood and Adolescence

Gerald P. Mallon

Homophobia and heterosexism impinge on the developmental tasks of gay, lesbian, and bisexual youth. This hostile environment and a sense of differentness comprise the context where youth are socialized to hide their sexual orientation, establish independence from parents, explore educational, career, and vocational choices, and establish intimate relationships. The decision to "pass" or to come out affects their self-concept and the success of completing the adaptive tasks of adolescence. Case examples and practice suggestions are presented.

Professionals are often reluctant to listen carefully to adolescent expressions regarding their sexuality. Historically, adults have tried to convince young lesbian, gay, or bisexual people that their same-sex desires and relationships were "just a phase" that they were going through. One young person spelled it out this way:

If you say you're gay you are told that you are not gay and that you're going through a phase because you are a teenager. Or you're told that you are mixed up and that once you come out of this stage (you know as a teenager you are supposed to go through these stages), then you will not be gay. That's their attitude! If we know, that we know, that we know, that we know, that we know, that we know, that we are gay, they still tell us that we're not, it's just a phase. I think that they don't want to believe that young people can be gay.[1] [February 1993]

The existence of lesbian, gay, or bisexual adolescents is a difficult issue for many professionals to acknowledge and to reconcile, but it at least establishes an important place to start in examining the actuality of lesbian, gay, or bisexual childhood and adolescence. In order to understand childhood and adolescent homosexuality, one must first acknowledge that it exists (Mallon 1998; Remafedi 1987a, 1987c). The issue of whether there is such a person as a homosexually oriented adolescent is a topic that has engendered a great deal of discussion among various professional communities. Isn't homosexuality just an adolescent phase? Isn't same-sex sexual behavior something that many adolescents go through? Can adolescents really know what their sexual orientation is? These are some of the questions that professionals have been asking themselves for years.

Indeed, it is the Western cultures' belief system that supports the negative myths, stereotypes, and misconceptions about gay and lesbian people—not the orientation itself—that is a major life stressor for young lesbian, gay, or bisexual people. Being attracted to someone of the same sex embodies a sense of fit that is not only expressed through same-sex sexual behavior but is also, through a sense of internal goodness of fit, expressed emotionally and affectionally. Being gay, lesbian, or bisexual is actually a normal variation of human sexuality. However, owing to society's sanctioned stigmatization of this sexual minority, a lesbian, gay, or bisexual youth may not be ready or able to acknowledge his or her homosexual orientation and may initially identify as heterosexual.

For lesbian, gay, or bisexual youth, the realization that they are attracted to someone of the same sex can initiate a very confusing time. Nonetheless, notes Schneider and Tremble (1985), confusion, although it may be an uncomfortable state, is a normal part of adolescent development. Though normative models of adolescent development (Offer 1980; Offer & Sabshin 1984) describe the conventional hallmarks of adolescence, human development at this phase of life is not always a linear process. As different environments may require new energies or new adaptations, many adolescents do not resolve the issue of sexual orientation until their early twenties when they are in college or in the world of work. Lesbian, gay, or bisexual young people do not choose their sexual feelings; but they do choose how they will act on them (Cain 1991b).

Although gay and lesbian young people share many common characteristics (as they are both members of a sexual minority), there are distinct differences between the two (deMonteflores & Schultz 1978), which are more likely attributed to gender than to sexual orientation. Hunter and Schaecher (1987) note that gay males tend to come out earlier and seem to focus on the physical aspects of sexuality; young lesbians, on the other hand, are more likely to come out later and to form intense relationships with each other.

Lesbian, gay, and bisexual adolescents come from all cultures, racial groups, religions, and socioeconomic backgrounds and are identical to their heterosexual peers in interests, behaviors, and appearance. The only difference is that gay and lesbian young people juggle two interrelated processes at the same time—growing up and coming out (Schneider 1989). Distressed lesbian, gay, and bisexual teenagers act like distressed heterosexual teenagers. Some may exhibit substance abuse, depression, antisocial behavior, or deteriorated school performance; others may not. Some may have troubled families, school problems, or any number of other concerns; others will not. Essentially lesbian, gay, and bisexual adolescents face all the familiar stressors of adolescence.

While homosexuality per se is no longer classified as a pathological condition, the consequences of social intolerance place lesbian, gay, and bisexual teenagers at extreme risk for many psychosocial problems. In addition, concern about sexual orientation, coupled with fears of disapproval or rejection from peers and from family members, often leaves them feeling they have no options and no one to turn to for help. In support of this point, an important aspect of Dank's (1971) study notes that gay and lesbian adolescents do not have opportunities to go through a period of what he calls "anticipatory socialization." Thus sexual minority adolescents have no familial referent to help them learn about their new role as a gay or lesbian person, and requiring him or her to turn to the gay and lesbian social network for support. One young woman in a session expressed it this way:

> If you think that you are a lesbian, you have three options: you can hide, you can kill yourself, or you can find a safe place to come out and deal with who you are. It's really hard though to come out and to accept yourself when so many people are telling you that what you think you might be is so terrible. That's why so many young people opt for the first two choices. All it takes though is one kind person to tell you that's it's all right, that's you're okay, to make you believe that you are not this terrible person that society is always saying you are. It's that one person who can literally save your life. [August 1994]

Unlike their heterosexual counterparts, most gay and lesbian adolescents do not have opportunities to learn about their emerging sexual identity in sex education classes in their school. Most sex education curriculums have either limited information about gay, lesbian, and bisexual sexual development or completely ignore these populations. Armed with very little accurate information about their emerging sexual identity, these young people frequently rely on an abundance of myths, stereotypes, and misinformation about gay, lesbian, and bisexual people as their only knowledge base. Although increasingly there are more visible gay and lesbian adult role models, historically, gay, lesbian, and bisexual young people have not had the benefit of seeing lesbian and gay adult role models in their lives. Without adult gay and lesbian role models, the negative stereotypes and attitudes toward homosexuality frequently espoused by significant adults and peers in the environment were often the only sources of information for the lesbian, gay, or bisexual teenager. Internalization of these negative messages and stereotypes leads to a weakening of self-esteem, self-pride, and pride in one's group. When young people are led to believe these negatives views, this phenomenon is called internalized homophobia (Malyln 1981) and can lead to a sense of internalized oppression (Pharr 1988:60).

As lesbian, gay, and bisexual young people strive for the best person:environment "fit," many find, as a consequence to their environment's intolerance, that the fit is not good. Due to this lack of complementary fit (Meyer 1996), these young people may exercise three adaptive options: they may actively decide to adapt by either changing themselves, modifying their environment, or by migrating to a new environment (Germain 1981; Hartmann 1958). Moreover, in addition to coping with the usual developmental processes of adolescence, Hetrick and Martin (1987) note that the lesbian, gay, or bisexual adolescent's primary developmental task is adjusting to a socially stigmatized role. Such stigmatization causes stress, which can lead to coping complications (Gitterman & Germain 1976).

This chapter, utilizing an ecological framework (Germain 1973, 1978, 1981), examines lesbian, gay, or bisexual adolescent development from a holistic viewpoint where individuals and environments are understood as a unit, in the context of their relationship to one another (Germain 1991:16). The chapter considers the primary reciprocal exchanges and transactions that lesbian, gay, and bisexual youths encounter as they confront the unique person:environmental tasks involved in being a lesbian, gay, or bisexual young person in a society that assumes all of its members are heterosexual. The focus here is limited to a discussion regarding the recognition of sexual identity; an examination of the adaptation process sexual minority youths go through to deal with the stress of an environment where there is not a "goodness of fit"; and a discussion of the overall developmental tasks of lesbian, gay, or bisexual children and adolescents. Recommendations for social work practice with lesbian, gay, and bisexual youths are presented in the conclusion.

Heterosexual Assumptions

There has always been a widespread assumption held by researchers and most practitioners that all children and adolescents are heterosexual. For children who are lesbian, gay, or bisexual, this assumption represents a major life stressor. The idea that a child or an adolescent can identify as a lesbian, gay, or bisexual individual is inconceivable to many. Savin-Williams (1995) suggests that this difficulty may stem from "uncertainty and confusion over the distinctions between sexual behavior and identity" (166). Similarly, Malyon (1981) points out that same-sex sexual behavior alone does not predispose one toward a homosexual orientation. Although Blos (1981), Erikson (1950), Marcia (1980), and Newman and Newman (1987) discuss concepts of sex-role identification that are concerned only with heterosexual development and presume heterosexual identity as an eventual outcome, they have also acknowledged that children and adolescents at times engage in a range of same-sex sexual behaviors.

Although many professionals might reluctantly accept that children are, as Freud (1938) noted, sexual beings, it is almost unquestionably assumed that they will be heterosexual beings. Most professionals have difficulty believing that a youngster could call him/herself gay, lesbian, or bisexual before they reach adulthood. The possibility of childhood or adolescent homosexuality is therefore usually dismissed. Malyon (1981) notes that "many theorists and clinicians have regarded all reports of homosexual fantasy or behavior" as an indication of "sexual identity confusion" and that they viewed any type of same-sex eroticism as no more than a transient developmental phenomenon (324). The traditional standard response to a child or adolescent who expresses same-sex sexual attraction has been to immediately reassure the youngster that his or her feelings are "just a phase" and that such feelings do not indicate the existence of a fixed homosexual orientation. But to always interpret adolescent same-sex sexual impulses as incidental, Malyon (1982) points out, is a therapeutic error. Such a response also sends the message to the young person that to be lesbian, gay, or bisexual is an undesirable and inferior sexual orientation (1982:324). Sullivan and Schneider (1987) describe such a response as "viewing homosexuality from a developmentally pejorative perspective" (22).

From a treatment perspective, Whitlock (1989) notes that some professionals either avoid addressing issues of sexual orientation altogether, out of fear that they would be seen as "encouraging" or "influencing" adolescents toward a homosexual orientation, while others treat one's emerging sexual identity as an antisocial behavioral pattern to be rectified immediately before it becomes too serious. What is paradoxical is that while most professionals were convinced that it was "too soon" for an adolescent to identify as lesbian, gay, or bisexual, the same professionals were equally convinced that every young person was heterosexual.

Nonetheless, the issue of whether a young person is "old enough" to self-identify as lesbian, gay, or bisexual has generated a great deal of professional and personal debate. Remafedi (1987b) says it best when he notes:

> Theoretically, the issue of adolescent homosexuality brings into direct conflict two fundamental sociocultural beliefs. One upholds the innate innocence and goodness of children, and the other decries homosexuals as "assertive, destructive, and deviant." The two perspectives are difficult to reconcile in the case of the adolescent who claims to be gay or lesbian.
>
> (Remafedi 1987b:224)

A Sense of Differentness

It has been well documented (Hersch 1991; Hetrick & Martin 1987; Hunter & Schaecher 1987; Schneider 1988; Schneider & Tremble 1985) that homosexual orientation may first be acted upon during adolescence. However, most researchers (Money 1980; Money & Ehrhardt 1972; Sullivan & Schneider 1987) agree that sexual orientation is set before the child enters school, and that it is not subject to change thereafter.

Although American society would generally prefer to think of children as innocent, nonsexual entities, the work of Jackson (1982), Constantine and Martinson (1981), and Martinson (1994) demonstrates that children are indeed sexual beings. Confirming these studies, Whitlock (1989) notes: "It is easy to lose sight of the fact that sexuality is a component of human personality that is already developing in a child's earliest years" (20). Retrospective studies (Bell, Weinberg, & Hammersmith 1981; Cantwell 1996; Hunter & Schaecher 1987; Mallon 1998) found that some lesbian, gay, and bisexual adults recalled experiencing a sense of "differentness" as early as age four. Given that ages four to five are the developmental ages when children begin to be socialized to recognize gender-role behavior (Constantine & Martinson 1981; Diamond 1979; Diepold & Young 1979; Newman & Newman 1987) and begin to develop interests in what "Moms do" and what "Dads do," it is plausible that a child who may later identify as lesbian, gay, or bisexual could also begin to sense an attraction to same-sex individuals during this period. Such children, some of whom (though not all, as gender-atypical behavior does not necessarily indicate one's sexual orientation) may exhibit gender nonconforming behaviors (i.e., boys wanting to play with dolls; girls refusing to wear a dress) or express gender nonconforming ideas (i.e., a desire to marry someone of the same sex, or verbalizing that they will never marry a person of the opposite sex), find that their behaviors and expression are quickly squelched by a distressed relative or parental figure. Although one explanation of this could be an expression of children reared in families that do not reinforce strict gender-conforming roles, another account for this occurrence could be that many gay and lesbian adults have felt since childhood that there was something different about them, something they couldn't name and didn't understand, but knew intuitively that they must not reveal. One young man recalled his family's reaction to his sense of differentness this way:

> I knew I was different from other boys when I was five years old. I remember my sister got a Barbie for Christmas and I really wanted one too. When I told my family that I wanted a Barbie, my uncle got furious with me and said, "Boys, do not play with dolls, girls do!" I didn't care what he said, I still wanted a Barbie, and for my birthday my grandmother bought me a Ken doll (Barbie's boyfriend). I was disappointed, I still wanted Barbie, but I felt better knowing that at least she tried. This time my uncle was even more enraged. He said, "You are as queer as a three dollar bill." I remember thinking I didn't even know they made three dollar bills, and I had no idea why he was so angry. But I quickly learned that whatever this was that I was feeling, I should keep it to myself because it just made people too upset. [April 1994]

In her survey of the childhood experiences of gay and lesbian adults, Cantwell (1996) provides further preliminary evidence of the experience of the sense of differentness. Responses to the question "At what age did you have an inkling that your emotions and interests did not match familial and societal expectations of your gender?" confirm that children were able to identify these feelings at early ages. Some respondents noted that they felt they were "born gay" (1996:56). This last response resonates with more recent thinking on the origins of homosexuality in individuals that it may be biologically determined (Baranaga 1991; Le Vay 1991).

The acquisition of a gay identity, however, occurs over a number of years. Although adult lesbian, gay, or bisexual persons often recall feeling different from their peers and from their family during childhood, this differentness is not attributed by these young people to sexuality until years later. Albeit the above concepts with respect to a sense of differentness are largely speculative and subjective and have not been fully measured in scientific terms, preliminary studies suggest that there is a need to conduct further research on this sense of differentness as described by some gay and lesbian people during their childhood.

Socialized to Hide

Most children internalize society's ideology of sex and gender at an early age and also have opportunities to observe society's dislike and disapproval of lesbian and gay people. Since even young children of four and five can readily pick up the negative feedback in their surroundings over feelings they have that may be different from what other members in the family or in society itself tacitly or implicitly convey as being generally acceptable, this discrepancy is likely to make the child feel extremely uncomfortable in his or her environment. As all children are eager to please their parental figures, most develop adaptations which assist them in masking any difference. This process, labeled as "passing" by some (Berger 1990; Brown 1991; Goffman 1963) but more appropriately described for children and adolescents as hiding (Mallon 1998; Martin 1982), represents a major person:environment life stress for the youngster.

Living in an environment that promotes stress and is hostile to their very existence causes many lesbian, gay, and bisexual youths to search for ways to cope with what Goffman (1963) would call their "spoiled" identity. Germain (1978) notes that "physical and social environments may fail to provide the protection, security, and the biological, cognitive, social and emotional nutriments individuals, families, and groups need" (540). As lesbian, gay, and bisexual youths are deprived from receiving *their* proper nutrients, owing to social opprobrium, they risk suffering from the consequences of entropy, so that biological, cognitive, emotional, and social development can be destroyed, delayed, or impaired. Martin (1982) identifies three possible choices that young people might utilize to nourish themselves in an environment almost devoid of nutrients:

> Every child learns not only what is accepted of the various identities he or she is being raised to, but also what society abhors. In adolescence, young homosexually oriented persons are faced with the growing awareness that they may be among the most despised. As this realization becomes more

pressing, they are faced with three possible choices: they can hide, they can attempt to change the stigma, or they can accept it.   (Martin 1982:57)

Noting that the third would be the most optimal, Martin states that society does all it can to encourage the homosexually oriented adolescent to adopt the first two strategies; naturally, in doing so, gay and lesbian youth are subject to powerful psychosocial stressors.

Hiding one's orientation—the choice that almost all young people initially select—leads to dysfunction and distortion of relationships, which leads to social, emotional, and cognitive isolation (Hetrick & Martin 1987) and feelings of extreme sadness and loneliness. Lesbian, gay, or bisexual adolescents may feel "inauthentic," as if they are living a lie, believing that others would not accept them if they knew the truth (Goffman 1963). Hiding becomes a destructive falsehood for the lesbian, gay, and bisexual young person. In his discussion about the socialization of hiding for gay and lesbian adolescents, Martin (1982:58) notes: "The socialization of the gay adolescent becomes a process of deception at all levels. This strategy of deception distorts almost all relationships the adolescent may attempt to develop or maintain and creates a sense of isolation."

One of the major aspects of this sense of isolation is the ever-present need to self-monitor. Gay and lesbian adolescents who hide are experts at self-monitoring their conscious and automatic behaviors. The stress of watching the way one talks, stands, carries one's books, uses one's hands, or dresses can become unbearable. Many gay and lesbian teenagers hide their feelings from others in order to "fit in"—to conform to the environment's expectations for them. One client put it this way:

Hiding was so exhausting. I always had to watch myself. I always had to make sure that I was not acting too butch or dressing too much like a dyke. I always felt like I was trying to be someone who I wasn't, always trying to fit in where I knew I didn't fit. It was really hard. I really felt all alone, I thought I was the only person in the world who felt this way. But then I finally came out and decided that I didn't have to hide anymore or keep myself in check. I just accepted the fact that I was a dyke. I was tired of hiding it and I got to a point where I didn't care who knew. [June 1995]

While a child may be successful in hiding his or her difference from significant adults while in elementary school or as a preadolescent, the need to obscure one's homosexual orientation during the teen years, when adolescents are expected to date opposite-gendered individuals and to develop romantic attachments, may make management of one's hidden identity even more problematical.

Several years or more may elapse before the lesbian, gay, or bisexual youth resolves this confusion and adopts a lesbian, gay, or bisexual identity. For some, this will not occur until they reach adulthood; still others may spend a lifetime hiding or at least may require additional time to integrate their sexual feelings into a positive self-identity. Unlike hiding, which consumes a considerable amount of psychic energy, acceptance is more positively characterized by personal satisfaction, an unwillingness to change one's sexual orientation, and sufficient energy to develop intimate relations. As noted earlier, the process of acquiring a gay identity is not a linear one of orderly progression; likewise, the process of coming out (described elsewhere in this book) is clearly a continuing process and not just a one-time event. Coming to terms with a gay, lesbian, or bisexual identity often entails a roller coaster of emotions as one struggles to find one's way to personal acceptance.

Adaptive Tasks of Adolescence and Coming Out

Those theoreticians who espouse the normative position of adolescence (Offer & Offer 1975; Offer, Ostrov, & Howard 1981) propose that youth is a time of physical and cognitive development, psychological growth, and the development of life plans. This perspective, which avoids focusing on the crisis mode of the developmental processes of this period, holds that most teenagers and their families cope successfully with the adaptive tasks of puberty and adolescence (Germain 1991:354).

Obviously, since heterosexist assumptions dominate the environment of the lesbian, gay, and bisexual adolescent, there is no acceptable way to achieve adulthood as defined by traditional theories and environmental expectations. While essentially lesbian, gay, and bisexual adolescents face all the familiar stressors of adolescence, they also face some that are unique to their status as a stigmatized individual in society. Adaptations are necessary to achieve a "goodness of fit" between the person and his or her environment. This dilemma serves as the theoretical framework for understanding lesbian, gay, and bisexual adolescents in a developmental context.

The most frequent adaptive tasks for youths making the transition from childhood to adulthood (from a Western perspective) include:

1. Creating an expanded self-concept which usually draws on identification with one's gender, family, and cultural group

2. Working toward changing relationships and increasing independence from parents

3. Building a social support network

4. Pursuing opportunities to explore educational, career, and vocational goals

5. Establishing intimate relationships.

These specific adaptive tasks will be examined in relation to the coming out process, with particular reference to lesbian, gay, and bisexual youth.

SELF-CONCEPT

For the young lesbian, gay, or bisexual person who is coming out, there is almost always a discrepancy between how they feel, think, and behave and the environmental definition of how "normal" adolescents should feel, think, and behave. Browning (1987) notes that a young lesbian, gay, or bisexual's identity "will emerge through the resolution of his or her perceived discrepancy and how he or she chooses to relate to his or her environment" (47).

Although the Internet and the World Wide Web (see *http://www.youth.org/ resources.html*; *http://www.qrd.org/qrd/youth*; and *http://www.vector.net/cariboo/ youth*) have liberated gay and lesbian young people from their extreme isolation by supplying them with limitless opportunities to communicate with other young gays and lesbians in chat-rooms and bulletin boards, most lesbian, gay, and bisexual adolescents have little access to information about their emerging identity and few adult role models from which to learn. These young people usually have a very limited view of what it means to be lesbian or gay. The fact that their identity is a subject of constant public debate provides additional stress in their lives. Young people of color often have an even more difficult time managing their sexual identity since they already have to deal with the onerous effects of racial or ethnic discrimination and must now also choose to openly address or hide their sexual identity.

Developing a positive self-concept in an environment that assumes you are heterosexual at the same time it denigrates your gay, lesbian, or bisexual identity is a stressful and fatiguing process. Hunter and Schaecher (1990) say it best when they note:

It is very difficult to grow up with a positive self-image when one's identity carries a stigma. People who are unable to conform to the standards society calls normal are disqualified from full acceptance and are, therefore, stigmatized. Part of that process has been to label homosexuals as deviant, sick, or sinful.

(Hunter & Schaecher 1990:300)

Young lesbian, gay, and bisexual people, however, have also had to learn resiliency skills and continually look for means to cope with the stresses inherent in belonging to a stigmatized group. Support groups for youths, particularly those where they can find peer support, and safe-space drop-in centers as well as trained and affirming school counselors, clergy, and parents can assist young people in developing a positive self-concept to help them move toward a healthy adulthood. Developing a positive self-concept is essential for healthy development.

INDEPENDENCE FROM PARENTS

The process of independence from parents, notes Browning (1987), "involves reevaluating parental values and expectations, adopting those which hold relevance, rejecting those that are not congruent with self-definition" (48). Most families convey powerfully positive heterosexual messages—that is, that heterosexual relationships are the only valid and appropriate life goals. Some families, particularly families with strong religious convictions, may openly condemn homosexuality, unaware that their own child is lesbian, gay, or bisexual. And although some families might not openly denounce homosexuality, "the absence of discussion sends a negative message" (Browning 1987:48).

Families provide many opportunities for their children to receive validating reinforcement and approval for a heterosexual orientation; indeed, heterosexual children rarely have their sexual identity challenged as unacceptable. But while it is to some degree understood and accepted in most cultures for an adolescent to rebel against his or her parents, what young lesbian, gay, or bisexual youths fear most in revealing their sexual orientation is that their own families will reject their very personhood, resulting in the destruction of their relationship with them. This fear, real or imagined, can prevent a lesbian, gay, or bisexual young person from fully developing his or her identity. The goal for the social worker becomes to help the young person to see him/herself as being separate from the parents, to acknowledge differences and similarities in values and attitudes, while still being able to maintain a relationship with the family. If the lesbian, gay, and bisexual young person feels secure, then he or she may choose to come out to his or her parents. Indeed, parental reaction to a child's disclosure can be a positive experience that increases the level of intimacy and honesty between child and parents. Unfortunately, it can also be a negative experience: parents may react with anger, denial, and guilt, perhaps even insisting on therapy to "change" the young person's orientation; and in some cases disclosure to parents results in verbal harassment or physical abuse (Savin-Williams 1994). Disclosure can also cause expulsion from the home, or the young person may decide to leave voluntarily to seek out a safer environment with a better fit. For these reasons many gay and lesbian adolescents often try to learn to live with their secret, which sometimes leads them to experience an abnormal distancing from their families out of fear that their parents will discover it. In worst-case scenarios, children who cannot handle the fear of disclosure or the inner humiliation of being a stigmatized individual or whose parents are overtly rejecting may be driven to suicidal thoughts or actions.

SOCIAL SUPPORT

Browning (1987) notes that "heterosexual adolescents have many opportunities to explore their heterosexual identity within a supportive peer group and cultural milieu" (49). The lesbian, gay, or bisexual youth, conversely, may find the process of developing social support to be a challenge. Heterosexual peers may be intolerant of differences, especially with respect to differences around sexual orientation, because it threatens their own identity. Social workers need to help lesbian, gay, or bisexual youths identify age-appropriate resources in the community in an effort to provide them with opportunities to socialize with their peers. Such young people will also need assistance in learning about the culture of lesbian, gay, and bisexual people, as most do not have an adequate knowledge of what it means to be lesbian, gay, or bisexual. Without a supportive peer system, the young lesbian, gay, or bisexual person may feel increasingly isolated and respond by becoming psychosocially compromised or by engaging in high-risk behaviors.

In the absence of appropriate social supports, young gay males in particular are at risk in resorting to transient, anonymous, and potentially abusive sexual contacts as their only outlet. Gonsiorek (1988) notes that this secret behavior can become a highly maladaptive coping mechanism. However, for some young people, even anonymous sex is preferable to the alternatives of extreme loneliness and isolation (Martin 1982).

The following case example illustrates some of the issues regarding the isolation and lack of intimacy experienced by many gay and bisexual male adolescents (there is no documentation of this phenomenon occurring in the lesbian community). One young man, seen in counseling by the author, spoke about how he had assumed that all gay males were promiscuous loners without the support of their families or friends.

> I thought that all there was to being gay was sex. I had no idea that there were gay relationships, gay people who were out to their families, and who had

children and friends. I thought that being gay meant that you lived a secret life, that you were shunned and that you had sex with as many people as possible. So of course I had a lot of sex in parks, at bookstores, in movie theaters, in back rooms, even with people whom I did not know. That's how it was for me when I first came out. It's different now. [June 1995]

As evidenced by the above exchange, even though these activities at first made this young man uncomfortable and also included a dangerous element of hiding and secretiveness, he found them to be a preferable alternative to the loneliness and lack of intimacy that he experienced in being a gay youth. Sessions with this young person focused on his isolation and feelings of loneliness. In an effort to decrease feelings of loneliness and promote appropriate social behavior, the counselor introduced him to a local gay and lesbian social service agency where the young man could engage in nonsexual, social activities and where he could meet other gay and lesbian young people. In the form of direct education, this young man was cautioned about the need to reduce risky sex, and the potential consequences of unsafe sex for himself and his partners were discussed (see Hunter & Schaecher 1994).

EDUCATIONAL/CAREER/VOCATIONAL EXPLORATION

Developmentally, the adolescent is consistently seeking means to achieve competence and to be viewed by significant adults as productive and mature. Young lesbian, gay, and bisexual youths face educational, vocational, and career issues, but these must be viewed in the context of antigay and anti-lesbian discriminatory attitudes and violence. Antigay and anti-lesbian discrimination clearly exists in almost every educational, workplace, and neighborhood setting. High school, for most young lesbian, gay, and bisexual people, is the most stressful of all environments. Many suffer self-doubt or loss of self-esteem because of the homophobia they experience from antigay/anti-lesbian comments, jokes, and negative stereotypes. Just as the majority of educational and workplace environments are not positive or affirming toward gays and lesbians, neither are most educators knowledgeable about homosexuality or gay and lesbian issues, especially in regard to children and adolescents.

Personal safety is an extremely important consideration for the homosexually oriented adolescent. Lesbian, gay, or bisexual young people are at high risk for verbal harassment and physical violence (Hunter 1990; Savin-Williams 1994). One eighteen-year-old Latino young man told this vivid story about verbal harassment and physical violence:

It was my sophomore year at Christopher Columbus HS in the Bronx. I had just finished up my last midterm exam and was heading for the bus when I heard people yelling. I turned around and saw a crowd running after me.

"Marica, homo . . ."

I started running, but it wasn't long until they got me. They tried to hit me but a lady driving in a car started yelling, "the cops, the cops." They disappeared.

That wasn't the first time I was harassed because of my sexuality. My fellow students hurled insults at me all the time. Other students had hurt me emotionally many times and I could deal with that. But once I realized that they might hurt me physically, that's when I drew the line. After that crowd chased me and I just barely escaped getting beat up, I was too scared to go back to school.   (Valenzuela 1996:45)

Clearly, although discrimination and threats of violence are a reality for them, most lesbian, gay, and bisexual young people do finish school, obtain employment, and live within every community. And while young lesbian, gay, and bisexual persons may need assistance in developing coping strategies to deal with hostile environments, and understanding adults to help them in this process, most learn to successfully incorporate these adaptations into their lives.

ESTABLISHING INTIMATE RELATIONSHIPS

"Falling in love," "having a crush," or "feeling attracted to someone" are all terms that are usually evoked in a heterosexual context. And all are essential components of adolescent development. As adolescence is a time to try on new behaviors, to experiment with relationships and to develop a sense of intimacy, many lesbian, gay, and bisexual youths are unable to openly participate in this important socializing process. Indeed, most lesbian, gay, and bisexual youths may feel pressure from peers or family to have heterosexual sex in order to "be like everyone else." In an effort to adapt to their environment, one that expects adolescents to date opposite-gendered individuals, lesbian, gay, and bisexual teenagers may date members of the opposite sex in order to fit in or to test their feelings. Young lesbian, gay, and bisexual people may pass as heterosexual until they feel safe to "come out" and develop relationships with people of the same sex. As one young person said:

I was dating this girl from my school; she was really nice, but, I don't know, something was missing. I mean the zing just wasn't there. Then one day I was at her house and I met her brother—I immediately knew that he was like me. We started hanging out and pretty soon I stopped seeing her and I started seeing her brother. I mean I dated girls, I dated boys, I dated some more girls, then some more boys. I decided that I felt more comfortable with boys. [March 1993]

Savin-Williams (1995) notes that the difficulties of same-sex dating during adolescence are numerous. The first is the difficulty that young people may experience just in finding one another, or if they do, such relationships may be restricted to purely sexual encounters which often lack romance, affection, and intimacy. Most lesbian, gay, and bisexual youths are closeted and may not even be out to themselves. Additionally, there is no environmental support for or recognition of those who are involved with a member of the same sex. Young lesbian, gay, and bisexual people are told that emotional, physical, and affectional intimacy can only be achieved with members of the opposite gender. Lesbian, gay, and bisexual adolescents may never know that same-sex relationships are possible. Remafedi (1987b) notes that "without appropriate opportunities for dating and peer socialization, gay youth frequently eschew intimacy altogether and resort to transient and anonymous sexual encounters with adults" (1173).

Some lesbian, gay, and bisexual youths do meet, date, and become involved in relationships that enhance self-esteem, assist in lifting feelings of depression, and increase feelings of self-worth. Young lesbians and bisexual women, according to Savin-Williams (1990), had more relationships and longer-lasting romances that began at a younger age than did gay or bisexual males. However, more often than not, these young people are denied opportunities to be involved with people of the same sex, which causes them to feel worthless and alienated. Grace (1977) theorized that such a loss—so important in heterosexual adolescent development—could predispose some young people to feelings of depression and self-esteem difficulties as adults and almost certainly as teenagers. This may also increase the risk for other self-destructive behaviors including suicide, substance abuse, and other high-risk behaviors (Hunter & Schaecher 1987; Remafedi, Farrow, & Deisher 1991).

Developing Adaptations to a Hostile Environment

The fact that so many lesbian, gay, and bisexual young people do survive and do go on to become successful functioning adults is a testament to their resilience. Real effort must be made to build on this resilience of gay youth, as expressed in their adaptability, perseverance in the face of adversity, interpersonal skills, introspection, and pride in their lesbian, gay, or bisexual culture.

Malyon (1981:326–27) provides a useful model for examining how lesbian, gay, or bisexual adolescents make adaptations to an emerging homosexual identity. His model identifies three possible solutions:

1. Repression of same-sex desires
2. A developmental moratorium in which homosexual impulses are suppressed in favor of a heterosexual or asexual orientation
3. Homosexual disclosure and the decision to mobilize same-sex desires.

The young person who represses same-sex sexual desires chooses the most primitive and least satisfactory adaptation to an emerging homosexual orientation. While the repressed youngster may successfully "push down" his or her gay, lesbian, or bisexual feelings during adolescence, in response to environmental pressures and stresses, these impulses almost assuredly resurface later in life. Malyon (1982) suggests that coming out later in life in all probability causes panic and a major disruption of "established coping mechanisms and life patterns, since there has been no opportunity to integrate the homosexual desires" (327).

The young person who suppresses homosexual impulses during adolescence declares a temporary developmental moratorium. These youngsters often exhibit problems of identity formation, which becomes truncated as they attempt to "fit into" the heterosexual culture by adopting its values and role expectations. Frequently this is expressed through overachievement— overcompensating for feelings of inadequacy and unacceptability. Some young people may attempt to brace this suppression of their gay or lesbian feelings by becoming involved in heterosexual marriage; others make superhuman efforts to become the "perfect" child or the "best little girl or boy in the world." Sexual feelings are sublimated into positive or negative obsessions such as sports, academics, and clubs, or use of drugs or alcohol, or by engaging in other high-risk behaviors. This kind of adaptation represents a state of chronic unrest and disequilibrium, and it is not uncommon to find identity issues reemerging later when a person is in his thirties or forties. After years of suppressing same-sex sexual desires, the adult who did not address these desires during adolescence could experience what Malyon labels "the second epoch of a biphasic adolescence" (1982:327). This second phase is, quite literally, a reliving of the adolescent period which had been suppressed through hiding during biological adolescence. Such suppression of one's lesbian, gay, or bisexual impulses during primary adolescence can result in an "interruption and mitigation of the process of identity formation" (328). Coming out after adolescence prompts another phase of growth (similar to that which is usually exhibited during age-appropriate adolescence), its goal being the integration of "previously compartmentalized and rejected sexual and intimate capacities" (328).

Since the Stonewall Rebellion of 1969, many young people have been coming out earlier (Herdt & Boxer 1993). The youngster who decides during adolescence to disclose his or her lesbian, gay, or bisexual identity often feels alienated and neglected by peers as well as by the larger heterosexual culture. As lesbian- and gay-affirming support services for lesbian, gay, or bisexual youths are in short supply (Dulaney & Kelly 1982), young people who are open about their sexual orientation must either try to complete their developmental process in a hostile and unnurturing heterosexist environment or seek support and opportunities in the adult lesbian, gay, or bisexual community.

Some lesbian, gay, or bisexual youngsters, realizing that they cannot adapt to change themselves or their current local environment, will opt to migrate to one of the more widely known lesbian, gay, or bisexual communities. While such a move might be seen as a step toward healthfulness in exiting the stressful local environment, such a move may also have deleterious effects in that it separates young people from their families and requires the premature assumption of adult responsibilities and social roles (Mallon 1998; Malyon 1981). A frequent consequence of this choice is either homelessness, foster care placement, or survival prostitution, none of which promises a very positive outcome for young lesbian, gay, or bisexual people (Mallon 1992). Disclosure, however, also has many positive features in that some (Hunter & Schaecher 1987; Malyon 1981; Sullivan & Schneider 1987) have indicated that coming out as an adolescent can assist young people in achieving—maybe for the first time in their lives—a goodness of fit with their environment. Clearly, the disclosure of one's homosexual orientation, facilitated by coming out, can be framed as coping, which is a rebalancing process between the youth and his or her environment (Germain 1978). As social workers become increasingly skilled at providing more lesbian- and gay-affirming services, and as support groups for lesbian, gay, and bisexual youths burgeon across the country, more young people are choosing to be forthright about their orientation as opposed to hiding.

A fourth adaptation for young people, not mentioned by Malyon, is the group that identifies as bisexual during their adolescence, and later as gay or lesbian when they become adults. While some youngsters are truly bisexual in their orientation and remain so throughout their life, other youngsters self-identify as bisexual either to describe their sexual experimentation with both sexes or because it is somehow less stigmatizing to be bisexual. For some young people, bisexuality offers a possibly more acceptable bridge from heterosexuality to homosexuality by implying that one is at least half-heterosexual; for others, bisexuality is and should be considered to be a genuine sexual orientation.

Social Worker Practice with Lesbian, Gay, and Bisexual Adolescents

Most social workers and clinicians no longer accept the outmoded cure theories (Bieber et al. 1962; Cautela 1967; Feldman 1966; Feldman & MacCullough 1965; Mayerson & Lief 1965), which before 1973 (when homosexuality was depathologized) attempted to change sexual orientation and to thereby insist that lesbian, gay, and bisexual individuals somehow acquire a heterosexual orientation that to them was an unnatural "fit" since they were actually not heterosexually oriented. The consensus at present is to help clients develop an attitude of self-acceptance and move to recover from the trauma of growing up in hostile heterosexist environments.

The following suggestions may also be helpful for those practitioners who are interested in working with lesbian, gay, or bisexual youths:

1. Lesbian, gay, and bisexual young people need social workers who are nonjudgmental, and who can assist them in dealing with the stigma and discrimination that they experience, as well as other problems which may or may not have to do with one's sexual orientation. Social workers should facilitate social services for lesbian, gay, and bisexual young people by providing them with accurate and relevant information about their emerging identity. Literature written by gay and lesbian young people for gay and lesbian young people is most helpful (Alyson 1991; Due 1995; Heron 1994; Kay, Estepa, & Desetta 1996; Miranda 1996; Monette 1992). Videos and guest speakers should also be utilized. This information should assist the homosexually oriented youngster in abolishing myths and stereotypes and correcting misconceptions. This information can also help educate straight teens about their gay and lesbian peers (Greene 1996).

2. Social workers should not pretend to have all the answers and should become more familiar with existing literature that addresses the needs of lesbian, gay, and bisexual youth from a social work perspective (see Cates 1987; De Crescenzo 1994; Mallon 1994; Morrow 1993; Needham 1977).

3. Social workers practicing with young lesbian, gay, or bisexual clients must not fall into the trap of trying to identify lesbian, gay, or bisexual clients;

instead, professionals must focus their energy on creating lesbian- and gay-affirming environments where it is safe for all young people to be themselves. Social workers working with lesbian, gay, or bisexual youths must also remember to accept the client as a total person; too often the fact that a young person is lesbian, gay, or bisexual obscures everything else about them.

4. A basic social work principle states that workers should meet the client on his or her own terms. Let the client know that it is okay to be bisexual, gay, or lesbian. That it is okay to be confused and to not get involved or enter into a relationship. That it is even okay for the client to go back and forth and change his or her mind. The role of the social worker is to facilitate the process, not to insist that the lesbian, gay, or bisexual youth come out.

5. Help clients to understand and clarify their feelings about their sexual orientation. Allow them to talk about their feelings, their frustrations, and their successes.

6. Provide or be able to refer youngsters to nonsexual, healthy peer support groups within their local communities or schools. Social interaction between other lesbian, gay, and bisexual youth will help to alleviate the extreme social isolation and loneliness that most gay and lesbian adolescents experience.

7. Help clients to develop other appropriate contacts within the gay and lesbian community, to develop a social support network. Social workers should know these resources and be able to refer clients to them.

8. Help the client to develop effective interpersonal coping mechanisms to deal with the negative effects of societal stigmatization. Assist young people in exploring and developing such mechanisms to deal with conflict, relationships, depression, safer sex, and peer pressures.

9. Be aware of the signs of stress, especially in regard to thoughts of suicide as well possible excessive use of alcohol and substance abuse. Know how to refer clients to those resources which can help them to deal with these issues.

10. Help the client to deal with a wide variety of family issues and be prepared to help families also. Whenever possible, young people should be encouraged to reunite or reconcile with their families; if this is not possible, then help them find a supportive gay-affirming, out-of-home placement and encourage them to develop life skills that will enable them to live independently. Social workers should proceed very cautiously in assisting lesbian, gay, or bisexual youngsters who want to disclose their orientation to their families. Workers must understand the risks involved since no one can know in advance how a family will respond.

11. Assist in the training of other professionals by providing them with

accurate and adequate information about lesbian, gay, and bisexual adolescent issues. Help other professionals to view homosexuality from a nonjudgmental, nonpejorative perspective.

12. Be prepared to be an advocate for youngsters who are having trouble at school, in the group home, or in their own family. Protection of gay and lesbian youths from homophobic attitudes or actions is an important task for the social worker.

13. Respect confidentiality at all times. The relationship must be based on trust, understanding, and respect.

Conclusions

The developmental issues that confront gay and lesbian adolescents are rooted in their adjustment to a stigmatized role in a society which teaches them that they belong to a despised and hated group. Gay and lesbian youths struggle with the same problems as other adolescents, but also with difficulties that are unique to anyone who is homosexually oriented. A sense of differentness, first developed in some lesbian, gay, and bisexual people during childhood, can compound the stress one may feel in striving to develop a goodness of fit between the person and his or her environment. The stress of societal stigmatization and of hiding one's orientation leads to social, emotional, and cognitive isolation and intense feelings of loneliness, depression, hopelessness, low self-esteem, and worthlessness. The stress of dealing with family rejection, verbal harassment, or just the threat of physical violence can cause lesbian, gay, and bisexual youths to feel even further estranged from their environment. As has been shown, in worst-case situations young lesbian, gay, or bisexual individuals are at least three times more likely to attempt or commit suicide (Remafedi 1987b).

The most effective means for working with gay and lesbian adolescents is to assist these young people in developing strategies to enhance their lesbian, gay, or bisexual identity, not to seek ways to eliminate it. To be effective in practice with lesbian, gay, and bisexual youths, social workers themselves must first become more comfortable and knowledgeable about homosexual orientation. Social workers must recognize that heterosexist society has created a hostile environment for lesbian, gay, and bisexual people. As a consequence to social opprobrium, lesbian, gay, and bisexual youths must continually make adjustments in learning to adapt to an environment almost completely devoid of the necessary nutrients one needs to grow into a well-balanced, productive adult. In attempting to help lesbian, gay, and bisexual adolescents find a "fit" that both affirms their lives and promotes health, social workers must be willing to move beyond the stereotypes and mythology that surrounds homosexuality.

Those who work with gay and lesbian adolescents need to be comfortable addressing issues of homosexuality as well as to be open to developing individualized treatment plans by using a variety of approaches designed to address the unique needs of each client. Helping young people grow up to be responsible, well-adjusted adults is one of the primary goals of social work. The major role of the social worker in this process is to assist in promoting a "good fit" between the young person and his or her environment. Most young people in our society already have affirming environments to assist and support them on this journey. Gay and lesbian young people, however, usually experience a marked estrangement from their environment and, in some cases, may even find themselves completely rejected by those around them. They need caring adults in their lives to help them successfully accomplish their own journey to adulthood.

5

Between Men, Between Women

Sexual and Intimate Relationships

> A central task of adult development is to form and maintain satisfying intimate relationships. Despite negative stereotypes, many gay and lesbian couples do have relationships that are rewarding and long-lasting. This chapter discusses same-gender sexual activity and dating; couple relationships, both gay and lesbian; the current controversy about marriage for same-gender couples; and bisexual relationships. The ways homophobia and heterosexism affect same-gender sexual and couple relationships are explained, and the implications for social work practice are emphasized.

A gay, lesbian, or bisexual identity is most often defined by the nature of the sexual and affectional ties that people form. In fact, it is often the initiation of same-gender sexual and/or intimate activity that precipitates the coming out process. However, there is great variation in the kinds of sexual and intimate relationships desired and formed by gay, lesbian, and bisexual people. The sexual activities and intimate relationships of gay, lesbian, and bisexual people are affected by all the influences that can impact on similar heterosexual relationships, including class, race, culture, age, religion, education, geography, family relationships, coping with issues of sexual compatibility and functioning, the negotiation of a mutually agreeable level of commit-ment, the definition of roles and mutual responsibilities, handling workplace pressures, determining how leisure time is spent, and the management of conflict within an intimate relationship. However, gay, lesbian, and bisexual people must deal with these issues without the social and institutional sup-ports available to those in legally and religiously recognized marital relation-ships. In addition, there are special challenges faced by people who meet their needs for sexual satisfaction and intimacy within a gay, lesbian, or bi-sexual context because of the heterosexism and homophobia they encounter on both an individual and institutional level. This chapter provides an over-view of what is currently known about sexual and intimate relationships among gay, lesbian, and bisexual people, emphasizing the issues that may pre-sent themselves to social workers.

Because sexual orientation itself is popularly defined only by whom a per-son has sex with, gay, lesbian, and bisexual people are all too often seen only as sexual beings or as people for whom sex is of overriding importance in their lives. However, sexual orientation is about more than just sex. It is about the whole person, including social, affectional, and intimate behavior other than sex. A gay, lesbian, or bisexual person who is not sexually active is still a gay, lesbian, or bisexual person. Therefore this chapter addresses not just sex-ual behavior but also how gay, lesbian, and bisexual people meet the common human need for affection and intimacy.[1]

Just as gay and lesbian sex and sexuality have been overemphasized, gay and lesbian couple relationships have been understudied.[2] In addition, many myths surround gay and lesbian relationships: that gays and lesbians don't want and/ or can't achieve long-lasting relationships; that gay and lesbian relationships are generally "unhappy, abnormal, dysfunctional, and deviant"; and that gay and lesbian relationships are modeled on the traditional role patterns of heterosex-ual relationships (Peplau 1993:399). Recent research on same-gender couple relationships has shown that gays and lesbians can and do seek and sustain long-term relationships that are healthy and fulfilling. Although there is great diver-sity among same-gender couples, most experts, like Peplau (1993), have con-cluded that "homosexual partnerships appear no more vulnerable to problems and dissatisfactions than their heterosexual counterparts, although the specific problems encountered may differ for same-sex and cross-sex couples" (414). Because bisexual people are involved with both same- and opposite-gender sex and relationships, gay and lesbian sexuality and relationships will be discussed first, and the little that is now known about bisexual sexuality and relationships will then be separately summarized.

Sexuality and Sexual Identity

Same-gender sex, like cross-gender sex, is affected by the views of sex and sexuality in the culture in general and what individuals have absorbed through their families and from the wider society. There are many sharply contrasting views of sex and sexuality across cultures and even within American society (Blumenfeld & Raymond 1988; Laumann et al. 1994). The *conservative* or *pro-creational* view of sexuality is based on "the assumption that the primary purpose of sexual activity is to reproduce " (Laumann et al. 1994:511). This perspective of sexuality leads to a political stance on homosexuality that Sullivan (1995) describes as *prohibitionist*. The *liberal* or *relational* view, emphasizing the right of personal privacy, sees nothing wrong with consensual sexual activity among adults in the belief that "sexual activity is a natural component of an intimate, living relationship" (Laumann et al. 1994). This point of view undergirds the political stance toward homosexuality that Sullivan (1995) also calls *liberal*. The *libertine* or *recreational* view emphasizes the pursuit of pleasure as the primary purpose of sexual activity, suggesting that sex is not an ethical issue, although sometimes limiting the statement to sexual activity between consenting adults. Sullivan (1995) describes the corresponding political perspective as *liberationist*. There is also the *feminist* view that emphasizes the need for consent, equality, and mutuality in all sexual interactions (Blumenfeld & Raymond 1988). The libertine view is a component of the gay liberation movement and "queer" activism, while the feminist view has had a specific influence among lesbian feminists.

These various attitudes about sex and sexuality have influenced gay, lesbian, and bisexual people as individuals, their communities and others in their social context, as well as the helping professionals with whom they may interact. Unlike heterosexual sex, however, same-gender sex and sexuality is generally seen as being by definition incompatible with the conservative view of sex, the view that informs much of the homophobic and heterosexist rhetoric that gay, lesbian, and bisexual people encounter.

An individual's first sexual activities usually occur as masturbation and/or in the context of play with other children. This is as true for same-gender sexual activity as it is for cross-gender sex. A young girl or boy may experience same-gender erotic fantasies while masturbating, or she or he may begin to experience sexual arousal in the presence of or during what had previously been asexual physical contact or play with a friend. These early experiences of same-gender attraction are usually confusing, surprising, and/or frightening—at least to some degree—as the individual seeks to understand what they mean.

Despite the conservative view of sexuality, the age at which young people are initiating sexual activity with others has been steadily declining in this century, especially for women (Laumann et al. 1994). In fact, there is a great discrepancy between what people actually do and the belief that sexual activity in adolescence is wrong (Laumann et al. 1994). Based on self-reported age at first sexual intercourse, national surveys, including the large-scale Laumann et al. (1994) study, have shown that the age of first sexual intercourse has been declining slowly but steadily in the latter half of this century. For example, the Laumann et al. (1994) study showed that for those born between 1963 and 1974, who are in their twenties and thirties in the 1990s, only about 39 percent of men and 42 percent of women reported having had *no* sex partners before the age of eighteen. Stated another way, 1990 statistics show that 71 percent of all eighteen-year-olds have had sexual intercourse by age eighteen (Guttmacher 1994).

As the initiation of sexual activity with others and the selection of sex partners occurs at younger ages, issues of sexual orientation for those who think about or engage in same-gender sexual activity are arising earlier, too. Adolescence is traditionally seen developmentally as a time of potential identity confusion and reconsolidation. For those teens whose ventures into intimate relationships involve same-gender sexuality, the developmental challenge may be intensified (see chapter 4).

Just as heterosexual males become sexually active on average earlier than heterosexual women do (Guttmacher 1994; Laumann et al. 1994), gay males are likely to have acted on their homosexual feelings at younger ages than lesbians. For example, Laumann et al. (1994) report that, among those who had any same-gender sexual activity, almost twice as many men as women reported that they had had such activity with a partner since puberty (7.1 percent of men and 3.8 percent of women). However, that study did not ask about the specific age at which people had had their first same-gender sex. Although the data on lesbian and bisexual youth in particular are very limited (Rotheram-Borus & Fernandez 1995), studies have suggested that men report beginning the coming out process and engage in same-gender sex at younger ages than women do (Dempsey 1994).

In addition, for males, it is same-gender sexual activity that is likely to precipitate questions about a gay or bisexual identity; for females, emotional attachment and questioning of their sexual orientation is more likely to precede same-gender sexual activity. As de Monteflores and Schultz (1978) point out:

> Women, it would appear, avoid identifying themselves as gay by emphasizing their feelings; men by denying their feelings. . . . Among lesbians, a first

homosexual experience is often seen as "special," that is, the event is roman-
ticized and explained in terms of intense love and meaningfulness . . . [as
about] "this particular woman." . . . A man is more likely to deny affective
involvement in order to minimize the importance of his sexual experiences
with men. He may neutralize his emotions by emphasizing money or sexual
gratification as the goal of sexuality . . . or he may deny responsibility for his
feelings or actions as in the "boy-was-I-drunk syndrome."

(de Monteflores and Schultz 1978:68)

This gender difference in the motivation for an initial sexual experience is not
much different for heterosexuals; for example, the Laumann et al. (1994)
study found that women were much more likely than men to report that they
were in love with the partner with whom they first had sex, while men were
more likely to report curiosity about sex as a reason for having intercourse
the first time.

Sexual behavior and sexual orientation rarely correlate perfectly. Some who
later develop an identity as gay, lesbian, or bisexual may not experience same-
gender attraction and/or activity until after some period of asexuality or of
heterosexual activity (Dempsey 1994). For example, Laumann et al. (1994)
report that among those in their survey who had experienced any same-gender
sexual activity, about 91 percent of men and 95 percent of women had had sexual partners of both genders at some point since puberty, meaning that only
about 9 percent of the men and 5 percent of the women had experienced same-
gender sexuality only. Sometimes young people may engage in a mixture of
same- and cross-gender sexual and affectional experiences during adolescence
and/or young adulthood, only later settling into a pattern of lesbian, gay, heterosexual, or bisexual identity (Rotheram-Borus & Fernandez 1995). Then a
process of "recasting the past" begins (de Monteflores & Schultz 1978), often
including reinterpreting and "owning" previously forgotten or disavowed same-
gender behavior and/or relationships and/or reevaluating and specifically devaluing cross-gender experiences. Others may engage in some mixture of
same- and opposite-gender sexual and intimate activity for a longer time,
meaning that the initiation of same-gender sexual activity and/or a commitment to same-gender or mixed-gender sex or sexual identity can occur at a
later stage of life.

SAME-GENDER SEX

Heterosexual sex is often thought of as limited to penile-vaginal activity. Even
scientific studies of sexuality tend to define the beginning of sexual activity

according to the initiation of penile-vaginal intercourse. Of course we know that while this activity is the most common and is generally seen as the apex of heterosexual activity, it is only one form of sexual expression in a large repertoire of possible sexual behaviors or ways of giving and receiving sexual pleasure. The discovery that female orgasm is the same whether it results from vaginal or from clitoral stimulation, for example, has helped to legitimate other forms of sexual activity for women even in the heterosexual context. In addition, one effect of the AIDS epidemic has been the need to educate people about safer sexual practices; while safer sex can involve the same activities with the use of a condom, it can also encompass the use of other activities that lead to the giving and receiving sexual pleasure but that do not, as heterosexual intercourse does, involve the exchange of bodily fluids.

Same-gender sexual activity is no different, then, than heterosexual activity. Same-gender sexual partners use the same methods that heterosexual people use, *other than* penile-vaginal intercourse, to give and receive sexual pleasure. These methods may and often do include kissing, stroking, cuddling, and/or body rubbing; manual stimulation of the genitals; oral sex (fellatio and cunnilingus); and anal sex. Even much less common sexual practices, such as the use of "sex toys" and pornography, and even those devices and behaviors associated with sadomasochistic sex, are associated with cross-gender as well as with same-gender sex. Most gays and lesbians engage in many forms of sexual activity, and strict adherence to a particular role in sexual activity is relatively uncommon (Bell & Weinberg 1978).

The pattern of sexual activity within a same-gender couple may be that one partner is more "active" and the other more "passive" in one or more of these activities or that there is symmetry in them. Among males, this pattern may be referred to as *top* and *bottom*; among females, it may be associated with a *butch/femme* stereotype. However, while it is often thought that the sexual behaviors in a same-gender couple tend to mirror a traditional male-female, active-passive stereotype or are designed to resemble penile-vaginal intercourse as closely as possible, these patterns *may or may not* apply. In addition, just as heterosexual couples differ in the narrowness or breadth of the range of sexual techniques that are known and used, some same-sex couples engage in a range of sexual behaviors while others are more limited in the ways they use to express physical affection and sexual pleasure (Roth 1985).

For the helping professional, comfort in dealing with issues of sexuality in general is essential, although it may not be easy to achieve. In the case of same-gender sexuality, for the heterosexual practitioner it is generally helpful to remember that one is dealing with sexual activities that are also part and parcel of the heterosexual repertoire and not with some set of activities that are unique to same-gender sex. However, there may be terms used to describe these activities that are unique to gay, lesbian, or bisexual culture and that may or may not be familiar, even if the activities they refer to are. Certainly, too, certain sexual acts are more common in the same-gender context, given that heterosexual penile-vaginal intercourse is not part of the repertoire.

FREQUENCY OF SEXUAL ACTIVITY

As already noted, there is a tendency to view gay, lesbian, and bisexual people exclusively as sexualized. However, the evidence for the idea that those who self-identify as gay, lesbian, or bisexual are more sexually active or more interested in sex than those who identify as heterosexual does not confirm this stereotype (Bell & Weinberg 1978; Isay 1989; Laumann et al. 1994). For example, men and women who identified as gay, lesbian, or bisexual reported having about two to three times as many sexual partners since age eighteen than those who identified as heterosexual. Part of this difference may be due to the fact (already noted) that most gay and lesbian people engage in opposite-gender sexual activity at some point in their lives in addition to their same-gender activity. By contrast, looking at self-reported frequency of sexual activity in the previous month, men who reported any same-gender sexual activity had consistently *lower* reported frequencies of sexual activity than those who described themselves as heterosexual either by identity or the absence of same-gender sexual activity (Laumann et al. 1994). (The data given in the Laumann et al. study for women who reported a lesbian identity or same-gender sexual activity were more limited and equivocal.) This conclusion is consistent with the Laumann et al. finding overall that those who are heterosexually married seem to report and enjoy the greatest opportunity for satisfying sexual activity in this society, perhaps because they do so in the context of a culturally approved and socially supported relationship.

PROBLEMS WITH SEX

Sexual problems can occur in gay or lesbian relationships just as they can in heterosexual ones. However, the kinds of problems encountered in lesbian and gay relationships appear to differ. Because male sexuality seems oriented to orgasm in both same- and opposite-gender contexts, problems surrounding the achievement of orgasm seem to be the most common sexual complaint in gay male relationships. Reece (1988) suggests that while "early ejaculation" may be the more common sexual dysfunction reported among men in cross-gender relationships, inhibited orgasm may be the more common complaint in gay male relationships. The patterns of sexual interaction in gay sex do not make one partner's orgasm dependent on the achievement of orgasm by the other; early ejaculation thus affects only one partner's satisfaction, not both. However, problems of arousal or in achieving orgasm may trouble both the man with the problem and the partner who wishes to please him. Such problems can have a medical basis, which should always be ruled out before assuming that the problem is an interpersonal one.

In addition, specific sexual behaviors can have specific symbolic meanings to people that can create problems. For example, some have reported that anal sex, particularly negotiations around who will be the "active" or inserting person and who will be the "passive" or receptive person, can be a source of problems for gay males. Being the more "passive" partner can be threatening to a sense of masculinity and hence create problems within a male-male sexual partnership (Blumstein & Schwartz 1983; Isay 1989).

AIDS can also have an impact on the sexual functioning of gay male couples. An issue that may occur in gay couples, as in heterosexual ones, is the inhibition of sexual functioning when safe-sex practices are being used (Mattison & McWhirter 1994). In addition, when one member of the couple is HIV-positive and the other is not, the infected partner may withdraw sexually out of fear of spreading the virus to his partner, which can be experienced by the partner as distancing or rejection. When both are infected, there may be an unspoken tension about who did what sexually to become infected and/or about who infected whom (Forstein 1994; Mattison & McWhirter 1994). In the face of these tensions, some HIV-positive gay men may experience the impulse to act out sexually outside of the relationship in unsafe ways, which can affect the couple's sexual relationship as well (Forstein 1994).

The most commonly discussed sexual problems in lesbian couples seem to be, by contrast, problems of desire or of infrequent or declining sexual activity over time (Bell & Weinberg 1978; Blumstein & Schwartz 1983; Magee & Miller 1992; Roth 1985). In fact, some romantic lesbian relationships are or become completely asexual (Rothblum & Brehony 1991). One explanation that has been offered for this observation relates to gender socialization: that women are socialized in the culture to be sexually receptive, not to be sexual initiators, and thus when two women are together, especially once the initial intense excitement that is characteristic of all early intimate relationships has waned, neither may be skilled or interested in getting sexual activity going (Blumstein & Schwartz 1983; Roth 1985; Slater 1995). As in all couples, a decline in sexual interest or activity may be symptomatic of other acknowledged or unacknowledged nonsexual difficulties in the couple (Blumstein & Schwartz 1983). For example, since many women have experienced sexual victimization at some point in childhood or adolescence, sexual inhibition or other sexual difficulties as a result of the victimization can affect women in a lesbian relationship, just as it can affect women in a heterosexual one (Murphy 1994; Nichols 1987; Slater 1995).

Heterosexism and homophobia may also play a role in sexual inhibition among lesbians: if one generally suppresses all visible expressions of affection or sexual attraction outside the bedroom, especially in public, in order to feel safe, it may be difficult to "turn on" the feelings that have been carefully "turned off," even when it is safe and desirable to do so (Roth 1985). This problem may affect women more than men because it is known that, even in the heterosexual context, women are on average more likely than men to want or need a continuum of expressions of caring, including gestures of romance and affection, prior to and surrounding sexual activity in order to respond sexually. Thus, the invisibility of lesbian relationships and their construction as "roommate" or "special friendship" relationships may weaken sexual bonds.

Finally, for both gay and lesbian couples, the demands of jobs, extended family, and/or child care responsibilities can compete for priority with romance and the need to keep a longer-term sexual relationship vital. Thus it is worth noting that while the problem of declining or absent sexuality may be more common in lesbian than in gay male relationships, it does happen in the gay male context as well (Blumstein & Schwartz 1983; Shernoff 1995a).

The same frameworks used to understand and treat problems in sexual functioning in heterosexual couples are generally considered useful in treating same-gender couples as well (as long as the treating sex therapist is not homophobic him/herself). However, especially when dealing with same-gender relationships between women, it may be important to consider that genital sexual expression has a different salience to women than to men, that erotic desire differs in "its relative importance to [an individual's] sense of identity" (Magee & Miller 1992). Since, however, sexual desire and activity seem to define a gay, lesbian, or bisexual identity, problems of sexual desire may raise anxieties about sexual orientation itself. In addition, of course, it is necessary to be knowledgeable about the varieties of gay sexual and socialization practices and alert to the ways in which internalized homophobia can contribute to anxieties and inhibitions that are related to the sexual dysfunction (Reece 1988).

Looking for Love

No discussion of sexuality and intimacy is complete without consideration of how people initially make connection with their partners. Both psychological and social factors play a role in how all people, whether involved in same-gender or cross-gender relationships, find ways to meet their sexual, affectional, and social needs. However, homophobia and heterosexism exert a powerful influence on those who are looking for same-gender love and intimacy, affecting both psychological and social aspects of this process.

Since gay, lesbian, and bisexual people cannot usually be recognized as such by their appearance, the first challenge that a person interested in same-gender sex or relationships must face is how to identify others who share that interest (Murphy 1994). Many of the social and cultural institutions that have developed in areas, typically in heavily populated urban centers, with a large identified gay and/or lesbian population have in fact been established to meet this need. Prominent among them have been gay and/or lesbian bars, gay and/or lesbian bookstores, bath houses for gay men, and various social clubs and organizations. These groups and institutions function as places where people can go to meet other people like themselves. Thus they meet the dating needs of those looking for sexual or intimate connection and for those in such relationships who seek safe places in which to socialize or to enjoy romantic recreation—to dance, for example. In some communities there may even be alternative newspapers that have personal advertisements designated as for "men seeking men" or "women seeking women" or dating services that cater to same-gender couples. Thus institutions parallel to those used by many heterosexual people have sprung up to try to meet this common human need for dating and romantic recreation in a social context of invisibility and/or potential harassment.

While recognizing the importance of these alternative institutions to gay, lesbian, and bisexual life, it is important to remember that gay, lesbian, and bisexual people also meet each other, get intimately involved, and/or fall in love in other kinds of contexts as well: at work; at school; through voluntary associations, clubs, and organizations centered around other issues (political, social, or recreational); and through friendship networks. Thus gay, lesbian, and bisexual people meet their partners in all the ways and places that heterosexual people do. However, on average, these kinds of contacts may be less available to them than to heterosexual couples (Murphy 1994), making identified gay or lesbian organizations and settings important for initiating these contacts, at least for some. Those men and women seeking a same-gender relationship who live in rural or other areas in which these gay-identified resources are limited thus may suffer greater isolation and loneliness as a result.

Whatever the context in which a relationship begins, the initiation of same-gender sexual or romantic relationships may be the occasion for greater visibility and thus for greater risk. The expression of affection in public, for example, such as holding hands or embracing, is still quite unusual in most areas and may cause a couple or individual to become the target of verbal or physical harassment. Biracial couples may be especially visible and thus at even greater risk (Greene 1994b; Murphy 1994). In addition,

> ethnic and racial minority gay men and lesbian women live in three communities: the gay and lesbian community, the racial/ethnic community, and the dominant, mainstream society. Although each community offers some support, each has its own expectations and demands which conflict with each other. The tension of living in these three communities, in all of which one feels marginalized, adds to identity difficulties, which can be particularly difficult if there are racial and cultural differences between the partners.
>
> (Murphy 1994:25)

For example, the expectations of some racial and ethnic groups, such as Latinos (Morales 1996) and East Asians (Liu & Chan 1996), may be that ties and responsibilities to the family of origin will be more important than those to a partner, perhaps creating tensions within the couple.

The community institutions designed to support lesbian and gay social life, such as gay or lesbian bars, may in fact be dangerous because some people intent on harassing or harming gay or lesbian people may go there to identify their victims (see chapter 10). Realistic assessment of this risk has an important influence on the strategies for stigma management—assimilation and passing, confrontation, ghettoization, or the embrace of a sense of special identity (de Monteflores 1986)—that an individual or couple may decide to adopt. In addition, gay, lesbian, and bisexual people who also identify as people of color often do not find gay and lesbian community institutions to be as hospitable or comfortable for them as whites do since whites tend to predominate in them.

Entering into an important intimate relationship may also be the occasion for disclosure of a lesbian, gay, or bisexual identity to family members or other significant people, such as heterosexual friends, in order to share one's joy in the relationship and to allow the new partner to become a part of the social and family events that the individual may previously have taken part in alone (Lee 1992). "Yet this may be the hardest task gay individuals face due to painful homophobic responses received and anticipated" (Lee 1992:17). In sum, entering into a same-gender sexual or romantic relationship may precipitate some degree of social crisis for the individual or couple.

Because of the link between same-gender sexual and romantic activity and the very nature of a gay, lesbian, or bisexual identity, the beginning of a sexual, romantic, or intimate relationship (especially a first or potentially important one) may precipitate an individual crisis as well:

> Coming out sexually/emotionally in a relationship . . . is usually a turning
> point in the coming out process. This can cause emotional turmoil as well as
> the positive feelings of joy, love, closeness, relief and authenticity. Finding
> and maintaining a partner relationship is a critical search and life task for
> many gay men and lesbian women.   (Lee 1992:16)

This infusion of a key pleasurable event with a sense of psychological, social,
and/or physical threat is a more common experience for lesbian, gay, or bisexual people than for those engaged in cross-gender relationships, especially
for men.

Relatively little research has been done on the social and interpersonal rituals of dating in either the cross-gender or same-gender context. However, using
the concept of the social script (see chapter 2), which is thought to have cultural, interpersonal, and intrapsychic elements, Klinkenberg and Rose (1994)
studied the dating behavior of a sample of gay men and lesbians. Much of the
behavior that the gay men and lesbians described as being part of a first date was
very similar to what heterosexual couples have described in other studies. However, there were some differences, such as the common report by both gay men
and lesbians of discussing coming out during the date. In addition, while young
heterosexual women often reported telling their parents about a first date, lesbian women did not. Within each couple interaction described, a gay man or
lesbian woman was less likely to describe gender-stereotypic interpersonal
behavior than a heterosexual man or woman. Although most elements of a first-
date script were common to both gay and lesbian couples, there were differences between the behavior of lesbians and gay men on a first date that seemed
to reflect gender issues, e.g., gay men were more likely to report sexual contact
on the first date while lesbians emphasized emotional issues (Klinkenberg &
Rose 1994). Thus both issues related to dealing with the social context, such as
coming out and a disinclination to share information about dating experiences
with family, and issues that seem related to the same-gender nature of the relationship, such as the differential emphasis on sex or emotional intimacy, have an
impact on even the very beginning of gay, lesbian, and bisexual relationships.

Beyond the first date, on average, the degree to which men and women seek
out and enjoy anonymous or casual sex differs markedly. This activity is often
termed *cruising* in the gay male community. For example, one survey of same-
gender couples showed that more gay men than lesbians met their partner at a
bar or via a sexually charged setting, such as through the personals column or
in a bath house (Bryant & Demian 1994). By contrast, more lesbians reported
meeting their partner through friends or at work (Bryant & Demian 1994;
Murphy 1994) or from establishing a friendship with a potential partner before

initiating a sexual relationship (Klinkenberg & Rose 1994; Murphy 1994; Slater 1995). For men, such contacts may be for sex only, not for a relationship. However, these gender issues affect gay, lesbian, and bisexual relationships after a sexual or dating situation becomes something a bit more permanent—that is, when the pair begin seeing themselves as a "couple."

Same-Gender Couples

As in heterosexual relationships, there are several distinct stages in the formation and development of gay, lesbian, and bisexual relationships. Even as more gay and lesbian couples now rear children (see chapter 6), the use of the terms *couple* or *relationship* on the one hand, or *family* on the other, to describe a gay or lesbian relationship seems to reflect a position about whether or not a family can be "complete" as a twosome. Even what to call the person to whom one relates as part of an established pair is a problem—*lover, partner, girlfriend*, and *boyfriend* being common options, each with its advantages and drawbacks. Chapter 6 will deal with gay and lesbian parenting issues; chapter 8, on midlife and older gay and lesbian people, will deal with how those life stages affect gay and lesbian couples and gay/lesbian family relationships. This section deals with the special issues involved in the formation of gay and lesbian couples and in negotiating ongoing relationships.

Slater (1995), in writing about lesbian relationships from a family systems perspective, has discussed "family formation," the negotiation of "ongoing couplehood," and, in some instances, the integration of children into the family; she has also examined the challenges of the individual life cycle during the middle and older years. Thus some stages are seen as being intrinsic to the life of the family or couple itself while others reflect the intersecting of the life stage of the individual(s) involved with the life of the couple itself. McWhirter and Mattison (1984), and others who have drawn on their work to study gay male couples, speak of "blending" in the first year, "nesting" or settling in to the relationship in the second and third years, followed by the "building" and "maintaining" stages in years four through ten; their last two stages of long-term relationships, "releasing" and "renewing," are addressed as much to the mid- and late-life tasks of the individuals as to the ways couples must find to deal with them (Kurdek 1995). Clunis and Green (1988) adapted these to lesbian couples, suggesting phases of prerelationship, romance (like "blending"), conflict (like "maintaining"), acceptance, commitment, and collaboration, when the couple seeks to create something together in the outside world.

One of the major controversies underlying all discussions of gay and lesbian relationships is whether same-gender relationships do or should resemble the cultural norms embodied in heterosexual marriage. A common heterosexist prejudice is that same-gender relationships are inherently flawed and thus cannot achieve health and stability; another is that gay and lesbian people in same-gender relationships usually play out roles within those relationships that mirror those of the traditional heterosexual marriage. Both of these beliefs are without foundation in fact (Peplau 1993; Green, Bettinger, & Zacks 1996).

Gay and lesbian liberationists often argue that the normative ideals of heterosexual marriage and the nuclear family embody so much that is both sexist and heterosexist that gay and lesbian couples should reject all the norms associated with it, such as monogamy, as a model for their own lives (Vaid 1995). Another way in which this debate has been framed is in terms of culture—that is, about whether there is (or are) a distinct gay and/or lesbian culture(s), which is(are) in turn reflected in gay or lesbian family forms, and, politically speaking, whether there even should be (Blumenfeld & Raymond 1988; Sullivan 1995; Vaid 1995; Weston 1991). Given the fact that gay and lesbian relationships are defined by the fact that they are same-gender relationships and because they currently do not receive the same social and legal support, however, legal marriage is not currently an option as it is for heterosexual pairs. Thus gay and lesbian relationships cannot by definition be the same as heterosexual ones in all respects, leading to what Brown (1989) has termed the "normative creativity" of gay and lesbian people as they invent lives and relationships outside the usual patterns. This creativity in couples has also been described as a high degree of healthy role flexibility within the relationship (Green, Bettinger, & Zacks 1996).

COUPLE FORMATION

There comes a point in any sexual or dating relationship when the partners must decide whether or not to define themselves as a couple. To do so generally implies some hope of developing an ongoing relationship, and this hope may or may not be mutually shared. In addition, the partners may have similar or different ideas about what the nature of a desirable relationship should be. In the heterosexual context, the progression may be from a steadily dating pair to a negotiation of the kinds of sexual behavior that are acceptable to both partners in the relationship to a commitment to marry, with or without a period of cohabitation prior to marriage. The decision to marry—the engagement—and the point of marriage itself are generally marked visibly and socially with rings, public announcements, and public ceremonies. These events themselves are ritualized and, in the case of marriage, marked within and outside the couple by ongoing ritual in the form of anniversary observances. Other more private markers of the progression of a relationship—the first intercourse, the first vacation together, introducing a new partner to friends and/or coworkers, introducing a partner to immediate and later to extended family members—are often equally important to the couple and to the individuals involved. However, much less ritual typically surrounds these events despite their importance. For example, the introduction of a new partner to friends and/or family is often an occasion for observation and feedback on the partner and for the partners to discover about each other how they negotiate potentially stressful events that are important to the other. These observations are often crucial to each partner in assessing the potential for the relationship to survive over the long run.

In addition to the lack of legal recognition, many of the social and religious rituals around couple formation that are available to heterosexual couples, especially the more public ones, are not available in gay and lesbian relationships (Murphy 1994). Cultural and social heterosexism is enacted in the fact that the rituals that help bind a heterosexual couple together are not available to those in same-gender relationships. Stated another way, the couple must invent its own social scripts, within the relationship as well as between the couple and others in the wider world (Murphy 1994). A substantial proportion of gay and lesbian couples, for example, make specific legal arrangements so as to be able to leave property to or to speak legally for a partner when needed (Bryant & Demian 1994).

Even the more private markers of couple formation, such as the introduction of a significant new partner to the family, may not be possible or may be made more complex and difficult if one or both partner's friends, coworkers, or family members do not feel positively about their sexual orientation, that is, by an encounter with individual homophobia or heterosexism. In fact, it is often the beginning of what a person views as an especially significant partner relationship that precipitates the disclosure of a gay, lesbian, or bisexual identity to family so that the partner may become integrated into extended family life. Thus a time of great joy—the beginning of an intimate and loving relationship—is often also a time of great pain arising from these encounters with heterosexism, and the stress on each partner from bearing this pain can have its effect on the beginning relationship itself. Because of the lack of other ways to mark a significant relationship, there is some evidence that gay and lesbian couples often decide to live together earlier in the course of a relationship than heterosexual couples do (Murphy 1994; Slater 1995). However, gay and/or lesbian social groups and friendship networks sometimes substitute for other friend and family relationships as places where a couple can announce and get support for its existence and its developing intimacy, where, for example, a decision to live together can be discussed and celebrated. Having such a supportive network of friends appears to be correlated with well-being in gay and lesbian couples (Green, Bettinger, & Zacks 1996).

The capacity to achieve intimacy with another, whatever the context, is a major psychological task of adult development (Erikson 1950). In the past, because same-gender relationships were seen as inherently flawed, it was also concluded that gay and lesbian individuals had failed by definition in achieving this milestone of adult development. However, the current view is that any relationship—same-gender or opposite-gender—offers the potential for true intimacy. There is a great deal of evidence that many gay and lesbian couples are able to achieve truly satisfying intimate and long-lasting relationships (Bell & Weinberg 1978; Bryant & Demian 1994; Kurdek 1988; Peplau 1993; Green, Bettinger, & Zacks 1996), relationships that are psychologically indistinguishable from successful heterosexual ones. Thus an individual in a mutually satisfying gay or lesbian couple relationship should be seen for what he or she is—a person who has achieved a major milestone in individual development. As Browning (1988) has noted, "the nature of intimate relationships depends a great deal upon the degree of development of the individual's identity. Developing intimacy requires the ability to take emotional risks by sharing one's *real* self and establishing a level of commitment between oneself and another" (51; emphasis in the original). It is on this basis—the nature of the intimate bond itself and the capacity of each member of the couple to be genuine within it—that same-gender relationships must be evaluated, not on their resemblance to or lack of resemblance to the norms of heterosexual marriage. Conversely, in acknowledging the social and cultural barriers to the establishment and maintenance of a same-gender relationship, gay, lesbian, and bisexual individuals can be seen as facing special challenges as they work to achieve this developmental goal.

ISSUES FOR GAY AND/OR LESBIAN COUPLES

One of the first issues that a gay, lesbian, or bisexual individual must face in becoming part of a couple and in talking about that experience within and outside the relationship is language (Healy 1993; Murphy 1994). What word shall be used to describe the partner—lover? partner? "wife" or "husband"? The way the relationship is named must be acceptable to both members of the couple. Sometimes it is talked about differently within the relationship than outside it, leading to issues of self-censorship and genuine confusion about how to talk about the relationship to others, especially those who are not themselves lesbian, gay, or bisexual, in ways that will communicate the meaning of the relationship effectively. While this problem may exist to some degree for cohabiting but unmarried heterosexual couples as well, it is not one that can be solved by the same-gender couple through the language of engagement and/or marriage.

The fact that there is no easy language with which to describe a same-gender couple relationship leads to another potential problem: invalidation of the relationship through invisibility or the "assumption of heterosexuality" (DePoy & Noble 1992). While many same-gender couples use strategies within and outside the home to protect themselves from identification as lesbian, gay, or bisexual, others seek recognition of their relationships and inclusion of their partners in at least some private or more public events. The task of communicating the nature and importance of the relationship, especially to those who are not themselves lesbian, gay, or bisexual, is often a difficult one.

Another way in which same-gender couples may not resemble most heterosexually married couples is in the nature of the contract between them about sexuality. The stereotype of the homosexual couple is of hypersexuality within and outside the relationship. In fact, it is much more common in gay male relationships, even in many enduring ones, to find that sexual monogamy is not part of the relationship (Bell & Weinberg 1978; Blumstein & Schwartz 1983; Bryant & Demian 1994; Murphy 1994; Kurdek 1988, 1995). However, it should be noted that most of the research on this issue was conducted before the onset of the AIDS epidemic (Murphy 1994). Shernoff (1995a) recently updated this discussion and proposed a system of classification of gay male couples based largely on the variation in "the roles sex plays in the development and maintenance of the relationship" (43), from sexual exclusivity to unacknowledged nonmonogamy to primarily monogamous relationships with a regular additional participant, and acknowledged "open" relationships. His classification system includes also "nonsexual lovers," most often couples whose relationship had been sexual but which is later maintained as primary although sexual activity is no longer a part of it. While it may be that there is similar variation in lesbian and/or heterosexual relationships, at least in centers of gay culture this variation may well be more common in gay male couples than in others. There is not enough information available to give any reliable estimates of how common or successful any of these patterns are among gays, or in any other type of couple for that matter.

Monogamy in general is more important to heterosexual than to lesbian or gay couples, even though monogamy is more common in lesbian than gay male couples (Bryant & Demian 1994; Murphy 1994; Kurdek 1988, 1995). Most observers agree with Blumstein and Schwartz's (1983) conclusion that the nonmonogamous nature of many gay relationships reflects the greater emphasis that men may place on sexuality as compared to women and the lesser emphasis that they place on the relational context of sexual activity (Green, Bettinger, & Zacks 1996). Even in other couples, it is often not the fact of outside sexual activity that is a threat; it is an outside *relationship* that is important to one partner that is intolerable to the other.

By contrast, the stereotype of the lesbian relationship is of fusion, that is, of two women whose emphasis on the importance of relationship and emotional intimacy leads to the development of an excessive closeness, termed fusion or merger. Again, studies of gay and lesbian relationships have indeed shown that "lesbian couples . . . are likely to emphasize the importance of power equality, intimacy, closeness, and communication" (Murphy 1994:20). To the extent that closeness may become sameness, it has been noted that some degree of perceived difference enhances desire; if desire diminishes, an important means of sustaining intimacy—sexual expression—can be lost (Nichols 1987). Issues of power, dependency, and nurturing are present in all

---

Several clinicians have noted the tendency of lesbian couples to respond to homophobia and a lack of recognition by adopting a "two-against-the-world" stance . . . [citing] a varied range of characteristic lesbian relational elements—including social isolation, exclusive emphasis on partners' similarities with little tolerance of differences, the interweaving of the sense of self with the couple relationship, low tolerance for conflict, and a preponderance of time spent on the relationship of the couple with little attention to individual relationships outside the couple—and labeled them "fusion." . . .

Such fusion is a potentially constructive and functional move for two reasons. First, . . . because women of all sexual identities tend to prefer relational structures that feature mutual interdependence, the evolution of identity through connection with others, and a high degree of intimacy, . . . it is therefore not surprising to find that couples in which both partners are women are naturally drawn to a relational structure that is characterized by greater fusion than are those of heterosexual or gay male couples. . . . Secondly, lesbians have used fusion to strengthen their boundaries and to challenge the culture's claim that they are not families at all. . . . We propose that fusion be viewed . . . as a primarily constructive and desirable relational feature which becomes problematic only when it is employed at extreme levels, high or low.

—Suzanne Slater and Julie Mencher (1991:378–79)

relationships but may play out in special ways in lesbian relationships because of the particular psychological challenges of female development and social-ization (Burch 1987; Murphy 1994; Peplau et al. 1978). However, it is impor-tant not to underestimate the effects of social isolation and homophobia/ heterosexism as a potential contributor.

It is important to remember, though, that attachment and autonomy are independent factors that must be balanced in all relationships, including les-bian ones (Peplau et al. 1978). Even in lesbian relationships, individuals differ in the importance they place on independence and attachment, on time to-gether and time apart (Peplau et al. 1978). However, a high value is general-ly placed on egalitarianism in lesbian relationships (Blumstein & Schwartz 1983; Peplau et al. 1978).

Entering into an important couple relationship alters each partner's wider relationships, including with friends and family. *Boundary maintenance*—that is, the capacity of the couple to find time, space, and other resources for its own life amid competing priorities and demands—is an important issue for all couples. Boundary maintenance is often a special challenge for same-gender couples either because others are less likely to perceive or understand the couple and its need for boundary maintenance as legitimate or because one or both partners may be keeping the existence of the relationship or the nature of it a secret as a way to keep from disclosing their own lesbian, gay, or bisex-ual identity (Johnson & Keren 1996). Any differences between members of a couple in stigma management strategies may therefore be more easily toler-ated at the beginning of a relationship than when the couple is moving toward a higher level of commitment or greater permanence. While each partner may feel that she or he is making a personal decision about disclosure (or the lack of it), that decision has an impact on the other member of the relationship as well (Murphy 1994). However, it should be noted that disclosure to the fam-ily of origin is not in itself a factor in the success of a lesbian or gay relation-ship (Green, Bettinger, & Zacks 1996; Berger 1990).

The following examples make clear that, whatever social or individual factors affect how a couple defines its boundaries, the fact that there are no social norms to provide a road map adds a special challenge for lesbian and gay couples.

The adult daughter of a lesbian mother is getting married. The mother divorced the father and began living with her lesbian lover about five years before; the daughter, who was then in college, remained with the father, although she continued to have close and frequent contact with her mother. The mother's lesbianism, that is, the nature of her new relationship, has not been openly discussed in her extended family. Both mother and father are paying for the large, traditional wedding. Although the daughter likes the mother's lover, she has had some difficulty coming to terms with her mother's lesbianism. As the guest list is being discussed, the daughter requests that her mother's lover not attend the wedding. Initially, both the mother and her lover agree with this request on the theory that it is the daughter's big day, although as the wedding date approaches, the mother's partner finds herself feeling increasingly resentful and devalued at being left out. However, were she to attend, neither partner is certain exactly what role she might play.

Joe, now thirty-two, is the youngest of five children. His father, eighty-two, has Alzheimer's disease and his mother, seventy-five, suffers from high blood pressure and rheumatoid arthritis. His father now requires constant supervision and nearly total care, but his mother is determined to continue to care for him at home. She has always relied on Joe for occasional help with heavy chores but now calls him almost daily and wants him to visit every weekend for help with his father's personal care and for emotional comfort. Joe's older brothers and sisters are all married with children. Even the two who still live in the same metropolitan area do not help out nearly as often. Joe has lived with his partner, Dan, for the last two years. Dan appreciates Joe's concern about his father's failing health and the increasing strain on his mother but wants Joe to place greater limits on his involvement in his parents' care so that he will be less tired himself and will have more time for their relationship. While Joe's parents know about Joe's relationship with Dan, Joe makes his Sunday visits "home" alone. However, as the weeks of visiting stretch into months, Joe himself feels increasingly drained, resentful, and uncertain about how best to meet everyone's needs.

In each of these examples, were the relationship that of a heterosexual marriage, it is likely that a quite different accommodation would have been reached. In addition, even when an established couple has succeeded in negotiating a mutually acceptable pattern disclosure and boundary maintenance for itself, crises and life cycle transitions in the extended family as well as within the couple itself often cause the issue to be reopened, resulting in new stresses and strains.

It sometimes happens that one member of a lesbian, gay, or bisexual couple (or both) is married, that is, simultaneously engaged in a committed heterosexual relationship (Forstein 1994; Green & Clunis 1989). In some cases this situation is seen as or expected to be a temporary one—that is, the married partner has yet to complete the coming out process, in which it is assumed that in the future the marriage will be dissolved and the partner will continue in the same-gender relationship, which is experienced as being more satisfying than the marital one. Just as when an individual becomes involved in a heterosexual extramarital affair, issues of secrecy or disclosure within the marriage, potential guilt, and questions for both extramarital partners about the relative levels of commitment to the marriage as compared to the other relationship are likely to arise. However, to these must be added the fact that the new relationship—the same-gender one—often raises all the identity issues of coming out and that the two same-gender partners may be at quite different stages in their own identity development or coming out process. Sometimes, however, the married partner may intend to remain married either because of a positive commitment to the marriage (see the section on bisexual relationships below) or because the idea of being identified as lesbian or gay is intolerable, or both. In this situation, both partners must be willing to accept the conditions in the same-gender relationship that remaining in the marriage will impose.

The Controversy About Legal Recognition

Although laws in most states have not specified that marriage must be between a man and a woman, marriage in the United States has been defined by custom, legal precedent, and judicial interpretation as being only for mixed-gender couples (Eskridge 1996; Sullivan 1995; Tully 1994). The fact that same-gender couples may not marry deprives them of an important ritual, both with respect to couple formation and to the maintenance of a long-term relationship; in the absence of a wedding to denote the occasion of commitment, what anniversary is the couple to mark—the first date? moving in together? In fact, many gay and lesbian couples invent and maintain many important private rituals of commitment and/or anniversary, even if these may not be readily noted and acknowledged by others. Even some religious organizations, although by no means all of them, are willing to perform rites of religious commitment for same-gender couples (Eskridge 1996; Sullivan 1995). However, civil marriage establishes many legal bonds between people, ranging from state-by-state rules about the sharing of material goods, inheritance, the capacity to make major decisions on behalf of the other, spousal benefits in private and public employment and insurance systems, the establishment of legal procedures necessary to dissolve the relationship, and immigration rights. Symbolically, these features of marriage express society's approval of the union; concretely, these aspects of marriage serve to reinforce the interpersonal and emotional bond and to confer important legal benefits on the partners. Even conventions of individual naming are associated with heterosexual marriage.

There is considerable controversy about same-gender marriage (Eskridge 1996; Sullivan 1995; Weston 1991). Some, like Tully (1994), argue that the religious and legal benefits of marriage should be as available to those same-gender couples who desire them as they now are to mixed-gender couples. Others emphasize the importance of civil marriage rights (Eskridge 1996; Sullivan 1995). Only in this way, it is argued, can the devaluing of same-gender relationships in particular and lesbian and gay people in general be overcome. The institution of marriage is seen as supporting and protecting the couple's loving commitment in the context of the family, the community, and society as well as within the couple itself. Gays and lesbians, it is argued, should have an equal right to participate. A parallel is often drawn to the anti-miscegenation laws, laws that made interracial marriage illegal, that were abolished earlier in the twentieth century. Those who support granting gays and lesbians the right to legal marriage generally also support domestic partnership arrangements, that is, alternative mechanisms available in some local jurisdictions and organizations that permit same-gender couples the right to share tenancy, employment benefits, and other (but generally not all) benefits of marriage if they meet certain criteria.

> The rationale for the justification of legalizing same-sex marriage is multifaceted and rooted in the current structure and definition of the family in this country, the concept of homosexuality itself, and the need for the courts to become involved with the legal rights of lesbian and gay couples.
> —Carol Tully (1994:82)

Opposition to the idea of gay and lesbian marriage from mainstream culture takes many forms, which have been reviewed in depth elsewhere (Eskridge 1996; Sullivan 1995; Vaid 1995). Even in the gay and lesbian community, however, there is no consensus on this issue. Opponents of the idea of gay and lesbian marriage within the gay community note that not all aspects of marriage, religious or civil, are benign. For example, they worry that gay and lesbian couples, if married, might lose some of the freedom they now enjoy to invent relationships that work outside of gender-based and heterosexual norms (Sullivan 1995). Arguing from a feminist or gay liberationist stance, they also suggest that working to attain equal access to a flawed system like marriage is a mistake. They generally do not believe that attaining these rights would indeed end discrimination and antigay prejudice; Vaid (1995), for example, suggests that the progress made in gay rights since Stonewall has resulted in a "virtual," not a real, equality. They would generally prefer to see traditional institutions and arrangements like marriage transformed into less normative and more egalitarian ones that both same-gender and mixed-gender couples would participate in, like domestic partnership arrangements.

The courts are now beginning to get involved in the controversy over same-sex marriage (Eskridge 1996; Tully 1994). In a case that began in 1990 when a lesbian couple applied for a marriage license and was turned down, state courts in Hawaii have been reviewing the issue. In 1993 the Hawaii Supreme Court overturned a lower court's ruling that this discrimination against a same-gender couple was justified; the case was retried in 1996. However, because states recognize each other's marriages, other states began passing laws specifically to exempt themselves from having to recognize a same-gender marriage performed elsewhere. In addition, in 1996 Congress passed and President Clinton signed the Defense of Marriage Act, making it lawful for states to do just that. In 1996 the original Hawaii ruling in favor of same-sex marriage was upheld, but its implementation was stayed pending appeal. In addition, many states were considering whether or not to act on the issue. Thus the legal and legislative controversy about same-sex civil marriage will likely continue for some time (see figure 5.1).

UNCOUPLING

Many lesbian and gay people are in intimate relationships and, just as with cross-gender couples, not all of these relationships endure. The dissolution of an important personal relationship is generally a major personal crisis for those involved whether the relationship was a same-gender or cross-gender one. However, just as there are no rules, norms, or rituals available to same-gender couples when they begin, there are no rituals or mechanisms available when they end (Hartman 1996). For example, someone who is married can talk with a coworker about the process of separating and getting a divorce; someone involved in a gay or lesbian relationship may find it more difficult to talk about or be understood when experiencing a similar life transition. There have been very few studies of the end of gay and lesbian relationships; those that exist suggest that the reasons for the breakup of gay and lesbian relationships are similar to those for the end of heterosexual ones, such as major difficulties with money, work, or sex (Kurdek 1995). Nor is there any reason to believe that the personal difficulties an individual may experience following the breakup of a gay or lesbian relationship are much

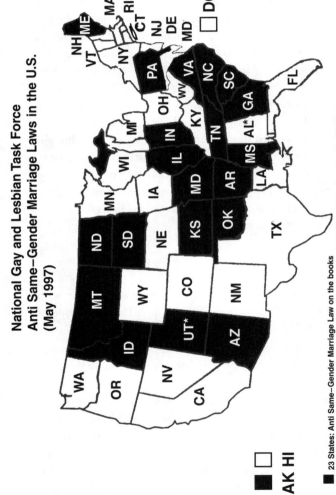

National Gay and Lesbian Task Force
Anti Same–Gender Marriage Laws in the U.S.
(May 1997)

■ □
AK HI

■ 23 States: Anti Same–Gender Marriage Law on the books

NOTE: In July 1996 Congress passed the so-called Defense of Marriage Act (DOMA). In September, President Clinton signed DOMA into law. DOMA limits the federal definition of marriage to exclude same-gender couples. DOMA bars legally married same-gender couples from receiving the federal economic protections and recognition afforded to straight couples. Gay and Lesbian couples are currently denied the right to legally marry anywhere in the U.S.; DOMA also makes it lawful for states to subvert the full faith and credit clause of the U.S. Constitution by denying marriage rights to same-gender couples legally married in other states.

Petition Drives exist in Maine and Oregon. Signatures in Maine have been approved to qualify for the November 1997 ballot.

* 1996 Governor Issued Executive Order barring same-gender marriage

Figure 5.1 Anti same-gender marriage laws in the United States (as of May 1997). Reproduced by permission of the National Gay and Lesbian Task Force Policy Institute, 2320 17th Street, N.W., Washington, DC 20009, (202) 332-6483; *http://www.ngltf.org.*

different from those that someone involved in an important cross-gender relationship would experience.

Because at some level the decision to end a couple relationship is a cost-benefit decision—that is, based on an assessment of the pains of parting compared with the pains of continuing—some have argued that the fact that same-gender relationships and same-gender relationship disruptions are not formalized legally may make deciding to end a gay or lesbian relationship easier (Murphy 1994). In addition, the norms and legal mechanisms that guide property and child custody decisions in divorce are not available to same-gender couples, for better or for worse (Hartman 1996). Only contract law can be used by the former partners to settle such disputes. However, recourse to the legal system in any way certainly requires that the privacy of the relationship be compromised, an issue of special salience if one or the other partner is somewhat closeted. Again, especially when one or the other partner has endeavored to keep the nature of the relationship a secret, there may be little opportunity to garner social and interpersonal support while negotiating the readjustment that the dissolution of a couple relationship requires.

Finally, because gay, lesbian, and bisexual people often function in rather small social networks of others like themselves, the breakup of a relationship and/or the beginning of a new one may disrupt these social groups. Although many may choose to remain friends after a breakup (Murphy 1994), for those who do not wish to do so it may not be as easy to establish new social networks or to avoid social contacts with a former partner as in the heterosexual context. In fact, it seems to be much more common among gay men and lesbians than heterosexuals for there to be continuing relationships of friendship or even "family" with "ex" lovers or partners. This pattern, while not well-studied, appears to involve a choice to preserve some aspects of a valued relationship, not just the difficulty of avoiding contact in a small social network. In fact, in some instances, ex-partners even become an important support system for new relationships.

Bisexuality and Relationships

So far, this chapter has addressed same-gender relationships, that is, gay or lesbian couples. This strategy is used because there is no reason to believe that the same-gender relationships of people who identify as bisexual are any different from those of people who identify as lesbian or gay. However, just as bisexuality itself has been understudied, very little is known about the relationships that bisexual people form and maintain beyond the fact that there are many different patterns of bisexual relationship.

People who identify as bisexual or who in fact have both same-gender and cross-gender intimate relationships while identifying as gay, lesbian, or heterosexual experience many sharply distinct patterns in their sexual relationships. Some identify with and practice bisexuality as a "defense" while in the process of coming into a lesbian or gay identity (Fox 1995). In this instance, their heterosexual relationship(s) are most likely destined to end as they get more comfortable with a gay or lesbian identity and/or when a fully satisfying gay or lesbian partner is found. Others practice "sequential" bisexuality (Fox 1995; Weinberg, Williams, & Pryor 1994); that is, they engage in one relationship at a time, but a same-gender relationship may be preceded or followed by either a same- or cross-gender one. In either of these patterns, the same-gender relationships they are in are likely to be much like any other same-gender relationship, except that the self-identification of the bisexual partner may be different from that adopted by the partner. For many of those in the sequential pattern, the quest seems to be for the most satisfying relationship, and the expectation is that they will settle into a same- or cross-gender relationship once a fully gratifying relationship has been found (Weinberg, Williams, & Pryor 1994).

Some who identify as bisexual, however, do engage simultaneously in same-gender and cross-gender relationships. A common pattern of simultaneous bisexuality is in the context of heterosexual marriage, in which case the same-gender relationships of the bisexual partner, who may or may not identify in that way, generally take place outside the context of the marital or family relationship (Fox 1995). In this instance, the marital relationship is seen as primary and the same-gender one(s) as secondary. However, there is great variation in how openly this situation is handled within the marital relationship and in how the same-gender relationship(s) are conducted. There are some people (although relatively few even among those who identify as bisexual) who in fact simultaneously engage in same- and cross-gender relationships that they consider of equal importance, with others who may also identify as bisexual or who may identify as gay, lesbian, or heterosexual (Fox 1995; Weinberg, Williams, & Pryor 1994). In these situations of simultaneous bisexuality, the major issue is how the sexual openness of the relationship is handled and whether the understanding developed within each relationship remains satisfactory to all concerned over time. Finally, in any nonmonogamous situation, safe-sex practices must be a primary concern. The major implication of this variety in the patterning of bisexual identity and relationships is that no assumptions should be made about either the same-gender or the cross-gender relationships of bisexual people. However, it should also be noted that those who are bisexual may be assumed to be "defensive" bisexuals in the gay and/or lesbian communities, in part because most gay and lesbian people have themselves been involved in cross-gender relationships before coming out as lesbian or gay. This reaction can be a source of stress and/or can result in isolation from others in same-gender relationships for those who are bisexual and their same-gender partners.

The Implications for Social Work Practice

The achievement of satisfying and stable intimate relationships is a major life task of adulthood, and the form that such a relationship takes is secondary to the functions it fulfills for the individuals involved and for the families and communities they are a part of. Thus the major goal of social work practice with gay and lesbian couples, just as with heterosexual ones, should be the safe-guarding of the conditions that support the development and maintenance of safe and healthy attachments and the optimal development of the couple unit and of the individuals who are part of it. The problem of violence, both within same-gender relationships and as visited upon them, is a serious one and is discussed in chapter 10; this section will discuss other major issues arising in social work practice with gay and lesbian couples.

The person-in-environment focus of social work practice is well suited to work with lesbian, gay, and bisexual people and their couple relationships (Gunther 1992). Personal developmental matters and contextual issues affect all couple relationships. The couple relationships that gay, lesbian, and bisexual people form illustrate that principle well. Only attention to issues at both levels will ensure that gay, lesbian, and bisexual people will be able to enjoy the dynamic sexual and intimate relationships that most adults aspire to.

One major pressure on sexual relationships that gay and lesbian people are generally more aware of than heterosexual people are stems from the fact that many states have sodomy laws that make certain common sexual acts, even

> Lesbian and gay male couples are viable family units that can benefit from counseling to build satisfying relationships. Social workers trained and skilled in couple counseling will quickly recognize the many similarities in counseling with heterosexual couples. Problem areas that become the focus of intervention likewise are similar. Differences come from the added stress lesbians and gay men experience in living a lifestyle that is unacceptable to the majority in society.
>
> —Travis L. Peterson & Josephine H. Stewart (1985:32)

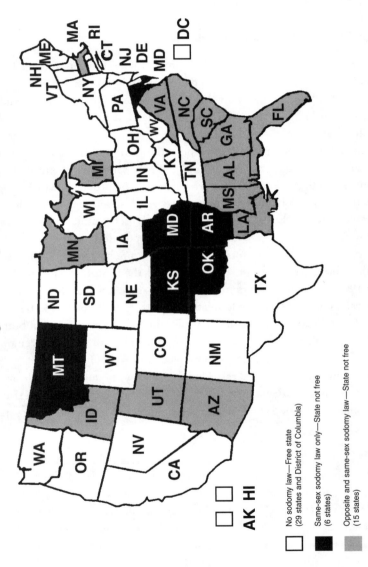

National Gay and Lesbian Task Force
The Right to Privacy in the U.S. (May 1997)

No sodomy law—Free state
(29 states and District of Columbia)

Same-sex sodomy law only—State not free
(6 states)

Opposite and same-sex sodomy law—State not free
(15 states)

Figure 5.2 The right to privacy in the United States (as of May 1997). Reproduced by permission of the National Gay and Lesbian Task Force Policy Institute, 2320 17th Street, N.W., Washington, DC 20009, (202) 332-6483; *http://www.ngltf.org.*

between consenting adults, illegal (see figure 5.2). These laws constitute a human rights problem for gay and lesbian people in particular, even though they are rarely enforced, because the acts proscribed are among the most common in the gay and lesbian context (Hartman 1996; Vaid 1995). These laws thus have implications for social and legislative action as well as for individual counseling with gay and lesbian people who are sexually active, and social workers must be aware of the laws that are in effect in the states where they practice.

These same laws and the attitudes they embody have also been a major obstacle to the development of effective safe-sex education, especially for young people (see chapter 11). The HIV/AIDS epidemic has made community-level as well as individual attention to safe-sex issues essential for all couples and individuals. To the extent that higher-risk sexual behaviors, including nonmonogamy, may be more common among gay male couples than heterosexual or lesbian ones, safe-sex information is even more important to them and those who work with them, although it is important for everyone who is sexually active.

Civil rights and antidiscrimination measures that include homosexuality as a protected category are essential in safe-guarding same-gender couples. For example, living together is common in gay and lesbian couples, but housing is an area in which gay and lesbian people fear discrimination if the nature of their cohabitation is known. Most states and local jurisdictions lack such basic protective measures; in many areas that do have them, efforts are under way to repeal or outlaw these measures (Vaid 1995). The political struggles for and against these measures have the potential both to threaten and to empower gay and lesbian people and couples (Baker 1995). Some cities and employers are beginning to offer same-gender (and, in some cases, nonmarried heterosexual) couples the opportunity to declare themselves "domestic partners," usually using a criterion of cohabitation for some period of time to qualify. Registering as a domestic partnership is designed to insure that a housing lease, for example, is shared equally and/or to qualify for "family" employment benefits, such as health insurance, on the same basis as a legally recognized spouse. Social workers often involve themselves in the fight to obtain such benefits as one way to combat discrimination against gay and lesbian people and to strengthen gay and lesbian couples and families. Certainly any social worker practicing with gay and lesbian couples must know about the laws and regulations, pro- and antigay, that obtain in their areas.

As has already been described, the recognition of same-sex civil marriage continues to be controversial. However, there are other ways that gay and lesbian couples may choose to celebrate their relationships through ritual.

Some churches will commemorate religious marriages or commitment ceremonies for same-gender couples, but the availability of this option varies widely regionally and among religious denominations (Blumenfeld & Raymond 1988; Vaid 1995), especially if the religious background of the two members of the relationship is different. Other couples choose to invent their own rituals of celebration, commitment, or anniversary, with or without a religious or spiritual element. Those social workers who work with gay and lesbian couples must inform themselves about the local religious community and its attitudes in order to help interested couples negotiate these matters as constructively as possible. The "chosen family" that surrounds the couple can often constitute a "mini-community" that confers vital recognition and sustaining support, a resource that a worker may well want to urge a couple to cultivate.

When it comes to direct practice with gay and lesbian couples, there is no reason to believe that the basic principles of couple or family practice that are useful with heterosexual couples should be employed differently with gay and/or lesbian ones. However, when assessing a gay or lesbian couple, it is important to remember that the context within which they function is not the same and that the heterosexism and homophobia that are normative in the society will have impacted upon the couple and its members in a variety of ways (Brown & Zimmer 1988). In particular, as has been noted, the beginning of a more stable and intimate couple relationship often makes one or both members of the couple more visible as lesbian or gay within the extended family and/or in the community than was true before. The two members of the relationship may or may not share the same identity management strategies, yet the decisions that each one makes will affect the other (Murphy 1994). In addition, they may inhabit individual workplace or family contexts that are not equally tolerant or supportive. Thus negotiation of these issues and the development of mutually agreeable strategies for living that both members of the couple find comfortable or at least tolerable and that neither experiences as invalidating of themselves individually or of the relationship is essential. A skilled social worker can often be of great assistance in normalizing these stresses for a gay or lesbian couple and in helping them discuss these matters in a nonjudgmental way with one another.

Of course there are other important ways in which gay and lesbian couples differ from heterosexual ones that affect how a social worker might practice with them. As noted above, in same-gender couples gender-role issues may emerge quite strongly (Brown & Zimmer 1988; Slater 1995). The typical differences between gay and lesbian couples outlined above are generally attributed to these gender issues. However, it is important not to overemphasize such differences either (Green, Bettinger, & Zacks 1996). Nor are real or ideal role models of successful, long-term gay or lesbian relationships usually as available to young or new gay or lesbian couples as they may be to hetero-sexual ones (Peterson & Stewart 1985; Slater 1995). The challenge in practice with any individual couple is to be able to see how it may be both like and unlike couples of other kinds.

For gay male couples, issues related to the HIV status of one or both mem-bers of the couple are likely to arise. When both members of the relationship are or become HIV-positive or ill with AIDS, issues of illness and a likely ear-lier death must be addressed. Individuals and couples must be helped with the financial and legal issues that chronic illness and/or impending death impose and, as already discussed, they must do so without the legal mechanism of marriage to help them attain their goals of providing adequately for one an-other. Because HIV is often (but not always) transmitted sexually, the disease status of one or both partners may raise issues of past or more current behav-ior that were previously unaddressed in the relationship, presenting an addi-tional crisis to cope with on top of the illness or threat of illness. Once a diag-nosis of AIDS has been made, issues of recurrent acute illness, decisions about treatment, and caregiving concerns become prominent.

Serodiscordant couples—that is, couples in which only one member is HIV-positive—must deal directly with safe-sex issues and with caregiving and bereavement issues once the illness progresses (Mattison & McWhirter 1994). As Forstein has observed:

> The threat of being infected or infecting others with HIV; the realities of liv-
> ing with a chronic, usually debilitating and fatal illness; and the emotional
> impact of living under siege present enormous challenges for any gay male
> relationship. . . . Some must now work hard to affirm their right to remain
> seronegative in the face of an infected partner, while at the same time remain
> intimate and emotionally connected. Others must negotiate life with a new
> set of parameters; a potentially shortened life span, the presence of an illness
> at a time of life that would typically be free of illness, and a heightened
> awareness of mortality that affects all aspects of individual psychological
> function.   (Forstein 1994:299)

The social worker involved with the couple may at least initially be more aware of these issues and their potential impact than the members of the cou-ple consciously are. Thus knowledge about HIV and AIDS and its multiple impacts on individuals, couples, and communities is essential to those who work with same-gender couples, especially male couples. However, it is crucial to be mindful, too, of how the crises of illness and even death and dying can mobilize individuals and couples in growth and be deeply meaningful though painful intimate experiences.

Summary and Conclusions

Social work, with its person-in-environment focus, is ideally suited to work with lesbian, gay, and bisexual couples because it is necessary to understand both the external stresses that homophobia and heterosexism impose on such couples as well as the individual differences in how people creatively adapt to life outside the heterosexual majority. As this chapter has illustrated, to work effectively with lesbian and gay relationships it is necessary to understand simultaneously how they may be the same as and different from heterosexual pairs. The most important similarity to remember is that same-gender relationships can be every bit as satisfying to the partners as heterosexual relationships can, and it is the job of every social worker who encounters these couples to assist them in achieving the maximum growth and happiness in the relationship that is possible.

6

Gay, Lesbian, and Bisexual Parents and Their Children

There are many more gay and lesbian parents than is commonly realized. Gays and lesbians enter into the bearing and rearing of children in a variety of ways, some of which may involve them with medical and child welfare service systems. Studies of the children of gay and lesbian parents are reviewed, showing that such children fare just as well as their counterparts reared by heterosexual parents. However, homophobia and heterosexism often affect the well-being of these families and their members. Implications for social work practice with gay and lesbian parents and their children in regard to schools, medical care, child welfare, and in the community and other settings are presented.

Many people who seem ready to accept gay, lesbian, and bisexual people as individuals unfortunately have difficulty with the idea of gay, lesbian, and/or bisexual people as parents. In fact, many gay, lesbian, and bisexual people are or want to be parents, just as many heterosexual adults do. This commitment of many gay men and lesbian women to childbearing and/or child-rearing stands in sharp contrast to the stereotype of gays, lesbians, and bisexuals as "narcissistic, self-absorbed, [and] irresponsible" (Weston 1991:19). In fact, the AIDS epidemic may be underscoring a wish for generativity and the affirmation of life among both gay men and lesbians, especially in those urban communities where the effects of the pandemic have been most pronounced (Weston 1991).

While reliable data on gay and lesbian parenting are limited, it has been estimated that there are between two and eight million gay and lesbian parents in the United States, with one and a half to five million of them estimated to be lesbian mothers (Falk 1993; Hare 1994; Martin 1993). Estimates of the number of children of gay or lesbian parents in the United States range from four to fourteen million (Hare 1994; Martin 1993; Patterson 1995b). Since there are no exact data on gay and lesbian parenting, the variation in these estimates is based in the continuing debate about how common a gay or lesbian sexual orientation is in the general adult population (see chapter 2). However, whether one accepts the lower or the higher estimates, we now know that gay and lesbian parents and their children are certainly more numerous than has generally been assumed.

Gay, lesbian, and bisexual people become parents in a variety of ways. With the advent of new birth control and other reproductive technologies in the twentieth century, the connection between heterosexual intercourse and reproduction has been changed, and new possibilities have emerged for controlling when and how to have children. Other alternative ways of forming families, such as through adoption, formal or informal, have existed for millennia. Finally, because most gay, lesbian, and bisexual people are involved in heterosexual relationships at some point in their lives, some of them have become mothers and fathers in a different relational context, and those same-gender partners that they subsequently become involved with may find them-

> Lesbians and gay men, as individuals, in couples, in families, and as parents are as healthy and, in some ways, perhaps more "functional" and "satisfied" than their heterosexual counterparts. Similarly, the children of lesbians and gay men also do as well as their peers along the many dimensions measured and, not surprisingly, tend to be more flexible and more tolerant of difference in others. The research has, of course, also emphasized the special problems lesbians and gays encounter, linking them to the impact of conducting their lives in environments that are disqualifying and hostile . . . and . . . we begin to see some of the special strengths of this invisible minority, strengths that, at least to some extent, come from standing at the margins and from having to be particularly alert to and critical of prevailing cultural and political discourses.
>
> —Joan Laird (1993:210)

selves also entering into a parental role. Great concern has been expressed about the many children of gay, lesbian, and bisexual people—about their development and adjustment as children and in later life. However, the limited but growing data that exist about the children of lesbians and gays[1] suggest that they are no different in their development and adjustment from the children of heterosexual parents.

This chapter will describe the various ways in which gay, lesbian, and bisexual people become parents. In same-gender relationships, both partners cannot be the biological parents of the same child. Thus "step-" or "adoptive" parenting, or parenting in the absence of biological procreation, is more common in same-gender couples than among heterosexual ones. The particular issues involved in the co-parenting role in the gay and lesbian context will be discussed. The literature available on the outcomes for children reared in gay and/or lesbian homes will be summarized to show how little the development of children is affected by the gender constellation or professed sexual orientation of the parent(s), despite common fears about this issue. Most importantly, however, those who surround gay, lesbian, and bisexual parents—including the extended family, schools, and helping professionals—often are either unprepared to deal with or are hostile to them and their children. Because of their person-in-environment focus, social workers are often in a position to make the interactions between gay and lesbian parents and their children and the larger social environment either better or worse. Therefore, implications for social work practice with or on behalf of gay, lesbian, and bisexual parents and their children will be emphasized.

Forming Families

The traditional definition of family has involved ties formed by marriage, procreation, or adoption. These ways of forming a "family" are differentially available to those in same-gender relationships than to those in heterosexual ones. Whether with regard to couple relationships, the bearing and rearing of children, or deciding who in an extended network of relatives and friends counts as "family," gay, lesbian, and bisexual people have a complicated relationship to the idea of "family" (Benkov 1994; Martin 1993; Weston 1991). Thus it is difficult to find language to describe the child-bearing and child-rearing units and roles that gays and lesbians create. Certainly the children of lesbians and gays generally become the center of some group of people committed to them and their welfare although the definition of these groups is more often consciously constructed than assumed. These groups are functionally "families" with all the potential for ongoing commitment and intimacy and their vicissitudes that the term ordinarily implies. Recognition of the existence of gay and lesbian "families," among other "alternative family forms," has been a major impetus behind the effort to rethink how family and kinship are defined in such fields as family therapy, family policy, and even sociology and anthropology (see, for example, Hartman 1996; Laird & Green 1996; Weston 1991). Thus while an uncritical use of the term *family* can be problematic in the gay and/or lesbian context, the term is still used here as shorthand for a set of important relationships that come into being when gays and lesbians bear, adopt, and rear children. In addition, since family is such a central concept and concern in social work theory and practice, the concept is retained because it helps to make practice with lesbian and gay parents and their children comprehensible within a framework that most social workers understand and care deeply about.

> Mainstream society declares that lesbians are inherently unfit mothers whose children must be rescued from their influence whenever their lesbian identity is discovered. Lesbian women are left, then, to believe simultaneously that as women they *must* mother, and as lesbians they must *not* mother.　—Suzanne Slater (1995:90; emphasis in the original)

Being a gay, lesbian, or bisexual parent is both the same and different from being a heterosexual one. Most societies, including ours, assume that most or all adults will become parents, the unstated assumption being that they will do so as heterosexuals. Thus, for example, being gay or lesbian and being a mother or father are thought to be contradictory states (Bigner 1996; Crawford 1987; Evans 1990; Muzio 1993; Lott-Whitehead & Tully 1993; Slater 1995). As Benkov (1994) notes, gay and lesbian parents have "faced two of the most powerful facets of homophobia: abhorrence of any association between homosexuals and children; and the belief that gay men and lesbians exist in opposition to family life" (31). In reality, however, there have always been gay, lesbian, and bisexual parents, although different cohorts of gay, lesbian, and bisexual people have become parents at different rates and typically have become parents in different ways (Slater 1995). Given this context, the choice to become a parent has special meaning to gay and lesbian people and likely presents some special challenges and considerations (Benkov 1994; Bigner 1996; Crawford 1987; Evans 1990; Martin 1993; Muzio 1993; Shernoff 1996; Slater 1995).

PARENTHOOD FROM A HETEROSEXUAL CONTEXT

Until recently, the most common way in which gay, lesbian, or bisexual people became parents was in the context of a heterosexual marriage or relationship (Bigner 1996; Slater 1995; Weston 1991). Some marry at a point in their
lives when they have no awareness of any same-gender sexual orientation.
Others who know or suspect they may be gay, lesbian, or bisexual enter into
marriage and childbearing as a sincere attempt to be or to become "straight."
Others do so in conflict over their sexual orientation, in what Bigner (1996)
has termed "identity foreclosure" (371). However they were formed, some of
these marriages result in children. When such a marriage comes to an end,
especially in the case of women, the parent who is or later comes to be
lesbian- or gay-identified may be the custodial parent or may share a significant ongoing noncustodial relationship with the child or children. Thus some
children of divorce or of single parents are also children of a gay, lesbian, or
bisexual parent.[2]

Although norms are changing, it is still more often the female parent than
the male parent who seeks and/or who is awarded child custody following a
separation or divorce. Thus the postdivorce or single-parenting scenario more
often involves lesbian women than gay men, but not exclusively. One of the
most important stresses on such parents is the fear that their sexual orientation will result in the loss of custody or contact with their children (Benkov
1994; Bigner 1996; Patterson 1995b; Slater 1995). In fact, there have been
court decisions in a number of jurisdictions which have awarded custody to
the heterosexual parent or even to the extended family because of the mother or father's homosexual sexual orientation (Badgett 1992; Benkov 1994;
Hartman 1996; Patterson 1995b). Although such cases are relatively rare,
knowledge of them is widespread in the lesbian, gay, and bisexual community. Given the importance of their relationship to a child or children, most parents are greatly disturbed by the fear that such a case might be brought. This
fear can have a profound effect on gay, lesbian, or bisexual parents and their
children, both on how they manage their lives within the household and on
how they interact with other people and institutions, even those institutions
that are ordinarily a child-rearing family's major sources of support, such as
the extended family, schools, churches, and various health care professionals
(Slater 1995).

Within or outside of marriage, serial monogamy is the most common
form of intimate relationship in America (Laumann et al. 1994); for this reason, many divorced or single parents subsequently enter into other intimate
relationships. Thus some gay, lesbian, and bisexual people become the parents

of children because they enter into committed relationships with a same-gender partner who is rearing children from a former relationship. Such a person may or may not bring children of his or her own into the new relationship as well.

The common term for this relationship in the lesbian and gay community is *co-parent* rather than stepparent; co-parent is also used for the nonbiological parent when a child is born into a lesbian relationship and for the nonadoptive parent in a gay or lesbian couple as well (see below). This terminology has developed to counter the negative stereotypes traditionally associated with the "stepparent." It is also used to signify—especially in the case of childbirth—that this "other" parent is not a replacement and is considered to be a full partner in parenting. However, when a person assumes a parenting role by entering into a relationship with someone who is already a parent, what results is what is generally termed a "blended" family (Crawford 1987). It should be noted that, whether in a same-gender or a cross-gender context, there is tremendous variation in how parenting roles in blended families are handled, talked about, and enacted. There are some issues that tend to occur more often for the biological or custodial parent and other issues that occur more often for the "step-" or "co-parent," which will be considered below.

When the parenthood of a gay, lesbian, or bisexual person is the result of former heterosexual involvements, the parent is likely to have to negotiate a coming out process while parenting (Bigner 1996). This raises the issue of deciding about coming out to one's children—whether, how, and when. In the past, rearing a child or children in a gay or lesbian context sometimes occurred without explicitly coming out to those children. However, one effect of several decades of gay activism and the gains that have been made in identifying homophobia as a form of prejudice and protecting some civil rights for gay and lesbian people has been that it is now much less common for a gay or lesbian parent to decide not to discuss his or her sexual orientation with his or her children. The decision to come out to one's children most often occurs at the time of redefining oneself as lesbian, gay, or bisexual (Benkov 1994; Bozett 1993) or at the time of entering into a committed primary relationship that will bring the new partner into more frequent contact with the children, when the presence, role, and/or meaning of that partner to the parent requires explanation. In the latter case, the risk is that the children's reactions to the parent's coming out will be confounded with their reaction to the entry of this person into (or the redefinition of the role of the person in) their lives. In general, gay fathers and lesbian mothers report that their children's reaction to learning of their parent's sexual orientation was positive (Bozett 1993; also, see below). Indeed, the divorce experience per se may have a greater impact than the fact of the parent's sexual orientation (Turner, Scadden, & Harris 1990).

It should be noted that, just as among heterosexuals, there are many lesbian, gay, and bisexual parents who do not live with or have custody of their biological children. Just as among heterosexuals, these parents may have minimal or may have quite intensive relationships with their children. They may also face issues of how and when to come out to their children, and they must negotiate this process without the built-in reassurance that coresidence and/or custody of the child brings. For such parents, the reactions of the custodial parent and the other members of the children's extended family with whom they have contact may be even more critical to the continuation and comfort of the parent-child relationship for both parent and children than it is in other situations.

LESBIAN AND GAY CHILDBEARING

Another way in which lesbian and gay people become parents is through childbearing (Benkov 1994; Flaks et al. 1995; Martin 1993; Muzio 1996; Patterson 1994a, 1994b; Shernoff 1996; Slater 1995). Because it is more common, the focus of this discussion will be on childbearing by lesbians in or not in a committed relationship.[3] However, as among heterosexual women, the decision to bear and rear a child is most often (but not always) taken in the context of an intimate or partnership relationship, as an expression of a shared wish for generativity as a couple that grows out of their mutual caring and/or because the material and nonmaterial resources of two people rather than of one person are seen as preferable for the job of childrearing. This kind of family formation grows out of the capacity of a woman to become pregnant and give birth and thus is generally more easily available to lesbian relationships than to gay ones. It relies on the common technique of *donor insemination*.

Many special issues arise in the use of donor insemination by lesbians (Benkov 1994; Martin 1993). All couples who decide to have children must decide together to do so, and the partners may not have the desire to do so to the same degree or at the same time (Crawford 1987; Martin 1993; Patterson 1994b). These issues are complex and often challenging for any couple, touching as they do on deep emotions and life goals on the one hand and pragmatic issues, such as finances, employment, and household work, on the other. However, when it is a lesbian couple that decides to enter into childbearing, there are a number of special issues that must be faced (Benkov 1994; Martin 1993).

First of all, who will become pregnant since both partners may be biologically able to do so? If one partner wishes to become pregnant, what role does
the other partner, who cannot be the impregnator, play in the decision to
become pregnant and in the act of impregnation? What commitment is the
other partner interested in making to the child-to-be and to the birth mother and is it the kind of commitment that the potential birth mother seeks?
Since legal parenthood is established by biology, marriage, or adoption, what
standing will the lesbian nonbirth mother have in the child's life, especially if
the couple's relationship should later end since these options are rarely or
never available to her? What if both women wish to become pregnant and to
bear a child? How will it be decided who is to attempt to become pregnant
and when? What if a partner's attempts to become pregnant fail? Since donor
insemination, like other reproductive technologies, tends to be costly and
may not be covered by any health insurance, how much is the couple willing
to invest in the process and/or in infertility services, especially since it is
unlikely that one partner can have access to the health (and other) benefits of
the other? Will a difficulty in achieving a pregnancy cause the couple to re-
assess the issue of who will become pregnant? How will each partner's extended family, friends, and/or employer react to a pregnancy or to the birth
of a child? When the child is born, who will be called "mother," or how will
the partners be addressed? These are issues that lesbian couples must face in
addition to those that all couples deal with in deciding to enter into childbearing or when they require medical assistance in achieving a pregnancy.
They spring uniquely from the two-woman nature of the relationship and
from the fact that the parenting of the nonbiological mother is not legitimat-
ed in the wider society or its social institutions. In fact, whatever the personal factors that enter into such decisions, the choices that lesbian (and gay) parents make about how to become parents place them and their children in very
different relationships to the state (Benkov 1994; Martin 1993).

Whether or not the pregnancy is undertaken in the context of a couple relationship, a major issue that must be faced is to decide how such a pregnancy
will be achieved—that is, how to obtain the necessary sperm (Benkov 1994;
Martin 1993). Some choose to do it the "old-fashioned" way, that is, through
"procreative, heterosexual" sex (Weston 1991:167). Others opt to use the
medical care system, that is, to work with a gynecologist or obstetrician to initiate the pregnancy just as a married heterosexual woman who wants to bear
a child despite her husband's infertility might do (Benkov 1994; Martin 1993).
For the lesbian woman, however, such a step requires access to a physician
knowledgeable and experienced in such procedures as well as one who will
provide this service to a lesbian woman. Since physicians and other health care

providers share many of the attitudes of the larger society, a lesbian woman seeking such a service is often concerned that she may encounter a nonsupportive or homophobic response. In those areas with a well-developed lesbian community, it is more often possible to identify in advance those health care providers—clinics and physicians—who offer such services without prejudice. However, in many parts of the country, such supportive services are much more difficult to identify.

If assisted insemination will be used, there are still major questions to be answered about the donor sperm (Benkov 1994; Martin 1993). Will the sperm of a known donor or of an anonymous donor be used? How will the donor be chosen? A major concern about any donor, especially a known donor, is the degree of contact with, commitment and/or obligation to the child and/or the woman that the donor and the woman who will obtain the donation both see as acceptable and desirable. Donor and potential recipient may not easily agree on these issues. The woman who receives the donation may feel that her connection to the child is in jeopardy because of the importance that the law places on biological procreation in determining the rights of parenthood. As several well-publicized cases surrounding surrogate pregnancy have illustrated, contract law has been determined to have limited applicability in some cases; thus even written legal agreements achieved between parties to a pregnancy may prove useless in court should later conflict arise. Thus an unknown or anonymous donor obtained from a sperm bank is often used when a woman wants to insure that there is no possibility of future legal or social connection between herself or her child and the donor.

There are two major health issues involved in seeking an unknown donor. The first is the necessity of access to the medical care system, the risks of which have already been noted, although in some areas ways have been found to access existing sperm banks with minimal involvement with the medical establishment. This arrangement is more likely to be possible when frozen sperm are used, but some women have more confidence in the safety and effectiveness of fresh over frozen sperm. The second is the degree of knowledge and/or control that the woman receiving the donation can or will have over the characteristics of the donor. It is common to be given some general information about the characteristics of an anonymous sperm donor, but this information is apt to be more limited, of course, than when the donor is well-known to the recipient. Whenever a biological parent is unknown over time to a child or to a parent, concerns about health, health history, and other genetic issues arise. To use an extreme but not unrealistic example in this age of medical technology, should the child in future need a kidney transplant or a marrow donation, the child of an unknown sperm donor (or of a closed adoption) is at a disadvantage in identifying a potentially compatible family donor. There is a major health concern facing all sperm donation: the threat of HIV transmission (Benkov 1994; Martin 1993). Like blood banks, reputable sperm banks screen donations for the HIV virus. However, even the most stringent testing is not infallible. When a woman seeks a donation from a known donor on her own, the issue of HIV testing must be raised. Finally, while lesbians as a group are statistically at relatively low risk for HIV infection, risk is determined by behavior, not by identity. There are lesbians who have engaged in unprotected sex involving the exchange of bodily fluids or who use injectable drugs. As is the case with any woman, a lesbian who contemplates becoming pregnant must make decisions about being tested herself as well as about the HIV status of the man who provides the sperm for her pregnancy in order to protect her own health and that of any child who might be born. Medical knowledge and practice and state public health policy surrounding the HIV virus and pregnancy are evolving rapidly, and all women, including lesbian women, who are considering becoming pregnant must actively seek out the latest information available on this and the many other health issues surrounding pregnancy. Any woman considering pregnancy must always seek out health care providers who are prepared to discuss HIV risk and protection frankly.

Finding gynecological and obstetrical care that is "lesbian-friendly," of course, is an issue that goes beyond insemination (Martin 1993). Once a pregnancy has been achieved, there is the need to obtain prenatal care and to identify facilities, such as childbirth classes and birthing centers, that will instill confidence in both the lesbian birth mother, her partner, and/or any other person who will accompany and/or assist her in giving birth. These concerns are added to those any person giving birth must address—choosing a physician or midwife and a hospital, birthing center, or home birth. Depending on where a woman lives, there are likely to be great differences in the number of seemingly comfortable and/or lesbian-friendly choices available to her.

While most heterosexual couples who bear a child with the help of donor insemination do not tell the child about her or his origins (Benkov 1994; Cook et al. 1995; Martin 1993), the strategy of letting the child assume that the social father is the biological father is not available to the lesbian couple; what will the child be told about his or her biological origins, and when? As in the closed adoption situation, Crawford notes:

> Not to know or have contact with one's father raises external cultural issues and internal identity issues. Practically speaking, a woman must ask

herself if she can provide her child with the maximum amount of information available in a way that acknowledges its importance. This may mean being quite conscientious and assertive about getting detailed information about the donor . . . [and his] reasons for donating sperm. At an emotional level the mother must be able to attend over the years to the changing questions and feelings about a child who may not be satisfied to know only about the family she has provided. There may be questions about the mother's choice as well as questions about the father. . . . [Nevertheless,] there is no reason why a child without a known father will not grow to a happy, healthy, and productive adulthood, especially if he or she is given the open help and support of his or her parent in dealing with this issue.

(Crawford 1987:208)

As Muzio (1993) notes, "It is not that the children born to lesbians do not have biological fathers; it is that they do not 'belong' to them in the same way children born to a heterosexual couple 'belong' to their fathers" (216). However, in some states a known sperm donor may be regarded as the father of the child for child support enforcement purposes should the mother and child request AFDC benefits (Hare 1994). Control of the obligations and involvement of the donor then passes out of the hands of the mother and into the hands of the state.

Gay Men Choosing Children
While becoming a parent through giving birth is more common among lesbians than gay men, some gay men do become biological parents outside heterosexual marriage (Benkov 1994; Bigner 1996; Martin 1993; Shernoff 1996). A gay man may, for example, enter into a joint parenting arrangement with a lesbian friend who gives birth to a child conceived with his sperm. And because she thinks a gay man might be more supportive of her wish to parent, a lesbian woman who wants to bear a child may seek out a gay friend as a donor. Other gay men, especially gay male couples, use paid surrogacy arrangements and then become the sole parents of the baby. Such men and their partners face many of the same personal and legal issues outlined above; however, surrogacy arrangements in particular are fraught with legal and moral dilemmas, and the rules governing them vary greatly from state to state (Benkov 1994; Martin 1993; Shernoff 1996). Should conflict arise over the child, these men may fear the preference traditionally given to mothers over fathers in the courts (although a lesbian who is a biological mother may fare no better in custody disputes than a gay man).

ADOPTIVE AND FOSTER PARENTING

One way to become a parent that is open to both gay men and lesbian women is to adopt a child (Benkov 1994; Hartman 1996; Martin 1993; Shernoff 1996). Other gay, lesbian, and bisexual people decide to become foster care providers and to care for the children of others. The complicated factors that go into any person's decision or any couple's decision to become a foster or especially an adoptive parent are well-known. However, there are special challenges that a gay, lesbian, or bisexual person who wants to become a foster or adoptive parent must face because of their sexual orientation, which is what this section will focus on. Shernoff (1996) reports that gay males who seek to adopt often feel that they must be "better than the equivalent heterosexual" in order to qualify to parent (44), a situation that affects lesbians as well.

The first issue to be faced is the fact that the potential adoptive or foster parent's sexual orientation, especially if it is exclusively gay or lesbian, may itself be a barrier to parenthood (Benkov 1994; Martin 1993). State foster care and/or adoption policies, regulations, and/or practices often either forbid or discourage gay and lesbian parenting, or at least give such parents lower priority than others when placing children. The National Association of Social Workers, the American Psychological Association, and other professional and human services organizations and associations have taken the position that sexual orientation in and of itself should have no bearing on child custody cases or on deciding whether a person is fit to be a foster or adoptive parent (Benkov 1994). Rather it is the capacity of the person to parent that should be the issue.

Because of discriminatory regulations and practices, gay or lesbian people seeking to adopt a child must first decide whether (and how) to attempt to conceal the fact of their sexual orientation (Martin 1993). Since single-parent adoptions and foster parenting are permitted in most states, one partner often decides to apply to become a foster parent or to adopt as an individual. If this strategy is used, the potential co-parent may become completely marginalized in the official process. Even when the adoptive or foster parent's sexual orientation is not concealed and both partners identify themselves as intending to rear the child together, the fact that gays and lesbians may not legally marry means that the adoption or foster care arrangement cannot by definition officially be entered into by the couple. Thus, as with lesbian pregnancy, the couple must negotiate who will be the foster or adoptive parent of record and who will be merely the "roommate" or "friend," even if the plan within a couple is to parent on an equal basis.

Another outcome in this situation is that such parents may decide to seek or may only be offered a child or children who are considered otherwise "higher risk" or "difficult to place," meaning older, with siblings, or with identified problems, medically (especially HIV/AIDS), by history, or in their current behavior. Most people who seek to be foster parents or especially who seek to adopt want to have a child who is young and healthy; deciding to take on a child with already identified problems can work out well but does raise additional challenges. Moreover, there is evidence that child welfare agencies have been placing adolescents known or thought to be gay in foster homes with gay couples for some time (Ricketts & Achtenberg 1990). This practice may reflect a wish to provide support and positive role models for a gay or lesbian adolescent or it may reflect reluctance to place any adolescent *except* a gay or lesbian one with lesbian- or gay-identified foster or adoptive parents (Ricketts & Achtenberg 1990).

For this reason as well as others, gay or lesbian people who wish to adopt a child may turn to cross-cultural or international adoption in the belief they may be more likely to obtain a young and/or healthy baby that way (Martin 1993). International adoption, however, like some forms of private adoption within the United States, is often very costly, thus making it available only to those who can afford it. In addition, it often raises issues of cross-racial and cross-cultural parenting (as domestic adoption may also do) that must be considered and addressed (Crawford 1987; Martin 1993).

Anecdotally, some child welfare workers do not agree with restrictive policies or simply become convinced on an individual basis that an identified or possibly gay or lesbian applicant for a child will make a good foster or adoptive parent. In other cases, because of the chronic shortage of good foster and adoptive homes available for children, the worker's dedication to obtaining viable and potentially permanent placements for children in need outweighs any reservations about such a placement that they may have based simply on sexual orientation. In this situation, the worker may consciously or unconsciously fail to inquire about or note sexual orientation or may be able to support the application effectively anyway (Ricketts & Achtenberg 1990). Gay and lesbian people who want to become foster and/or adoptive parents often become quite knowledgeable about the child welfare systems and agencies in their area and attempt to seek out those agencies and workers whose attitudes are known to be less restrictive. Despite stringent legislation and regulations, they know that they can become foster or adoptive parents, and they do. Increasingly, gays and lesbians who seek to become licensed as foster parents or to adopt a child are choosing to be candid about their sexual orientation in order to prevent disruption of the placement later should the information about their sexual orientation emerge (Ricketts & Achtenberg 1990). Finally, as among heterosexual parents, some lesbian and gay parents take on the rearing of a child as the result of a kinship, guardianship, or other formal or informal arrangement—that is, through private foster care or adoption agreements (Benkov 1994; Martin 1993).

CHOOSING CHILDREN

One thing that both lesbian childbearing and adoption by self-identified lesbians and gays have in common is the fact that the decision to bear and/or rear a child or children was entered into in a context that was known to be lesbian or gay. These arrangements are therefore more controversial both among heterosexuals and even among some lesbians and gays. Some heterosexuals as well as some older gays and lesbians, for example, feel that "a person should get married or at least renounce gay involvements if he or she wants children" while others have argued that "having one or two strikes against you (race or class oppression) was sufficient, without asking children to bear the added stigma of a gay or lesbian parent" (Weston 1991:167). These attitudes are the product of homophobia—internalized or externalized—since those gays and lesbians who do decide to parent clearly have chosen to do so in the conviction that they can be as good or better than the average heterosexual as parents (Patterson 1994a).

Gay and lesbian people who choose to become parents must overcome many structural and concrete obstacles as well as many intangible ones in order to bear and/or rear children. They cannot become parents "by accident" or simply as the product of a pronatalist and unexamined life script as some heterosexual people do. This factor is especially important to consider given the fact that a wanted child is apt to be better taken care of than an unwanted or ambivalently regarded one. As the literature on the children of lesbians and gays has shown, there is no objective reason to believe that children reared by lesbian or gay parents fare any more poorly than children reared by those who identify as heterosexual (see below).

Defining Parenthood: Who Counts?

The childbearing and child-rearing situation regarded as normative in our society—of a married woman and man who live with their own child or children under eighteen—is only one of many family forms that now exist in our society. In fact, in the United States today, the so-called normative ideal is actually a minority household constellation, comprising only 25 percent of American households in 1996 (Bureau of the Census 1997). To anyone who bears and/or rears children in some other family form in our society, defining parenthood has become an important concern. It takes on added salience for gays and lesbians, however, because they have traditionally been seen by definition as being incapable of parenting or as being unfit parents. In addition, when two gay or lesbian people parent together, the lack of a mixed-gender model for assigning parental (as well as household) roles and responsibilities calls for creativity and thoughtfulness in defining and naming the parenting that takes place.

The single most common problem that parenting gay and lesbian couples face is the potential and/or actual invisibility of the nonbiological or non-adoptive parent (Benkov 1994; Crawford 1987; Muzio 1993; Martin 1993). As Slater (1995) puts it in relation to lesbians, "lesbian co-parents dramatically illustrate the outlaw status of all lesbian families" (99). This problem occurs in all gay and lesbian parenting situations: when the children are from one (or both) partner's former heterosexual ties; when the child or children were born into the relationship; and when the child or children are adopted. However the family is formed, such families still seem to struggle with the issue of whether they really are a family (Hare 1994).

The first way that this invisibility manifests itself is in language because the names we have for parents are gendered: one is a mother and the other is a father (Ainslee & Feltey 1991; Benkov 1994; Martin 1993; Muzio 1993). What are the parents to be called when both are of the same gender? Will the biological or adoptive parent get the traditional name—mother or father—while the other parent is called something else? Will both be called by the gender-appropriate parenting name (e.g., "Mama Sue" and "Mama Jane")? Or perhaps "Mama" and "Mom"; or "Daddy" and "Papa"? Or will the traditional parent-naming be rejected altogether in favor of given names? Will the naming of the parent(s) be the same inside and outside the "family" (Ainslee & Feltey 1991)? How widely some of these naming conventions can be used outside the household depends, of course, on how open the parents and children are or can safely be in the world outside the family—with physicians and other health care providers, at day care, at school, to employers, to the adoption agency, with extended family, with mental health and social service agencies and professionals.

Another naming issue concerns the child's surname. Lesbian couples often elect to give a child born to them the surname(s) of one or both of them (Martin 1993; Muzio 1993). Others find ways to incorporate names associated with both families into the full array of first, middle, and last names that the child will carry. This naming issue is often seen as important not just for the nonbirth mother but also for the relatives of both families, as acceptance and belonging for the child in both extended families is usually the wish and the goal. Some of these naming strategies, especially those involving surnames, may be less available to those who adopt and who feel a need to conceal their gay or lesbian relationships.

Perhaps the greatest effect that invisibility has is on the co-parenting gay or lesbian partner (Benkov 1994; Crawford 1987; Martin 1993; Muzio 1993). Parental rights in our society are legally defined most often by procreation, adoption, or marriage. Therefore a nonbiological or nonadoptive parent in the gay and lesbian context—as in other nonmarital situations—has no formal legal parental rights. Such a parent cannot legally authorize medical care for the child and has no right of custody following the death of the other parent, for example. In addition, whether or not such an employed nonbiological or nonadoptive parent can purchase a family medical insurance plan for the child or for the partner who may not have such a plan available depends entirely upon how the employer and the insurance company define family, the definitions often being restrictive rather than inclusive. Furthermore, maternal or paternal leave at the time of birth or adoption may not be available as it would be in the context of marriage. Should the couple's relationship come to an end, there is often no legal basis for custody or for further contact with the child, even if the co-parent is still providing economic support. All these rights are determined without reference to the parental *functions* that the nonbiological or nonadoptive parent may have and his or her economic, social, or emotional importance to the child. These extrafamilial influences can impact on the dynamics between the parents within the relationship, and in relation to the child or children as well, since one parent is so much more empowered outside the relationship than the other. Although there is some evidence that lesbian co-parents are more involved with children in a family when the children are born or adopted into it than when the children come from a previous marriage (Hare 1994), there is ample evidence that all gay and lesbian co-parenting partners are very involved with the children they live with and help to rear, making this anxiety about their legitimacy as parents very painful (Benkov 1994; Evans 1990; Martin 1993). One study found that lesbian co-mothers have a higher level of parenting skills than heterosexual fathers do on average (Flaks et al. 1995)

One solution that some co-parents have sought as a means of stabilizing and legitimating their parenting of the child is to adopt the child born to or adopted by the other (Benkov 1994; Cullum 1993; Martin 1993; Shernoff 1996). Adoption confers many legal benefits, such as financial stability for the child, access to private and public benefits such as health insurance and Social

Security for the child, and full legal status as a parent for the co-parent. This legal recourse is not easily available in all jurisdictions, especially in those unfamiliar with the procedure. It also, of course, requires the consent of the biological or adoptive parent, and there are ways for the biological parent in the gay or lesbian couple to express consent to such an adoption without jeopardizing his or her own rights in any way (Benkov 1994; Cullum 1993; Martin 1993). Co-parent adoptions are more easily arranged in the case of birth by donor insemination when the biological father is unknown or when there has been a legal adoption in which both biological parents have relinquished rights to the child. Especially in jurisdictions where co-parent adoptions are unfamiliar, it is often useful to seek assistance from legal advocacy groups, such as the National Center for Lesbian Rights and the Lambda Legal Defense and Education Fund (Cullum 1993; Martin 1993; Patterson 1994b).

Other couples seek to balance the relationship by taking turns in adoption or childbearing, a solution that works, of course, only when multiple children are desired and, in the case of lesbian childbearing, when both members of the couple are physically able to do so (Martin 1993). Some lesbian couples who are bearing a child may seek a sperm donation from a relative of the nonbirth mother so that she will be able to claim some degree of biological relationship to the child in the event of the birth-mother's death, since courts (and others) often give preference in custody to relatives over nonrelatives. However, this option raises all the potential problems that can arise when a known sperm donor also knows the child; the fear of course is that the biological father can or will assert parental rights at some later point in time. Hare (1994) describes a lesbian couple in which each partner had given birth from the same unknown donor, making the children biologically half-siblings. As ovum donation becomes more common, lesbian couples will use it creatively to create joint ties to the infant, as when one partner carries a pregnancy based on the ovum of the other.

There are more legal mechanisms available that help the nonadoptive or nonbiological parent provide for the child than there are to protect the parent. However, all of them are more limited than those provided by co-parent adoption (Cullum 1993; Hare 1994; Martin 1993). Children who are by law defined as "nonrelated" can be named as beneficiaries in life insurance policies or wills, and a biological or adoptive parent can make the co-parent the guardian of the child in the event of her or his death. Contracts in which a nonbiological or nonadoptive parent commits to the financial support of the child can be developed. Legal mechanisms to insure that, at least in the absence of the biological or adoptive parent, the co-parent can authorize medical care for the child, for example, can also be put in place. These allow a co-parent to function as a parent on behalf of the child. However, other mechanisms that allow a nonbiological or nonadoptive parent to provide for a child, such as including him or her as a beneficiary of health or other employment-related benefits, are not so widely available as they depend entirely on the definition of "family" or "dependent" that the employer and/or the insuring entity adopt. Nominations of guardianship in the event of the biological parent's death may be made (Cullum 1993). Even with the mechanisms that can be put in place, extra steps must be taken to ensure that they are there, rather than being able to assume that the co-parent's rights as a parent or the child's rights to care from that parent are in fact in place.

The biggest fear that most co-parents suffer from is that their standing in law as a parent is not protected, meaning that should the couple's relationship be disrupted or in the event of the adoptive or biological parent's death, the co-parent's rights to contact with the child can easily be terminated (Benkov 1994; Crawford 1987; Martin 1993; Shernoff 1996). Child custody disputes are meant to be decided on the legal principle of the best interests of the child (Benkov 1994; Falk 1993; Martin 1993), and extended family members can be and have been awarded custody of children in preference to a co-parent. For example, courts often assume that a lesbian mother is by definition mentally ill, unstable, or less maternal than other women; they may also assume that a child reared by a lesbian will have difficulties with sexual orientation or sexual identity development or with peer relationships because of the stigmatization of the mother (Benkov 1994; Falk 1993). In this way, custody rulings involving a gay father or lesbian mother are handled very differently from those involving heterosexual parents; in the latter case, it is well accepted that the sexual conduct of the parent outside of marriage is not a negative factor in custody decisions unless it can be shown that the conduct has produced specific harm to the children in question (Badgett 1992). Thus the "best interests of the child" are often automatically thought to mean the rearing of that child by a heterosexual person or persons rather than by a gay, lesbian, or bisexual one. However, all the research on this issue to date indicates that the developmental outcomes for children reared by lesbian and/or gay parents are as good or better than those reared in comparable heterosexual households.

Outcomes for Children of Lesbians and Gays

Interestingly, it has been the concern of courts about resolving legal issues surrounding lesbian and gay parenthood that has given rise to much of the limited research that has been done on children reared by lesbian and gay parents (Patterson 1995b). Despite its heterosexist and homophobic roots, this research has generally shown that there is little or no difference in the developmental outcomes among children reared by lesbian or gay parents and those reared in comparable heterosexual households (Falk 1993; Lott-Whitehead & Tully 1993; Patterson 1995b; Strickland 1995; Tasker & Golombok 1997; Turner, Scudden, & Harris 1990). However, because of the controversies that continue to surround this issue, it is useful to examine the research results in relation to the specific developmental outcomes that have most often been examined. Moreover, because childbearing has only recently become a viable option for lesbians and gays, most of the published studies address children born to lesbians and gays who were formerly married; the emerging research on children born into lesbian families will also be described. The information presented here draws principally on recently published reviews of research done in this area over the past two decades.

Judicial and policy decisions discriminating against gay and/or lesbian parents in child custody, foster care, and adoption decisions often begin from the still common but mistaken belief that homosexuality per se represents a mental illness. This point of view assumes that a gay or lesbian parent is unfit based on the idea that he or she is mentally ill. However, all the studies to date on this issue have found that lesbian and gay parents function just as well as their heterosexual counterparts in their parenting roles (Bigner 1996; Patterson 1995a, 1995b), and twenty-five years of research have shown that lesbian, gay, and bisexual people in the general population are as well adjusted as heterosexual people are (Strickland 1995). Nor have any studies of emotional and behavioral problems, moral maturity, self-concept or other measures of psychological functioning (most of which were done on children of lesbian mothers) shown any significant differences between them and comparable children reared by heterosexual mothers (Gottman 1990; Patterson 1992, 1994a; Tasker & Golombok 1997).

One of the most common fears about developmental outcomes in children reared by lesbian and/or gay parents is that such children lack the role models necessary for the development of "normal" gender-role behavior and/or the development of a stable gender identity. Studies of gender identity and gender-role behavior in such children have repeatedly found them to be no different from that among children reared by heterosexual parents (Gottman 1990; Patterson 1992, 1994a). Most of these studies have been done on children of lesbian parents since they are more numerous than those being reared by gay ones. Most of the children studied to date have been those reared by formerly married women, and there is some evidence that children of lesbian mothers may have more regular contact with their fathers and with other adult males on average than those of divorced heterosexual mothers (Patterson 1992). However, the findings of the studies on psychological development have important implications for theories of child development which suggest that a two-gender parental constellation is necessary for the development of gender identity and gender role (Patterson 1992; Tasker & Golombok 1997; Strickland 1995).

Another commonly asked question has been about the sexual orientation of adolescents and adults reared by gay and lesbian parents. Sexual orientation has been assessed from the standpoint of the child's fantasy life and sexual interests as well as simply by asking the child about his or her self-identification. The distributions of gay and/or lesbian sexual orientation in the hundreds of children studied to date was not significantly different from that in comparable samples or in the general population (Bailey et al. 1995; Patterson 1992). This result is not surprising given the often-noted fact that most gays, lesbians, and bisexuals were themselves reared by heterosexual parents and that sexual orientation is currently thought to have both a genetic and an environmental genesis (Bailey et al. 1995).

Peer and other social relationships in children of lesbians and gays have also been studied because of the fears that living with gay or lesbian parents will be so stigmatizing that the children will suffer socially. In fact, studies have found that the peer relationships of such children are not significantly different in nature and quality from those of comparable children reared by heterosexuals (Bigner 1996; Patterson 1992; Tasker & Golombok 1997). Nor is there any evidence that children reared by gay or lesbian parents are at risk of sexual abuse; in fact, the evidence suggests that most child sexual abuse is perpetrated by adult heterosexual men on female children (Bigner 1996; Patterson 1992).

However, there is some preliminary evidence that children of divorced lesbian mothers are more likely than those of divorced heterosexual mothers to be living in a household that includes a mother's partner and that such households had a "richer, more open and stable family life" than those that did not (Patterson 1992:1035). In addition, the division of household and child care work within the family is likely to be more even in lesbian than in heterosexual couples with children, and there is some evidence that the higher the non-biological or nonadoptive mother's involvement with the child, the better the child's adjustment is likely to be (Patterson 1995a). Studies like these suggest that supporting and protecting a co-parent's relationship and involvement with the child should be important policy and practice goals.

There is evidence that many children of lesbian, gay, or bisexual parents do not always disclose their parent's sexual orientation to their friends, perhaps leading to some degree of social isolation (Patterson 1992). As one respondent in a study of adolescent children of lesbian mothers observed, "First your mother comes out to you, and then you have to come out about your mother" (O'Connell 1993:289). In particular, it has been suggested that when a biological father has a negative attitude toward a mother's lesbianism, the self-esteem of the children may suffer (Patterson 1992). In other words, the attitudes surrounding a gay, lesbian, or bisexual family may create the biggest problems, not anything within the family itself (Bigner 1996; Rothberg & Weinstein 1996). As Supreme Court Justice Burger remarked in another context, "Private biases may be outside the reach of the law, but the law cannot, directly or indirectly, give them effect" (quoted in Badgett 1992:189).

Much more research on the children of lesbian, gay, and bisexual parents is needed—specifically, research that addresses the variations within and among gay, lesbian, and bisexual families, most of which has been based to date on white middle-class samples in general and on divorced lesbian mothers in particular. One of the leading researchers on the children of gay, lesbian, and bisexual families has summed up what we know about the children of gay, lesbian, and bisexual parents, as follows:

> Research on children of gay and lesbian parents has reached a significant turning point. Having addressed heterosexist and homophobic concerns represented in psychological theory, judicial opinion, and popular prejudice, child development researchers are now in a position also to explore a broader range of issues raised by the emergence of different kinds of lesbian and gay families. Results of future research on such issues have the potential to increase our knowledge about nontraditional family forms and about their impact on children, stimulate innovations in theoretical understanding of human development, and inform legal rulings and public policies relevant to children of gay and lesbian families.   (Patterson 1992:1039)

Specifically, the research findings to date emphasize the greater importance of family and parent-child processes compared to structural variables, such as the sexual orientation of the parent or the number of adults present in the household, on child development outcomes. This conclusion is the same as that drawn from research on other alternative family forms, with family theory, and with psychological theories such as ego psychology, attachment theory, and the self-psychology. Thus these findings are fully compatible with the knowledge base of social work practice as well.

Boundary Maintenance

One special challenge that all members of gay, lesbian, and bisexual families face is that of boundary maintenance. This challenge arises for a variety of reasons.

The first is that some people may not even believe that such families exist as childbearing or child-rearing units (Benkov 1994; Hare 1994). As a result, the relationships that exist among family members—parent-child, co-parent–child, brother and/or sister—may not be seen or acknowledged for what they are or may even be questioned or challenged. Thus extra effort must be made to protect, defend, name, or define them. Martin (1993) speaks of frequently "being on the spot with strangers" (311), that is, of having ordinary encounters and "small talk" out in the world—at the supermarket, at the playground, at the airport—call relationships into question. A gay father buying diapers with his infant hears, "How lucky your wife is that you help out." A lesbian couple with their toddler gets asked, "Who's the mother?" or "Where's the father?" These common encounters call for constant decision making about what to say and how to say it. Such problems can be greatly alleviated or greatly exacerbated depending upon the social and community resources and attitudes that surround the family unit itself. Hence (as ecological theories of adaptation would suggest), when possible, gay and lesbian parents often actively seek out those living environments and community institutions in which their families will feel most comfortable.

Another set of boundary maintenance problems can arise from the various identity management strategies that gay, lesbian, or bisexual family members may adopt on the continuum of coming out (Bigner 1996; Hare 1994; also see chapter 2). It must be remembered that stigma is "sticky" or "contagious"; those who are associated with stigmatized individuals—in this context, the children and other relatives of people known to be lesbian, gay, or bisexual—may find themselves stigmatized as well or may worry that they will be, leading them to be concerned with identity management strategies similar to those that gay, lesbian, and bisexual people themselves cope with (Benkov 1994; Hare 1994; Martin 1993). These identity management problems can affect all family members' transactions within the family—although they are even more likely to influence transactions between family members and those in the family's wider world: the extended family; other community members; schools; and health, mental health, and social welfare organizations (Bigner 1996; Martin 1993). Religious beliefs and political ideas as well as racial and ethnic variations (both in how a gay or lesbian sexual orientation is typically viewed and managed and in how "family" and children are typically responded to) are other important factors affecting how boundary issues are understood and managed and on the adaptation of the family as a whole (Rohrbaugh 1992).

Writing about lesbian families from a family systems perspective, Slater (1995) has articulated well some the particular identity issues that families headed by gays and lesbians face:

In addition to protecting their children, lesbian parents must also articulate a clear and affirming family identity to their children. . . . Difficult for any family that mainstream society devalues, lesbian families' task is compounded by the fact that not all members of the family are lesbians. While family members within nondominant racial, religious, and ethnic groups all share their minority identity, lesbian parents cannot assume their children will grow up to be gay. In that sense, they are not "lesbian families" at all, but rather families with lesbian parents. The child's likely identification with heterosexual peers complicates naming the family's shared group identity and potentially threatens the family members' experience of belonging.

(Slater 1995:105)

This situation, of course, is in some ways the reverse of that of the child or adolescent who realizes he or she is gay, lesbian, or bisexual at the cost of a threatened or reduced sense of belonging or identification within his or her family of origin. The point is not that a family cannot include and embrace differences in the sexual orientation of its members; rather, the point is that all members of any family with one or more gay, lesbian, or bisexual members must engage in stigma management when relating to the wider world. When writing further of this problem as it affects lesbian parents, Slater (1995) observes that "lesbian parents must . . . also face the ongoing concern that people will ostracize or harass their children to protest the parents' lesbian identity. Every parent's nightmare is that they will be unable to protect their children, and society's homophobia leaves lesbian parents preoccupied with this worry" (108). These concerns have a great deal to do with how gay and lesbian parents manage the coming out process with their children.

COMING OUT TO CHILDREN

One boundary issue that gay, lesbian, and bisexual families must face *within* the household or family unit is that of how the father or mother's sexual orientation will be represented to the children. In a heterosexist society, a heterosexual orientation is assumed and thus is also assumed not to need identification or explication. However, a lesbian, gay, or bisexual parent, whether or not he or she lives with or has custody of the child, must decide if and when to reveal or discuss that fact with a child. This process is commonly described as coming out to one's children. Those parents who come to or openly affirm a gay, lesbian, or bisexual identity after bearing children often fear this process greatly, worrying about potential rejection by their children and/or worrying about the effect that this fact may have on a child (Hare 1994).

Most of the studies of coming out to children have been done on lesbian families, particularly those formed by one or more previously married women rearing children. Despite their fears, most gay and lesbian parents do discuss their sexual orientation with their children, a course widely recommended by mental health professionals because it generally leads to more open and honest relating between parent and child (Rohrbaugh 1992).[4] In fact, continued and ongoing discussion of the parent's sexual orientation is generally needed because, as children grow and mature, their own concerns, questions, and capacity to understand the issues involved change as well. In addition, what parents think children know and what children actually understand may not always be the same (Rohrbaugh 1992). There is some preliminary evidence that children first told of their parent's gay or lesbian sexual orientation in early adolescence, as opposed to at younger or older ages, may have a more difficult time adjusting to the information (Patterson 1992). Adolescents do not like to feel different in any way (O'Connell 1993). In addition, a parent who comes out during a child's adolescence may make it more difficult for the child because of the developmental issues adolescents face; these include the pressure of peer relationships and the consolidation of one's own sexual identity, each of which may seem initially threatened by the parent's stigmatized identity (O'Connell 1993). However, this finding does not suggest that secrecy is a better strategy, even during early adolescence; family secrets of any kind have long been discussed by family therapists and family theorists as destructive to family bonds and relationships. Rather it suggests that a parent may have to anticipate and be prepared to deal with a more negative reaction from a child of that age than of a different age and stage of development.

Children have a variety of reactions to the news that a parent is lesbian or gay.[5] Most respond favorably (Bigner 1996; Lott-Whitehead & Tully 1993). Many assert that this information makes no difference or that they "knew all that already" (Turner, Scadden, & Harris 1990). While this initial response may be reassuring to a parent, it should not be taken literally to mean that there are not or never again will be any questions about the issue. Other children will react more as the parent may fear: with distress, anxiety, anger, or sorrow, expressed perhaps in tears or possibly even in statements quite rejecting of the parent. Some adolescent male children of lesbian mothers have reported that they feared her lesbianism meant that she was "anti-male" and thus might not love them any more (O'Connell 1993). In addition, because children identify with their parents, a child who is told that a parent is lesbian or gay, especially an older child or adolescent who is likely to be overtly or covertly concerned with his or her own sexuality, may wonder if the parent's sexual orientation means that she or he will be lesbian or gay as well. What must always be remembered, whether the initial response is positive or negative, is that a child's first response is unlikely to be the only or enduring one.

Because most gay or lesbian people have have had mixed feelings about themselves while coming to the point of identifying as lesbian or gay, the fact that their children will have complicated feelings about the issue and will need repeated and continuing opportunities to discuss it will come as no surprise. However, the responses of children to the information about their parent's gay or lesbian identity may reactivate in parents some their own negative feelings about themselves, just as with many other issues that children negotiate as they grow and develop.

Parents often initiate a coming out process with their children to help them understand some related change in the parent's or the family's situation. When a married man or woman decides to get a divorce because he or she is now embracing a gay or lesbian self-identification, a parent may come out to a child to explain the divorce. To some children, the parent's coming out to them may signal the end of the hope, common among all children following a divorce, that the divorcing parents may someday reconcile (O'Connell 1993).

A single or divorced gay or lesbian parent may come out to a child at the point when a new same-gender lover has become important enough to him or her that more contact with the children will take place or even that the lover may be joining the household. It may, however, occur because of some other event that has caused a child to ask about the issue for the first time. In any of these circumstances, the reaction of the child to these other major events will color their reaction to the issue of the parent's being gay or lesbian. For example, if the coming out occurs on the occasion of a new lover entering on the scene, children may blame the lover or imagine that if the lover were to go away, so would the parent's sexual orientation. In fact, the response of the child to the issue of the parent's sexual orientation may be colored as much by the surrounding issues—a divorce or the arrival of a new adult in the household—as by the child's response to sexual orientation issues themselves.

Gay and lesbian parents are likely to be aware that their children will need help in identifying who else in their social network knows and does not know about the parent. And, just like their mothers and fathers, children of gay fathers and lesbian mothers can also become caught in the dilemma of when and how to attempt to "pass" and when and how to disclose fully their identities as children of gay and/or lesbian parents (Bigner 1996; O'Connell 1993). In fact, it may be helpful for parents to let other trusted adults know when they are sharing this information with their children so they can specifically reassure the children that there are other people available they can further talk to about the issue. To the extent that the parents are not open about their lesbian or gay identity, these contexts and possible strategies for dealing with them should be identified for the children as well (Crawford 1987).

On balance, however, most children respond to a gay or lesbian parent's coming out with loyalty and protectiveness (O'Connell 1993). Because social workers may be called upon to help in the coming out process, it is important to understand the variety of meanings such an event can have to a child at one time or another. However, the positive effects must not be overlooked as well. For example, O'Connell quotes an anonymous adolescent who participated in her study of children reared by lesbian mothers as saying about her mother: "I saw her as a model to be open and honest. She has nourished me and loved me while taking big risks in her life. That she was a lesbian, that she could be brave . . . allowed me to understand that I could be brave too" (O'Connell 1993:281).

Because of the many challenges that can arise in the process of coming out to children, some gay or lesbian parents may even seek professional help for themselves or their families during this pivotal time. This move should be seen as one representing great concern for the children involved and as an admirable effort to cope with a situation made difficult by a homophobic and heterosexist society rather than as a sign of personal vulnerability. A social worker seeking to be helpful in such a situation, of course, must be knowledgeable about sexual orientation issues, about gay and lesbian families (especially co-parenting issues where relevant), and about how homophobia and heterosexism may be manifested in the interpersonal interactions that a family may encounter in their particular social context. Otherwise, the methods used to assess the needs of and to intervene with a family in the process of coming out do not differ from those that might be used when helping any family deal with a process of change in self-definition or composition. When there is a gay or lesbian community available to the family, parent support groups (and/or chances to participate in other groups), social gatherings, or opportunities for similar contacts with other children of gay or lesbian parents are likely to prove invaluable. Many lesbian parents in particular have identified contacts with an organized lesbian community as a positive support in coping (Rohrbaugh 1992), but not all families will have such resources open to them (especially in some regional, religious, or ethnic or racial communities).

The Ecology of Families Headed By Lesbians and Gays

So far, this chapter has addressed various situations and options of gay and lesbian parents and their children within the family system itself. In addition, some of the legal and policy issues that impact on such families have also been discussed. However, there are other elements of the environment that are critical to the well-being of families headed by gay, lesbian, or bisexual people. These include the extended family, the "chosen family" (Weston 1991), and the child care, educational, employment, and health care organizations with which members of the family interact, often on a daily basis. Finally, where they exist, gay and lesbian communities are important sources of support (and sometimes strain) on gay and lesbian parents. It should be noted that some of these crucial transactions between gay, lesbian, and bisexual parents and their children take place in a macrosystems environment in which the basic civil rights of gay and lesbian people are protected; but many of them do not, which has a profound and pervasive effect on the family, especially where such basic issues as employment and housing are concerned.

EXTENDED FAMILY

The entry of a child into a family is ordinarily an occasion of great joy. While the extended families of many gay, lesbian, and bisexual people have that reaction, responses can in fact be quite varied (Martin 1993; Slater 1995). Sometimes the arrival of a longed-for grandchild, niece, or nephew can draw the grandparents and other relatives closer to the couple having the child. However, if negative attitudes have previously kept extended family members distant, old wounds may need to be worked through before a comfortable closeness can result. Sometimes the wish of the extended family for more contact and/or closeness following the arrival of a child may exclude a co-parent and extend only to a related birth or adoptive parent, thus creating a loyalty conflict in that parent, who may want the closeness for the child but also wants to include the partner as well. When the child has two parents, the reactions of the two extended families may be the same or they may be different, an imbalance that may create resonances within the couple as well. Hence homophobic reactions from extended family may be complicated or eased by the arrival of a child on the scene. Just as in other types of families, when a child becomes part of the family some extended family members may be more intrusive and others may be more distant than the parents might like (Slater 1995). However, either problem can be made worse when the family form is different. Unlike heterosexual parents, then, gay, lesbian, and bisexual parents cannot more or less automatically count on extended family as a source of unqualified support for their childbearing and child-rearing. In fact, a "chosen family," especially other gay and lesbian friends, may be as important or more important as sources of support to gay, lesbian, and bisexual parents and their children than family members are.

SCHOOLS

Schools and other child care institutions, such as day care organizations, are key points of contact between gay, lesbian, and bisexual parents and their children and the wider community (Martin 1993). Schools, other child care organizations, and health care institutions reflect the norms of their communities. Although, when they can, gay, lesbian, and bisexual parents seek out schools and day care providers who are comfortable with the kind of family from which the child comes and where the child will therefore feel comfortable, there are certain issues that typically arise in dealing with them.

Gay, lesbian, and bisexual parents, just like other families, often take great care in deciding where to live, in part to increase their odds of finding schools and communities that will be comfortable for them and their children. However, others find themselves in settings that are less hospitable and in circumstances that they cannot easily change. For example, while an affluent couple in an urban setting might be able to seek out a private school or child care facility in which they feel welcome, those with more limited means or who live far from any school alternative will most likely have to make do with the public schools and facilities available. Some parents may cope with schools and other institutions by representing themselves as single parents, letting others make the assumption of heterosexuality and working with their children to identify where it is and is not safe to talk about their families in other ways. Other parents who decide to be more open about their families, just like many parents of children with special needs, may find themselves in the position of having to educate school and child care personnel about themselves and their circumstances and about how to handle questions that might arise about themselves and their families in the classroom and in the community, even though their children are themselves without special needs of any kind.

Whatever the strategy the family adopts, it should be noted that the subject of "family" is ubiquitous in schools. Children of all ages are continuously asked about their families, in the classroom and in social situations, in pictures and in words. The depictions of families that children are likely to encounter in the school environment—as in the culture in general—are likely to reflect what is considered the norm, even though most children are likely to live in one or another type of "alternative family form" at some time during their growing up. The children of gay, lesbian, and bisexual parents are not as likely as other children to see themselves depicted positively as part of their everyday learning and social environments. In addition, books and other materials for children that do depict gay and lesbian families are often the subject of heated and public controversy and are even banned from some school settings. Children of gay, lesbian, and bisexual parents, then, like children who live in other "alternative families," have to be helped by their parents and other caring adults to cope with social and learning environments that range from indifferent to hostile when it comes to their families.

All schools and child care organizations must determine who is responsible for each child as part of their efforts to protect them. Only designated parents and guardians may pick up a child from school or write a note explaining an absence, for example. Only designated parents and guardians may visit a child's classroom, meet with a child's teacher, or act as an official advocate for the child in the event of any problems. Designated parents and guardians are also welcome to join the school's parent or parent-teacher organization. Thus gay and lesbian parents must decide about identifying a nonbiological, nonadoptive and/or noncustodial parent to the school simply to function on behalf of the child on a day-to-day basis. Many schools will not have a ready category for such a parent, and their registration forms are generally not set up to record the existence of such a parent except as a "stepparent," which may not be appropriate to the situation. Parents and children may have to do a lot of explaining about who they are as a family—to teachers, to administrators, and even to other parents and children. Aside from the logistics of child care and providing parental support for a child's education, when school and child define and describe a child's family in the same way, the child's day-to-day functioning in the classroom may be easier. However, gay, lesbian, and bisexual parents must assess any school situation carefully to decide for themselves and their children what strategy or degree of disclosure will best serve the social and educational needs of the child.

Health Care

In health care settings, as in schools, only legally recognized parents and guardians can speak for the child (Benkov 1994; Martin 1993). In the case of medical care, in emergency or critical care circumstances, this can seem a life-or-death situation. Actually, in life-threatening emergencies, there are ways to deliver the care needed with or without parental consent, although consent is always preferred. Thus the greater problems may actually arise in the everyday efforts to obtain competent care that is easily authorized and that permits all those people important to the child to be part of the caregiving process.

For example, when a child is hospitalized, both parents, not just the biological or adoptive one, may want to room with the child, to be there beyond official visiting hours and the like. Both may want to meet with medical personnel to hear the confidential information about the child's test results, diagnosis, and treatment options. While pediatric care these days is generally more attentive to the social and emotional needs of the child as essential to health and well-being, parents or even the child may be fearful of the consequences of disclosing the nature of their family life to strangers:

> A teenager arrives in the emergency room of a major tertiary care hospital with a suspected brain tumor. After examining the patient, the neurologist and neurosurgeon to whom the family has been referred come into the crowded waiting room, where the mother, the mother's long-time lesbian partner and co-parent of the teen, and the divorced father all wait anxiously. Concerned about confidentiality, the neurologist stops to ask who the co-parent is before giving the diagnosis and making a recommendation about admission and treatment. The mother makes a split-second decision and identifies her partner as co-parent, and the medical report is then given to all three parents present. In fact, from that moment forward all three parents are included by the physicians in all information-giving and planning for the child. However, at a time of great personal stress, the co-parent has to experience a questioning of her legitimacy, and the lesbian parents have to face a rapid coming out decision to people and in a setting previously unknown to them.

There is a great deal that health care organizations can do to ease such fears. For example, the patient registration forms that must be filled out can be constructed in such a way that every family can find a way to describe itself accurately and comfortably. Staff can be educated about gay and lesbian parents and their children, which may not only reduce negative responses but may render such families less often "invisible" to them. An invitation from a health care professional to include a co-parent in the information-sharing and caregiving, for example, often makes it much easier for parents and children to be who they are comfortably. For example, in the vignette above, the positive reaction of the physicians to the parents' emergency room coming out certainly made it easier on the child in question who was subsequently hospitalized for some time (although in a less pressured situation it would have been better for all—parents and child—to discuss and decide together how to proceed). However, health care organizations are constrained by state law when issues bearing on the authorization of treatment arise; parents and co-parents, then, must use the legal mechanisms available to them for this problem (see the section on co-parents, above).

CHILD WELFARE

The involvement of child welfare agencies with gay and lesbian parents and their children when these families are formed by adoption or foster care has already been discussed. However, it should be noted that, just like among the children of heterosexuals, problems can arise that will bring the child of a gay or lesbian parent to the attention of these agencies (Faria 1994). However, lesbian and gay parents may face some special challenges in resolving them, and child welfare workers must be knowledgeable about gay and lesbian parenting in order to be effectively helpful. Fearing a negative reaction, parents may not find it easy to be completely candid about their situation, which may further complicate an agency's efforts to help.

A case described by Faria (1994) illustrates some of these issues. A twenty-six-year-old woman with several serious chronic health problems gave birth to a daughter. Her physician referred her to the child welfare agency after the birth because of his concerns that she might not be able to adequately care for her daughter because of them. A family preservation worker met with the mother and her lesbian partner, assessed the mother's ability to care for the baby, determined that the baby was healthy, and connected the family to supportive services in the community. The parents did not give a convincing explanation of how the mother had become pregnant, but the worker was sensitive to indirect evidence that the pregnancy had been proactively planned. The worker also assisted the mother's partner in obtaining legal guardianship over both the mother and the baby because the mother's health problems were such that greater disablement or her premature death were distinct possibilities; in this way, continuous custody and care for the baby was ensured. This case illustrates how a positive attitude toward lesbian (and gay) parenting must be an integral part of responsible child welfare practice.

COMMUNITY

For gay, lesbian, and bisexual parents and their children, at least two communities must be considered—the gay and/or lesbian community and the general community in which the family lives (Martin 1993). Not all gay, lesbian, and bisexual parents actually have access to an identifiable gay or lesbian community. Those in rural areas, for example, usually do not. Gay, lesbian, and bisexual parents who are not white or who are part of a nondominant religious group, for example, may feel more connected to their own racial, ethnic, or religious community than to any community defined by sexual orientation. However, for some gay, lesbian, and bisexual parents and their children, the gay and/or lesbian community is an important source of support.

Reference has already been made to the fact that the gay and lesbian community and gay/lesbian advocacy and legal rights organizations are important sources of information and resources for lesbian, gay, and bisexual people considering becoming parents or needing assistance in doing so (Martin 1993; Shernoff 1996). These specialized services have been developed because of the discrimination that gay and lesbian parents and their children can encounter elsewhere. In addition, within the gay and lesbian community in general, gay, lesbian, and bisexual parents and their children may be able to identify, meet, and socialize with other families like themselves, reducing their sometimes burdensome sense of difference and uniqueness. Often, "extended family networks" (Ainslee & Feltey 1991) or "chosen families" (Weston 1991) form around gay or lesbian parents and their children, perhaps because of a recognition that support from the extended family of origin of the parent(s) may not be as reliably given as in other family forms. In addition, the rearing of children within gay and lesbian communities is thought to have generative and political meaning for members of the community who do not themselves choose to do so (Weston 1991), leading them to want to support in tangible and intangible ways the children and parenting of others. For example, at least one study has suggested that the lesbian community often offers much tangible support to women who are parents, such as through attention to the child care needs of women who want to participate in organized community events (Ainslee & Feltey 1991). However, another study of lesbian mothers found that emotional support from friends was the most consistently helpful coping strategy identified (Levy 1992).

Parenting can, however, give rise to tensions between gay and lesbian parents and the gay and/or lesbian community. Some parents, who had previously been very involved in "the community," may feel that they are more distanced from it when they become parents since the majority of others within the community do not have children. The lifestyles of parents and those of nonparents are indeed quite different on a day-to-day basis. Because of this, gay or lesbian parents may be surprised or disconcerted to find that they sometimes feel that they have more in common with or get more support from the heterosexual families that they meet through their children than they do with or from members of "their own" community (Martin 1993; Slater 1995). Levy's study (1992) found that support from personal friends was much more often rated as helpful in coping than involvement in the lesbian community was. At the pediatrician's office, at school, and at the ball field, gay and lesbian parents are more likely to meet, relate to, and share experiences with heterosexual parents than with other gay, lesbian, or bisexual ones. The child's community and the parent's community may seem more different from each other than is the case for other families. Continuous attention, therefore, is needed on the part of the parents to the issue of private versus public identities, on assessing the community environment for safety, and on boundary maintenance strategies that will maximize the opportunities for connection and support and minimize the risk of harm to all family members.

Gay and lesbian parents typically have more control over the mesosystems they inhabit—the extended or chosen family members they relate to, their friendship networks, their choice of neighborhood—than they do over the larger systems—schools, work settings, and macro policy systems—that also affect their daily lives. As in heterosexual families, the decision to have children may move gay, lesbian, or bisexual parents to become more active in collective efforts to change school, workplace, and other policy systems than they had been before. On the other hand, depending on their assessment of the safety of the environment and on how best to meet the needs of all members of the family, they may elect to become less involved with activism for a time while they are most intensely involved with child-rearing. Nevertheless, the policies that surround gay, lesbian, and bisexual parents and their children have a profound effect on family life. For example, those who live in the states that have laws protecting gay and lesbian people from discrimination in employment, housing. and public accommodations, for example, may well feel more comfortable requesting parental leave at the time of birth or adoption, in pushing for inclusion of domestic partnerships and the offspring of them in eligibility for employment benefits, or in working openly with schools for the inclusion of information about gay, lesbian, and bisexual people in diversity training (Martin 1993). Thus civil rights protections can translate very directly into the daily lives of gay, lesbian, and bisexual people and their children as they affect relationships with the larger community.

Implications for Social Work Practice

Gay, lesbian, and bisexual parents and their children are more numerous than is usually supposed, and their numbers are most likely growing. Gay, lesbian, and bisexual people become parents in a variety of ways and manage their lives in different ways as well as they adapt to immediate and broader social contexts that exhibit very different degrees of tolerance and/or acceptance of them. However, heterosexism and homophobia tend to make all these families invisible to practitioners and policymakers alike.

> To provide effective and positive services to gays and lesbians, the social worker must have a knowledge base and skills that not only engage a client, but must understand the gay or lesbian person's position within the social environment. Social workers have been educated to give practice attention to the multiple factors that influence an individual's well-being and achievement of life's needs and goals. . . . Work with gays and lesbians cannot be successful if taken out of the context of the social environment. Nor can it be effective if diverse family groupings and lifestyles are not addressed as being valid systems that may need and seek professional help.
>
> —Patricia Gunther (1992:105–106)

The first principle of practice with lesbian, gay, and bisexual parents and their families, then, is to *recognize that they exist*. Such families will be encountered in medical, educational, social service, child welfare, and mental health settings. Professionals of any discipline in any of these settings who have not considered that these families exist are unlikely to recognize one when the situation arises. Nor are such practitioners likely to feel comfortable in working with such a family without some prior preparation. Not to do so, however, is likely to result in mistakes in assessment of family resources and possibly even in the unintentional wounding of family members by lack of inclusion. How families are depicted even in one's office decorations conveys a message, intended or unintended. Making sure that all social agencies have records that both permit and invite families to describe themselves as they actually are, for example, will not only make such families feel more welcome, they will invite the staff who function in them to consider their existence. However, this approach must be used with caution in policy contexts that do not protect against discrimination—in states that do not protect the civil rights of lesbian and gay people or that have child welfare policies and practices that actively discriminate against gay and lesbian parents, for example. The best interests of the client must always come first. Thus policies that discriminate against lesbian, gay, and bisexual people take a toll on professional workers committed first to client well-being as well as on the clients themselves because such policies conflict with core professional values and ethics, placing all workers in a bind that they must negotiate daily in their practice.

The second principle of practice with lesbian, gay, and bisexual parents and their children is *not to assume that it is the sexual orientation of the parent(s) that is the problem*. In fact, such parents and their children may have any of the common problems of childbearing and child-rearing that any family may have—

infertility, illness in any family member, special educational needs, employment or income problems, difficulties with child behavior, problems in parenting, child custody issues, and/or separation of a couple. While these problems may be compounded by identity management issues and/or by lack of access to resources that other couples may enjoy, they may otherwise be no different from those experienced by other types of families. However, in the case of families headed by lesbian, gay, or bisexual parents, careful assessment is needed that does not minimize the potential problems that heterosexism and/or homophobia may be creating for them but that does not assume that the sexual orientation of the parent(s) is the problem either.

Even when civil rights protections exist, it is essential *not to overlook the real fears, risks, and harms of homophobia and heterosexism.* Gay, lesbian, and bisexual people and their children are likely to have encountered such harm in the past, even if they have managed to construct a relatively safe and supportive immediate environment around themselves. Dealing with this discrimination is likely to have had some psychological effects, both positive and possibly negative, on the individuals in the family. As with other issues of difference between an individual and the majority community and/or between social worker and client, sexual orientation and the worker's attitudes toward it may need to be acknowledged and discussed in any professional-client relationship that is significant. As with other issues of difference, all social workers need to examine their own attitudes about sexual orientation, especially as they relate to childbearing and child-rearing, and to be prepared to deal with them with clients and in supervision or consultation when needed. *Knowledge of community resources* (including but not limited to professional services) that are not discriminatory and that are gay- and lesbian-affirmative is essential. It is also essential to be familiar with—or at least to be ready to learn about—resources within any local gay, lesbian, or bisexual community, including gay and lesbian advocacy organizations that are local or even national in scope. Such organizations can be an invaluable resource to the professionals who work with them as well as to the families themselves.

Finally, it is vital to recognize the *variety of ways in which families headed by lesbian, gay, or bisexual parents define themselves, function, and adapt.* This chapter has offered an introduction to gay, lesbian, and bisexual parents and their children. While all such families likely face certain challenges in common, these challenges and the resources to meet them also differ markedly among families. Just as individual gay, lesbian, and bisexual people choose different strategies for managing a gay, lesbian, or bisexual identity, families with one or more lesbian, gay, or bisexual members do too. Both the gay or lesbian community and majority society may convey a message that there is only one right way to be such a family, even though those messages differ sharply. A social work professional can play a pivotal role: to know about the variations among families headed by lesbian and gay parents and to help all family members realize that there are many options available to them for successful adaptation and a flourishing family life.

7

Gay, Lesbian, and Bisexual People in the World of Work

Homophobia and heterosexism affect gay, lesbian, and bisexual people in their work lives as well as in their private lives. Discrimination in hiring and firing, limitations on career and occupational choices, inequities in employment benefits, and social marginalization on the job may all occur. Ways to combat homophobia and heterosexism in the workplace are discussed. Particular attention is paid to gay, lesbian, and bisexual people in social work and other helping professions; also outlined are the special issues that can arise in relationships between clients and workers when both are lesbian, gay, or bisexual.

Most lesbian, gay, and bisexual people participate in the labor force—that is, they earn money as employees or through self-employment. There are no national data available on the employment participation rates of lesbian, gay, or bisexual people. However, because all of the income-sharing, assets-sharing, and benefits-sharing advantages that marriage provides are not usually available to lesbian and gay couples, it is generally assumed that a higher percentage of lesbians and gays are employed than holds true among heterosexuals (Elliott 1993; Fassinger 1995; Morgan & Brown 1991). For example, for women data show that 85 to 92 percent of lesbians were employed outside the home in the 1980s when only about 50 percent of women in general were

(Elliott 1993; Morgan & Brown 1991). Anyone who works with clients, especially those in employee assistance programs (EAPs) and other settings that focus on employment issues, therefore must be knowledgeable about career development, work role performance, and workplace issues as they affect lesbian, gay, and bisexual people.

In addition, it is very likely that anyone who is employed works with lesbian, gay, or bisexual people whether they are aware of that fact or not. The social work profession itself has many self-identified, or "out," lesbian and gay members and likely an even larger number of lesbian, gay, and bisexual members who do not identify themselves as such in the workplace or in the wider community. Thus, anyone in the profession of social work is likely to work with lesbian, gay, and/or bisexual social workers whether or not their sexual orientation is known. In addition, those social workers who are supervisors, managers, or administrators need to be knowledgeable about employment issues for lesbian, gay, and bisexual people.

This chapter offers an overview of career development and workplace issues as they affect lesbian, gay, and bisexual people. The emphasis will be on lesbian and gay workers because bisexual people who are married, for example, do not face the same institutionalized discrimination in employment and benefits that those in same-gender relationships do and because less is known about bisexual employees as a group. However, bisexual people who identify as such or who seek benefits for same-gender partners, for example, encounter the same workplace problems as gay and lesbian people do. The chapter will then summarize what little is known about the situations of lesbian, gay, and bisexual people in social work and related fields specifically. It should be noted at the outset, however, that essentially all the information available about gay, lesbian, and bisexual people in the workplace addresses the experiences of whites of European descent, mostly in the United States, which is a serious limitation in our knowledge base.

Discrimination Against Lesbian, Gay, and Bisexual People in the Workplace

> Sexual orientation does not affect a person's ability to contribute to society. . . . Gay people have an overall potential to contribute to society similar to that of heterosexual people, including in the workplace.
> —Brief of amicus curiae, American Psychological Association in *Watkins v. United States Army* (Gary B. Melton 1989:936)

Discrimination in employment is a reality for lesbian, gay, and bisexual people (Badgett 1996; Ellis 1996). For example, in 1991 a roadside restaurant chain in the South and Midwest fired all of its known lesbian, gay, and bisexual employees because they "failed to demonstrate normal heterosexual values" (Elliott 1993:217). This order was later rescinded as a result of picketing by gay and lesbian activists and their friends and family members. However, the pain caused to those who lost their jobs and to those gay, lesbian, and bisexual workers not known as such to their employer (and who had to decide whether to cross picket lines to go to work or to identify themselves and lose their jobs) was considerable (Elliott 1993).

Most of the data available on workplace discrimination against lesbian, gay, and bisexual people[1] come from self-report surveys asking respondents about their experiences on the job. Since 1980 there have been about two dozen such surveys, all of which have concluded that discrimination at work affects a substantial proportion of gay and lesbian people—reported as between 13 and 62 percent of respondents depending on the specific survey, the gender and occupation of the respondents, and the way the question was asked (Badgett 1996; Woods 1993). These same surveys reveal that most gay and lesbian people did not reveal their sexual orientation at work specifically because they believed that they would be discriminated against at work were they known to be lesbian or gay (Woods 1993). The master status of homosexual is thought to be so pejorative that the effect on the work role would be negative and immediate. These fears seem well founded: some employers state in surveys that they would not hire, would fire, or would not promote a gay or lesbian employee (Woods 1993).

While most (but not all) of the surveys of workers ask only about whether or not a respondent's sexual orientation has cost him or her a job or promotion, antigay prejudice in the workplace is often more subtle and pervasive (Friskopp & Silverstein 1995; Powers 1996).

> In prejudicial compensation practices, the forced invisibility of gay employees, the social validation of heterosexual mating rituals, the anti-gay commentary and imagery that circulate through company channels, even the masculine nature of the bureaucratic organization itself, a certain kind of heterosexuality is routinely displayed and rewarded . . . [resulting in] more subtle, unseen ways in which lesbians and gay men are stigmatized, excluded, and denied the support given their heterosexual peers.   (Woods 1993:9–10)

Thus, when surveys ask whether a gay or lesbian sexual orientation ever "creates stressful situations at work," a great majority of respondents indicate that it is always or often a stress (Woods 1993).

Whether or not lesbian, gay, and bisexual people identify as such at work, they may well face personal antigay attack. At one extreme of the continuum of expression of antigay attitudes at work is overt harassment, threats, and intimidation (Kitzinger 1991). As one expert in leading anti-homophobia training in the corporate sector put it:

> In one corporation, several people associated publicly with the gay and lesbian employee support group have received death threats on their office telephone answering machines or in letters sent to both office and home. Threats are also made in bathroom graffiti or even, remarkably enough, face-to-face. At the other end of the homophobia continuum, we have the occasional joke that someone tells at the lunchroom table, the offensive anti-gay cartoon taped to an office door, or the limp-wristed impersonation when talking about homosexuals.   (McNaught 1993:55)

Fortunately, the latter manifestations of antigay prejudice are much more common than the former.

Although many people believe that the general guarantees in the Bill of Rights offer sufficient protection against employment discrimination based on sexual orientation, federal laws have been enacted in the latter half of the twentieth century to underscore the fact that these basic Constitutional guarantees cannot be limited by race and gender, among other statuses. However, as Badgett (1996) explains, "Gay[, lesbian,] and bisexual people have no explicit protection from employment discrimination in the private sector" (32). Federal employees and public-sector employees in eighteen states that have executive orders in effect to protect them are somewhat better protected (Badgett 1996). However, employment protection for lesbian, gay, and bisexual workers in all sectors is explicitly guaranteed by law in only a few states, counties, and localities, although the number is gradually increasing (Badgett 1996; Elliott 1993; Ellis 1996).

Corporate employers vary widely in their official policies toward lesbian, gay, and bisexual employees. Some state explicitly that they do not discriminate on the basis of sexual orientation; others have policies stating that they hire and promote strictly on ability, making no mention of sexual orientation, or that they do not inquire about an employee's sexual orientation. However, some companies state explicitly that they do take action based on sexual orientation in a variety of ways, such as "when sexual orientation interferes with job performance, disrupts other employees or adversely affects the company" (Elliott 1993:217). Other companies do not express any willingness to adopt company nondiscrimination policies even when they operate in localities where there is no legal protection for their gay, lesbian, and bisexual employees (Elliott 1993).

Employee activists, however, have been successful in some settings in lobbying to change discriminatory workplace policies. For example, employees at Apple Computer, IBM, Xerox, and the Rand Corporation have successfully changed discriminatory hiring policies; at Digital Equipment Corporation, employees formed a support group and then went on to persuade the company to offer educational programs to employees about lesbian and gay life as a method of reducing workplace discrimination (Ellis 1996; McNaught 1993; Seck et al. 1993). The number of major corporations enacting such antidiscrimination policies, especially those in high-tech industries competing for highly qualified workers, is gradually increasing. Colleges and universities are also settings where stated antidiscrimination policies that protect lesbians and gays are more common, although by no means universal.

OCCUPATIONAL CHOICE AND CAREER DEVELOPMENT

Like others who face systemic discrimination, gay, lesbian, and bisexual people may not be confident that the opportunity structure—that is, the normal pathways to occupational success and career advancement—is as open to them as it may be to others (Morgan & Brown 1991; Pope 1996). Three common strategies that may be used to cope with antigay discrimination include: opting for self-employment; "job-tracking" (meaning choosing to work in fields, settings, or localities that are more accepting of a lesbian or gay sexual orientation and/or avoiding those that may be especially hostile); or deciding not to reveal or to actively conceal one's sexual orientation at work (Morgan & Brown 1991). The first two strategies affect occupational choice and career development directly.

Gay, lesbian, and bisexual people may begin the process of acknowledging a gay, lesbian, or bisexual orientation or identity at any point in the life span (see chapter 2). If they do so as adolescents, the whole process of educating themselves and developing their occupational identities will be affected by the fact of their sexual orientation. However, a gay, lesbian, or bisexual identity may be adopted at a later point in the process of education, vocational choice, and/or career development, which may in turn result in a new and perhaps different appraisal of the previous choices made in occupation, vocation, or career, or involving a specific job or employer (Pope 1996). The occupation-

al impact of coming out later in adult development has not yet been systematically studied.

Because of potential employment problems, it has been suggested that gay
men and lesbians may have more difficulty deciding upon a career or choosing an occupation and may experience greater anxiety both in choosing an
occupation or job and on the job (Etringer, Hillerbrand, & Hetherington
1990). One small-scale study of undergraduate students in the Midwest suggested that gay men showed a higher degree of uncertainty about their career
choice than others and lesbians showed a lower level. Interestingly, gay men
and heterosexual women showed the highest levels of dissatisfaction with
their career choices (Etringer, Hillerbrand, & Hetherington 1990). Chung
(1995) and Hetherington and Orzek (1989), for example, suggest that gay
men and lesbians may face a "Catch-22" situation in career choice: those pursuing nontraditional careers for their genders may face the risk of being assumed to be homosexual, while those who pursue more traditional careers
may face negative attitudes from conservative heterosexual colleagues and
lack the social support of many gay or lesbian colleagues. For lesbians the
stereotype is that they work in such nontraditional jobs as auto mechanic,
plumber, and truck driver (Hetherington & Orzek 1989), while for gay men
it is photographer, interior decorator, and nurse (Hetherington, Hillerbrand,
& Etringer 1989). However, the evidence as to if sexual orientation actually
affects occupational or vocational choice overall is limited and contradictory,
and more research in this area is urgently needed (Chung 1995; Gonsiorek
1993b; Pope 1996).

One effect of discrimination may be "to isolate lesbian and gay people in
certain professions" (Elliott 1993:216). Many studies of public attitudes have
documented the fact that, while people generally feel that all workers should
be treated fairly, there are some kinds of work in which people are uncomfortable with gay and/or lesbian people. For example, few members of the
general public think that gay or lesbian people should be employed as school
teachers or in other roles where they deal with vulnerable or impressionable
groups, such as young people or the mentally ill (Kitzinger 1991). Where legislation specifically forbids presenting "positive images of homosexuality" in
the classroom, pressures on those gay, lesbian, and bisexual people who are
employed as teachers can be especially intense (Kitzinger 1991).

Contrary to the stereotype and given the gender segmentation of the labor
market in general, most gay men, lesbians, and bisexual people work in jobs
that are typical for their genders. That is, contrary to the stereotype, most gay
men do *not* work in "gay-dominated" jobs, and most lesbians do *not* work in
"nontraditional" jobs (Kitzinger 1991; Woods 1993). In addition, even when

gay men or lesbians do aspire to stereotypic or nontraditional occupations, their work goals in relation to status and prestige are no different from those of heterosexuals (Chung 1995). However, given concerns about workplace discrimination and safety, some gay men in particular may prefer to work in fields that are thought in general to be more hospitable to the "out" gay man, such as hairdressing, interior design, or the arts (Chung 1995; Kitzinger 1991). Gays and lesbians, especially those who are more public in their self-identification, may develop or seek out self- or independent-employment opportunities in order to avoid the problems they have encountered in traditional settings or to develop the workplace supports and comfort they desire.

One unique work value for lesbian, gay, and bisexual individuals may be the importance of being lesbian, gay, or bisexual in relation to work. As Chung (1995) notes, for gay, lesbian, and bisexual people, another "important consideration is whether individuals can express their sexual orientation at or outside of work" (181). This factor may be more important for gay, lesbian, and bisexual people because it is one generally taken for granted by heterosexual people. Some individuals may place a high value on being able to express their sexual orientation through work, such as in artwork, writing, and political action (Chung 1995). Helping activities in relation to the gay and lesbian community may be another example of this particular kind of work value.

On the other hand, there are some careers and occupations in which lesbian, gay, and/or bisexual people may be more likely to encounter fear and discrimination than in others. Educators at a variety of levels—from preschool through higher education—may be confronted with fears that they will influence the impressionable young to become lesbian or gay, in fact, that they may molest or seduce them (Fassinger 1993; Kitzinger 1991). Similar attitudes affect child care and child welfare workers as well. These fears persist despite long-standing evidence that child molesters are most commonly heterosexual males (De Young 1982; Groth 1978; Groth & Birnbaum 1978; Newton 1978) and that homosexuality is not "caused" by any kind of interpersonal influence in childhood (see chapter 2). Therefore lesbian, gay, or bisexual people who work in education and other child-related fields, especially those who work with younger children, may choose to conceal their sexual orientation and/or to limit the closeness and social contact they allow themselves to have with their students and others (Fassinger 1993; Griffin & Zuckas 1993; Kitzinger 1991).

Similarly, there is evidence that the general public is more uncomfortable with gay and lesbian physicians (especially pediatricians) and other health care providers, who may be involved in physically touching their patients, than with gays and lesbians in other occupations (Fassinger 1993).[2] Even some physicians themselves do not think a gay or lesbian person should be admitted to medical school or, in particular, go into pediatrics (Fikar 1992; Parker 1994). Again, this attitude persists despite the data that show decisively that the overwhelming majority of complaints about sexual contact and/or exploitation of patients by health care professionals involves heterosexual contact between men and women who are their patients, and the same is true for child sexual abuse. However, most of the data available about sexual orientation and the medical and related professions has addressed health care providers' attitudes toward lesbian and gay people and toward people with AIDS than about how lesbian, gay, and bisexual people are faring within these professions (McAnulty 1993), or the problems that gay and lesbian health care providers themselves may be facing in their work. Some data suggest, however, that a substantial proportion of physicians are unwilling to refer patients to homosexual colleagues, especially pediatricians (McAnulty 1993). At least one study has shown that self-identified gay physicians have a higher proportion of gay patients in their caseloads than others do, and there is also some evidence that many gay and lesbian people, including gay and lesbian teens, would prefer a gay or lesbian health care provider (Bradford & Ryan 1988; Fikar 1992). Therefore, any barriers to practice encountered by gay and lesbian health care providers are also likely to harm health care to gay, lesbian, and bisexual consumers.

Two occupations that have specific histories of the outright exclusion of known gay and lesbian people from their ranks are the clergy and the military (Anderson & Smith 1993; Chung 1995; McSpadden 1993). In both of these occupations as well, the role of women has also been systematically limited, suggesting that lesbians face a "double whammy" in such careers. Different religious organizations and denominations vary widely in their attitudes toward gay and lesbian people (and women) in the clergy and within their congregations (McSpadden 1993). Policy toward gay and lesbian people in the military has been widely debated in politics and in the media in the early 1990s, but movement toward a nondiscriminatory policy has been slow. Since substantial discrimination against lesbians and gays still exists in both these fields, what advice should be given to the young person who is interested in joining the clergy or the military, and how might that advice be different if the young person were known to be heterosexual, to be questioning his or her sexual orientation, or to be lesbian, gay, or bisexual (Elliott 1993; Pope 1996)?

Concern about career choice and the discrimination that may be encountered in specific occupations or fields is not the only way in which the career development of lesbian, gay, and bisexual people can be negatively affected. It has been suggested that many adult gay, lesbian, and bisexual people in the United States often relocate in order to live in communities that provide an identifiable gay community, a protective civil rights environment, and/or enhanced employment and social opportunities (Chung 1995; Hetherington, Hillerbrand, & Etringer 1989). While there are undoubtedly many benefits to such a pattern of living, over time career or job mobility (employment or promotion) may be affected: "For example, a person who lives in a liberal, progressive part of the country might view a job move to a more restrictive area where there is more discrimination with great anxiety" (Elliott 1993:213). Like members of other minority groups, gay and lesbian employees "may reach a plateau far too early in their careers" (Seck et al. 1993), in part in some cases because they may not see geographic mobility as an option for them. Partner relocation may also be an issue (Hetherington, Hillerbrand, & Etringer 1989; Hetherington & Orzek 1989). Thus, even those gay, lesbian, and bisexual people who are employed worry about a "lavender ceiling" that may prevent them from reaching their full potential on the job (Friskopp & Silverstein 1995).

An essential strategy in eliminating workplace discrimination against lesbian, gay, and bisexual people is to expose the argument that their sexual orientation is destructive or "disruptive" in the workplace for what it is: prejudice. As Woods (1993) states, it is a "brutal, circular form of prejudice: a gay man's sexuality is disruptive because others despise him for it" (244). Understanding the circularity of this argument makes clear that the focus of workplace change must be on reducing heterosexism and homophobia among all employers and employees rather than on keeping the peace by keeping lesbian, gay, and bisexual employees away or keeping them hidden. Acceptance based on presumptive "asexuality," as in the "don't ask, don't tell" policy of the U.S. military (Hartman 1993; Woods 1993), is also not adequate because it results in other forms of workplace discrimination and stress.

SOCIAL MARGINALIZATION AT WORK

One result of heterosexism and homophobia is the assumption of heterosexuality—that is, no one is assumed to be gay, lesbian, or bisexual in the absence of specific social cues or information. While the assumption of heterosexuality may be statistically correct, it creates many social and personal strains and difficulties at work for those who do not fit it. The result is often a feeling of social marginalization and interpersonal stress (Chung 1995; Powers 1996).

Most places of work have at least occasional social events to which workers are permitted or encouraged to bring their husbands, wives, or dates. Invitations are generally not worded to be inclusive of a same-gender partner. The gay, lesbian, or bisexual worker, even if in a well-established couple, must decide in this context whether to go alone, to bring the same-gender partner, or even to bring a friend of the opposite gender who will function as the "date." Thus these occasions, and the usual social questions about the upcoming or just-past event, underline the dilemmas surrounding coming out at work: whether to attempt actively to deceive, whether to simply omit reference to, or whether purposely to reveal a gay, lesbian, or bisexual orientation. The strategies chosen by lesbian and gay workers vary, and both disclosure and nondisclosure appear to be adaptive for different people in different situations (Hetherington & Orzek 1989).

This dilemma presents itself at work in many different ways. Any social invitation from a coworker—to get together after work, to go out or come over for dinner, or even to chat over lunch—can present the same problem. Some gay, lesbian, or bisexual workers decide to come out to selected coworkers, to those with whom they elect to establish closer, friendship-oriented relationships, even when they do not come out in the work setting as a whole. However, such workers are likely aware that, in doing so, they are not in control of the information about themselves (or their partners) once it is shared. In addition, members of a gay or lesbian couple may not agree on being open even with selected coworkers and/or may encounter greatly differing degrees of comfort or safety in their different workplaces. These differences in turn can lead to strains within the relationship (Morgan & Brown 1991).

Whether or not a gay, lesbian, or bisexual worker decides to socialize with coworkers, with or without his or her partner, the many casual conversations that take place at work often address themselves to private and social life. Questions about activities over the long weekend just past, about relationships and dating, about the home or living situation, in fact any information elicited or offered about one's life outside of work are very difficult to respond to for the lesbian, gay, or bisexual worker attempting to conceal his or her sexual orientation. Identity management strategies used include inventing a heterosexual cover story, depicting oneself as asocial, telling stories of home life with the pronouns changed, having separate telephone lines at home, or being more open and genuine, often selectively and/or gradually, about one's real life. When a partner is sick or dies, when a partner's child is ill or in crisis, or deciding what to say about one's own HIV status or AIDS-related illnesses (Powers 1996; Woods 1993)—these situations not only call into question workplace policies about family care and bereavement leave but present intense social and emotional challenges as well. Deciding how to handle these situations involves assessing the safety of the setting as a whole as well as the attitudes of the individuals with whom the person is interacting directly (see "Coming Out" section below). When workers relate on a face-to-face basis with customers, consumers, clients, or "the public" in their work roles, these same dilemmas can and do occur regularly.

At yet another level, there are many messages about sexual orientation conveyed in the workplace (Powers 1996). Coworkers' engagements and marriages may be celebrated at or after work. Pictures of husbands, wives, and children may be prominent parts of office decor. The jokes and stories that are told in social moments can convey antigay and/or pro-heterosexuality messages. On the other hand, there are instances of workplaces where coworkers will celebrate an upcoming commitment ceremony or grieve with a bereaved lesbian or gay coworker in the same way that they might in a heterosexual situation. Gay, lesbian, and bisexual people can control the social attitudes and behaviors of their friends and can elect to spend time in safe and friendly surroundings in their personal lives; they have much less control over those things at work. Nevertheless, work space is also personal space, and the lesbian, gay, or bisexual worker may encounter strains in the work and social interface that others do not.

COMING OUT AT WORK

Whether or not to "come out," that is, to reveal a lesbian, gay, or bisexual identity to a supervisor or coworker, is a major preoccupation of lesbian, gay, or bisexual workers. Many gay, lesbian, and bisexual people who have come out in their private lives are not "out" at work, believing many aspects of private life, especially sexuality (Woods 1993), to be irrelevant in that setting. However, the strains associated with active or passive concealment are considerable (Powers 1996). As Hall has described it for lesbians:

> All the forms of non-disclosure, whether the occasional substitute of "he" for "she" when describing a week-end outing with a lover or the complete fabrication of a heterosexual life, leave a lesbian in a morally untenable position. Not only is she lying . . . she is ignoring the strong exhortations of the lesbian community to come out.   (Hall 1986:73)

Coming out is never a one-time event; as clients or customers, coworkers and supervisors change over time, the decision about what to say or not say about a lesbian, gay, or bisexual identity must continually be made and remade (Griffin & Zuckas 1993; Hall 1986; Kitzinger 1991; Powers 1996). Moreover, the self-identification can be made directly or indirectly (Pope 1996). An employee may actively hide a gay or lesbian orientation, such as by bringing a "date" of the opposite gender to work-related social events; conversely, an employee may openly announce a lesbian, gay, or bisexual identity and/or bring a same-gender partner to such events. In between is the strategy of not concealing the facts of one's life, even to the extent of speaking up for gay rights in the work context, but also not definitely declaring a gay, lesbian, or bisexual identity. Thus lesbian, gay, and bisexual workers are often in some intermediate or "borderline" state of knowing that some people at work know about their sexual orientation while being uncertain about what others do or do not know or assume about them (Griffin & Zuckas 1993; Kitzinger 1991). This uncertainty also leads to difficulties in interpreting workplace events; if one is snubbed in the lunchroom or overlooked for a promotion, it is especially difficult to determine whether or not antigay prejudice is a factor if it is uncertain as to whether or not the fact itself is known or understood (Gonsiorek 1993b).

One study suggested that openness about a lesbian or gay orientation at work was correlated with job and life satisfaction; that is, those survey respondents who were open with both coworkers and supervisors had generally higher levels of job satisfaction (Ellis & Riggle 1995). However, those who were less open were more satisfied with their pay and had marginally higher salaries. Job satisfaction was also higher when the employer had a nondiscrimination policy. Since the sample in this study was drawn from two cities, one with and one without a city ordinance protecting gay civil rights, the effect of this difference in locale was also examined. Workers who lived in the city with civil rights protection were more likely to report that their employers had antidiscrimination policies that protected lesbian, gay, and bisexual workers than those who did not. In addition, those in the city with the civil rights protection were more likely to be open about their sexual orientation at work and to have higher levels of life satisfaction when *more* open; however, those in the city without civil rights protection had higher levels of life satisfaction when they were *less* open on the job. Thus, not surprisingly, both employers and employees were shown to be very sensitive to the general legal climate in which they worked.

Decisions about coming out at work (and elsewhere) are not decisions that a gay, lesbian, or bisexual worker makes in a vacuum. Those who are in stable couple relationships must also consider the other member of the couple, whose own employment situation may be similar or different in its tolerance or safety level. Often, then, there are two sets of decisions to be made about identity management in two usually different work situations. Issues of being out on the job can be confounded with issues of commitment to the relationship, especially if one member of the couple is more open at work than the other (Morgan & Brown 1991).

Disclosing one's sexual orientation on the job is distinct from deciding to become professionally concerned with gay, lesbian, and bisexual rights or interests. In a study of academic sociologists, being active on sexual orientation issues—that is, advocating for gay rights on campus or in professional organizations or pursuing scholarship on gay or lesbian issues—as opposed to simply being open about one's sexual orientation, was correlated with reports of negative career consequences, including job discrimination in hiring, promotion, and even harassment and intimidation (Taylor & Raeburn 1995). However, in an intensive study of male and female schoolteachers in the Netherlands, gay men and lesbians adopted quite different strategies of self-presentation in the school setting. More (but not all) of the gay men were overtly or behaviorally "out," and some of them also saw themselves as actively engaged in the political struggle for gay rights in the workplace. The lesbians were more often concerned with issues of gender equity in the setting rather than with sexual orientation issues in the workplace and saw themselves as responding to the needs of students and/or of the work group as a whole rather than as pursuing personal concerns (Dankmeijer 1993). The author concluded that "the political demand that teachers come out professionally ignores the central professional and political concerns of . . . teachers and their need for professional survival. . . . Coming out fitted the lifestyle only of those who took on the role of crusaders for gay liberation" (95). These studies highlight the variability in style and behavior even among those gay, lesbian, and bisexual people who self-identify as such at work and the consequences that may follow from the different identity management strategies employed.

DIFFERENCES BETWEEN GAY MEN AND LESBIANS

To the extent that heterosexism and homophobia are the basis for workplace discrimination, lesbians and gay men may encounter similar problems at work. However, there are also ways in which workplace problems are different for gay men and lesbians. Miller (1995) has observed that the "corporate definition of competency" is of a white, attractive, affluent, Protestant, married (with children) male (15). It has long been acknowledged that women in general are therefore at a disadvantage in the world of work. Lesbians thus are likely to encounter gender discrimination on the job—in hiring, compensation, benefits, and advancement (NASW 1997a). This gender discrimination can occur along with or apart from discrimination issues related to sexual orientation (Badgett 1996; Elliott 1993; Fassinger 1995; Friskopp & Silverstein 1995; Schneider 1987). As a result, lesbians typically earn less than gay men (Badgett 1996; Elliott 1993). In addition, since lesbians are more likely to designate themselves as heads of a household than gay men are (Elliott 1993), exclusion of domestic partnerships from and limitations on ways to claim a child as a dependent for employment-related benefits (as in the case of a partner's child not related by biology or adoption to the employee) more often affect lesbians than gay men. Surveys suggest that lesbians may be less likely than gay men to be "out" at work, perhaps because of their concerns about gender discrimination (Badgett 1996).

There is some evidence that lesbian workers may be more likely than heterosexual women to define and to condemn unwanted sexual remarks and advances at work as sexual harassment than heterosexual women do (Schneider 1982). In addition, one form of sexual harassment is particular to lesbians at work (and elsewhere): sexual harassment or assault by men designed to impose heterosexual sex upon them because they are lesbians (Kitzinger 1991). Although most lesbians, like most other women, work in jobs typically held by women, women, including lesbians, in nontraditional work roles face higher levels of harassment on the job, often harassment that specifically targets their sexual orientation. For example, media accounts show that women athletes in tennis and golf are often suspected of being lesbians, and those who do come out as lesbians have been accused of discrediting their sport. As another example, women in the military are discharged because of their sexual orientation much more often than men, in part because of the sexism that views military service as inherently and properly "masculine" (Anderson & Smith 1993). Lesbians in all kinds of work roles, therefore, may take pains to appear quite "feminine" as a method of avoiding disclosure of their lesbianism or simply to avoid harassment based on sexual orientation. However, one study suggests that lesbians who are more open about their sexual orientation may actually experience fewer incidents of sexual harassment than those who are less open because most workplace sexual harassment is based on the idea that a woman is heterosexually available (Schneider 1982).

Gay men also may face forms of discrimination at work particular to them. Gay men are still associated in many people's minds with HIV and AIDS; thus gay men at work may encounter irrational fears and even harassment based on their assumed HIV status (McNaught 1993; Poverny & Finch 1988), a problem much less likely to be encountered by lesbians. Few employers have written policies about AIDS, and although the Americans with Disabilities Act forbids discrimination against persons with AIDS, many such instances indeed occur (Miller 1995; Roth & Carman 1993; see also chapter 11). Gay men in occupations considered quintessentially masculine, most notably the military (Anderson & Smith 1993) and professional sports (Barret 1993), may be subject to particularly intense harassment and may take extraordinary measures to keep their sexual orientation hidden. The fact that these occupations regularly bring men together in all-male living and/or bathing situations may make the gay male especially threatening to coworkers, leading, for example, to the argument that gay men in the military inevitably harm "combat effectiveness" by disrupting "morale, discipline and good order" (Anderson & Smith 1993:70). However, studies of attitudes toward gay men and lesbians serving in the military suggest that negative attitudes are correlated with general conservatism in a variety of areas and not on the substance of the argument (Harris & Vanderhoof 1995).

Gay men in such situations (and lesbian women in similarly targeted situations) have developed a variety of ways to cope with fears and experiences of discrimination, including "passing" and other forms of invisibility and over-achievement (Anderson & Smith 1993; Kitzinger 1991). Since sexual orientation per se has been shown not to affect job performance, even in the military, the goal must be to eliminate such discrimination wherever it occurs.

RACE AND RACISM

Very little is known about gay, lesbian, and bisexual workers of color. In general, a nonwhite racial or ethnic identity and a gay, lesbian, or bisexual one are not simply additive; they interact in complex gender- and culture-specific ways (Badgett 1996; de Monteflores 1986; Rosabal 1996). Because so little is known about gay and lesbian workers, Friskopp and Silverstein's (1995) study of graduates of the Harvard Business School oversampled respondents of color. In general, the workers interviewed felt themselves to be at risk of multiple discrimination, although their race was more often a problem to them than their sexual orientation largely because the latter aspect of their identities could often be successfully concealed. Moreover, being gay or lesbian sometimes compromised their ability to draw support outside the workplace from their racial or ethnic communities, and being a person of color sometimes limited the support available to them from the gay or lesbian community. Some in this highly privileged group, however, viewed their ability to draw support from both groups as an asset. For gay and lesbian workers of color, concerns with safety and survival at work must be eliminated, progressing to concerns with learning how to thrive on the job (Rosabal 1996).

EMPLOYMENT BENEFITS

A major focus of antidiscriminatory policies in the workplace must be the heterosexist bias that defines employment benefit packages, especially the definitions of "family" used in law, in company policy, and in insurance policies (Poverny & Finch 1988; Seck et al. 1993; Spielman & Winfeld 1996). Domestic partnerships and co-parenting relationships must be recognized not only in health and dental care but also in child and other dependent care, and in pension, insurance, and other survivors' rights—that is, in both "hard" and "soft" benefits (Seck et al. 1993; Spielman & Winfeld 1996). When they are excluded, not only are benefits denied to the children and partners affected; when the value of employee benefits is added to the value of wages, "the result is total compensation lower than that of married co-workers performing the same job" (Eblin 1990). In 1996 it was known that more than sixty corporations and public agencies, at least thirty colleges, universities, and professional schools, and about twenty not-for-profit organizations in the United States were offering employee benefits to domestic partners (Spielman & Winfeld 1996; Zuckerman & Simons 1996). Although this number clearly represents only a very small fraction of the employing organizations in the United States, it does demonstrate that offering such benefits is an economically and socially viable business practice.

Most of the objections to and fears about including domestic partnerships in employment benefit packages have been found to have little basis in fact, based on study of those cities and companies that were in the forefront of providing domestic partnership benefits. The first objection is usually cost, and employee benefits as a whole do indeed represent a significant proportion of payroll costs. Often about half of those electing to take advantage of domestic partner benefits have been heterosexual couples who, for one reason or another, are not married (Eblin 1990). Many eligible gay and lesbian employees do not in fact choose to utilize available partnership benefits because it is often cheaper for each member of the couple to use his or her own employment benefits when both are employed, as is often the case (Spielman & Winfeld 1996). However, including more employees in benefit programs does indeed increase total employer expenses, although doing so in this case reduces the inequity in total compensation between gay and lesbian employees and heterosexual ones. However, fears that domestic partnership benefits and/or claims might be more costly than those accorded to marital couples have proven to be unfounded (Eblin 1990; Winfeld & Spielman 1995), including fears that AIDS-related costs might drive expenses up (Spielman & Winfeld 1996). Any concern about fraud can be easily handled through regulations on the benefits program and may be outweighed by the reluctance of employees to apply for these benefits, especially in state contexts in which the civil rights of gay and lesbian people are not protected and/or where specific sexual acts are criminalized (Eblin 1990; Spielman & Winfeld 1996). The city of Berkeley, California, for example, requires a signed statement to register a domestic partnership in which the signers swear that

1. The two parties have resided together for at least six months and intend to do so indefinitely.
2. The two parties are not married, are at least eighteen years of age, are not related closer by blood than would bar marriage in California, and are mentally competent to consent to the contract.
3. The two parties declare that they are each other's sole domestic partner and they are responsible for their common welfare.
4. The two parties agree to notify the employer if there is any change in the circumstance attested to in the affidavit.
5. The two parties affirm, under penalties of perjury, that the assertions in the affidavit are true to the best of their knowledge.

(McNaught 1993:79–80)

Similar definitions and procedures are used in other jurisdictions and can be used by employers in areas where such provisions do not exist (Spielman & Winfeld 1996). However, the employer who decides to offer such benefits must consider the tax consequences both for the business or company itself and for any employee receiving such benefits in a rapidly changing IRS regulatory climate (Eblin 1990; Spielman & Winfeld 1996).

Implications for Practice

Because work is so central to self-maintenance and self-esteem as well as to meaning in life, *practice with lesbian, gay, and bisexual people that recognizes both the importance of work and the special problems that gay, lesbian, and bisexual workers may encounter as workers* is a major way to contribute to the well-being of lesbian, gay, and bisexual people (Elliott 1993; Ellis 1996; Morgan & Brown 1991). However, theories about work and career development, even those that have been adapted to women and their work, have only recently been systematically applied to lesbian or gay workers (Morgan & Brown 1991; Pope 1996). Thus there is little specific knowledge to guide the practitioner in dealing with issues related to work. However, those who work in employee assistance programs (EAPs) or whose practice focuses specifically on issues of employment and training have an especially important role to play (Poverny & Finch 1988; Van Den Bergh 1994).

People engaged in career and employment counseling must be educated about and trained in handling lesbian and gay issues and about heterosexism and homophobia and their effects (Elliott 1993; Fassinger 1995; Hetherington, Hillerbrand, & Etringer 1989; Hetherington & Orzek 1989; Morgan & Brown 1991; Pope 1996; Poverny & Finch 1988; Prince 1995; Van Den Bergh 1994). They cannot afford to fall into the assumption that all their clients are heterosexual. They must also be aware that sexual orientation can affect educational and occupational decision making and can complicate career development and advancement. Identity management issues, which can be an area of conflict or of relative comfort, can be more intense at work or can be handled quite differently than in other aspects of a client's life. Helping a client to appraise a work-related situation—to decide if discrimination and/or social marginalization have occurred and to decide how to respond—is often important, especially when the client is in a "borderline" state of openness on the job. Practitioners must therefore be aware of the facts about workplace discrimination and about the provisions, if any, that may protect the rights of a lesbian, gay, or bisexual worker in his or her locale or work organization.

The pervasiveness of workplace discrimination must not be underestimated. However, there is great variability in the responses that lesbian, gay, and bisexual people employ to cope with it. This stance of course includes becoming aware of and managing one's own heterosexism and homophobia.

It is suggested that employment counselors regard "lesbian and gay clients as members of a nonethnic cultural minority group" (Elliott 1993:211) and thus *include gay and lesbian issues in the diversity training being offered in the workplace and to employment counselors* (Hetherington, Hillerbrand, & Etringer 1989; Hetherington & Orzek 1989). However, private attitudes are not the focus of workplace training; behavior in the workplace is (McNaught 1993). Goals of such workshops might include understanding the employer's policies on nondiscrimination and whether they address sexual orientation; exploring and articulating participants' attitudes about gay, lesbian, and bisexual people; replacing myths about gay, lesbian, and bisexual people with accurate information; exploring the effects of heterosexism and homophobia on all employees; and strategizing about ways to reduce or eliminate destructive behaviors and policies related to sexual orientation from the workplace (McNaught 1993).

However, employee support groups and workshops are not enough. Because homophobia and heterosexism exist on both individual and institutional levels, *efforts to eliminate discrimination against lesbian, gay, and bisexual people in employment must include action on a variety of levels:*

1. An explicit employment policy that prohibits discrimination based upon sexual orientation;
2. Creation of a safe work environment that is free of heterosexist, homo-phobic, and AIDS-phobic behaviors;
3. Company-wide education about gay issues in the workplace and about AIDS;
4. An equitable benefits program that recognizes the domestic partners of gay, lesbian, and bisexual employees;
5. Support of a gay/lesbian/bisexual employee support group;
6. Freedom for all employees to participate fully in all aspects of corporate life;
7. Public support of gay issues.

(McNaught 1993:66)

Taken together, these are the things that gay, lesbian, and bisexual employees want in the workplace (McNaught 1993).

In addition, if an employee has been discriminated against because of gen-der or sexual orientation, *an EAP professional must be prepared to assist a client, perhaps in a broker or mediator role, in using whatever grievance mechanisms may exist* (Van Den Bergh 1994). It is also necessary to keep current about local and national legal and legislative developments that may enhance or threaten the rights of gays and lesbians on the job and about community resources and advocacy groups that can assist gay and lesbian employees personally or voca-tionally (Morgan & Brown 1991). Gay and lesbian employees may find that connecting with community-based support groups and identifying gay or les-bian role models can also be helpful (Hetherington, Hillerbrand, & Etringer 1989; Hetherington & Orzek 1989). Action at all these levels will be neces-sary for equal employment opportunities and optimal productivity for les-bian, gay, and bisexual people to become a reality.

Gay, Lesbian, and Bisexual Social Workers

There has been no large-scale systematic study of how lesbian, gay, and bisex-ual people are faring as social workers. Nor do we know how many gay, les-bian, and bisexual social workers there are. However, based on issues that have been found to matter to other helping professionals—physicians, nurses, and psychologists, for example—it is possible to outline issues that gay, lesbian, and bisexual social workers face as workers. Anecdotally, it has been reported that nurses manage a gay or lesbian identity at work in a variety of ways and report a range of reactions, both positive and negative, to "coming out" (Sharkey 1987), which is likely to be true of social workers as well. Gay and lesbian clinical social work interns also vary in how open they choose to be about their sexual orientation in their field placements (Lewis 1990). In addition, there is some information from the mental health field that addresses the special dilemmas that can arise when identified gay and lesbian mental health professionals work with gay, lesbian, and bisexual clients (which will also be outlined here).

One major difference between social work and some other helping professions is the strong value stance that the profession has taken in support of gay rights (see chapter 1). The public commitments of a profession and of a specific employer make a real difference to employees and to clients. The stated value stance of the social work profession is empowering to those within the profession who work to serve lesbian, gay, and bisexual people and their family members and to those in the profession who are themselves lesbian, gay, or bisexual. However, there is also evidence of heterosexism and homophobia within the profession (DeCrescenzo 1984; Wisniewski & Toomey 1987), including the suppression of knowledge about the key roles lesbians in particular have played in the history of social work, in the settlement house movement and elsewhere (Aronson 1995; Humphreys 1983). In fact, as in society as a whole, there are major differences in points of view on gay and lesbian civil rights within the social work profession, even though only one point of view predominates in the public documents of the profession (Van Soest 1996).

WORKPLACE ISSUES

Despite the public pronouncements of the profession as a whole, gay, lesbian, and bisexual social workers often face the same dilemmas as workers that others do. Concern expressed for gay, lesbian, and bisexual clients and their families may not extend to those who serve them. However, it is likely that gay, lesbian, and bisexual clients will feel only as safe and comfortable in a setting as the lesbian, gay, and bisexual workers there do. However, to date there has been no research on the employment experiences and careers of lesbian, gay, or bisexual social workers.

There has been no large-scale study of social work practice with lesbian, gay, and bisexual clients comparable to that done of psychologists by the

American Psychological Association (APA 1991). Nor has there been much research describing social workers' attitudes towards gay, lesbian, and bisexual people (Reiter 1991; Tievsky 1988). However, most social workers are women, and general studies of attitudes toward lesbian, gay, and bisexual people have shown that women tend to be less prejudiced against lesbians and gays than men are (Eliason 1995). Recent studies have shown that social workers and psychologists are on average more knowledgeable about and less prejudiced against gay and lesbian people than, for example, nurses, even when gender and other factors, such as the amount of contact with lesbian or gay friends and acquaintances, are taken into account (Harris, Nightengale, & Owen 1995). However, there are also a significant number of social workers who do hold negative attitudes (Berkman & Zinberg 1997; DeCrescenzo 1984; Wisniewski & Toomey 1987) and/or who lack knowledge in areas related to sexual orientation (Harris, Nightengale, & Owen 1995; Tievsky 1988).

One general study of lesbian self-disclosure in the workplace suggests that being employed in the human services, which included describing oneself as a social worker, increased the degree to which a lesbian employee was open about her sexual orientation with fellow employees (Schneider 1987). In the same study, the percentage of women workers in the work setting was also correlated with both the amount of socializing lesbians did with coworkers and with disclosure of their sexual orientation (Schneider 1987). However, none of these findings were specific only to social work as a profession (including also "therapists," "counselors," and the like), although they do suggest that for women, employment in social work may be experienced as more comfortable than other work settings. The larger the total number of employees in the organization, the less open lesbian workers tended to be, suggesting that in smaller organizations it may be easier to assess the consequences of sharing (Schneider 1987). In addition, there were several other factors that predicted reductions in the amount of openness of lesbians at work: higher income, working with children rather than just adults, and having previously experienced a job loss due to one's lesbianism (Schneider 1987). Although this study focused only on lesbians, these inhibiting factors are likely to apply to gay men as well since they reflect what Schneider terms "risk" factors related to commonly held homophobic attitudes, including holding more powerful or professional jobs and especially having contact with children.

This special concern about helping professionals who work with children is not confined to social work. Physicians are more negative about a gay person entering pediatrics than other areas of medical practice, despite the urgent need for medical practitioners to work with gay and lesbian teens, a

> Prejudice toward lesbian, gay, and bisexual social workers results in discriminatory personnel practices and unnecessary stress. It should be noted that even within the profession, lesbian, gay, and bisexual social workers do not necessarily feel safe to openly and publicly declare their sexual orientation. It is imperative, therefore, that all social workers examine their attitudes and feelings about homosexuality and their understanding of lesbian, gay, and bisexual cultures and work toward full social and legal acceptance of lesbian, gay, and bisexual people. Ongoing self-examination will ensure that social workers remain aware of the negative impact that prejudice and discrimination have on their lesbian, gay, and bisexual clients and colleagues and can minimize homophobic responses that may arise in treatment or professional settings.
>
> —National Association of Social Workers (1997b:202)

group at very high risk (Fikar 1992). School administrators as well as the general public are very concerned about gay and lesbian teachers, especially those who are active politically on behalf of gay civil rights (Olson 1987).

Gay and lesbian teachers themselves have reported that they frequently encounter stereotypes of gay and lesbian people at work that few feel they can address directly without risking their jobs (Olson 1987). Teachers identify choosing to conceal their sexual orientation, distancing themselves socially from coworkers, making sure that their job performance is exemplary, choosing the communities where they work carefully, seeking support from other gay and lesbian friends both within and outside the profession, and looking for support from unions and professional organizations as common survival strategies (Olson 1987; Fassinger 1993). A few, however, describe coming out both as a personal survival and a social change strategy (Olson 1987; Spraggs 1994). A teacher's right to teach rests on legal arguments about "fitness to teach" and "disruption of the educational environment" (Fassinger 1993:124). In a parallel to some recent arguments regarding gays and lesbians in the military, it is possible that "the negative attitudes of only a few people can generate enough 'disruption' to 'impair' the effectiveness of a gay/lesbian teacher" (Fassinger 1993:125). Because of statutes in some states that criminalize certain forms of sexual behavior that include common same-gender practices and because of the "moral character" aspects of state-based licensing and credentialing, similar risks likely apply to lesbian, gay, and bisexual social workers and their right to practice, especially in those states that lack civil rights protection for gay, lesbian, and bisexual people.

One small-scale study of agency personnel who work with clinical social work interns suggests that gay and lesbian students vary greatly in the degree to which they are open about their sexual orientation in their field placements (Lewis 1990). While the expressed attitudes of supervisors and training directors in the settings were generally positive toward "out" gay and lesbian students, the ways they described and understood the educational issues were quite diverse and even somewhat contradictory. For example, some asserted that an intern's sexual orientation was a "personal issue"; his or her "ability to learn and develop clinical skills" was all that mattered (Lewis 1990:45). Another, however, noted that a gay or lesbian intern who was not "out" to his or her supervisor was to some degree having an "as if" supervisory experience, running the risk of key issues for the intern being overlooked (Lewis 1990:50). The supervisors also described great variability in the degree to which staff were out in their agencies and in the perceived personal and career risks to being out in their own work settings.

There has been a bit more attention paid to gay and lesbian social workers in academia than in other sectors of social work practice (Aronson 1995; Cain 1996; Martin 1995). For social workers in academia, considerable energy goes into identity management, especially before the granting of tenure, the period "when university faculty are particularly subject to public scrutiny and critique . . . . when [they] are most exposed and most vulnerable, in terms of material job security and basic credibility" (Aronson 1995: 15). As a result, and because many social work educators live and/or work in states and municipalities that do not provide legal protections for them, many social work educators do not choose to disclose a lesbian, gay, or bisexual identity (Martin 1995).

I believe I should . . . tie the disclosure [of a gay identity] more explicitly to my teaching philosophy . . . [and] provide a rationale and a context for students in understanding the purpose of the personal disclosure. I would also emphasize the connection between homophobia, heterosexism, and power relationships in general. . . [to] help students to develop a broader political analysis and thus better understand other forms of oppression. I also believe that I need to consider further the question of student safety in the classroom. For example, I need to say clearly that people must judge for themselves when it is safe to disclose personal information, and to stress that they should not feel pressured by my decision to come out.

—Roy Cain (1996:75–76)

It has often been argued that a gay or lesbian educator's choice to disclose a gay or lesbian identity is especially important to gay, lesbian, and bisexual students. Most often, such students' reactions are positive because of the affirmation and role modeling that it makes possible. However, it should also be noted that some of these students who are not choosing to acknowledge their own identities in the classroom may feel criticized or anxious in the face of a teacher's self-disclosure (Aronson 1995; Cain 1996). Needless to say, however, faculty in general are in more powerful positions in colleges and universities than students are, which likely affects the identity management decisions they make. In addition, gay and lesbian faculty who come out can play important roles in reaching out informally to and supporting individual gay, lesbian, or bisexual students and in advising gay, lesbian, and bisexual student associations and organizations (Martin 1995). Nevertheless, coming out in the classroom raises many dilemmas for faculty and students that have to be carefully considered (Aronson 1995; Cain 1996). Like all decisions in professional practice, it is a disclosure that must be made for a professional purpose.

Content on gay and lesbian issues is more likely to be included systematically in the classroom and on course reference lists when faculty are less homophobic and when faculty members report having more frequent social contact with lesbians and gays, suggesting that gay and lesbian colleagues may have an important influence on their heterosexual peers (Humphreys 1983). Because there is evidence that engaging in specific training experiences can increase knowledge about and reduce negative attitudes toward gay, lesbian, and bisexual people (Newman 1989), schools of social work need faculty members willing and able to teach and develop curriculum on gay, lesbian, and bisexual issues. Mackelprang, Ray, and Hernandez-Peck (1996) found that schools of social work that had greater inclusion of content on gay, lesbian, and bisexual issues also placed greater emphasis on recruiting and retaining both students and faculty who identified as lesbian or gay.

Aside from its impact on students in the classroom, gay, lesbian, and bisex-

---

Two inseparable tasks seem to lie ahead: first, giving attention to the particular needs of lesbians as they encounter social services and social welfare institutions, and putting into the picture the presence of lesbian service providers and educators, as well as clients; and second, developing a fundamental critique of the heterosexist assumptions and exclusions of the standard social work curriculum.

—Jane Aronson (1995:19)

ual educators who acknowledge their identities publicly often find a need to address curriculum issues of various kinds. Thus they may find themselves in a position similar in some ways to that of women who are feminist social work educators and to social work educators of color who take on academic and curricular work in relation to sexism and racism. While most colleges and universities endorse antidiscriminatory policies and practices, scholarly teaching and curricular work on issues of difference, including gay, lesbian, and bisexual issues, is often controversial. Faculty members often fear that such work may be dismissed as less important than work in other areas, thus affecting tenure and promotion decisions. Those gay and lesbian social work educators who have commented on these problems generally state that they are uncertain about whether or not their coming out or their work on lesbian, gay, and bisexual issues has affected their university careers, either positively or negatively (Aronson 1995). There is one study of academic sociologists that suggests that such "identity politics" can indeed have negative career consequences (Taylor & Raeburn 1995). Also, because of continuing glass ceiling problems for women in social work education (Petchers 1996), lesbian and bisexual women may face additional problems.

Thus it must be emphasized that gay, lesbian, and bisexual faculty members can only be effective on behalf of students, in curriculum development and in scholarship on lesbian, gay, and bisexual issues, to the extent that they feel, and are, safe as workers themselves (Tierney & Rhoads 1993). To this end, current contradictions often hidden in educational and institutional standards and practices, including value conflicts between schools and departments of social work and their host institutions, must be acknowledged and addressed (Van Soest 1996). Whether employed in human services agencies or in academic settings, then, there are certain things that all gay, lesbian, and bisexual social workers want and need in the workplace:

1. Responsiveness to the needs of lesbian, gay, and bisexual clients and students
2. Valuing of work with gay, lesbian, and bisexual clients and on lesbian, gay, and bisexual issues
3. Explicit service delivery and employment policies that prohibit discrimination based on sexual orientation
4. A working atmosphere free from the expression of homophobia and heterosexism
5. An equitable program of compensation, promotion, and benefits
6. Freedom for all employees to participate fully in the formal and informal social life of the work organization

7. Organization-wide education and training on lesbian, gay, and bisexual issues

8. Public support of lesbian and gay civil rights.

Work organizations exist both for their clients and for their employees. In the case of groups that are often discriminated against, the well-being of workers and clients in such groups are inextricably linked. Only when the workplace is safe for lesbian, gay, and bisexual employees will they be free to serve and to advocate effectively for services to lesbian, gay, and bisexual clients.

GAYS AND LESBIANS WORKING WITH GAYS AND LESBIANS

There are special concerns that can arise for gay, lesbian, and bisexual social work professionals when they work with gay, lesbian, and bisexual clients. Most of these issues involve boundary maintenance issues that arise because both worker and client share membership in a minority culture and community in the context of societal homophobia and heterosexism. While the literature on these issues tends to come from the mental health field, the principles discussed have relevance for social work as well.

When the social worker is providing direct service to an individual or family, a major question that often arises is whether to reveal a gay, lesbian, or bisexual orientation to the client(s). Some studies have suggested that many gay and lesbian people prefer a gay or lesbian health or mental health care provider (Bradford & Ryan 1988; Lease, Cogdal, & Smith 1995; McDermott, Tyndall, & Lichtenberg 1989). However, to many others the sexual orientation of the provider is not as important a factor or is important principally when the problem involves sexuality or sexual orientation (Lease, Cogdal, & Smith 1995; McDermott, Tyndall, & Lichtenberg 1989). Those clients for whom the sexual orientation of the worker is important will either ask directly or try to determine in other ways the worker's orientation. Knowing the worker's sexual orientation may be most important to those clients struggling with high levels of internalized homophobia (Lease, Cogdal, & Smith 1995; McDermott, Tyndall, & Lichtenberg 1989; Schwartz 1989).

Gay, lesbian, and bisexual professionals, when deciding how open to be about their orientation, must consider the impact on present and future clients. "Out" providers of mental health services, for example, can find that they are serving a largely gay, lesbian, or bisexual clientele because of clients who seek them out or because of intra-agency case-assignment procedures. In many cases, however, the sexual orientation of the worker will be unknown to the client (McDermott, Tyndall, & Lichtenberg 1989) and will be a subject of direct or indirect inquiry. How these questions are answered, of course, must be determined by the same considerations that guide all matters of self-disclosure by the social work professional: the best interests of the client(s). The overt question—about the sexual orientation of the worker—may really be a question about the worker's attitudes toward a gay, lesbian, or bisexual identity and the provider's attitudes and knowledge about it (Schwartz 1989).

When a client and worker share a gay, lesbian, or bisexual identity, they may also participate in the same social and cultural community (Schwartz 1989). This participation may increase the likelihood that client and worker will encounter each other at social and community events. This presents the risk of entering into what the NASW's *Code of Ethics* defines as a dual relationship. Dual relationships should be avoided whenever possible because of the risk of discomfort, harm, or exploitation to the client. When this situation cannot be avoided, it is the responsibility of the social work professional to ensure that no harm comes to the client as a result. For example, if there is only one gay- and lesbian-oriented church in the community to which both of them belong, it is probably unreasonable to expect either client or worker to give up the opportunity of religious worship because one is using the professional services of the other. However, the worker must conduct him/herself in such a way as to make such contacts as comfortable and easy for the client as possible and to ensure that any risk of exploitation of the client is minimized. However, because of the various psychological meanings of these extratherapeutic encounters to the client, their impact on the professional relationship cannot always be predicted (Schwartz 1989).

In mental health practice, because the professional social worker, like the client, has likely been exposed to homophobic and heterosexist attitudes and beliefs while growing up and even in professional training, internalized homophobia can be an influence in working with lesbian, gay, and bisexual clients even for the worker who shares their sexual orientation (McHenry & Johnson 1993; Schwartz 1989). These can lead to various "blind" spots (Schwartz 1989:49) in the effort to help. These can affect the referral process, perhaps by overvaluing the sexual orientation of the worker as opposed to the fit between the service needs of the client and the worker's specific areas of expertise (McHenry & Johnson 1993). As with any shared concern, assessment can be complicated when the worker and the client share areas of conflict related to a gay or lesbian identity, especially because determining the degree of the internalized homophobia in a client can be difficult. This influence can either be undervalued or overemphasized by the worker. As with all issues of bias in professional practice, continuous self-evaluation and good supervision and consultation are the best safeguards. Thus gay, lesbian, and bisexual social workers who practice with gay, lesbian, and bisexual people need a supportive and gay-affirmative employment in order to practice effectively.

STRATEGIES FOR AN INCLUSIVE WORKPLACE[3]

Those charged with the management of any organization do not typically address a problem until two things happen. First, they become reasonably sure that a problem exists, and second, they become convinced that trying to solve the problem will be good for agency growth and survival. Winfeld and Spielman (1995) suggested that public and private organizations are attempting to adapt to the changing demographics of both their clients/consumers and their employees. One current strategy is diversity management, which is now viewed more as a core administrative issue and less as strictly a human resources one. The distinction is crucial. Although administrators have not doubted that proper management and support programs are important, those programs have not been tied into performance outcomes. Some vague relationship between caring for staff and their resulting performance has always been acknowledged, but it was never considered an empirical cause and effect. That is changing in industry and in some sectors of the public arena. If the point of a diversity management effort is to create a harassment-free, satisfactory, cooperative, productive, and profitable/effective workplace for all, then it must include sexual orientation as a diversity factor.

A significant factor in managing a diverse environment is the very real issue of productivity. Work is a task, but it is also a social activity. People need and expect to be able to express themselves to the fullest, and when they can't, they are unhappy. That unhappiness may eventually sabotage the efforts of the work group and by extension weaken the performance of the whole organization.

There are other reasons to include lesbian and gay employees into an overall diversity strategy: law, service effectiveness, and common sense. The legal landscape in relation to gay rights changes continually. As of this writing gay rights are not protected by the U.S. Constitution. No federal job protection exits in this country. In 1997 eleven states offered full civil rights legal protection to gay and lesbian people, approximately eighteen others covered some degree of protection, and another one hundred and sixty-five cities and counties had ordinances. The Employment Non-Discrimination Act (ENDA), which would provide such protection, had yet to be passed by Congress (National Gay and Lesbian Task Force 1996). While present local laws and ordinances vary in power, each represents a building block upon which precedents are being set. Many of these precedents have implications for employers. A business or agency that operates in a state, city, or county with a sexual orientation nondiscrimination law or order (United Airlines in San Francisco, for example) is in violation of that law if it does not include sexual orientation as a protected characteristic in the company's written nondiscrimination policy. Violators can be sued or brought before the state's human rights commission.

> Organizations can expect more of their gay employees to insist upon discrimination protection and equitable benefits in the workplace. And those organizations would do well to listen. The reason is simple. In those places where the law does not protect and provide for inclusion of sexual minorities, gay people work under enormous strain. They cannot perform at their best under these oppressive circumstances. In many cases discrimination is unlawful; it is always unproductive and unprofitable.
>
> (Winfeld & Spielman 1995:11)

Effectiveness is another reason for organizations to take a proactive stance. The experience of industry suggests that adopting discriminatory policies is detrimental to economic health. Human rights are never far divorced from economics. According to a 1996 *Newsweek* poll, nearly 84 percent of Americans support equal employment rights for gay men and lesbians. The Human Rights Campaign found that, in 1994, 70 percent of the voting population did not realize that antigay job discrimination is still widespread and predominantly legal (Goldberg 1996). Organizations that support gay and lesbian employees and their requirements will be rewarded, and those that resist inclusion will see the results in their annual reports, decreased service caseloads, and funding sources.

Common sense is perhaps the most compelling reason for including gay and lesbian workers in the agency's diversity mix. They are already there. About 10 percent of the population is believed to be gay or lesbian, yet a much higher but unconfirmed percentage is estimated for the health and social services workforce. About 21 million (conservative estimate) lesbians and gay men live and work in the United States. Some studies estimate that they are the single largest minority in the workforce (Williamson 1993). They need and want the quite ordinary freedom of visibility without reprisals.

It must be acknowledged that some agencies, either through religious conviction or homophobia or both, are hesitant or want to avoid this subject altogether. Some fear that they will lose clients or community support if they take an ethical/legal stance. They are afraid that having an inclusive policy will be interpreted as giving tacit approval, and that clients who hold the opposite view will seek services elsewhere. This argument would have little merit if the discussion were to focus on racism or sexism, but homophobia is so institutionalized that this contradiction is seldom raised. Leaving the ethics of this situation aside, the answer is simple: acknowledgment of and education about something does not equal endorsement of it. Providing for the concerns of a particular constituency in the agency does not mean that you endorse the members of that constituency, their behavior, or their beliefs. Rather, it is quite pragmatic in that it simply signals that the agency is committed to all its employees, with no exceptions.

The agency can do many things to secure and maintain the best efforts of its employees. In return for equitable benefits, programs, and policies, the employer has the right to expect dedication, loyalty, self-motivation, and cooperation from all employees at all times. From a gay and lesbian perspective, the trade is a simple one, the same as is expected by and granted to heterosexual employees: a safe working environment, equitable benefits, and appropriate public support (Winfeld & Spielman 1996).

A safe work environment is demonstrated and encouraged by three things: (1) a nondiscrimination policy that expressly includes sexual orientation, (2) diversity education that includes a comprehensive module on sexual orientation, and (3) equitable human resource policies, and the support of a gay/straight employees alliance. Equitable benefits means providing to the partners of lesbian and gay employees the same benefits, including health coverage, that are accorded the families of other employees—in essence, equal pay for equal work.

CLIENT ADVOCACY AND SELF-ADVOCACY

It is too easy to overestimate the climate of acceptance. Collective action is more effective than individually playing Don Quixote and fighting windmills. The process of building the support of other minorities and like-minded allies will prove more fruitful. Gay men and lesbians have been successfully working side by side with heterosexuals throughout the nation's history. What is different today is that many people now openly live out their sexual orientation. This challenges straight and gay people alike to deal with their fears and prejudices on the job so that all can be creative and productive together.

The following steps are recommended in the process of assisting agencies to become nurturing environments that champion the civil rights and the well-being of lesbian and gay employees:

1. Start with an educational program related to sexual orientation for all employees

2. Follow this up with supportive programs that offer mentoring by someone with organizational status (or arrange an opportunity to work with a
   coming out coach who has a proven record of success), as well as programs that encourage joining support groups and networks of lesbians,
   gay men, and their allies.

Understandably, such a support group or network might itself become the
main constituency group, the medium for self-advocacy most invested in
pressing for a safe work environment, equitable benefits, and appropriate
public support.

Summary and Conclusions

Workplace issues for lesbian, gay, and bisexual people have not received the
attention they deserve despite the popular belief that job discrimination
based on sexual orientation is fundamentally unfair. While employment discrimination based on sexual orientation is sometimes hard to document, it is
clearly widespread, especially in relation to employment benefits. There are
some occupations, however, where antigay or anti-lesbian attitudes are very
clear, such as military service, work with children, or in the clergy in some
religious groups.

Managing a lesbian, gay, or bisexual identity at work is a nearly universal
issue for lesbian, gay, and bisexual clients and for lesbian, gay, and bisexual
social workers. For lesbians and bisexual women, gender discrimination may
present an additional problem; for gay and bisexual men, anti-AIDS attitudes
may present special challenges; and for gay men and lesbians of color, racism
presents additional problems. Sussal (1994), drawing upon extensive research
on organizational structures and their psychosocial impact, directed specific
attention to the employees of social service agencies. A convincing case was
made for the workplace having the potential to promote feelings of personal
validation and a source of mental health. The workplace itself, however, can
also become a source of emotional distress. Menzies-Lyth (1988) studied ways
the workplace can become destructive. She noted that anxieties not handled
openly through discussion may result in an increased likelihood that rigid and
injurious defenses against conflictual interactions may be developed. These
include "prohibitions against talking about uncomfortable anxiety-producing
topics, unnecessarily harsh disciplinary practices, rigid lines of hierarchical
relationships, and scapegoating. The impact on the individual employee in
these circumstances can result in feelings of worthlessness and self-devalua-
tion" (91). She suggested that lesbians and gays are subjected to a breadth of

discriminatory feedback in their daily lives that no other segment of the population must undergo.

> It is not uncommon for public policies and practices to disregard lesbian and gay special needs, while at the same time not even acknowledging their existence. [This is an exercise of the most destructive defense—denial.] A conspiracy of silence exists which is anxiety producing and painful.
>
> (Sussal 1994: 90–91)

Only when formal and informal discriminatory workplace policies and practices of all kinds are eliminated can gay, lesbian, and bisexual workers and clients reach their full human potential and contribute fully to society as a whole. This is an immediate challenge for gay, lesbian, bisexual, and heterosexual but lesbian and gay-affirming managers, supervisors, social workers, faculty and students to use their organizational change and advocacy skills on behalf of their clients and themselves.

8

Middle-Aged and Old Gay, Lesbian, and Bisexual Adults

Nancy A. Humphreys and Jean K. Quam

This chapter explores issues of aging as they affect lesbian, gay, and bisexual people. Consideration will be given to how those who share a same-gender sexual orientation differ among themselves, noting the biases in the current scant empirical record. Attention will be given to those issues that have particular relevance to gays and lesbians in the later years of life. The special social service needs of old gay, lesbian, and bisexual adults will be emphasized.

Until recently, old gays and lesbians have been invisible in the literature on sexual orientation. Similarly, homophobia in the social gerontology literature is reflected in the fact that sexual orientation has largely been ignored (Reid 1995). Some texts on aging continue to list homosexuality under sections on "deviant behavior" or isolate it as a form of sexual behavior without considering its social and psychological aspects. The paucity of information on middle-aged and old gays, lesbians, and bisexuals is even greater if one seeks empirical studies of any of these groups. In addition, the empirical studies that do exist tend to be biased in the direction of urban, white, middle-class adults who live in New York, Los Angeles, or San Francisco. Information and studies about old bisexuals are almost nonexistent, and some argue that such a group does not really even exist as an oppressed population. This invisibility of gays and lesbians in gerontology is striking since it is estimated that there are 3.5 million gay men and lesbians over sixty in the United States (Slusher, Mayer, & Dunkle 1996).

What study there has been of gay and lesbian aging has involved substantial controversy (Berger & Kelly 1996b; Lee 1990; Reid 1995). The first social psychological studies of older gay men were undertaken to refute the stereotype that old gays and lesbians would inevitably be isolated and unhappy. Since then, it has been suggested that these early gay-affirmative studies, with samples largely limited to affluent whites, have painted too rosy a picture. In actuality, it is likely that there is great variation in the late life adaptation of gay, lesbian, and bisexual people, just as there is among heterosexuals (Reid 1995). There is still debate about the importance of age itself as compared with cohort-specific historical experiences and about sexual orientation as compared with gender in understanding old gays and lesbians. In addition, we clearly need to know much more about old lesbians, about gays and lesbians in midlife, and about gay and lesbian people of color in midlife to old age (Berger & Kelly 1996a, 1996b; Jacobson 1995; Kimmel & Sang 1995; Reid 1995).

Despite the limits in our knowledge base, this chapter will present what we now know about helping middle-aged and old gays, lesbians, and bisexuals achieve what gerontologists term *successful aging* (Reid 1995). Ingredients of successful aging include length of life, physical health, mental health, cognitive efficacy, social competence and productivity, personal control, and life satisfaction. It includes the ability to compensate for losses and diminishing capacities and/or to optimize those capabilities that remain. Because of the oppression that they have had to face and overcome in their lives, it has been suggested that gay, lesbian, and bisexual people may be especially well equipped to achieve successful aging through what has been termed "crisis competence" or crisis "mastery" (Berger 1980; Kimmel 1978), "gender-role flexibility" (Friend 1980, 1990), a willingness to question negative stereotypes including those of aging (Friend 1990), or a resilience born of struggle. However, old gays and lesbians, like their younger counterparts, face many structural obstacles to achieving an optimal adaptation at the end of the life course. This chapter will focus on ways of working with middle-aged and old gay, lesbian, and bisexual people to help them achieve successful aging.

Issues in Terminology

AGE AND AGING

A word about language and definitions is needed in relation to age. Many articles about people in the last phase of life use the terms *older* or *aging*. Some argue that these adjectives imply a fear and a stigma associated with old age.

> The OLOC brochure says that although "old has become a term of insult and shame . . . we refuse the lie that it is shameful to be an older woman." We are neither "older" (than whom?), nor "elder," nor "senior." We name and proclaim ourselves as OLD for we no longer wish to collude in our own oppression by accommodating to language that implies in any way that old means inferior, ugly , or awful. . . . By naming ourselves as old, we give up the attempt to pass. And as we break our silence, we empower ourselves and each other.
>
> —Shevy Healy (1993:52)

When the term *old* is used, a clearer picture is presented. The Old Lesbian Organizing Committee (OLOC), a national organization of lesbians over the age of sixty, has led the way in helping old lesbians confront ageism in our society. Healy (1993) states that talking about being old is new for lesbians. Old lesbians are used to denying their age and feel scared and repulsed by the aging process.

The definition of specific age cohorts is not easy either. What is middle age? When does it begin and when is it over? When does the next phase—old age— begin? The beginning and ending of old age used to be much clearer. For many years sixty-five was the generally accepted beginning of old age. Today, however, no such distinct boundary exists. Mandatory retirement age has been raised to seventy or eliminated altogether. In addition, average life expectancy now makes it possible for most elderly adults to remain active well into their seventies, which leads to further discussions about increasing the retirement age and delaying the age at which individuals can collect retirement, social security, or pension benefits. Thus there are many markers of aging, and it is impossible to attach a specific age to the beginning of old age. For example, as early as age fifty one can join AARP (the American Association of Retired Persons). At age sixty-two one is eligible for Medicare. But some people do not retire until they are in their seventies or eighties.

Deciding when middle age begins can be just as tricky as pinpointing the onset of old age. Suggest to a thirty-something friend or relative that they have become middle aged and you are likely to need to apologize later. Many forty-year-olds continue to define themselves as young adults while others may feel their first debilitating chronic illness. Many lesbian couples are now parenting for the first time given the advances made in fertility and reproductive technologies. A forty-year-old parent of young children is more likely to see herself as a young adult regardless of her aches and pains.

The distinction of the frail elderly as a separate group within old age has led to the suggestion that there are many stages associated with old age. Gerontologists generally agree that there is a "young-old" age in which members are still physically healthy and active, relatively financially well off (compared to their working years), and eager to pursue a variety of activities during their leisure time. Some find part-time jobs or volunteer work while others enjoy hobbies and sports for which they now have time. This phase is a time in which members are able to take care of themselves and enjoy life, albeit at a slower pace.

The age at which one becomes a part of the "old-old" age phase may be harder to discern and much harder to attach to a particular age. Usually this stage is the time in which a person experiences a crisis in terms of health, income, or both. Frequently, losses are compounded by fewer resources available as support. Loss of family, friends, neighborhood, home, and reduced outside activities only exacerbate deteriorating health. Women over the age of eighty are the fastest growing cohort of any age cohort in the United States (Hooyman & Kiyak 1993).

Finally, there is the issue of lumping all "old" people together in the research. In trying to find people to study, some research has included anyone over the age or forty-five or fifty in the old category despite the fact that we know there may be wide differences between fifty-year-olds, seventy-year-olds, and ninety-year-olds.

WHO ARE MIDDLE-AGED AND OLD GAYS, LESBIANS, AND BISEXUALS?

Unfortunately, most studies and demographic analyses of the aged fail to differentiate gays, lesbians, and bisexuals. This fact is not surprising given the difficulties associated with the need for self-definition and dangers of disclosure. The categories of "single" and "not married" are used in many different ways in the social gerontology literature. It would be safe to assume that a large proportion of the never married group might also be gay or lesbian. However, often these terms refer to the status individuals hold when they are old rather than describing a life-long status (i.e., those individuals who never married). Thus even extrapolation from existing data on the aged in general to gay, lesbian, and bisexual populations is difficult since data on those individuals who never married is often not separately reported. Therefore, despite sampling limitations, data about gays, lesbians, and bisexuals as a separate and discreet population among the aged are generally the best source of information about these populations currently available.

Berger (1983) has proposed a model of gay or lesbian identity which involves completion of three interdependent tasks, including a same-sex sexual encounter and social labeling by outsiders. Gay or lesbian identity, and presumably the identity of bisexuals, develops over time and is uneven in the formative period as the individual comes to grips with his or her sexual orientation and society's reactions to that fact. The desirable outcome of the identity formation process is a mentally healthy gay, lesbian, or bisexual individual who accepts his or her own sexual orientation and manages his or her identity in the face of the social oppression of the particular life situation (see also chapter 2). Old gays and lesbians often point to coming out as one of their most significant life experiences (Berger 1984). The issue of who are middle-aged and old bisexuals, gays, and lesbians is complicated by the fact that identity defined by sexual orientation is not always clear-cut or stable over the life course. For example, when does one move from being bisexual to being gay or lesbian? Are you a lesbian couple if you live in a nonsexual "Boston marriage"? These issues are complicated by the fact that there are many different ways in which old gay, lesbian, and bisexual adults have lived their lives.

> Amanda always considered herself to be heterosexual. She married at a young age, had three children, and never questioned her sexuality. At fifty-three, when her children were grown and her marriage was encountering some problems, she attended a women's support group at a local church. Amanda found herself attracted to and increasingly curious about Elizabeth, who identified herself as a lesbian. Amanda and Elizabeth eventually became romantically involved.

> Harvey and Richard, aged eighty-two and seventy-nine, respectively, are schoolteachers who have lived together for over fifty years in a "closeted" relationship. They define themselves as roommates to family and friends and were very fearful of losing their jobs if the true nature of their relationship had ever been discovered.

> Henry, age sixty-four, is married. He has had hundreds of sexual encounters over the years in gay bars and bathhouses. He travels regularly and engages in most of his relationships away from home. He is looking forward to his retirement years with his wife and expects that his encounters with other men will diminish as his traveling decreases.

> Barbara, age sixty-nine, knew she was a lesbian at a young age and has been active in gay and lesbian organizations, churches, and social

activities. She has been in three long-term relationships with women as well as in several other shorter relationships. Her most recent relationship ended after sixteen years owing to the death of her partner. Barbara is concerned that at her age it will be difficult to find someone new.

By the time of middle age and beyond, gays, lesbians, and bisexuals have generally achieved an identity that acknowledges their sexual orientation although they often do so in different ways (Adelman 1990). First, there are those who have known and accepted their sexual orientation for some time. This group is further divided between those who are "out" (i.e., publicly identifying themselves as gay, lesbian, or bisexual) and those who remain closeted and "pass" in everyday life (Friend 1990). This division is not pure since one may be "out" in some areas of life while passing in others. For some, the career accomplishments and anticipated retirement of middle age and late life permits more openness or flexibility in managing a gay, lesbian, or bisexual identity.

> "While some of my perspectives have changed, I'm essentially the same person I always was. I've had a few hardships along the way (gotten ill, lost loved ones to AIDS, ended unhappy relationships), but maybe I survived *because* I continued to be the same person. The single constant denominator has been my identity, my sense of self. This is who I am, nothing has ever changed that, and nothing will—so perhaps I'll get through this life after all."
>
> —Ray Berger, author of *Gay and Gray*, quoted in Reyes and Farrell (1993:20)

Another group with a quite different identity are those who come to identify as lesbian, gay, or bisexual for the first time during their middle or older years. These individuals find a whole new identity in their middle or later years that can be very invigorating and sets the stage for the remainder of their lives.

Naming the Identity

The problems in defining the terms *gay*, *lesbian*, and *bisexual* have been previously discussed (see chapter 2). What to call oneself has particular significance for those who have lived a long time and have experienced different interpretations and preferences in the use of language. Generational life space, or cohort, issues are particularly significant with the old. Most old gays, lesbians, and bisexuals living today have lived the bulk of their lives before the advent of the gay and lesbian liberation and civil rights movement. Thus those who are old today have lived through several distinctly different phases in the naming and labeling of sexual orientation.

The names by which one identifies oneself will differ depending on how much stigma or acceptance is prevalent in the larger social environment. Other redefinitions of social labels will also influence the terms individuals use to refer to themselves. For example, some lesbians, particularly those who are old or unaffiliated with the modern women's movement, continue to refer to themselves as "gay" rather than the more commonly used "lesbian" as reference to self. In interacting with old gays, lesbians, or bisexuals in a helping relationship, it is important to use the terms that are most comfortable for the client.

Gaps and Issues in Research

While little is known about gay and lesbian behavior in general, even less is known about gay and lesbian behavior in midlife and old age. In addition, there are serious methodological problems in what has been published. Originally, some studies used subjects who were in therapy, often as a result of their confusion regarding their sexual orientation. These clinical samples gave a distorted and often negative view of gay and lesbian development over the life span. At the other extreme, some researchers drew convenience samples of adults who felt comfortable with their sexual orientation and were open to questioning. Frequently, these studies consisted of small groups of retired professionals who knew each other and intentionally wanted to project a "positive image of gay and lesbian aging" (Berger & Kelly 1996b).

An intriguing question is how to interview or study the lives of individuals who are closeted and do not want to have their sexual orientation known. Many old gay men, lesbians, and bisexuals have lived through times in which they lost jobs or lost family because their behavior was considered to be immoral, illegal, or simply wrong. They believe that they cannot disclose their sexual orientation for fear of reprisals.

Further complicating the definitional problem is the fact that many lay and professional people assume that all individuals, regardless of gender, who share the same sexual orientation can be understood as a single common group. In this way of thinking, old gays and lesbians have more in common than lesbians do with other women or gays do with other men. However, Quam and Whitford (1992) discovered that, in some instances, gender was a defining factor such that old lesbians were more like other old women in their concerns than they were like old gay men. Gender as well as sexual orientation is a key variable in understanding middle-aged and old people. Therefore when encountering a gay, lesbian, or bisexual individual, particularly if she or he is a client, it is imperative that the age, gender, and sexual orientation along with class, race, and ethnicity of the individual all be considered as independent and interdependent factors which shape the life experience and behaviors of people.

Some have raised questions as to who should do research about old gay, lesbian, and bisexual adults (Healy 1993; Jacobson 1995; MacDonald 1986). Should only gay, lesbian, or bisexual researchers do this work? Should they only do the work if they are also old themselves? Should bisexuals be included in research on gays and lesbians? Or should bisexuals be studied separately? How should researchers relate to those being studied so as to reach as diverse and representative a group as possible?

The research in the field of gay, lesbian, and bisexual aging is going through its own developmental transitions and changes similar in some ways to research on gender and racial differences. In the first stages of research, there are only a few articles published in smaller, less well-known journals. While the research is welcomed by the subjects and advocates of gay and lesbian issues, mainstream research marginalizes the new area as trivial and inconsequential. Most of the early studies also tend to see the subjects in a very positive light in contrast to mainstream literature which has only seen the subjects as "other."

After a while, the second stage emerges in which enough articles have been published in multiple disciplines that the area of research begins to take shape. Researchers begin to focus on areas of more specificity in their subjects (e.g., rather than just research on gay and lesbian aging, we now see articles about old Latino males, lesbian grandmothers of adolescents, and lesbians who have lost their partners of twenty-five years or more). The literature begins to be critical about the subjects as well as positive. Journal boards seek submissions about gay and lesbian aging and add experts in the area to their editorial boards. This stage comes closest to describing the current state of research with gay and lesbian adults who are old.

What we could perhaps strive for is the stage in which all gerontologists naturally include sexual orientation as a part of their inquiry in the same manner as they would ask about gender, age, or race. Similarly, those doing research on gay, lesbian, and bisexual adults should never exclude adults who are old. In addition, funding must become available to longitudinally study this population in which large data sets emerge that can answer questions we have not yet considered. Most of this, however, assumes a society that is far more open to acceptance of diversity in sexual orientation than the society we have now.

Theories of Late Life Development

The middle years and old age are unique phases in the adult life span. The theories most often used in social work to understand these life stages are those of Erik Erikson (1963) and Daniel Levinson (1978). Erik Erikson's theory posits stages of psychosocial development, each of which is marked by a central set of critical issues, a crisis, which challenges one toward progress or regression. Erikson notes that when an individual lacks the ability to come to grips with who he or she is, a sense of stagnation and personal impoverishment results. Bisexuals, gays, and lesbians may face special challenges in their identity development in any part of the life span, especially if stigmatization based on sexual orientation has been intense. In writing about the adjustment of old gays and lesbians, Adelman (1990) underscored this point: "It is stigma and stigma management that make gay development so perilous" (28). Her study found a significant positive relationship between adjustment to later life and satisfaction with being gay or lesbian whatever the style of identity management employed.

According to Erikson, *middle age* is a time of crisis in the development of a sense of what Erikson called *generativity versus stagnation*. During this phase of development middle-aged individuals are primarily concerned with guiding the next generation and being productive and creative. Most commonly this critical issue is met in parenting, but many middle-aged individuals guide the next generation in ways other than parenting.

While a growing number of gays and lesbians are parenting and while bisexual people often bring children into same-gender relationships, the majority of gays and lesbians are childless and must find other ways to contribute to the development of future generations. Child substitutes such as nieces, nephews, godchildren, and other children in the family and friendship network take on great significance to childless adults. The advent of the gay, lesbian, and bisexual rights movement has offered a new organizational arena for contributing to future generations. Individuals and couples may link themselves to the larger struggle for gay, lesbian, and bisexual rights which aims to improve the life chances and minimize the social vulnerability of future generations.

Another avenue for generativity are the many service-oriented professions and occupations. Slater (1995) notes that the overrepresentation of women in the traditional service professions, including social work, allows many lesbians to focus their generative activities in their work setting. Many gays, lesbians, and bisexuals are active in a variety of social change and political organizations. The human devastation and cost as well as the public health crisis associated with the AIDS pandemic has mobilized a multitude of social action and service initiatives which, in a very direct way, have had an impact on the future of young people. Because old gays, lesbians, and bisexuals have survived a hostile environment and lived a nonconforming lifestyle, they have the inner resources to challenge the status quo and thus they make good activists (Slater 1995).

In Erikson's framework, the central crisis for *old age* is the issue of *ego integrity versus despair*. Ego integrity implies an emotional integration, an acceptance of who one is and what one has had to cope with. For gay, lesbian, and bisexual individuals, acceptance of self is made more complicated because of their sexual orientation, which is deemed deviant by many. On the other hand, coping with and managing society's definition of them, or what Goffman (1963) calls "managing spoiled identities," can be very liberating and can leave people feeling that they have fought a good fight and even if they didn't always or mostly win, at least they equipped themselves well.

The contrasting outcome of despair brings many older individuals to social service agencies of many kinds. A common form of despair among those with a different sexual orientation is a sense that much of their life has been wasted because of their own discomfort with their sexual orientation. This may be magnified by losses of severed relationships because parents, siblings, children, spouses, and friends were unable to accept them. Despair expresses a fear of death and the feeling that life is now too short and the life that has been lived was not what it could or should have been. The very real oppressive forces that confront gays, lesbians, and bisexuals can easily result in a life of constant and insurmountable struggle which can challenge ego integrity and can increase the likelihood of despair. Old gays, lesbians, and bisexuals share with all old people a growing number of losses of friends and family members. Similarly, they share issues associated with retirement and a time of reduced income and increasing health concerns. And like other old people they face the loss of their partners. Unlike other old individuals the special significance of these losses may not be acknowledged and the mourning that must be done alone without the support of others can add to the struggle between despair and ego integrity.

However, presenting these challenges does not do justice to the vitality, strength, and emotional health that is common among these groups. Slater (1995) notes that many lesbian couples successfully "navigate their way through their middle years" and become old with "neither peril nor on-going drama" (195). She goes on to say that the pressures imposed by a homophobic culture often force younger lesbians to steel themselves for a hostile environment. The outcome of such challenges often are great maturity and insight. The same outcomes are no doubt true for many old gays and bisexuals as well.

Daniel Levinson's (1978) theory of adult development posits periods of transition involving the active development of new "life structures" interspersed with periods of relative stability. Kimmel (1993), while noting that the theory was developed using only middle-class, white, college-educated and heterosexual males, suggests that Levinson's descriptions of a period of "midlife transition" (ages forty to forty-five), of "age 50 transition" (ages fifty to fifty-five), and of "late adult transition" (ages sixty to sixty-five) have relevance to at least some gay men. Those who embrace a gay, lesbian, or bisexual identity for the first time in late life, for example, often seem to do so during one of these "transitions." Others may change how they manage their gay, lesbian, or bisexual identity at these times, often becoming more open about it in significant aspects of their lives. This theory does not extend, however, beyond the beginning of old age as currently understood.

However, Kimmel (1993) notes that it is very important to consider how these phases of adult development have intersected with specific historical changes depending on when a person was born. This may be even more important when thinking about gay and lesbian lives than others because of the dramatic social changes that have occurred in gay and lesbian life in the United States in the late twentieth century. For example, the choices available to someone experiencing the "midlife transition" before or after the Stonewall Rebellion have been significantly different. In addition, Levinson's theory is not well-developed in relation to women, gay or straight, or to people of different cultures and ethnicities (Jacobson 1995).

Understanding the interaction of individual life cycle and family life cycle issues is an important concern in need of further investigation both in clinical work as well as through formal research with lesbians, gays, and bisexuals. Slater (1995) notes that much of what is known about family life cycles is largely irrelevant to the experiences of gay, lesbian, and bisexual adults since it is predicated on the idea of the heterosexual couple at the apex and a family bonded by blood and/or marriage. None of these conditions exist in the lives of gays, lesbians, and many bisexuals. She further notes that the understandings of those who work with lesbian couples and families can inform all family work by expanding the horizons of family life and emphasizing the family life cycle of childless couples. Understanding the intersection of family life cycle issues, sexual orientation, and the individual life cycle will expand our general knowledge while specifically enhancing what we know about middle-aged and old gays, lesbians, and bisexuals.

Challenges in Gay and Lesbian Aging[1]

While many gay and lesbian people negotiate middle age and old age with great resiliency and success, they do so despite certain structural obstacles that do not affect their heterosexual counterparts. Although they may know about these obstacles, many gay and lesbian people, like others, enter midlife and old age not having actually made the plans and arrangements necessary to make their hopes for old age a reality (Waite 1995). This section will outline some of the areas critical to successful aging in which special challenges must often be overcome. It will also discuss those areas in which the issues of gay men and lesbians often differ.

HEALTH CARE NEEDS

As the aging process continues, most old people become increasingly concerned about their health. Overall, studies of old gay and lesbian adults show a positive feeling toward the aging process and high scores on life satisfaction as one ages (Deevey 1990; Whitford 1997). Quam and Whitford (1992) found a particularly strong relationship between the support of gay and lesbian friends and less fear of the aging process.

Fear of how a physician and other health care workers will treat a gay, lesbian, or bisexual patient is very strong (Reid 1995). In a study of 178 lesbians, ages eighteen to fifty-five, Lucas (1992) discovered that most of the subjects preferred lesbian care providers and did not want their sexual orientation listed in their medical record.

These fears can lead to poorer medical care if gay and lesbian patients avoid needed medical care. Deevey (1990) found that lesbians went to see physicians less frequently for breast exams and, despite excess weight gains, were less likely to see a physician about their weight. Berger (1982) makes the point that older homosexual men may be too embarrassed to request information about complicated medical conditions unique to homosexual men such as pharyngeal and anal gonorrhea and anal fissures resulting from rectal penetration. Older adults are less likely to use condoms because they are seen as a method of birth control, and old adults do not believe they are at risk for sexually transmitted diseases (Drost 1996). Almost 10 percent of all adult cases of AIDS in the United States have occurred in people over fifty; 25 percent of those are in adults over sixty, and 4 percent of those over age seventy (Drost 1996).

Fear of AIDS has created many new problems for the aging gay male particularly. Misunderstanding has led to decreased sexual activity and an unnecessary fear of intimacy. The enormity of losses of personal friends and colleagues in the gay community is devastating for all. Some old gay men have lost dozens of friends to AIDS. The constant, unremitting sense of loss and fear can lead to despair at a much earlier age than one might normally expect.

An additional concern is the fear of institutionalization if one is unable to care for oneself (Waite 1995). For an old gay man, lesbian, or bisexual this may mean that a decision has to be made as to whether or not to come out to nursing home staff. Despite the fact that some nursing homes are becoming more progressive in allowing sexual expression and sexual interaction in private spaces among heterosexual residents, there is no evidence that this privilege has been extended to gay, lesbian, and bisexual residents. What is most needed is staff development training such that nursing personnel will understand and support the sexual expression of residents as a healthy part of the aging process regardless of their sexual orientation.

Finally, while substance abuse issues are somewhat more common among gay men and lesbians of all ages than among others (see chapter 9), there is some evidence that old gays and lesbians may be at particular risk of alcoholism. The number of people who drink at all and the number who engage in problem drinking generally declines with age. However, these numbers do not decline as much among older gay men and lesbians, leading to higher rates of alcohol-related problems (Bradford, Ryan, & Rothblum 1994; McKirnan & Peterson 1989a; Skinner 1994). Substance abuse problems, including alcoholism, are generally underdiagnosed and undertreated among the elderly. Gay- and lesbian-affirmative alcohol treatment services may thus be especially important for middle-aged and old gay men and lesbians.

HOUSING

In addition to the need for adequate health care, old gay men, lesbians, and bisexuals are concerned about adequate housing as they age. In most studies of aging gay and lesbian adults, high percentages of the subjects live alone. The lowest percentage was 38 percent (Berger 1980), with most studies finding about 50 percent (Friend 1980; Kehoe 1989; Lee 1987; Quam & Whitford 1992; Weinberg & Williams 1974) and some studies finding much higher rates (Kimmel 1978; Minnigerode & Adelman 1978).

While many dream of ideal housing in old age, in reality few opportunities exist for specialized housing for old gay, lesbian, and bisexual adults. There are selected examples from around the country as to lesbian-only nursing homes or gay and lesbian apartment complexes or women-only trailer courts. Kehoe (1989) found a strong preference among old lesbians for a lesbian-only retirement facility. In one of the more extensive sets of questions asked about housing, Quam and Whitford (1992) found that 80 percent of old lesbians wanted lesbian-only housing available while 60 percent wanted gay and lesbian only housing and 53 percent wanted women-only housing. Old gay men were much more interested in a gay and lesbian mixed housing option (63 percent) than they were in housing for gay men only. It seems clear that in all the research, old gay men and lesbians want at least a housing choice in which they can feel comfortable living their lives openly and in which they can have the opportunity to meet other old gay men and lesbians. Old age is a time of feeling vulnerable, and one wants to feel safe in one's own home regardless of one's age.

RELIGION

Because sexual orientation is often stigmatized as morally wrong, religion has an important place in the lives of those with different sexual orientations. It is also recognized that religion tends to take on an increased importance as one ages. As suggested by Erikson's model, the search for meaning often intensifies (Sang 1993), and spirituality and religion may be areas of increasing interest.

Most religious organizations have been vigorously debating their views on sexuality given current changes in our culture and in our politics. The more conservative religious groups reject gay and lesbian behavior/lifestyles as part of the deterioration of morals in our society, while more liberal religious groups embrace gays and lesbians in all aspects of religious life (Whitford & Quam 1995). Many gay and lesbian adults have left churches that were unaccepting and either joined "reconciled" congregations or started their own church groups.

Tensions between religion and homosexuality do exist. As early as 1948, Kinsey reported that male homosexual contacts occurred most frequently among males who were not active in their respective religious organizations. The differences between those who were active and inactive were not always great but were consistently in the same direction. It is also important to note that Kinsey defined religiosity as active participation in religious organization, a definition that is not used as much by researchers since that time.

Weinberg and Williams (1974) questioned more than 2,400 gay males in three locations (the United States, the Netherlands, and Denmark). Anywhere from 10 to 25 percent were over the age of forty-five. They believed that because the "Judeo-Christian tradition condemns homosexuality, homosexuals who ascribe importance to religion face a dilemma" (363). Measuring religiosity as "the personal importance attributed to formal religion"

(363), they found that religious gay men were more concerned with passing, more worried about exposure, more likely to attribute importance to the opinion of others, less socially involved with other gay men, more likely to believe that they were born homosexual, and the least committed to their homosexuality.

More recent studies have found a trend of gay and lesbian adults reconciling their religion and their sexual orientation and finding strength in their religion and religious organizations (Berger 1984). Quam and Whitford (1992) found that almost a third of their sample of old gay men and lesbian women regularly attended churches that supported their sexual orientation. Despite the tensions, then, it is likely that old gays and lesbians are concerned with issues of religion and spirituality like their heterosexual peers.

Social Support

In old age there is a great diversity in behavior, physical strength, mental health, and personality. It may be that years of being closeted or fearful lead to loneliness and isolation in old age. But several authors have found that involvement in the gay community increases the self-esteem of old gays and lesbians (Johnson & Kelly 1979; Raphael & Robinson 1980; Whitford 1997). It also appears that younger cohorts of gay, lesbian, and bisexual adults will expect more opportunities for social interaction in the gay community such as churches, social and professional organizations, sports leagues, and educational groups. Younger cohorts seem to be more concerned about the need for these activities as one ages and expect them to be in place as they grow older.

Social isolation, however, can be a problem. In a large study of old lesbians, Kehoe (1989) uncovered many "coupled" lesbians who were very isolated and tended to socialize only in their own homes. These women were at great risk of increased isolation when their partners died. Some writers have called for more intergenerational activities among gays, lesbians, and bisexuals to mitigate against the losses of same-age peers. Dorrell (1990) describes a particularly poignant example of seven young lesbians who form an informal support group to care for an eighty-four-year-old terminally ill lesbian.

Old gays and lesbians often find social support among both heterosexual and homosexual friendship networks (Berger 1984). However, social support and mutual aid from other lesbians and gays may be especially vital (Adelman 1986). As Berger (1984) put it: "Association with other homosexuals is an important part of self-acceptance. Not only does it relieve the sense of being 'the only one in the world who is different,' it also exposes the individual to a set of beliefs that counter prevalent negative social attitudes" (59).

Having learned to question the prevailing negative stereotypes of being lesbian or gay may also help middle-aged and old gays and lesbians to resist stereotypes of aging and thus adapt more successfully (Berger 1980, 1984; Friend 1990; Reid 1995). Similarly, having learned to proactively develop social support systems outside the family system can be a vital asset in late life (Kimmel & Sang 1995).

LEGAL ISSUES

Old gays and lesbians may encounter some specific legal problems based on the fact that their partner relationships are not legally recognized (Berger & Kelly 1996a; Kelly 1977; Kimmel 1993; Reid 1995). A surviving gay or lesbian person does not automatically inherit or receive tax shelter for property left when a partner dies the way a legally married spouse does. Surviving biological relatives may even challenge property left through a will (Berger & Kelly 1996a). While anyone can be made the beneficiary of a life insurance policy, there is no provision available to gay and lesbian people to provide survivor's benefits for a partner in Social Security benefits the way married heterosexuals can do for each other. The value of some private pensions may be available to a partner through inheritance at the time of the death of the individual covered or may permit benefits to be allocated to a nonrelative by the beneficiary. However, careful estate planning and assertive action on the part of the beneficiary are necessary; since self-disclosure is required, closeted individuals or couples may not be able to take advantage of such arrangements even when they are available. Thus gay and lesbian couples face significant obstacles in planning for their mutual financial well-being in old age.

In addition, a gay or lesbian partner is not legally empowered to make medical and end-of-life decisions the way a spouse can without specific provision through an advanced directive or durable power of attorney. Relatives may care for or be awarded guardianship for a disabled lover (Hartman 1996; Kimmel 1993). In some settings, a gay or lesbian person may even have difficulty gaining access to the bedside of a partner in an intensive care setting because the nature of the relationship is not recognized. In all of these areas, advanced planning and special legal arrangements may be necessary in order that the personal, medical, and property rights of both members of the relationship will be protected in the way that both partners desire. Social workers need to be knowledgeable about the legal resources available in their areas to assist gay and lesbian people in planning their personal care and inheritance arrangements. Such planning should ideally begin in midlife. However, many of these issues could easily be resolved if gay and lesbian people who wanted to were permitted to marry (see chapter 5).

BEREAVEMENT

> This was going to be the best part of my life but my lover died of cancer at 60. So, I'm retired and alone for five years now. We were in the closet so I don't have any gay friends. I do everything alone.
> —Charles, quoted in Ryan and Bogard (1994:14)

Just as partners are legally invisible, the loss of a beloved partner in mid- or late life may also be an invisible event (Berger & Kelly 1996a; Kelly 1977; Kimmel 1993; Lee 1990; Reid 1995). In addition, to the extent that "chosen family" (Weston 1991) forms a vital part of the support networks of many gay and lesbian people, the loss of a "friend" may have an impact more like that of the loss of a sibling or partner to others. Although peer support has been found to be one of the most effective means of helping those who are grieving, generic bereavement groups may or may not seem or be welcoming to a lesbian or gay member mourning the loss of a lover (Kimmel 1993). This area may be one in which the use of gay- or lesbian-specific services can be most valuable (see below).

DIFFERENCES BETWEEN LESBIANS AND GAYS

Despite our limited knowledge base and the considerable diversity within each group, it is possible to describe a few ways in which middle-aged and old gay men and lesbians are likely to differ from one another (Kimmel 1993). Lesbians are more likely than comparable gay men to have experienced fluidity in their sexual orientation in adulthood, perhaps even to have been heterosexually married. At least in current middle-aged and elderly cohorts, lesbians are more likely to have children than gay men (but less so than heterosexual women). In addition, they are more likely to be living in a long-term relationship than gay men are, perhaps in part because of the longer average life expectancy of women than men. These differences are likely to affect the social supports available to lesbians and gay men in old age.

Another important difference between old gay men and lesbians is in finances. Few old gay men express concern about finances (Berger & Kelly 1996b) while a substantial proportion of lesbians do (Sang 1993). This difference is not surprising. Significant gains have been made in recent decades in reducing poverty among the elderly, which was cut in half between 1966 and 1974. Despite these general improvements, poverty and near-poverty are still problems for many older Americans, especially people of color and women of all racial and ethnic groups. For example, Miller (1995), using 1991 data, reports that the poverty rate was 15 percent for older women and only 9 percent for older men.

Income levels in old age are the result of earnings and employment experience in all of adulthood. Thus Crawley (1995) notes that the average income of older women is only 57 percent of that of older men; the average Social Security benefit of women is only 76 percent of that of men. Older men are much more likely to receive private pensions than older women are (Miller 1990; Tracy & Ozawa 1995). For women, income in old age is also the result of policies that allow married women (and some widows) to qualify for pension and Social Security benefits based on the higher lifetime earnings of their male spouses. Thus poverty rates among single women in old age are much higher than those for married women, and lesbians are much less likely to have been married than their heterosexual counterparts. For the reasons outlined above, despite well-established patterns of participation in the paid labor force, old lesbians are likely to have earned less, to have less often qualified for private pension benefits, and thus to have less available to them in retirement income than their gay male counterparts. Changes both in gender discrimination in pay and advancement and in the recognition of gay and lesbian partner relationships in public and private pension programs will be necessary to safeguard the economic well-being of lesbians in midlife and old age.

Specialized Versus Generic Services

Gays, lesbians, and bisexuals face special service needs around retirement and end-of-life planning given that the nature and extent of their personal partnerships are not legally sanctioned and often not fully accepted and respected by family and friends. Unless clients who are gay, lesbian, or bisexual feel free to share their true identities and relationships, obtaining social services may be a useless act or one that leads to further discrimination.

Historically, there is a debate about the advantages and disadvantages of age-integrated versus age-segregated service for old adults. Equally debatable are the advantages and disadvantages of generic services for all old adults, such as Social Security or senior centers, as opposed to specific services for selected groups of old adults usually based on income or need, such as Medicaid or public housing (Hooyman & Kiyak 1993). There is also disagreement over whether to create separate services for gay, lesbian, and bisexual adults who are old in a time of scarce and declining resources (Berger 1984). For some adults these programs will be extremely important and represent a "safe" place in which to have needs met. For others who feel safer "in the closet," it will be perhaps even more important to make sure that generic social service providers be sensitive to the needs of old gay men, lesbians, and bisexuals regardless of their own sexual orientation or their own attitudes toward homosexuality.

Gays, lesbians, and bisexuals share with other elderly people many of the same needs for sensitive, available, and accessible social services. However, gays, lesbians, and bisexuals need to be recognized as distinct subgroups in all considerations of social service needs of the elderly. Whether the services are aimed at assisting elderly clients with retirement planning, housing assistance, relationship problems, loneliness, or any of a variety of needs for supportive social services, status as a gay, lesbian, or bisexual adult is a major factor in providing meaningful and relevant social services. Failure to recognize this fact or to take it into consideration can and does result in serious omissions and mistakes in services to these groups of elderly clients. The social work profession's commitment to serving gays and lesbians requires a strong affirmative stance in recognizing and meeting the special needs of gays and lesbians.

Agencies do exist that serve primarily gay, lesbian, and bisexual clients who are old. Founded in 1978, SAGE (Senior Action in a Gay Environment) in New York was one of the first agencies to serve an exclusively gay and lesbian aging client group. It provides counseling, information and referral, friendly visiting for shut-ins, support groups, and a wide array of workshops and social events. It is a nonprofit organization with more than seven thousand members (Freedman 1995). SAGE has now begun to affiliate with other organizations around the country into an organization called SageNet.

Other examples are GLEAM (Gay and Lesbian Elders Active in Minnesota) in Minneapolis; GLOE (Gay and Lesbian Outreach to Elders) in San Francisco; LOAF (Lesbians Over the Age of Forty) in New York; OLOC (Old Lesbian Organizing Committee) in Chicago; SOL (Slightly Older Lesbians) in Denver, San Francisco, and Santa Cruz; GEMS in Hartford; and Vintage in Denver. Hubbard, Allen, and Mancini (1992) and Grenwald (1984) describe how these programs can function to meet many of the social service needs of old gay and lesbian adults. The history of the different phases of development of a support group that has met monthly for more than seven years is described by Slusher, Meyer and Dunkle (1996).

Middle-aged and old gays and lesbians differ in their preferences for gay-and-lesbian, gay-only, lesbian-only, or generic service providers in old age. Thus it will be necessary to develop and support both specialized and generic elder services to adequately meet the needs of this group.

PRINCIPLES OF PRACTICE WITH OLD GAY, LESBIAN, AND BISEXUAL PEOPLE

"I was reminded once again of the significance of the extended family for lesbians and gay men. We know 'family values' very well. We preserve them. Too, we understand fully the words in the traditional marriage ceremony, 'in sickness and in health.' For older gays the extended family renders possible a sense of community and its corollary of shared experiences. Being secretive about one's gayness and remaining in the closet mitigates against the possibility of joining an extended family, celebrating life with happiness and fulfillment."
—Malcolm Boyd, quoted in Reyes and Farrell (1993:42)

For those agencies that want to be sensitive to the needs of all their old clients regardless of their sexual orientation, there are several steps that can be taken. First and foremost is to *respect a client's right to privacy and confidentiality*. Because a client feels safe enough to come out to one worker may not necessarily mean that he or she wants everyone in the agency to know about them. Agencies need to review all language used in their public documents, including assessments, intake forms, brochures describing the agency, and contracts. Do intake forms ask about marital status rather than who the client considers to be his or her family? Do we use gender-neutral terms such as "partner" or "friend" if someone talks about a relationship that is important to them? Realize that, particularly for an old gay man or lesbian, the idea of talking about one's sexuality may be a forbidden topic. It is possible that an old lesbian, for example, may not be able to use the word *lesbian* or talk about her sexuality to someone she has just met.

Second, *recognize that there is diversity within the gay, lesbian, and bisexual community*. Different individuals are at different levels of comfort with their sexual orientation. While a social worker might label a client as bisexual based on his or her sexual history, a client who is old may not use this term. Some clients are out to everyone while others may never have acknowledged to anyone that they are gay. The age at which someone discovered they were gay could have been at twenty or at fifty. Some may have a history of acceptance from family and friends while others may have experienced humiliating discrimination.

As noted earlier, there are important differences in the historical experiences of gay men and lesbians depending on the era in which they were born and on when they acknowledged a lesbian, gay, or bisexual orientation. Differences in how open or closeted a middle-aged or old gay man or lesbian is have already been described. It is important to note, however, that middle-

aged and old gay men and lesbians may also use different terminology in referring to themselves and to their sexual orientation than younger gay men and
lesbians do (Jacobson 1995). Those who work with lesbian, gay, and bisexual
older adults must inquire about and use whatever terminology the person is
most comfortable with.

Third, *recognize that not all problems a person has are associated with being gay
or lesbian or with being old*. It is relatively easy to fall into an ageist trap of thinking that because someone is old, they are tired or frail. In the same manner,
depending on a practitioner's view of gay and lesbian adults, there may be a
homophobic bias in seeing clients as frightened or depressed. An old gay man,
for example, can be depressed about many different things other than his sexuality or his age.

Fourth, *treat identified family as family*. Most gay or lesbian adults have created their own families, which may consist of some or all of their biological
family and some or all of their partner's family and other friends who are supportive of their sexual orientation. One of the greatest fears of old gay and
lesbian adults is that when the time comes for critical decisions to be made
about one's health by "family members," physicians and health care providers
will not recognize gay or lesbian partners as family. Rather, they will turn to
sons or daughters who, while they have the legal right to make choices, may
or may not be the chosen decision-maker for the patient.

Five, *plan activities and discussions that are neutral with respect to sexual orientation*. In one senior center, for example, a discussion group that had offered a
Valentine's Day discussion about "husbands and wives" changed the topic to
"those I have loved." Another senior center started having round dances and
ethnic dancing that did not involve male-female partners.

Last, *create an atmosphere among staff that is open to discussion about difference
but that does not tolerate discrimination based on sexual orientation*. Although many
agencies do very good work with staff training and sensitivity to diversity, including sexual orientation, personnel change over time. New questions are
raised particularly as new clients and circumstances may challenge the norms
of an agency. To create an environment in which staff members can safely express their ignorance of an issue is difficult but not impossible.

Politics and Policy: Creating the Future

Citizens in the upper ranges of the middle-aged and the old are becoming widely recognized as one of the most effective and empowered political constituencies in the United States. In the 1992 presidential election, 71 percent of those
over the age of sixty voted, while only 58 percent of people ages twenty-five to

forty-five voted, and the voting rate for the newly enfranchised young was lower still. The voting behavior of the old is matched by their participation in lobbying groups that seek to represent their interests. The old are generally active and effective advocates for their own interests. Fernando M. Torres-Gil, a social worker and assistant secretary for aging in the Department of Health and Human Services (HHS), and Michelle Puccinelle (1995) note that the "politics of the new aging" will change dramatically in the twenty-first century. Specifically, they cite increasing longevity, greater diversity among the old, and escaping generational tensions as the dominant themes that will influence the relations between the generations in the political and public policy arena.

The modern gay and lesbian movement has gained great strength since the 1969 Stonewall Rebellion, generally recognized as the benchmark of the modern gay and lesbian civil rights movement (Duberman 1993). The social movement for gay and lesbian civil rights has helped to soften social attitudes and the stigma of different sexual orientations. Shilts (1993) notes that the gay and lesbian rights movement was most effective on college campuses and as a result college-educated people had a greater chance of learning about different sexual orientations in a less hostile and stigmatized environment. In addition to helping to soften public attitudes, this civil rights movement has helped mobilize the political power of gays and lesbians. Currently, several openly gay and lesbian people are serving in elected office and the strength of this constituency is growing. This burgeoning strength has significantly affected the public policy debate, including the defeat of various antigay and anti-lesbian initiatives in several states.

Nevertheless, the successes of the gay and lesbian liberation movement, while significant, are not yet enough. Urvashi Vaid (1995), a longtime national leader, cautions that the movement has yielded not freedom and full citizenship but rather a state of what she calls "virtual equality":

> In this state [of virtual equality], gay and lesbian people possess some of the trappings of full equality but are denied all of its benefits. We proceed as if we enjoy real freedom, real acceptance, as if we have won lasting changes in the laws and mores of our nation. Some of us even believe that the simulation of equality we have won represents the real thing. But the actual facts and conditions that define gay and lesbian life demonstrate that we have won "virtual" freedom and "virtual" equal treatment under "virtually" the same laws as straight people.
>
> In this state of virtual equality, gay and lesbian people are at once insiders, involved openly in government and public affairs to a degree never before

achieved, and outsiders, shunned by our elected officials unless they need our money or votes in close elections.   (Vaid 1995:4)

Both the aged lobby and the gay and lesbian rights movement have overlapping issues and membership. Each of these social movements recognizes that greater diversity is in their interests. Both would be enriched by greater contact and cooperation, and together they could amplify the clout of their individual constituencies (Lee 1990). For this to happen, very conscious action and some risks will need to be taken by both sides. Recognizing the special place and perspective of old gay, lesbian, and bisexual people, especially those who are politically active, would enrich the policy agendas and advocacy efforts of both groups.

Part 3

ぉ

Special Issues

9

Mental Health and Substance Abuse

Mental health and substance abuse issues have been among the most controversial in relation to lesbian, gay, and bisexual people. Homophobia and heterosexism have been major influences in both fields. This chapter briefly reviews these controversies and presents current evidence about the prevalence of mental health and substance abuse disorders among gay, lesbian, and bisexual people. Principles of *affirmative practice* with gay, lesbian, and bisexual people related both to mental health and substance abuse are emphasized.

In the past a gay, lesbian, or bisexual orientation was often seen by definition as a mental health problem, and lesbian, gay, and bisexual people and their families sometimes sought mental health treatment for that reason alone. Similarly, excessive alcohol and even drug use were seen as part of a pattern of more general personality problems, of gender maladjustment, or of the deviant lifestyle of the demimonde that was only to be expected when a person was lesbian, gay, or bisexual. These views have been successfully challenged in recent decades, and a lesbian, gay, or bisexual orientation per se is no longer seen as related to any type of mental health problem or as inherently leading to substance abuse. This change in point of view resulted from the combined efforts of enlightened professionals and researchers and of activists, many of them lesbian or gay, who challenged medical, mental health, and substance abuse professionals on both scientific and ethical grounds. However, these earlier views and the battles to change them have left scars—among some mental health professionals who still defend discredited practices and among gay, lesbian, and bisexual people and their advocates who remain suspicious of mental health and substance abuse professionals and services. These earlier views, coupled with society's homophobia and heterosexism, have also delayed the development of sound and reliable knowledge about mental health and lesbian, gay, and bisexual people (Dunkle 1994).

This book is focused on common life stage issues, problems in living, and psychosocial stresses experienced by gay men, lesbians, and bisexual people—not major psychiatric problems. Thus the problems discussed exclude those involving serious psychopathology or gross social dysfunction requiring intensive psychiatric intervention. References useful for these more serious problems include Alexander (1996), Falco (1991), Gonsiorek (1985), Ross (1988), or the *Journal of Gay and Lesbian Psychotherapy*. Therefore this chapter addresses the more common mental health and substance abuse problems encountered in this population.

This chapter is written in the conviction that mental health and substance abuse services can be effective for lesbian, gay, and bisexual people who happen to have mental health or substance abuse problems *when such services are delivered in a nonheterosexist, nonhomophobic, well-informed, and gay-affirmative fashion*. In fact, we now understand that many of the mental health and substance abuse problems of lesbian, gay, and bisexual people result from the stresses that come from living in a homophobic and heterosexist society.

Social workers are the largest professional group delivering mental health services in the United States today, and they are increasingly involved in alcohol and drug abuse treatment as well. Therefore it is likely that lesbian, gay, and bisexual people who seek out and use mental health and substance abuse services will receive help from social workers. Since a higher proportion of lesbian and gay individuals seek out mental health services compared to heterosexuals (Rudolph 1989a), it is also likely that social workers in mental health and substance abuse regularly encounter lesbian, gay, and bisexual people among the clients and families that they serve even though sexual orientation itself is unlikely to be the focus of service.

This chapter will briefly review the painful history that still colors encounters between lesbian, gay, and bisexual people and the mental health system; review current information about the ineffectiveness of mental health interventions to change sexual orientation; discuss what is now known about the incidence and prevalence of mental health and substance abuse problems among lesbian, gay, and bisexual people; and describe the principles that underlie affirmative mental health and substance abuse practice with lesbian, gay, and bisexual people.

Mental Health: From Dysfunction to Difference

Most contemporary discussions of mental health and homosexuality point to a watershed event: the 1973 decision of the American Psychiatric Association to eliminate homosexuality as a recognized psychiatric disorder, a decision soon endorsed by the American Psychological Association (Deutsch 1995; Lewes 1988). Unlike the American Psychiatric Association, which publishes the *Diagnostic and Statistical Manual of Mental Disorders* (1994), the National Association of Social Workers (NASW) does not produce an official listing of mental illnesses; however, in 1977 NASW, the nation's largest organization of social workers, adopted an official policy statement (subsequently revised and expanded) endorsing the actions of the American Psychiatric and Psychological Associations and calling for an end to all forms of discrimination against gay and lesbian people (NASW 1991). In 1980 the NASW's *Code of Ethics* was revised to include sexual orientation in its nondiscrimination clause (NASW 1980), a change retained in its latest revision (NASW 1996). However, both homosexuality itself and ego-dystonic homosexuality (see below) are still included in the World Health Organization's International Classification of Diseases despite evidence that homosexuality is defined very differently in different cultures and societies, is stigmatized in only a relatively small percentage of societies, and in any case cannot meet the criteria that define a mental disorder (Ross, Paulsen, & Stalstrom 1988). Despite the time that has passed since this change in diagnostic thinking was formally enacted, the decision remains controversial among a minority of mental health practitioners (Deutsch 1995; Gonsiorek 1991; Smith 1988), and the prior history of being pathologized still affects the attitudes of many lesbian, gay, and bisexual people toward mental health care and mental health care providers.

Psychoanalytic theory is often blamed for the past practice of pathologizing a same-gender sexual orientation. A more sophisticated examination of that theory, however, suggests that there has been variation over time and among psychodynamic and psychoanalytic thinkers and practitioners in the humaneness of their approach to gay and lesbian clients (Cornett & Hudson 1985; Deutsch 1995; Friedman 1988; Lewes 1988). All psychodynamic thinkers seek the roots of their beliefs in the work of Sigmund Freud. Because he wrote so extensively and over such a long period of time, there is generally variation in what Freud said on any given topic, which is true of his writing about homosexuality as well (Deutsch 1995; Friedman 1988; Lewes 1988; O'Connor & Ryan 1993). Therefore, both those with more humane views and those with more negative views could invoke Freud to support their positions. In fact, a case can be made that it was specifically neo-Freudians of the midcentury in the United States, not Freud himself, who had the most negative views of homosexuality and who had the greatest influence on oppressive practices in psychiatry toward gay and lesbian people (Cornett & Hudson 1986; Lewes 1988). Although few practice psychoanalysis as a form of treatment these days, because psychoanalytic thinking has been so influential in American mental health treatment in general and in clinical social work practice in particular, a brief review of the changes in psychoanalytic views of same-gender sexual orientations is useful in understanding mental health issues today as they affect lesbian, gay, and bisexual people and their families.

It should be noted, too, that most of the discourse and research on same-gender sexual orientation in psychiatry and psychology was directed to male homosexuality (O'Connor & Ryan 1993). While women who expressed a same-gender sexual orientation were also pathologized (Deutsch 1995; Magee & Miller 1992; Suchet 1995), in general much less was said or written about them (O'Connor & Ryan 1993). Views of homosexuality, especially lesbianism, were profoundly influenced by negative views of women (Magee & Miller 1992; Suchet 1995). Bisexuality has even less often been addressed, and it has sometimes been described in relation to homosexuality and sometimes in relation to heterosexuality (Friedman 1988). Most often it has been described as a state that is likely temporary as a person moves to a heterosexual or homosexual orientation.

There were several themes in past thinking about the inherent pathology of a same-gender sexual orientation. Many of them arose from what was an unexamined moral overlay that condemned any sexuality that was by definition not related to procreation (Lewes 1988; Suchet 1995), clearly a heterosexist assumption. Choosing an object of desire of the opposite gender was seen as an essential part of developing a "normal" gender identity (Cornett & Hudson 1986; Deutsch 1995; Lewes 1988; O'Connor & Ryan 1993; Suchet 1995), a heterosexist idea. The term *inversion* was therefore sometimes used to describe lesbian or gay people (O'Connor & Ryan 1993; Pillard 1991), confounding their object choice with their gender identity (Suchet 1995).

A gay or lesbian identity per se has also been regarded as evidence of psychopathology (Gonsiorek 1991; Suchet 1995). In particular, disorders involving paranoia, masochism, and narcissism were hypothesized to be associated with homosexuality (Friedman 1988). Lesbians were often described as "infantile, orally fixated, sadomasochistic, and envious of those who possess what they really desire—the penis" (Deutsch 1995:23), in terms of diagnosis as "borderline at best" (Deutsch 1995:19). Confusion with "the perversions," with psychosexual phenomena such as transsexualism, pedophilia, or fetishism, also occurred (Deutsch 1995; O'Connor & Ryan 1993; Smith 1988). One legacy of this last phenomenon has been tensions between those who define themselves as transgendered (including those who would be called transsexuals and transvestites by psychiatrists) and those who define themselves as lesbian, gay, and/or bisexual but who want to establish the intellectual and political claim that their own gender identity and role behavior is merely a variation of the "normal" and to distance themselves from the incorrect thinking of the past and of the pejorative psychiatric label of "perversion."

The concept of bisexuality has also been surrounded with controversy within psychoanalytic theory. Based on an evolutionary perspective, Freud posited an innate bisexuality that in individuals would tend to resolve into, most often, a heterosexual object choice (Cornett & Hudson 1986; Fox 1995). Since homosexuality, male or female, was the label generally applied to anyone who expressed any degree of same-gender desire or behavior, there was some acknowledgment that same-gender and opposite-gender sexuality could and did exist at times in the same individual. Many, however, even in the field of lesbian and gay identity theory, saw bisexuality as a transitional state that should be resolved into a predominantly homosexual or, usually preferably, exclusively heterosexual identity (Fox 1995). Thus the bisexual person was often seen as inadequately heterosexual *and* inadequately homosexual. While contemporary thinking acknowledges that the number of people who identify as bisexual is quite small, sexual orientation is less often seen as dichotomous and immutable, making room for the possibility of bisexuality as "a distinct sexual orientation and identity" (Fox 1995:53) that is no more connected by definition to mental disorder than any other sexual orientation is. In fact, research done in the 1970s paralleling that done on homosexuality found that men and women who identified themselves as bisexual showed no evidence of elevated levels of psychopathology or psychological maladjustment (Fox 1995).

The clinical experience that informed much past writing about gay, lesbian, and bisexual people cannot be wished away. Certainly there are lesbian, gay, and bisexual people who suffer from psychological disorders such as narcissistic and borderline personality problems, severe depression, and even psychotic disturbances. These individuals suffer and, seeking relief, often enter psychiatric or other forms of mental health treatment. One of the great logical flaws in the psychoanalytic argument about the pathology of homosexuality arose from the basic fact that these observations were based on *clinical populations*, that is, on people who had mental health problems and were seeking mental health treatment (Gonsiorek 1991; Suchet 1995). They were not descriptive of the great majority of lesbian, gay, or bisexual people who, at any one point in time, are functioning very well psychologically and socially (Gonsiorek 1991). Therefore a major new line of research was needed to document the existence of "the happy homosexual" that theory said could not by definition exist, a line of research that began with Evelyn Hooker's work on gay men in the late 1950s (Hooker 1957). Subsequent psychological research conducted over the next twenty-five years on both males and females repeatedly found that there were no significant differences in psychological functioning between homosexual and heterosexual individuals (Gonsiorek 1991).

Another line of research that has had an effect on professional thinking about the mental health of lesbian and gay people has been research on sexuality. The famous Kinsey studies conducted in the late 1940s demonstrated that homosexual behavior was far more common, especially among men, than had previously been thought (Kinsey, Pomeroy, & Martin 1948; Kinsey et al. 1953). If one in ten men could be called homosexual, it was hard to imagine that such a high proportion of men should also be called psychiatrically impaired. The Masters and Johnson (1966, 1976) studies of the female sexual response had a major effect in a different way: by establishing that there was no difference between a clitoral and a vaginal orgasm, their work undercut prevailing arguments that heterosexual sexuality was "better than" same-gender sexual expression (and also affected many heterosexual women previously deemed "frigid" based on the way they achieved orgasm, the group that Masters and Johnson was in fact interested in helping). However, their work suggesting that behavioral techniques could be used to alter sexual orientation has been discredited (see next section, below).

Modern psychoanalytic and psychodynamic thinkers emphasize the capacity for intimacy, not the nature of the partner in such intimacy, as the hallmark of psychological health. As Deutsch (1995) expresses it when writing about women, "establishing a lesbian identity represents a developmental *accomplishment*: . . . developing an authentic sexuality embedded in an intimate relationship" being the goal (34; emphasis in the original).

In sum, contemporary psychodynamic and social psychological thinking have converged in the understanding that, both for men and for women, there are a variety of "homosexualities" (Bell & Weinberg 1978; Lewes 1988; O'Connor & Ryan 1993). The same psychological disorders and dysfunctions occur in both homosexual and heterosexual people, and there is similarly a wide range of psychological functioning among gay and lesbian people from quite healthy to quite impaired (Friedman 1988; Lewes 1988). However, there is no apparent difference in current rates of psychiatric disorder between homosexual and heterosexual people (Friedman & Downey 1994).

"REPARATIVE AND CONVERSION" THERAPIES

If a same-gender sexual orientation is not in itself an illness, then there is no logic in the idea that becoming heterosexual should be a goal of mental health treatment or a sign of optimal psychological functioning and development. Nevertheless, there are still some mental health practitioners, most of them psychiatrists or psychologists but some clinical social workers, who continue to practice reparative or conversion therapies that have as their explicit goal helping lesbian and gay people to become heterosexual. Therapies of this type have been tried throughout this century and have involved all kinds of techniques, from psychoanalytic approaches through sexual and/or behavioral treatments, including painful "aversion" therapies involving "negative reinforcements" such as the application of electrical shocks to the patient at any sign of sexual arousal to a same-gender stimulus. Despite decades of research on them, because there is no evidence that any such "reparative," aversion or conversion therapies can work—except perhaps in shifting the balance of same-gender and opposite gender fantasies and behavior in persons attracted to both genders (Friedman & Downey 1994)—it is considered unethical to engage in such practices today (Haldeman 1991; Stein 1988) (see figure 9.1). It should also be noted that, outside the formal mental health treatment system, there are many religion-based programs that offer to "cure" homosexuality. These programs are often based on arguments already discredited in the mental health establishment, and there is no evidence that the religion-based "conversion" treatments work either (Haldeman 1991).

Understanding the lack of logic and lack of success of such "treatments" should make suspect as well the more common and subtle forms of therapy to treat what has sometimes been termed "ego-dystonic homosexuality," no longer an official diagnosis since the mid-1980s (Gonsiorek 1991). Because of the pervasiveness of heterosexism and homophobia and their destructive effects on lesbian, gay, and bisexual people, "Ego dystonicity is not helpful in evaluating whether homosexual patients should be considered healthy or unhealthy. . . . Homosexual individuals should not be considered psychologi-

Figure 9.1

Position Statement

"REPARATIVE" OR "CONVERSION" THERAPIES FOR LESBIANS AND GAY MEN

The National Association of Social Workers' Code of Ethics states, "The social worker should not practice, condone, facilitate or collaborate with any form of discrimination on the basis of . . . sexual orientation."

Prepared by NASW—National Committee on Lesbian and Gay Issues

The National Association of Social Workers' National Committee on Lesbian and Gay Issues (NCOLGI) is greatly concerned about the public attention being drawn to so-called reparative or conversion therapies which purport to change the sexual orientation of lesbians and gays. NCOLGI is particularly concerned that persons confused about their sexual orientation may be drawn into allegedly therapeutic work which cannot and will not change sexual orientation, but which can lead to severe emotional damage. Proponents of reparative therapies claim—without documentation—many successes. They assert that their processes are supported by conclusive scientific data which are in fact a little more than anecdotal. NCOLGI protests these efforts to "convert" people through irresponsible therapies which can more accurately be called brainwashing, shaming, or coercion. These therapies, and those who espouse these, are evidence that homophobia is a continuing threat to the psychological well-being and civil liberties of lesbian and gay persons.

By adopting reparative therapy methods advanced by Nicolisi, Bieber, Socarides et al. (whose theories about the cause and consequences of homosexuality have been discredited by empirical studies), a social worker may apply techniques which can cause considerable psychological anguish for a client and, in the process, reinforce external and internal homophobia, and prejudice and stereotypes about lesbians and gays. The assumptions and directions of reparative therapies are theoretically and morally wrong. The desired outcome of the reparative therapies are either a commitment to celibacy, or heterosexual marriage.

That same-sex relationships can be fulfilling or are natural for lesbians and gays is consistently denied. Sweeping generalizations are made in the name of science, but without any of the rigor science requires. Empirical research does not demonstrate that homosexuality is more likely than heterosexuality to be associated with psychopathology, or that sexual orientation (heterosexual or homosexual) can be changed through these so-called reparative therapies.

Social workers practicing with lesbian and gay clients may need to be especially aware of the value of non judgmental attitudes towards sexual orientation. If a client is uncomfortable about his/her sexual orientation, the sources of discomfort must be explored, but without a prior assumption that same-sex attraction is dysfunctional. Open and non judgmental attitudes by social workers enhance their ability to offer optimal support and services to lesbians and gays. Social workers must encourage development of supportive practice environments for lesbian and gay clients, and social workers.

The National Committee on Lesbian and Gay Issues believes that the use of reparative or conversion therapies by social workers violates the National Association of Social Workers policy statement on lesbian and gay issues (1987), particularly with regard to discrimination and oppression of lesbians and gays. NCOLGI further believes that the use of these therapies violates the professional *Code of Ethics* which specifically states:

> The social workers should act to prevent and eliminate discrimination against any person or group on the basis of race, color, sex, sexual orientation, age, religion, national origin, marital status, political belief, mental or physical handicap, or any other preference or personal characteristic, condition or status (Code of ethics), VI, paragraph 1, page 9, emphasis supplied.

Since 1977, the National Association of Social Workers has advanced a policy opposing discrimination directed against lesbians and gays. All social workers have an ethical obligation to work actively against oppression in all of its forms, including the oppression and homophobia so explicit in the so-called reparative therapies.

NOTE: Members of NCOLGI are available to provide consultation to individuals or chapters on the issue addressed in this statement, or on other issues pertaining to lesbian and gay concerns.

Members may be reached by calling the national office of NASW and asking for staff members for NCOLGI.

For information on research on sexual orientation, practitioners will find value in Gonsiorek & Weinrich eds. (1991). *Homosexuality: Research implications for public policy*, New York: Sage. Martin Duberman (1991) offers a personal account of the destructive effects of conversion therapies in his *Cures: A gay man's odyssey.* (New York: Dutton).

Prepared in 1992 by the National Association of Social Workers' National Committee on Lesbian and Gay Issues, 750 First Street, NE, Suite 750, Washington, DC 20002-4241.

cally ill simply because of their perceptions of and judgments about their homosexuality" (Lewes 1988:186). Smith (1988) has stated that siding with a patient's wish to change his or her sexual orientation "constitutes siding with the defensive structure of the patient, and impedes natural development of conflict-free adjustment as homosexual. . . . Their psychopathology is not their homosexual thoughts, feelings and behaviors, but rather their internalized and self-directed homophobia which impairs self-acceptance and the establishment of adaptive and sexually fulfilling lifestyles" (68–69). This point of view is the predominant one in psychodynamically informed clinical social work practice today. As Deutsch (1995) puts it:

> Attempts to alter sexual orientation violate basic tenets of psychoanalysis in favor of social control; they are a harmful misuse of analytic authority. The therapeutic solution is a neutrality that includes recognition of reality: prejudice against lesbians is pervasive in the culture and in analytic relationships. In the case of lesbian, gay, and bisexual patients, the reality includes coercion, oppression, and societal hatred that is defensively internalized.
>
> (Deutsch 1995:32)

Thus one emphasis in modern psychodynamic thinking is shifting toward an analysis of the toll that homophobia and heterosexism can take on psychological and social development (Deutsch 1995; Friedman 1988). Another, based in feminist and postmodernist thinking, is toward positing bisexuality as innate, especially for women, emphasizing the independence of gender identity and object choice (Suchet 1995).

The definition of psychotherapy varies considerably among different schools of therapy: psychoanalytic or psychodynamic, behavioral, and humanistic. There also exists a wide range of interventions or approaches among these various schools which may be confusing to the individual seeking psychotherapy. There does not appear, however, to be any inherent characteristic of a given theoretical school which in its nature is antithetical to conducting psychotherapy in a helpful manner with gay men and lesbians, once the belief is removed that homosexuality is by definition an expression of pathology (Stein 1988). He also reports that no particular mode of psychotherapy appears to be any more effective than another in working with gay men and lesbians if the characteristics of this population are viewed by a therapist as consistent with the treatment offered within a given mode.

The personal characteristics of the therapist, including a nonhomophobic, nonheterosexist attitude, and especially the capacity to establish an empathic relationship with the client, may constitute the most important factors in determining the ultimate effectiveness of the therapeutic endeavor rather than the theoretical school of the therapist (Goldstein 1992; Kottler 1991; Stein 1988).

Substance Abuse: Psychological or Social?

While the mental health field is now recognizing that there is little difference in the mental health status of gays and lesbians compared to heterosexuals, in the substance abuse field the available evidence continues to suggest that substance abuse problems, especially problems with alcohol overuse, may be more common among gay and lesbian people than among heterosexuals[1] (Friedman & Downey 1994; Ratner 1993). This finding may hold true only for different age cohorts. Jazwinski (1994), in a study of gay, lesbian, and heterosexual college students and drinking, found that no relationship existed between sexual orientation and alcohol use. The only difference was that gay, lesbian, and bisexual students were more likely than their heterosexual counterparts to drink in bars—but this did not result in any increase in any of the drinking measures or problems due to drinking for gays and lesbians. In part, the higher levels of drinking previously noted may result from the use of gay bars as a sample source (Friedman & Downey 1994). While previous views of the problem tended to equate this greater level of substance use with the assumed pathology of a lesbian or gay sexual orientation, contemporary views of the problem emphasize the vulnerabilities that arise from the social stresses imposed by heterosexism and homophobia, the limited opportunities for open same-gender dating and socializing that may lead gays and lesbians into environments such as bars that support or encourage substance use, and the obstacles to effective and gay- or lesbian-friendly substance abuse treatment that still exist (Ratner 1993). Thus the view of substance abuse problems among gay and lesbian people has evolved from psychological to social.

MENTAL HEALTH AND SUBSTANCE ABUSE PROBLEMS AMONG LESBIANS AND GAYS

Adding to the debates about the mental health of lesbian, gay, and bisexual people, there are only limited epidemiological data on the incidence and prevalence of mental health and substance abuse problems in these groups (Rothblum 1994). Large-scale population studies of the epidemiology of mental and emotional disorders do not ascertain if respondents are lesbian, gay, and/or bisexual because they do not ask questions about the full range of sexual behaviors necessary to make such a determination. Nor is there a commonly accepted definition of sexual orientation, or even agreement about whether it should be treated as a set of dichotomous possibilities or as a continuum. Even surveys designed specifically to determine how many people are lesbian, gay, or bisexual have involved controversy about how sexual orientation is defined and about whether respondents actually and accurately disclose their same-gender sexual activities, past and/or present (see, for example, Laumann et al. 1994; also see chapter 2). These studies of sexual orientation or behavior do not, in turn, include information on mental health.

The alternatives to studies of the general population are unsatisfactory in different ways. Studies based on clinical populations—that is, on people in treatment—do not by definition include lesbian, gay, and bisexual people who are not suffering psychologically and therefore do not seek treatment. Studies based on populations of people who self-identify as lesbian, gay, or bisexual are limited by the difficulties inherent in reaching the full range of lesbian, gay, and bisexual people, especially those who shy away from identifying themselves as such, who live in low population-density areas, and/or who may also identify as members of racial and/or ethnic minority groups (see, for example, Bell & Weinberg 1978; Gonsiorek 1991; and Rothblum 1994 as well as Herek et al. 1991, for good discussions of these sampling difficulties).

Despite these limitations in the data, it is important to review the information that is currently available about the incidence and prevalence of defined mental health and substance abuse disorders among lesbian, gay, and bisexual people. The studies that do exist have been done in a variety of ways and on a variety of different populations. *Taken together, the results of these studies show that mental and emotional disorders are in general no more common or uncommon in lesbian, gay, and bisexual people than among those who are heterosexual.* However, there are certain *specific* disorders that have been shown in several studies to occur with greater frequency among lesbian and/or gay people, and these are described here.

Despite the fact that there is no discernible difference in the overall mental health of lesbian and gay as compared to heterosexual people, there is some evidence that gay and lesbian people may seek out psychotherapy services somewhat more often than others (Bradford, Ryan, & Rothblum 1994; Gonsiorek 1991; Rudolph 1989a). However, in surveys, more of them report "dissatisfaction with their treatment" than heterosexuals do (Rudolph 1989a:8). Therefore it is essential that mental health providers know realistically about the mental health risks that do—and do not—seem to occur with greater frequency among lesbian, gay, and bisexual people and about how to work more effectively with them.

Some authors conclude that there is a difference in the lifetime prevalence of depression (Friedman & Downey 1994) or possibly in chronic depression or dysthymic disorder (Gonsiorek 1991; Smith 1988). This difference has generally been explained in relation to painful childhoods and/or other stressors connected with homophobia, including victimization, that are translated into painful internal states in some way (Friedman & Downey 1994; Odets & Skinner 1996). Rofes (1996) describes a sense of doom and terror in the gay community because of AIDS. The human system is overwhelmed beyond capacity and it simply shuts down. The immersion in an environment of sickness and death fractures thinking and obscures vision. Many gay men and lesbians are "shell-shocked" for protracted periods of time, similar to post-traumatic stress disorder (PTSD). Some suggest that this phenomenon is also related to a higher lifetime prevalence of suicide attempts, especially among young people (Bradford, Ryan, & Rothblum 1994; Friedman & Downey 1994; Gonsiorek 1991; Savin-Williams 1994; Smith 1988). One study of risk factors for suicide attempts among gay, lesbian, and bisexual youth found that self-reports of family relations, social environment, and self-perceptions, including symptoms of depression, were all related to the likelihood that a teen might think about or actually attempt suicide (Proctor & Groze 1994). Thus social stresses and lack of parental support are implicated. A survey of lesbian women suggested that the risk of attempted suicide may be higher for African-American and Latina women than for whites (Bradford, Ryan, & Rothblum 1994). Whether or not suicide is an issue, isolation and/or estrangement, both in their own racial or ethnic community and in the gay or lesbian community, can be problems for gay and lesbian clients of color (Greene 1994a).

Problems with alcohol and the use of drugs such as marijuana and cocaine have been found to be more prevalent among gays and lesbians than among heterosexuals (Bradford, Ryan, & Rothblum 1994; Gonsiorek 1991; McKirnan & Peterson 1989a; Skinner 1994; Smith 1988). Several reasons have been advanced for the higher prevalence of alcohol problems observed among both lesbian and gay people. One is the high level of stress and anxiety that can be generated in living as a member of a socially stigmatized group and the fact that alcohol and other drugs can be used in response (McKirnan & Peterson 1989b; Smith 1988). In addition, bars have historically been the most readily identifiable location for the more open same-gender social and sexual interaction often needed for partnering and for socialization (Smith 1988), leading perhaps to lower rates of abstaining from alcohol (McKirnan & Peterson 1989a) or to more frequent or problematic drinking (McKirnan & Peterson 1989b). In general, alcohol use declines with age, but several studies have shown that this decline does not occur as frequently in lesbian and gay populations (Bradford, Ryan, & Rothblum 1994; McKirnan & Peterson 1989a; Skinner 1994), which is clearly one source of the overall difference. Thus older lesbians and gays may be at particular risk, either because their patterns of socialization do not change much or because they drink in response to social isolation (Bradford, Ryan, & Rothblum 1994). In addition, it is important to note that, while not an official disorder, cigarette smoking appears to be more common among lesbians and gay men than in the general population (Skinner 1994). Cigarettes are not only a "gateway" drug; their use also involves substantial and well-known health risks, clearly a significant public health problem in the lesbian and gay community. Finally, the amount and patterns of licit and illicit substance use, including both cigarettes and alcohol, differ somewhat between men and women, and thus there are significant differences in the amount and pattern of use of specific substances between lesbians and gay men (McKirnan & Peterson 1989a, 1989b; Skinner 1994). Therefore both gender and sexual orientation need to taken into account when dealing with the use of alcohol and other drugs.

Any discussion of mental health and substance abuse is not complete without at least mention of HIV/AIDS, especially for gay men. There are many mental health implications of HIV/AIDS (as will be discussed in chapter 11). Problems with substance abuse and/or impulse control in general can have lethal implications when it comes to being able to practice safe sex (Smith 1988). Being tested, being HIV-positive, or having AIDS can place severe stresses on the person with the illness and on those who care about him, and AIDS itself can produce neurologic and psychiatric symptoms as an inherent part of the illness's effects on the brain (Friedman & Downey 1994). However, apart from these neurologically-based difficulties, there is no firm evidence that rates of depression and suicide are any higher among AIDS sufferers than among others (Friedman & Downey 1994) despite the discrimination they often experience. Odets and Shernoff (1995) warn that while profound psychiatric disorders are distributed equally among sexual orientations, the AIDS-related problems amenable to therapy include safer sex maintenance, drug relapse, serodiscordant and HIV-positive couples coping with AIDS, family conflicts, parental expectations for HIV-infected women, bereavement, care and custody planning, long-term survivors' guilt, support for the worried well, and grief counseling for caregivers as well as a range of adjustment needs throughout the life cycle of HIV disease.

Clearly the list of mental health and substance abuse disorders that may be more common among lesbian and/or gay people is short. Given the prior prejudices of psychiatry and the other mental health professions toward lesbian, gay, and bisexual people, it is important to emphasize certain particular conditions that do *not* occur any more frequently among gays and lesbians than among heterosexuals. These include psychosexual disorders such as pedophilia (Smith 1988) and personality disorders, including narcissistic, borderline, masochistic, or other disorders (Gonsiorek 1991; Smith 1988). Nor is there any evidence of a higher rate of the childhood victimization of women among lesbians, including child sexual abuse (Bradford, Ryan, & Rothblum 1994). Thus theories that suggest these as either outcomes or causes of a same-gender sexual orientation are without foundation in fact.

PROTECTIVE FACTORS

As limited as the research on risk factors for psychiatric disorders among lesbian, gay, and/or bisexual people has been, even less attention has been given to those factors that place *heterosexual* men and women at risk for psychiatric disorders that do *not* apply to homosexual men and women. This absence of risk might be termed a set of "protective factors" that are part of a lesbian or gay way of life (Rothblum 1994). These risk and protective factors are gender-specific. For example, for women, being heterosexually married is a risk factor for a variety of problems, such as depression, anxiety, and abuse (Rothblum 1994). Similarly, having young children at home is related to stress among women. The role problems that are thought to explain these risks among heterosexual women do not obtain in lesbian relationships, even when children are present in the home, which occurs less often (Rothblum 1994). Gay men may enjoy greater access to high-quality health care given the higher incomes of men and the lower number of gay men supporting children than among heterosexuals, both factors that may be protective when it comes to stress and mental health as well (Rothblum 1994). The resilience of lesbian, gay, and bisexual people in the face of heterosexism and homophobia has often been cited in relation to the epidemiological findings with respect to mental health. *How* this resilience is achieved—that is, the identification of specific additional adaptive capacities or protective factors—has not yet been studied systematically at all.

Implications for Affirmative Practice—Mental Health

Even though there is no evidence of greater maladjustment among lesbian, gay, and bisexual people than among heterosexuals, lesbian and gay people have been found to use mental health, specifically, psychotherapeutic, services more often than others (Bradford, Ryan, & Rothblum 1994; Gonsiorek

1991; Rudolph 1989a). This difference in service utilization is usually attributed to the stresses that result from living in a heterosexist and homophobic society. Therefore it is essential that mental health services be accessible to and effective for lesbian, gay, and bisexual people. Minimally, those providing mental health services, including psychotherapy services, must be able to serve lesbian, gay, and bisexual people without bias or discrimination. Increasingly, however, the concept of *gay- or lesbian-affirmative practice* is becoming the goal to which those practicing in the mental health and substance abuse fields are striving. There is no particular theoretical approach to psychotherapy or other forms of mental health treatment nor any particular modality of treatment—individual, couple, family, or group—that cannot be made useful for lesbian, gay, or bisexual people if approached affirmatively (Dunkle 1994; Stein 1988).

Unfortunately, however, heterosexism and homophobia continue to affect mental health and psychotherapeutic services. While there has been no comparable study specifically of social work practitioners, a major large-scale survey of clinical psychologists conducted by the American Psychological Association's Committee on Lesbian and Gay Concerns (1991) identified a range of "biased, inadequate, or inappropriate practice[s]" (10) occurring in psychotherapy with lesbian and gay clients.[2] These documented instances of inappropriate practice included practicing based on the belief that homosexuality per se constituted evidence of pathology; actively discouraging a client "from having or adopting a gay or lesbian orientation" (12), seeking to change such an orientation even when not requested by the client; making the renouncing of a gay or lesbian orientation a condition of treatment, and/or expressing beliefs that "trivialize and/or demean" gay and/or lesbian experience or orientation (13); incorrectly attributing a client's problem to his or her sexual orientation and/or then focusing the intervention on sexual orientation rather than on the problem the client sought to address; overlooking the client's own negative attitudes toward homosexuality as a source of psychological distress that needed to be addressed or as an influence on development; terminating treatment because a client disclosed a gay or lesbian orientation; and disclosing a client's sexual orientation without permission or inappropriately. Many more practices stemming from insensitivity to or lack of accurate knowledge about gay and lesbian development and life experiences, including underestimating the homophobic or heterosexist behaviors that gay and lesbian clients are often exposed to, were also outlined. These occurred most often in relation to the intimate and family relationships of clients. Specific cases illustrating the forms of bias outlined were included in the report. In fact, homophobic attitudes on the part of a therapist, conscious or unconscious, can affect every aspect of the treatment process—from referral through history-taking and diagnosis, as well as the treatment process itself and its outcome (McHenry & Johnson 1993).

The APA report, however, also sought specific examples of knowledgeable and sensitive practice with gay and lesbian clients. Based on therapist responses, the report suggested that practitioners understand that a gay or lesbian sexual orientation does not in itself constitute evidence of psychopathology, is fully compatible with living a fulfilled and happy life, and is but one of many important attributes that a client has. However, the therapist should also not overlook the impact that homophobia and heterosexism may have on the life of the client or on his or her development, especially when combined with an ethnic or racial minority status. In addition, the therapist should be knowledgeable about gay and lesbian couple and family relationships, including the variability in them, and about community resources that may either be hostile to or helpful to lesbian and gay people.

Both the biased and the exemplary practices identified in this study of psychologists could also likely be found among social workers and others who practice in the mental health field. In addition, there are some issues that the study's authors acknowledge were not covered, such as HIV infection or AIDS, differences in the experiences of gay men and lesbians in therapy, the impact of the sexual orientation of the therapist, and a range of boundary issues, especially those that may arise when both the therapist and client are gay and/or lesbian, especially when they reside in the same community (Garnets et al. 1991). Nondiscrimination in practice, the primacy of client welfare and self-determination, and the commitment to competence, among others, are the ethical principles common to social work and psychology that undergird these practices and their definition as either positive or negative. Moreover, the study underscores the fact that the absence of misinformed and negative or biased practice is not enough for sensitive and effective practice with lesbian, gay, and bisexual clients.

It is not enough to support affirmative psychotherapy through verbal "should," and it is not enough to "just" practice what you preach. . . . Without research, affirmative psychotherapy may be passed over as unsubstantiated beliefs or even propaganda. In contrast, rigorous research may advance the scope and depth of current affirmative models and may broaden their acceptance among professional communities.

—Ann E. MacEachron (1995:25)

Although there has been little research on affirmative models of psychotherapy, some principles of gay- and/or lesbian-affirmative practice are being articulated. The principles that are part of affirmative mental health and/or psychotherapeutic practice closely reflect the ideas described as "exemplary" practice in the APA (1991) study described above. As Malyon (1982b) puts it, "The goals of gay-affirmative psychotherapy are similar to those of most traditional approaches to psychological treatment and include both conflict-resolution and self-actualization" (81).

The experiences of one clinician in a community mental health agency serving older adults illustrates the resistance that can be encountered in trying to serve gay and lesbian people. As she writes,

> when we began an outreach program for older gay men and lesbians, . . . we decided to start a support group. . . . When our proposal was first presented to the program staff, we were met with comments and questions such as: We don't have gay and lesbian clients; Why do gays and lesbians need a special support group? What if other clients feel uncomfortable? . . . Staff began to relay stories about current and previous clients: One was a gay man who had lost his lover of 28 years and wanted a bereavement group. The peer counselor who was leading the group felt uncomfortable having the gay man in the group. . . . Another staff member told of two women who had lived together as "sisters" and "friends" and yet didn't feel comfortable with in-home supportive services our agency could provide them due to extreme fear and shame. . . . When we first started putting flyers of our support group in the lobby, the stack of flyers would disappear within a day or two. This occurred a few times until I asked the receptionist what was happening. She told me a staff member was removing them. I met with the staff person and she admitted being concerned about having the flyers "so openly displayed."
>
> (Finzer 1997:4)

Staff responses like these are clear signals that education about gay, lesbian, and bisexual people and their needs, about overcoming heterosexism and homophobia, and about affirmative practice are needed.

Affirmative therapy has several other characteristics that are unique to work with lesbian, gay, and bisexual people. First of all, in most instances, a client in the mental health system does not begin the process of seeking help explicitly revealing a sexual orientation of any kind. In affirmative practice, the service provider *does not automatically assume that a client is heterosexual* (Hancock 1995). To do so generally makes it more difficult for a client who may be questioning his or her sexual orientation or who identifies as lesbian, gay, or bisexual to feel safe in disclosing important things that may or may not be related to whatever the presenting problem is but that are necessary to know in assessing and treating the client.

The assumption of heterosexuality is often expressed not only in the words of the treating practitioner; it is often also embedded in the total experience of the client, from the forms that he or she may be asked to fill out as part of the service delivery routine (which do not have a category to describe the relationship of a gay or lesbian couple or the co-parent of a child) to the office decor which may include images of only traditional couples or families. It is always difficult to ask for help; it is especially difficult to do so when the environment does not signal acceptance of the client.

Affirmative mental health practice assumes that it is "homophobia within the patient and in society that is the problem rather than . . . homosexuality" (Hanley-Hackenbruck 1988:32). *Same-gender sexual desires and behaviors instead are viewed as a normal variation in human sexuality* (Cohen & Stein 1986; Hall & Fradkin 1992). A belief that homosexuality per se represents pathology or developmental arrest is not compatible with gay- or lesbian-affirmative mental health practice (Hall & Fradkin 1992; Hanley-Hackenbruck 1988, 1989; Stein 1988). Because of homophobia and heterosexism, some people who experience same-gender sexual desires or behaviors or who begin to wonder if they are lesbian, gay, or bisexual experience feelings of fear, self-doubt, guilt, or "badness," which are clearly sources of psychological distress and even, perhaps, connected with psychiatric symptoms, such as depression and/or anxiety (Cabaj 1988; Hanley-Hackenbruck 1988, 1989). As Gonsiorek and Rudolph (1991) put it, "Negative feelings about one's sexual orientation may be overgeneralized to encompass the entire self" (166). Malyon (1982b) explains this dynamic as the incorporation of antigay prejudice into a negative self-image, which may also include a "self-imposed limit on aspirations," personal or vocational (Cabaj 1988:18). However, it is essential that any distress or negative self-image be understood on an individual basis and not be assumed to represent an inevitable part of a lesbian, gay, or bisexual identity.

An affirmative therapist or practitioner *accepts the adoption of a lesbian, gay, or bisexual identity as a positive outcome* of any process in which an individual is questioning or working on developing his or her sexual identity (Dunkle 1994; Hall & Fradkin 1992; Hanley-Hackenbruck 1988, 1989). Both attitudes toward and information about gay, lesbian, and bisexual identity formation contribute to affirmative practice. For example, knowing that studies of various kinds have demonstrated that the personal adjustment of lesbians and gay men do not differ in any significant way from that of heterosexual men and women is knowledge that can encourage a practitioner in his or her affirmative practice. Practicing with the assumption that the adoption of a lesbian, gay, or bisexual identity is positive may have special relevance to practice with adolescents: it has been noted that the practitioner who responds to an adolescent's disclosure of same-gender feelings, fantasies, or acts with the "reassurance" that they represent "confusion" typical of his or her age forecloses a chance to explore what meaning a gay, lesbian, or bisexual orientation has to the client, gay or straight, and likely leaves a gay, lesbian, or bisexual teen feeling abandoned and misunderstood (Teague 1992).

Accepting the development of a lesbian, gay, or bisexual identity as positive means that *a goal of affirmative practice is to reduce any internalized homophobia that a client may experience.* Some gay, lesbian, or bisexual clients may rather readily disclose feelings of shame or self-loathing that they connect to their same-gender sexual or affectional feelings or behavior or to their self-identification as lesbian, gay, or bisexual. Others may not. No one knows how widespread such feelings are among lesbian, gay, or bisexual people (Shidlo 1994). Internalized homophobia may be extreme or it may be more moderate and subtle in its manifestations (McHenry & Johnson 1993; Shidlo 1994). For example, Margolies, Becker, and Jackson-Brewer (1987) list such features as fear of exposure, discomfort with readily identifiable or overtly self-identified lesbian or gay people, defensive rejection or denigration of heterosexuals (although de Monteflores [1986] points out that this stance is usually transitory), uneasiness with the idea of children being reared by lesbian or gay parents, and low expectations for intimate relationships as being common indirect manifestations of internalized homophobia in lesbian clients. However, internalized homophobia also has to be distinguished from realistic perceptions of the challenges of being lesbian, gay, or bisexual in a heterosexist and homophobic society and from such other issues as fear of intimacy (Shidlo 1994). Internalized homophobia has been shown to be related to a variety of psychological and interpersonal problems, including alcoholism and other substance abuse, depression, and other forms of psychological distress (Malyon 1982b; Odets & Skinner 1996; Shidlo 1994). In addition, internalized homophobia affects gay and lesbian clients' expectations of treatment (Lease, Cogdal, & Smith 1995) and tends to make it more difficult for them to talk openly with their mental health providers, especially about their sexual orientation (McDermott, Tyndall, & Lichtenberg 1989).

For these reasons, affirmative mental health treatment should include efforts to identify and reduce internalized homophobia (Cohen & Stein 1986; Malyon 1982b; Shidlo 1994), which will then increase the range of emotional expression and personal choices available to clients, in treatment and in general (Margolies, Becker, & Jackson-Brewer 1987). As Margolies, Becker,

& Jackson-Brewer (1987) put it, "Clients need to discover and express discomfort, doubt, mourning, and fear, as well as pride and delight" (237).

Affirmative practitioners must be *knowledgeable about the coming out process, its variations, and its stages,* as well as about the typical differences in the process for men and women (Browning, Reynolds, & Dworkin 1991; Cohen & Stein 1986; de Monteflores 1986; Hanley-Hackenbruck 1988, 1989; Hall & Fradkin 1992; Hancock 1995; Shannon & Woods 1991). Knowledge about the coming out process aids in identifying the specific issues typically involved at each stage of the process and the factors that may predispose a client to having more difficulty in the process, such as a rigid, critical, or especially religious family of origin, early experiences of feeling "deviant" or different, and experiences of specific instances of homophobic discrimination, as well as other previous trauma history or other unrelated psychological difficulties (Hanley-Hackenbruck 1989). Whether a client seeks supportive mental health services for negotiating a developmental "crisis" around coming out or whether the process is complicated for him or her because of these or other factors, knowledge about coming out is essential for the therapist who is trying to help. Culture, ethnicity, class, and geographical location all influence the process (de Monteflores 1986; Hancock 1995; Shannon & Woods 1991; see also chapter 2). Since the coming out process usually involves overcoming some degree of internalized homophobia, psychotherapy and other mental health services, such as group treatment, can often be helpful during this process. Self-help groups and psychoeducational approaches of various kinds are also often useful.

There are other areas of knowledge that will help any mental health practitioner working with lesbian, gay, or bisexual clients to practice affirmatively. These include knowledge about antigay prejudice and identity management strategies and the skill to help clients distinguish between realistic and unrealistic fears about family reactions, workplace issues, and other potential homophobic reactions from others (Browning, Reynolds, & Dworkin 1991; Cabaj 1988; Hancock 1995; Shannon & Woods 1991). It is also important to know about lesbian and gay coupling, how it may be like and unlike the usual patterns of heterosexual relationships, how it may differ for men and women, and how HIV infection and/or AIDS may impact upon a relationship (Browning, Reynolds, & Dworkin 1991; Cabaj 1988; Hancock 1995; Shannon & Woods 1991; Stein 1988). Parenting issues may also be relevant (Stein 1988), and knowledge about the options currently available to gay men and lesbians in this area is also essential (Hancock 1995). Those who are seriously and persistently mentally ill and who are also lesbian or gay may benefit from group treatment that addresses their simultaneous need for help with sexual orientation issues and for psychoeducation related to their illness and its treatment (Helfand 1993).

Knowledge about HIV/AIDS issues is also essential, especially for work with gay men (Shannon & Woods 1991; see also chapter 11). However, it is important to note that

> The risk of a psychiatric disorder in a person who is HIV-positive apparently depends less on symptoms of the disease itself than on other personal characteristics and life circumstances, such as limited social supports, low income, unemployment, homelessness, family history of mental illness, recent bereavement, or trauma. Recent studies indicate lower rates of emotional distress and psychiatric disorder than earlier reports. . . [perhaps] due to the improved scientific understanding of the natural history of the disease, better medical and psychosocial treatment, and community support networks, all of which reduce the burden of isolation and uncertainty.
>
> (Appleby 1995:14)

Nevertheless, initial diagnosis or a change in health status, dealing with long-term care and the strains that chronic illness and long-term care can put on a relationship, or actual or impending bereavement, are issues for which mental health services can often be helpful (Dunkle 1994).

Finally, an essential part of affirmative mental health practice with lesbian, gay, and bisexual people is that *the practitioner must learn to deal with his or her own homophobia and heterosexual bias* (Cabaj 1988; Hall & Fradkin 1992; Hancock 1995; McHenry & Johnson 1993; Stein 1988). This needs to be done *whatever the sexual orientation of the practitioner* is since everyone in the United States has grown up and has been professionally educated in the context of a homophobic and heterosexist society to one degree or another (McHenry & Johnson 1993; Stein 1988). In addition, it is essential that the practitioner feel comfortable with his or her own sexuality and in working with sexual issues that the client may bring to treatment (Cabaj 1988; Fassinger 1991).

Many gay and lesbian people express a preference for a gay or lesbian mental health professional, but many others do not (McDermott, Tyndall, & Lichtenberg 1989). Knowing or not knowing the sexual orientation of the practitioner, whatever it is, can have a variety of meanings to the lesbian, gay, or bisexual client which may need to be carefully examined (Stein 1988). Even when client and therapist differ in sexual orientation, it is important for both to be able to feel that they are more alike than different while not overlooking any differences in experiences and attitudes which may in fact exist. In some ways, this process is not likely to be much different from dealing with other issues of difference, such as gender, race, or ethnicity, that may obtain in the therapeutic relationship. However, to the extent that feelings of closeness or sexuality may arise in a therapeutic relationship, the therapist, especially a heterosexual one, must be prepared to deal with them in the same-gender context.

In summary, key features of affirmative therapy with lesbian, gay, and bisexual clients can be outlined. Studies of treatment process or outcome with lesbian, gay, or bisexual clients, however, are few (Dunkle 1994). In addition, most of the theoretical and empirical literature that does address therapy with gay and lesbian clients does not include bisexuality. Clearly, more research is needed, both process and outcome studies, focusing on therapy with lesbian, gay, and bisexual clients and on the training and education needed for those who provide mental health services to them (Browning, Reynolds, & Dworkin 1991; Dunkle 1994; Gonsiorek & Rudolph 1991; Hancock 1995; Mac-Eachron 1995).

Issues in Substance Abuse Treatment

Unlike mental health problems, substance abuse problems, particularly problems with alcohol, are thought to be more prevalent among lesbian and gay people than among heterosexuals (Bickelhaupt 1995; Bradford, Ryan, & Rothblum 1994; Friedman & Downey 1994; Gonsiorek 1991; McKirnan & Peterson 1989a, 1989b; Ratner 1993; Skinner 1994). Whatever the cause of this phenomenon, which is currently poorly understood, this fact makes it essential that those who work with substance abuse problems be knowledgeable about gay, lesbian, and bisexual people and about how to work successfully with them since it is very likely that they will find them among their clients. All the principles related to affirmative mental health practice apply as well to the substance abuse field, but there are some special issues to consider in practice in the substance abuse field as well. These issues have been described by some activist substance abuse professionals in terms of *denial*, a key concept in the substance abuse field:

> The gay and lesbian communities have long been in denial of alcoholism and drug addiction as problems. They have often not acknowledged its epidemic proportions and ignored the truths that alcoholism and drug abuse cripple and kill. And the alcoholism and drug addiction treatment fields have long been in denial of their own homophobia and resulting destructive behavior. Too often they have ignored and not dealt with the major issues of sexuality, sexual orientation, sexual identity and as a result have failed at times to give proper treatment. (Finnegan & McNally 1995:84)

There has not been to date any large-scale study of substance abuse practice with lesbian, gay, and/or bisexual people comparable to the one done by the American Psychological Association on psychotherapy. Anecdotally, however, there are "instances of counselors who, when they discover that their clients are gay or lesbian, set about trying to change their orientation rather than treating their addiction . . . [assuring their patients] that, once sober, they'll find themselves 'normal.' . . . Committed relationships of many years' duration are ignored, while distant relatives are selected to participate in family treatment programs" (Bissell 1995:xxv). Gay, lesbian, or bisexual clients seeking treatment may fear problems in generic substance abuse treatment programs. However, they may fear exposure of their sexual orientation, including in their medical records, if they seek help from facilities or programs specifically designed for lesbian or gay clients (Bissell 1995).

The first thing that a lesbian, gay, or bisexual person with substance abuse problems needs is to have the substance abuse problem—*not* his or her sexual orientation—treated. In this way, lesbian, gay, and bisexual clients are no different from heterosexual clients who need similar treatment. Denial of the problem, its seriousness and/or the magnitude of its consequences, is usually the first problem that must be overcome (Ratner 1988). Treatment providers cannot assume that "alcohol and drugs are just naturally a part of the lesbian/gay 'scene' " (Finnegan & McNally 1996). In fact, denial of the substance abuse problem may lead some clients to collude with treatment providers who want to make sexual orientation, not addiction, the focus of treatment. As Ratner (1988) notes, "a treatment environment that affirms the lesbian and gay lifestyle" and works toward "increased self-awareness and self-acceptance" is the first requirement of affirmative treatment (34).

Even when it is understood that substance abuse is the problem, however, there are some issues that may affect the substance abuse treatment of lesbian, gay, and bisexual clients differently from others, issues that can have an impact on the process of achieving recovery. First of all, *the climate and practices of the treatment agency and the attitudes of the staff should make it easy for gay, lesbian, or bisexual clients to disclose and discuss issues related to sexual orientation.* As in mental health treatment, currently the gay, lesbian, or bisexual client seeking substance abuse services is not likely to reveal his or her sexual orientation immediately, although more will do so during the course of treatment (MacEwan 1994; Nicoloff & Stiglitz 1987). While the substance abuse problem, not sexual orientation, should be the focus of treatment, failure to take a person's sexual orientation into account can lead to the exclusion of partners and lovers from family aspects of treatment (Nicoloff & Stiglitz 1987). It can also result in failure to discuss relapse prevention effectively because of lack of accurate knowledge about the client's social milieu. Statements that suggest that a gay, lesbian, or bisexual orientation per se is a cause of a substance abuse problem are unwarranted and will make it more difficult for such a client to reveal his or her sexual orientation. Such practices likely contribute to the fact that gay and lesbian clients consider the substance abuse treatment they have had to have been less effective than their heterosexual counterparts do (MacEwan 1994). Therefore substance abuse professionals need to be familiar with the issues surrounding self-disclosure for lesbian, gay, and bisexual people.

In addition, a family history of substance abuse is often thought to be related to substance abuse problems among lesbian, gay, and bisexual people and/or their partners, just as it may be among heterosexuals (Black 1990; Ubell & Sumberg 1992). However, homophobic scapegoating within the family during childhood (Ubell & Sumberg 1992) may have added to the difficulties experienced. In addition, Black (1990), who originated the concept of the "Adult Child of Alcoholics" syndrome, asserts that at the very least a lesbian or gay person who grew up in a family with an addicted parent has been dealing with her or his lesbian or gay identity issues in a family of origin that is by definition dysfunctional. *Shame and a sense of being different or deviant are often associated both with growing up in an alcoholic or addicted family and with being gay or lesbian* (Black 1990; Rothberg & Kidder 1992). Thus there are likely to be complications for the gay, lesbian, or bisexual person in dealing with identity issues and family substance abuse. The recovery process often involves taking steps toward increased honesty in relationships, which might include coming out to family members for the first time (Kus & Smith 1995). Substance abuse professionals must therefore know something about the process of coming out to family members—how it can go well and how to assist a client when it does not.

The understanding of family and/or codependency issues most common in the addictions treatment community, which emphasizes dysfunction, overlooks the different salience of family to people in different racial, ethnic, and social class groups. As Tallen (1990) puts it in relation to lesbians, for example, "It . . . is ironic that often the very families defined as 'dysfunctional,' such as the single-parent, African-American family, might be more functional for women, as well as a refuge from the racism of a larger society" (404). Lesbian, gay, and bisexual people who come from racial, ethnic, or other devalued groups may have different experiences of and attitudes toward their families of origin and toward disclosure of their sexual orientation to their families than are commonly assumed among others, attitudes and identity management strategies that must be respected. Flores-Ortiz and Bernal (1990) suggest that contextual family therapy—that is, an intergenerational approach aimed at including all available individuals (extended family) into its preventive strategy for the benefit of current and future generations—might be more effective for Latino clients. It is assumed that in this ethnic group, drug abuse is rooted in generational conflicts.

A history of sexual abuse is thought by some to be related to substance abuse problems among gay men and lesbians (Neison & Sandall 1990; Ratner 1988), just as it may be among heterosexual people (Roshenow, Corbett, & Devine 1988). One study of clients treated in a twenty-eight-day in-patient program exclusively serving gay men and lesbians found that 70 percent of the women and 42 percent of the men reported a sexual abuse history (Neisen & Sandall 1990). The consequences of the abuse, which may include low self-esteem, affective disorders, and interpersonal problems of various kinds, may leave the victim more vulnerable to the development of substance abuse problems and is also likely to complicate the process of recovery. Treatment professionals must have at minimum the capacity to ask routinely about and to deal openly with any sexual abuse history that a substance abuse client may disclose. *While a history of childhood sexual abuse may affect vulnerability to substance abuse problems, there is currently no evidence to suggest that it is implicated in the development of a lesbian, gay, or bisexual orientation or identity, although clients themselves may wonder if it is.* Therefore, it is recommended that a sexual abuse history be approached as another source of stigma and challenge to recovery but one that can be overcome (Neisen & Sandall 1990).

Practice wisdom in the substance abuse field suggests that personal development is changed or interrupted once an active addiction begins. As McNally and Finnegan (1992) have put it, based on an intensive study of lesbians in recovery from addiction: "Some drank to deny fears about sex and the possibility of lesbian feelings; some drank to be *not* lesbian; some drank to *be* lesbian" (94). Whatever the motivation to drink, once sober most lesbians in the study spoke about having to renegotiate or to continue the process of developing their lesbian identity as a sober person. This speaks to the concept of living sober, the idea that recovery from addiction is more than just not using any addictive substances but is also developing a new way of living. *For the lesbian, gay, or bisexual person, then, learning to live a clean and sober life may also require revisiting and reworking "coming out" or sexual identity issues.* While this very rarely includes a change in orientation, it may often mean changing one's style of life, circle of friends, and/or pattern of intimate relationships. Even sexuality may be affected: those who needed alcohol or some other disinhibiting substance in order to "anesthetize internalized homophobia . . . may need reassurance that this is a normal state of affairs and should eventually pass with continued sobriety" (Kus & Brown 1995:97). On the positive side, it may only be when sobriety has been achieved that a recovering alcoholic can truly accept and affirm a gay self (Kus 1989). Recovering from internalized homophobia must go hand in hand with recovery from addiction (Ratner 1988).

AIDS and HIV infection have relevance to substance abuse treatment in several ways (Pohl 1995). Gay men are still the social group with the highest incidence and prevalence of HIV infection in the United States. Thus anxiety about one's HIV status, knowledge of being HIV-positive, or the stresses of being sick with AIDS may be factors in the life of a gay or bisexual man seeking substance abuse treatment that must also be taken into account when working with him. Although HIV infection is not very common among lesbians, it is *behavior*, not status, that determines HIV risk; lesbians have become infected with the HIV virus through injectable drug use with dirty needles, engaging in heterosexual sex, being artificially inseminated, having received blood products (especially before the screening of the blood supply), and even in a few cases through unprotected woman-with-woman sexual activity (Glassman 1995). Especially in the substance abuse treatment setting, then, HIV issues may be prominent for lesbians.

One way that the HIV virus is transmitted is through the needle use associated with the use of injectable illegal drugs. When a substance abuse client, male or female, has a history of needle use, especially needle sharing, the possibility of HIV infection must be taken seriously. Many recommend that a risk-reduction strategy be used with such clients, emphasizing abstinence from all mind-altering substances if possible. If not, eliminating needle use is the next most effective step; for example, in methadone programs the rate of HIV infection has been lowered (Pohl 1995). If neither of these strategies is working for an individual client, education about risk reduction, such as participation in needle exchange (or "clean needle") programs, and the use of bleach to clean needles may help somewhat (Pohl 1995). Finally, HIV infection also can occur through certain forms of sexual contact. *Use of any mind-altering substance, including alcohol, has been found to affect people's capacity to employ the safer sex practices they have learned about* (Kus & Smith 1995; Pohl 1995). Helping gay, lesbian, and bisexual people to live clean and sober lives will also help to slow the spread of the HIV infection among them.

One of the treatment modalities most often suggested and utilized for substance abuse problems are the twelve-step self-help programs, specifically Alcoholics Anonymous and Narcotics Anonymous, in addition to the similar groups formed for those who identify as partners or children of those with addictions. As helpful as these programs have been for many people, *certain potential limitations of twelve-step programs for lesbian, gay, and bisexual people have been noted* (Glaus 1989; Hall 1993; Heyward 1992; Kus 1992; Tallen 1990).

Because twelve-step groups are organized around personal addiction issues only and do not include a social analysis of addiction or other problems, some problems of women may not be well understood (Heyward 1992; Tallen 1990). As Tallen (1990) notes, the twelve-step programs conceptualize power as related to personal feeling, not to political and/or social oppressions and privilege, which may not make sense to the client struggling to confront the effects of the oppression of gay, lesbian, and bisexual people. In addition, the origins of Alcoholics Anonymous had a pronounced emphasis on the privileged white heterosexual male, which was discouraging to women, while at the same time white middle-class married women whose husbands had alcohol problems were the ones encouraged to participate in Al-Anon, perhaps overlooking their own drinking problems. While the programs of AA and similar groups have been altered over the years to increase inclusiveness, traces of the history remain and are bothersome to some members. Finally, the spiritual dimension of the twelve-step programs, which is connected in most people's minds with a Christian conception of God, may constitute a barrier to the participation of lesbian, gay, and bisexual people who identify Christianity or other religions with heterosexism and homophobia, and who have experienced condemnation or rejection because of their sexual orientation by religious people or organizations with whom they have been involved, or who belong to other religious traditions (Tallen 1990).

In some areas of the country, special interest groups have formed within AA and other twelve-step organizations (Hall 1993; Kus & Latkovich 1995). Some find lesbian-only, gay-only or gay-lesbian 12-steps groups, or male- or female-only groups, more congenial even though the underlying program model is still the same. Some use special interest groups exclusively; others use them in conjunction with more traditional groups (Kus & Latkovich 1995) or with psychotherapy (Hall 1993). Certainly the substance abuse professional should know about such resources where they exist, but they should also be prepared to discuss with clients who use traditional *or* special twelve-step groups the problems or ambivalence they may have about them related specifically to their sexual orientation in a supportive rather than dismissive fashion (Kus 1992; Kus & Latkovich 1995). For example, reminding clients that alternative conceptions of spirituality exist that are fully compatible with twelve-step programs is often helpful (Kus 1992). Finally, it is often helpful to know about substance-free settings in which gay and lesbian people in recovery can socialize (Finnegan & McNally 1996).

In discussing mental health and substance abuse problems separately in this chapter, we reflect a problem affecting both fields: the tendency *not* to work across diagnostic and treatment system boundaries. This separation in the study and treatment of mental health and substance abuse problems serves both clients and the helping professions poorly because there are many people who have both substance abuse and mental health problems, such as depression (Finnegan & McNally 1996). This population, often termed a "dual diagnosis" group, is currently receiving growing attention as studies are finding an increased risk for psychiatric disorder among those identified as substance abusers and the reverse—a higher risk of substance abuse among those identified as having a psychiatric disorder. When sexual orientation issues arise in a dual diagnosis case, skilled assessment and affirmative treatment are essential to a good treatment outcome (Finnegan & McNally 1996; Hellman 1992).

However, to date there is still very little available to guide the practitioner in dual diagnosis work specifically with gay, lesbian, or bisexual people. When working with lesbian, gay, and bisexual clients with substance abuse problems, it must be remembered that "in most chemically dependent clients, depression and other forms of emotional disease fade away in sobriety. Sometimes, however, depression and other problems may turn out to be independent of the chemical dependency treatment" (Kus & Brown 1995:95). In such cases, competent and affirmative mental health and substance abuse treatment may both be needed, especially because untreated mental health problems can trigger relapse into substance use (Finnegan & McNally 1996). Finally, even when symptoms of a mental illness like depression may be part of the addiction, when they are severe enough they need immediate attention (Finnegan & McNally 1996).

Summary

Unfortunately, the mental health and substance abuse fields have in the past been rife with myths and misconceptions about gay, lesbian, and bisexual people. Thus, although lesbian, gay, and bisexual people are frequent consumers of these services, they are not always well and effectively served in many mental health and substance abuse programs. Social workers understand that practice is informed by a combination of knowledge, attitude, and skill. This chapter has reviewed current knowledge about mental health and substance abuse problems among lesbian, gay, and bisexual people. While this knowledge is incomplete in many areas, especially in relation to bisexual people, there is a great deal that is now known about how to work more effectively with lesbian, gay, and bisexual people who seek mental health and/or substance abuse services. However, it has also been emphasized that attitudes are just as important as knowledge in delivering services in a nondiscriminating and affirmative manner.

Education and training has been shown to improve practitioners' attitudes toward and knowledge about lesbian and gay people and most likely their effectiveness in working with them as clients, especially when that training includes contact with identified lesbian, gay, and/or bisexual people along with didactic content (Rudolph 1989a). Clearly there is a continuing need for further training and education in this essentially important sector of social work practice. Social work and social workers can continue to provide vital leadership in furnishing that training and in the development and delivery of affirmative mental health and substance abuse services to lesbian, gay, and bisexual people.

IO

Violence in the Lives of Lesbians and Gay Men

Violence manifests itself at a variety of levels—the cultural, the institutional, and the individual. This chapter focuses on violence perpetuated against gay and lesbian individuals. Its most common form is "gay-bashing," that is, violence against gay and lesbian people by others. How such violence affects its victims and how social workers can respond will be emphasized. The somewhat different problem of domestic violence in lesbian and gay relationships will also be discussed.

Violence against lesbians and gay men as well as violence within gay and lesbian relationships are not new problems. However, these are two distinct and separate issues. The first is a phenomenon in which violence of many kinds is perpetuated against lesbians and gay men by society. The second form of violence is directed at an individual group member by an individual group member. Gay and lesbian "bashing" is quite pervasive in American society while gay and lesbian domestic violence appears to be a well-kept secret in both the straight and gay communities. Each form of violence will be dealt with separately. Antigay/lesbian violence will be discussed first because it is the more common and because of the widespread attention it has recently gained in the professional literature and in the popular media. Little reference will made to anti-bisexual violence because so little is known about this problem, although it is assumed that violent acts perpetrated against bisexuals occur when it is thought that the victim is lesbian or gay.

Violence Against Gay and Lesbian People

People whose sexual partner is of their own gender have long been subjected to physical brutality. Gay and lesbian historians note that violence has often represented official governmental policy; for example, sodomy was punishable by castration, torture, and death in Colonial America (Boswell 1980; Katz 1976). In Germany before and during the Second World War, approximately 15,000 homosexuals were forced to wear the pink triangle before they were slaughtered in Nazi concentration camps (Adam 1987). Twentieth-century observers detail the collusion of police who often looked the other way while young men preyed on gay people. In everyday life, family members, coworkers, and schoolmates have harassed and brutalized lesbian and gay people.

Anti-gay/lesbian violence was frequently a subtext in the gay and lesbian literature of the 1970s and 1980s. Comstock (1991:31–32) described this as a recurring theme in autobiographical and biographical statements, political and social commentaries, novels, short stories, poetry and plays, and articles in the social sciences. Columnists reported incidents of violence in great detail and editorialists disapproved of the leniency with which the criminal justice system tended to treat perpetrators. This information was mostly anecdotal and descriptive without sufficient data to make general observations. However, in the 1980s lesbian and gay organizations and antiviolence projects, lesbian and gay scholars, and service administrators devoted significant attention to the task of systematically collecting data on this violence. More recently, the pervasiveness of antigay violence has been blamed by the media on the fear and hatred associated with AIDS. However, AIDS is probably less a cause of antigay sentiment than it is a new focus and justification for expressions of antigay prejudice (Farley 1996; Herek & Glunt 1988).

Unfortunately, violence against gay and lesbian people can occur at any age. An example of extreme antigay violence was reported nationally from Chicago court transcripts of the murder of a four-year-old boy by his mother and her live-in boyfriend. During the summer of 1987 the boy was starved, burned, stuck with pins and needles, beaten with various implements, scalded with steaming water, tied up and hung upside down, and gagged for hours because he was perceived to be homosexual. His brother was tortured for the same reason. The boy was eventually killed by a blow to his head (*St. Louis Post-Dispatch* 1990). The irrationality of acts like these makes it clear that violence against gay and lesbian people (or those who are thought to be) must be understood as manifestations of heterosexism and homophobia (see chapter 1).

Gregory Herek and Kevin Berrill (1992) in *Hate Crimes: Confronting Violence Against Lesbian and Gay Men*, probably the most thorough study of anti-gay crime, suggest that victims have often been prevented from reporting these crimes because of the stigma not only of the victim but of family and friends. Public officials and law enforcement personnel have often remained indifferent to the problem. Comstock (1991) suggests that assault has been the price paid for visibility, and seeking to remain invisible has been a common strategy of the vast majority of lesbians and gay men to avoid stigma and violence.

Since the Stonewall Rebellion in 1969 (the modern birth of the gay liberation movement), gays and lesbians have organized around the demand for political and social equality and have attempted to advance public education so as to counter negative stereotypes. With these actions came public visibility and the increasing probability of becoming a target of those who hate and hope to harm. In the 1990s, as gay men and lesbians became more visible than ever before in American society, an unprecedented number of attacks against them have been reported.

During the 1980s and 1990s, antigay violence paralleled the increased attacks against women and against ethnic, religious, and racial minorities. These attacks included episodes of murder, arson, bombings, assault, vandalism, cross-burning, and harassment. The National Institute of Justice reported that the most frequent victims of hate crime were blacks, Latinos, Southeast Asians, Jews, and gays and lesbians—gays and lesbians in fact being the most frequent victims (Finn & McNeil 1987). During this same period, the AIDS epidemic inflicted considerable losses on gay people. Stigma was assigned to those who were infected with the virus, those thought to be infected, and often those who were the caregivers of the infected. The increase in prejudice, discrimination, and violence against lesbian and gay people was supposedly justified because of society's fear of AIDS.

Violence against gay and lesbian people does not just affect the individual victim; it affects all gay and lesbian people.

> Every such incident carries a message to the victim and the entire community of which he or she is a part. Each anti-gay/lesbian attack is, in effect, a punishment for stepping outside culturally accepted norms, that is the prevailing pattern of power and privilege, and a warning to all gay and lesbian people to stay in their place, the invisibility and self-hatred of the closet.
>
> (Herek & Berrill 1992:3)

More recently, gay men and lesbians have refused to tolerate these antigay attacks and, in so doing, have refused to collude in the enforcement of the cultural codes of silence and invisibility, two significant components of homophobia and heterosexism discussed in chapter 1.

Assessment based on a thorough understanding of the problem and psychosocial interventions designed to end antigay violence should be grounded in the knowledge of the cultural and social context (cultural heterosexism), as well as the individual consequences of normative behavior and attitudes (psychological heterosexism). To develop theory for practice, then, this chapter will draw heavily on the findings of New York City's Gay and Lesbian Anti-Violence Project (Herek & Berrill 1992), national projects (Larcom & Weiss 1990; *New York Native* 1995), periodic reports from the National Gay and Lesbian Task Force Policy Institute, the *National Lesbian Health Care Survey* (Bradford & Ryan 1988), and Comstock's (1991) summary of twenty national antigay/lesbian violence surveys. While these studies contribute much to our knowledge, there are significant limitations in that samples are drawn in the United States from populations that are primarily white, male, and middle-class adults.

INCIDENCE AND PREVALENCE

It is essential to understand the extent and nature of violence against gay and lesbian people. Berrill's (1992) summary of several antigay violence studies is a good place to begin: 19 percent of the respondents reported having been punched, hit, kicked, or beaten at least once in their lives because of their sexual orientation; 44 percent were threatened with physical violence; 94 percent experienced verbal abuse, physical assault, abuse by police, assault with a weapon, having their property vandalized, or being spat upon, chased or followed, and pelted with objects; and 84 percent knew other lesbian or gay people who had been victimized. Ninety-two percent were targets more than once. Also reported was the impact of the threat of antigay violence: 83 percent believed that they might be victims in the future; 62 percent feared for their safety in general; and 45 percent changed their behavior (took self-defense classes, avoided certain locations, or shunned physical contact with friends or lovers in public) to reduce the risk of attack. All surveys reported found harassment (80 percent) and violence (44 percent) to be widespread.

Studies of antigay violence suggest that there are some differences in the kinds of violence and oppression experienced by gay men and lesbians. Males generally experienced greater levels of antigay verbal harassment by nonfamily members, threats, victimization in school and by police, and most types of physical violence and intimidation. Lesbians generally experienced higher rates of verbal harassment by family members and reported greater fear of antigay violence. However, lesbians encountered significantly more discrimination of other kinds than gay men.

Anti-lesbian violence is closely connected to violence against women in general. Bradford and Ryan (1988) report that over one-third of their sample confirmed having been severely beaten or physically abused at some point in their lives. Six percent had been physically abused both in childhood and adulthood. Those abused in childhood were abused by a male relative. One-fifth of the sample had been raped or sexually attacked as children and 15 percent as adults. Although the rate of sexual abuse in adulthood was similar among whites, African-Americans, and Latinas, a third of all African-American women, one-fourth of Latinas, and one-fifth of white women had been abused as children. It becomes difficult to distinguish between the status of lesbian or woman as the motivator for many of these crimes.

In addition, there are data that suggest that gay men and lesbians of color may more frequently be the victims of antigay violence than others. For example, Comstock (1989) found that lesbians and gay men of color were more likely than were white subjects to be chased or followed (43 percent vs. 29 percent), pelted with objects (31 percent vs. 17 percent) or physically assaulted (21 percent vs. 18 percent). In a San Francisco study of four hundred lesbians, von Schulthess (1992) found that lesbians of color were more likely than white lesbians to report having experienced physical violence, threats, vandalism, or rape. These higher levels of victimization may be associated with the higher risk levels of African-Americans and Latinos in general. Only a small percentage of this violence is reported to any type of agency.

Teenagers can also be victims (Remafedi 1994). Hunter (1992), in a study of five hundred youths, found that 40 percent reported they had experienced violent physical attacks, 46 percent reported the assault was gay-related; 61 percent of the gay-related violence occurred in the family. Suicidal thoughts were found among 44 percent of those experiencing violent assaults; 41 percent of the girls and 34 percent of the boys reporting violent assaults had tried to kill themselves (1992:78–79).

The level of violence reported in many antigay attacks is often extreme. A study by the Gay and Lesbian Anti-Violence Project found that nearly 60 percent of the 151 antigay slayings reported in twenty-nine states involved extraordinary and horrific violence of a sort fueled by rage and hate. While guns are used in 68 percent of all murders in this country, only 26 percent of antigay/lesbian murderers shot their victims. Instead, knives, baseball bats, clubs, and hammers were the weapons of choice. The level of violence in these homicides is gruesome. The study also found that anti-homosexual violence is underreported because families of some victims try to keep it quiet and police frequently refuse to give details. There are on record at least eight serial murderers who prey on lesbians and gay men, and the study reports that six are still at large (*New York Native* 1995).

THE PERPETRATOR

Most authors who study anti-gay/lesbian violence have also focused on the psychosocial characteristics of the perpetrator of violence. The general profile of the gay-basher that emerges from these data is a young male, often acting in conjunction with other young males, all of whom are strangers to the victim (DeCecco 1985; Herek & Berrill 1992; Renzetti 1992). The general literature on violence sees these acts as defensive behaviors against shame with complex biological, psychological, and social features. The risk factors for a person who is more apt to resort to violent behavior include previous episodes of violence, substance abuse, head trauma, seizures, information-processing problems, and environmental stressors. The greater the number of risk factors and the fewer perceived avenues to replace shame, the more likely violence will be chosen. However, many of these studies employ small samples and are fraught with limitations. For example, contrary to other studies, Comstock (1991) in his empirical study of violence against gays and lesbians, found that the perpetrators of violence were predominantly average young men whose behavior is socially sanctioned and consistent with the role expectations of the aggressive male rather than individual actions intrapsychically determined. Finn and McNeil (1987) observed that the majority of hate crimes do not appear to be committed by individuals who are affiliated with hate groups (i.e., the Ku Klux Klan, skinheads, Aryan Nation, Family Values Alliances, Neo-Nazis, or the religious right). However, many offenders may be encouraged by the rhetoric of these hate groups.

On a community level, while the police are responsible for protecting lesbians and gay men, many view hate crimes as harmless pranks or as an acceptable form of behavior. Still other police are themselves perpetrators of antigay harassment and violence. The National Gay and Lesbian Task Force (NGLTF) Policy Institute (1991) documented numerous cases of police verbal and physical abuse, entrapment, blackmail, unequal enforcement of the law, and deliberate mishandling of antigay violence cases. The Anti-Violence Project previously cited said, in essence, that police were often indifferent to gay-lesbian related homicides and operated from a blame-the-victim perspective.

Berrill's (1992) analysis of numerous studies counters the view that violence is primarily a street crime committed by strangers. Hate crimes occur in schools, colleges, the home, and prisons and jails where victims are acquainted and often intimate with the perpetrator.

While all researchers point to the limitations of their studies, each starts from a different theoretical perspective and interprets his or her data differently. All offer ample evidence that the problem is severe. The human cost of anti-gay/lesbian bigotry, however, cannot be captured in these various measures, in that they fail to convey the fear and anguish experienced not only by the survivors of violence but also by the communities of which they are a part.

ANTIGAY VIOLENCE IN CONTEXT

To understand violence against gay men and lesbians, one needs to understand the problem of violence in general. Why some people act in a violent manner is still an unanswered question in the social sciences. We do not know under what conditions specific forms of violence are evoked. Nor do we know why, under ostensibly the same conditions, one person will act violently and another will not. We know that not all prejudiced people act out their prejudices violently.

Violence is woven into the social fabric. Ours is a violent society. Most Americans have lived through at least one war, several military actions, a number of urban or police riots, and terrorist attacks. Most have watched hundreds if not thousands of hours of violence on TV and in the movies and have heard untold hours of violent song lyrics. Thus each of us has some recollection of group conflicts or national acts of violence. The conspiracy of silence around violent, criminal conduct by members of a family, such as spouse battering, marital rape, child abuse, and abuse of the elderly, commonly referred to as family violence, has an exceptionally long history. Even, today, a large percentage of Americans actually condone violence in the family by their belief that such matters are private. Straus (1983) observed that a majority of American children are physically punished until the time they leave their parent's home. Thus most Americans regard some forms of violence as socially acceptable in some situations. This shared cultural history does not explain the disproportionate violence directed at gay, lesbian, and bisexual people. Van Soest and Bryant (1995) have reconceptualized violence as (1) cultural, (2) institutional, and (3) individual actions. Figure 10.1 is a graphic display of their formulations.

National Association of Social Workers
Social Workers Redefine Violence

Individual Violence. Harmful actions against people or property; visible, easy to condemn, immediate consequences; perpetrator (and motivations) and victim (and injuries) are easy to identify; considered a punishable crime.

Individual Violence

Examples
- murderers, rape, gang fights, drive-by shootings, terrorism, spouse abuse, child abuse, assault.

Violence We See
Unseen Violence

Institutional Violence. Harmful actions within institutions that obstruct the spontaneous unfolding of human potential; occurs in bureaucracies such as government agencies, businesses, prisons, mental institutions, welfare systems, schools, the military; often caused by policies considered necessary for profit or control; usually subtle, indirect, covert, regrettable but not a crime.

Examples
- leveraged buy-out by corporation results in layoffs and reduced wages
- company defaults in pensions and retirement health coverage
- nursing home patients are strapped to their beds because the home lacks sufficient staff
- development assistance is withheld from poor communities and countries
- banks fail to make loans in certain inner-city neighborhoods
- wars between countries and within countries
- female genital mutilation practices

Institutional Violence

Cultural Violence. Harmful actions that result from the way society thinks, conventional values, everyday practice; often sinister, difficult to discern; usually accepted as "normal."

Examples
- avoidable differences between groups within a country/between countries: infant mortality rates, premature death rates, cancer rates, little political representation, few development opportunities
- passively accepting inequities and deprivations such as poverty, racism, sexism
- denigration of minorities, refugees, unfamiliar cultures and countries, ethnic groups, women, gays and lesbians, the disabled
- the easy acceptance of violence and threat of violence as a solution to problems

Cultural Violence

Adapted from *Violence Reconceptualized for Social Work: The Urban Dilemma*. Accepted for publication in *Social Work Journal* 1995 by Dorothy Van Soest, DSW and Shirley Bryant, DSW

Figure 10.1 Social workers redefine violence

Thus the antigay and anti-lesbian violence that is generally discussed is at the top of the pyramid: the visible acts committed against individuals. However, this violence is part of a continuum that includes all of the structural and less visible oppression of gay and lesbian people. Unseen violence supports and influences responses to individual violent acts, and visible acts of individual violence frighten people and reduce resistance to its less visible forms. Thus the various forms of violence reinforce each other.

Patterns of prejudice are maintained because they are in keeping with the current social norms. Ehrlich's (1973) standard-setting work on the social psychology of prejudice and his subsequent studies (1978; 1992:105–11) on antigay/lesbian violence support Herek's notion that there is a well-developed social heritage of prejudice:

> This heritage is a body of cultural practices, social norms, values, attitudes, and beliefs that is "there" for every child and young adult to learn. Habits of prejudice are communicated within the family. People develop attitudes similar to those of those who socialized them. Parents communicate attitudes as explicitly as they teach the child other modes of behavior. They also control the child's opportunities and experiences and, not least, provide models of behavior for the growing child.   (Ehrlich 1973:106)

While the family may facilitate the development and transmission of prejudice, larger social forces must legitimate specific "out-groups" as appropriate targets of prejudice. The motivations for violence appear to be much more complex, with elements of power, affiliation, conformity, and expressiveness.

Cultural Heterosexism

Hate crimes against lesbians and gay men must be understood in context: antigay/lesbian violence is a logical extension of cultural heterosexism (Herek 1985). In chapter 1 heterosexism was defined as an ideological system that denies, denigrates, and stigmatizes any nonheterosexual form of behavior, identity, relationship, or community. Cultural heterosexism requires that homosexuality be largely hidden and, when publicly recognized, be condemned or stigmatized. An example may help to illustrate the point about the privatization and invisibility of homosexuality:

> A new social work graduate excited about her first "real" job with her own office decides to place a picture of her husband on her desk. In the photo the couple smiles at one another while in an affectionate embrace. This photo

conveys information explicitly about the relationship and implicitly about her private sexual behavior. The fact that she is heterosexual is taken for granted. Most people would not think of her partner (husband) in primarily sexual terms. They would most likely focus on his physical appearance, personality, occupation, and social status. At no point would our social worker think that displaying this photo constitutes an inappropriate intrusion of the private life into public life.

If this were a photo of two women in the same pose, everyone would take notice. It conveys information about a relationship and because there is another woman in the photo, it overwhelms all other information about her. The sexual component of the relationship is not benign and implicit as with the heterosexual spouse. There is now a violation of intrusion of the private into the public. Thus the simple act of displaying a photo fundamentally defines an employee's status and relationships.

Sexism is also an influence on antigay and anti-lesbian violence. The language of anti-gay/lesbian prejudice mirrors the culture's gender ideology, which is essentially sexist and indicative of traditional attitudes and gender-role norms. The core belief, male superiority, turns gays and lesbians into ideological renegades because their existence is seen as a rejection of the "appropriate" hierarchy of beliefs, attitudes, and behaviors. Male socialization entails constant pressure to prove his commitment to male gender roles. Sexual and violent acts are often the means to prove male commitment. Comstock (1991), as previously noted, found that the perpetrators of antigay violence are predominantly average young men whose behavior is socially sanctioned and consistent with the role expectations of the aggressive male rather than the result of individual actions intrapsychically determined.

SOCIAL INSTITUTIONS

Anti-gay/lesbian violence persists not solely because of individual psychology but also because of the structure of society in which we live. Patterns of prejudice are normative, the result of social and historical processes. Herek (1992b) notes that there are four major social institutions that are the glue of these processes: (1) religion, (2) law, (3) psychiatry/psychology, and (4) mass media. In them there is ample evidence both of a pressure for invisibility and of a rationale for out-and-out hostility.

Religion
First, an analysis of religion leads us to the observation that many Americans are

admittedly, proudly, and militantly anti-homosexual. Many people are self-righteous about their hatred because their churches have taught them that homosexuality is intrinsically sinful or evil. Religion as a system of beliefs, values, and customs that form a group's worldview or perception of social reality is an effective vehicle for learning both love and hate. Judeo-Christian tradition values patriarchy, male power and privilege, hierarchical gender roles, and narrowly defined sexual relations and approved behaviors. This, then, is a powerful foundation for culturally induced hatred, discrimination, and violence.

Ehrlich (1992) illustrates through a quotation how religious rhetoric introduces the classic themes of power and control and then adds another important element, dehumanization:

> Homosexuals are . . . committed to destroying the traditional Christian values on which this nation is founded. . . . If these deviates chose to keep their sins to themselves, perhaps it could be tolerated. But as it is, they are seeking rights that are reserved for normal citizens . . . such as marriage and adoption. These people are unfit to live, let alone to raise children.
>
> (Quoted in Ehrlich 1992:108)

In the world of bigotry, the enemy must be defined as less than human. Violence is then rationalized by "blaming the victim"; that is, the victim's actual or anticipated behavior is defined as an unwanted provocation, leaving the perpetrator no other response but violence, all in the name of God.

Most institutional religions prescribe rules and procedures for moral living, often stressing the "inherent" virtues of a committed marital relationship through which children are conceived and raised in the faith. According to Boswell (1980), marriages are by definition heterosexual; homosexuality is widely condemned; same-sex relationships and families are not recognized. The Catholic church, for example, in its Vatican statements opposed extending civil rights protection to lesbians, bisexuals, and gay people.

Law

Gay men and lesbians remain largely outside the law. At this writing, there are only eleven states and a handful of cities where discrimination based on sexual orientation is prohibited in employment, housing, and public accommodations or services (see chapter 3 for a more extensive discussion). Gay relationships generally have no legal status, and lesbian and gay parents often lose legal custody of their children when their sexual orientation is known. Nearly one half of the states outlaw private consenting homosexual acts and their right to do so was upheld by the U.S. Supreme Court in 1986 (*Bowers v. Hard-*

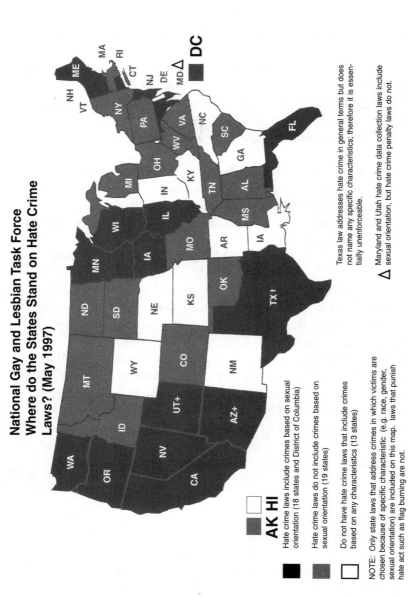

Figure 10.2 Where states stand on hate crimes (as of May 1997). Reproduced by permission of the National Gay and Lesbian Task Force Policy Institute, 2320 17th Street, N.W., Washington, DC 20009, (202) 332-6483; http://www.ngltf.org.

wick 1986). The justices refused to find a constitutional legal right for privately consenting homosexual behavior because the proscriptions against sodomy have ancient origins in Judeo-Christian tradition. Herek (1992b) sees this as a clear illustration of the linkage between legal philosophies and religious teachings.

Law, through what it forbids and what it does not, is also a significant force when justifying violence against gays and lesbians. Violent acts committed against individuals because of other status characteristics, such as their race, ethnicity, or gender, are often classified as civil rights violations or given the special legal status of hate crimes, which often lead, in turn, to stiffer sentences for offenses. However, in 1995, while only a handful of states lacked any hate crime statute at all, crimes against people based on sexual orientation had the status of a hate crime in only eighteen states and the District of Columbia (see figure 10.2). In addition, as already noted, the response of law enforcement officials to violence against gay and lesbian people when it is reported has been variable at best.

Psychiatry

Psychiatry has assumed responsibility for the protection of the moral and social order as religion faltered in the twentieth century. Psychiatry and the other mental health professions have historically pathologized homosexuality (see chapter 9). Bayer (1987) notes that despite Freud's refusal to label homosexuality a sickness, mainstream American psychiatry and psychoanalysis spent much of the twentieth century seeking its cure. In the 1970s the National Association of Social Workers, the American Psychological Association, and the American Psychiatric Association, after a considerable review of the available clinical and social science research, stopped classifying homosexuality as a psychiatric illness or as an emotional problem. Gonsiorek (1982a, 1991) notes that when the theory that homosexuality is linked to psychopathology is subjected to rigorous scientific testing, the theory is proved to be without basis. More than twenty years have passed since this policy was enacted by the three leading mental health professional associations. In the meantime, the other mental health professions of psychiatric nursing, marriage and family therapists, and counselors of various backgrounds have followed suit.

Unfortunately, there are still those who in the name of mental health continue to add to the discrimination against lesbians, gay men, and their families by revisiting discredited theory and damaging practice. The language of pathology still infuses public perceptions and popular debate, as evidenced by the antihomosexual initiatives being introduced in state legislatures and congressional hearings related to gays and lesbians in the military, lesbian and gay civil rights, and federal funding for AIDS education, service, and research.

Media

The mass media is the fourth social institution that both reflects and perpetuates cultural heterosexism. Media images of gays and lesbians are still quite infrequent. Few portrayals give any sense of depth or realistic diversity. It is important to remember that the vast number of Americans have been exposed to images of people who were purposely presented as weak, pathetic, and often doomed. Therefore, it would be from these negative depictions that perceptions have been formed. For example, Russo (1981) concluded in his study of American films that most homosexuals died from suicide or murder before the end of the movie. In addition, their characterization often implied a gender-role violation or nonconformity, and thus they were the brunt of ridicule, contempt, and violence. Bronski (1984), in his study of culture, notes that it is easier to dismember a lesbian on TV or in a movie than it is to present two lesbians kissing. An honest portrayal of gay or lesbian life in school textbooks or educational films is often greeted with school board protest. A frank presentation of gay or lesbian sex in AIDS educational material will result in threats to end funding.

All minorities have recognized the power of mass media in maintaining stereotypes and perpetuating bigotry. Each has targeted the media when engaging in political action to improve society's response to them. Gay and lesbian people, too, are beginning to concern themselves with the elimination of negative portrayals and with findings ways of portraying gay and lesbian people realistically and positively in the media. The Gay and Lesbian Alliance Against Defamation (GLAAD) is an example of a media watchdog group that has gained some prominence and now rewards, in a very public way, positive media efforts to affirm gay and lesbian people.

PSYCHOLOGICAL HETEROSEXISM

Herek (1992a, 1993a) views the manifestation of heterosexism in individuals' antigay attitudes and violent actions as psychological heterosexism. His formulations are an important contribution to theory for practice with many implications for strategies of social work intervention. In his framework, violence is seen as often functional for the perpetrator although the function it serves may differ for each person, depending upon his or her psychological needs. The translation of individual needs into antigay attitudes and behaviors involves a complex interaction among deep-seated personality characteristics, factors related to the immediate situation, and cultural definitions of sexuality and gender.

People, according to this functional approach (see table 10.1), hold and express particular attitudes because they get some sort of psychological benefit from doing so. From this perspective people can have very different motivations for expressing their feelings. There are three different functions these attitudes serve: (1) an *experiential function*, whereby an attitude helps in making sense of previous interactions with a gay person; (2) an *anticipatory function* that helps an individual to understand how the world works and to develop strategies for maximizing rewards and minimizing negative experiences; and (3) a *social identity function* that demonstrates that an individual is like some people and unlike certain other people. Thus attitudes and behavior may not be based on past experience but on anticipation of future interactions with lesbians and gay men and/or with heterosexuals. Most Americans do not think they personally know a lesbian, bisexual, or gay man and thus understand homosexuality and gay, lesbian, or bisexual people primarily as symbols. The social identity function of attitudes helps people to increase their self-esteem by expressing what sort of person they believe themselves to be by distancing themselves from or even attacking people who they believe to be the sort of person they are not or do not want to be.

A social identity can contribute to positive or negative attitudes. For example, one social identity would be an individual who had been raised to be accepting, nonjudgmental, and open to human difference, thus reacting to homosexuality as a personal matter that does not represent a deficit in personality or character. By contrast, a social identity of a fundamentalist Christian who believes that the Bible is correct, that it states that homosexuality is a sin, and that he or she must follow every word to be a good Christian would be reflected in judgmental and distancing attitudes toward gay and lesbian people (see table 10.1).

Within the category of the social identity function of heterosexism, Herek (1992a) makes several interesting distinctions between value-expressive, social-expressive, and ego-defensive functions, all of which share a common characteristic: anti-gay/lesbian prejudice helps people to define who they are by directing hostility toward gay people as a symbol of what they are not. Anti-lesbian/gay attitudes help to define the world in terms of good and evil, right and wrong; by opposing gay and lesbian people, the supposed embodiment of evil, a person reaffirms his or her own morality and virtue. These attitudes help designate the in-group and the out-group; by denigrating gays a person affirms his or her status as an insider. As Herek (1992a) puts it, negative attitudes toward "gay people help to affirm and 'own' the good or accept-

TABLE 10.1   *The Psychological Functions of Heterosexism*

Name of Function	Description	Benefits to Individual
Evaluative functions:		
Experiential	Generalizes from past experiences with specific lesbians or gay men to create a coherent image of gay people in relation to one's own interests	Makes sense of past experiences and uses them to guide behavior
Anticipatory	Anticipates benefits or punishments expected to be received directly from lesbians or gay men	In absence of direct experience with gay men or lesbians, plans future behavior so as to maximize rewards and minimize punishments
Expressive functions:		
Social identity:		
Value-expressive	Lesbians or gay men symbolize an important value conflict	Increases self-esteem by affirming individual's view of self as a person who adheres to particular values
Social-expressive	Lesbians of gay men symbolize the in-group or out-group	Increases self-esteem by winning approval of others whose opinion is valued; increases sense of group solidarity
Defensive	Lesbians or gay men symbolize unacceptable part of the self	Reduces anxiety associated with a psychological conflict by denying and externalizing the unacceptable aspect of self and then attacking it

NOTE: With the evaluative functions, benefit is contingent upon direct experience with lesbians and gay men. With the expressive functions, benefit is contingent upon the consequences of expressing the attitude.

Source: From G. M. Herek and K. T. Berrill, eds., *Hate Crimes: Confronting Violence Against Lesbians and Gay Men*, 157 (Newbury Park, Calif.: Sage, 1992). Reprinted by permission of Sage Publications, Inc.

able parts of the self while denying the bad or unacceptable parts. Unacceptable feelings (such as homoerotic desires, 'feminine' tendencies for men, or 'masculine' tendencies for women) are projected onto gay people, who are then disliked. In this way, individuals can symbolically (and often unconsciously) prove to themselves that those unacceptable feelings are not their own" (Herek 1992a:156).

Social identity theory holds promise as theory for practice in that it advances our understanding of violence against gay and lesbian people, especially youthful violence. Developmental theory tells us that individuals desire positive self-esteem. Their self-esteem is tied to the way their in-group status is evaluated relative to other groups. These social groups supply not only a worldview but a system of orientation for self-reference. Through this self-reference they create and define their place in society (Tajfel & Turner 1986:16). "Because an individual's self-concept is based on the image and evaluation of the group(s) with which he or she identifies, people can build up their own self-esteem by promoting their in-group's evaluation. This is accomplished by comparing one's in-group with and differentiating it from relevant out-groups" (Hamner 1992:179–80). Heterosexism makes gay people a potentially relevant out-group for everyone who identifies as a heterosexual, regardless of his or her membership in other in-groups.

According to Tajfel and Turner (1986) differentiation of the in-group from the out-group both fosters and is generated by group conflict. Conflict prompts individuals to deal with each other not as individuals but as representatives of their respective groups. Anti-gay/lesbian violence and other hate-motivated crimes can be understood to represent intergroup conflicts rather than simple interactions among a few individuals. Social identity theory allows us to understand why lesbians and gay men are especially likely to be victims of hate-motivated violence. Society's socioeconomic structure, with its hierarchy of social statuses, limits the access to high social standing in-groups. As a group generally held in low regard by society, lesbians, bisexuals, and gay men are likely to represent a relevant out-group for all quarters of society, particularly for individuals lower in the social system. As Herek (1992b) points out, "Psychological heterosexism can serve these functions only when an individual's psychological needs converge with the culture's ideology" (156). This is the connection between psychological and cultural heterosexism.

Heterosexist attitudes may not result in violence, but they are an important component of the action when violence occurs. The functions of psychological heterosexism described above may serve as an explanation of antigay crimes. However, other theorists see violence as an "expressive act," that is, an end in itself (Ehrlich 1992). In any case, most conclude that it is essentially "instrumental," that is, a habitual pattern of behavior adopted to achieve a set of personal needs or ends. This type of violence is motivated often by attempts to gain power and control.

Harry (1992) explains that there is a value-based justification for anti-gay/lesbian violence, reflecting society's norms related to gender. Perpetrators may rationalize that lesbians and gay men are worthy of punishment; therefore they see themselves as rendering gender justice and reaffirming the natural order of gender appropriate behavior. Whatever the function of the violence for those who engage in it, however, the consequences for victims can be quite severe.

THE PSYCHOLOGICAL CONSEQUENCES FOR VICTIMS

The widespread prevalence of anti-lesbian/gay prejudice and violence has not led to psychological dysfunction in the lesbian and gay communities. These communities do not differ significantly in mental health from the heterosexual population (Gonsiorek 1982a, 1991). While this is testimony to the resilience of lesbians and gay men as a group, individuals who are victims of violence may suffer from a variety of short-term and long-term effects. The psychological aftermath of victimization can include sleep disturbances and nightmares, headaches, diarrhea, uncontrollable crying, agitation and restlessness, increased use of drugs, and deterioration in personal relationships. Garnets, Herek, and Levy (1993) note that victimization creates psychological distress because it interferes with the normal process of denial through which people feel secure and invulnerable; it interferes with the perceptions of the world as an orderly and meaningful place; and it leads people to question their own worth. Survivors will often engage in self-blame for some specific behavior related to the crime as a coping strategy to feel a sense of control over their own lives and as a way for avoiding revictimization. This approach is contrasted to characterological self-blame, a perceived character flaw associated with low self-esteem (Janoff-Bulman 1979, 1982). When victims question their own self worth, it is often followed by a devaluation process wherein they perceive the self as no longer autonomous—they are helpless first at the hands of the perpetrator and then at the hands of others who help (the social stigma of being a victim). Herman's (1992) extensive study of trauma is informative. The victim may have a severe psychological response, which may be of short or long duration, beginning at the onset or delayed for years after the crime. Severe reactions are diagnosed as posttraumatic stress disorder (PTSD), presenting persistent symptoms for at least one month following the crime: (a) a constant reexperiencing of the victimization (e.g., via memories, intrusive thoughts, dreams, or intense distress from activities or events triggering recollection of the event); (b) complete avoidance of trauma-associated stimuli or a numbing of general responsiveness (e.g., diminished interest in significant activities, feelings of detachment from others, restricted affect, sense of foreshortened future); and (c) ongoing symptoms of increased arousal (e.g., sleep disturbances, exaggerated startle response, difficulty concentrating). The following case illustrates some of these effects as well as the inadequacy of the systemic response to the violence:

The literature related to victimization is well developed and constitutes an appropriate reference when working with lesbian, bisexuals, and gay men who have experienced violence. However, it must be remembered that because of heterosexism, specifically the ideologies of sex and gender, gays internalize some degree of negative feelings when they first become aware of their homosexuality. This internalized homophobia creates a "basic mistrust of one's sexual and interpersonal identity" (Stein & Cohen 1984a:61) and interferes with the process of identity formation (Malyon 1982). When a person is

SURVIVOR'S STORY*

My name is Bob Gravel and my family has lived in Lewiston, Maine's second largest city, for seventy-five years. Until last year I had lived there all my life, working for the last fourteen years as a shipping clerk for a shoe manufacturer.

In April 1985 three young men whom I'd seen around the neighborhood began to call me names. At first they called me "Faggot" and "Queer." By summer the harassment had escalated. One night they threw a bottle at me; on another, they chased me in their van. One night on July I noticed this van on the street and left a note on the windshield: "We all live in the same neighborhood. You live your life, I'll live mine." I even called the mothers of two of the young men and asked them to tell their sons to stop bothering me.

It did no good. On August 14, the same guys stopped me while I was taking groceries out of my car. They chased me, knocked me down, and kicked me. One said, "I'm going to kill you, faggot. I don't care how long it takes." He said it with such hatred that I knew he meant it.

On November 1, 1985, after eight months of harassment and threats, these people waited for me to come home. I spotted them in the alley near my home and stayed in my car. They pelted my car with rocks and bottles, but I was able to escape. I saw a police car and informed them of the attack.

The police were getting impatient with me because this was my fifteenth complaint against this group. I was getting no positive response from the police. They seemed upset at me. One officer told me to stay home. Another told me I should move, but I didn't feel I should leave my home. I went to a lawyer and had a harassment notice served on the leader of the group and I continued to plead with the police to stop these people from harassing me.

I then borrowed a gun. I'd never had a gun and I don't like them. I was scared that these guys were going to come to my house. At 9:00p.m. on November 3, 1985, they did come to my home. I looked out the window and saw one of them in my driveway. I called the police. One of them knocked at the front door and yelled obscenities at me. I was frightened. Suddenly another one began kicking the back door. They kicked and kicked at my door until the door began to break apart. I went to the bedroom and got the gun and called the police again. I could see them all outside. I felt cornered. I lost it. I ran downstairs and when one of them came at me, I fired one shot into the air. He kept coming. I shot again and killed him.

I became a different man. I became very ill, was unable to function, and lost myself esteem. It's a terrible thing to have killed a man. I have spoken with his family and visited his grave, but this feeling continues. I cannot enjoy life again.

The same guys came to my home again in March of 1986, just four months after the shooting. Again they hollered and threw objects in my apartment window. I called the police. The cop told me, "Gravel, you have to understand that these guys will go out and get drunk and start thinking about what you did to their friend."

My landlord asked me to move because he was scared of this group. Where was I to go? If I moved to another street, these people would just track me down again. I couldn't go out. I couldn't even go to the market. So the best solution was for me to move far away. I had to leave most of my furnishings. I lost my job. I lost the comfort of being with my family and friends. I was forced from my home.

My life is now hell. I had to begin at the bottom and take a janitor job. I am earning $100 less a week than at my former job. I have $4,000 in attorney's fees. I paid for damages around my former home, damages to my car, hospital and psychiatrist bills. The most severe damage to me was emotional; I cannot believe I had to kill to live free.

The leader of this group finally went to court. He received a $35 fine. The court told me they plea-bargained because the court didn't have time for a trial.

One man lost his life. Another man lost the will to live; the court assessed $35.

* Reprinted from Anti-Gay Violence (Hearing before the Subcommittee on Criminal Justice on the Committee on the Judiciary House of Representatives, 99th Congress, Second Session on Anti-Gay Violence; October 9, 1986). Washington, D.C.:GPO, Serial No. 132.

attacked because he or she is perceived to be gay, the consequences of victimization converges with those of cultural heterosexism to create a unique
set of challenges for the survivor. The victim is not prepared for victimization.
Hopefully, he or she has developed a gay or lesbian identity, psychological
resilience and coping skills, along with supportive networks, community
resources, and nonheterosexist interpretation of the experience so as to buffer the feelings of helplessness, depression, and low self-esteem.

In the aftermath of an assault, the lover and friends of a victim are also at
risk for secondary victimization as they assist the survivor in negotiating the
legal, health, and social service systems. For example, friends and lovers may
be denied access to hospital visitation because they are not immediate family. When staff do not recognize the relationship, it serves to remind the gay
couple and their friends that the larger society is hostile to them as gay or lesbian people.

Not all assaults are just physical; some are *sexual*. Lesbians may be directly
targeted for sexual assault by perpetrators who view them as "open targets"
who deserve punishment because they are not under the protection of a man:

> Because many lesbians are not accustomed to feeling dependent on or vul-
> nerable around men, a sexual attack motivated by male rage at their life-style
> constitutes a major assault upon their general sense of safety, independence,
> and well-being. In addition to the humiliation and degradation that are com-
> mon components of all sexual victimization, anti-lesbian rape may also in-
> clude attempts by the perpetrator to degrade lesbian sexuality.
>
> (Garnets, Herek, & Levy 1993:584)

Thus there are special meanings to the assault when sexual orientation is
involved.

Male-male sexual assault is largely an invisible problem assumed to occur
only in prisons and other closed institutions, although Anderson (1982) and
Myers (1989) report that it is more serious outside of institutions. Male gender-role socialization creates distinct problems for gay male rape survivors.
Because most men have internalized the belief that sexual assault of men is
beyond the realm of possibility, the male victim's sudden confrontation with
"his own vulnerability, helplessness, and dependence on the mercy of others"
can be devastating (Anderson 1982:150). Both perpetrators and victims may
regard themselves as gay or straight. As with a lesbian sexually assaulted by a
man, a man who has been sexually assaulted by another man must deal not
only with the effects of the violation of basic autonomy but also with the
meaning of the assault from a sexual orientation standpoint.

Anti-lesbian/gay *verbal* abuse constitutes a symbolic form of violence and is a common reminder of the ever-present threat of physical assault. It also challenges the victim's routine sense of security and invulnerability, making the world seem more malevolent and less predictable (Garnets, Herek, & Levy 1993:215). This effect can be readily understood when violence itself is understood on a continuum from the ordinarily invisible to the visible as figure 10.1 has illustrated.

In this way, the entire gay and lesbian community is victimized by these crimes against individuals. These crimes create a climate of fear that forces some to conclude that it is safer to hide their sexual orientation. Another response can be victim blaming, focusing on "obvious" behaviors, gestures, or clothing as having provoked an attack. This response reinforces cultural heterosexism, the prescription to conform to highly restrictive gender-role behavior and the belief that being gay or lesbian is wrong and worthy of punishment. It parallels, of course, the common tendency to blame women who are victims of verbal or sexual harassment for having provoked the attack through their behavior or appearance and with the self-protective measures many women take to restrict their own activities at night to avoid victimization. The alternative is to demand safe streets at all times for all people—that is, to make violence prevention in general a priority.

Social Work Practice with Victims of Antigay Violence

> The incidents of violence against lesbians and gay men are endless. These are
> the stories of our lives: the horror of walking down the street, perhaps with a
> loved one, and being beaten or abused by complete strangers solely because we
> are gay or lesbian; the shame of being harassed, threatened or assaulted by our
> neighbors or co-workers because they don't want "our kind" around; the fear
> of reporting the incident to the police, getting medical attention, or seeking
> counseling services because they may blame our sexual orientation on the
> attack or accuse us of "coming on" to the attacker.   —Bea Hanson (1996:97)

Social workers can help victims of hate crimes by drawing upon the professional literature related to crisis intervention, rape, assault, trauma, and violence. However, before working with the lesbian or gay victim, the therapist must be aware of his or her own heterosexist biases and know about gay male and lesbian identity as well as about related mental health issues. Many of the comments made elsewhere in this book related to therapeutic bias would be appropriate for review as a guide to defining the problem and establishing a therapeutic alliance in a nonheterosexist manner.

Bard and Sangrey (1979) conceptualize intervention as moving through the impact, recoil, and recovery phases. Crisis intervention, a focus on safety, and medical care are the appropriate interventions during the *impact phase*. Assessment must address the meaning of this experience, feelings about self, and the degree to which the victimization is associated with being lesbian or gay. Assessment of the internal and external coping resources targets (a) learned coping skills, (b) support networks, such as a lover, family, or friends who can help meet immediate needs, and (c) existing or potential involvement in gay and lesbian community networks.

The survivor needs to ventilate the horror and terror of the crime during the *recoil phase*. The feelings of alienation and isolation must also be given free vent. The goal is to support victimized clients as they regain their self-confidence and sense of competence and wholeness while their feelings of guilt, shame, helplessness, and embarrassment diminish (Garnets, Herek, & Levy 1993:588–89). Survivors should be encouraged to feel and express anger toward the assailant, especially survivors who are blaming themselves or are depressed (Bard & Sangrey 1979; Bohn 1984). The practitioner should help the victim review the decisions made before, during, and after the assault to prevent self-blame and guilt; the intent is to help thwart the distorted perceptions that lead to self-blame. Other strategies include systematic desensitization, flooding, and stress inoculation (Barker 1987; Hepworth 1993; Mattaini 1997). Reexposure to the memory of the traumatic event may be accompanied by cognitive restructuring of false assumptions about oneself or the world (Frank et al. 1988).

Negative feelings about their sexual orientation are typical of survivors of hate crimes whether the perpetrator is heterosexual or homosexual. These feelings must be explored to separate the assaultive experience from the all-too-often regression to the coming-out experience. The aim is to reestablish the client's positive identity as a lesbian or gay man. Consciousness-raising to place the crime in a social context, group work to permit identification with other lesbian and gay male victims, and increased involvement with the gay community are likely to be particularly helpful in achieving the necessary psychosocial reorganization and recovery.

Anti-lesbian/gay sexual assault requires the practitioner to help the survivor separate the crime from the experience of sexuality and intimacy. "Gay male survivors are at special risk for phobic or aversive feelings toward male sexuality because their normal sexual behavior will superficially resemble the sexual assault. . . . Lesbian survivors also may experience fear reaction and flashbacks to the assault triggered by normal sexual contact" (Bard & Sangrey 1979:221). The therapist's support for the survivor and partner will allow fear to diminish and healing over time. Clients will need encouragement as they initiate sexual contact in stages. This is the *recovery phase*, which is to help the client regain a sense of being in charge of one's own body and to counter the fear and powerlessness experienced during the crime.

Support will be needed by lovers, family, and friends who will experience losses and pain associated with the crime; who will need to make sense of this experience; and who will have to regain a sense of the world as stable and predictable. Psychoeducational intervention for the significant other as related to the dynamics of violence, homosexuality, victimization, and hate crimes is helpful in this process of reorganization. Many of these strategies will entail development of new programs as well as changes in agency policy (Sloan & Edmond 1996).

The criminal justice and the medical systems may pose an additional threat to gay and lesbian victims of hate crimes because of their heterosexist bias. Police are often hostile, perhaps rejecting the idea that male-male rape occurs or suggesting that gay victims themselves deserved or instigated the attack (Anderson 1982; Hanson 1996). Medical professionals may assume that a lesbian sexual assault victim is heterosexual and display insensitivity in their questions (Orzek 1988). The social worker can play an important role as consultant, educator, and advocate for the survivor and his or her significant other within law enforcement and medical treatment systems.

Social workers should join with other mental health professionals to mobilize the community to confront hate crimes and the cultural and psychological heterosexism that fuels them. Anti-hate legislation and victimization programs are needed by the lesbian and gay community, which may come about with community education and organizing and with coalition-building. Legislative action might focus on the expansion of civil rights to cover gay men, bisexuals, and lesbians as well as to classify antigay and anti-lesbian-bashing as hate crimes. The legal argument might more appropriately focus on current public accommodations laws and laws pertaining to freedom of religion, as opposed to justifications built on privacy laws and laws relating to freedom of speech.

Empirical research on the social and familial determinants of anti-lesbian/gay violence, the motivations for individual acts of this type of violence, the characteristics of perpetrators, and the problems experienced by victims is needed. Ehrlich (1992) notes that Johann Galtung, the sociologist, once described violence as

anything that prevents an individual from fully developing her or his full potential. That definition comes closer than any to identifying the essence of violence. . . . We should not let legal norms or custom define our problem. To do so would be not just to ignore but to delegitimize the pain of thousands of survivors of violence in this society.   (Ehrlich 1992:111)

How people learn antigay violence, when they learn it, and whether they accept or reject the heritage of violence are important questions to answer if a successful program of attitude and behavior change and social transformation is to be instituted.

Lesbian and Gay Domestic Violence

So far, violence against gay and lesbian people has been discussed as it occurs in public, generally between strangers. Violence between gay and lesbian people who are lovers or partners—that is, within the private domestic space of their couple relationships—is a different kind of problem in many ways. However, there are similarities between them. Each is a form of individual violence (see figure 10.1) that can be understood as related to more pervasive dynamics of power and powerlessness, domination and subordination. In addition, violence against gay and lesbian people can be easily dismissed as a problem by many because it expresses widely held attitudes; similarly because gay and lesbian relationships are either invisible (these are just "roommates" or "friends" who got into a fight) or are seen as dysfunctional anyway, the problem of domestic violence in gay and lesbian relationships has long gone unrecognized. When it comes to domestic violence, however, the gay and lesbian communities themselves have also been slow to acknowledge the problem despite the fact that it is now suggested that domestic violence may be as common in gay and lesbian relationships as it is in heterosexual ones (Hanson 1996).

Research related to the nature of domestic violence in lesbian and gay relationships is thwarted by many false assumptions commonly accepted in gay and lesbian communities. Two of these assumptions are that domestic violence is only physical abuse and that any abuse perpetrated by a lesbian or gay man is not that dangerous or harmful because of the relatively equal size and strength of same-gender partners. Other myths and misconceptions have been identified as reasons why gay-on-gay domestic violence is most often not recognized or labeled as such:

Only straight women get battered; gay men are never victims. Domestic violence is more common in straight relationships than in gay male relationships. Gay domestic violence is a "fight" and when two men fight it is a fair fight between equals. It is not really violence when two men fight; it is nor-

mal; it is boys being boys. Gay men's domestic violence is just a lovers' quar-
rel. The batterer will always be bigger and stronger; the victim will always be
smaller and weaker. Men who are abusive while under the influence of drugs
or alcohol are not responsible for their actions. Gay men's domestic violence
has increased as a result of the AIDS epidemic, alcoholism, and drug abuse.
Gay men's domestic violence is sexual behavior, a version of sado-
masochism; the victims actually like it. The law does not protect victims of
gay men's domestic violence.   (Island & Letellier 1991:15–20)

These myths keep the gay community as well as the community at large from
taking responsibility and action. The myths also serve as powerful forces for
keeping gay men and lesbians in abusive relationships. However, these myths
and assumptions run counter to the empirical data gleaned from survivors and
research participants.

Another reason that the gay and lesbian community has resisted acknowledging the problem of domestic violence is because it is believed that widespread knowledge of this problem would add to already high levels of antigay
discrimination. As Island and Letellier (1991) put it with respect to gay men:

> Gay men generally believe they are more affluent than their straight broth-
> ers, are better educated, are in better physical shape, and make a significant
> effort to lead a more enlightened lifestyle. But, if the gay community really
> did take its own domestic violence seriously, it would mean that gays them-
> selves [would be required to give up a powerful defense mechanism, denial,
> and] would have to recognize that gay men truly are not only ordinary peo-
> ple but also have [their] proportionate share of violent individuals in their
> midst who bash other gay men in startlingly high numbers.
>
> (Island & Letellier 1991:10)

For the lesbian community, the issues are similar in that recognizing that
lesbians are both victims and perpetrators constitutes an uncomfortable fact.
Denial also serves to maintain the false assumption that only men are batterers and only women are victims. Men are supposed to be in control of their
lives and therefore immune to victimization. A narrow definition of sexism
does not allow for lesbian abusers. Finally, denial attempts to negate heterosexist assumptions that gay and lesbian relationships are inherently sick and
seeks to reduce any further justification for devaluing gay and lesbian lives or
for escalating violence and discrimination.

Unfortunately, however, lesbians and gay men can be and are battered or
abused by a family member, roommate, lover, ex-spouse, or ex-lover. Anec-

dotal evidence suggests that some victims seek help and tell authorities the real reason they are doing so and some victims seek help without revealing the real reason. However, most victims don't tell anyone at all, and the authorities fail to ask if a reported assault is domestic violence. Nearly all batterers do not tell anyone and do not seek help voluntarily. This pattern is much like that seen in heterosexual domestic violence, although gay and lesbian people fear the heterosexism and homophobia of potential helpers along with all the other barriers to seeking assistance that all domestic abuse victims experience.

THE EXTENT OF THE PROBLEM

Although gay men's domestic violence is a newly recognized problem, it has existed since gay men began coupling and living together. What is new about it is that all over the country gay men are coming forward to seek help as victims of domestic violence. These estimated half million battered men, along with an equal number of perpetrators, face a gay community and a society in general that are ill-prepared to help them. It is estimated that "only substance abuse and AIDS adversely affect more gay men, making domestic violence the third largest health problem facing gay men today" (Island & Letellier 1991:1). The actual numbers are hard to come by because domestic violence is a taboo subject. For authorities to show interest by collecting data would mean that something should be done. Because sodomy is still a crime in many states and because gay-bashing is still widely ignored, there are many disincentives for reporting the problem, and legal intervention on behalf of battered gay men has little political capital.

Similarly, battering and other forms of physical violence in lesbian relationships is not a new phenomenon but a rather newly recognized one. Although the women's shelter movement is recently increasing its attention to serving women who are being abused in their relationships with other women, it is not clear that lesbian women feel comfortable seeking help in these settings (Renzetti 1996), and it is only by reporting the problem or seeking help with it that the prevalence of the problem will become known. Isolation is often a major problem; as Waldron (1996) notes, "Often, because of a reluctance to identify as a lesbian, the battering lesbian partner is the only other lesbian with whom the battered lesbian has extensive contact" (44). Nevertheless it has been estimated that 22 to 46 percent of all lesbians have been involved in a lesbian relationship in which physical violence occurred (Elliott 1996). Where there is acceptance that gay and lesbian domestic abuse exists, there is often the assumption that it affects only certain groups within the gay and lesbian community. Violent and abusive behavior are found in all segments of the gay and lesbian community, without regard for race, class, ethnicity, age, ability, education, politics, or religion. However, some subgroups within the community, such as gay men and lesbians of color, may find it even more difficult than others to identify sources of help that they can trust (Mendez 1996; Waldron 1996). The few studies of gay and lesbian domestic abuse that do exist concluded that neither the victim nor the perpetrator are easily identified. These misconceptions are often similar to those held about heterosexual abusive relationships.

Abuse within an intimate relationship actually can take on a variety of forms, many of which are found along with physical violence when it occurs. Walber (1988:251) identified the following forms of domestic violence reported by lesbians and gay men: physical abuse (hitting, choking, slapping, burning, shoving, using a weapon, neglecting, locking up in a room); isolation or the restriction of freedom (controlling personal/social contacts, access to information, and participation in groups and organizations); psychological and emotional abuse (criticizing constantly, ridiculing, trying to humiliate or degrade, lying, undermining self-esteem); threats and intimidation (threatening harm; threatening children, family, or friends; threatening to make reports to authorities that would jeopardize relationships to children, child custody, immigration, or legal status); heterosexist control (threatening to reveal gay or lesbian identity to family, neighbors, employers, ex-spouses, or city, state, and/or federal authorities); economic abuse (controlling resources, fostering dependency, stealing money, running up debts); sexual abuse (forcing sex or specific acts, assaulting "sexual parts," withholding sex, criticizing performance); property destruction (destroying mementos, breaking furniture or windows, throwing or smashing objects, threatening or hurting pets, trashing clothes). Figure 10.3 (which posits a female victim in the context of a heterosexual marriage or relationship) illustrates how all these facets of abuse relate to each other whatever the nature of the relationship. It also points out the fundamental dynamic of power and control within the relationship whatever specific form the abuse may take.

Understanding the Problem

Many of the models for understanding and stopping domestic violence come from the battered women's movement and are applied to the gay and lesbian communities. Whether this framework is adequate is currently being debated. These current general understandings of domestic violence are worth reviewing for their relevance to gay and lesbian victims and batterers. However, study of gay and lesbian domestic violence to date, though limited, has suggested ways

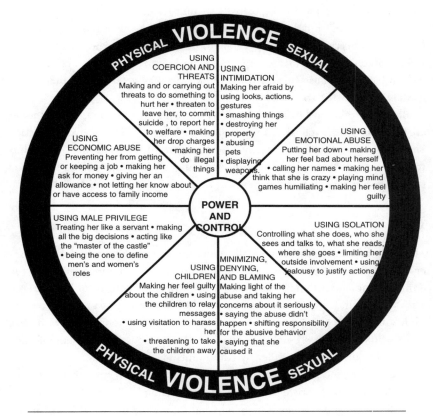

Figure 10.3 Power and control in the cycle of physical and/or sexual violence

in which theory and practice may need to be modified (see, for example, Bera
& LeTourneau 1994; Marrujo & Kreger 1996; Merrill 1996; Renzetti 1992).

Domestic violence is currently understood as any pattern of behavior
designed to dominate, coerce, or isolate within a relationship. It is an exercise
of any form of power that is used to maintain control or to dominate. This is
thought to be another manifestation of sexism, an ideology of unequal power
not necessarily based on gender. Since battery (according to the dominant
thinking in this field) is caused by the cultural belief that hierarchical rule and
coercive authority are natural, then all relationships tend to be based on
power and domination. All forms of battery are linked (hooks 1984).

This lesson is strongly reinforced in the socialization of men and women;
gay men, bisexuals, and lesbians are no exception. Regardless of sexual orientation, certain lessons are learned within the family. The family is a place
where unequal power is evident and where that power can be used, without

consequences, to control. Lesbians, like non-lesbians, often desire control over the resources and decisions in family life that power brings and that violence can assure when control is resisted. Lesbians have learned that violence works in achieving partner compliance. Therefore, Hart (1986) asserts that lesbian batterers abuse for much the same reason as heterosexual men do— namely, to get what they want.

Battering relationship are rarely only abusive. Love, caring, and remorse are often part of a cyclical pattern of abuse (Walker 1979). Survivors are convinced that the situation will change for the better. They want the relationship to continue but the violence to end. As in any relationship, shame, isolation, and economic or emotional dependency can be major barriers to leaving.

THE BATTERERS

Most scholars and practitioners fail to identify a common profile of a batter-er/abuser. Most would agree that there is no provocation or justification for domestic violence. Psychotherapists when working with a lesbian batterer start with a fundamental assumption: she (the batterer) must accept responsibility for her actions and the consequences of her actions because she has chosen violence. They emphasize that the lesbian abuser is accountable not only to the survivor but to the gay community.

Theory for practice related to male domestic abuse suggests that batterers have a learned, progressive psychological disorder and will continue to act out their dysfunction until they obtain help and follow the prescribed treatment. Violence is a choice. *Social learning theory* suggests that batterers actually believe that they will "get their way" if they create an environment and atmosphere of intimidation and terror for their lover. People, according to this theory, will take repeated instances of a lesser punishment to avoid an extreme punishment that has been threatened. Positive reinforcement is involved because at the end of the violent episode, "making up" often includes sex and other expressions of affection. Once the rage has passed, the cessation of the perpetrator's violence is a reinforcement to the violent act. For the abuser, violence itself may be self-reinforcing because it serves as a tension release.

Developmental and cognitive theories are referenced by those who view the perpetrator as having experienced some developmental impairment. Specifically, the perpetrator did not learn to choose a nonviolent solution but learned to be violent toward those who do not do what he or she wants. This cognitive, developmental flaw was acquired through parental neglect, inappropriate modeling, or inept teaching by adults around them. *Personality theory* might suggest that male batterers overexaggerate their masculinity so as to validate their maleness. *Communication theory* suggests that male abusers have failed to acquire adequate communication skills, that is, the ability to verbalize anger without resorting to violence. A number of theorists view batterers as psychologically unhealthy, with a mental disorder (Gondolf 1985; Hamberger & Hastings 1988; Island & Letellier 1991). They contend that batterers have several characteristics that differentiate them, to some degree, from men in general. They note that batterers who were abused as children are more likely to present personality disorders and are highly resistant to treatment.

This mental health perspective on gay and lesbian domestic violence is highly controversial because it counters the prevailing view that battering is not a psychiatric issue, that if society were to change, the battering would stop. From this perspective, if domestic violence were pathologized, as has been the case with homosexuality historically, and with drug abuse and alcoholism more recently, the field would be taken over by professionals with little experience with the problem. Island and Letellier (1991) reject what they see as sexual politics, the position posed by "some women [who] fear that the use of mental disorder categories by therapist treating lesbian batterers will lead to further victimization of women, a group already damaged by incompetent, sexist, or homophobic therapists and institutions for hundreds of years" (59). They argue that by not properly labeling the batterer as disordered, it can be interpreted that the community is aiding and abetting the perpetrator in avoiding accountability for his or her conduct.

Practice wisdom in the domestic violence field, however, assumes a contrary stance; that is, most men are viewed as violent and inherently aggressive since in 80 percent of the marriages, husbands are abusive toward their wives. This position is disputed by Gelles and Straus (1988:104); they contend that some men follow a negative societal prescription for masculinity while others do not. Those who follow blindly the popular American notions of acting tough at all times, not showing tender feelings at all (e.g., the lean, mean, super cool, stoic cowboy type), those who get their way by flexing their muscles, drinking to excess, getting angry and hitting people are heading toward pain, trouble, and possible domestic violence. The behavioral idea of masculinity for some men is to intimidate, to dominate, and to do what they damn well want to, no matter what the consequences to themselves and to other people. Masculinity to these men is reflected in their attempt to control others so that they are sure that no one controls them, since being influenced by others is considered unmasculine (Island & Letellier 1991:50–51). Island and Letellier view this as further evidence of psychological disorder and propose a rather elegant and original theory of perpetrator behavior which is summarized here:

There is a pre-existing tendency to desire and attempt to manipulate, control and dominate others, especially the partner. There is a pattern for the violence and abuse to become progressively more serious. The abuser shows a pronounced difficulty managing his own frustration, anger, patience, and impulses toward the victim. The abuser has a specific tendency to restrict the autonomy of people with whom he has a close relationship, especially the partner. There is a pattern in the batterer to use cruel, demeaning, and aggressive behavior toward and actual violence against the partner. Before the violence, there is a discernible decision-making pattern in the perpetrator which reveals a premeditated intent to commit violence. The batterer has a pressing need to keep secret the fact and extent of the violence. The batterer shows a strong pattern of always justifying his violence by blaming the victim for having provoked it. The batterer usually shows a certain personality profile, including, but not limited to, a tendency toward: low self-esteem; self-hatred, perhaps with internalized homophobia; depression, perhaps chronic depression; minimizing and trivializing his own violent action; an ability to deny responsibility for his own violent actions; holding exceedingly high expectations for self, partner, and relationships; suspiciousness; jealousy, perhaps pathological jealousy; extreme criticism and judgment of others; extreme insecurity and inability to trust others; lying; a fascination with violence of all kinds, weapons, martial arts, injury and torture; a "Jekyll-and-Hyde" type of personality; strong feelings of guilt and failure. There is a pattern of extreme emotional dependency by the perpetrator on the victim. The perpetrator has a strong tendency to obsess about the victim such that over time a significant proportion of the perpetrator's thinking is consumed with thoughts about the victim. The abuse has an identifiable life history, a history that fits some or all of the elements in the pattern below. The abuser may show a pattern of some or frequent life disappointment or perceived failure in relationships, school, occupation, finance, love, family, and the general circumstance of living. There is a pattern of poor communication skills, especially in relation to feelings and conflict resolution. There is a specific tendency in the batterer to have unusually rigid and unachievable, stereotyped concepts of masculinity and sex-roles. The batterer has some mental disorder, state or condition, from many possible causes or origins, as indicated by episodes of domestic violence of which he is the perpetrator. There is strong tendency in the abuser not to display violence or his violent tendencies toward people in position of authority or higher status. The batterer has a strong resistance to receiving or seeking help from outside sources and instead evidences a need for, and over-reliance on, help and support from the victim.   (Island & Letellier 1991:76–80)

America is a violent culture and a patriarchal society at its roots, yet millions of men who experience all these pervasive forces reject all of them, adopt only some of them, or dramatically neutralize most of them. *Sociopolitical theory*, which identifies causation as solely gender-role socialization and patriarchy, lets the individual violent man off the hook by not giving sufficient attention to his psychological makeup, his interpretation of "masculinity," his dysfunctional choices, and his responsibility for the criminally violent act.

The Victims

Lesbians and gay men are aware of the mistaken belief of mental health providers that the survivor's behavior reflects masochism or personal weakness or that it is caused by substance abuse, intimacy problems, family influences, stress, childhood violence, or provocation. While these may be related factors in some cases, they are not causes. Some have even questioned the division of roles in abusive relationships into a simple dichotomy of victim and perpetrator (Marrujo & Kreger 1996). However, most commentators find that those who are abused within an intimate relationship often manifest certain characteristics in common *at least in the context of that relationship*, such as being dependent, overly responsible, concerned with the needs and feelings of others, and feeling inferior or inadequate in the relationship. The abuse they suffer tends to reinforce and magnify these same traits. However, there is no evidence that victims of domestic abuse share any common mental health disorder or problem in every case.

Island and Letellier (1991) depart from the consensus position that there is no victim profile. They propose a victim theory which postulates that

> the prospective victim will tend to have relatively sound mental health without a prior history of, or contact with, abuse of any kind. This person has a history of handling life's problems in a reasonably confident and effective manner. Many tend to blame [themselves] for most interpersonal problems with others and to absolve others. This [abused] individual may tend to want to please others and sometimes submit to control and influence by others . . . may tend to mistrust his own judgment about people and to be uneasy with disagreement, to be conciliatory, though argumentative, in response to interpersonal disagreements. This individual may tend toward taking responsibility for others; a strong sense of independence; low self-worth; a fatalistic world-view; a considerable reservoir of guilt; liking people; trust and lack of suspicion; insecurity; high ego strength; and trivializes or denies the negative or unpleasant.   (Island & Letellier 1991:105–106)

These authors challenge current thinking in the domestic violence field, first by rejecting the popular notion that domestic violence is codependency, second by extending the analysis of power in relationships beyond the traditional male/female dyad, and finally by postulating that the victim and the batterer have very separate psychologies.

Views like these suggest that power, not gender, underlies lesbian and gay male abuse. Our previous discussion of cultural heterosexism helps us to understand that most gay men and lesbians were raised in heterosexual homes where power differences between men and women, parents and children fueled the gender-role socialization patterns that they may then have modeled in their own relationships. While these and other authors who write about gay and lesbian domestic violence draw heavily from all the current domestic violence literature, they differ markedly from many of the theoretical, clinical, and political positions of the pioneers in this field in that they emphasize that many propositions do not apply to lesbians and gay men (Island & Letellier 1991; Marrujo & Kreger 1996; Merrill 1996). A more sophisticated understanding of domestic violence in general and in gay and lesbian relationships in particular is clearly needed in order to intervene more sensitively and effectively.

Implications for Practice

Social workers must begin practice with gay and lesbian domestic abuse with an analysis of sexism and heterosexism, so that the psychological implications for individuals and couples are viewed within an appropriate context. The potential conflict between activists and professional providers must be recognized. Therapeutic interventions directed solely at changing "self-defeating personality disorder" or "sadistic personality disorder" may heighten this conflict. Interventions that do not include group analysis and action about the larger issues of violence may be viewed as strategies to help clients to adapt to unjust situations and thus as missing the mark.

The key issue for survivors of domestic abuse is empowerment. Breaking down the profound sense of isolation experienced by survivors is the intervention challenge. Social work assessments must include the possibility of domestic violence when accepting any lesbian and gay man's request for services. *As is the case with all domestic abuse, the survivor must be helped to evaluate his or her physical and emotional safety first.* Knowledge of appropriate resources, such as self-help groups, hotlines, or shelters and safe home programs is essential. Within such programs clients can develop their own options, generate short- and long-term goals, and draw upon successful coping and adaptation skills. The battered women's movement has long held the position that couples' counseling or mediation through the courts are inappropriate since these interventions assume an equal power relationship between parties. A survivor's fear of reprisals may prevent authentic participation in counseling, especially when the possibility of physical and emotional safety may be compromised.

When dealing with domestic abusers, Walber (1988), whose primary focus is lesbians, recommends that service providers adopt a community education role, emphasizing that battering and abuse are social problems in the gay and lesbian community and are part of the social context that fosters hierarchical relations between people. Education directed toward increasing sensitivity while changing social norms is a primary task. Providers must develop an understanding of the cyclical nature of abuse, the escalation of violence, barriers that exist for all survivors in the criminal justice system, and specifically the heterosexist attitudes within domestic violence programs. Batterers/abusers must be accountable for their behavior and its impact on survivors and on the community. The community must be helped to respond with support for those that speak out. Services for women are often limited while programs for abused gay men are nonexistent in most areas; therefore basic community organization will need to stimulate program development.

Services for gay and lesbian batterers have not been widely studied. Interventions that emphasize psychoeducational groups addressing issues of power, control, and sexism, rather than of anger management and personal psychology, may be more effective than an individual approach. Providers, however, observed that abusers typically ignore or deny their actions and move on to new relationships, often aggressively blaming the survivor for any problems while seeing themselves as the real victim. "The pattern of abuse is then repeated, reinforced by societal norms and condoned through community denial" (Walber 1988:254). Byrne (1996) suggests that a combination of individual and group treatment may be ideal. Since these observations are based on prescriptive studies, the clinician is cautioned to evaluate her own interventions in a systematic fashion.

The mental health approach of Island and Letellier (1991) is very different in that it proposes that gay male batterers are in serious psychological, legal, and interpersonal trouble, and therefore are in need of a full range of interventions involving therapy, treatment, imprisonment, education, and/or counseling over the course of one to two years. A summary of their detailed treatment guidelines follows: (1) couple counseling is inappropriate and dangerous (Frank & Houghton 1987); (2) the therapist must understand domestic violence issues; (3) the therapist must be gay-affirmative; (4) the therapist must not use sociological and/or social learning theories to excuse or justify battering behavior: and (5) the therapist must not view male violence as innate and natural. Treatment resources should include several components: (1) therapy; (2) community support services; (3) safe houses with lay helpers; and (4) access to law enforcement and the justice system. The reader is encouraged to review the richness of the suggested activity for each of the above components and to carefully consider the full range of intervention levels that are needed (Hamberger 1996).

Finally, the literature related to the treatment of domestic violence or battered women is extensive and may be used as a model for intervention with lesbians and gay men. Gondolf (1985) offers a cautionary note by pointing out that there is an 85 percent recidivism rate and the few evaluations that exist reveal the limited impact of current treatment programs. Therefore, the reader, when using this approach with gay and lesbian people involved in domestic abuse, is reminded that this is new theory and is cautioned to evaluate each intervention because of the limited clinical appraisal to date.

Conclusion

Both gay/lesbian-bashing and lesbian and gay domestic violence are wrong, they are criminal, and they must stop. The pervasiveness and seriousness of both of these problems are only recently being recognized. Because of the biopsychosocial and ecological perspectives that are so central to how they approach their work, social workers are well positioned to contribute both to an enriched understanding of these problems and to be helpful to gay and lesbian people who have been affected by them. As this chapter has emphasized, however, the first task for the profession and for the gay and lesbian community will be to overcome the denial that has so far impeded both adequate recognition of these problems of violence and the development of an adequate and effective response.

HIV Disease

A Social Work Response

Social workers are central to the delivery of health and social services to gay men, bisexuals, and lesbians infected with HIV disease, as well as others affected by the epidemic. Effective practice is built upon knowledge of the impact of homophobia and heterosexism on the social construction and response to AIDS, the process of HIV infection, medical treatment and the health care delivery system, core psychosocial issues, the impact on social functioning, and AIDS dementia as well as the concerns of the "worried well." Understanding the social and economic effects of the epidemic, on society in general and the gay and lesbian communities specifically, is important in the planning of micro and macro social work interventions.

Acquired Immunodeficiency Syndrome (AIDS)[1] is this nation's most serious pandemic. Historians will classify this among the most devastating global epidemics since the black plague of the Middles Ages, the cholera epidemics of the 1800s, and the great influenza pandemic of 1918–19. In 1996 Human Immunodeficiency Virus (HIV) disease was the chief cause of death among men and women in the United States between the ages of twenty-four and forty-five years of age. HIV disease is responsible for enormous psychological, social, and economic distress. It is a disease that affects not only the individual but the significant others, family, friends, coworkers, the community, and society at large.

HIV disease and substance abuse are now understood to be closely related. Substance abuse, another major social problem, is both influenced by and influences the social construction of and the societal response to HIV disease.

Since AIDS was first recognized in 1979–1981 through 1995, more than 400,000 cases had been reported nationwide, with more than 200,000 deaths during that period. In 1995 worldwide there were well over two million reported cases of AIDS, with an estimated 13 million people infected with the virus. In 1995 the World Health Organization projected that by the year 2000 there will be 40 million to 100 million people infected with HIV (Centers for Disease Control 1995).

The demographics of the epidemic in the United States, now into its second decade, have changed. In many medium and large cities on both coasts drug users and their partners and children represent the largest percentages; the fastest growing categories now are women and adolescents. In 1986 African-Americans comprised 24 percent of overall reported AIDS cases, Latinos 15 percent, and whites 60 percent; however, in 1995 a dramatic shift was apparent: 39 percent African-American, 19 percent Latino, and 40 percent white. By the year 2000, AIDS may no longer be considered a gay white man's disease; African-Americans will account for more than half the reported cases in the United States. In 1995 African-Americans reported 93 cases for every 100,000 people while whites logged in 15 per 100,000. AIDS is killing more African-American men than murder, heart disease, and accidents combined. And black women account for two-thirds of all U.S. women with the disease. Statistics from the Centers for Disease Control (CDC) show that 70 percent of white men who contracted AIDS during the period July 1995 to June 1996 were infected through men with men sex, while only 33 percent of black men contracted AIDS sexually. Among black women, 36 percent of the cases were attributed to drug use and 37 percent to heterosexual sex (Smith 1996). When HIV disease, or AIDS, was first reported in the United States, its related opportunistic infections were first found among gay men living in San Francisco. AIDS was therefore viewed primarily as a "gay disease" and was called Gay Related Immune Disease (GRID) and thus assumed the social stigma attached to homosexuality. Stigma intensified when injection drug users (a small percentage of whom were gay, lesbian, or bisexual) were identified as another group at risk for infection. During the first half of the 1990s, public health officials in the United States reported increasing proportions of cases in heterosexuals and those addicted to IV drugs. In 1995, however, 53 percent of the cases in the United States still occurred in gay men. Therefore, the HIV epidemic is intimately involved in the lives of most gay men, their lovers, friends, families, communities, and many bisexuals and lesbians as well.

Presently, because of homophobia and negative attitudes toward drug use and addiction, HIV disease is one of the most emotionally charged public health issues faced by society (Altman 1987; Conrad 1986). Regardless of one's source of infection, the result is stigmatization for the client and secondary stigmatization for those in his or her supporting social systems. Stigma, in turn, affects HIV-related policy development, service delivery, and funding. Infected women, some lesbians and bisexual women, and their children experience public fear and discrimination. Many of those infected have been abandoned by family and friends. Some health care and social service practitioners, including social workers (in violation of the *Code of Ethics*), have refused to provide care to patients with HIV disease (Appleby 1995).

HIV disease affects all areas of biopsychosocial functioning. Its literature is therefore enormous, drawing upon a broad spectrum of academic and professional disciplines, including the arts and sciences, education, health care, law and advocacy, social services, and mental health. Each has chronicled the hopelessness and despair, as well as the resilience and the heroism, of people living with HIV disease. Social workers have contributed significantly to the psychosocial and mental health literature related to HIV. Appleby (1989), Christ and Wiener (1985), Dansky (1994), Dilley and Goldblum (1987), Land (1992), Leukefeld and Fimbres (1987), Lynch, Lloyd, and Fimbres (1993), Odets and Shernoff (1995), Reamer (1993a, 1993b), Shernoff and Scott (1988) are just a few of the many who have published practice-oriented texts on this topic. These authors and many other social workers have addressed HIV disease in all the leading professional journals. It is beyond the scope of this chapter to do justice to all that has been written on HIV disease in the United States. The reader is reminded to review the references in this chapter as well as professional journals in social work and other allied professions, specifically *The Active Voice+* (published by people with AIDS), *AIDS Education and Prevention, Focus: A Guide to AIDS Research and Counseling, HIV Frontline*, the *Journal of Gay and Lesbian Psychotherapy*, and the *Journal of Gay and Lesbian Social Services* for the depth necessary to serve HIV-infected gay, bisexual, and lesbian people and their affected children and families. This chapter provides an overview and basic understanding of, first, an individual's progression through the disease; second, the impact on the family; third, the impact of the epidemic on society; and, fourth, the toll the epidemic has taken on the gay, bisexual, and lesbian communities.

AIDS and HIV Infection

AIDS is the common name for the final stage of HIV disease, when the body's immune system is seriously compromised or breaks down. HIV disease is believed to be caused by a virus called the human immunodeficiency virus. The virus invades and destroys T-4 white blood cells, which are necessary for the body to resist infections. Without T-4 cells, the natural defense or immune system of the body cannot produce antibodies to overcome foreign organisms. Without a fully functioning immune system, organisms that usually would be harmless or relatively easily dealt with by the body's defenses can cause life-threatening infections and illnesses. Those infections are called "opportunistic" because the weakened immune system gives the invading organisms the opportunity to grow and thrive. Opportunistic infections and diseases, such as pneumocystis carinii pneumonia (PCP) and Kaposi's sarcoma (KS), and not the virus itself, cause death.

A mild malaise or flu-like symptoms may or may not occur following exposure to the virus. After exposure there is a "window period" of six to twelve weeks (possibly longer) when the virus cannot be detected in the blood. Antibodies to HIV can be detected in the blood by testing after the "window period." HIV-positive[2] (infected) individuals can remain asymptomatic and seemingly in good health for many years, sometimes for five to ten years or perhaps longer. However, during that time they can infect others, and their own immune systems can be slowly weakening.

To be diagnosed with AIDS, a patient must have one of the following along with evidence of HIV infection:

1. Presumptive or proven opportunistic infection including those caused by protozoa, virus, fungus, and certain bacteria
2. One of several forms of cancer, specifically lymphoma, cancer of the cervix, or Kaposi's sarcoma
3. HIV encephalopathy (problems with thinking, judgment, memory, mood, and other brain functions) with resulting cognitive dysfunction, caused by HIV infection of the brain
4. Wasting syndrome with weight loss, fever, and diarrhea, or
5. Less than two hundred T-4 cells (CDC 1992).

However, people with AIDS represent only a small proportion of those who are suffering from HIV disease.

TRANSMISSION AND PREVENTION

The HIV virus is transmitted through having unprotected (i.e., without a condom or other barrier protection) vaginal, anal, or (perhaps) oral sexual intercourse; through sharing drug injection equipment with an infected person;

from infected mother to child transmission during pregnancy or birth; or through transfusions with infected blood or blood products. HIV cannot be acquired through casual contact such as shaking hands, sharing utensils, water glasses, coughs or sneezes, or through toilet seats or mosquito bites (Friedland & Klein 1987; see also figure 11.1 for risk factors for infection from exposure to HIV). The practice of engaging in sexual acts that minimize the exchange of infected body fluids (e.g., semen or vaginal secretions) constitutes "safer sex." These methods include the use of barrier devices, such as condoms for either men or women and dental dams, along with a spermicide like Nonoxynol-9. During vaginal intercourse women are encouraged to use multiple forms, such as a diaphragm or sponge with a foam that contains Nonoxynol-9, while the male should use a condom (Voeller 1986).

As noted in chapter 2, sexuality was presented as fluid over time for many people, even those who identify as exclusively heterosexual, lesbian, or gay. Too often health and human services workers operate with stereotypes about sexuality and sexual history. A lesbian may be inappropriately assumed to be not at risk for HIV infection because there have been few reported cases among lesbians until recently (Glassman 1995). She may have been in a heterosexual relationship where safe sex was not practiced. She may have been in a relationship where she or her partner were using intravenous drugs without cleaning their works. A gay man may be in a monogamous relationship for the past five years but may have had unprotected sex with many of his previous partners. A self-identified heterosexual male may not disclose that he has anonymous sex with other men. A heterosexual couple may become involved periodically with "threesomes" or visits to "straight" sex clubs. Therefore, the worker should be clear about the potential range of sexual practices any given client might be involved in by asking and not presuming. Understanding that sexual identity and sexual practices are not the same and can be highly variable over time is essential to effective prevention efforts.

This confusion about sexual orientation and behavior has had a major impact on data-gathering about the incidence of HIV disease among lesbians (Glassman 1995; Stevens 1993). As Stevens (1993) notes:

> The official figure clearly underestimates the incidence of AIDS among lesbians . . . because it is based on a rigid and arbitrary CDC definition of who lesbians are. Only women who have had sexual contact *solely* with women partners since 1977 are considered lesbians, but this definition does not represent the contemporary experience of lesbians. The CDC has no specific exposure category for woman-to-woman transmission of HIV, classifying it in the "no identified risk" category. (Stevens 1993:290; emphasis in the original)

Risk Factors for Infection from Exposure to HIV

Potential For Infection	TRANSMISSION FACTORS			
	Fluid Type	Route of Absorption	Fluid Dose	Health Status
HIGH RISK	Blood Semen	Injection Rectum Vagina Placenta	Large volume Repeated exposures	Ill Infected with other agents
	Vaginal/ Cervical secretions Breastmilk	Break in skin Penis Mouth	Occasional exposures	Malnourished Drug use (including alcohol and tobacco) Stressed Pregnant
	Saliva Tears Urine	Newly inflicted wound Eyes Nose	Small volume One exposure	Healthy
NO RISK	Sweat Feces	Intact skin	No exposure	

Figure 11.1 Risk factors for infection from exposure to HIV

Despite changes in the official definition of AIDS in 1993 to include such woman-specific manifestations of the illness as cervical cancer, women's health activists argue that signs of HIV infection and immune compromise common in women are still excluded from the official definition of AIDS. Thus while the incidence of HIV infection among lesbians is indeed lower than that among other groups, it is most likely not as low as the figure published by the CDC, i.e., less than one percent of AIDS cases (CDC 1993). These definitions matter because resources—for individuals and communities—flow from them. Once again, the real experiences and risks of lesbians are rendered invisible.

Pohl (1995) notes that because HIV is found in blood, sharing an intravenous drug-injecting apparatus is a very efficient way of transmitting the virus. Transmission-reduction techniques, including the "harm reduction model" practiced in many cities, involves a hierarchical approach to risk reduction that will prove helpful to bisexual, lesbian, and gay chemically dependent clients (Cates & Hinmann 1992):

1. Abstinence from all mood-altering drugs through treatment is optimal.
2. If a person is unwilling or unable to become abstinent, eliminating needles would be a reasonable goal. In methadone maintenance programs, there is a lower rate of HIV infection associated with being in treatment (Cooper 1989). Unfortunately, amphetamine and cocaine addicts do not benefit from maintenance drugs at this time.
3. Injecting, but not sharing, needles is the next best goal. Making needles available more readily, as with needle exchange programs, may result in decreased transmission of HIV (Selwyn 1987).
4. If sharing a needle, sterilizing the needle with 10 percent bleach may be effective in killing the virus. However, the efficiency of viral eradication is not 100 percent with this method (Vlahov el al. 1991).

In addition to transmission through needle use, the use of alcohol and others drugs is disinhibiting, which makes it difficult to adhere to risk reduction and safer sex practices. There is also some evidence that alcohol and other drugs may even make one's cells more susceptible to infection upon exposure to the HIV virus (Pohl 1995). This information about risks and risk reduction is vital to every program that serves or treats substance-using people.

Gabriel Rotello (1997) presents a controversial message in *Sexual Ecology: AIDS and the Destiny of Gay Men* wherein he argues that the current AIDS prevention paradigm has been less than successful in ending the transmission of the virus. He builds a case for ecological thinking, the recognition that human disease and health are reflections of the complex relationships between human populations and their habitats. To a medical ecologist, no infectious disease simply happens. Infectious diseases are largely caused by specific microbes, and diseases are more than the simple sum of their microbial causes. He urges that scientists should focus on the ecology of sex, which would consist of the entire spectrum of causes and effects that influence the spread of sexually transmitted diseases, the way these enter the body, the way these reproduce and interfere with the normal working of cells, thereby causing disease. Also considered would be the role specific behaviors play in transmitting microbes from one person to another, any biological cofactors, and whether, once exposed, infection takes place, and once infected, illness occurs. The way in which the course of illness itself impairs or enhances a person's ability to pass the infection to others would be studied.

Rotello (1997:46–47) argues that AIDS erupted into an epidemic only when cultural changes, including the gay male sexual revolution of the 1970s, created ideal conditions for its evolution and spread. Weaving ecological theory, epidemiology, and sexual politics, he shows that the epidemic results as much from human behaviors as from specific microbes. Ignoring the politically correct position on the etiology of AIDS, sexual ecology focuses on the behavior of "core groups" or "risk groups" who suffer from and transmit the virus at much higher rates than the rest of the population. The dynamics of "core groups" are important to understand. First, people in core groups have significantly higher numbers of partners than those outside. Second, those partners also have significantly higher numbers of partners within the core group, creating a kind of biological feedback loop that is primed to magnify disease. Third, core group members tend to engage in forms of sex that are conducive to transmission (exchange of fluids). Finally, core group members tend to suffer from a complex of health problems related to poverty, substance abuse, lack of adequate medical care, and heightened exposure to diseases like tuberculosis as well as repeated sexually transmitted disease infections (STDs).

The combination of multiple sex partners and anal sex in relatively intense core groups had already created an unstable sexual ecology for some gay men even before Stonewall. Rotello (1997) argues that sexual versatility (insertive and receptive anal sex), core group behavior centered in commercial sex establishments, widespread recreational drug abuse, repeated waves of STDs, and constant intake of antibiotics and concurrent sexual relationships became a sexual pattern for a significant number of men after gay liberation. "From the virus's point of view, the ecology of liberation was a royal road to adaptive triumph. From many gay men's point of view, it proved a trapdoor to hell on earth" (89).

CLINICAL COURSE AND TREATMENT

The clinical course of HIV infection varies over time in different people. The CDC identifies a spectrum of HIV disease comprised of four stages or levels. The first stage is *acute onset of infection*, followed by *asymptomatic incubation*, the second stage; the third stage, *chronic symptoms*, is followed by the end stage, *AIDS*. Initially, infection appears as a viral illness with fever, swollen glands, body aches, and a rash. Many people infected with HIV remain asymptomatic for many years. Subsequently, approximately 50 percent of people over ten years, according to Moss and colleagues (1988), go on to develop more serious signs and symptoms of infection, including fevers, night sweats, diarrhea, mild infections such as thrush, weight loss, swollen glands, fatigue, lymphadenopathy, non-life-threatening infections, and eventually progressively serious and debilitating illness, such as wasting syndrome, AIDS dementia, secondary infections, rare cancers, and interstitial pneumonia.[3]

Although the worst cases of HIV disease eventually cause disability and death, many people live fairly healthy lives for many years (Pohl 1995). Powrie (1995) cautions against accepting the death notice of an HIV-positive diagnosis, noting the large number of persons living with AIDS or at the end stage of HIV disease who are asymptomatic long-term survivors, as well as those who have seroconverted and are healthy.

Seroconversion is the development of antibodies to a particular antigen. When people develop antibodies to HIV or an experimental HIV vaccine, they "seroconvert" from antibody-negative to antibody-positive. In the above situation, however, we are referring to a smaller and much debated population who have seroconverted from antibody-positive to antibody-negative.

Over the last decade, several cofactors[4] for disease progression have been identified: reinfection with HIV; intercurrent infections, such as herpes viruses, hepatitis B, other sexually transmitted diseases, and tuberculosis; use of alcohol and other drugs, such as prescription drugs, nicotine, steroids, and illicit substances; excessive or poorly managed stress; unstable self-esteem; intimacy problems and loneliness; little or no social support; preexisting diseases like cancer or diabetes; trauma, surgery, and accidents; vaccinations using "live" materials; hormone fluctuation in women; poor nutrition or sanitation; allergies; pregnancy and giving birth; and genetic vulnerability (Andrews & Novick 1995). While the relationships among these cofactors and disease progression is still unclear, their promise for public health and psychosocial intervention, such as psychoeducation and clinical support for lifestyle changes, are evident.

While there have been significant medical discoveries and advances in HIV-related biomedical research, there still is no cure, no vaccine, and no medical solution for this deadly disease. However, in the mid-1980s, the average life span for somebody diagnosed with AIDS was nine months. By 1989, 61 percent of people with AIDS were alive eighteen months after diagnosis, signifying increased efficacy of treatments. The presence of thousands of long-term survivors, many of whom have not used medical intervention, promises to be another productive research endeavor. Apparently, researchers have found a genetic mutation, CKR5, found only in Caucasians, that confers total immunity to one in one hundred whites and, once infected, resistance in progressing to AIDS in one in five whites (*Advocate* 1996a). In 1996 the introduction of combination therapies involving protease inhibitors seemed to be reducing symptoms and lengthening life. Because there is no cure and no vaccine against HIV disease, efforts have been directed at changing high-risk behavior as a means of controlling the spread of the virus. These are not medical treatments but psychosocial interventions. There is much encouraging and promising research being undertaken on all fronts of HIV treatment.

The treatment goals for all people who are HIV-positive are to (1) prevent disease transmission; (2) decrease viral replication; (3) boost the immune system; and (4) enhance quality of life. The medical treatments fall into five categories:

1. *Antiviral drugs* are designed to attack the virus by halting its ability to reproduce or transcribe itself by inhibiting reverse transcriptase (RT). In this category are zidovudine (AZT) or retrovir. The other RT inhibitors include DDI (Didanosine), DDC (Dideoxcytidine), and D4T (Stavudine).

2. *Immunomodulators* stimulate T-cells and other immune system components to enable the system to more effectively fight off infection. These include interferon and other experimental substances.

3. *Anti-infection agents* encompass another category of drugs available to treat the variety of infections called opportunistic infections because they take the opportunity to attack patients with impaired immune systems. As of this writing, there are over forty drugs being investigated for their efficacy in treating fungal, bacterial, protozoal, and viral infections such as herpes, pneumocystis pneumonia, and *Ccytomegalovirus* as well as various cancers.

4. *Prophylaxis* is a category of medical treatment that includes the preventive use of sulfa drugs or pentamidine for anyone with a T-4 count under 200–300 (CDC 1995).

The fifth class of treatments, *protease inhibitors*, belongs to a new family of antiviral drugs created specifically for the treatment of HIV infection. The optimism based on research around these drugs has allowed for the concept of HIV eradication (Prescott 1996). HIV viral load tests show that these drugs are more effective than previously approved antiretroviral drugs (AZT, DDI, DDC, D4T, 3TC) in reducing the amount of HIV and in increasing the number of CD4 cells (immune system blood cells) in the body. Protease inhibitors block the action of one of the enzymes that HIV uses to replicate itself. The protease enzyme is found in HIV-infected cells, where it cuts viral protein chains into usable lengths for the production of new virus particles. The use of protease inhibitor drugs (Invirase, Norvir, Crixivan, Viracept, VX-478) results in the formation of defective viruses that cannot infect cells.

No single strategy for the treatment of HIV infection is right for everyone (Baker 1996). All of these medical interventions have a range of side effects which can be quite toxic or debilitating or that may stimulate the onset of other chronic diseases. The costs of these drugs are incredibly high, often requiring patients to spend beyond medical insurance limits and/or to supplement their insurance with a state-managed AIDS drug-assistance program. (This will be discussed in greater detail under the Ryan White CARE Act, below.) Thus the promise of improved treatments for HIV disease also raises the challenge of making these treatments accessible and affordable for all who might benefit from them.

Psychosocial Issues

Because of the social stigma associated with this disease as well as its association with marginalized groups such as gay men, minorities of color, and substance abusers, the patient with HIV disease—more than any other population of acutely ill patients—suffers a dramatic change in self-esteem, activities of daily living, and general lifestyle in response to the onset of the illness. There are numerous psychosocial crisis points throughout the life cycle of this disease for the person infected with HIV as well as a parallel process for those affected in that person's social support system (lover, family, and friends) and his or her professional caregivers—social workers, primary care providers, and the numerous volunteers and staff in the AIDS service organizations (ASOs) who offer an array of services: initial HIV-positive diagnosis; initial hospitalization; care through the onset of chronic problems; and help and care through the stages of dying, death, and after. For example, many gay men with HIV disease describe their initial reaction to diagnosis as a second coming out process, and this will be experienced again many times over as the disease progresses and new social support systems become involved. A series of issues are typically revisited again and again throughout these crises: revealing of secrets, shame, impact on sexuality, need for information, changing behaviors, psychological reactions, the management of distressing feelings, psychological adjustment of others, loss and isolation, assaults to body image and identity, loss of status, social stigma, balancing hope and denial, maintaining employment and other valued social roles, and the conflicting needs of the various systems with which the person living with HIV disease must interact. These systems include community supports, religion, employment, finances and insurance, government entitlements, health care and social services, and cultural systems. It is important to keep in mind the potential significance of race and ethnic identity, social class, gender, and the degree of gay/lesbian identity when making an assessment (see chapter 3). The major issues in psychological and social functioning commonly identified by clients with HIV disease (Appleby 1989; Herek & Glunt 1988; Robinson 1994) will be discussed briefly: psychological and social isolation; alteration in quality of life; shame and lowered self-esteem; intensity of emotion; issues of control; denial; and social stressors.

Psychological and social isolation result from the lack of or withdrawal of social supports. The person with the illness may withdraw, or his friends or family members may withdraw from him. Often this withdrawal is based on a fear of mortality among friends and family as well as their sense of helplessness because they are unable to effectuate change. When working with friends and families, it is common to hear themes related to their inability to "make the patient feel better" or to establish realistic expectations of what can be done physically or psychologically. Overidentification with the patient is a common occurrence when friends are of the same age and share the same lifestyle, interests, and patterns of daily living. This arouses a sense of vulnerability and fragility. A fear of contagion will also result in withdrawal. This can be seen in both persons with HIV and with AIDS as well as among friends and associates who may fear contracting the HIV virus. Sometimes the individual with HIV disease is concerned about contracting an illness from others which will further compromise his immune system. Both types of fear are exacerbated by conflicting and sometimes unscientific media reports making it difficult to separate appropriate from inappropriate anxiety. Social isolation is also experienced in health care settings wherein the patient may be isolated among hospital patients because of the homophobia of staff or the infection-control precautions needed to protect the patient as well as others. The psychological toll this isolation takes on a person living with HIV disease is devastating, especially in light of the social and psychological support needed when coping with acute disease (Bean et al. 1989; Levi 1992; Meyer, Tapley, & Bazargan 1996; Pies & Helquist 1989).

The patient's *quality of life* is significantly altered because of crisis, disruption, and disorganization in thinking and in daily habits. Too often he or she experiences bankruptcy, boredom, isolation, and social withdrawal. Patients may be too sick to work but too well to stay at home. Fatigue may limit vocational and social participation. Medical restrictions may result in limiting sexual practices or in abstinence, as well as withdrawal from social outlets. Patients describe this as viewing themselves as a leper, in a social sense, and as living in a sexual void.

Self-esteem is affected by the stigma of AIDS. *Shame* may result from internalized homophobia resurfacing with an HIV diagnosis. Patients begin to feel guilty and dirty. The infected may engage in an internal dialogue: "What did I do to deserve this?" "I have AIDS because I am gay." "I'll go straight if only I am cured." Self-condemnation concerning the client's sexual practices may be replaced by a view of the self as toxic to others. In chapters 1 and 2, shame was discussed as a consequence of homophobia and heterosexism and also as a family of emotions that lesbians and gay men confront in the earliest stages in the process of "coming out." These emotions range from feeling awkward, self-conscious, apologetic, and embarrassed to feeling ridiculous, degraded, humiliated, naked, and unexpectedly exposed. Shame is revisited by the HIV-infected gay man, bisexual, or lesbian as a judgment against the self, a feeling that one is bad, defective, incompetent, inadequate, weak, unworthy, unlovable, stupid, or disgusting. Normal shame is a painful, but passing, experience. Shame becomes pathological when it is internalized, when one identifies oneself, in essence, as permanently and totally flawed as a human being (Kaufman 1992). Sabar (1995) warns that shame is a powerful emotion which can strip us of our pride, our sense of entitlement to feelings and needs, and our belief in our own autonomy, control and competence. It can lead to isolation and spiritual despair. Among HIV-infected gay men and lesbians, stigmatized for both their sexuality and their illness, shame may be triggered by the ever-present acts of heterosexism, homophobia, and religious condemnation.

The *intensity of emotion* can include obsessive preoccupation, emotional vacillation, and anger. The absence of customary diversions, distractions, and daily habits becomes a void often filled by ruminative or repetitive thinking. The frequent vacillation between anger, guilt, rage, depression, fear, and easy tears is described as a "roller coaster" effect. There is an alternation between hopeful highs and helpless lows due to changes in medication, medical condition, doctors' reports, and media coverage of the "latest cure" or of an AIDS-related tragedy. Perceptions of a lack of justice or righteousness in life, as well as in response to realistic and concrete frustrations, results in anger. Demands for answers and effective treatments are not satisfied. The lack of a humane and effective government response is reported on the evening news, while victimization by the medical establishment is well established in AIDS folklore. The inability to retain personal control, the bouts of media hysteria, and the abandonment of friends and family make anger appear as a reasonable response.

Issues of control are important to the age group most affected by this disease. The patient experiences a general sense of lack of control over the disease, over his or her body, over his or her life. Medical professionals reinforce a passive, helpless patient role and seldom present an effective treatment plan, each of which adds nothing to a patient's sense of competence and control. The patient seems to be in a constant struggle to regain control, scrambling from doctor to doctor for disconfirmation of the diagnosis or in the selection of new treatment options. He questions the help of his counselors and challenges their relevance. On the other hand, some medical treatments demand an extremely high degree of regularity and compliance with demanding regimens of care.

Denial is an important and healthy defense mechanism to assist someone through a crisis; it helps keep them intact. It is manifest in patient themes: "Not me, it can't be true." "I'll be the first to overcome this disease." Denial can be an avoidance of active coping, a component of depression, and an essential ingredient of hope. Reiss (1994) suggests that denial can be seen as an unconscious process or as a conscious cognitive strategy. It is therefore a challenge for clinicians to differentiate between denial's adaptive and maladaptive aspects. Denial becomes dysfunctional when it compromises medical treatment and should then be confronted. The worker's task will be to distinguish between conscious and unconscious denial, the purpose it serves, and to help the client to understand the fine line between denial and hope.

The *social stressors* associated with HIV disease are tremendous. The cost of treatment is exorbitant, ranging from $50,000 to more than $100,000 over the course of the disease, thus requiring sophistication with third-party reimbursement (insurance) and government entitlements. Employment—and thus access to economic resources and health insurance—is generally compromised at later stages of the disease. Knowledge and self-advocacy skills are necessary to access and coordinate the complex array of health care, legal, housing, mental health, and social services required during the course of this illness.

IDENTITY ISSUES

Homophobia and heterosexism, experienced by gay, lesbian, and bisexual people as heterosexual hostility and discrimination, erode a person's sense of identity, psychological integrity, and sense of coherence (Antonovsky 1979, 1987). Homophobia and heterosexism increase the range and strength of stressors in life, which in turn compromise wellness, thus placing a person at greater risk of psychological and physical illness, including HIV disease.

Berzon (1992) reminds us that

> we are greatly affected by external events. We, in turn, affect those events by the way we relate to them. Our lives involve a constant interplay of feeling and behavior, past and present, fantasy and reality. We are the sum of all our parts, but only for a moment. Identity is a moving, changing process, not a fixed, established point.   (Berzon 1992:3)

This is what personal identity is about. It is not immutable. It is not totally fluid. It is somewhere in between. While identity development within the context of heterosexism and homophobia has been discussed in chapters 1 and 2, gay and lesbian identity in the era of HIV disease is fraught with pitfalls and challenges that arise specifically from the epidemic.

"Healthy gay identity" means a fusion of homosexual sexuality and emotionality into a meaningful whole. Developmental theory reveals that humans develop the ability to attain an integrated sense of self during adolescence. For the most part, as we were reminded in chapter 4, gay men and lesbians have not had supportive or affirmative opportunities to foster a gay or lesbian identity during adolescence. Positive role models are not readily available to gay and lesbian adolescents. No opportunity is offered for learning to deal with social stigma or isolation, which are often the by-product of homophobia. These barriers to development are significant because it is through the mutual and reciprocal processes of shared reactions, perceptions, and interpretations that identity is formed and maintained. For these reasons, developing effective ways to reach adolescents, especially high-risk youth, with treatment and prevention services is an urgent priority (Campbell & Peck 1995).

The maintenance of self and identity is contingent upon one's ability to remain humanly connected. Paradis (1990) observes that how one thinks and feels about oneself is in part related to one's intimate and personal involvements with others. Disruption in intimate ties to others, as is the case of a gay person with HIV or AIDS, leads to alienation, self-fragmentation, and fears of disintegration. Identity also relates to meaning, and illness often causes one to reexamine what life and relationships mean. Illness also raises a range of spiritual issues: differing views of spirituality and illness; concerns about death and suffering; desire for forgiveness; desire for spiritual support; reconciliation with God or a Higher Power; need for hope; and the need to express a nontraditional spirituality (Dansky 1994; Johnston 1995; Shernoff 1995b).

MENTAL HEALTH ISSUES

Homophobia chips away at the psychological integrity of gay men and lesbians as it justifies the hostility and discrimination of heterosexuals (Boykin 1991; Hetrick & Martin 1987), thus placing homosexuals at greater health risk. The high levels of stress and the reactive or compensatory behavior of gay men to discrimination are often barriers to mental and physical health. These are also viewed as cofactors in contracting HIV and in progressing rapidly to full-blown AIDS (Cadwell 1991). Stress compromises the immune system while reactive, avoidant (Martin & Knox 1995), or compensatory behavior will cloud judgment in relation to healthy lifestyles and safer sex. Coupled with this general feeling of rejection, former supports such as the family and the church may also shun the gay person with HIV due to his perceived "immoral" lifestyle. In turn, family and friends often fade away, while others have already severed ties with HIV-infected family members stemming from conflicts regarding what they view as an "alternative," "psychologically dysfunctional," or "immoral"—that is, nonheterosexual—lifestyle. The HIV diagnosis makes these groups more vulnerable still to acts of discrimination and even violence (as was discussed in the preceding chapter).

The risk of a psychiatric disorder in a person who is HIV-positive apparently depends less on symptoms of the disease itself than on other personal characteristics and life circumstances, such as limited social supports, personal history of psychiatric disorders, low income, unemployment, homelessness, family history of mental illness, recent bereavement, or trauma. Recent studies indicate lower rates of emotional distress and psychiatric disorder among people with HIV disease than earlier reports (Rabkin & Rabkin 1995). This may be due to the improved understanding of the disease, improved medical treatment, and improved community support, which have reduced the burden of isolation and uncertainty (*Harvard Mental Health Letter* 1994). This optimistic view is not shared by all (Odets 1995b; Rofes 1996). Researchers at the University of California, San Francisco, show that HIV-positive men are 67 percent more likely to die of AIDS complications if they are chronically depressed. Clinicians must realize that if they treat depression, the risk goes down (*Advocate* 1996b). Many believe that gay men are responding with a generalized numbness to a crisis in the meaning of life or with symptoms of posttraumatic stress disorder because of the constant psychic assault with death and disease.

Many of the psychosocial stressors discussed previously can be experienced, in almost a parallel fashion, by the significant other, the family of choice and/or origin, and by the support network of friends and colleagues. In chapter 1 it was noted that stigma and shame may be experienced by families and others as a generalization of the marginalized status of the person who is lesbian, gay, or bisexual; the same is true of those connected to someone living with HIV disease. This is a form of social contagion which may diminish the social statuses and role performance of those around the HIV-infected client. These issues may be addressed by the worker with family and group intervention.

Temoshok et al. (1990) identify certain characteristics correlated with long-term survival with AIDS, including assertiveness, accepting the diagnosis, demonstrating a strong reality orientation, having a positive attitude, taking personal responsibility for life, having a sense of purpose and commitment to life (Antonovsky's sense of coherence [1987]), collaborating with the treatment team, being able to nurture oneself, working with others who are infected, and being emotionally connected with others. Therefore, enhancing immune function and quality of life correlates with strategies that will reinforce these coping behaviors. These strategies are well within the domain of social work practice, specifically through psychoeducation, coaching, and modeling interventions effective in addressing these concerns.

AIDS DEMENTIA

Patients with HIV disease can suffer with delirium, an acute confusional state. This is often reversible and must be ruled out as a part of the mental status workup. AIDS dementia complex (ADC) and depression are the two most common neuropsychological manifestations of HIV. Development of ADC can be insidious, with symptoms developing gradually over a period of months. Depression can involve many similar symptoms and can coexist with ADC. However, making a distinction between them is important in treatment planning.

Buckingham and Van Gorp (1994) raise concern about HIV-related dementia and the worker's assessment skills necessary for early detection, diagnosis, and intervention. This issue is addressed here primarily because cognitive disorders may be the *only* symptoms presented by at least 20 percent of HIV-infected clients in the earliest stages of the disease, often before HIV testing has taken place. The worker might also give consideration to helping the significant other or family in managing ADC. Andrews and Novick (1995) have offered some helpful tips for counselors doing this work.

An infected client may present for a concern or problem unrelated to HIV infection; thus this client-worker episode may be the first opportunity for raising issues about infection and possible testing. Therefore, it is important that unexplained difficulties in regard to forgetfulness, slowed speech, visuo-spatial confusion, depression and social withdrawal, concentration problems, inattentiveness or distractibility, or problems with sequential reasoning or multistep tasks be thoroughly explored and then associated with the correct disease etiology and with subsequent medical referral and pharmacological and psychosocial interventions. There are several neuropsychological tests that can be administered by individuals with limited training: the Trail-Making Test, Symbol Digit Modalities Test, Stroop Neuropsychological Screening Test, and Dementia Rating Scale are all useful for screening cognitive impairment. The Folstein Mini Mental Status Exam, which appears as figure 11.2, is easy to administer (Andrews & Novick 1995:117–24).

Depression presents as apathy or hopelessness, changes in affect, sleep or appetite change, and psychomotor retardation. Depression in HIV-symptomatic gay males has been found to relate to the degree of disability and illness being experienced; however, it is also related significantly to social functioning, social support, and previous mental health treatment. All patients who are depressed should be asked about suicidal or homicidal thoughts, intentions, or plans. The important factors are:

1. Plan: Is it detailed, lethal, and available?
2. Mental state: Is the patient hopeless? Conversely, does the patient have a new and unexplained sense of peace or serenity, with no apparent change of circumstances?
3. Precipitating crisis: Has the patient recently experienced a significant loss?

Whether or not there is a risk of suicide, depression can and should be treated. A psychiatric referral may be appropriate for medication that will relieve some of the symptoms.

THE "WORRIED WELL"

Odets (1995a) warns that all gay men now live with a "dark companion," the complex social and psychological epidemic among those who are still uninfected with HIV and who might survive the epidemic itself:

We have denied and underestimated virtually every aspect of the AIDS epidemic: how long it would last, how many it would take, how awful the process

The Folstein Mini Mental Status Exam

			points
1. What is the:	year	_____	(1)
	season	_____	(1)
	date	_____	(1)
	month	_____	(1)
2. Where are we:	state	_____	(1)
	county	_____	(1)
	town	_____	(1)
	hospital	_____	(1)
	floor	_____	(1)

3. Name three objects   _____ (3)
4. Serial 7's [counting by 7s]
   (5 answers) or spell "world"
   backwards   _____ (5)
5. Recall three objects   _____ (3)
6. Name a pencil, a watch   _____ (2)
7. Repeat "no ifs, ands, or buts"   _____ (1)
8. Follow 3-step command: Take
   a paper in your right hand, fold
   it in half, and put it on the floor   _____ (3)
9. Write a sentence   _____ (1)
10. Copy the design   _____ (1)

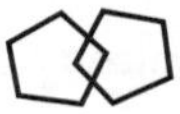

    TOTAL SCORE   _____

Level of Consciousness [subjective observation]: Alert Drowsy Stupor Coma

Figure 11.2 The Folstein Mini Mental Status Exam

would be, and what legacy it would leave for survivors. . . . We now have in the gay male and bisexual communities of uninfected men a second, completely uncontrolled epidemic—a psychological one—that threatens the health and welfare of millions of Americans. . . . Broad social denial colludes powerfully with the denial of those who live in the middle of the epidemic and who must protect themselves from seemingly unbearable psychic pain. . . . Denied or not, being gay and being uninfected is now a condition, not the absence of one. Being uninfected is a personal and social identity, like being gay, and it must be similarly clarified, consolidated, and acknowledged in the world. Being uninfected thus involves precisely the kind of "coming out" process that being gay does.   (Odets 1995a:204–14)

Survivor guilt is being experienced in increasing numbers in the gay community (Boykin 1991). Guilt-mediated depression and anxiety can seriously complicate the grieving process. Expressions of guilt include deliberate binges of unprotected sex, substance abuse, self-generated financial problems, difficulty planning for the future, and the avoidance of personal and romantic relationships. Odets (1995b) notes that guilt-mediated depression and survivor guilt are often responsive to psychotherapeutic intervention.

Much has been written concerning the impact of the family on a member who is HIV-infected (Dansky 1994; Geballe, Gruendel, & Andiman 1995; Odets & Shernoff 1995) but less has been discussed about the impact of HIV on the family (Walker 1995). Walker (1995) suggests that the family must confront and resolve issues related to fear, shame, and the social stigma associated with AIDS because these have a demoralizing effect on its functioning. The family will need to expand its natural support system, thus minimizing the psychosocial stress of the disease. Drawing upon the coping skills and the tradition of mutual aid, families must be engaged to work through a broad range of tasks, such as medical management, infection-related fears, disclosure guidelines, maintaining a normal life in the context of this disease, parenting infected children, coping with siblings, developing a support system with extended family; and planning for imminent illness or death.

The clinician can assist the family and the client by providing case management intervention; by helping the client and the family to decide when and how to disclose the client's HIV status to others; by helping family members to adapt to the strains of caretaking and fears of loss; by opening communication pathways within the family; and, finally, if death occurs, by supporting and helping the family through the bereavement process (Walker 1995:85–99). Long-term survival for the HIV caretaker appears to be associated with learning about grief (reading or in-service training), attending a caregivers' bereavement support group, and giving oneself permission to grieve. The tasks of bereavement are to accept the reality of the loss, to experience the pain of grief, to adjust to an environment in which the deceased is missing, and to emotionally relocate the deceased and move on with life (Worden 1976). The specifics of therapeutic intervention are addressed in those texts cited at the beginning of this chapter and in the practice courses taken in graduate school.

THE COMMUNITY IMPACT OF THE EPIDEMIC

The HIV epidemic has had a profound impact not only on many gay, lesbian, and bisexual individuals but also on the gay, lesbian, and bisexual community. In fact, the HIV epidemic presents a serious danger to the functioning and survival of the gay and lesbian communities. Early in the epidemic, serious discussions in the gay community ensued about whether the gay male population was doomed for extinction. Rofes (1996) reminds us that gay men found solace in two oft-repeated beliefs: (1) a treatment that would save their lives would be found soon; (2) gay men in urban centers had implemented safe sex practices and halted sexual transmission in the population. "These beliefs became the theoretical and spiritual foundation of our collective lives in the health crisis" (2), providing the focus for community activism and mutual aid efforts.

Overshadowing everything is the terrible tragedy of AIDS with the inexpressible personal sorrow it has brought to so many. Paradoxically, however, there have simultaneously been significant improvements in the social, legal, and political place of gays and lesbians in America. The HIV epidemic has galvanized the gay and lesbian community to adopt more of a political action agenda not only for HIV-related services and research but also for a full range of civil rights. Many previously closeted individuals realized that they had little to lose in light of the epidemic and decided to come out to family and coworkers and to fight for legal protection of their constitutional rights. Thus the fight against homophobia and heterosexism has made some of its most important advances while the nation was confronting the HIV epidemic (Berzon 1992).

In general, 1981–1984 were years of denial and shock; 1985–1990 was a period of agitation and anger with periodic bargaining with an external power. Gay men seemed to be enacting the belief that "we would not get sick if we volunteered in AIDS service organizations and donated a lot of money, and if we did the nightmare would swiftly end. . . . Like a holy prayer, we chanted over and over that HIV is a chronic and manageable illness, hoping no one else would have to die" (Rofes 1996:3).

Between 1993 and 1996 there was great collective hope and great collective depression. Hope was rekindled with new drug treatments, specifically AZT and later protease inhibitors. Meanwhile, however, epidemiologic evidence confirmed that new infections among gay and bisexual men were on the upswing after years of decline, and significant numbers of men were engaging in anal intercourse without a condom. Collective hope alternated with collective depression. It appeared as if the gay community might have entered a new stage where its members had reached the limits of their ability to mourn and to mobilize. Many felt that the normal cycles of grief were no longer occurring.

Despite these historical fluctuations in perceptions amid preoccupations, there have clearly been many positive community developments as a result of the HIV epidemic. These have included the coalitions formed between gay men and lesbians to fight the disease.

> The AIDS epidemic has generated an unprecedented working together of gay and lesbian communities through volunteer and community-based agencies, political activism, and shared grief. Historically, it has been difficult to build and sustain alliances between lesbians and gay men in the face of our differences. The AIDS epidemic challenges all of us to find ways to consolidate and maintain the integrity of our communities and our differences, while building coalitions to fight this devastating epidemic.
> —Judy Macks & Caitlin Ryan (1988:198)

Just as individual adaptation to a lesbian, gay, or bisexual identity in an oppressive social context calls upon individual human resiliency, so the response of the gay community to this epidemic calls upon it on a collective level. The time, energy, money, and talent expended by the gay and lesbian community in response to this epidemic is a model for the rest of society, specifically the demonstration of community responsibility and group solidarity during a time of crisis. The network of AIDS service organizations in cities of all sizes throughout the country; the AIDS task forces on national, state, and local levels; the AIDS units found in public health departments, hospitals, and health clinics; the confidentiality and nondiscrimination codes, statutes, and laws; the Ryan White CARE Act, and (to a lesser degree) the Americans with Disabilities Act, as well as the increases in AIDS-related public education, biomedical research, and treatment development, can all trace their origins, development, and maintenance to the advocacy of gay men and lesbians. Two decades of organizing, fund-raising, lobbying, advocating, program and policy development, and serving have increased our understanding of acute and chronic disease processes and what should constitute effective health care and social service delivery. All this was accomplished within the sociopolitical context of heterosexism and homophobia.

Nevertheless, there has been intense frustration as well, especially because the epidemic has not been conquered. Larry Kramer (1989), a founder of the Gay Men's Health Crisis (GMHC) and the AIDS Coalition to Unleash Power (ACT-UP), captures the sense of anger and despair so many feel with the following:

> There's got to be a higher vision for your reason for being. You've got to want to end *this!* Instead, I see layer upon layer of bureaucracy, hordes of employees, and thousands of volunteers spending hours and days at endless useless meetings, just like all the bureaucrats in Washington. Plus, all those useless board members, who have absolutely no sense of urgency, no sense of urgency, no sense of urgency that 40 million people are going to die in a few short years' time.
> (Kramer 1989: introduction; emphasis in original)

The challenge is to continue to translate frustration into effective action. While the gay community has much to be proud of and to celebrate, there is also much to mourn because the dark side of society has been exposed. Anti-gay violence is a logical extension of the heterosexism that pervades American society, and HIV disease continues to be used to rationalize prejudice, discrimination, and violence against gay men and lesbians. Most of all, a careful analysis of the societal response to the HIV epidemic in the United States has revealed how inadequate it has been, to the great peril to any citizen whose behaviors may put them at risk of HIV infection.

SOCIETAL RESPONSE

The vast personal loss is compounded by the loss of talents and skills in numerous occupations and professions. These losses are difficult to translate into the overall costs to society. The estimated billions of dollars spent since the passage of the 1990 Ryan White Comprehensive AIDS Resources Emergency (CARE) Act alone, on medical treatment, research, and human services, has been staggering. What does this mean to society?

The early stages of recognition and identification of an epidemic are characterized by social denial, a group reaction similar in many ways to an individual's reaction of denial of a threatening event. Social denial, like its individual counterpart, is an unconscious mechanism of defense that protects against fear and anxiety. If it is not rapidly resolved, denial can endanger the group by inhibiting appropriate responses to the epidemic. Several factors may impede the resolution of social denial, including geographic distance or a belief that those at risk represent a different group as defined by age, race, religion, social class, gender, sexual orientation, or other identifiers. These factors allow the group to develop social and psychological distance and thus to perceive the threatening individual or group as "outsiders" or "others."

Social denial has been amply demonstrated throughout the AIDS epidemic and is a major component of the social construction of this disease (Herdt 1992a; Levine 1992). Those people predominantly affected by AIDS were already labeled by society as different and marginal. These were the racial and sexual minorities traditionally discriminated against in U.S. society. The dominant group's perception of the infected and affected as different, "other," or "outsider" slowed the response to the epidemic. This social denial of the importance of the threatening event, the epidemic, was also fed by hostility for both the infected and his or her caregiver. Social scientists and medical historians suggest that societies have ignored (and will continue to do so) the complexity and weight of scientific evidence about diseases or social issues and will seek simplistic explanations, or at best, a confirmation of preexisting beliefs or attitudes. The result most often is to blame marginal individuals ("others") for the health crises and social problems. Thus the AIDS epidemic was attributed to gay men who the general public believed transmitted HIV casually.

Historically, ethnic minority groups or very poor individuals have commonly been blamed for the spread of diseases. Society tends to fix the responsibility for a disease on groups seen as socially marginal and to ostracize the group it scapegoats in an attempt to distance itself from the problem. Even now these responses, influenced by cultural values and religious beliefs, allow many U.S. citizens to believe that they are not at risk of contracting HIV. Some people have referred to AIDS as the "wrath of God" for those who deserve punishment because of who they are or how they lead their lives—although the failed logic of this argument is never extended to all the people suffering from cancer, leukemia, heart disease, or any other innumerable illnesses. Bigotry, racism, and homophobia resulted in antipathy and obstruction of the development of effective prevention and treatment programs. These fearful responses frequently lead some to call for various prompt but ineffective actions, such as quarantine of those infected with the disease. This action is almost always questionable and often violates the civil rights of those infected and affected. Actions based on belief systems and resulting prejudice, however, often continue long after they have been proven to be useless (McDonell 1993).

While there may be other reasons for the continuing rise in the number of cases of HIV disease in various populations in this country, one consequence of social denial in this the second decade of the epidemic is that heterosexual women and adolescents are increasingly vulnerable to infection. This might have been avoided with a national commitment to prevention. However, such an action would have required confronting society's homophobia and adopting a public health strategy (Mays, Albee, & Schneider 1990).

The evidence of neglect and the less than adequate response by our government to the HIV epidemic warrants elaboration. Three dimensions of health care policy clearly reflect the obvious connection between AIDS and homophobia/heterosexism. These were the delays in developing public health policy and intervention, the lack of funding for programs, and the injection of moral and political motives into the public response.

In the case of any infectious disease, swift and effective action to prevent its spread is critical. The U.S. Department of Health and Human Services responded rapidly and effectively to episodes of Legionnaires' disease and toxic shock syndrome. The groups affected by these diseases were not considered different or marginalized. This was not true in the case of AIDS. The magnitude of the epidemic today can be traced to the long and unprecedented *delays* in early AIDS education and prevention activities. The first risk-reduction guidelines published by the Public Health Service (PHS) did not appear until March 1983, nearly two years into the epidemic (Perrow & Guillen 1990). It was not until 1985 that the first official "prevention program" was initiated by PHS, and its focus was on HIV testing rather than public education (Bailey 1991). It took the federal government five years to unveil a mass media campaign, *America Responds to AIDS*. In 1987 the United States was the only major Western nation without a national HIV/AIDS education program (Rowe & Ryan 1987); some would say none really existed even in the early 1990s.

The *lack of federal funding* for AIDS education and services paralleled the lack of funding in other areas, most notably research. Bayer (1989) noted in his review of the reports of the PHS and Congress's Office of Technology Assessment that efforts to prevent AIDS through education had received minimal funding, especially efforts targeted at groups at highest risk, such as gay men. In the early years of the epidemic, Congress earmarked money for AIDS although neither the president's budget nor any PHS request had allocated any money to AIDS. In subsequent years Congress voted substantially larger budgets for AIDS than the Reagan administration, which sometimes failed to spend all the funds appropriated. As late as 1985 the PHS was redirecting funds (most often from funds allocated to fight sexually transmitted disease) in order to begin minimal AIDS education.

How little had been done to underwrite the efforts of the gay community groups that had borne the burden of educating homosexual men about the risk of AIDS was tellingly underscored by the fact that in fiscal year 1984 the PHS made an award of $1,500,000 to the U.S. Conference of Mayors so that it might fund community groups engaged in prevention activities. In the 1990s, however, the federal commitment to AIDS-related services became more obvious, the CDC stepped up their efforts to support research and prevention and education programs, and Ryan White funding for outpatient health care and social services has increased each year up to 1997.

The *moral and political motives* of political and cultural elites were often implicit and sometimes explicit in the battles over the content of educational materials to be used in prevention efforts. These battles, in turn, prevented an effective federally funded AIDS prevention campaign for the entire first fifteen years of the epidemic.

From the beginning the PHS has resisted providing frank information to the general public about how transmission of HIV could be avoided, based on misguided concerns over the "offensiveness" of such material. For example, in 1983 the PHS published risk-reduction guidelines that failed to mention basic protection such as the use of condoms and in the same year established an AIDS hotline with the provision that sexual matters and condom use could not be discussed (Perrow & Guillen 1990). In 1986 the CDC published restrictions on the explicitness of the educational materials that could be developed with the use of federal funds and required that local "review panels" determine the appropriateness of their content. In 1987 these restrictions became law when an amendment to an appropriations bill introduced by conservative Sen. Jesse Helms (R–NC) passed both House and Senate with overwhelming majorities. The amendment precluded the use of CDC funds for educational materials that "promoted" or encouraged homosexual activities. However, in May 1992 a federal court judge ruled in a suit brought by the Gay Men's Health Crisis (GMHC) that the CDC had "exceeded its authority in promulgating the restriction on 'offensive' material, and that the rule was unconstitutionally vague" (McFadden 1992). The judge stated that Congress "has made clear its intent: the federal government must not interfere with or hamstring public health efforts to educate all Americans, including gay or bisexual men, about AIDS." However, again in 1995 and 1996 Senator Helms gave vent to his rabid homophobia by attempting to cut off all funding for the Ryan White CARE Act, the primary source of federal funds for state and community-based health care and social services. While his efforts were unsuccessful, the floor of the Senate became a well-televised public platform for right-wing antigay rhetoric.

This history of controversy reflects a battle between public health professionals and social scientists on the one hand and representatives of the religious and radical right on the other. By 1989 these two camps were labeled the "public health realists" and the "moralizers" (Ehrhardt 1992). Both groups want to stop the spread of the disease, but the moralists assess prevention measures against a narrowly selective moral standard rather than a health standard. This battle has been perhaps the most formidable obstacle to effective AIDS education.

A third position is presented by Rotello (1997), who argues that the application of sexual ecologies approach would require a transformation of gay culture, specifically ending much of the behaviors associated with the gay liberation movement. Human cultures are far more than just "lifestyles" comprised of rituals and rules with symbolic meaning for their members. Cultures are adaptive strategies for survival, ways of life that allow their members to cope with the complex obstacles that nature, and other people, place in their way. A collective gay response to AIDS must begin with a sober evaluation of the ways the sexual culture of the 1970s produced the AIDS epidemic. This very discussion will be considered by some as offensive, homophobic, self-loathing. On the contrary, it is a call to reexamine the code of the condom, the assumptions related to relapse and harm reduction, and to apply an understanding of sexual ecology to strategies of prevention.

In summary, societal and institutional heterosexism and homophobia have left us without a national policy, a comprehensive service delivery system, or the necessary resources to respond effectively to HIV disease. The real devastation, however, is experienced on personal and interpersonal levels. It is at these levels that the hatred of homosexuals and the stigma of AIDS converge. Collectively, the infected and the affected experience this disease as a culture of death, dying, grief, mourning, and—too often—internalized homophobia and a loss of meaning in life. Thus a range of responses are required from the helping professions.

The Response of the Professions

Unfortunately, the stigmatization of gay, lesbian, and bisexual people and the fear of AIDS are as widespread among health and mental health professionals as they are in the general population. These attitudes are significant because these are the professionals who have responsibility for assisting the infected gay male, lesbian, and bisexual client cope with the personal and social consequences of homophobia and the course of HIV disease. It is often difficult to differentiate negative attitudes toward homosexuality from those related to AIDS (Riley &

Greene 1993). The persistent homophobia of health and mental health professionals was discussed in chapter 1. The elimination of homosexuality from the nosology of the APA's revised (1994) *Diagnostic and Statistical Manual of Mental Disorders* (DSM III-R; see chapter 9) did not immediately eradicate homophobic attitudes (Eliason 1995; Harris, Nightengale, & Owen 1995). As Forstein (1988) and Dulaney and Kelly (1982) note, this elimination has not changed the personal opinion of many in the professional mental health community. Specifically, Wallach (1989) reported that 9 percent of the nurses and physicians in his study agreed that AIDS is God's punishment to homosexuals, and 6 percent agreed that patients who choose a homosexual lifestyle deserve to get AIDS. Knox and Clark (1993) reported that 55 percent of community mental health center staff members preferred to avoid working with HIV-infected clients. Social workers who are more comfortable in working with gay and lesbian clients are also generally more comfortable working with people with HIV disease (Mancoske & Lindhorst 1995).

It would be foolish to assume that HIV-infected clients are not aware of this sometimes active avoidance of their presence. In fact, this fear of discrimination and stigma prevents many individuals from being tested for HIV, let alone sharing information regarding their drug use or sexual history. It is also understandable that an HIV-infected gay man or lesbian, when confronted with the neglect of our government and the homophobia of professionals, may rebel by rejecting conventional medical advice and demanding different clinical trials and nontraditional or alternative treatments,[5] and by using the pharmaceutical underground. What may be viewed by some as paranoia, inappropriate use of resources, or noncompliance with medical advice is viewed by others as healthy distrust, survival tactics, or attempts at gaining personal control.

Implications for Social Work Practice

It is not surprising that many social workers have provided services to people infected and affected by HIV disease almost from the first days of the epidemic. This response occurred first because of the significant presence of lesbians and gay men in the profession whose vulnerability and compassion led them to action and, second, because of the diversity of settings in which social work is practiced: mental health agencies (36 percent), health promotion programs, hospitals, and clinics (18 percent), children, youth, and family services (32 percent), and substance abuse and corrections (6 percent) (Gibelman & Schervish 1993). In addition to their paid employment, social workers have been from the start and continue to be actively engaged as public interest advocates, as volunteers on agency boards, and as unpaid staff support for community-based AIDS agencies. Micro and macro practice skills enable many social workers to contribute to the development and growth of community-based AIDS service organizations. Although many of these organizations began in the gay and lesbian community to meet the needs of infected gay men, most eventually expanded their mission to serve anyone infected or affected, including those with substance abuse histories, their families and significant others.

> Social workers were among the very first professionals to respond to the AIDS crisis. Gay and lesbian social workers are prominent among those early heroes and heroines of this plague. We all should remember and be proud of this history. The challenge remains: How do we sustain ourselves and each other for what appears to be the reality that AIDS will be with us for at least the rest of our professional lives?
>
> —Michael Shernoff 1995b:88

It should be noted, however, that the social work response to HIV disease has been made primarily by individual practitioners. Unfortunately, as with other professional disciplines, social work as a corporate entity (as represented by the National Association of Social Workers, the Association of Black Social Workers, the Association of Clinical Social Workers, or any other national body) limited its response to advocacy for adequate care and professional education and training. Although there are many population groups affected by the HIV epidemic with which social workers are concerned, the focus here will be on practice with gay, bisexual, and lesbian people in particular.

Anecdotally, faculty at various schools of social work, especially those with an urban community focus, have seen a steady increase in HIV-related services that their student interns are providing. In the largest cities a majority of social work interns are engaged in practice with clients who are infected and affected by HIV disease.

INTERPERSONAL INTERVENTION

There are several key points where social work intervention may be required: at the level of client reaction to the threat of HIV disease and how the HIV epidemic is shaping the client's behavior; when, after infection, the person is coping with its psychological effects and adjusting his or her attitudes toward health care treatment and healthy behavior; when the client is using the various health and social services defined in his or her treatment plan; and when the person with AIDS is coping with disability and/or approaching death. Throughout these four points the client will need assistance in accessing and coordinating various ancillary health and social services (Macks 1987). These services are not found in a single coordinated and comprehensive system and thus demand the organizational and self-advocacy skills seldom demonstrated by a client in crisis due to acute medical need. Case management is necessary to insure that clients get the services they need in a timely and coordinated fashion, especially when there are multiple health and social care needs and diminished personal, informal, or formal resources. In addition, researchers estimate that 30 to 70 percent of people diagnosed with HIV disease may experience some degree of cognitive impairment or AIDS-related dementia, thus limiting their ability to negotiate these complicated systems without assistance (Buckingham & Van Gorp 1994; Dilley & Goldblum 1987; Lowenstein & Shartstein 1983). A social work practice approach that encompasses attention to the intrapersonal, the interpersonal, and the environmental is clearly a useful one in this context.

PRACTICE RELATED TO RISK REDUCTION

An essential task during the assessment of any gay, lesbian, or bisexual client is to help the client evaluate his or her level of HIV risk, history of coping, and history of physical or sexual abuse. Therefore, it is incumbent upon the social worker to take a thorough sexual and substance use history, which then will serve as a baseline for subsequent prevention education and for future maintenance or relapse counseling (see figures 11.3 and 11.4 for assessment protocols). This information is useful not just for prevention but also in counseling those already infected with the HIV virus in reducing risk to others. Psychoeducation for the family and significant others addressing the course of the disease (both the medical and psychosocial aspects which will be of concern for the client and the family) should be given priority early in the intervention process. Prevention programs targeting all segments of the gay, lesbian, and bisexual community and emphasizing risk reduction, relapse prevention, and stigma management should be of primary concern.

Most psychotherapists, no matter the discipline, have had minimal or no training in human sexuality and sex counseling. It is therefore not surprising that they are uncomfortable and not knowledgeable about how to discuss sexual matters. Shernoff and Scott (1988) warn that to eliminate high-risk behaviors requires that all responsible health care professionals introduce an aspect of sex education into clinical practices where at all possible:

Conducting a Client Risk-Assessment History

A risk-assessment history can assist a client in personalizing his/her risk of HIV infection, particularly with respect to such sensitive areas as sexual and drug-using behaviors. The following six-step check list should be used as a tool for conducting such a history.

Step 1:   Explain to client the purpose of a risk-assessment history is to:
- gain"ownership" of one's risk
- understand why certain activities have put one at risk
- prepare for ways to reduce risk in future

Step 2:   Ask client to explain what he/she understands about the three modes of HIV transmission ("start where the client is"):
- sexual activity
- injection drug use
- perinatal exposure

Be sure to correct any misperceptions

Step 3:   Ask the client to assess his/her own drug history.
Areas worth exploring include:
- type of drug (including alcohol) used
- approximate dates of first use and abuse
- route of administration (orally, injected, sniffed, etc.)
- sharing of injection equipment
- disinfection of injection equipment (e.g., bleach)
- frequency and duration of use
- effect of drug use on sexual activity
- geographic location in which drug use ocurred
- medical problems related to drug use
- treatment experience/history

Step 4:   Ask the client to assess his/her sexual history.
Areas worth exploring include:
- type of body fluid exposed during sexual activity (semen, blood, vaginal/cervical secretions, saliva, etc)
- route of entry into body (vagina, penis, mouth, etc.)
- frequency of fluid exposure (e.g., single versus repeated exposures)
- use and effect of any drugs during sexual activity
- history/treatment of any sexually transmitted diseases (chlamydia, gonorrhea, syphilis, herpes, hepatitis B, etc.)

Step 5:   Ask client to review assessment of HIV risk and discuss concerns.

Step 6:   Bridge to risk-reduction planning

Figure 11.3 Conducting a client risk-assessment history

Conducting a Risk Assessment

A risk assessment interview can assist a client in coming to "own" his/her risk, if it addresses the "assessable" content and the counselor uses a process that actively engages the client's participation.

Content

The content of an HIV-transmission risk assessment concentrates on those things that can be known by the client—his/her beliefs, his/her behaviors, including partners known to be at high risk, and, where applicable, symptoms:

1. Beliefs about the modes of HIV infection

2. Sharing of drug injection equipment with any other person

3. Unsafe sexual activity

4. Other exposures (to blood, semen, contaminated instruments)

5. Involvement of these behaviors with persons infected or/in from locations of | high HIV disease prevalence

6. Physical symptoms suggestive of HIV disease

Process

The process suggested for conducting a risk assessment is designed to maximize the client's active involvement in examining the content areas listed above with appropriate introduction and closure. Towards this end, you may find it helpful to use a tool such as "AWARE Scorecard" to directly engage the client in performing an "anatomy" of his/her risks.

Step 1: Explain the purpose of the risk assessment.

Step 2: Ask the client to explain what he/she believes about the three modes of transmission risk.

Step 3: Ask the client to assess his/her IV works-sharing history.

Step 4: Ask the client to assess his/her sexual history.

Step 5: Ask the client to assess his/her "other" risks.

Step 6: Ask the client to review his/her assessments and discuss concerns.

Step 7: Bridge to risk-reduction planning.

Figure 11.4 Conducting a risk assessment

The issue of sexual practices in relation to AIDS prevention should be raised with every individual who is already sexually active, contemplating becoming sexually active, is not absolutely certain that he or she has been in a monogamous relationship for at least the past [fifteen] years, and who is not absolutely certain that his/her partner has not used drugs intravenously or been transfused during the same time period. . . . Thus, professionals working with adolescents, individuals in sexually non-exclusive relationships, newly separated or divorced adults and any person even contemplating having sex with a gay or bisexual man, I.V. drug user or transfusion recipient must learn about safer sexual practices.   (Shernoff & Scott 1988:131)

Their guidelines and counseling resources are helpful because of their realistic appraisal of clients' strong emotional responses to sexual questions, and the skill and sensitivity needed to eroticize safer sex and proper condom use. The practitioner will also find figure 11.5 helpful in gauging the level of risk associated with a specific sexual activity. Safer sex education and psychoeducational interventions focusing on healthy lifestyles and strategies for enhancing the immune system should be addressed when working with gay men, bisexuals, and lesbians.

Paradis (1990, 1991) notes that most gay men (and lesbians) have confronted the tasks of managing socially devalued and stigmatizing identities across the life cycle. Through the often painful but necessary developmental processes of coming out, gay men (and lesbians) struggle with balancing their need for intimacy while simultaneously consolidating a healthy gay self. The resilience of gay men and lesbians in the face of such obstacles is truly remarkable. Clinical work with gay men in the era of AIDS must focus on the differentiation between internal conflict associated with difference and internalized homophobia and the external threat of AIDS.

Internalized homophobia impedes the ability to cope and adapt, leaving the individual less apt to practice safer sex, thus avoiding HIV infection. It also interferes with efforts to maintain a healthful lifestyle when infected, thus avoiding relapse behavior and reinfection and slowing the progression to full-blown AIDS. Many young gays and lesbians manifest internalized homophobia in what appears to be a very strong and self-destructive denial of HIV risk (Blankenship 1993; Silven 1993). Others who constitute the "worried well" may become anxious, depressed, immobilized by guilt and shame, or experience sexual dysfunction even though they have not engaged in risk behaviors. Therapy can reduce self-blame by examining the origins of shame and intervening to stop the process of "internal shame spiral" (Sabar 1995).

Social workers are encouraged to engage in outreach to high-risk groups,

Scale of Risk for HIV in Regard to Various Sexual Activities

No-Risk Sexual Activities
involve no exchange of blood, semen, vaginal secretions, urine, or feces and pose no risk of transmitting HIV. These include:

flirting	mutual masturbation with external (on me not in me) organs
fantasy	light s/m without bleeding or bruising
solo masturbation	phone sex
hugging, body rubbing	talking "dirty"
dry kissing	watching another person
massage	being watched
showering together	

Probably Safe Sexual Activities
are safe as long as the barrier used remains intact there may be danger of transmitting HIV if the barrier slips or breaks. Using barriers properly increases the safety. These include:

Anal or Vaginal Intercourse with a Condom and using a water-based lubricant; even safer if a spermicide is also used for vaginal intercourse and/or the penis is withdrawn before ejaculation.

Fellatio with No Exchange of Semen; a condom can be used and/or ejaculation can take place outside the mouth.

Cunnilingus or Anilingus (rimming) through a Barrier; a latex sheet (dental dam) or plastic wrap around the vulva or anus.

Sharing Sterile Sex Toys; cover the toy with an unused condom or latex barrier and put a new one on before sharing it with someone else.

Brachioproctic/Brachiovaginal sex (fisting) with a latex glove; will protect the hand of the inserter, but can still cause damage to internal tissue.

Possibly Risky Sexual Activities
are those during which exchange of body fluids might create some danger of transmitting HIV, but from which no known cases of transmission have occurred to date. These include:

Deep kissing; particularly if there are cuts or sores where blood might be present in the mouth.

Oral, Anal, or Vaginal Intercourse Without a Condom and Withdrawing prior to Ejaculation.

Cunnilingus may be more risky when the woman is menstruating.

Sharing Sex Toys or Enema Equipment that have come in contact with vaginal secretions, semen, or blood.

Fisting, if the hand has cuts or sores in it. The risk is increased if internal tears are produced and there is subsequent intercourse.

Mucous Membrane or Broken Skin Contact with Urine/Feces.

Rimming can spread bacteria, viruses, and parasites that are harmful to one's health.

Risky Sexual Activities
are clearly linked to HIV transmission in some cases.

Fellatio with ejaculation in the mouth can be dangerous for the receptive partner.

Definitively High-Risk Sexual Activities
are known to provide a major route of transmitting HIV. These include:

Anal and Vaginal Intercourse Without a Condom and Internal Ejaculation: riskiest for the receptive partner, but dangerous for both partners.

Figure 11.5 Scale of risk for HIV in regard to various sexual activities

in peer training with hard to reach populations, and in psychoeducation and prevention counseling with all their clients. This can only be accomplished by involving agencies in new program arenas and in well-planned public health campaigns directed at the population they serve. For example, because of the increasing numbers of people of color infected with HIV, Ryan, Longres, and Roffman (1996) suggest that anonymous telephone risk-reduction counseling in agencies located in and serving communities of color should be developed.

CLINICAL PRACTICE

It should be clear by now that those who have HIV disease and those who care about them are confronted with a wide array of issues, challenges, and problems during the course of the illness that social workers can be helpful with. Therefore, while this depends in part on the setting and the purpose of the worker-client encounter, the assessment of such a client must span the range and interrelationship of psychological, sociocultural, and physiological aspects of HIV disease. Data must be gathered regarding the client's premorbid personality, coping skills, strengths and weaknesses, risk of decompensation, occupational and social functioning, family history, substance abuse, self-esteem, sense of coherence, feelings about AIDS and particular risk factors, as well as available formal and informal supports. The worker must attend to cultural, religious, social class, and spiritual values and attitudes, especially in relation to sexual orientation, the use of drugs, and death, dying, and grief, as well as notions related to accepting help (Chersky & Siever 1994; Dowsett 1994; Gold 1995). These are factors that affect both the client's definition of the problem and the worker's choice of interventions.

A primary goal of social work as well as most allied health and mental health professions is to support people in meeting their developmental tasks so as to achieve an optimal level of psychosocial functioning, integration, and a sense of integrity. When working with lesbian, gay, and bisexual clients with or affected by HIV disease, the goal is to assist in the development and ongoing maintenance of self-esteem and a healthy gay identity. This is often done by helping the client to confront the personal damage of heterosexism and homophobia, to develop the necessary coping skills and social supports for healthful functioning, and to nurture positive interactions within both the gay community and the wider social system. Whether or not a client has HIV disease, the meaning of the HIV epidemic to lesbian, gay, and bisexual people collectively and to any gay, lesbian, and bisexual person individually, especially its potential negative effect on self-esteem, must be considered.

Social workers can often assist greatly with the exploration of painful feelings associated with having HIV disease. As Mancoske and Lindhorst (1995) note:

> Discussion of emerging issues and the shifting feelings of the persons infect-
> ed with HIV is particularly helpful . . . especially in an environment that
> holds that "positive thinking" is a road to health. Mental health providers who
> are able to balance the anxiety that discussion of uncontrollable loss, progres-
> sion of illness, and death creates are able to offer the opportunity to those
> affected with HIV to fully examine their lives, empowering the client to
> make healthful choices.   (Mancoske & Lindhorst 1995:36)

However, this work can take a toll on the practitioner as well (Cadwell, Burn-ham, & Forstein 1994).

Practitioners must also recognize the difficulties gay men face in balancing public and private expressions of their "gayness" (Paradis 1990:260–61). Fears of intimacy will be complicated by shared fears of disease and death. Many clients with AIDS require assistance in dealing with these distressing feelings (Dworkin & Kaufer 1995; Macks 1987; Robinson 1994). As already noted, contracting HIV disease is often an occasion that forces people to reconsider and renegotiate coming out issues and the public/private boundary. However, some who are "closeted" remain "hidden grievers" and thus beyond the reach of helping professionals (Dworkin & Kaufer 1995).

Stulberg and Smith (1988) found that HIV disease has severely strained family relationships. While an AIDS diagnosis persuades some families to work through conflicts and accusations about sexual orientation and thus to become willing to care for their HIV-infected member, many families remain unavail-able as caregivers, removed by their own distress, denial, and disapproval (Abell & Miller 1991; McDonell 1993). Delgado and Rose (1994) found that in their research close friends and significant others did their best to fill the void of formal and familial support. Accustomed to institutional and person-al discrimination, the gay community has a history of developing alternative resources and family structures, which explains the large number of gay and lesbian caregivers identified in their study. Meeting with the significant other, family and friends will help the clinician to assess the level of social support, the potential for caregiving, and the collateral interventions that might be necessary during the course of HIV disease (Lloyd & Kuszelewicz 1995).

HIV disease of course raises special issues for the lovers and partners of those affected whether or not they have the disease themselves (Livingston 1996). It is also necessary to establish a safer sex strategy for serodiscordant couples who must be helped to adjust to their situation while building on their bonds of love and caring (Bryant & Demian 1994; Mattison & Mc-Whirter 1994; Robinson 1994; Shernoff 1995a). However, partner notification issues can raise important ethical dilemmas in practice that require careful attention and knowledge of state statutes that may be relevant (Silverman & Rice 1995). Groups for the partners of those with HIV disease have often proved helpful (Livingston 1996). Work with couples facing multiple losses might include expanding family and other social supports in the community (Nord 1996).

For the gay person infected with HIV, the impact is magnified when confronted by the homophobia of medical and mental health professionals. Reamer (1993b) notes that "one of the most tragic by-products of the AIDS crisis is the frighteningly large number of health care professionals who are reluctant or unwilling to treat infected individuals" (414). Referrals to gay- and lesbian-affirming and AIDS-knowledgeable providers would be a necessary first step. The previously cited studies of homophobia and the fear of AIDS among professionals, as well as the studies of biased, inadequate, or inappropriate clinical practice with lesbian and gay clients, call attention to the need for social work consultation and a continuing education or in-service training requirement for all health and human services professionals. These educational programs should be designed to increase knowledge and clinical skills related to AIDS and homophobia while dealing with participants' fears, biases, and their perceptions of their professional competence working with this population. Advocacy and staff education are thus appropriate macrosystem interventions designed to change those nonnurturing environments upon which clients are dependent.

HIV SERVICE DELIVERY SYSTEM

Based on more than a decade's experience working with persons living with HIV disease and their health and social service providers, the following comprehensive service delivery model is presented. This ideal health and social care system would be comprised of five major components:

1. *Health services* consisting of both acute and chronic care; HIV testing; outpatient clinics; psychiatric care; dental care; and community nursing care. These health services would also provide diagnostic capabilities; designate a primary health care provider (physician, nurse practitioner, or physician assistant); allow access to alternative treatments and experimental drug therapy trials.

2. *Psychosocial services* consisting of pre- and post-HIV-test counseling; case management; crisis intervention; support, counseling, and psychotherapy;

family and group treatment; self-help groups; spiritual and/or pastoral counseling; psychoeducation; staff training and support (all of which would be enhanced by evaluation); partner notification; and peer counseling.

3. *Social services* consisting of information and referral; social insurance, such as Medicare, Medicaid, and Supplemental Security Income (SSI) benefits; legal assistance; food, clothing, transportation; housing, such as independent, group, or supervised apartments; home health assistance; respite care; foster care; child care; case and class advocacy; geriatric services; employment and vocational counseling; "buddy" programs; funeral and burial arrangements; and chore and food delivery.

4. *Substance abuse treatment* consisting of detoxification; a range of treatment options which would also including counseling and aftercare support; maintenance programs; and AA, NA (Narcotics Anonymous), and related programs for the patient as well as for significant others and family members.

5. *Extended care* consisting of community-based home care; intermediate home care; skilled nursing care; and, when necessary, home-based and residential hospice care (Appleby 1992).

Psychological and social interventions are an integral part of medical treatment, for without adequate coping strategies and environmental supports, patients are easily lost from follow-up care, in which case their health will deteriorate more rapidly. Because there are many different services needed over the course of this disease, this system of services needs to be coordinated in a timely fashion, keeping all caregivers involved and thus avoiding service fragmentation and access problems. An effective interpersonal (micro) and systems development (macro) modality is case management, a core social work skill.

SUBSTANCE ABUSE

Substance abuse is not only a risk factor for contracting HIV disease; it can affect the course of the illness as well. Practice with gay, lesbian, and bisexual clients affected by both HIV disease and substance abuse requires keen awareness, knowledge, and intervention skills in response to a number of unique issues, including client stigmatization and marginalization; racial, ethnic, and cultural diversity of client groups; multitude of client educational, psychosocial, and resource needs; mobilization of client social networks; multidisciplinary care planning; and the emotional toll experienced by care providers. Social workers when working with clients with HIV disease and substance abuse may be required to address in practice discrimination; loss of housing and other staples of client survival; inability of clients to afford quality health care; deterioration of already dysfunctional family support systems; further decline in health status; limited availability or access to needed resources such as substance abuse treatment, medical care, and clinical trials; client relapse to substance use or unsafe sex in response to stress associated with HIV disease; exacerbation of HIV disease management by addiction; unfamiliarity and bias by health and social service providers in treating both diseases concurrently; and unformulated public policies to protect both individual rights and the public health (Lloyd et al. 1991). Many of the social and psychological services listed in the preceding section (and which are well within the recognized domain of generalist and clinical social work practice) will be needed at some point in time. Finally, the hallmarks of lesbian- and gay-affirmative substance-abuse treatment were covered in chapter 9.

COMMUNITY CONCERNS

Gay men and lesbians have already experienced the death of lovers, friends, associates, and clients to a staggering degree and, given the numbers of those infected but not yet ill, this experience will no doubt continue until a cure is found (Nord 1996). Many have not had adequate opportunity to process these multiple losses (Stulberg & Smith 1988). Social workers need to be prepared to deal with bereavement issues at the individual, family, and community levels (Dworkin & Kaufer 1995), as well as to be ready for the impact these issues will have on their professional colleagues and themselves.

There is a pervasive sense of mourning and depression in the gay community which affects many aspects of life, including sexuality, and a real risk exists of reverting to more negative attitudes about sexual orientation among gays and lesbians themselves, as well as among heterosexual people. This backlash has resulted in some bitterness and despair in the gay community and to fear that hard-earned gains and increased acceptance may slip away in the face of AIDS. The clinician must be aware of this dynamic when working with a lesbian or gay client on interpersonal issues, as must the community organizer or social work consultant who is attempting to facilitate AIDS organizational efforts (Dworkin & Kaufer 1995). The unresolved grief, anger, and depression may be issues that must be confronted before other work proceeds. Also the increase in gay/lesbian bashing, possibly stimulated by the fear of AIDS, must be addressed through assault counseling and neighborhood safety campaigns.

Self-help efforts have proven their healing power (empowerment) for the participants. Support groups as well as self-help groups focusing on community and resource development should be given priority.

> The only bright note in this grim reality is that because of homophobia and neglect, lesbian and gay communities mobilized in unprecedented numbers and ways to develop community-based AIDS service organizations for gay men. As is evident in the histories of other oppressed groups, crisis can inspire collaboration and mutual aid.
>
> —Gary A. Lloyd (1992:93)

Although the development of community-based AIDS service organizations (ASOs) has been a positive outcome of the epidemic, like their patients these agencies may themselves become imperiled (Wilson 1995). As the demographics of the epidemic shift, they are challenged to develop new services and broadened community relationships, including with groups who have not always been seen as gay-friendly and who have not always seen ASOs as responsive to their needs. However, as Wilson (1995) notes, "The nature and magnitude of the HIV/AIDS epidemic outstrips the capacity of any one type of organization such as ASOs to respond adequately" (124). Thus these vital organizations must be preserved even as new ones develop to meet other special population needs and mainstream services for people with AIDS are expanded.

The tasks ahead require psychological and cultural transformation of the structures that support homophobia and heterosexism. This assignment for the hardy would be to use skills of community organizing and community development to help gay and lesbian communities (and the agencies that serve them) to come to terms with the meaning of AIDS on intellectual, social, psychological, spiritual, and existential levels (Nord 1996) and to "revive the tribe" (Rofes 1996). As Rofes notes:

> Some HIV-negative men fear social condemnation as they consider reconstructing their lives to include some separation from the epidemic. It is as if leaving professional or volunteer work with people with AIDS is equivalent to turning one's back on the cause. Until survivors of the first fifteen years of the epidemic achieve significant progress in recovery from grief and trauma, formulation [reviving the tribe] will continue to be a place of great struggle and internal ambivalence.   (Rofes 1996:246)

The appeal of victimization and powerlessness in contemporary culture in the United States is tremendous. Healthy adaptation is antithetical to this diminished identity. Rofes (1996:262–80) makes several recommendations for reconstructing community: (1) we must de-AIDS gay/lesbian identity,

community, and culture; (2) the gay/lesbian political movement must priori-
tize a broad agenda; (3) the community must begin to discuss sex; (4) support
must come for both separate and mixed spaces for HIV-positive and HIV-negative people; (5) the community must support gay men's involvement with
children and youth; (6) encourage the celebration of life; (7) encourage gay
men and lesbians to seek spiritual outlets; (8) gay men and lesbians must find
opportunities for witnessing; (9) encourage the rebirth of gay/lesbian identity; (10) explore multiple identities; (11) the community's commitment to
combating AIDS must continue; and (12) love between men and love between
women must be treasured and promoted. The positive aspects of community-
building to end isolation and alienation, and the negative aspects of pseudo-
communication and a false sense of connection, must become the focus of gay
and lesbian activists and those social workers who would join them.

POLICY AND PROGRAM CONCERNS

The information in regard to laws, policies, and AIDS-related programs is vast
and thus beyond the scope of this chapter. There are several policies that will
be briefly covered because of the importance to agency-based services for
those who are HIV-infected. First, the overarching policies presently in flux
are welfare reform and managed care. Federal and state policies concerning
financial support and medical coverage are basic to the well-being and/or the
survival of a majority of HIV-infected clients. Welfare policy establishes who
will be covered, for how long, at what level of funding, and under what circumstances. Many working clients or those who have limited private insurance rely on a state's AIDS Drug Assistance Program because of their more
generous insurance caps. Those welfare policies related to continued eligibility, such as twenty-four months of assistance and then termination, to lower
income levels for access to coverage, or to various types of Medicaid coverage
and housing supplements are increasingly important to clients as the disease
progresses. As states deal with block grants and can no longer rely on categorical assistance from the federal government, all these programs become
competitive with other human needs.

Second, the Ryan White CARE Act, the federal government's largest dollar
investment for the provision of services for the HIV-infected, is intended to
help hard-hit communities and all states to increase the availability of outpatient primary health care and support services in order to reduce utilization of
more costly inpatient care, increase access to care for the underserved population, and improve the quality of life of those affected by the epidemic. Title I
of the measure directs emergency funding to urban areas with a cumulative

total of two thousand or more AIDS cases. There were, as of 1996, fifty-six cities mandated by law to receive funds for primary medical care, pharmaceuticals, dental care, home health care, hospice care, rehabilitation, substance abuse treatment, and inpatient personnel as well as for case management, adoption/foster care assistance, buddy/companion services, day/respite care, emergency assistance (rent and utilities), food/home delivered meals, housing-related services, client advocacy, transportation, and other local priorities. Dollars supporting these services have been directed to community agencies. Title II provides formula funding to each state to improve the quality, availability, and organization of health and support services for people and families with HIV/AIDS. Many of these funds support the collaborative efforts of community agencies. Title III supports outpatient early intervention to reduce the risk of transmission and to link people to care. Title IV supports demonstration projects for children, youth, women, and families with the disease. This act is discussed because of its policy implications at all levels. On the federal level, the expansion or redefinition of benefits and the level of funding resurface in Congress every three to five years; policy advocacy and coalition-building are important interventions at this level. At state and local levels, the service priorities and the amount of funding are established by a community council. Membership on a council is an excellent venue for influencing and developing policy. Agencies benefit by advocating for local needs and by offering AIDS-related services.

Third, another policy of importance to all agencies is the Americans with Disabilities Act (ADA), which prohibits public accommodation, credit, and job-related discrimination against persons *perceived* to be HIV-infected and those actually infected. Agency policy related to the type of service provided to HIV-infected and affected clients and those procedures insuring access to these services must be developed. Agency personnel policies and procedures should be formulated with reference to clients and employees who are HIV-infected.

Finally, there are so many areas that are or may, in the future, be covered by federal, state, and agency policy. Since these issues are treated differently depending upon the locality and because they may change over time, the remainder of this section will briefly note the more significant policy domains and then identify resources that will allow the reader to stay abreast of future developments.

Policies related to prevention and education—and dealing with issues such as degree of explicitness, cultural and linguistic appropriateness, target audience, types of media, and funding—are necessary to prevent infection or in lowering the risk to disease progression. At the point of diagnosis, AIDS testing and reporting policies become important. Whether these tests are confidential or anonymous has significance. Mandatory testing of all people at risk or of pregnant women or even of health care providers themselves strikes at the constitutional issue of privacy and due process. Who will receive this information and under what circumstances are central to the confidentiality debate. Policies related to partner notification or duty to warn—notifying the spouse, partner, or drug-using companions when HIV is reported—becomes another constitutional concern. As the disease progresses, policies related to patient visitation, guardianship, power of attorney, advance directives, and inheritance need legal attention. Other related issues of importance to people living with the virus concern who will be authorized to provide health care and mental health services; whether permanency planning, co-parenting, partner adoption, and subsidized adoption will be encouraged and funded; funding for explicit safer sex and clean needle use prevention campaigns; antidiscrimination laws and access to legal recourse and compensation; authorization and support for needle exchange programs and drug treatment as well as for the medical use of marijuana; access to experimental drug trials; and the decriminalization of assisted suicide. Each of these concerns have been and will be translated into policy. Appropriately, these policy issues should have the input of social workers and health care providers and, finally, the active support of provider and client coalitions to insure passage and implementation.

In an attempt to stay current, there are several World Wide Web sites that are excellent resources because they provide consistently high-quality, well-organized, and frequently updated material. Usually these sites contain "links" to other sites with complementary information. The Body collects an impressive amount of articles and fact sheets regarding legal issues from reputable sources. (The Body's site address is *http://www.thebody.com*.) The University of California's (San Francisco) Center for AIDS Prevention Studies (CAPS) provides a great deal of prevention-related research and information with links to other prevention-related sites which are helpful for policy development. (The CAPS site address is *http://www.caps.ucsf.edu/capsweb/index/html*.) The Centers for Disease Control (CDC) National AIDS Clearinghouse contains a storehouse of information, ranging from HIV-related epidemiological data (including the *HIV/AIDS Surveillance Report*) to fact sheets that can be downloaded from the site. Also posted at this site is the CDC's *AIDS Daily Summary*, which includes abstracts of articles from major U.S. publications (the site address is *http://www.cdcnac.org*). The *Journal of the American Medical Association*'s (JAMA) Web site is an excellent resource for scientific information and contains a link to the National Library of Medicine AIDS Database. (The JAMA site address is *http://www.ama.assn.org/special/hiv/hivhome*.) ARIC (AIDS Research Information Center) is geared toward empowering people with HIV disease by making medical information accessible to lay people (the ARIC site address is *http://www.critpath.org/aric*). Other treatment publications are *GMHC Treatment Issues* (*http://www.gmhc.org*), the *Bulletin of Experimental Treatments for AIDS* (*BETA*) (*http://www.sfaf.org/beta.html*), the consumer-developed *Project Inform Perspectives* (*http://www.projinf.org/pub/pip_index.html*), and *AIDS Treatment News* (*http://www.immunet.org/atn* or *http://www.aidsnews.org/index.html#Home*).

Conclusion

The practice tasks described above require case management and clinical skills, community mobilization and resource development, advocacy on both case and class levels, program planning and development, task force and board work, policy development, evaluation, and a broad array of psychosocial interventions, all of which are part of social work education and training. However, this general information must be supplemented with specific knowledge about HIV disease and its multiple impacts on individuals, couples, families, communities, and society as a whole. This chapter's overview of knowledge for practice with gay, lesbian, and bisexual people with and affected by HIV disease should serve as a sound starting point for practice. The social work profession is challenged to maintain and improve upon the leadership shown by many individual social workers in responding to HIV disease until it has been eradicated in all of our communities.

Part 4

Conclusion

Affirming Lesbian, Gay, and Bisexual Lives

To summarize the knowledge for and about social work practice that has been presented, this chapter is organized around the five curriculum areas defined in social work education: human behavior and the social environment; research; social welfare policies and services; social work practice; and fieldwork and the social work workplace. While acknowledging the significant problems that continue to challenge gay, lesbian, and bisexual people today, it presents a vision for a future in which a gay, lesbian, or bisexual sexual orientation will be regarded as a dimension of human difference that is no longer devalued.

Gay, lesbian, and bisexual people in the United States today still clearly face significant challenges to their growth and development because of the heterosexism and homophobia that they all too commonly encounter. These forces have affected how sexual orientation itself is defined and experienced and the cultures and communities, gay and straight, in which people live. For gay, lesbian, and bisexual people, each major life task—growing up, developing satisfying sexual and intimate relationships, having children, working and supporting oneself, and negotiating middle and old age—is profoundly affected. Gay, lesbian, and bisexual people often also face specific barriers in finding adequate mental health and substance abuse services. Many, especially among gay and bisexual men, are dealing with the impact of the HIV epidemic. And, unfortunately, all too many have experienced violence simply because of being gay or lesbian. The profession of social work purports to be at the forefront of addressing issues of discrimination against traditionally oppressed groups (NASW 1997b). However, more than 50 percent of social work educational programs lag significantly when is comes to addressing heterosexism in the curriculum, in academic, personnel, or admission policies, or in scholarship (Morrow 1996). The Council on Social Work Education's (CSWE) Curriculum Policy Statement (1988, 1993) mandates practice and theoretical content on gay and lesbian issues at both the baccalaureate and master's level. Such inclusion is essential because it is highly unlikely that social work students will have been exposed to curriculum addressing gay, lesbian, and bisexual issues earlier in their education (Newman 1989). CSWE in July 1995 implemented a new curriculum policy that provides greater specificity in relation to gay and lesbian content, but this has been vigorously resisted by a vocal and well-organized few. This academic resistance appears to be comparable to what Hartman (1993) and Newman (1989) have characterized as backlash in the broader political arena, that is, efforts to abridge gay and lesbian rights that have intensified. Even on liberal college campuses with nondiscrimination policies related to sexual orientation, gay, lesbian, and bisexual people commonly encounter problems (Norris 1991).

Pursuing another vein of reasoning, Epstein and Zak (1993) identify several factors that appear to limit the inclusion of lesbian and gay content in the social work curriculum: (1) homophobia and heterosexism; (2) the traditional family-oriented value system of the profession; (3) breadth and depth of race and gender content already in the curriculum; and (4) uncertainty about the gay and lesbian content to be included. For example, Mackelprang, Ray, and Hernandez-Peck (1996) found that, before the implementation of the new CSWE guidelines, inclusion of curriculum content on race and gender in graduate and undergraduate social work programs was much greater than content on sexual orientation.

Tierney and Rhoads (1993) describe another constraint, which is a component of institutionalized heterosexism: the lack of credibility and support for faculty to pursue research on gay, lesbian, and bisexual issues. Faculty fear that pursuing this line of research will have a detrimental impact on their professional advancement, or that they will be accused of having a lesbian or gay agenda. Finally, as we go to press, the profession is still hotly debating the CSWE mandate, particularly whether issues of religious freedom, especially for those programs that are housed in religiously affiliated colleges and universities, should limit it (Parr & Jones 1996). Whatever the reason, the current mandate is quite specific and nonnegotiable, and even were an exemption-granting process for religious schools to be accepted, the vast majority of schools would still need to do a great deal more than they are currently doing to prepare their students to serve gay, lesbian, and bisexual people and their families adequately.

This concluding chapter is organized around core social work curriculum areas. Major points made throughout the text will be selectively summarized with the intent of integrating knowledge for use in practice, as well as identifying where there are gaps in our understanding or where more research is needed. Specific attention is given to empowerment interventions that promise to be most affirming and effective with lesbian, gay, and bisexual people in all their diversity. In addition, by organizing our concluding points in this way, students, professional social workers, and educators can evaluate the education they are receiving, or have received, for its adequacy in preparing them to serve gay, lesbian, and bisexual people. However, because the summary is relatively brief, it is by no means exhaustive of areas to consider when planning curriculum and educational activities to address gay, lesbian, and bisexual concerns.

HUMAN BEHAVIOR AND THE SOCIAL ENVIRONMENT

The *theories for practice* commonly presented in the human behavior and social environment curriculum sequence have proven quite useful in guiding assessment and intervention, and they complement the theory and knowledge presented in the preceding chapters as unique to gays, bisexuals, and lesbians. This text's ecological and empowerment framework serves as a wide-angle lens for viewing the functioning of gay, lesbian, and bisexual people, their families, and their communities from various vantage points: intrapersonal issues, the dynamics of the person-environment interaction, and knowledge about the social context. Theory and knowledge related to all of these are needed to inform interventions to address problems, issues, and needs at all systems levels. The *biopsychosocial* framework so often cited as the basis for understanding human behavior seems especially relevant in looking at gay, lesbian, and bisexual lives. Assessment with gay, lesbian, and bisexual people requires a "dual focus"; as Hall (1978) put it, "The practitioner must be able to see the ways in which the client's presenting problem is both affected by and separate from her sexual orientation" (380). As we have written elsewhere:

> Damage to self-esteem resulting from oppression and stigmatization must always be considered, but at the same time the client probably occupies roles,

works on developmental tasks, and experiences feelings in which being gay, lesbian, or bisexual is incidental. For example, [some gay, lesbian and bisexual teens are rejected by their families. These] teens have the same developmental needs for the support and approval of adults and peers that others do and would be seeking a way to separate and differentiate themselves from their families even if rejection based on their sexual orientation had not occurred. Thus a worker . . . might expect to hear both a longing for the love and approval of their parents despite their rejecting behavior and a simultaneous longing to be completely free of parental restraint or control.

(Appleby & Anastas 1992:366)

In addition to understanding these normative conflicts, however, specific knowledge about how teens can develop a positive gay, lesbian, or bisexual identity is also needed. As with other dimensions of difference, the challenge is to hold and enact the simultaneous understanding that gay, lesbian, and bisexual people are both the same as and different from their heterosexual counterparts. Including course content on human sexuality in general that includes information on gays and lesbians specifically has been suggested as an effective way to increase social workers' knowledge and positive attitudes toward gay and lesbian people (Newman 1989), another example of the usefulness of the dual focus.

Several areas of theory and knowledge presented in the preceding chapters are especially significant and thus worth repeating. *Identity development* has been a major part of the discussion in the first four chapters, wherein we focused on its definition, its relationship to self-concept, the structure of identity, changes that occur as identity develops, and internal and external factors affecting such changes. Some attention was given to theoretical differences in understanding gay and lesbian identity development, particularly the degree to which identity is viewed as an individualistic and inherent phenomenon or as a more socially based phenomenon (see chapter 2). In the absence of definitive answers to many major questions, along with most contemporary scholars we conclude that gay, lesbian, and bisexual identity development and identity management strategies are best understood as the product of both internal and external, individual and social, personal and interpersonal processes. In fact, the study of gay and lesbian identity development serves as an ideal case example of why the biological, the psychological, and the social (biopsychosocial) all must be considered for adequate understanding of human behavior.

On a macro level, theory about groups in conflict, including conflict between subordinate (in this case, gay, lesbian, and bisexual people) and dominant ones, is also useful. Because society is separated into social groups that possess different amounts of power and prestige, social groups must decide which dimensions will be used to differentiate themselves from other groups. The group identity enhancement strategies used must be understood: (1) social mobility—that is, entrance of an outgroup member into the dominant group via passing, capitulating, or covering (Troiden 1989); and (2) social change—that is, social creativity in altering the status quo between the outgroup and the dominant group, either by changing the basis of the comparisons (cognitive change) or through social competition, as in social protests, lobbying, and social action. The objective is to get both the subordinate group and the dominant group to accept a changed status relationship between the groups. "Each strategy is useful, but for different people in particular circumstances" (Cox & Gallois 1996:22).

In addition, *the reality of gay, lesbian, and bisexual identities and identity management strategies is not the same as the political vision of it.* For example, research does not support the position that identity is unidirectional, unidimensional, or effectively managed in only one way at all times. Here is one important place where the professional and the political understanding diverge.

Social identity theory (Cox & Gallois 1996; Tajfel 1982) is both compatible with our ecological orientation and sensitive to the possible multiple identities (including racial, ethnic, and cultural identities) that gay, lesbian, and bisexual people participate in. There are two processes in this theory: self-categorization and social comparison. The process of self-categorization ("identity development") has been discussed extensively. The social comparison process is raised here, however, because it serves as a clearer link to the person-environment formulation and as a challenge for practice and policy thinking. In addition, an appreciation of *human diversity* is needed for cultural competency, including knowing that there is tremendous diversity among lesbian, gay, and bisexual people. There are also great differences among them in their levels of acculturation and cultural identities, both in their racial, ethnic, and cultural worlds and in relation to gay, lesbian, and bisexual communities and cultures.

Social self-esteem is derived by comparing the social groups one belongs to with other groups. Groups are motivated to improve their comparability through attaining more prestige, power, and status. Cox and Gallois (1996) tell us that dominant groups are in the position of being able to control the status quo. Social groups thus jostle for position in the society, with members of the dominant group attempting to maintain a status quo favorable to themselves, while subordinate groups seek to alter the status quo in some way so as to better their own position. This theory helps us to understand the individual emphasis on upward social mobility of various minority groups and some of the bigotry gay and lesbian people experience at the hands of other minorities. It also offers a framework for exploring the interaction that occurs between a person's multiple identities.

There are other areas of knowledge worth briefly reviewing. Research on mental health has documented that as individuals, couples, and as a social community, lesbians, gay men, and bisexuals do not show lower levels of adjustment than their heterosexual counterparts. Also, common beliefs about the harmful effects on children of having a gay or lesbian parent are all mistaken. Additionally, the idea that gay and lesbian relationships are overly sexualized, shallow, brief, or unstable is ill-informed; such relationships have been found to be as variable (functional and dysfunctional) as heterosexual ones, including unfortunately their potential to be violent. It has even been suggested that the coping skills required of gay and lesbian people may equip them particularly well to deal with the challenges of midlife and old age despite structural problems that they face. Thus the resiliency of gay, lesbian, and bisexual people, in light of heterosexist bias and homophobia within American society, is remarkable. In fact, this resiliency deserves further study to inform risk-reduction and health-promotion efforts for all people.

There are also some special challenges that gay, lesbian, and bisexual people face that have been reviewed. Although a gay, lesbian, or bisexual orientation is no longer viewed as pathological, misguided and oppressive mental health treatments still linger. The problem of substance abuse among gay and lesbian people is not yet adequately understood or treated. Despite recent changes in the epidemiology of the epidemic in the United States and in treatment of the illness, HIV disease is still taking a terrible toll, especially on gay and bisexual men, their families, friends, and communities. Violence against individual gay and lesbian people is still unfortunately widespread.

Oppression, power and privilege, heterosexism and homophobia form the environmental context in which lesbians and gay men develop and function. These abstract social dynamics are experienced as nonnurturing social behaviors (discrimination, prejudice, bias, and violence), which present major barriers to optimal social functioning. There are some signs of positive change; 84 percent of Americans think that discrimination on the basis of sexual orientation is wrong according to a 1996 *Newsweek* poll that asked if gays and lesbians should enjoy the same access to job opportunities as heterosexuals. However, Singer and Deschamps (1994:55–57) have been analyzing public opinion data since 1973 and concluded that while support for nondiscrimination in the workplace has increased dramatically (59 percent to 84 percent), over the same period acceptance of homosexuality itself has increased only marginally (34 percent to 38 percent). Thus the environment is hardly predictably nurturing to gay, lesbian, and bisexual people and is more likely to be a source of pressure and stress. Social workers need to know about heterosexism, homophobia, and heterosexual privilege and how to recognize them, in others and in themselves.

While a wealth of theoretical and empirical information has been presented, there are many significant gaps in our knowledge. The gay and lesbian community is diverse in ethnicity, gender, race, and social class; however, most of what is known is based on the study of urban, white, and well-educated people. Much of what we know about psychosocial adaptation of rural and suburban clients is primarily anecdotal, which is also true for other small subpopulations, such as the physically and mentally challenged. Many of the new immigrant populations have yet to be studied. Berger (1992) and Tully (1992) note that much of what we know about older lesbians comes from small samples and thus makes conclusions difficult and also that much of our understanding of older gay men precedes the AIDS epidemic. Brooks (1992), who amply notes many of the methodological problems with lesbian- and gay-focused research, encourages the next generation of social work researchers to increase our understanding of the survival strategies, the coping and adaptive skills of lesbians, gay men, and bisexuals in the context of a heterosexist society. There is limited research regarding the resilience of gay, lesbian, and bisexual individuals under exceptional conditions, trauma, domestic violence, chronic illness, substance abuse, homelessness, or other significant social problems. The psychological, social, and political effects of AIDS (multiple losses, sexuality, sense of community) on individuals and communities are still unknown (Rofes 1996). The relationship between adolescent sexual orientation and suicide is still not clear. There is a paucity of empirical or qualitative information available about this population in general. Increased knowledge in all these areas (and others) is necessary for adequate social work assessment to occur.

RESEARCH

As has just been noted, there is a great need for more research on gay, lesbian, and bisexual people, their problems and their adaptive successes. In addition, there is essentially no research available on effective practice with gay, lesbian, and bisexual people or on what constitutes gay- and/or lesbian-affirmative practice (MacEachron 1995). As the preceding chapters have shown, social workers have been among the leaders in research areas such as AIDS and HIV disease, gay and lesbian families, gay and lesbian aging, and lesbian health (Newman 1989). Published studies by social work researchers in these areas should be more widely known as they illustrate well how the social work person-in-environment perspective is useful in studying a variety of important and complex topics.

Heterosexism and homophobia, however, can also have an effect on research. Anastas and MacDonald (1994), Brooks (1992), and others (Herek et al. 1991) warn us about the abuses of research methodology in relation to studies of minorities in general and gay and lesbian populations more specifically. "A research study may be technically in order as related to data analysis and statistical procedures, and yet be irrelevant or misleading in its conclusions about a particular problem or population. Just as we cannot solve problems if the definition of the problem has been inaccurate, research cannot contribute to our knowledge base if it is formulated around faulty premises" (Brooks 1992:201). Following Eichler (1988), bias in research on gay, lesbian, and bisexual people can result in invisibility, overgeneralization, insensitivity, dichotomism, and/or the use of double standards (Anastas & MacDonald 1994). When studying populations at risk and that are hard to identify, special ethical challenges can arise (Woodman, Tully, & Barranti 1995). Social workers must be able to detect these biases and potential hazards in the studies that they read and know how to avoid them in the research that they do.

In all research, especially research involving gay, lesbian, and bisexual people, it is necessary to first address the assumptive ideology—in this case, heterosexism—to see if majority norms have influenced the formulation of the research question itself. Like sexist and racist bias, heterosexist bias can be influential in the selection of the problem and the sample to be studied, as well as in the way data are gathered (or not gathered) and in the interpretation of research results. For example, in the past, research conducted on clinical populations—that is, using samples of gay and lesbian people seeking psychiatric help—was too often used to draw conclusions about *all* gay and lesbian people, contributing to the now discredited view that being gay or lesbian was incompatible with good adjustment and psychological health. However, as was noted in the chapter on middle and old age, too much social and psychological research is still being done in which the sexual orientation of the research participants is taken for granted as being heterosexual, leaving major gaps in our knowledge about gay, lesbian, and bisexual people, especially about normal populations. This heterosexist assumption renders the gay, lesbian, and bisexual experience still largely invisible. Except for studies of parenting or the children of gay and lesbian parents, studies of gay men are more numerous than those of lesbians (Newman 1989). As with social work practice, we do not believe that gay- or lesbian-specific research methods are needed. However, research on gay, lesbian, and bisexual people urgently needs to be improved in both quality and quantity.

As has been true for other groups, it might be useful for gay and lesbian researchers to carve out their own terrain by defining their own frameworks and priorities. Gay and lesbian researchers might have their own questions to ask related to identity development, disclosure, assertiveness, androgyny, interpersonal attraction, self-image, alienation, evaluation of social service needs, coupling, parenting, aging, health and illness, and intergroup relations (Brooks 1992). Gay, lesbian, and bisexual identity coexists with many other identities, resulting in functional adaptations in some cases and conflict in others. Since identifications with social groups are a fundamental influence on behavior, it is important to examine individuals within certain groups. It is equally important to examine the effect of the group on the individual, that is, how group-based categorization and social comparison substantially affect behavior. Some have suggested that involving research participants in designing the study itself can be very helpful (Renzetti 1995). The various gay and lesbian journals cited in the references and previous chapters continue to identify emerging and promising issues and concerns deserving of further research.

SOCIAL WELFARE POLICY AND SERVICES

The broad objective of social welfare is to provide resources, services, opportunities, and social support to people with needs who are unable to meet them in other social institutions, such as the family and the economic or political systems. Significant gaps in the resources, opportunities, and support services generally available to lesbian, gay, and bisexual people have been identified throughout.

Core values of the social work profession include social justice, independence and freedom, diversity, community life, empowerment, self-determination, and change. Justice must be accessible to all on an equal basis; it must be impartially applied. Social conditions must be just. People want to feel a sense of self-importance and have a real ability to make decisions that affect their own lives and not to be manipulated by an intrusive government or an impersonal bureaucracy. Independence and freedom are needed to experiment, reflect, and change. People generally want to create their own community as a chance to experience support and a feeling of belonging, to have greater power over their lives, and to find ways of resolving problems. On the other hand, when people are isolated, they may more easily become victims of exploitation and alienation, feel powerless, vulnerable, and unimportant.

The NASW's *Code of Ethics* encourages all social workers to further the cause of social justice by promoting and defending the rights of persons suffering injustice and oppression. Gay, lesbian, and bisexual people certainly meet this definition. Social workers are enjoined to view discrimination and prejudice directed against any minority group as a breach of their civil rights and an assault on the mental health of the affected minority, as well as a detriment to society as a whole. Furthermore, through its social policy statement specifically addressed to lesbian, gay, and bisexual people, social workers are urged to work to combat discriminatory employment practices and any other form of discrimination that imposes something less than equal status on gay or lesbian individuals:

> NASW affirms its commitment to work toward full social and legal acceptance and recognition of lesbian, gay, and bisexual people. . . . To this end, NASW supports legislation, regulation, policies, judicial review, political action, and changes in social work policy statements and the [NASW's] *Code of Ethics* and any other means necessary to establish and protect the equal rights of all people without regard to sexual orientation. NASW is committed to working toward the elimination of prejudice and discrimination both inside and outside the profession.   (NASW 1997b:202)

These commitments, in turn, translate into a variety of social policies and social change strategies:

> NASW works in coalition with mental health and other human services professions to help enact antidiscrimination legislation at national, state, and local levels and actively campaigns against any laws allowing discriminatory practices against lesbian, gay, and bisexual people, primarily in immigration, employment, housing, professional credentialing, licensing, public accommodation, child custody, and the right to marry.

> NASW opposes policies that exclude lesbian, gay, and bisexual people from the military and other forms of government services.

> NASW and its chapters need to develop and participate in coalitions with other professional associations to lobby for the civil rights of lesbian, gay, and bisexual people and other oppressed groups; to defeat efforts to limit the civil rights of lesbian, gay, and bisexual people; and to advocate for increased funding for programs designed to eliminate hate crimes and anti-gay violence, and to provide education, treatment services, and research that increases our understanding of the lesbian, gay, and bisexual community.

NASW supports working toward implementation of domestic partnership and marriage legislation at local, state, and national levels that includes lesbian, gay, and bisexual people. It endorses the development and dissemination of model antidiscrimination and domestic partnership and/or marriage legislation that can be used in municipal, state, and national legislatures.

NASW encourages adoption of laws that recognize inheritance, insurance, same-sex marriage, child custody, property, and other rights in lesbian, gay, and bisexual relationships.

NASW encourages self-identified lesbian, gay, and bisexual individuals to seek election in all political jurisdictions.
— NASW, "Lesbian, gay, and bisexual issues" (1997b:203–204)

Thus a wide range of policy issues relevant to gay, lesbian, and bisexual people have been identified as social work concerns.

All *civil rights* movements represent the collective decision of individuals from groups of stigmatized Americans who refuse any longer to regard themselves through the majority's eyes and who therefore cease to accept the understanding that deprives them of their rights. Equal treatment before the law should be afforded to all lesbians and gay men, which is basic to U.S. citizenship. It is worth emphasizing that these are not new or special rights but rather the extension of existing rights guaranteed to all American citizens by the Constitution and identified by the Declaration of Independence as the purpose, and not the gift, of government.

In addition, the history of the gay liberation movement, especially as it emerged following the Stonewall Rebellion of 1969, is a prime example of effecting social change through a *grass-roots social movement*. During the HIV epidemic, other grass-roots organizations emerged to force political, scientific, and medical attention to the illness, and a major self-help movement involving both gay and lesbian people created the needed services when they did not exist. Formal social service organizations were established, and major health and public health institutions, organizations, and procedures were forever changed by their actions. While these efforts have not been without controversy and while the problems are not all solved by any means, learning about the history and ongoing development of these movements illustrates human and community capacity in the face of oppression and adversity and may have lessons for other groups as well.

The constitutional *right of privacy* free from government regulation or intrusion is also fundamental. Privacy means that people make choices other people have to respect. The choice lesbians and gay men make to *express* their sexual orientation is quintessentially the kind of choice government has no business interfering with. That is exactly what privacy means, and this understanding of privacy is grounded in the natural-rights philosophy of our constitutional government. Such privacy is also exactly what gay, lesbian, and bisexual Americans do not enjoy. Our private choices as individuals are not protected, and thus, as a group, we do not enjoy equal protection of the laws. The chapters related to youth (4), family (6), relationships (5), culture (3), aging (8), violence (10), AIDS (11), and the workplace (7) presented ample evidence of this claim. The shared characteristic of sexual orientation thus routinely excludes us from full citizenship (Nava & Dawidoff 1994).

Criminalization of homosexual acts is another violation of the right of individual privacy. Criminal statutes proscribing adult homosexual behavior create an environment of oppression arising from fear of prosecution and provide the means of blackmail. Such statutes are most reprehensible when linked to enforcement by entrapment. These laws perpetuate discrimination against homosexuals. Discrimination on the basis of homosexuality violates an individual's right of privacy and denies the person equal protection of the law. The fight for gay and lesbian civil rights is, then, the reassertion of the rights to personal freedom and to personal choice about personal life (Nava & Dawidoff 1994; Sullivan 1995; Vaid 1995).

The legal landscape in relation to lesbian/gay rights changes continually. As of this writing, gay rights are not protected by the U.S. Constitution. No federal job protection exits in this country. The Human Rights Campaign found that, in 1994, 70 percent of voters did not realize that antigay *job discrimination* is still widespread and predominantly legal (Goldberg 1996). The Employment Non-Discrimination Act, which would provide such protection, has yet to be passed by Congress. The Defense of Marriage Act (anti-lesbian/gay marriage) was passed by Congress and signed into law by President Clinton in 1996. By 1997 only eleven states (California, Connecticut, Hawaii, Maine, Massachusetts, Minnesota, New Hampshire, New Jersey, Rhode Island, Vermont, and Wisconsin) and the District of Columbia offered full civil rights legal protection to lesbian, gay, and bisexual people. Between fifteen and eighteen others cover some degree of protection with very tenuous executive orders. Approximately 165 cities and counties have ordinances, which do not carry the weight of law (National Gay and Lesbian Task Force 1996). While these laws and ordinances vary in power, each represents a building block upon which precedents are being set. Many of these precedents have implications for employers who are experiencing pressure from lesbian, gay, and bisexual employees for a safe work environment, equitable benefits, and appropriate public support.

Achtenberg (1988:244) reminds us that to favor lesbian and gay rights or to support an end to discrimination must mean to deplore the ways in which society undermines the formation, preservation, and protection of the *lesbian and gay family*. Gay rights must also include support for custody and visitation statutes that ensure strict neutrality with regard to the sexual orientation of the parent. Advocacy for adoption and foster parenting laws and administrative practices that are strictly neutral should become a related activity. Joint adoptions by same-sex couples should be permitted when it is in a child's best interests. Laws permitting delegation of personal and health care duties to nonrelatives should be created, as well as provision for fair determination of the guardian or conservator for an ill person. The same sentiment should inform the laws of interstate succession. Equity, not sexual orientation or marital status, should become the value undergirding the distribution of work-related and governmental benefits.

Pierce (1992) cautions us to look beyond social policy in its most general and abstract forms to *agency and program policy, regulation, and procedures* as well. There are a number of steps that can be taken to enhance gay, lesbian, and bisexual people's capacities, specifically those that recognize and support cultural and lifestyle differences; promote natural helping and support networks;

In a case in which NASW was an *amicus* last year [1996], school officials in Ashland, Wis., agreed in November to pay $900,000 to settle a federal lawsuit by a young gay man who charged that school officials failed to protect him from anti-gay abuse by his middle- and high-school peers. . . . The settlement . . . followed a federal jury's decision that two school principals and an assistant principal were liable for not protecting Jamie Nabozny, now 21, from abuse by other students between 1988 and 1992. . . . Nabozny's lawsuit stated he was the victim of several demeaning incidents that typically involved male students insulting and physically assaulting him because of his sexual orientation. . . . Nabozny testified that abuse by other students included being shoved, spat upon, beaten and urinated upon. . . . Nabozny said he had been kicked in the abdomen so many times he later required surgery. Nabozny and his mother also testified that his pleas to school officials for help were met with comments like, "Boys will be boys," and "If you're going to be gay, you have to learn to expect such abuse." . . . Nabozny had received services from county social workers, but none of them informed school principals of problems related to his sexual orientation.   —*NASW News* (February 1997) provide support to individuals who find themselves in transitional situations; teach or inform others about new information and skills; further people's involvement in decision making and developmental opportunities; and encourage self-help opportunities (172–84). A recent example of working in coalition to affect school policies to prevent violence against gay and lesbian teens is given in the following box. The story illustrates both initial professional indifference and later professional action in coalition to end violence against gay and lesbian people—in this case to make institutions like schools comfortable for the gay, lesbian, and bisexual people who make use of them.

Knowledge development related to social welfare policy and gay, lesbian, and bisexual people is urgently needed. The impact of gay- and lesbian-inclusive policy initiatives has yet to be implemented, much less evaluated in most areas of social welfare, and the opportunities to do so are unlimited. Those areas where laws, policy, or procedural change have taken place (such as the passage of civil rights legislation in eleven states, the inclusion of domestic partnership benefits in industry, or the expansion of adoption and foster care procedures to include lesbians and gays, to name only a few) require evaluation. It is conceivable that these experiences may inform policy development in other areas. The impact of anti-gay/lesbian or affirmative procedures and regulations related to the delivery of services demand attention. The debate as to whether to adopt gay or lesbian specialty versus integrated social services must be given a hearing. If there is commitment to do this type of analysis, social work researchers, doctoral students, and policy analysts will have many professional opportunities to make a difference.

Social Work Practice

Each chapter of this book has presented information designed to enhance the reader's understanding of client environments, interpersonal processes, and life tasks related to practice with gay, lesbian, and bisexual people. This was done to increase both assessment skills and intervention options. Specific practice implications were framed in terms of lesbian, gay, or bisexual strengths, competencies, and challenges. After an extensive review of the empirical and clinical practice literature, not withstanding the pioneer work of Berger (1983), we conclude that there is no need to develop a new model or theory of social work practice with lesbians, gays, and bisexuals. Models that are effective and affirming for other minority clients appear to be promising for this stigmatized group. Translating these principles of practice into the specific context of working with lesbian, gay, and bisexual clients and their families is called *lesbian/gay-affirmative practice*.

Dubois and Miley (1996) note that it is the social worker who transforms the abstract values of the profession into principles for practice. Then they translate these principles into concrete actions in specific situations. Values abstractly shape social workers' ways of thinking and concretely direct their actions in practice. Professional activities mirror the dual purpose of social work "directed at empowering consumers in all social systems to realize their own potential and create responsive social structures. Empowerment is achieved to the extent that people gain mastery over their lives and to the extent that institutional structures respond humanely and equitably to human needs" (1996:458–59). Practice that is characterized by focusing on strengths, working collaboratively with clients, and linking personal and political power resonates well with those who have been stigmatized and marginalized. While all models of practice incorporate core social work values and principles, not all models empower clients equally. Ideally, social work is an empowering profession. The process of social work is ostensibly empowering, and the product of professional intervention may be empowerment. When social workers work with clients in partnerships that affirm clients' strengths and competencies, empowerment is the product.

The history of gay, bisexual, and lesbian oppression warrants a practice approach that emphasizes *empowerment*, a "process of increasing personal, interpersonal, or political power so that individuals, families, and communities can take action to improve their situations" (Guitierrez 1994:202). Empowerment may be defined as the enabling of a client population to handle problems on their own, with the feeling of a growing capacity to take their lives into their own hands. Guitierrez (1990) explains empowerment as a process of increasing personal, interpersonal, or political power so that individuals can take action to improve their situation. It is a process necessary to cope in a hostile world and may mean (1) increasing self-efficacy; (2) developing a sense of mastery, initiative, and action; and (3) fostering group consciousness and a "sense of shared fate." Swift and Levin (1987) note that as an outcome, empowerment defines the end state of achieving power. Empowerment refers to a state of mind, such as feeling worthy and competent or perceiving power and control; it also refers to a reallocation of power that results from modifying social structures. In other words, empowerment involves subjective elements of perception, as well as more objective elements related to resources within social structures.

Empowerment implies exercising psychological control over personal affairs as well as exerting influence over the course of events in the interpersonal and in the sociopolitical arena (Moreau 1990). Empowerment facilitates a person's ability for reducing self-blame and seeing many problems as being collective, rather than just the individual's alone. Morales (1995) identifies problems as more often the function of societal power arrangements. Self-blame for society's definition of the problem is often responsible for feelings of depression and immobilization. When people feel competent and self-assured, they are more capable of assuming personal responsibility for change.

The model framed by DuBois and Miley (1996) shares elements of most contemporary paradigms: forming partnerships, articulating challenges and strengths, defining directions, exploring resource systems, analyzing resource capabilities, framing solutions, activating resources, expanding opportunities, recognizing success, and integrating gains. It appears to capture the core of the empowerment and the strengths-building approaches. Those models that achieve an empowerment end are preferred because they explicitly attempt to address the effects of social injustice, one of the prime purposes of social work and often a major issue for gay, lesbian, and bisexual people and their families.

The current NASW policy statement on gay, lesbian, and bisexual issues has a lot to say about services for and practice with gay, lesbian, and bisexual people and their families. In addition, social workers are guided by the NASW's *Code of Ethics* (1996), which bans discrimination on the basis of sexual orientation and encourages social workers to act to expand access, choices, and opportunities for oppressed people and groups.

> It is the position of NASW that same-gender sexual orientation should be afforded the same respect and rights as opposite-gender orientation. Discrimination and prejudice directed against any group are damaging to the social, emotional, and economic well-being of the affected group and of society as a whole. NASW is committed to advancing policies and practices that will improve the status and well-being of all lesbian, gay, and bisexual people.

> Nonjudgmental attitudes toward sexual orientation allow social workers to offer optimal support and services to lesbian, gay, and bisexual people. The profession supports and empowers lesbian, gay, and bisexual people through all phases of the coming out process and beyond. Discriminatory statutes, policies, and actions that diminish the quality of life for lesbian, gay, and bisexual people and that force many to live their lives in secrecy should be prevented and NASW supports the right of the individual to self-disclosed sexual orientation and encourages the development of supportive practice environments for lesbian, gay, and bisexual clients and colleagues. The rights and well-being of the children of lesbian, gay, and bisexual people should be an integral part of all these considerations.

NASW endorses policies in both the public and private sectors that ensure nondiscrimination; that are sensitive to the health and mental health needs of lesbian, gay, and bisexual people; and that promote an understanding of lesbian, gay, and bisexual cultures. Social stigmatization of lesbian, gay, and bisexual people is widespread, and is a primary motivating factor in leading some people to seek sexual orientation change. . . . Sexual orientation conversion therapies . . . assume that homosexual orientation is both pathological and freely chosen. No data demonstrate that reparative or conversion therapies are effective; and in fact [they] may be harmful. . . . NASW believes social workers have the responsibility to clients to explain the prevailing knowledge concerning sexual orientation and the lack of data reporting positive outcomes with reparative therapy. NASW discourages social workers from providing treatments designed to change sexual orientation or from referring [to] practitioners or programs which claim to do so. . . .

NASW strongly advocates for the availability of culturally appropriate comprehensive psychological and social support services for lesbian, gay, and bisexual people and for families. . . . NASW recognizes the increasing number of lesbian, gay, and bisexual people who are making reproductive choices, and it strives to establish legal, medical, and psychological supports for these families through its constituencies. . . .

NASW continues to advocate for the implementation of programs that address the health and mental health needs of lesbian, gay, and bisexual youths, including human immunodeficiency virus (HIV) prevention, psychosocial stress and dysfunction prevention and treatment, and suicide prevention. This population is often denied services because without parental consent they cannot access insurance, and they often feel disenfranchised from adult lesbian, gay, and bisexual cultures. . . .

NASW recognizes the health and mental health needs of older lesbian, gay, and bisexual people and advocates for programs that address these needs.
—NASW, "Lesbian, gay, and bisexual issues" (1997b:202, 204)

In this document, the many social work scholars cited were not suggesting a new model of practice with lesbian, gay, and bisexual people. The values, knowledge, methods, and skills taught in generalist or clinical practice or in administration, policy development, or community organizing, when appropriately applied, were seen as potentially effective and affirming.

Even though there is no evidence of greater maladjustment among lesbian, gay, and bisexual people than among heterosexuals, it was noted in chapter 9 that lesbian and gay people have been found to use mental health, specifically psychotherapeutic, services more often than others. The vulnerability gays, lesbians, and bisexuals routinely experience places them at high risk for an number of problems for which they will require an array of services. It is because of this vulnerability that Cain (1991b), Levy (1992), Newman (1989), and Tievsky (1988) and others conclude that it is likely that a much higher percentage of gays and lesbians than heterosexuals are seen by human services providers, most likely social workers. This difference in service utilization is usually attributed to the stresses that result from living in a heterosexist and homophobic society. On the other hand, the higher rates of some forms of substance abuse among gay and lesbian people remain poorly understood and inadequately addressed in treatment and prevention programs. Therefore it is essential that mental health, substance abuse, and other social services be accessible to and effective for lesbian, gay, and bisexual people. Minimally, those providing mental health and substance abuse services, including psychotherapy services, must be able to serve lesbian, gay, and bisexual people without bias or discrimination.

Failure to consider that a client may be gay or lesbian is the most common mistake made by social worker practitioners. As we have written elsewhere:

> Most lesbian and gay clients are not visually identifiable as such, and many may not identify themselves as gay or lesbian at first, especially when the problem for which they are seeking assistance may not have much to do with sexual orientation. . . . The friend or roommate who brought the heart attack victim to the hospital and who seeks to visit him or her on the intensive care unit; the parent of the first-grader with a visual impairment who meets with the school social worker to discuss the child's adjustment to school; the middle-aged woman attending a support group for those caring for an elderly parent with Alzheimer's disease; the adolescent referred to the mental health center because he or she is feeling depressed or suicidal—any of these may or may not be a client who is lesbian or gay. . . .
>
> However, the social worker is unlikely to get a full enough picture of the client's situation in order to be helpful without keeping an open mind to the possibility of a gay or lesbian identity. . . . Therefore, having an attitude and using language that conveys an openness to both a heterosexual or a homosexual possibility are critically important. If the assumption of heterosexuality is made, as it usually is, or if it is assumed that the client's most important family ties are only biological ones, it can be actively if unwittingly painful and alienating to the client seeking help. Exploring the situation with an open

mind to whatever identity the client chooses to convey will be both more comfortable for the client and more fruitful for the worker who genuinely wishes to understand the client's reality.

(Appleby & Anastas 1992:365–66)

The usual assumption of heterosexuality, a key feature of heterosexism, must be avoided.

Germain (1991) and Germain and Gitterman (1980), in their advancement of the ecological model, treat stress as a psychosocial condition "generated by discrepancies between needs and capacities, on the one hand, and environmental qualities on the other. It arises in three interrelated areas of living: life transitions, environmental pressures, and interpersonal processes" (7). Parts 2 and 3 of the present volume have been designed to describe the normative life tasks and transitions and common environmental pressures, such as the HIV epidemic and violence, as they are experienced by gay, lesbian, and bisexual people. Social work interventions often appropriate for dealing with needs of this kind are support, resource referral, empowerment, psychoeducation, consultation, case advocacy, and self-help. Case management and advocacy might be the chosen interventions if the gay, lesbian, or bisexual client needed numerous social services but was limited either in their capacity to access formal or informal resource systems (cognitive deficits, cultural practices, or ineffective social skills) or experienced significant barriers or resistances from within the systems themselves. "Oppression is a social disease. Stress, alienation, powerlessness, and isolation from the societal mainstream as well as inequality with the customary entitlements of life can exacerbate any crisis for the lesbian and gay individual" (Terry 1992:121).

As with other minority groups, the oppression that may be visited upon gay and lesbian people because of their sexual orientation can be destructive to individual self-esteem and well-being. At early stages of the coming out process, many people actively resist acknowledging even to themselves that they are sexually attracted to or active with others of their own gender. This resistance is often a product of negative attitudes toward homosexuality they have themselves absorbed, as everyone does, from the society as a whole or of negative reactions they fear from significant others, such as parents, children, friends, associates, or authority figures, such as teachers, coaches, or religious leaders. This strong reaction results from the implicit challenge to traditional understandings of gender and sex roles and to the power and privilege of heterosexuality. It is essential that the social work services gays and lesbians receive be free of the homophobia that would add to or reinforce these fears and attitudes.

The process of coming out can be a time of intense personal stress or crisis as well as joyful self-discovery. Feelings of acute anxiety or depression may occur, or behavioral problems such as excessive use of substances or other forms of acting out can develop or intensify. Professional help may be sought or recommended to better "manage the stigma," and the responses of the social worker to an individual in crisis—who may or may not initially identify coming out as an issue—are critically important to the client's comfort and progress toward a more comfortable self-definition and self-acceptance.

General principles of gay- and lesbian-affirmative practice have been presented previously but warrant repeating for emphasis. In affirmative practice, the social worker:

- *does not automatically assume that a client is heterosexual.*
- assumes that it is likely to be homophobia within the client and in society that is the problem rather than sexual orientation. *Same-gender sexual desires and behaviors instead are viewed as a normal variation in human sexuality.*
- *accepts the adoption of a lesbian, gay, or bisexual identity as a positive outcome* of any process in which an individual is questioning or working on developing his or her sexual identity.
- accepts the development of a lesbian, gay, or bisexual identity as positive, meaning that *a goal of affirmative practice is to reduce any internalized homophobia that a client may experience.*
- is *knowledgeable about the coming out process and its stages*, as well as about the typical differences in the process for men and women.
- *deals with his or her own homophobia and heterosexual bias*, whatever the sexual orientation of the practitioner is.

Practice with gay, lesbian, and bisexual people requires a nonjudgmental attitude toward sexual orientation, allowing social workers to offer optimal support and services, thus empowering clients through all phases of the coming out process and beyond.

There are other areas of knowledge that will help any social worker practicing with lesbian, gay, or bisexual clients to practice affirmatively. These include knowledge about anti-gay/lesbian prejudice and identity management strategies, including the skill to help clients distinguish between realistic and unrealistic fears about family reactions, workplace issues, and other potential homophobic reactions from others. Because of the potential for mutual aid and for reducing isolation, group treatment and mutual aid are often useful modes of intervention to consider. There is also an emerging literature addressing couple work and family practice with gay, lesbian, and bisexual people and their families that should be consulted (Laird & Green 1996; Slater 1995). The same principles of affirmative practice, while developed in the context of individual intervention, have relevance for these forms of intervention as well.

Macro practice with this population continues to be important. Social workers might help gay and lesbian activists to organize their communities with the intent of developing educational and political strategies and of forming coalitions with national advocacy groups, such as the American Civil Liberties Union, the Lambda Legal Defense and Education Fund, and the National Gay and Lesbian Task Force. Efforts are still needed to advance civil rights legislation; to defeat efforts to limit civil rights; to advocate for programs to eliminate hate crimes and antigay violence; and to enhance education, treatment services, and research related to lesbians, gay men, and bisexuals. The opportunities seem endless.

For the immediate political future, however, same-sex marriage and equal treatment in the military are likely to continue as major battlegrounds for civil rights activism. While neither issue has captured widespread support in the gay and lesbian communities, both, however, engage core social institutions where blatant discrimination and flagrant breach of a gay citizen's rights to privacy and equal protection persist. The 1997 State Supreme Court decision in Hawaii permitting legal marriage between same-sex couples, which was anticipated by lawmakers, resulted in the Defense of [Heterosexual] Marriage Act (DOMA) and subsequent state actions. While "domestic partnership" recognition has been advanced in industry and in some municipalities, others argue that this new status as an alternative to marriage will only accord "second class" rights and privileges in comparison to those awarded with marriage (see chapter 5). The current "Don't ask, don't tell" military policy is being challenged successfully in the federal courts because of its apparent violation of the Constitution's equal protection and privacy clauses. Legal progress is slow, and gains appear to be made at the margins, such as in more states promulgating administrative policy allowing for gay and lesbian foster parenting and adoptions. Yet these advances are hardly secure because the religious right and political conservatives have aggressively targeted gay men and lesbians in the same manner they fought communists and Jews only a decade ago. Whatever an individual social worker's personal and private opinions on these issues, the profession's stance in relation to client self-determination and antidiscrimination is clear, even though opinion about how best to make equality a reality, as in the dispute about legalizing same-sex marriage, may be divided.

Finally, social work practice interventions designed to remove stigma and to change bias, bigotry, and discrimination on both interpersonal and institutional levels have been presented, but at this point we do not know if they are effective (Gunther 1992; Lenna 1992; MacEachron 1995; Terry 1992). Affirmative practices have been described, but are they appropriate for all gays, lesbians, and bisexuals (race, ethnicity, class, culture, age, etc.) and under what circumstances? Are these affirmative practices equally helpful (however defined) during all phases of the helping process or if delivered by a gay, lesbian, or straight practitioner? All social work practice should stand the rigors of evaluation, but, as in most other areas of practice, most of what we know about social work practice with lesbian, gay, and bisexual people has yet to be adequately studied in a systematic way. Therefore, the practice researcher has tremendous challenges ahead.

FIELDWORK AND THE SOCIAL SERVICE AGENCY

Effective practice is strongly influenced by its context—the work setting. The field internship required in all social work programs is a critical experience for all social workers. Fieldwork is where practice principles come to life in actual work with clients and where professional identity is shaped. The values and knowledge conveyed in the field practice setting tell students what really matters in professional practice. However, the field agency also reflects the realities of social work practice back to students and to schools. Just as with other areas of diversity, the field agencies used by social work schools should be examined for how they handle diversity related to sexual orientation as they affect both clients and workers, an issue that draws our attention to the influence of work issues for gay, lesbian, and bisexual people in general and in the social work profession and the human services in particular.

Sussal (1994), in her study of social services, observes that the workplace has the potential for promoting both feelings of validation and emotional distress. When anxieties (homophobia and heterosexism) are not handled openly, there is the likelihood that defenses will develop against conflictual interaction and anxiety-provoking discussions, which may result in scapegoating. The employee—the social worker or the client—as a result may feel worthless and devalued. Thus, as chapter 7 has emphasized, it is important to assess the workplace issues of gay, lesbian, or bisexual clients as well as those of gay, lesbian, and bisexual social workers and social work students.

The policy of NASW on these matters is clear:

> NASW supports curriculum policies in schools of social work that eliminate discrimination against lesbian, gay, and bisexual people. In conjunction with the Council on Social Work Education, the schools of social work are expect-

ed to address the issue of discrimination; to articulate this position in curriculum policy and standards; to require course content on lesbian, gay, and bisexual cultures and concerns . . . ; to integrate this material throughout the curriculum; to provide field opportunities for students interested in working with lesbian, gay, and bisexual people; to offer research opportunities for investigating issues of relevance to this population (while also integrating lesbian, gay, and bisexual people into general research) . . . and to develop and provide training for classroom instructors, field supervisors, and field advisors regarding lesbian, gay, and bisexual issues.

NASW encourages the implementation of continuing education programs on practice and policy issues relevant to lesbian, gay, and bisexual people and cultures, and human sexuality. . . . Training should focus on the complexity of power dynamics, on negotiating relationships, and on sexual behaviors.

NASW aims to increase awareness within the profession of oppression, heterosexism, and internalized homophobia. . . . Additionally, NASW is concerned with increasing awareness of the multiple dilemmas and stigmas that lesbian, gay, and bisexual clients and social workers of color experience.

NASW strongly supports all social work organizations and associations in their use of inclusive, gender-neutral language and their inclusion of questions specific to lesbian, gay, and bisexual issues in social work licensing exams.

NASW strives for full representation and establishment of means to affirm the presence of lesbian, gay, and bisexual people at all levels of leadership and employment in social work and in NASW.

NASW supports all social agencies, universities, professional associations, and funding organizations in their efforts to broaden statements of nondiscrimination to include sexual orientation.

All social work practitioners, administrators, and educators are encouraged to take action to ensure that the dignity and rights of lesbian, gay, and bisexual employees, clients, and students are upheld and that these rights are codified in agency policies.

   —NASW, "Lesbian, gay, and bisexual issues" (1997b:202–203)

In fact, we might pose a question: If the topic were race or ethnicity, would we feel comfortable with a statement about "provid[ing] field opportunities to students interested"? Or might we prefer a goal of requiring some level of exposure to and competence in working with these issues from all of our students?

Attitudes about homosexuality in the helping professions have been changing for the better since the 1970s. Unfortunately, however, social workers, students, and clients may still be affected by the residue of outmoded psychological theory that until the mid-1970s viewed homosexuality as a pathology in and of itself. Studies still show significant levels of homophobia among social workers, social work students, and social work faculty (Eliason 1995; Harris, Nightengale, & Owen 1995). Thus it is not surprising that the experiences of gay and lesbian students in social work field placement agencies is indeed quite variable (Lewis 1990). Social workers' feelings, attitudes, and level of comfort with gay, lesbian, or bisexual orientations must be examined; they require self-exploration over time. It is the homophobia and heterosexism gays and lesbians encounter that are likely to be problems, not the homosexuality itself. Rather than seeking causes or explanations for homosexuality, the social worker is directed to explore and help the client to overcome the oppression (discrimination and bigotry), specifically those obstacles, internalized or external, that may stand in the way of healthy functioning as a lesbian, gay, or bisexual person.

The social agency setting, while an appropriate system to understand or possibly to intervene in when working with clients, requires professional assessment before delivering services. The outcomes of interpersonal intervention are contingent upon the agency's environment, e.g., its administrative practices, policies, and procedures (Hidalgo 1992). Social workers must first focus on the level of staff knowledge and commitment before introducing gay-affirming programs. All workers need a safe workplace environment, equitable benefits, and appropriate public support from their employers. Agency policies, procedures, and practices must address the needs of lesbian, gay, and bisexual clients *and* staff, as clients are likely only to feel as safe and affirmed as staff do. Until all social agencies have achieved these levels of safety and commitment for their gay, lesbian, and bisexual clients and workers, the need for agencies specializing in services to gay, lesbian, and bisexual people and their families will continue.

When it comes to selecting field agencies and experiences for social work students, then, one might ask the following questions: How does the agency demonstrate its commitment to serving clients without discrimination with regard to sexual orientation? What are its policies and practices with regard to gay and lesbian staff? Has each student had some experience in working with sexual orientation issues as part of their professional training? How can

schools of social work assist their faculty, their field faculty, and their affiliated agencies in meeting these standards and in staff training on these issues?

Visions for the Future

In the last several decades, a revolution has taken place in gay and lesbian people's perception of themselves. The notion of homosexuality as an individual
illness has been discredited and replaced with a political and social definition
which posits that to be gay is to be a member of an oppressed minority, similar in some ways to racial and ethnic minority groups. In response to oppression, lesbians and gays have organized to reinforce this new self view and to
press for the civil rights that are currently denied to them. The future political agenda of lesbian, bisexual, and gay communities will include state and
national activity around each of the following issues:

1. Civil rights (e.g., the repeal of state sodomy laws, passage of antidiscrimination statutes, and legal recognition of relationships, i.e., marriage or
   domestic partnership)
2. Violence/hate crimes (e.g., protections against gay- bashing, harassment,
   and abuse)
3. Substance abuse (e.g., increased awareness of, access to, and the development of drug and alcohol services that are sensitive to the needs of gay,
   lesbian, and bisexual clients)
4. Health care (e.g., ensuring access to as well as the quality of gay-sensitive
   services in regard to sexually transmitted diseases, AIDS care, reproductive rights, equity for women's health issues, and new reproductive technologies such as alternative insemination)
5. Mental health services based on affirming models
6. Community, family, and social life (e.g., custody, child and foster care
   rights)
7. Youth services (e.g., education, support services, suicide prevention, and
   legal protections)
8. Elder care (e.g., expansion of services to reflect the increase in numbers
   and the different life histories and expectations of the gay and lesbian
   elders of the future)
9. Equity in taxes, insurance, and retirement benefits.

In the private sector lesbians, gay men, and bisexual people will continue to
organize around (1) employment rights and health and pension benefits equitable with those of married heterosexual employees; (2) nondiscrimination,

anti-harassment, and promotion policies, and (3) marriage or domestic partner entitlement. Lesbian, gay, and bisexual people will continue to press for an expansion of resources and services that meet their specific needs in all these areas.

At the same time, schools of social work will have to do more to prepare their students for this future and for contemporary social work practice. Summarizing the helpful work of Morrow (1996) is a good way of understanding the steps that will be needed for minimizing heterosexism and including gay and lesbian content in the social work curriculum: (1) faculty should develop an institutional philosophy that establishes safety and freedom for an inclusive curriculum and a policy of nondiscrimination; (2) the program philosophy of the school of social work should reinforce the institutional philosophy; (3) gay-, lesbian-, and bisexual-related research and scholarship should be actively encouraged and given comparable standing with other areas of research; (4) language used in class and in curriculum materials should be reviewed for its heterosexist content and changed (e.g., *gay* and *lesbian* in preference to *homosexual*, or adding partner or significant other to the list of husband, wife, and spouse); and (5) faculty should, at the least, adopt textbooks and other curriculum materials that include gay, lesbian, and bisexual concerns in addition to case studies and supplementary materials that focus on coming out, identity development, identity management, homophobia and heterosexism, gay and lesbian relationships, families, and practice issues at all systems levels or units in a required course or a designated elective. Progress in these areas would typically require periodic review by relevant bodies, such as the educational policy or curriculum committee, the undergraduate and/or graduate program committees, the field education committee, other curriculum or program area committees, the school-community advisory board, and ultimately the full faculty. The school will also have to consider recruitment and retention issues as they affect both students and faculty as well (Mackelprang, Ray, & Hernandez-Peck 1996).

Finally, we must remember what we have learned from increasing our knowledge of human diversity in all respects: that all people benefit from knowing more about the range of human adaptation and resiliency. In this way, as Strickland (1995) notes, "Research on gay and lesbian people provides new and enhanced paradigms and ways of thinking about the whole of human behavior" (139). For example, when gay and lesbian adolescents in out-of-home care are treated humanely (Mallon 1998), their heterosexual counterparts who may be unconventional in some other way will also benefit. From studying the wide variety of family forms in contemporary society, it is increasingly clear that it is the functional qualities of the parenting that matter to the child, not any particular demographic or status characteristic of the person giving the care. Similarly, a mutually satisfying and nonexploitative couple relationship is certainly not guaranteed by the legal or religious recognition that marriage confers, and despite the obstacles it is quite possible to achieve long-lasting and successful intimacy in other kinds of relationships. We are therefore challenged to find ways to deliver needed social supports and social benefits to people that do not rely on the shorthand of social statuses.

In the future, workplaces and communities throughout the country will see an expanded presence of identified lesbians, bisexuals, and gays. Social acceptance and integration will be illusory in some sectors of society while a reality in others. The distinctions between public and private discrimination will be clarified in law and organizational practice as a concession to the religious right and political conservatives. Social work professionals are in a position to have an influence on many of the issues facing lesbians and gays today and in the future—civil rights, access to health and mental health services, child custody, and adoption and foster care, to name but a few. We will all be challenged to use that influence for the good.

Appendix 1

Resources

The resources that follow are appropriate for gay, lesbian, or bisexual clients as well as for gay/lesbian/bisexual faculty, students, and practitioners or those that are gay/lesbian/bisexual-affirming.

Books and Journals

The number of books and journals related to gay and lesbian studies is vast and constantly increasing. Important journals include the *Journal of Gay and Lesbian Social Services*, *Journal of Homosexuality*, *Journal of Lesbian Studies*, and the *Journal of Gay and Lesbian Psychotherapy*. The Haworth Press is the publisher of many of these journals and also has an extensive gay, lesbian, and bisexual book list. Call 1-800-342-9678 or Fax 1-800-895-0582 or e-mail *getinfo@haworth.com*.

Lambda Rising is a large gay/lesbian/bisexual bookstore in several cities that will send a free catalog of published works. Contact: Lambda Rising, 1625 Connecticut Ave. NW, Washington, D.C. 20009-1013; phone 1-800-621-6969; fax 202-462-7257; or e-mail *lambdarising@his.com* on the Internet.

General Interest Lists and Web Sites

ACTION ALERT: A resource by which you can respond to attacks on the gay/lesbian/bisexual community. To subscribe, e-mail *majordomo@vector.castl.com*.

BISEXU-L: Offers a mailing list for discussion of bisexual issues and bisexuality. Membership is open to all orientations. To subscribe, e-mail *listserv@ brownvm.brown.edu.*

GAYNET: A national discussion and news network for gay, lesbian, and bisexual concerns. To subscribe, e-mail *majordomo@queernet.org.*

GLBPOC: Offers a mailing list for lesbian, gay, and bisexual people of color. To subscribe, e-mail *glbpoc-request@ferkel.ucsb.edu.*
———. GLB-NEWS: A read-only repository of information for gay, lesbian, bisexual, transsexual, transgender, and sympathic persons. To subscribe, e-mail *listserv@brownvm.brown.edu.*

NGLTFCAMPUS: A list devoted to supporting the work and programs of the National Gay and Lesbian Task Force (NGLTF) Campus Project. E-mail *ngltf-campus-request@nenet.org.* Your subject line must read "subscribe."

Pridenet: Contact *http//:www.pride.net/pridenet.*

QUEERCAMPUS: A list devoted to organizing and networking among gay/ lesbian/bisexual campus communities. To subscribe, e-mail *majordomo@ vector.cast.com.*

The Queer Resources Directory: E-mail *gopher: vector.casti.com* or contact *http://www.qrd.org/QRD.* QRD offers one of the most comprehensive collections of information and referral sources on the Internet for lesbian/gay/ bisexual activists. It is also accessible by e-mail, for those who have limited Internet access. To use this service, e-mail *ftpmail@qrd.org.* Send a message with no subject title and containing only *help* on a line by itself.

SAPPHO: A forum and support group for lesbian and bisexual women. Membership is strictly limited to women. To subscribe, e-mail *sappho-request@ fiesta.intercon.com.*

UCB Queer Infoserver System: E-mail *gopher:server.berkeley.edu/communitytopic/ mblga* or contact *http//:www.server.berkeley.edu/mblga.*

Pamphlets and Posters

Pamphlets and posters are helpful in designing a gay/lesbian/bisexual-affirming office or waiting room for clients and staff.

The Campaign to End Homophobia: PO Box 819, Cambridge, MA 02139; phone (617) 868-8280.

Diversity Works: Order *Straight Talk About Homosexuality* (pamphlet) from Diversity Works, Inc., PO Box 2335, Amherst, MA 01004; phone (413) 256-1868.

Gay and Lesbian Alliance Against Defamation (GLAAD): 80 Varick Street, Suite 3-E, New York, NY 10013; phone (212) 966-1700.

Lesbian and Gay Public Awareness Project: PO Box 65603, Los Angeles, CA 90065; phone (818) 990-8000.

Parents and Friends of Lesbians and Gays (P-FLAG): PO Box 27605, Washington, D.C. 20038; phone (202) 636-4200.

Posters that focus on some of the major stigmas or myths about gay/lesbian/bisexual people can be ordered from: The Stonewall Center, Crampton House/SW, University of Massachusetts, Amherst, MA 01003; phone (413) 545-4824.

Anti-Violence and Anti-Harassment Resources

Anti-Defamation League, Department of Campus Affairs, 823 United Nations Plaza. New York, NY 10017; phone (212) 490-2525.

Center for Democratic Renewal: PO Box 50469, Atlanta, GA 30302; phone (404) 221-0025.

Lambda Legal Defense and Education Fund: 666 Broadway, New York, NY 10012; phone (212) 995-8585.

National Gay and Lesbian Task Force (NGLTF): 2320 17th Street, N.W., Washington, D.C. 20009; phone (202) 332-6483.
———. Also, contact the NGLTF Policy Institute for an excellent selection of fact sheets and policy statements and position papers, as well as to obtain *Lesbian, Gay, Bisexual, and Transgender Campus Organizing: A Comprehensive Manual*: 2320 17th Street, NW, Washington, D.C. 20009-2702; phone (202) 332-6483, ext. 3327, or e-mail *publications@ngltf.org* or contact *http://www.ngltf.org/ngltf*.

National Institute Against Prejudice and Violence: 31 South Greene Street, Baltimore, MD 21201.

Southern Poverty Law Center: PO Box 548, Montgomery, AL 36195-5101; phone (205) 254-0286.

Employment Resources

American Civil Liberties Union—Gay and Lesbian Rights Project, 132 West 43rd Street, New York, N.Y. 10036, or call (212) 807–1700.

Human Rights Campaign, 1101 14th Street, NW, Suite 200, Washington, D.C. 20005, or call (202) 628–4160.

Lambda Legal Defense and Education Fund, 666 Broadway, 12th floor, New York, N.Y. 10012, or call (212) 995–8585.

National Committee on Lesbian, Gay, and Bisexual Issues of the National Association of Social Workers (NASW). *Contact:* Luisa Lopez, NASW, 750 First Street, NE, Suite 700, Washington, D.C. 20002–4341, or call (202) 408–8600.

National Gay and Lesbian Task Force—Workplace Project, 2320 17th Street, NW, Washington, D.C. 20009, or call (202) 332–6483, ex. 3361.

WorkNet has been amassing information aimed at persuading Congress to pass ENDA. It also shares the tools necessary to lobby for fairness at work and information on employers with nondiscrimination policies, domestic partnership policies, and employee support groups. A referral service is available for workers who need legal assistance regarding job discrimination. WorkNet can be reached at the Human Rights Campaign's Web site (*http://www.hrcusa.org*) or by calling (202) 628–4160.

National Organizations for Networking and Resources

Black Gay and Lesbian Leadership Forum/AIDS Prevention Team: 1219 S. La Brea Avenue, Los Angeles, CA 90010; phone (213) 964-7820, fax 213-964-7830.

Gay and Lesbian Latinos Unidos: PO Box 85459, Los Angeles, CA 90072: phone (213) 660-9681.

Gay and Lesbian National Hotline (talk directly with volunteers): E-mail *glnh@ msn.com web* or contact *http://www.escape.com/˜7Eirany/index.html*.

Gay, Lesbian, and Straight Teachers Network: PO Box 390526, Cambridge, MA 02139-0006; phone (617) 536-3597 or e-mail *glstn@aol.com.*

Human Rights Campaign: 1101 14th Street, NW, Washington, D.C. 20005; phone (202) 628-4160, TTY 202-628-4169, fax 202-347-5323, or contact *http://www.hrcusa.org.*

National Center for Lesbian Rights: 870 Market Street, Suite 570, San Francisco, CA 94102; phone (415) 392-6257, fax 415-392-8442.

National Lesbian and Gay Health Association: 1407 S Street, NW, Washington, D.C. 20009; phone (202) 939-7880, fax 202-234-1467.

Parents and Friends of Lesbians and Gays (P-FLAG): 1101 14th Street NW, Suite 1030, Washington, D.C. 20005; phone (202) 638-4200.

Youth

Bridge Project, c/o American Friends Service Committee, 1501 Cherry Street, Philadelphia, PA 19102; phone (215) 241-7133, fax 213-241-7119, or e-mail *bridgespro@aol.com.*

Hetrick-Martin Institute (home of Harvey Milk School): 2 Astor Place, New York, NY 10003-0998; phone (212) 674-2400, fax 212-674-8650.

National Advocacy Coalition on Youth and Sexual Orientation: 1711 Connecticut Ave, NW, Suite 206, Washington, D.C. 20009-1139; phone (202) 319-7596, fax 202-319-7365, or e-mail *nacyso@aol.com.*

Project 10, Fairfax High School: 7850 Melrose Avenue, Los Angeles, CA 90046; phone (213) 651-5200, ext. 244, or (818) 577-4553.

Additional Resources: HIV Disease

ACT-UP New York (*http://www.interchg.ubc.ca/aids11/aids96html*)
AIDS Action Committee (*http://www.aac.org*)
AIDS Care Givers Support (*http://www.vive.com/connect/acsn/acsnhome.htm*)
CDC AIDS Page (*http://www.cdc.gov/diseases/aids.html*)
Gay Men's Health Crisis (*http://www.gmhc.org*)
IAPAC (*http://www.IAPAC.org*)

The Names Project (*http://www.aidsquilt.org*)
NAPWA (*http://www.the cure.org*)
Positive Nation (*http://www.positivenation.co.uk*)

Exercises for the Classroom (see Appendix 2)

How Homophobia Hurts Everyone: A Theoretical Foundation (summary and classroom exercise) by Warren J. Blumenfeld is a good place to start.

"Homowork": Ways to increase LGBT Visibility and Reduce Homophobia by Warren J. Blumenfeld offers an opportunity for active learning.

"Heterosexual Questionnaire" is an excellent ice-breaker which should be followed by a discussion.

High School Curriculum and Staff Development Projects offers a catalogue of materials that can be modified for the university classroom or social agency inservice programs; phone (617) 491-5301.

"Attitude Checklist: Homosexuality" is an interesting questionnaire which should be followed by discussion or given as a before and after measure after students have attended a workshop or course on gay/lesbian/bisexual issues.

Contact the *Gay, Lesbian, and Straight Teachers Network (GLSTN)* (as noted above) for additional teaching/training materials.

Appendix 2
Exercises for the Classroom

How Homophobia Hurts Everyone:
A Theoretical Foundation[*]
Warren J. Blumenfeld

Within the numerous forms of oppression, members of the target group (sometimes called "minority") are OPPRESSED, while on some level members of the dominant or agent group are HURT. Although the effects of oppression differ qualitatively for specific target and agent groups, in the end everyone loses.

1. Homophobia locks all people into rigid gender-based roles that inhibit creativity and self-expression.
2. Homophobic conditioning compromises the integrity of heterosexual people by pressuring them to treat others badly, actions contrary to their basic humanity.

---

[*] Unless otherwise noted, the materials by Warren J. Blumenfeld are from Warren J. Blumenfeld (Ed.), *Homophobia: How We All Pay the Price* (Boston: Beacon Press, 1992). Copyright by Warren J. Blumenfeld; reprinted by permission. Warren J. Blumenfeld, PO Box 929, Northampton, MA 01061; phone (413) 585-9121, fax 413-584-1332, or e-mail *blumenfeld@educ.umass.edu*.

3. Homophobia inhibits one's ability to form close, intimate relationships with members of one's own sex.

4. Homophobia generally restricts communication with a significant portion of the population and, more specifically, limits family relationships.

5. Societal homophobia prevents some lesbian, gay, bisexual, and transgender (LGBT) people from developing an authentic self-identity, and adds to the pressure to marry, which in turn places undue stress and oftentimes trauma on themselves as well as their heterosexual spouses and their children.

6. Homophobia is one cause of premature sexual involvement, which increases the chances of teen pregnancy and the spread of sexually transmitted diseases (STDs). Young people, of *all* sexual identities, are often pressured to become *heterosexually* active to prove to themselves and others that they are "normal."

7. Homophobia combined with sexphobia (fear and repulsion of sex) results in the elimination of any discussion of the lives and sexuality of LGBT people as part of school-based sex education, keeping vital information from all students. Such a lack of information can kill people in the age of AIDS.

8. Homophobia can be used to stigmatize, silence, and, on occasion, target people who are perceived or defined by others as gay, lesbian, or bisexual, but who are, in actuality, heterosexual.

9. Homophobia prevents heterosexuals from accepting the benefits and gifts offered by LGBTs: theoretical insights, social and spiritual visions and options, contributions in the arts and culture, to religion, to family life, indeed to all facets of society.

10. Homophobia (along with racism, sexism, classism, sexphobia, etc.) inhibits a unified and effective governmental and societal response to AIDS.

11. Homophobia diverts energy from more constructive endeavors.

12. Homophobia inhibits appreciation of other types of diversity, making it unsafe for everyone because each person has unique traits not considered mainstream or dominant. Therefore, we are *all* diminished when any one of us is demeaned.

"Homowork": Ways to Increase LGBT Visibility and Reduce Homophobia

Warren J. Blumenfeld

1. Be aware of the generalizations you make. Assume there are LGBT people where you go to school, where you work, in your family, etc.
2. Notice the times you disclose your heterosexuality.
3. For sensitization, hold hands with someone of the same sex in a SAFE public place.
4. Wear pro-LGBT buttons and T-shirts.
5. Read positive LGBT books and periodicals, and include them in your school or workplace libraries and offices.
6. Attend LGBT cultural and community events.
7. Challenge homophobic jokes and epithets.
8. Use inclusive, affirming, or gender-neutral language when referring to sexuality and human relationships in everyday speech, on written forms, etc. Say the words "lesbian," "gay," "bisexual," "transgender" each day in a positive way.
9. Include "Sexual Orientation" as a protected category in your antidiscrimination policies.
10. Extend "Domestic Partnership" benefits to LGBT employees on par with heterosexual employees.
11. Develop support groups for LGBT people and heterosexual allies.
12. Monitor politicians, the media, and organizations to ensure accurate coverage of LGBT issues.
13. Work and vote for candidates taking pro-LGBT stands.
14. Coordinate discussions and workshops, and include material in educational curricula on the topic of homophobia and LGBT experiences.
15. Implement and participate in a "Safe Space" program in your school or workplace.

Gender and Sexual Identity
Warren J. Blumenfeld

Though sometimes connected and overlapping, the following categories of sexual and gender identity are often distinct and unique.

BIOLOGICAL (sometimes referred to as CHROMOSOMAL) SEX: This can be considered as our "packaging" and is determined by our chromosomes (XX for females, XY for males); our hormones (estrogen and progesterone for females, testosterone for males); and our internal and external genitalia (vulva, clitoris, vagina for females, penis and testicles for males). About 4 percent of the population can be defined as "intersexuals" born with *biological* aspects of both sexes to varying degrees.

(CORE) GENDER IDENTITY: This is the individual's innermost concept of self as "male" or "female"—what we perceive and call ourselves. Individuals develop this generally between the ages of eighteen months and three years. Most people develop a (core) gender identity aligning with their biological sex. For some, however, their gender identity is different from their biological sex. We sometimes call these people "transsexuals," some of whom hormonally and/or surgically change their sex to more fully match their gender identity.

GENDER ROLE (sometimes called SEX ROLE): This is the set of socially defined roles and behaviors assigned to females and males. This can vary from culture to culture. Our society recognizes basically two distinct gender roles. One is the *masculine*: having the qualities or characteristics attributed to males. The other is the *feminine*: having the qualities or characteristics attributed to females. (A third gender role, rarely, though possibly increasingly, condoned in our society, is *androgyny*, combining assumed male [*andro*] and female [*gyne*] qualities.) Some people step out of their socially assigned gender roles or "crossdress" (wear the clothing traditionally reserved for the other sex). Though not universal or even precise, some of the terms used to identify these individuals include "cross-dressers" (formerly termed "transvestites")—often heterosexual males and females who crossdress—"Drag Queens" (male homosexuals who crossdress), "Drag Kings" (female homosexuals who crossdress). "Transgender" is increasingly becoming an umbrella term referring to people who cross gender barriers.

AFFECTIONAL ORIENTATION: This is determined by whom we feel comfortable "hanging out" with, whom we are close to in a primarily nonerotic way.

Most people seem to have a "bi-affectional" orientation—with individuals of both sexes.

SEXUAL (or EROTIC) ORIENTATION: This is determined by whom we are sexually (or erotically) attracted—our sexual/erotic drives, desires, fantasies. Categories of sexual orientation include *homosexuals*—gay, lesbian—attracted to some members of the same sex; *bisexuals*, attracted to some members of both sexes to varying degrees; *heterosexuals*, attracted to some members of the other sex; and *asexuals*, attracted to neither sex. Some sexuality researchers suggest that *pederasts* (adults sexually/erotically attracted to children) might be considered a separate sexual orientation.

Sexual orientation is believed to be influenced by a variety of factors including genetics and hormones, as well as unknown environmental factors. Though the origins of sexual orientation are not completely understood, it is generally believed to be established during early childhood, usually before the age of five.

SEXUAL BEHAVIOR: This is what we do sexually and with whom. Though we are not certain what influences determine a person's primary sexual attractions (sexual orientation), our culture can heavily influence peoples' actions and sexual behaviors. For example, one may have a "homosexual" orientation, but due to overriding condemnations against same-sex sexual expression may "pass" by having sex only with people of the other sex.

Sexuality researcher Alfred C. Kinsey and his colleagues devised a seven-point scale to chart the full spectrum of human sexual *behavior*, with "0" representing those whose histories are exclusively heterosexual, and "6" for those who are exclusively homosexual in behavior. Others were placed along the scale depending on the percentage of heterosexual (other sex) or homosexual (same sex) sexual expression in relation to overall behavior. Kinsey's findings and other studies also suggest that sexuality is indeed more fluid and complex than once believed.

SEXUAL IDENTITY: This is what we call ourselves. Such labels include "lesbian," "gay," "bisexual," "bi," "queer," "questioning," "undecided," "undetermined," "heterosexual," "straight," "asexual," and others. Sexual identity evolves through a multistage developmental process that has been charted by a number of researchers. This progression varies in intensity and duration depending on the individual.

Our sexual *behavior* and how we *define* ourselves (our identity) can be chosen. Though some people claim their sexual orientation is also a choice, for others this does not seem to be the case.

Internalized Homophobia: From Denial to Action
An Interactive Workshop
Warren J. Blumenfeld

What We Heard

What we heard about homosexuality, bisexuality, transgenderism, and LesBi-GayTrans people growing up: (1) *Nothing*, (2) *Positive/Factual Information*, (3) *Misinformation/Stereotypes*.

Terminology

"Internalized . . ." (or "Shame due to . . .")

1. "Homophobia"
2. "Biphobia"
3. "Heterosexism"
4. "Homonegativism"
5. "Transphobia"
6. "Sexual Orientationalism or Orientationalism"

is the internalization of conscious or unconscious attitudes regarding inferiority or differentness by the victims of systematic oppression.

Manifestations

This internalization, created by oppression from the outside, plays itself out where it has seemed "safe" to do so in two primary places: (a) *On Members of Our Own Group*; (b) *Upon Ourselves*. Some of the forms it takes:

1. Denial of one's sexual orientation (one's sexual and emotional attractions) to oneself and others
2. Attempts to alter or change one's sexual orientation
3. Feeling one is never "good enough" (sometimes a tendency toward "perfectionism")
4. Engaging in obsessive thinking and/or compulsive behaviors
5. Underachievement or overachievement as a bid for acceptance
6. Delayed or retarded emotional and/or cognitive development
7. Low self-esteem and body image
8. Contempt for the more "open" or "obvious" members of the LesBiGay-Trans community

9. Contempt for those at earlier stages of the "coming out process" (the "queerer than thou" attitude)

10. Denial that homophobia/heterosexism/biphobia/sexism are, in fact, serious social problems

11. Contempt for those who are not just like ourselves; and/or contempt for those who seem like ourselves

12. Projection of prejudice onto another target group (reinforced by society's existing prejudices)

13. Becoming psychologically and/or physically abusive; or remaining in an abusive relationship

14. Attempts to "pass" as heterosexual, sometimes marrying someone of the other sex to gain social approval, or in hopes of being "cured"

15. Increased fear and withdrawal from friends and relatives

16. School truancy and/or dropping out of school

17. Continual self-monitoring of one's behaviors, mannerisms, beliefs, and ideas

18. "Minstrelizing" or clowning as a way of acting out society's negative stereotypes

19. Mistrust and destructive criticism of LesBiGayTrans community leaders ("Eating One's Own")

20. Reluctance to be around or have concern for children for fear of being considered a "pederast"

21. Conflicts with the law

22. Unsafe sexual practices and other destructive risk-taking behaviors (including risks for pregnancy and HIV infection)

23. Separating sex and love, and/or fear of intimacy

24. Substance abuse (including food, alcohol, drugs, and others)

25. Suicidal ideation, attempts, completion

Assumptions

1. Homophobia/Heterosexism/Biphobia/Transphobia are forms of *oppression*; they are not simple fears.

2. Homophobia/Heterosexism/Biphobia/Transphobia are pervasive throughout the society.

3. It is difficult not to internalize society's negative notions of homosexuality, bisexuality, and transgenderism.

4. Internalizing these negative notions is not our fault.

5. There are steps we can take to reduce, or even eliminate, internalized oppression.

6. Working to end internalized oppression is a long—often lifetime—process.

Stage Model

- Denial
- Awareness
- Acceptance
- Action

Making Schools Safe for Gay, Lesbian, Bisexual, and Transgender Students and Staff
Warren J. Blumenfeld

1. *Hearings*: Hold public hearings in your community and/or your state to access the needs, concerns, and life experiences of LGBT youth, their families, and school staff.

2. *Policies*: (A) Schools are encouraged to develop policies protecting LGBT students from harassment, violence, and discrimination; (B) Include "Sexual and Gender Orientation" as protected categories in your antidiscrimination policies; (C) Extend "Domestic Partnership" benefits to LGBT employees on par with heterosexual employees.

3. *Personnel Trainings*: (A) Schools are encouraged to offer training to school personnel in violence prevention, suicide prevention, and specifically to the needs and problems faced by LGBT youth; (B) Implement and participate in a "Safe Space" program in your school.

4. *LGBT Support Groups*: Schools and communities are encourage to offer school- and community-based support groups for LGBT and heterosexual youth ("Gay/Straight Alliances").

5. *Counseling*: Schools and communities are encouraged to provide affirming school- and community-based counseling for LGBT youth and their families.

6. *Information in School Libraries*: School and community libraries are encouraged to develop and maintain an up-to-date collection of books, videos, journals, magazines, posters, and other information on LGBT issues.

7. *Curriculum and School Programs*: Schools are encouraged to include accurate, honest, up-to-date, and age-appropriate information on LGBT issues at *every* grade level, across the curriculum, and in other school programs and assemblies. Include LGBT issues in your school newspapers.

8. *Adult Role Models*: Schools are encouraged to recruit "open" LGBT faculty and staff to serve as supportive role models for all youth.

9. *Teacher Certification*: Include information and trainings on LGBT youth issues in college and university teacher education programs.

10. *Be an Ally*: (A) Educate yourself to the needs and experiences of LGBT youth and their families; (B) Attend LGBT cultural and community events; (C) Wear pro-LGBT buttons and T-shirts, and display posters; (D) Interrupt homophobic jokes and epithets; (E) Be aware of the generalizations you make. Assume there are LGBT people at your

school; (F) Notice the times you disclose your heterosexuality; (G) Monitor politicians, the media, and organizations to ensure accurate coverage of LGBT issues; (H) Work and vote for candidates (including school board members) taking pro-LGBT stands; (I) Use inclusive, affirming, or gender-neutral language when referring to sexuality and human relationships in everyday speech, on written forms, etc. Say the words *lesbian*, *gay*, *bisexual*, *transgender* each day in a positive way.

Making Colleges and Universities Safe for Gay, Lesbian, Bisexual, and Transgender (GLBT) Students and Staff*

Warren J. Blumenfeld

I. Policies

1. Enact nondiscrimination policies on the basis of sexual orientation in matters of hiring, tenure, promotion, admissions, and financial aid.
2. Have policies and procedures for dealing with homophobic violence and harassment.
3. Have a written, inclusive, and affirming definition of "couples" that is nondiscriminatory towards same-sex couples in a way that is appropriate for each institution.
4. Ensure equal access and equality of all benefits and privileges granted to all employees and students.
5. Have policies of active outreach in hiring openly GLBT and/or GLBT-sensitive faculty, staff, and administrators in all segments of the campus community.
6. Actively recruit openly GLBT prospective students.

All of the above policies should be written, clear, consistent, accessible, and well-publicized throughout the campus.

II. Training and Development

1. Homophobia and other "diversity" workshops should be implemented for the entire campus community to sensitize and educate staff, faculty, and administrators.

III. Services

1. Colleges and universities provide official recognition, support, and funding of campus GLBT student organizations.

---

*From *Making Colleges and Universities Safe for Gay and Lesbian Students: Report and Recommendations of the Governor's Commission on Gay and Lesbian Youth*, Warren J. Blumenfeld, Principal Author, 1993. For a free copy, write: The Governor's Commission on Gay and Lesbian Youth, Room 111, State House, Boston, Mass. 02133.

2. Physically safe, secure, and appropriate space with a welcoming, emotionally safe atmosphere should be available to GLBT organizations for meetings, social events, coffee houses, lectures, fora, workshops, and other events.

3. Legal and fund-raising support services should be available to GLBT students.

4. Campus housing should included GLBT living options.

5. University Leadership should make strong, clear, public statements on a regular basis that state the college's commitment to ending discrimination, conviction that violence and harassment are entirely unacceptable, and appreciation of the value of diversity on campus, including diversity of sexual identity.

6. Colleges and universities hire openly GLBT or GLBT-sensitive therapists/counselors, faculty, staff, and administrators.

7. Peer counselors and/or campus crisis hotline volunteers be adequately trained in sensitivity to sexuality, sexual orientation/identity, and "coming out" issues.

8. Effective AIDS education, imperative for all people of all sexual orientations, must be available and widespread.

9. Social activities through residence halls, Offices of Student Activities, and other organizations must be not only inclusive of all sexual orientations and identities, without pressures toward heterosexuality, but actively welcoming of GLBT people as well as same-sex couples.

10. College and university presidents have a standing advisory committee, panel, or board, appointed or elected in consultation with GLBT students, staff, and faculty members.

11. Student opinion should be assessed regularly, by the above-mentioned panel or in some other manner, in order to gauge the effectiveness of implemented changes.

12. Campus publications should take care to provide adequate and fair coverage of GLBT events and issues, both on and off campus.

13. Colleges and universities should aid students in alumni outreach.

14. Internship opportunities may also be cultivated among local GLBT-owned businesses and GLBT activist and community service organizations.

15. The diversity within the GLBT community should be recognized and affirmed.

16. The location and availability of resources of value to GLBT people should be published in materials distributed to all students, faculty, staff, and alumni.

17. Personnel at the Career Planning/Placement Center, like personnel in every college area, should be sensitive to GLBT issues and be aware of employment opportunities in GLBT-owned or GLBT-friendly businesses and community service organizations.

18. While needs differ greatly at each of the hundreds of institutions of higher education, it seems clear that for many, if not most, the most critically important and invaluable resource is a GLBT campus resource center with a paid administrator, staff, and resources.

19. In institutions where financial resources do not allow for centers and/or administrative support for any "minorities," there should at least be an ombudsperson or other clearly recognized, identified, and publicized as an official liaison to the campus GLBT community.

IV. Curriculum / Educational Materials / Academic Affairs

1. Issues relating to GLBT people should be formally and permanently integrated into existing courses across the curriculum.

2. Speakers on GLBT topics, and particularly those who present scholarly research on GLBT topics, should be brought to campus regularly.

3. Courses dealing specifically with GLBT issues in the humanities, natural sciences, education, social sciences, and other disciplines should be established.

4. A visiting scholar position in GLBT studies should be created and supported on a continuing basis.

5. College and university libraries should increase their holdings of GLBT books, periodicals, and computer networking systems.

6. Campus facilities should be available for regional GLBT studies conferences, with administrative support provided.

7. Fellowship opportunities should be created and funded for teaching and research of GLBT topics.

8. Scholarship and research into GLBT history, culture, and theory should be encouraged and supported in faculty and students.

9. All multicultural education should be inclusive of the issues, history, culture, and experiences of GLBT people in the United States and worldwide. Multicultural awareness (social diversity) courses should be mandatory for all students at some point during the undergraduate years.

10. An archive and history of GLBT organizations on campus should be created.

V. Employee Concerns

1. Policies regarding equal benefits and nondiscrimination should be made clear in recruiting brochures, informational materials, campus publications, and orientation sessions.
2. The university should aid, support, and fund the creation of GLBT faculty and staff discussion, support, and networking groups.
3. Trade unions and professional organizations should have inclusive policies and supportive services available to their members.
4. There should be equality in all benefits, including, for example: bereavement leave, insurance coverage, library privileges, access to gym and other recreational facilities, listings in directories if spouses are customarily listed, housing for GLBT couples where the qualifications are analogous to the qualifying basis for heterosexuals, "couple" rates must be made available to GLBT couples, access to any and all other privileges and benefits by GLBT partners if access is available to heterosexual spouses.
5. There should be ongoing sensitivity training and staff development on GLBT issues for all employees.
6. Colleges and universities should cover the expenses of employees attending conferences on GLBT issues.

VI. Community / Off-Campus Concerns

1. Community GLBT groups should be invited to attend campus events as participants, guests, and event leaders and facilitators.
2. Information regarding social, religious, and other community resources should be made easily accessible to all students, staff, faculty, and administrators.
3. Counselors, administrators, and faculty should be available to parents or other community members to alleviate any concern that may arise out of the implementation of any of the above recommendations, as well as any concerns arising during their child's "coming out" process, if that is the case.
4. Representatives of GLBT student groups from different schools should meet regularly to keep each other appraised of upcoming events, plan events together, and strengthen the GLBT community.
5. Publications, fund-raising materials, and all other publications distributed to parents and alumni should include relevant and appropriate stories, essays, and news regarding GLBT issues, organizations, and events.

6. Corporations, public agencies, and government, religious, and community agencies and institutions that do not have official written policies against discrimination based on sexual orientation should be strongly discouraged or prohibited from on-campus employment or enlistment recruiting.

Heterosexual Questionnaire

1. What do you think caused your heterosexuality?

2. When and how did you first decide you were a heterosexual?

3. Is it possible your heterosexuality is just a phase you may grow out of?

4. Is it possible your heterosexuality stems from a neurotic fear of others of the same sex?

5. If you've never slept with a person of the same sex, is it possible that all you need is a good Gay lover?

6. To whom have you disclosed your heterosexual tendencies? How did they react?

7. Why do you heterosexuals feel compelled to seduce others into you lifestyle?

8. Why do you insist on flaunting your heterosexuality? Can't you just be what you are and keep it quiet?

9. Would you want your children to be heterosexual, knowing the problems they'd face?

10. A disproportionate majority of child molesters are heterosexuals. Do you consider it safe to expose your children to heterosexual teachers?

11. Even with all the societal support marriage receives, the divorce rate is spiraling. Why are there so few stable relationships among heterosexuals?

12. Why do heterosexuals place so much emphasis on sex?

13. Considering the menace of overpopulation, how could the human race survive if everyone were heterosexual like you?

14. Could you trust a heterosexual therapist to be objective? Don't you fear he/she might be inclined to influence you in the direction of his/her own leanings?

15. How can you become a whole person if you limit yourself to compulsive, exclusive heterosexuality, and fail to develop you natural, healthy homosexual potential?

16. There seem to be very few happy heterosexuals. Techniques have been developed which enable you to change if you really want to. Have you considered trying aversion therapy?

Attitude Checklist: Homosexuality
Developed by Deryck Calderwood

Female_____

Male_____

Read the statements below and respond according to how you personally feel about the suggested situations. Circle the letter under the description of the response you feel most closely represents your current attitude—or in some situations your projected future attitude.

FOR ME PERSONALLY . . .	*Acceptable*	*Not Sure*	*Unacceptable*
1. To have homosexuals hold any job or position for which they qualify is:	A	NS	U
2. Changing the laws to allow sexual relations between consenting adults is:	A	NS	U
3. To allow homosexual individuals to serve in the armed forces is:	A	NS	U
4. To have a homosexual individual serve as president of the United States would be:	A	NS	U
5. Having two people of the same sex hold hands, kiss, or hug in public places is:	A	NS	U
6. To belong to an organization or group where there were known homosexual members would be:	A	NS	U
7. To learn that a business associate participated in homosexual acts would be:	A	NS	U
8. To have a gay counselor help me with a problem that involved interpersonal relationships would be:	A	NS	U
9. To share a room overnight with a gay person would be:	A	NS	U
10. To be treated or examined by homosexual medical personnel would be:	A	NS	U
11. To have a gay teacher for my children is:	A	NS	U
12. To have a gay individual for a close personal friend would be:	A	NS	U
13. The thought of two people of the same sex having sexual relations together is:	A	NS	U
14. To discover that my son or daughter was involved in homosexual acts would be:	A	NS	U
15. To discover that my son or daughter was gay would be:	A	NS	U
16. To learn that a brother or sister was gay would be:	A	NS	U

17. To learn that my marital partner was also involved in
homosexual behavior would be: A NS U

18. To share the knowledge with a friend of my own past
involvement during childhood or adolescence in homosexual
behavior is: A NS U

19. To think about participating myself in homosexual
acts is: A NS U

20. Homosexual behavior

_____ indicates a basic personality maladjustment.

_____ is immoral under any circumstances.

_____ is acceptable between consenting adults.

_____ is acceptable between consenting partners of any age.

_____ is a normal healthy variation in sex outlet for adults.

FACTFILE

POPULATION

Age of Awareness   Many gay men and lesbians sensed something "different" about them selves as early as age four or five. The age at which most acknowledge their homosexuality is between 14 and 16 years for males and between 16 and 19 years for females.

Source: Saghir MT, Robins E, Walbian B, Male and Female Homosexuality, Baltimore, MD: Williams & Wilkins, 1973.

Among Adolescents   The Kinsey study found that from puberty to age twenty, 28% of boys and 17% of girls had one or more homosexual experiences.

Source: Kinsey AC, Pomeroy WB, Martin CE, Sexual Behavior in the Human Male, 1948 and Sexual Behavior in the Human Female, 1953, Philadelphia: W.B. Saunders.

Among Adults   During adulthood, 37% of Americans have homosexual experiences. Ten percent are predominantly homosexual. (This is the source of the commonly accepted 10% figure.)

Source: Kinsey, op cit.

STRESS FACTORS

Isolation   Eighty percent of lesbian, gay, and bisexual youth report severe isolation problems. They experience social isolation (having no one to talk to), emotional isolation (feeling distanced from family and peers because of their sexual identity), and cognitive isolation (lack of access to good information about sexual orientation and homosexuality).

Source: Hetrick ES, Martin AD, "Developmental Issues and Their Resolution for Gay and Lesbian Adolescents," Journal of Homosexuality, 14(1/2):25-43, 1987.

Family Difficulties   Half of all lesbian and gay youth interviewed report that their parents reject them due to their sexual orientation.

Source: Ramafedi G, "Male Homosexuality: The Adolescent's Perspective," Pediatrics, 79:326-330, 1987.

Substance Abuse   In a study of gay male adolescents, 68% reported alcohol use (with 26% using alcohol once or more per week), and 44% reported drug use (with 8% considering themselves drug-dependent). Among lesbians, 83% had used alcohol, 56% had used drugs, and 11% had used crack/cocaine in the three months preceding the study.

Source: Rosario M, Hunter J, Rotheram-Borus MJ, Unpublished data on Lesbian adolescents, HIV Center for Clinical and Behavioral Studies, New York State Psychiatric Institute, 1992.

SUICIDE

Incidence   Gay youths are two to three times more likely to attempt suicide than heterosexual young people. It is estimated that up to 30% of the completed youth suicides are committed by lesbian and gay youth annually.

Source: Gibson P, LCSW, "Gay Male and Lesbian Youth Suicide", Report of the Secretary's Task Force on Youth Suicide, U.S. Department of Health and Human Services, 1989.

Multiple Attempts   In a study of 137 gay and bisexual males, 29% had attempted suicide, almost half of whom reported multiple attempts.

Source: Remafedi G, Farrow JA, Delsher RW, "Risk Factors for Attempted Suicide in Gay and Bisexual Youth," Pediatrics, 87(6), June 1991.

HIV/AIDS

Prevalence in Youth

Sixty percent of young adult cases of AIDS are among men who have had sex with men. Because HIV has an average incubationperiod of 10.5 years before the onset of AIDS, this statistic indicates that these young people were infected as teenagers.

Source: Centers for Disease Control, 1992.

A San Francisco Study of gay and bisexual men revealed that 14% of the men between ages 17 and 22 were HIV positive—a figure four percent higher than young men in the 23 to 25 age group.

Source: AIDS Office, Bureau of Epidemiology and Disease Control, San Francisco City Clinic Special Programs for Youths and San Francisco Department of Welfare, "The Young Men's Survey: Principal Findings and Results." San Francisco, CA, June 1991.

Risk of Infection

The factors that place lesbian and gay youth at a very high risk for HIV transmission include: having to exchange sex for money, unsafe sex, substance abuse, and denial of sexual identity.

Source: HIV Center for Clinical and Behavioral Studies, New York State Psychiatric Institute, 1992.

VIOLENCE

Physical Assault

In a study of self-identified lesbian and gay youth in New York City, 41% reported suffering violence from their families, peers, or strangers. One of the violent incidents, 46% were directly gay-related and primarily perpetrated by family members.

Source: Hunter J, "Violence Against Lesbian and Gay Male Youths," J. of Interpersonal Violence, 5(3), Sept. 1990.

In the Schools

Forty-five percent of gay males and 20% of lesbian females experience verbal or physical assault in high school. Twenty-eight percent of these youths are forced to drop out of school because of harassment resulting from their sexual orientation.

Sources: National Gay and Lesbian Task Force "Anti-Gay/Lesbian Victimization," New York, 1984; and Remafedi G, "Male Homosexuality: The Adolescent's Perspective," Pediatrics, 79:326-330, 1987.

HOMELESSNESS

Expulsion from families

Twenty-six percent of gay youths are forced to leave home because of conflicts with their families over their sexual identities.

Sources: National Gay and Lesbian Task Force, "Anti-Gay/Lesbian Victimization," New York, 1984; Remafedi G, "Male Homosexuality: The Adolescent's Perspective," Pediatrics, 79:326-330, 1987.

Survival Sex

Up to half of the gay/bisexual males forced out of their homes engage in prostitution to support themselves, greatly increasing their risk for HIV infection.

Source: Savin-Williams RC, "Theoretical Perspectives Accounting for Adolescent Homosexuality," J. Adol. Health Care, 9(2):95-104, March 1988.

ABOUT THE HETRICK-MARTIN INSTITUTE Founded in 1979, the Hetrick-Martin Institute is an education, social service, and advocacy organization that offers services to lesbian, gay and bisexual youth, ages 13 to 21, in New York City and nationally.

Notes

1. Understanding the Context of Gay, Lesbian, and Bisexual Lives

1. Bisexuals are not included here because the studies on which these conclusions are based asked about gay and/or lesbian people, not about bisexual people. However, it is likely that patterns of attitudes toward bisexual people would be similar.

2. Gay, Lesbian, and Bisexual Identities

1. These two contrasting points of view are described in the social sciences as *essentialist* on the one hand and *social constructionist* (DeCecco and Elia 1993) or *poststructuralist* (Eliason 1996) on the other.

2. When the question is confined to partners in the last year, 75 percent of the women and 74.7 percent of the men reported having same-gender partners only (Laumann et al. 1994:311).

3. As Tremble, Schneider, and Appathurai (1989) have noted, everyone has an ethnicity, and everyone has a culture, too. However, the terms *ethnicity* and *culture* will be used here to indicate an identification with a set of customs and traditions (and perhaps a language) that has its roots in a country other than the one in which the person is living or that is connected to a community of color.

3. Culture and Community

1. Although some would argue that a bisexual community has been forming in the last few years, this discussion will address gay and/or lesbian community and culture, which is much more well-established at this point in time.

4. Lesbian, Gay, and Bisexual Orientation in Childhood and Adolescence

1. All quotations are from interviews conducted by the author with gay and lesbian adolescents (dates of interviews are bracketed). All names have been changed to protect the confidentiality of the clients.

5. Between Men, Between Women

1. Bisexual people have both same- and opposite-gender sexual desires and experiences. But because more is known about gay and lesbian sexuality, the portions of this chapter that deal with sex and sexuality will address same-gender sex only. The intimate relationship patterns of bisexual people will be discussed separately.

2. Because less is known about bisexual relationships, the summary of findings in this chapter pertains to lesbian and gay—that is, to same-gender—relationships. It is assumed (but not known) that the same-gender relationships that bisexual people engage in are similar.

6. Gay, Lesbian, and Bisexual Parents and Their Children

1. Because bisexuality is relatively rare and has only recently been studied in any depth, there is only sketchy and anecdotal information available about the children of self-identified bisexuals. Thus the discussion of children reared in the context of same-gender relationships must be limited to the children of lesbians and gays.

2. Of course, it is also possible that a blended family can result from prior single parenthood, through birth or adoption, as well as from the death of a previous partner. Given the increasing rates of childbearing outside of marriage in the society as a whole, the former scenario is likely to become more common in the future. However, at this point, the divorce scenario just described is still the most common way that gay and lesbian families are formed from previously heterosexual ones.

3. Some gay men enter into childbearing through the use of a surrogate pregnancy, although this practice does not appear to be as widespread as lesbian childbearing (Benkov 1994; Bigner 1996; Martin 1993; Patterson 1995b).

4. Because of changing norms within and outside the gay community, it should be noted that today's *adult* children of gay and lesbian parents may or may not have been reared with the same openness about the sexual orientation of the parent(s).

5. As at other points in this chapter, this section includes only lesbian and gay parents because there is as yet no research base on which to describe the children of parents who identify as bisexual.

7. Gay, Lesbian, and Bisexual People in the World of Work

1. Most surveys did not ask about or sample bisexual people.

2. Actually, touch may be an issue at work for gay, lesbian, and bisexual people in all kinds of situations, even those involving ordinary social interactions with coworkers (Kitzinger 1991).

3. The following strategies are adapted from Appleby, G. (in press). In G. Mallon (Ed.), *Foundations of social work practice with gay and lesbian people*, 1–25. New York: Harrington Park Press.

8. Middle-Aged and Old Gay, Lesbian, and Bisexual Adults

1. This section does not include mention of bisexual people because there is at present no published research specifically addressing bisexual aging. To the extent that older bisexual people

are engaged in same-gender relationships or openly identified with the gay, lesbian, or bisexual community, the challenges they face may well be similar. To the extent that they are heterosexually married or integrated into heterosexual life, the challenges may be different.

9. Mental Health and Substance Abuse

1. This section addresses lesbian and gay people and does not include bisexual people because there is currently not enough research available to support a systematic discussion of their substance abuse problems and treatment needs. Clearly more research is badly needed in this area.

2. The study asked only about lesbian and gay clients and thus has no specific information to offer about bisexual clients.

11. HIV Disease: A Social Work Response

1. The term AIDS is obsolete; HIV infection more correctly defines the problem. *HIV disease* has replaced AIDS as the preferred term for the complex or syndrome that follows the diagnosis of specific diseases and conditions. The medical, social service, public health, political, and community leadership should focus on the full course of HIV infection rather than concentrating on the later stages of the disease (formerly termed ARC and AIDS). Continual focus on the later stages rather than the entire spectrum of HIV infection has left our nation unable to deal adequately with the epidemic. However, the term AIDS is sometimes used in this chapter, especially when referring to events and literature from the time when it was standard terminology or to late stages of the illness.

2. Being HIV-seropositive (HIV-positive) is determined by the presence of the HIV antibody, indicating retroviral infection, based on reactive screening through serologic testing. Each of the Western blot and enzyme-linked immunosorbent assay (ELISA) blood tests determines the presence of the antibody to HIV. Approximately 95 percent of individuals seroconvert within six months from exposure. An HIV-positive diagnosis can be asymptomatic (without any infections) or symptomatic (with infections associated with HIV disease).

3. Because the treatments for HIV disease are evolving rapidly, the reader should review resources such as the *Bulletin of Experimental Treatments for AIDS* e-mail: beta@thecity.sfsu.edu. It is also useful to contact the HIV/AIDS Treatment Information Service (ATIS) of the U.S. Department of Health and Human Services, Public Health Service e-mail: atis@cdcnac.aspensys.com.

4. *Cofactors* are substances, microorganisms, or characteristics of individuals that may influence the progression of a disease or the likelihood of becoming ill. For example, a cofactor can be a substance, such as a metallic ion or coenzyme, that must be associated with an enzyme for the enzyme to function. Or a cofactor can be a situation or activity that may increase a person's susceptibility to AIDS.

5. These include acupuncture, herbal remedies, chiropractic therapy, massage, meditation, vitamins, exercise, diet, and empowerment programs (Andrews & Novick 1995).

References

Abell, N. & J. Miller. 1991. Family members' willingness to care for people with AIDS: A psycho-social assessment model. *Social Work* 36(1): 43–53.

Achtenberg, R. 1988. Preserving and protecting the families of lesbians and gay men. Shernoff & Scott (Eds), *The sourcebook on lesbian/gay health care*, 237–45. Washington, D.C.: National Lesbian and Gay Health Association.

Adam, B. D. 1987. *The rise of a gay and lesbian movement*. Boston: Twayne.

Adelman, M. 1990. Stigma, gay lifestyles, and adjustment to aging: A study of later-life gay men and lesbians. *Journal of Homosexuality* 20(3–4): 7–32.

Adelman, M. (Ed.). 1986. *Long time passing: Lives of older lesbians*. Boston: Alyson.

Advocate. 1996a (November 12). Health: Reports from the medical front: Are some people immune? (p. 20). Los Angeles.

———. 1996b (December 10). Health: Reports from the medical front: Chronic depression (p. 18). Los Angeles.

Ainslee, J. & K. M. Feltey. 1991. Definitions and dynamics of motherhood and family in lesbian communities. *Marriage and Family Review* 17(1–2): 63–85.

Alexander, C. J. (Ed.). 1996. *Gay and lesbian mental health: A sourcebook for practitioners*. New York: Harrington Park Press.

Allport, G. 1958 (original ed., 1954). *The nature of prejudice*. Garden City, N.Y.: Anchor/Doubleday.

Altman, D. 1971. *Homosexual: Oppression and liberation*. New York: Outerbridge and Dienstfrey.

———. 1982. *The homosexualization of America*. Boston: Beacon Press.

———. 1987. *AIDS in the mind of America: The social, political, and psychological impact of a new epidemic*. New York: Anchor Doubleday.

———. 1993. *Homosexual oppression and liberation*. New York: New York University Press.

Alyson, S. (Ed.). 1991. *Young, gay, and proud*. Boston: Alyson.

Amendment 2, State Constitution (1996). State of Colorado. In the U.S. Supreme Court (*Remer v. Evans et al.*, No. 94–1039), October term, 1994.

American Psychiatric Association (APA). 1980, 1994 (4th ed.). *Diagnostic and statistical manual of mental disorders* (III-R). Washington, D.C.: American Psychiatric Press.

American Psychological Association (APA), Committee on Lesbian and Gay Concerns. 1991. *Bias in psychotherapy with lesbians and gay men*. Final Report. Washington, D.C.: APA.

Anastas, J. W. & M. L. MacDonald. 1994. *Research design for social work and the human services*. San Francisco: Jossey-Bass.

Andersen, M. 1983. *Thinking about women: Sociological and feminist perspectives*. New York: Macmillan.

Andersen, M. 1996. Foreword. In E. N.-L. Chow, D. Wilkinson, & M. B. Zinn (Eds.), *Race, class, and gender: Common bonds, different voices*, ix–xii. Thousand Oaks, Calif.: Sage.

Anderson, C. L. 1982. Males as sexual assault victims: Multiple levels of trauma. *Journal of Homosexuality* 7(2–3): 145–62.

Anderson, C. W. & H. R. Smith. 1993. Stigma and honor: Gay, lesbian, and bisexual people in the U.S. military. In L. Diamant (Ed.), *Homosexual issues in the workplace*, 65–89. Washington, D.C.: Taylor & Francis.

Andrews, L. J., L. B. Novick, & associates. 1995. *HIV care: A comprehensive handbook for providers*. Thousand Oaks, Calif.: Sage.

Antonovsky, A. 1979. *Health, stress, and coping*. San Francisco: Jossey-Bass.

———. 1987. *Unraveling the mystery of health: How people manage stress and stay well*. San Francisco: Jossey-Bass.

Appleby, G. A. 1992. AIDS: A social work response (course syllabus and materials). New Haven: Southern Connecticut State University.

———. 1995. AIDS and homophobia/heterosexism. *Journal of Gay and Lesbian Social Services* 2(3–4): 1–34. Reprinted in Lloyd & Kuszelewicz (Eds.), *HIV disease*, 1–24. New York: Harrington Park Press.

———. 1996. Homophobic attitudes of MSW and BSW students: A longitudinal study on SCSU students. Unpublished paper.

Appleby, G. (in press). Social work practice with gay men and lesbians within the context of organizations. In G. Mallon (Ed.), *Foundations of social work practice with gay and lesbian people*, 1–25. New York: Harrington Park Press.

Appleby, G. A. (Ed.). 1989. *Teaching AIDS to adults: A resource guide for acquired immune deficiency syndrome instruction*. Hartford: State of Connecticut, Department of Education.

Appleby, G. A. & J. W. Anastas. 1992. Social work practice with lesbians and gays. In Morales & Sheafor (Eds.), *Social work*, 347–81. 6th ed. Boston: Allyn & Bacon.

———. 1998. Social work practice with lesbian, gay, and bisexual people. In Morales & Sheafor (Eds.), *Social work*, 313–45. 8th ed. Boston: Allyn & Bacon.

Aronson, J. 1995. Lesbians in social work education: Processes and puzzles in claiming visibility. *Journal of Progressive Human Services* 6(1): 5–26.

Atkinson, D. R., G. Morten, & D. W. Sue. 1979. *Counseling American minorities*. Dubuque, Iowa: William C. Brown.

Badgett, C. R. 1992. Sexual orientation: Should it affect child custody rulings? *Law and Psychology Review* 16: 189–200.

Badgett, M. V. L. 1996. Employment and sexual orientation: Disclosure and discrimination in the workplace. *Journal of Gay and Lesbian Social Services* 4(4): 29–52.

Bagley, C. 1996. Viewpoint. *Advocate* (November-December): 44.

Bailey, J. M., D. Bobrow, M. Wolfe, & S. Mikach. 1995. Sexual orientation of adult sons of gay fathers. *Developmental Psychology* 31(1): 124–29.

Bailey, J. M. & R. C. Pillard. 1991. A genetic study of male sexual orientation. *Archives of General Psychiatry* 48: 1089–1096.

Bailey, J. M., R. C. Pillard, M. C. Neale, & Y. Agyei. 1993. Heritable factors influence sexual orientation in women. *Archives of General Psychiatry* 50: 217–23.

Bailey, M. E. 1991. Developing a national HIV/AIDS prevention program through state health departments. *Public Health Reports* 106: 695–701.

Baker, K. 1995. *A legal guide for gay and lesbian couples in Ontario*. Toronto: Legal Work Press.

Baker, R. 1996. Overview of the HIV protease inhibitors and new HIV treatment strategies. *Bulletin of Experimental Treatments for AIDS* (July): 1–2.

Baranaga, M. 1991 (August 31). Is homosexuality biological? *Science* 252(5023): 945–58.

Bard, M. & D. Sangrey. 1979. *The crime victim's book*. New York: Basic Books.

Barker, R. L. 1987. *The social work dictionary*. Silver Spring, Md.: NASW Press.

Barret, R. L. 1993. The homosexual athlete. In L. Diamant (Ed.), *Homosexual issues in the workplace*, 161–78. Washington, D.C.: Taylor & Francis.

Barzan, R. 1995. *Sex and spirit: Exploring gay men's spirituality*. San Francisco: White Crane.

Basch, M. 1975. Toward a theory that encompasses depression: A revision of existing causal hypotheses in psychoanalysis. In J. Anthony & T. Benedek (Eds.), *Depression and human existence*. Boston: Little Brown.

Bayer, R. 1987. *Homosexuality and American psychiatry: The politics of diagnosis*. 2d ed. Princeton: Princeton University Press.

———. 1989. *Private acts, social consequences: AIDS and the politics of public health*. New York: Free Press.

Bean, J., L. Keller, C. Newberg, & M. Brown. 1989. Methods for the reduction of AIDS social anxiety and social stigma. *AIDS Education and Prevention* 1: 194–221.

Bell, A. P. & M. S. Weinberg. 1978. *Homosexualities: A study of diversity among men and women*. New York: Simon & Schuster.

Bell, A. P., M. S. Weinberg, & S. K. Hammersmith. 1981. *Sexual preference: Its development in men and women*. Bloomington: Indiana University Press.

Bellos, N. S. & M. C. Ruffolo. 1995. Aging: Services. In R. L. Edwards (Ed.), *Encyclopedia of Social Work*, 173–83. 19th ed. Washington, D.C.: NASW Press.

Bem, S. L. 1983. Gender schema theory and its implications for child development: Raising gender-aschematic children in a gender-schematic society. *Signs* 8(4): 598–616.

Benkov, L. 1994. *Reinventing the family: The emerging story of lesbian and gay parenting*. New York: Crown.

Bera, W. H. & D. LeTourneau. 1994. *Male sexual abuse: A trilogy of intervention strategies*. Thousand Oaks, Calif.: Sage.

Berger, R. M. 1980. Psychological adaptation of the older homosexual male. *Journal of Homosexuality* 5(3): 161–75.

———. 1982. The unseen minority: Older gays and lesbians. *Social Work* 27(3): 236–42.

———. 1983. What is a homosexual? A definitional model. *Social Work* 28(2): 132–35.

———. 1984. Realities of gay and lesbian aging. *Social Work* 29(1): 57–62.

———. 1990. Passing: Impact on the quality of same-sex couple relationships. *Social Work* 35(4): 328–32.

———. 1992. Research on older gay men: What we know, what we need to know. In Woodman (Ed.), *Lesbian and gay lifestyles*, 217–34. New York: Irvington.

Berger, R. M. & J. J. Kelly. 1986. Working with homosexuals of the older population. *Social Casework* 67(4): 203–10.

———. 1996a. Gay men: Overview. In R. J. Edwards (Ed.), *Encyclopedia of Social Work*, 1064–75. 19th ed. Washington, D.C.: NASW Press.

———. 1996b. Prologue: Gay and gray revisited. In Berger, *Gay and gray: The older homosexual man*, 1–22. 2d ed. New York: Harrington Park Press.

Berger, R. M. & R. Federico. 1982. *Human behavior: A social work perspective*. New York: Longman.

Berkman, C. S. & G. Zinberg. 1997. Homophobia and heterosexism in social workers. *Social Work* 42(4): 319–32.

Bernard, D. 1992. Developing a positive self-image in a homophobic environment. In Woodman (Ed.), *Lesbian and gay lifestyles*, 23–32. New York: Irvington.

Berrill, K. T. 1992. Anti-gay violence and victimization in the United States: An overview. In Herek & Berrill (Eds.), *Hate crimes*, 19–45. Newbury Park, Calif.: Sage.

Berube, A. 1990. *Coming out under fire: The history of gay men and women in World War II*. New York: Free Press.

Berzon, B. 1992. *Positively gay: New approaches to gay and lesbian life*. Berkeley, Calif.: Celestial Arts.

Besses, L. 1994. The relationship between racial identity attitudes and internalized homophobia. Master's thesis, California State University, Chico.

Bhugra, D. 1988. Homosexuals' attitudes to male homosexuality: A survey. *Sexual and Marital Therapy* 3(2): 197–203.

Bickelhaupt, E. E. 1995. Alcohol and drug abuse in gay and lesbian persons: A review of incidence studies. *Journal of Gay and Lesbian Social Services* 2(1): 5–14.

Bieber, I., H. J. Dain, P. R. Dince, M. G. Drellich, H. G. Grand, R. H. Gundlach, M. W. Kremer, A. H. Rifkin, C. B. Wilbur, & T. B. Bieber. 1962. *Homosexuality: A psychoanalytic study*. New York: Basic Books.

Bigner, J. J. 1996. Working with gay fathers: Developmental, postdivorce parenting, and therapeutic issues. In Laird & Green (Eds), *Lesbians and gays in couples and families*, 370–403. San Francisco: Jossey-Bass.

Billy, J. O. G., K. Tanfer, W. R. Grady, & D. H. Klepinger. 1993. The sexual behavior of men in the United States. *Family Planning Perspectives* 25(2): 52–60.

Binson, D. et al. 1995. Prevalence and social distribution of men who have sex with men: United States and its urban centers. *Journal of Sex Research* 32(3): 245–54.

Bissell, L. 1995. Foreword. *Journal of Gay and Lesbian Social Services* 2(1): xxi–xxv.

Black, C. 1990. *Double duty: Gay or lesbian*. New York: Ballantine.

Blackwood, E. 1995. Breaking the mirror: The construction of lesbianism and the anthropological discourse on homosexuality. *Journal of Homosexuality* 11(3–4): 1–17.

Blankenship, W. 1993. Relapse prevention interventions. *Focus: A Guide to AIDS Research and Counseling* 8(2): 5–6.

Blos, P. 1979. *The adolescent passage: Developmental issues*. New York: International Universities Press.

———. 1981. *The adolescent passage: Developmental issues*. New York: International Universities Press.

Blumenfeld, W. J. 1992. Children, families, and homophobia. In Blumenfeld (Ed.), *Homophobia*, 95–130. Boston: Beacon Press.

———. 1992. Introduction. In Blumenfeld (Ed.), *Homophobia*, 1–78. Boston: Beacon Press.

———. 1992. Other societal manifestations of homophobia. In Blumenfeld (Ed.), *Homophobia*, 217–48. Boston: Beacon Press.

Blumenfeld, W. J. (Ed.). 1992. *Homophobia: How we all pay the price*. Boston: Beacon Press.

Blumenfeld, W. J. & D. Raymond (Eds.). 1988, 1993 (updated and expanded ed). *Looking at gay and lesbian life*. Boston: Beacon Press.

Blumstein, P. W. & P. Schwartz. 1983. *American couples: Money, work, sex*. New York: Morrow.

———. 1993. Bisexuality: Some social psychological issues. In Garnets & Kimmel (Eds.), *Psychological perspectives on lesbian and gay male experiences*, 168–83. New York: Columbia University Press.

Bly, C. 1982. *Letters from the country*. New York: Penguin.

Bohn, T. R. 1984. Homophobic violence: Implications for social work practice. In R. Schoenberg, R. S. Goldberg, & D. A. Shod (Eds.), *With compassion toward some: Homosexuality and social work in America*, 91–112. New York: Harrington Park Press.

Bonilla, L. & J. Porter. 1991. A comparison of Latino, black, and non-Hispanic white attitudes toward homosexuality. *Hispanic Journal of Behavioral Sciences* 12(4): 437–52.

Boston Lesbian Psychologies Collective (Ed.), *Lesbian psychologies: Explorations and challenges*. Urbana: University of Illinois Press.

Boswell, J. 1980. *Christianity, social tolerance, and homosexuality: Gay people in Western Europe from the beginnings of the Christian era to the fourteenth century*. Chicago and London: University of Chicago Press.

———. 1995. *Same-sex unions in pre-modern Europe*. New York: Vintage Books.

Bowers v. Hardwick, 478 U.S. 186 (1986).

Boykin, F. F. 1991. The AIDS crisis and gay male survivor guilt. *Smith College Studies in Social Work* 61(3): 247–59.

Bozett, F. W. 1993. Gay fathers: A review of the literature. In Garnets & Kimmel (Eds), *Psychological perspectives on lesbian and gay male experiences*, 437–57. New York: Columbia University Press.

Bradford, J. & C. Ryan. 1988. *The national lesbian health care survey*. Washington, D.C.: National Lesbian and Gay Health Association.

Bradford, J., C. Ryan, & E. D. Rothblum (Eds.). 1994. National lesbian health care survey: Implications for mental health. *Journal of Consulting and Clinical Psychology* 62(2): 228–42.

Bronfenbrenner, U. 1979. *The ecology of human development*. Cambridge: Harvard University Press.

Bronski, M. 1984. *Culture clash: The making of gay sensibility*. Boston: South End Press.

Brooks, W. K. 1992. Research and the gay minority: Problems and possibilities. In Woodman (Ed.), *Lesbian and gay lifestyles*, 201–16. New York: Irvington.

Brown, L. S. 1989. New voices, new visions: Toward a lesbian/gay paradigm for psychology. *Psychology of Women Quarterly* 13: 445–58.

———. 1995. Lesbian identities: Concepts and issues. In D'Augelli & Patterson (Eds.), *Lesbian, gay, and bisexual identities over the lifespan*, 3–23. New York: Oxford University Press.

Brown, L. S. & D. Zimmer. 1988. An introduction to therapy issues of lesbian and gay male couples.

Brown, P. 1991. Passing: Differences in our public and private self. *Journal of Multicultural Social Work* 1(2): 33–50.

Browning, C. 1987. Therapeutic issues and intervention strategies with young adult lesbian clients: A developmental approach. *Journal of Homosexuality* 13(4): 45–53.

Browning, C., A. L. Reynolds, & S. H. Dworkin. 1991. Affirmative psychotherapy for lesbian women. *Counseling Psychologist* 9(2): 177–96.

Bryant, A. S. & Demian. 1994. Relationship characteristics of American gay and lesbian couples: Findings from a national survey. *Journal of Lesbian and Gay Social Services* 1(2): 101–17.

Buckingham, S. L. & W. G. Van Gorp. 1994. HIV-associated dementia: A clinician's guide to early detection, diagnosis, and intervention. *Families in Society* 75: 333–45.

Burch, B. 1987. Barriers to intimacy: Conflicts over power, dependency, and nurturing in lesbian relationships. In Boston Lesbian Psychologies Collective (Eds.), *Lesbian psychologies*, 126–41. Urbana: University of Illinois Press.

——. 1993. Heterosexuality, bisexuality, and lesbianism: Rethinking psychoanalytic views of women's sexual object choice. *Psychoanalytic Review* 80(1): 83–99.

Bureau of the Census, U.S. Department of Commerce. 1997. Household and family characteristics: March 1996 (update). Washington, D.C.: U.S. Department of Commerce.

Byrne, D. 1996. Clinical models for the treatment of gay male perpetrators of domestic violence. *Journal of Gay and Lesbian Social Services* 4(1): 107–16.

Cabaj, R. P. 1988. Homosexuality and neurosis: Considerations for psychotherapy. *Journal of Homosexuality* 15(1–2): 13–23.

Cabaj, R. P. & T. S. Stein (Eds.). 1995. *The textbook on homosexuality*. New York: American Psychiatric Press.

Cadwell, S. A. 1991. Twice removed: The stigma suffered by gay men with AIDS. *Smith College Studies in Social Work* 61(3): 236–46.

Cadwell, S. A., R. A. Burnham, & M. Forstein (Eds.), *Therapists on the front line: Psychotherapy with gay men in the age of AIDS*. Washington D.C.: American Psychiatric Press.

Cain, R. 1991a. Disclosure and secrecy among gay men in the United States and Canada: A shift in views. *Journal of the History of Sexuality* 2(1): 25–45.

——. 1991b. Stigma management and gay identity development. *Social Work* 36(1): 67–73.

——. 1996. Heterosexism and self-disclosure in the social work classroom. *Journal of Social Work Education* 32(1): 65–76.

Campbell, C. A. & M. D. Peck. 1995. Issues in HIV/AIDS service delivery to high-risk youth. *Journal of Gay and Lesbian Social Services* 2(3–4): 159–77.

Cantwell. M. A. 1996. *Homosexuality: The secret a child dare not tell*. San Rafael, Calif.: Rafael Press.

Carrier, J. M. 1985. Mexican male bisexuality. In Klein & Wolf (Eds.), *Two lives to lead*, 75–85. New York: Harrington Park Press.

Cass, V. C. 1979. Homosexuality identity formation: A theoretical model. *Journal of Homosexuality* 4(3): 219–35.

Cates, J. A. 1987. Adolescent sexuality: Gay and lesbian issues. *Child Welfare* 66(4): 353–63.

Cates, W. & A. Hinmann. 1992. AIDS and absolutism: The demand for perfection in prevention. *New England Journal of Medicine* 327(7): 492–94.

Cautela, J. 1967. Covert sensitization. *Psychological Reports* 20(2): 459–68.

Centers for Disease Control (CDC). 1992. Revised classification systems for HIV infection and expanded surveillance case definition for AIDS among adolescents and adults. *Morbidity and Mortality Weekly Report* 41(RR-17): 1–19.

——. 1993. *HIV/AIDS surveillance: U.S. cases reported through August 1993*. Atlanta: CDC.

——. 1995. *HIV/AIDS surveillance: U.S. cases reported through August 1995*. Atlanta: CDC.

Chan, C. S. 1993. Issues of identity development among Asian-American lesbian and gay men. In Garnets & Kimmel (Eds.), *Psychological perspectives on lesbian and gay male experiences*, 376–87). New York: Columbia University Press.

——. 1995. Issues of sexual identity in an ethnic minority: The case of Chinese American lesbians, gay men, and bisexual people. In D'Augelli & Patterson (Eds.), *Lesbian, gay, and bisexual identities over the lifespan*, 87–101. New York: Oxford University Press.

Chauncey, G. 1994. *Gay New York: Gender, urban culture, and the making of the gay male world, 1890–1940*. New York: Basic Books.

Chersky, B. & M. D. Siever. 1994. Counseling working-class gay men. *Focus: A Guide to AIDS Research and Counseling* 9(3): 4–8.

Chestang, L. 1984. Racial and personal identity in the black experience. In B. W. White (Ed.), *Color in a white society*, 83–94. Silver Spring, Md.: NASW Press.

Chow, E. N. L., D. Wilkinson, & M. B. Zinn (Eds.). *Race, class, and race: Common bonds, different voices*. Thousand Oaks, Calif.: Sage.

Christ, G. & L. Wiener (Eds.). 1985. *AIDS: Etiology, diagnosis, treatment, and prevention*. Philadelphia: Lippincott.

Chung, Y. B. 1995. Career decision making of lesbian, gay, and bisexual individuals. *Career Development Quarterly* 44(2): 178–90.

Chung, Y. B. & M. Katayama. 1996. Assessment of sexual orientation in lesbian/gay/bisexual studies. *Journal of Homosexuality* 30(4): 49–62.

Clark, J. M. 1989. *A place to start: Toward an unapologetic gay liberation theology*. Dallas: Monument Press.

——. 1990. *A defiant celebration: Theological ethics and gay spirituality*. Garland, Tex.: Tanglewood Press.

Clunis, D. & G. D. Green. 1988. *Lesbian couples*. Seattle, Wash.: Seal Press.

Cohen, C. J. & T. S. Stein. 1986. Reconceptualizing individual psychotherapy with gay men and lesbians. In Stein & Cohen (Eds.), *Contemporary perspectives on psychotherapy with lesbians and gay men*, 27–54. New York: Plenum Medical.

Cohen, E. 1991. Who are "we"? Gay "identity' as political (e)motion (a theoretical rumination). In D. Fuss (Ed.), *Inside/out: Lesbian theories, gay theories*, 71–92. New York: Routledge.

Coleman, E. 1982. Developmental stages of the coming out process. In Paul, Weinrich, Gonsiorek, & Hotvedt (Eds.), *Homosexuality*, 149–58). Beverly Hills, Calif.: Sage.

——. 1985. Bisexual women in marriage. In Klein & Wolf (Eds.), *Two lives to lead*, 87–89. New York: Harrington Park Press.

Compton, B. R. & B. Galaway. 1989. *Social work processes*. Belmont, Calif.: Wadsworth.

Comstock, G. D. 1989. Victims of anti-gay/lesbian violence. *Journal of Interpersonal Violence* 4(1): 101–106.

——. 1991. *Violence against lesbians and gay men*. New York: Columbia University Press.

Conrad, P. 1986. The social meaning of AIDS. *Social Policy* 17(1): 51–56.

Constantine, L. & F. M. Martinson (Eds.). 1981. *Children and sex.* Boston: Little, Brown.

Cook, R., S. Golombok, A. Bish, & C. Murray. 1995. Disclosure of donor insemination: Parental attitudes. *American Journal of Orthopsychiatry* 65(4): 549–59.

Cooper, J. R. 1989. Methadone treatment and acquired immunodeficiency syndrome. *Journal of the American Medical Association* 262: 1664–68.

Cornett, C. W. & R. A. Hudson. 1985. Psychoanalytic theory and affirmation of the gay lifestyle: Are they necessarily antithetical? *Journal of Homosexuality* 12(11): 97–108.

Council on Social Work Education (CSWE), Commission on Accreditation. 1988. *Handbook of accreditation standards and procedures.* Washington, D.C.: CSWE.

———. 1993. *Handbook of accreditation standards and procedures.* Washington, D.C.: CSWE.

Cox, S. & C. Gallois. 1996. Gay and lesbian identity development: A social identity perspective. *Journal of Homosexuality* 30(4): 1–30.

Crawford, S. 1987. Lesbian families: Psychosocial stress and the family-building process. In Boston Lesbian Psychologies Collective (Ed.), *Lesbian psychologies*, 195–214. Urbana: University of Illinois Press.

Crawley, B. 1995. Older women: Policy issues for the twenty-first century. In Davis (Ed.), *Building on women's strengths*, 159–77. New York: Haworth Press.

Creekmur, C. K. & A. Doty (Eds.). 1995. *Out in culture: Gay, lesbian, and queer essays on popular culture.* Durham, N.C.: Duke University Press.

Crocker, J. & B. Major. 1989. Social stigma and self-esteem: The self-protective properties of stigma. *Psychological Review* 96(4): 603–30.

Cross, W. E., Jr. 1991. *Shades of black: Diversity in African-American identity.* Philadelphia: Temple University Press.

Cruikshank, M. 1992. *The gay and lesbian movement.* New York: Routledge.

Cullum, C. S. 1993. Co-parent adoptions: Lesbian and gay parenting. *Trial* (June): 28–36.

Dank, B. 1971. Coming out in the gay world. *Psychiatry* 34: 180–97.

Dankmeijer, P. 1993. The construction of identities as a means of survival: Case of gay and lesbian teachers. *Journal of Homosexuality* 24(3–4): 95–105.

Dansky, S. F. 1994. *Now dare everything: Tales of HIV-related psychotherapy.* New York: Harrington Park Press.

D'Augelli, A. 1989. The development of a helping community for lesbians and gay men: A case study in community psychology. *Journal of Community Psychology* 17: 18–29.

D'Augelli, A. R. & C. J. Patterson (Eds.). 1995. *Lesbian, gay, and bisexual identities over the lifespan: Psychological perspectives.* New York: Oxford University Press.

D'Augelli, A. R. & L. Garnets. 1995. Lesbian, gay, and bisexual communities. In D'Augelli & Patterson (Eds.), *Lesbian, gay, and bisexual identities over the lifespan*, 293–320. New York: Oxford University Press.

Davis, L. V. (Ed.). *Building on women's strengths: A social work agenda for the twenty-first century.* New York: Haworth Press.

de Anda, D. 1984. Bicultural socialization; Factors affecting the minority experience. *Social Work* 29(2): 101–107.

DeCecco, J. P. (Ed.). 1985. *Bashers, baiters, and bigots: Homophobia in American society.* New York: Harrington Park Press.

DeCecco, J. P. (Ed.). 1988. *Gay relationships.* New York: Harrington Park Press.

DeCecco, J. P. & D. A. Parker. 1995. The biology of homosexuality: Sexual orientation or sexual preference? In DeCecco & Parker (Eds.), *Sex, cells, and same-sex desire: The biology of sexual preference*, 1–27. New York: Harrington Park Press.

DeCecco, J. P. & J. P. Elia. 1993. A critique and synthesis of biological essentialism and social constructionist views of sexuality and gender. *Journal of Homosexuality* 24(3–4): 1–26.

DeCecco, J. P. & M. G. Shively. 1984. From sexual identities to sexual relationships? A contextual shift. *Journal of Homosexuality* 9(2–3): 1–26.

DeCrescenzo, T. A. 1984. Homophobia: A study of attitudes of mental health professionals toward homosexuality. In R. Schoenberg, R. S. Goldberg, & D. A. Shod (Eds.), *With compassion toward some: Homosexuality and social work in America*, 115–36. New York: Harrington Park Press.

DeCrescenzo, T. (Ed.). 1994. *Helping gay and lesbian youth: New policies, new programs, new practices.* New York: Haworth.

Deevey, S. 1990. Older lesbian women: An invisible minority. *Journal of Gerontological Nursing* 16(5): 35–39.

DeHoyos, G. & C. Jensen. 1985. The systems approach in American social work. *Social Casework* 66(8): 490–97.

Delgado, J. R. & M. K. Rose. 1994. Caregiver constellations: Caring for persons with AIDS. *Journal of Gay and Lesbian Social Services* 1(1): 1–14.

D'Emilio, J. 1983. *Sexual politics, sexual communities: The making of a homosexual minority in the United States, 1940–1970.* Chicago: University of Chicago Press.

D'Emilio, J. & E. B. Freedman. 1988. *Intimate matters: A history of sexuality in America.* New York: Harper & Row.

de Monteflores, C. 1986. Notes on the management of difference. In Stein & Cohen (Eds.), *Contemporary perspectives on psychotherapy with lesbians and gay men*, 73–101. New York: Plenum Medical. Reprinted (1993) in modified form in Garnets & Kimmel (Eds.), *Psychological perspectives on lesbian and gay male experiences*, 218–47. New York: Columbia University Press.

de Monteflores, C. & S. J. Schultz. 1978. Coming out: Similarities and differences for lesbians and gay men. *Journal of Social Issues* 34(3): 59–72.

Dempsey, C. L. 1994. Health and social issues of gay, lesbian, and bisexual adolescents. *Families in Society* 75(3): 160–67.

DePoy, E. & S. Noble. 1992. The structure of lesbian relationships in response to oppression. *Affilia* 7(4): 49–64.

Deutsch, L. 1995. Out of the closet and on to the couch: A psychoanalytic exploration of lesbian development. In Glassgold & Iasenza (Eds.), *Lesbians and psychoanalysis*, 19–37. New York: Free Press.

DeVore, W. & E. Schlesinger. 1981. *Ethnic-sensitive social work practice.* St. Louis: C. V. Mosby.

De Young, M. 1982. *The sexual victimization of children.* Jefferson, N.C.: McFarland.

Diamond, M. 1979. Sexual identity and sexual roles. In V. Bullough (Ed.), *The frontiers of sex research*, 234–41. New York: Prometheus.

Diaz, T., S. Chu, M. Frederick, P. Hermann, A. Levy, E. Mokotoff, B. Whyte, L. Conti, M. Herr, P. Checko, C. Rietmeijer, R. Sorvill, & M. Quaiser. 1993. Sociodemographics and HIV risk behaviors of bisexual men with AIDS: Results from a multistate interview project. *AIDS* 7(9): 1227–32.

Diepold, J. & R. D. Young. 1979. Empirical studies of adolescent sexual behavior: A critical review. *Adolescence* 14(53): 45–64.

Dilley, J. W. & P. B. Goldblum. 1987. AIDS and mental health. In V. G. Gong & N. Rudnick (Eds.), *AIDS: Facts and issues*, 246–77. New Brunswick, N.J.: Rutgers University Press.

Dorrell, B. 1990. Being there: A support network of lesbian women. *Journal of Homosexuality* 20(2–4): 89–98.

Douglas, C. J., C. M. Kalman, & T. P. Kalman. 1985. Homophobia among physicians and nurses: An empirical study. *Hospital and Community Psychiatry* 36(12): 1309–11.

Dowsett, G. W. 1994. Working-class gay communities and HIV prevention. *Focus: A Guide to AIDS Research and Counseling* 9(3): 1–4.

Drescher, J. In press. *Psychoanalytic attitudes toward homosexuality*. New York: Contemporary Psychoanalysis.

Drost, M. 1996. Older adults' knowledge and attitudes about HIV/AIDS. *Outword* 2(4): 6–8.

Duberman, M. 1993. *Stonewall*. New York: Dutton.

DuBois, B. & K. K. Miley. 1996. *Social work: An empowering profession*. 2d ed. Boston: Allyn & Bacon.

Due, L. 1995. *Joining the tribe: Growing up gay and lesbian in the 90's*. New York: Anchor Books.

Dulaney, D. & J. Kelly. 1982. Improving services to gay and lesbian clients. *Social Work* 27(2): 178–83.

Dunkle, J. H. 1994. Counseling gay male clients: A review of treatment efficacy research: 1975–present. *Journal of Gay and Lesbian Psychotherapy* 2(2): 1–19.

Dupras, A., J. Levy, & J. M. Samson. 1989. Homophobia and attitudes about AIDS. *Psychological Reports* 64(1): 236–38.

Dworkin, J. & D. Kaufer. 1995. Social services and bereavement in the lesbian and gay community. *Journal of Gay and Lesbian Social Services* 2(3–4): 41–60.

Eblin, R. L. 1990. Domestic partnership recognition in the workplace: Equitable employee benefits for gay couples (and others). *Ohio State Law Journal* 51(4): 1067–87.

Ehrhardt, A. A. 1992. Trends in sexual behavior and the HIV pandemic (editorial). *American Journal of Public Health* 82: 1459–61.

Ehrlich, H. J. 1973. *The social psychology of prejudice*. New York: Wiley.

——. 1978. Dogmatism. In H. London & J. Exner (Eds.), *Dimensions of personality*, 129–64. New York: Wiley.

——. 1992. The ecology of anti-gay violence. In Herek & Berrill (Eds.), *Hate crimes*, 105–12. Newbury Park, Calif.: Sage.

Eichler, M. 1988. *Nonsexist research methods: A practical guide*. Boston: Urwin Hyman.

Eliason, M. J. 1995. Attitudes about lesbians and gay men: A review and implications for social services training. *Journal of Gay and Lesbian Social Services* 2(2): 73–90.

——. 1996. Identity formation for lesbian, bisexual, and gay persons: Beyond a "minoritizing" view. *Journal of Homosexuality* 30(3): 31–58.

Eliason, M. J. & S. Raheim. 1996. Categorical measurement of attitudes about lesbian, gay, and bisexual people. *Journal of Gay and Lesbian Social Services* 4(3): 51–65.

Elliott, J. E. 1993. Career development with lesbian and gay clients. *Career Development Quarterly* 41(3): 210–26.

Elliott, P. 1996. Shattering illusions: Same-sex domestic violence. *Journal of Gay and Lesbian Social Services* 4(1): 1–8.

Ellis, A. L. 1996. Sexual identity issues in the workplace: Past and present. *Journal of Gay and Lesbian Social Services* 4(4): 1–16.

Ellis, A. L. & E. D. D. Riggle. 1995. The relation of job satisfaction and degree of openness about one's sexual orientation for lesbians and gay men. *Journal of Homosexuality* 30(2): 75–85.

Elze, D. 1992. "It Has Nothing to Do with Me." In Blumenfeld and Raymond (Eds.), *Looking at Gay and Lesbian Life*, 95–113. Boston: Beacon Press.

Epstein, A. L. & P. D. Zak. 1993. The master of social work core curriculum: Inclusion of gay, lesbian, and bisexual content. Paper present at the Council on Social Work Education Conference in New York City.

Erikson, E. 1950. *Childhood and society*. New York: Norton.

———. 1963. *Childhood and society*. 2d ed. New York: Norton.

Eskridge, W. N. 1996. *The case for same-sex marriage: From sexual liberty to civilized commitment.* New York: Free Press.

Espin, O. M. 1987. Issues of identity in the psychology of Latina lesbians. In Boston Lesbian Psychologies Collective (Ed.), *Lesbian psychologies*, 35–55. Urbana: University of Illinois Press.

Espin, O. M. 1993. Issues of identity in the psychology of Latina lesbians. In Garnets & Kimmel (Eds.), *Psychological perspectives on lesbian and gay male experiences*, 348–63. New York: Columbia University Press.

Etringer, B. D., E. Hillerbrand, & C. Hetherington. 1990. The influence of sexual orientation on career decision-making: A research note. *Journal of Homosexuality* 19(4): 103–111.

Evans, A. 1978. *Witchcraft and the gay counterculture*. New York: Fag Rag Books.

Evans, B. K. 1990. Mothering as a lesbian issue. *Journal of Feminist Family Therapy* 2(1): 43–52.

Faderman, L. 1984. The "new gay" lesbians. *Journal of Homosexuality* 10(3–4): 85–95.

———. 1991. *Odd girls and twilight lovers: A history of lesbian life in twentieth-century America.* New York: Columbia University Press.

Falco, K. L. 1991. *Psychotherapy with lesbian clients: Theory into practice.* New York: Brunner/Mazel.

Falk, P. J. 1993. Lesbian mothers: Psychosocial assumptions in family law. In Garnets & Kimmel (Eds.), *Psychological perspectives on lesbian and gay male experiences*, 420–36. New York: Columbia University Press.

Faria, G. 1994. Training for family preservation work with lesbian families. *Families in Society* 75(7): 416–22.

Farley, N. 1996. A survey of factors contributing to gay and lesbian domestic violence. *Journal of Gay and Lesbian Social Services* 4(1): 35–42.

Fassinger, R. E. 1991. The hidden minority: Issues and challenges in working with lesbian women and gay men. *Counseling Psychologist* 19(2): 157–76.

———. 1993. And gladly teach: Lesbian and gay issues in education. In L. Diamant (Ed.), *Homosexual issues in the workplace*, 119–42. Washington, D.C.: Taylor & Francis.

———. 1995. From invisibility to integration: Lesbian identity in the workplace. *Career Development Quarterly* 44(2): 148–67.

Federico, R. C. 1979. Human behavior in the social environment within a diversity framework. In B. Baer and R. Federico (Eds.), *Educating the baccalaureate social worker* 2:181–208. Cambridge, Mass.: Balinger.

Feldman, M. 1966. Aversion therapy for sexual deviation: A critical review. *Psychological Bulletin* 65: 65–69.

Feldman, M. & M. J. MacCullough. 1965. The application of anticipatory avoidance learning to the treatment of homosexuality: Theory, technique, and preliminary results. *Behavior Research and Therapy* 2: 165–83.

Fellows, W. 1996. *Farm boys: Lives of gay men from the rural Midwest*. Madison: University of Wisconsin Press.

Fikar, C. R. 1992. The gay pediatrician: A report. *Journal of Homosexuality* 23(3): 53–63.

Finn, P. & T. McNeil. 1987. *The response of the criminal justice system to bias crime: An exploratory review*. Cambridge, Mass.: Abt Associates.

Finnegan, D. G. & E. B. McNally. 1995. The National Association of Lesbian and Gay Alcoholism Professionals (NALGAP): A retrospective. In Robert J. Kus (Ed.), *Addiction and recovery in gay and lesbian persons*, 83–90. New York: Harrington Park Press.

———. 1996. Chemical dependency and depression in lesbians and gay men: What helps? *Journal of Gay and Lesbian Social Services* 4(2): 115–29.

Finzer, K. 1997. Implementing gay-sensitive services. *Dimensions* 4(2): 4.

Fitzgerald, F. 1986. *Cities on a hill: A journey through contemporary American cultures*. New York: Simon & Schuster.

Flaks, D. K., I. Ficher, F. Masterpasqua, & G. Joseph. 1995. Lesbians choosing motherhood: A comparative study of lesbian and heterosexual parents and their children. *Developmental Psychology* 31(1): 105–14.

Flores-Ortiz, Y. & G. Bernal. 1990. Contextual family therapy of addiction with Latino. In Flores-Ortiz & Bernal (Eds.), *Minorities and family therapy*, 123–41. New York: Haworth Press.

Forstein, M. 1988. Homophobia: An overview. *Psychiatric Annals* 18(1): 33–36.

———. 1994. Psychotherapy with gay male couples. In Cadwell, Burnham, & Forstein (Eds.), *Therapists on the front line*, 293–318. Washington D.C.: American Psychiatric Press.

Foucault, M. 1980. *The history of sexuality*. 2 vols. Vol. 1, *An Introduction*, trans. Robert Hurley. New York: Random House; reprint, New York: Vintage Books.

Fox, R. C. 1995. Bisexual identities. In D'Augelli & Patterson (Eds.), *Lesbian, gay, and bisexual identities over the lifespan*, 48–86. New York: Oxford University Press.

Frank, E., B. Anderson, B. D. Stewart, C. Danou, C. Hughes, & D. West. 1988. Efficacy of cognitive behavior therapy and systematic desensitization in the treatment of rape trauma. *Behavior Research and Therapy* 19: 403–20.

Frank, P. B. & B. D. Houghton. 1987. Confronting the batterer: A guide to creating the spouse abuse educational workshop. New York: Volunteer Counseling Service of Rockland County.

Freedman, M. 1995. Diversity with a difference: Gay and lesbian aging. *Aging Today* 16(5): 7.

Freud, S. 1938. *Basic writings of Sigmund Freud*. Translated by A. A. Brill. New York: Random House (The Modern Library).

Friedland G. H. & R. S. Klein. 1987. Transmission of the human immunodeficiency virus. *New England Journal of Medicine* 317: 1125–35.

Friedman, R. C. 1988. *Male homosexuality: A contemporary psychoanalytic perspective*. New Haven: Yale University Press.

Friedman, R. C. & J. I. Downey. 1994. Homosexuality. *New England Journal of Medicine* 331(14): 923–30.

Friend, R. A. 1980. Gayging: Adjustment and the older gay male. *Alternative Lifestyle* 3(2): 231–48.

———. 1990. Older lesbian and gay people: A theory of successful aging. *Journal of Homosexuality* 20(3–4): 99–118.

Friskopp, H. & S. Silverstein. 1995. *Straight jobs, gay lives: Gay and lesbian professionals, the Harvard Business School, and the American workplace*. New York: Scribner.

Garnets, L. D. & D. C. Kimmel (Eds.). 1993. *Psychological perspectives on lesbian and gay male experiences*. New York: Columbia University Press.

Garnets, L., G. M. Herek, & B. Levy. 1993. Violence and victimization of lesbians and gay men: Mental health consequences. In Garnets & Kimmel (Eds.), *Psychological perspectives on lesbian and gay male experiences*, 579–98. New York: Columbia University Press.

Garnets, L., K. Hancock, S. D. Cochran, J. Goodchilds, & L. A. Peplau. 1991. Issues in psychotherapy with lesbians and gay men: A survey of psychologists. *American Psychologist* 46(9): 964–72.

Geballe, S., J. Gruendel, & W. Andiman (Eds.). 1995. *Forgotten children of the AIDS epidemic*. New Haven: Yale University Press.

Gelles, R. J. & M. A. Straus. 1988. Intimate violence. New York: Simon & Schuster.

George, S. 1993. *Women and bisexuality*. London: Scarlet Press.

Germain, C. B. 1973. An ecological approach in casework practice. *Social Casework* 54(7): 323–30.

———. 1978. General-systems theory and ego psychology: An ecological perspective. *Social Service Review* 52(4): 535–50.

———. 1981. The ecological approach to people-environment transactions. *Social Casework* 62(6): 323–31.

———. 1991. *Human behavior and the social environment: An ecological view*. New York: Columbia University Press.

Germain, C. B. & A. Gitterman. 1980. *The life model of social work practice*. New York: Columbia University Press.

Gibelman, M. & P. H. Schervish. 1993. *Who we are: The social work labor force as reflected in the NASW membership*. Washington, D.C.: NASW Press.

Gitterman, A. & C. B. Germain. 1976. Social work practice: The life model. *Social Service Review* 4: 601–10.

Glassgold, J. M. & S. Iasenza (Eds.). 1995. *Lesbians and psychoanalysis: Revolutions in theory and practice*, 39–61. New York: Free Press.

Glassman, C. 1995. Lesbians and HIV disease. *Journal of Gay and Lesbian Social Services* 2(3–4): 61–74.

Glaus, K. O. 1989. Alcoholism, chemical dependency, and the lesbian client. *Women and Therapy* 8(1–2): 131–44.

Gochros, J. S. 1995. Bisexuality. In R. L. Edwards (Ed.), *Encyclopedia of Social Work*, 299–304. 19th ed. Silver Spring, Md.: NASW Press.

Goffman, E. 1963. *Stigma: Notes on the management of spoiled identity*. Englewood Cliffs, N.J.: Prentice-Hall.

Gold, R. S. 1995. Rethinking HIV prevention strategies for gay men. *Focus: A Guide to AIDS Research and Counseling* 10(3): 1–4.

Goldberg, S. B. 1996. No special rights: Supreme Court's Amendment 2 decision has long-range implications. *HRC Quarterly* (Summer): 4–5.

Golden, C. 1987. Diversity and variability in women's sexual identities. In Boston Lesbian Psychologies Collective (Ed.), *Lesbian psychologies*, 18–34. Urbana: University of Illinois Press.

Goldstein, H. 1992. If social work hasn't made progress as a science, might it be an art? *Families in Society* 73(1): 48–55.

Gondolf, E. 1985. *Men who batter: An integrated approach to stopping wife abuse.* Holmes Beach, Fla.: Learning Publications.

Gonsiorek, J. C. 1982a. Results of psychological testing on homosexual populations. *American Behavioral Scientist* 25: 385–96.

———. 1982b. The use of diagnostic concepts in working with gay and lesbian populations. In Gonsiorek (Ed.), *Homosexuality and psychotherapy: A practitioner's handbook of affirmative models*, 9–20. Beverly Hills, Calif.: Sage.

———. 1985. *A guide to psychotherapy with gay and lesbian clients.* New York: Harrington Park Press.

———. 1988. Mental health issues of gay and lesbian adolescents. *Journal of Adolescent Health Care* 9(2): 114–22.

———. 1991. The empirical basis for the demise of the illness model of homosexuality. In Gonsiorek & Weinrich (Eds.), *Homosexuality: Research implications for public policy*, 115–36. Newbury Park, Calif.: Sage.

———. 1993a. Mental health issues of gay and lesbian adolescents. In Garnets & Kimmel (Eds.), *Psychological perspectives on lesbian and gay male experiences*, 469–85. New York: Columbia University Press.

———. 1993b. Threat, stress, and adjustment: Mental health and the workplace for gay and lesbian individuals. In L. Diamant (Ed.), *Homosexual issues in the workplace*, 243–64. Washington, D.C.: Taylor & Francis.

———. 1995. Gay male identities: Concepts and issues. In D'Augelli & Patterson (Eds.), *Lesbian, gay, and bisexual identities over the lifespan*, 24–47. New York: Oxford University Press.

Gonsiorek, J. C. & J. D. Weinrich. 1991. The definition and scope of sexual orientation. In Gonsiorek & Weinrich (Eds.), *Homosexuality: Research implications for public policy*, 1–12. 2d ed. Newbury Park, Calif.: Sage.

Gonsiorek, J. C. & J. R. Rudolph. 1991. Homosexual identity: Coming out and other developmental events. In Gonsiorek & Weinrich (Eds.), *Homosexuality: Research implications for public policy*, 161–76. Newbury Park, Calif.: Sage.

Gottman, J. S. 1990. Children of gay and lesbian parents. *Marriage and Family Review* 13(3–4): 177–96.

Green, G. D. and D. M. Clunis. 1989. Married lesbians. *Women and Therapy* 8(1–2): 41–49.

Green, R. J., M. Bettinger, & E. Zacks. 1996. Are lesbian couples fused and gay male couples disengaged? Questioning gender straight jackets. In Laird & Green, (Eds.), *Lesbians and gays in couples and families*, 185–230. San Francisco: Jossey-Bass.

Greene, B. 1986. When the therapist is white and the patient is black: Consideration for psychotherapy in the feminist heterosexual and lesbian communities. In D. Howard (Ed.), *The dynamics of feminist therapy*, 41–65. New York: Haworth.

———. 1994a. Ethnic-minority lesbians and gay men: Mental health and treatment issues. *Journal of Consulting and Clinical Psychology* 62(2): 243–51.

———. 1994b. Lesbian women of color: Triple jeopardy. In L. Comas-Diaz & B. Greene (Eds.), *Women of color: Integrating ethnic and gender identities in psychotherapy*, 389–427. New York: Guilford.

Greene, B. & G. M. Herek (Eds.). *Lesbian and gay psychology: Theory, research, and clinical applications.* Thousand Oaks, Calif.: Sage.

Greene, R. R. (Ed.). 1994. *Human behavior theory: A diversity framework.* New York: Aldine de Gruyter.

Greene, Z.. 1996. Straight, but not narrow-minded. In Kay, Estepa, & Desetta (Eds.), *Out with it*, 12–14. New York: Youth Communications.

Grenwald, M. 1984. The SAGE model for serving older lesbians and gay men. *Journal of Social Work and Human Sexuality* 2(2–3): 53–61.

Griffin, C. & M. Zuckas. 1993. Coming out in psychology: Lesbian psychologists talk. *Feminism and Psychology* 3(1): 111–33.

Groth, A. N. 1978. Patterns of sexual assault against children and adolescents. In A. W. Burgess, A. N. Groth, L. L. Holmstrom, & S. M. Sgroi (Eds.), *Sexual assault of children and adolescents*, 3–24. Lexington, Mass.: Lexington Books.

Groth, A. N. & H. J. Birnbaum. 1978. Adult sexual orientation and attraction to underage persons. *Archives of Sexual Behavior* 7(3): 175–81.

Guitierrez, L. 1990. Working with women of color: An empowerment perspective. *Social Work* 35(2): 149–52.

——. 1994. Beyond coping: An empowerment perspective on stressful life events. *Journal of Sociology and Social Welfare* 21: 201–19.

Gunther, P. 1988. Rural gay men and lesbians in need of services and understanding. In Shernoff & Scott (Eds.), *The sourcebook on lesbian/gay health care*, 49–53. Washington, D.C.: National Lesbian and Gay Health Association.

——. 1992. Social work with non-traditional families. In Woodman (Ed.), *Lesbian and gay lifestyles*, 87–109. New York: Irvington.

Guttmacher Institute. 1994. *Sex and America's teenagers.* New York: Alan Guttmacher Institute.

Haldeman, D. C. 1991. Sexual orientation conversion therapy for gay men and lesbians: A scientific examination. In Gonsiorek & Weinrich (Eds.), *Homosexuality: Research implications for public policy*, 149–60. Newbury Park, Calif.: Sage.

Halifax, J. 1979. *Shamanic Voices.* New York: Dutton.

Hall, A. S. & H. R. Fradkin. 1992. Affirming gay men's mental health: Counseling with a new attitude. *Journal of Mental Health Counseling* 14(3): 362–74.

Hall, J. E. 1993. Lesbians and alcohol: Problems and paradoxes in medical notions and lesbians' beliefs. *Journal of Psychoactive Drugs* 25(2): 109–19.

Hall, M. 1978. Lesbian families: Cultural and clinical issues. *Social Work* 23(5): 380–85.

——. 1986. The lesbian corporate experience. *Journal of Homosexuality* 12(3–4): 59–75.

Hamberger, L. K. 1996. Intervention in gay male intimate violence requires coordinated efforts on multiple levels. *Journal of Gay and Lesbian Social Services* 4(1): 83–91.

Hamberger, L. K. & J. E. Hastings. 1988. Characteristics of male spouse abusers consistent with personality disorders. *Hospital and Community Psychiatry* 39(7): 763–70.

Hamer, D. & P. Copeland. 1994. *The science of desire: The search for the gay gene and the biology of behavior.* New York: Simon & Schuster.

Hammersmith, S. K. 1989. A sociological approach to counseling homosexual clients and their families. In E. Coleman (Ed.), *Integrated identity for gay men and lesbians: Psychotherapeutic approaches for emotional well-being*, 174–79). New York: Harrington Park Press.

Hamner, K. M. 1992. Gay-bashing: A social identity analysis of violence against lesbians and gay men. In Herek & Berrill (Eds.), *Hate crimes*, 179–90. Newbury Park, Calif.: Sage.

Hancock, K. A. 1995. Psychotherapy with lesbians and gay men. In D'Augelli & Patterson (Eds.), *Lesbian, gay, and bisexual identities over the lifespan*, 398–432. New York: Oxford University Press.

Hanley-Hackenbruck, P. 1988. "Coming out" and psychotherapy. *Psychiatric Annals* 18(1): 29–32.

———. 1989. Psychotherapy and the "coming out" process. *Journal of Gay and Lesbian Psychotherapy* 1(1): 21–39.

Hanson, B. 1996. The violence we face as lesbians and gay men: The landscape both outside and inside our communities. *Journal of Gay and Lesbian Social Services* 4(2): 95–113.

Hare, J. 1994. Concerns and issues faced by families headed by a lesbian couple. *Families in Society* 75(1): 27–35.

Harris, M. B., J. Nightengale, & N. Owen. 1995. Health care professionals' experiences, knowledge, and attitudes concerning homosexuality. *Journal of Gay and Lesbian Social Services* 2(2): 91–107.

Harris, M. B. & J. Vanderhoof. 1995. Attitudes towards gays and lesbians serving in the military. *Journal of Gay and Lesbian Social Services* 3(4): 23–51.

Harry, J. 1992. Conceptualizing anti-gay violence. In Herek and Berrill (Eds.), *Hate crimes*, 113–22. Newbury Park, Calif.: Sage.

———. 1993. Being out: A general model. *Journal of Homosexuality* 26(1): 25–39.

Hart, B. 1986. Lesbian battering: An examination. In K. Lobel (Ed.), *Naming the violence*, 173–89. Seattle: Seal.

Hartman, A. 1993. Out of the closet: Revolution and backlash. *Social Work* 38(3): 245–46, 360.

———. 1996. Social policy as a context for lesbian and gay families: The political is personal. In Laird & Green (Eds.), *Lesbians and gays in couples and families*, 69–85. San Francisco: Jossey-Bass.

Hartmann, H. 1958. *Ego psychology and the problem of adaptation*. New York: International Universities Press.

Harvard Mental Health Letter. 1994. AIDS and mental health—Part I (January): 1–4.

Harvey Milk Institute (HMI). 1997. Message from the executive director. *HMI Report Card* (Winter): 2.

Healy, S. 1993. Confronting ageism: A MUST for mental health. *Women and Aging* 5(1): 41–54.

Healy, T. 1993. A struggle for language: Patterns of self-disclosure in lesbian couples. *Smith College Studies in Social Work* 63(3): 247–64.

Hearn, G. 1969. Introduction. In G. Hearn (Ed.), *The general systems approach: Contributions toward an holistic conception of social work*, 1–4. New York: Council on Social Work Education.

Helfand, K. L. 1993. Therapeutic considerations in structuring a support group for the mentally ill gay/lesbian population. *Journal of Gay and Lesbian Psychotherapy* 2(1): 65–76.

Heller, D. 1985. *Power in psychotherapeutic practice*. New York: Human Services Press.

Hellman, R. E. 1992. Dual diagnosis issues with homosexual persons. In Weinstein (Ed.), *Lesbians and gay men*, 105–17. New York: Harrington Park Press.

Hepworth, D. H. 1993. *Direct social work practice, theory, and skills*. 4th ed. Belmont, Calif.: Wadsworth.

Hepworth, D. H. & J. Larsen. 1993. *Direct social work practice: Theory and skills*. Pacific Grove, Calif.: Brooks/Cole.

Herdt, G. 1992a. Introduction. In Herdt & Lindenbaum (Eds.), *The time of AIDS*, 3–26. Newbury Park, Calif.: Sage.

Herdt, G. (Ed.). 1992b. *Gay culture in America: Essays from the field*. Boston: Beacon Press.

Herdt, G. 1997. *Same sex, different cultures: Gays and lesbians across cultures*. Boulder, Colo.: Westview.

Herdt, G. & A. Boxer. 1991. Ethnographic issues in the study of AIDS. *Journal of Sex Research* 28(2): 171–88.

———. 1993. *Children of horizons: How gay and lesbian teens are leading a new way out of the closet.* Boston: Beacon Press.

Herdt, G. & S. Lindenbaum (Eds.). 1992. *The time of AIDS: Social analysis, theory, and method.* Newbury Park, Calif.: Sage.

Herek, G. 1985. Beyond "homophobia": A social psychological perspective on attitudes toward lesbians and gay men. In J. P. DeCecco (Ed.), *Bashers, baiters, and bigots: Homophobia in American society*, 1–21. New York: Harrington Park Press.

———. 1990. The context of anti-gay violence: Notes on cultural and psychological heterosexism. *Journal of Interpersonal Violence* 5(3): 316–33.

———. 1992a. Psychological heterosexism and anti-gay violence: The social psychology of bigotry and bashing. In Herek & Berrill (Eds.), *Hate crimes*, 149–69. Newbury Park, Calif.: Sage

———. 1992b. The social context of hate crimes: Notes on cultural heterosexism. In Herek & Berrill (Eds.), *Hate crimes*, 89–104. Newbury Park, Calif.: Sage.

———. 1993a. The context of antigay violence: Notes on cultural and psychological heterosexism. In Garnets & Kimmel (Eds.), *Psychological perspectives on lesbian and gay male experiences*, 89–107. New York: Columbia University Press.

———. 1993b. Sexual orientation and military service: A social science perspective. *American Psychologist* 48(5): 538–47.

———. 1995. Psychological heterosexism in the United States. In D'Augelli & Patterson (Eds.), *Lesbian, gay, and bisexual identities over the lifespan*, 321–46. New York: Oxford University Press.

Herek, G. & E. Glunt. 1988. An epidemic of stigma: Public reaction to AIDS. *American Psychologist* 43: 886–91.

Herek, G. M. & K. T. Berrill (Eds.). 1992. *Hate crimes: Confronting violence against lesbians and gay men.* Newbury Park, Calif.: Sage.

Herek, G. M., D. C. Kimmel, H. Amaro, & G. B. Melton. 1991. Avoiding heterosexist bias in psychological research. *American Psychologist* 46(9): 957–63.

Herman, J. 1992. *Trauma and recovery.* New York: Basic Books.

Heron, A. (Ed.). 1994. *Two teenagers in twenty.* Boston: Alyson.

Herrell, R. K. 1992. The symbolic strategies of Chicago's Gay and Lesbian Pride Day Parade. In Herdt (Ed.), *Gay culture in America*, 225–52. Boston: Beacon Press.

Hersch, P. 1991. Secret lives. *Family Therapy Networker* 15(1): 36–43.

Hetherington, C. & A. Orzek. 1989. Career counseling and life planning with lesbian women. *Journal of Counseling and Development* 68: 52–57.

Hetherington, C., E. Hillerbrand, & B. Etringer. 1989. Career counseling with gay men: Issues and recommendations. *Journal of Counseling and Development* 67: 452–54.

Hetrick, E. S. & A. D. Martin. 1987. Developmental issues and their resolution for gay and lesbian adolescents. *Journal of Homosexuality* 14(1–2): 25–42.

Heyward, C. 1992. Healing addiction and homophobia: Reflections on empowerment and liberation. In Weinstein (Ed.), *Lesbians and gay men*, 5–18. New York: Harrington Park Press.

Hidalgo, H. A. 1984. The Puerto Rican lesbian in the United States. In T. Darty & S. Potter (Eds.), *Women-identified women*, 105–15. Palo Alto, Calif.: Mayfield.

———. 1992. Integrating lesbian and gay content in program planning, administration, and community practice. In Woodman (Ed.), *Lesbian and gay lifestyles*, 123–32. New York: Irvington.

Hidalgo, H. A. (Ed.). 1995 (Special Edition). Introduction: Lesbians of color—a kaleidoscope. *Journal of Gay and Lesbian Social Services* 3(2): 1–5.

Hodge, J. 1975. *Cultural bases of racism and group oppression.* New York: Time Readers Press.

Hooker, E. 1957. The adjustment of the male overt homosexual. *Journal of Projective Techniques* 21: 18–31.

hooks, b. 1984. *Feminist theory: From the margin to the center.* Boston: South End Press.

Hooyman, N. R. & H. A. Kiyak. 1993. *Social gerontology: A multidisciplinary perspective.* 3d ed. Boston: Allyn & Bacon.

Hubbard, W. S., K. R. Allen, & J. A. Mancini. 1992. The GLOE program: Social services and support for older gay men and lesbians. *Generations* 16(3): 37–42.

Humphreys, G. E. 1983. Inclusion of content on homosexuality in the social work curriculum. *Journal of Social Work Education* 19(1): 55–60.

Humphries, L. 1972. *Out of the closets: The sociology of homosexual liberation.* Englewood Cliffs, N.J.: Prentice-Hall.

Hunter, J. 1990. Violence against lesbian and gay male youths. *Journal of Interpersonal Violence* 5(3): 295–300.

———. 1992. Violence against lesbian and gay male youths. In Herek & Berrill (Eds.), *Hate crimes*, 76–82. Newbury Park, Calif.: Sage.

Hunter, J. & R. Schaecher. 1987. Stresses on lesbian and gay adolescents in schools. *Social Work in Education* 9(3): 180–88.

———. 1990. Lesbian and gay youth. In M. J. Rotherram-Borus, J. Bradley, & N. Obolensky (Eds.), *Planning to live: Evaluating and treating suicidal teens in community settings*, 297–316. Norman: University of Oklahoma Press.

———. 1994. AIDS prevention for lesbian, gay, and bisexual adolescents. *Families in Society* 75(6): 93–99.

Icard, L. D. 1986 (Special Issues). Black gay men and conflicting social identities: Sexual orientation versus racial identity. In J. Gripton and M. Valentich (Eds.), *Journal of Social Work and Human Sexuality: Social work practice in sexual problems* 4(1–2): 83–93.

———. 1996. Assessing the psychosocial well-being of African American gays: A multidimensional perspective. *Journal of Gay and Lesbian Social Services* 5(2–3): 25–50.

Isay, R. A. 1989. *Being homosexual: Gay men and their development.* New York: Farrar, Straus & Giroux.

Island, D. & P. Letellier. 1991. *Men who beat the men who love them: Battered gay men and domestic violence.* New York: Harrington Park Press.

Jackson, S. 1982. *Childhood and sexuality.* London: Basil Blackwell.

Jacobson, S. 1995. Methodological issues in research on older lesbians. *Journal of Gay and Lesbian Social Services* 3(1): 43–56.

Janoff-Bulman, R. 1979. Characterological versus behavioral self-blame: Inquiries into depression and rape. *Journal of Personality and Social Psychology* 37: 1798–1809.

———. 1982. Esteem and control bases of blame: "Adaptive" strategies for victims versus observers. *Journal of Personality and Social Psychology* 50: 180–92.

Jay, K. (Ed.). 1995. *Dyke life.* New York: Basic Books.

Jay, K. & A. Young (Eds.). 1977. *Out of the closets: Voices of gay liberation.* New York: Jove.

Jazwinski, R. M. 1994. A study comparing lesbian, gay, and heterosexual college students on drinking, problem-related drinking, and on the impact of several psychosocial variables on drinking behaviors. Ph.D. diss., New York University (DA-9502373 Dissertation Abstracts International 55[9]).

Johnson, M. T. & J. J. Kelly. 1979. Deviate sex behavior in aging: Social definition and the lives of older gay people. In O. J. Kaplan (Ed.), *Psychotherapy of aging*, 243–58. New York: Academic Press.

Johnson, T. W. & M. S. Keren. 1996. Creating and maintaining boundaries in male couples. In Laird & Green (Eds.), *Lesbians and gays in couples and families*, 231–50. San Francisco: Jossey-Bass.

Johnston, W. I. 1995. *HIV-negative: How the uninfected are affected by AIDS*. New York Insight Books.

Katz, J. 1976. *Gay American history: Lesbians and gay men in the U.S.A.* New York: Crowell.

———. 1995. *The invention of heterosexuality*. New York: Dutton.

Kaufman, G. 1992. *Shame: The power of caring*. Rochester, Vt.: Schenkman Books.

Kay, P., A. Estepa, & A. Desetta (Eds.). 1996. *Out with it: Gay and straight teens write about homosexuality*. New York: Youth Communications.

Kehoe, M. 1989. *Lesbians over 60 speak for themselves*. New York: Harrington Park Press.

Kelly, J. 1977. The aging male homosexual: Myth and reality. *The Gerontologist* 17(4): 328–32.

Kimmel, D. C. 1978. Adult development and aging: A gay perspective. *Journal of Social Issues* 34(3): 113–30.

———. 1993. Adult development and aging: A gay perspective. In Garnets & Kimmel (Eds.), *Psychological perspectives on lesbian and gay male experiences*, 517–34. New York, Columbia University Press.

Kimmel, D. C. & B. E. Sang. 1995. Lesbians and gay men in midlife. In D'Augelli & Patterson (Eds.), *Gay, lesbian, and bisexual identities over the lifespan*, 190–214. New York: Oxford University Press.

Kinsey, A. C., W. B. Pomeroy, & C. E. Martin. 1948. *Sexual behavior in the human male*. Philadelphia: W. B. Saunders.

Kinsey, A. C., W. B. Pomeroy, C. E. Martin, & P. H. Gebhard. 1953. *Sexual behavior in the human female*. Philadelphia: W. B. Saunders.

Kitzinger, C. 1991. Lesbians and gay men in the workplace: Psychosocial issues. In M. J. Davidson & J. Earnshaw (Eds.), *Vulnerable workers: Psychosocial and legal issues*, 223–57. New York: Wiley.

Klein, F. 1993. *The bisexual option*. 2d. ed. Binghamton, N.Y.: Haworth.

Klein, F. & T. J. Wolf (Eds.). 1985. *Two lives to lead: Bisexuality in men and women*. New York: Harrington Park Press.

Klinkenberg, D. & S. Rose. 1994. Dating scripts of gay men and lesbians. *Journal of Homosexuality* 26(4): 23–35.

Knox, M. & F. Clark. 1993. Early HIV detection: A community mental health care role. *AIDS Patient Care* 7: 169–72.

Kottler, J. A. 1991. *The complete therapist*. San Francisco: Jossey-Bass.

Kramer, L. 1989. *Reports from the holocaust: The making of an AIDS activist*. New York: St. Martin's.

Krieger, S. 1982. Lesbian identity and community: Recent social science literature. *Signs* 8: 91–108.

Kurdek, L. A. 1988. Perceived social support in gays and lesbians in cohabiting relationships. *Journal of Personality and Social Psychology* 54(3): 504–509.

———. 1995. Lesbian and gay couples. In D'Augelli & Patterson (Eds.), *Lesbian, gay, and bisexual identities over the lifespan*, 243–61. New York: Oxford University Press.

Kus, R. J. 1989. Alcoholism and the non-acceptance of the gay self: The critical link. *Journal of Homosexuality* 15(1–2): 25–41.

——. 1992. Spirituality in everyday life: Experiences of gay men of Alcoholics Anonymous. In Weinstein (Ed.), *Lesbians and gay men*, 49–66. New York: Harrington Park Press.

Kus, R. J. & G. B. Smith. 1995. Referrals and resources for chemically dependent gay and lesbian clients. *Journal of Gay and Lesbian Social Services* 2(1): 91–107.

Kus, R. J. & M. A. Latkovich. 1995. Special interest groups in Alcoholics Anonymous: A focus on gay men's groups. *Journal of Gay and Lesbian Social Services* 2(1): 67–83.

Laird, J. 1993. Lesbians and lesbian families: Multiple reflections. *Smith College Studies in Social Work* 63(3): 209–13.

——. 1994. Lesbian families: A cultural perspective. *Smith College Studies in Social Work* 64(3): 263–96.

Laird, J. & R. J. Green (Eds). 1996. *Lesbians and gays in couples and families: A handbook for therapists*. San Francisco: Jossey-Bass.

Land, H. (Ed.). 1992. *AIDS: A complete guide to psychosocial intervention*. Milwaukee, Wis.: Family Service of America.

Larcom, B. & J. C. Weiss. 1990. The national group violence project. Unpublished MS.

Laumann, E. O., J. H. Gagnon, R. T. Michael, & S. Michaels. 1994. *The social organization of sexuality: Sexual practices in the United States*. Chicago: University of Chicago Press.

Lease, S. H., P. A. Cogdal, & D. Smith. 1995. Counseling expectancies related to counselors' sexual orientation and clients' internalized homophobia. *Journal of Gay and Lesbian Psychotherapy* 2(3): 51–65.

Lee, J. A. 1992. Teaching content related to lesbian and gay identity formation. In Woodman (Ed.), *Lesbian and gay lifestyles*, 1–22. New York: Irvington.

——. 1990. Foreword: Special issue on gay midlife and maturity. *Journal of Homosexuality* 20(3–4): 1–6.

——. 1987. What can homosexual aging studies contribute to theories of aging? *Journal of Homosexuality* 13(4): 43–71.

Lenna, H. R. 1992. The outsiders: Group work with young homosexuals. In Woodman (Ed.), *Lesbian and gay lifestyles*, 67–86. New York: Irvington.

Leukefeld, C. & M. Fimbres (Eds.). 1987. *Responding to AIDS: Psychosocial initiatives*. Silver Spring, Md.: NASW Press.

Le Vay, S. 1991 (August 31). A difference in hypothalamic structure between heterosexual and homosexual men. *Science* 253(5023): 1034–37.

Levi, J. 1992. Homophobia and AIDS public policy. In Blumenfeld (Ed.), *Homophobia: How we all pay the price*, 217–32. Boston: Beacon Press.

Levi, A. J. 1993. Stigma management: A new clinical service. *Families in Society* 74(4): 226–31.

Levine, M. P. 1992. The implications of constructionist theory for social research on the AIDS epidemic among gay men. In Herdt & Lindenbaum (Eds.). *The time of AIDS*, 185–98. Newbury Park, Calif.: Sage.

Levinson, D. J. 1978. *Seasons of a man's life*. New York: Knopf.

Levy, E. F. 1992. Strengthening the coping resources of lesbian families. *Families in Society* 73(1): 23–31.

Lewes, K. 1988. *The psychoanalytic theory of male homosexuality*. New York: Simon & Schuster.

Lewis, D. 1990. Gay and lesbian social work interns "coming out" in field placements. Master's thesis, Smith College School for Social Work, Northampton, Mass.

Lewis, M. 1992. *Shame: The exposed self*. New York: Free Press.

Liu, P. & C. S. Chan. 1996. Lesbian, gay, and bisexual Asian Americans and their families. In Laird & Green (Eds.), *Lesbians and gays in couples and families*, 137–52. San Francisco: Jossey-Bass.

Livingston, D. 1996. A systems approach to AIDS counseling for gay couples. *Journal of Gay and Lesbian Social Services* 4(2): 83–93.

Livingston, J. 1991. *Paris Is Burning* (Miramax, 78 min.).

Lloyd, G. A. 1992. Contextual and clinical issues in providing services to gay men. In Land (Ed.), *AIDS*, 91–105. Milwaukee, Wis.: Family Service of America.

Lloyd, G. A. & M. A. Kuszelewicz (Eds.). 1995 (AIDS Special Issue). HIV disease: Lesbians, gays, and the social services. *Journal of Gay and Lesbian Social Services* 2(3–4): 1–194.

———. 1995. *HIV disease: Lesbians, gays, and the social services*. New York: Harrington Park Press.

Lloyd, G. A., N. I. Lipscomb, & R. N. Johnson. 1991. *Social work and the HIV / substance abuse connection*. New Orleans: Tulane University School of Social Work Institute for Research and Training in HIV / AIDS Counseling and the Center for AIDS and Substance Abuse Training.

Lockard, D. 1985. The lesbian community: An anthropological approach. *Journal of Homosexuality* 11(3–4): 83–95.

Loiacano, D. K. 1993. Gay identity issues among black Americans: Racism, homophobia, and the need for validation. In Garnets & Kimmel (Eds.), *Psychological perspectives on lesbian and gay male experiences*, 364–75. New York: Columbia University Press.

Longres, J. F. 1981, 1995 (2d ed). *Human behavior in the social environment*. Itasca, Ill.: F. E. Peacock.

Longres, J. F. (Ed.). 1996 (Special Edition). Preface: Men of color—A context for service of homosexually active men. *Journal of Gay and Lesbian Social Services* 5(2–3): xix–xxiii.

Lord, K. B. & C. A. Reid. 1995. Drawing lines in the dirt: Rural lesbian communities—Models of self-definition and self-determination. *Journal of Gay and Lesbian Social Services* 3(4): 13–22.

Lott-Whitehead, L. & C. T. Tully. 1993. The family lives of lesbian mothers. *Smith College Studies in Social Work* 63(3): 265–80.

Lowenstein, R. J. & S. S. Shartstein. 1983. Neuropsychiatric aspects of AIDS. *Journal of Psychiatry in Medicine* 13: 255–60.

Lucas, V. A. 1992. An investigation of the health care preferences of the lesbian population. *Health Care for Women International* 13(1): 221–28.

Lukes, C. A. & H. Land. 1990. Biculturality and homosexuality. *Social Work* 35(2): 155–61.

Lynch, V. J., G. Lloyd, & M. F. Fimbres. (Eds.). 1993. *The changing face of AIDS; Implications for social work practice*. Westport, Conn.: Auburn House.

Lynn, D. 1966. The process of learning parental and sex-role identification. *Journal of Marriage and the Family* 28(4): 466–70.

MacDonald, A. P., Jr. 1981. Bisexuality: Some comments on research and theory. *Journal of Homosexuality* 6(3): 21–35.

MacDonald, B. 1986. Beyond the sisterhood: Ageism in women's studies. In J. Alexander, D. Berrow, L. Domitrovich, M. Donnelly, & C. McLean (Eds.), *Women and aging*, 20–25. Corvallis, Ore.: Calyx Books.

MacEachron, A. E. 1995. Potential use of single-system designs for evaluating affirmative psychotherapy with lesbian women and gay men. *Journal of Gay and Lesbian Social Services: Research Issues* 3(1): 19–28.

Mackelprang, R. W., J. A. Ray, & M. Hernandez-Peck. 1996. Social work education and sexual orientation: Faculty, students, and curriculum issues. *Journal of Gay and Lesbian Social Services* 5(4): 17–32.

MacEwan, I. 1994. Differences in assessment and treatment approaches for homosexual clients. *Drug and Alcohol Review* 13: 57–62.

Macks, J. 1987. Meeting the psychosocial needs of people with AIDS. In Leukefeld & Fimbres (Eds.), *Responding to AIDS*, 25–38. Silver Spring, Md.: NASW Press.

Macks, J. & C. Ryan. 1988. Lesbians working in AIDS: An overview of our history and experience. In Shernoff & Scott (Eds.), *The sourcebook on lesbian/gay health care*, 198–201. Washington, D.C.: National Lesbian and Gay Health Association.

Magee, M. & D. C. Miller. 1992. "She foreswore her womanhood": Psychoanalytic views of female homosexuality. *Clinical Social Work Journal* 20(1): 67–87.

Maguire, L. 1983. *Understanding social networks*. Beverly Hills, Calif.: Sage.

Mallon, G. P. 1992. Gay and no place to go: Assessing the needs of gay and lesbian adolescents in out-of-home care settings. *Child Welfare* 71(6): 547–56.

——. 1994. Counseling strategies with gay and lesbian youth. In De Crescenzo (Ed.), *Helping gay and lesbian youth*, 75–91. New York: Haworth.

——. 1998. *We don't exactly get the welcome wagon: The experiences of gay and lesbian adolescents in North America's child welfare system*. New York: Columbia University Press.

Malyon, A. K. 1981. The homosexual adolescent: Developmental issues and social bias. *Child Welfare* 60(5): 321–30.

——. 1982a. Biphasic aspects of homosexual identity formation. *Psychotherapy: Theory, Research, and Practice* 19(3): 335–40.

——. 1982b. Psychotherapeutic implications of internalized homophobia in gay men. *Journal of Homosexuality* 7(2–3): 59–69.

——. 1993. Psychotherapeutic implications of internalized homophobia in gay men. Reprinted in C. Cornett (Ed.), *Affirmative dynamic psychotherapy with gay men*. 77–92. Northvale, N.J.: Jason Aronson.

Mancoske, R. J. & T. Lindhorst. 1995. The ecological context of HIV/AIDS counseling: Issues for lesbians and gays and their significant others. *Journal of Gay and Lesbian Social Services* 2(3–4): 25–40.

Maniaci, T. & F. M. Rzeznik. 1993. *One nation under God* (video). New York: First Run Features.

Marcia, J. E. 1980. Identity in adolescence. In J. Adelson (Ed.), *Handbook of adolescent psychiatry*, 159–87. New York: Wiley.

Marcus, E. 1992. *Making history: The struggle for gay and lesbian equal rights, 1945–1990*. New York: HarperCollins.

Marcuse, H. 1962. *Eros and civilization*. New York: Vintage.

Margolies, L., M. Becker, & K. Jackson-Brewer. 1987. Internalized homophobia: Treating the oppressor within. In the Boston Lesbian Psychologies Collective (Eds.), *Lesbian psychologies*, 229–41. Urbana: University of Illinois Press.

Marrujo, B. & M. Kreger. 1996. Definition of roles in abusive lesbian relationships. *Journal of Gay and Lesbian Social Services* 4(1): 23–34.

Martin, A. D. 1982. Learning to hide: The socialization of the gay adolescent. In S. C. Feinstein,

J. G. Looney, A. Schartzberg, & A. Sorosky (Eds.), *Adolescent psychiatry: Developmental and clinical studies*, 52–65. Vol. 10. Chicago: University of Chicago Press.

———. 1993. *The lesbian and gay parenting handbook: Creating and raising our families.* New York: HarperCollins.

Martin, A. D. & E. S. Hetrick. 1988. The stigmatization of the gay and lesbian adolescent. *Journal of Homosexuality* 15(1–2): 163–82.

Martin, J. I. 1995. Gay and lesbian faculty in social work: Roles and responsibilities. *Journal of Gay and Lesbian Social Services* 3(4): 1–12.

Martin, J. I. & J. Knox. 1995. HIV risk behavior in gay men with unstable self-esteem. *Journal of Gay and Lesbian Social Services* 2(2): 21–41.

Martinson, F. M. 1994. *The sexual life of children.* Westport, Conn.: Bergin & Garvey.

Masters, W. H. & V. E. Johnson. 1966. *Reproductive Research Foundation* (Conference Proceedings). Boston: Little Brown.

———. 1976. *Ethical issues in sex therapy and research* (Conference Proceedings). Boston: Little Brown.

Mattaini, M. A. 1997. *Clinical practice with individuals.* Washington, D.C.: NASW Press.

Matteson, D. R. 1985. Bisexual men in marriages: Is a positive homosexual identity and stable marriage possible? In Klein & Wolf (Eds.), *Two lives to lead*, 149–71. New York: Harrington Park Press.

Mattison, A. M. & D. P. McWhirter. 1994. Serodiscordant male couples. *Journal of Gay and Lesbian Social Services* 1(2): 83–100. Reprinted in L. A. Kurdek (Ed.), *Social services for gay and lesbian couples*, 83–99. New York: Harrington Park Press, 1994.

Mayerson, P. & H. Lief. 1965. Psychotherapy of homosexuals: A follow-up study of nineteen cases. In J. Marmor (Ed.), *Sexual inversion.* New York: Basic Books.

Mays, V. M., G. W. Albee, & S. F. Schneider (Eds). 1990. *Primary prevention of AIDS: Psychosocial approaches.* Newbury Park, Calif.: Sage.

McAnulty R. D. 1993. The helping professions: Attitudes toward homosexuality. In L. Diamant (Ed.), *Homosexual issues in the workplace*, 105–18. Washington, D.C.: Taylor & Francis.

McDermott, D., L. Tyndall, & J. W. Lichtenberg. 1989. Factors related to counselor preference among gays and lesbians. *Journal of Counseling and Development* 68: 31–35.

McDonell, J. 1993. Judgements of personal responsibility for HIV infection: An attributional analysis. *Social Work* 38(4): 403–10.

McFadden, R. D. 1992. Judge overturns U.S. rule blocking "offensive" educational material on AIDS. *New York Times*, May 12, B3.

McHenry, S. S. & J. W. Johnson. 1993. Homophobia in the therapist and gay or lesbian client: Conscious and unconscious collusions in self-hate. *Psychotherapy* 30(1): 141–51.

McIntosh, P. 1988. *White privilege and male privilege: A personal account of coming to see correspondences through work in women's studies* (pamphlet). Wellesley, Mass.: Center for Research on Women, Wellesley College (19 pp.).

McKirnan, D. J. & P. L. Peterson. 1989a. Alcohol and drug use among homosexual men and women: Epidemiology and population characteristics. *Addictive Behaviors* 14: 545–53.

———. 1989b. Psychosocial and cultural factors in alcohol and drug abuse: Analysis of a homosexual community. *Addictive Behaviors* 14: 555–63.

McMillan, D. W. & D. M. Chavis. 1986. Sense of community: A definition and theory. *Journal of Community Psychology* 14: 6–23.

McNally, E. B. & D. G. Finnegan. 1992. Lesbian recovering alcoholics: A report on research and applications to treatment. *Journal of Clinical Dependency Treatment* 5(1): 93–103.

McNaught, B. 1988. *On being gay*. New York: St. Martin's.

———. 1993. *Gay issues in the workplace*. New York: St. Martin's.

McNeill, J. 1993. *The church and the homosexual*. Boston: Beacon Press.

McSpadden, J. R. 1993. Homosexuality and the church. In L. Diamant (Ed.), *Homosexual issues in the workplace*, 91–103. Washington, D.C.: Taylor & Francis.

McWhirter, D. P. & A. M. Mattison. 1984. *The male couple: How relationships develop*. Englewood Cliffs, N.J.: Prentice-Hall.

Melton, G. B. 1989. Public policy and private prejudice: Psychology and law on gay rights. *American Psychologist* 44(6): 933–40.

Mendez, J. M. 1996. Serving gays and lesbians of color who are survivors of domestic violence. *Journal of Gay and Lesbian Social Services* 4(1): 53–60.

Menzies-Lyth, I. 1988. *Containing anxiety in social institutions: Selected essays*. London: Free Association Press.

Merrill, G. S. 1996. Ruling the exceptions: Same-sex battering and domestic violence theory. *Journal of Gay and Lesbian Social Services* 4(1): 9–22.

Meyer, C. H. 1993. *Assessment in social work practice*. New York: Columbia University Press.

———. 1996. Reflection. *Reflections: Narratives of professional helping* 2(2): 49–65.

Meyer, I. H. 1995. Minority stress and mental health in gay men. *Journal of Health and Social Behavior* 36: 38–56.

Meyer, P., E. K. Tapley, & M. Bazargan. 1996. Depression in HIV symptomatic gay and bisexual men. *Journal of Gay and Lesbian Social Services* 5(4): 69–85.

Miller, D. C. 1995. What is needed for true equality: An overview of policy issues for women. In Davis (Ed.), *Building on women's strengths*, 27–56. New York: Haworth Press.

Miller, G. V. 1995. *The gay male's odyssey in the corporate world: From disempowerment to empowerment*. New York: Harrington Park Press.

Mills, C. W. 1959. *The sociological imagination*. New York: Oxford University Press.

Minnigerode, F. A. & M. R. Adelman. 1978. Elderly homosexual women and men: Report on a pilot study. *Family Coordinator* 27(4): 451–56.

Miranda, D. 1996. I hated myself. In Kay, Estepa, & Desetta (Eds.), *Out with it*, 34–39. New York: Youth Communications.

Monette, P. 1992. *Becoming a man: Half a life story*. New York: Harcourt Brace Jovanovich.

Money, J. 1980. Genetic and chromosomal aspects of homosexual etiology. In J. Marmor (Ed.), *Homosexual behavior: A modern appraisal*, 233–49. New York: Basic Books.

Money, J. & A. A. Ehrhardt. 1972. *Man and woman, boy and girl: The differentiation and dimorphism of gender identity from conception to maturity*. Baltimore: Johns Hopkins University Press.

Moraga, C. 1983. *Loving the war years: Lo que nunca paso por sus labios*. Boston: South End Press.

Morales, A. T. & B. W. Sheafor (Eds.). 1992. *Social work: A profession of many faces*. 6th ed. Boston: Allyn & Bacon.

Morales, E. 1996. Gender roles among Latino gay and bisexual men: Implications for family and couple relationships. In Laird & Green (Eds.), *Lesbians and gays in couples and families*, 272–97. San Francisco: Jossey-Bass.

Morales, J. 1992. Community social work with Puerto Rican communities in the United States.

In F. Rivera & E. Erlich (Eds.), *Community organizing in a diverse society*, 89–106. Needham Heights, Mass.: Allyn & Bacon.

——. 1995. Gay Latinos and AIDS: A framework for HIV/AIDS prevention curriculum. *Journal of Gay and Lesbian Social Services* 2(3–4): 89–105. Reprinted in Lloyd & Kuszelewicz (Eds.), *HIV disease*, 89–105. New York: Harrington Park Press, 1995.

Morales, J. & M. Bok (Eds.). 1992. *Multicultural human services for AIDS treatment and prevention: Policy perspectives and planning.* New York: Haworth.

Moreau, M. 1990. Empowerment through advocacy and consciousness-raising: Implication of a structural approach to social work. *Journal of Sociology and Social Welfare* 17(2): 53–67.

Morgan, K. S. & L. S. Brown. 1991. Lesbian career development, work behavior, and vocational counseling. *Counseling Psychologist* 19(2): 273–91.

Morrow, D. F. 1993. Social work with gay and lesbian adolescents. *Social Work* 38(6): 655–60.

——. 1996. Heterosexism: Hidden discrimination in social work education. *Journal of Gay and Lesbian Social Services* 5(4): 1–16.

Moses, A. E. & R. O. Hawkins. 1982. *Counseling lesbian women and gay men: A life-issues approach.* St. Louis: C. V. Mosby.

Moss, A. R. et al. 1988. Seropositivity for HIV and the development of AIDS or AIDS-related conditions: Three-year follow-up of the San Francisco general hospital cohort. *British Medical Journal* 296: 745–50.

Murphy, B. C. 1994. Difference and diversity: Gay and lesbian couples. *Journal of Gay and Lesbian Social Services* 1(2): 5–31.

Murray, S. O. 1992. Components of gay community in San Francisco. In Herdt (Ed.), *Gay culture in America*, 107–46. Boston: Beacon Press.

Muzio, C. 1993. Lesbian co-parenting: On being/being with the invisible (m)other. *Smith College Studies in Social Work* 63(3): 215–29.

——. 1996. Lesbians choosing children: Creating families, creating narratives. In Laird & Green (Eds.), *Lesbians and gays in couples and families*, 358–69. San Francisco: Jossey-Bass.

Myers, H. F. 1989. Urban stress and mental health in black youths: An epidemiological and conceptual update. In R. Jones (Ed.), *Black adolescents*, 123–52). Berkeley, Calif.: Cobb & Henry.

NASW News. 1997 (February). Abused gay student wins case (p. 7).

National Association of Social Workers (NASW). 1977. Gay issues. *Social Work Speaks: NASW Policy Statements.* Washington, D.C.: NASW Press.

——. 1980, 1996. *Code of Ethics.* Washington, D.C.: NASW Press.

——. 1991. Lesbian and gay issues. *Social Work Speaks: NASW Policy Statements*, 147–51. Silver Spring, Md.: NASW Press.

——. 1997a. Gender-, ethnic-, and race-based workplace discrimination. *Special Work Speaks: NASW Policy Statements*, 146–154. Washington, D.C.: NASW Press.

——. 1997b. Lesbian, gay, and bisexual issues. *Social Work Speaks: NASW Policy Statements*, 198–209. Washington, D.C.: NASW Press.

National Association of Social Workers, National Committee on Lesbian, Gay, and Bisexual Issues. 1992. *Position Statement: "Reparative" or "Conversion" therapies for lesbians and gay men.* Washington, D.C.: NASW Press.

National Gay and Lesbian Task Force (NGLTF), Policy Institute. 1991. Anti-gay/lesbian violence: Victimization and defamation in 1990. Washington, D.C.: NGLTF.

——. 1996 (January). *Beyond the beltway: State of the states 1995.* Washington, D.C.: NGLTF.

Nava, M. & R. Dawidoff. 1994. *Created equal:Why gay rights matter to America.* NewYork: St. Martin's.

Needham, R. 1977. Casework intervention with a homosexual adolescent. *Social Casework* 58(7): 387–94.

Neisen, J. H. 1990. Heterosexism: Redefining homophobia for the 1990s. *Journal of Gay and Lesbian Psychotherapy* 1(3): 21–35.

Neisen, J. H. & H. Sandall. 1990. Alcohol and other drug abuse in a gay/lesbian population: Related to victimization? *Journal of Psychology and Human Sexuality* 3(1): 151–68.

Newman, B. M. & P. R. Newman. 1987. *Development through life: A psychosocial approach.* 4th ed. Belmont, Calif.: Dorsey Press.

Newman, B. S. 1989. Including curriculum content on lesbian and gay issues. *Journal of Social Work Education* 25(3): 202–11.

Newton, D. E. 1978. Homosexual behavior and child molestation: A review of the evidence. *Adolescence* 13(49): 205–15.

NewYork Native (editorial). 1995 (January 2). Gay anti-violent project survey: Killers of gay men and lesbians more brutal, police less effective (p. 6).

Nichols, M. 1987. Lesbian sexuality: Issues and developing theory. In Boston Lesbian Psychologies Collective (Ed.), *Lesbian psychologies*, 97–125. Urbana: University of Illinois Press.

Nichols, M. & S. R. Leiblum. 1986. Lesbianism as a personal identity and social role: A model. *Affilia* 1(1): 48–59.

Nicoloff, L. K. & E. A. Stiglitz. 1987. Lesbian alcoholism: Etiology, treatment, and recovery. In the Boston Lesbian Psychologies Collective (Eds.), *Lesbian psychologies*, 283–93. Urbana: University of Illinois Press.

Nicolosi, J. 1991. *Reparative therapy of male homosexuality: A new clinical approach.* Northvale, N.J.: Aronson.

Nord, D. 1996. Assessing the negative effects of multiple AIDS-related loss on the gay individual and community. *Journal of Gay and Lesbian Social Services* 4(3): 1–34.

Norris, W. P. 1991. Liberal attitudes and homophobic acts: The paradoxes of homosexual experience in a liberal institution. *Journal of Homosexuality* 22(3–4): 81–120.

O'Connell, A. 1993. Voices from the heart: The developmental impact of a mother's lesbianism on her adolescent children. *Smith College Studies in Social Work* 63(3): 281–300.

O'Connor, N. & J. Ryan. 1993. *Wild desires and mistaken identities: Lesbianism and psychoanalysis.* New York: Columbia University Press.

Odets, W. 1995a. *In the shadows of the epidemic: Being HIV-negative in the age of AIDS.* Durham, N.C.: Duke University Press.

——. 1995b. Survivor's guilt in HIV-negative gay men. In Odets & Shernoff (Eds.), *The second decade of AIDS*, 201–18. New York: Hatherleigh Press.

Odets, W. & M. Shernoff (Eds.). 1995. *The second decade of AIDS: A mental health practice handbook.* New York: Hatherleigh Press.

Odets, W. & W. F. Skinner. 1996. The prevalence of victimization and its effects on mental well-being among lesbian and gay people. *Journal of Homosexuality* 30(3): 93–121.

Offer, D. 1980. Adolescent development: A normative perspective. In S. I. Greenspan & G. H. Pollock (Eds.), *The course of life*, vol 2, *Latency, adolescence, and youth.* U.S. Department of Health and Human Services Publication No. (ADM) 80–999. Washington, D.C.

Offer, D. & J. B. Offer. 1975. *From teenage to young manhood: A psychological study*. New York: Basic Books.

Offer, D. & M. Sabshin. 1984. Adolescence: Empirical perspectives. In Offer & Sabshin (Eds.), *Normality and the life cycle: A critical integration*, 84–113. New York: Basic Books.

Offer, D., E. Ostrov, & K. Howard. 1981. *The adolescent: A psychological self-portrait*. New York: Basic Books.

Olson, M. R. 1987. A study of gay and lesbian teachers. *Journal of Homosexuality* 13(4): 73–81.

Orzek, A. M. 1988. The lesbian victim of sexual assault: Special considerations for the mental health professional. *Women and Therapy* 8(1–2): 107–17.

Ozawa, M. N. 1995. The economic status of vulnerable older women. *Social Work* 40(3): 323–31.

Padilla, A. (Ed.). 1980. *Acculturation theory, models, and some new findings*. Boulder, Colo.: Westview.

Paradis, B. A. 1990. The psychological implication of positive HIV test results for gay men. Ph.D. diss., Simmons College, Boston.

——. 1991. Seeking intimacy and integration: Gay men in the era of AIDS. *Smith College Studies in Social Work* 613: 260–74.

Parker, S. G. 1994. Curing homophobia. *The New Physician* 43(3): 13–19.

Parr, R. G. & L. E. Jones. 1996. Should CSWE allow social work programs in religious institutions an exemption from the accreditation nondiscrimination standard related to sexual orientation? *Journal of Social Work Education* 32(3): 297–313.

Patterson, C. J. 1992. Children of lesbian and gay parents. *Child Development* 63: 1025–42.

——. 1994a. Children of the lesbian baby boom: Behavioral adjustment, self-concepts, and sex role identity. In Greene & Herek (Eds.), *Lesbian and gay psychology*, 156–75. Thousand Oaks, Calif.: Sage.

——. 1994b. Lesbian and gay couples considering parenthood: An agenda for research, service, and advocacy. In L. A Kurdek (Ed.), *Social services for lesbian and gay couples*, 33–55. New York: Harrington Park Press.

——. 1995a. Families of the lesbian baby boom: Parents' division of labor and children's adjustment. *Developmental Psychology* 31(1): 115–23.

——. 1995b. Lesbian mothers, gay fathers, and their children. In D'Augelli and Patterson (Eds.), *Lesbian, gay, and bisexual identities over the lifespan*, 262–90. New York: Oxford University Press.

Paul, W., J. D. Weinrich, J. C. Gonsiorek, & M. E. Hotvedt (Eds.). 1982. *Homosexuality: Social, psychological, and biological issues*. Beverly Hills, Calif.: Sage.

Pearlman, S. F. 1987. The saga of continuing clash in lesbian community, or will an army of ex-lovers fail? In Boston Lesbian Psychologies Collective (Ed.), *Lesbian psychologies*, 313–26. Urbana: University of Illinois Press.

Pellegrini, A. 1992. S(h)ifting the terms of hetero/sexism: Gender, power, homophobias. In Blumenfeld (Ed.), *Homophobia: How we all pay the price*, 39–56. Boston: Beacon Press.

Peplau, L. A. 1993. Lesbian and gay relationships. In Garnets & Kimmel (Eds.), *Psychological perspectives on lesbian and gay male experiences*, 395–419. New York: Columbia University Press.

Peplau, L. A., C. Cochran, K. Rook, & C. Padesky. 1978. Loving women: Attachment and autonomy in lesbian relationships. *Journal of Social Issues* 34(3): 7–27.

Perrow, C. & M. F. Guillen. 1990. *The AIDS disaster: The failure of organizations in New York and the nation*. New Haven: Yale University Press.

Petchers, M. K. 1996. Debunking the myth of progress for women social work educators. *Affilia* 11(1): 11–38.

Peterson, J. L. & G. Marín. 1988. Issues in the prevention of AIDS among black and Hispanic men. *American Psychologist* 43(11): 871–77.

Peterson, T. L. & J. H. Stewart. 1985. The lesbian or gay couple as a family: Principles for building satisfying relationships. In H. Hidalgo, T. Peterson, & N. J. Woodman (Eds.), *Lesbian and gay issues: A resource manual for social workers*, 27–32. Silver Spring, Md.: National Association of Social Workers.

Pharr, S. 1988. *Homophobia: A weapon of sexism*. Little Rock, Ark.: Chardon Press.

Phelan, S. 1993. (Be)Coming out: Lesbian identity and politics. *Signs* 18(4): 765–90.

Pierce, D. 1990. Who speaks for lesbian/gay adolescents: Voices to be silenced, voices to be heard. *Women and Language* 13(920): 37–41.

———. 1992. Policies of concern for practice with lesbian women and gay men. In Woodman (Ed.), *Lesbian and gay lifestyles*, 171–90. New York: Irvington.

Pies, C. & M. Helquist (Eds.). 1989. *Face to face: A guide to AIDS counseling*. San Francisco: AIDS Health project, University of California, San Francisco.

Pillard, R. C. 1991. Masculinity and femininity in homosexuality: "Inversion" revisited. In Gonsiorek & Weinrich (Eds.), *Homosexuality: Research implications for public policy*, 32–43. Newbury Park, Calif.: Sage.

Pinderhughes, E. 1989. *Understanding race, ethnicity, and power*. New York: Free Press.

Pohl, M. I. 1995. Chemical dependency and HIV infection. *Journal of Gay and Lesbian Social Services* 2(1): 15–28.

Pope, M. 1996. Gay and lesbian career counseling: Special career counseling issues. *Journal of Gay and Lesbian Social Services* 4(4): 91–105.

Poverny, L. M. & W. A. Finch. 1988. Integrating work-related issues on gay and lesbian employees into occupational social work practice. *Employee Assistance Quarterly* 4(2): 15–29.

Powers, B. 1996. The impact of gay, lesbian, and bisexual workplace issues on productivity. *Journal of Gay and Lesbian Social Services* 4(4): 79–90.

Powrie, R. 1995. HIV: Death sentence or opportunity? *Journal of Gay and Lesbian Social Services* 2(2): 113–16.

Prescott, L. M. 1996. HIV therapy after Vancouver. *Medical Alert (NAPWA)* 3(9): 1–6.

Prince, P. 1995. Influences on the career development of gay men. *Career Development Quarterly* 44(2): 168–77.

Proctor, C. D. & V. K. Groze. 1994. Risk factors for suicide among gay, lesbian, and bisexual youths. *Social Work* 39(5): 504–14.

Quam, J. K. 1993. Gay and lesbian aging. *SIECUS Report* 21(5): 10–12.

Quam, J. K. (Ed.). 1997. *Social services for older gay men and lesbians*. Binghamton, N.Y.: Haworth Press.

Quam, J. K. & G. S. Whitford. 1992. Adaptation and age-related expectations of older gay and lesbian adults. *The Gerontologist* 32(3): 367–74.

Rabkin, R. & S. Rabkin. 1995. Management of depression in patients with HIV infection. In Odets & Shernoff (Eds.), *The second decade of AIDS*, 11–26. New York: Hatherleigh Press.

Raphael, S. M. & M. K. Robinson. 1980. The older lesbian: Lover relationships and friendship patterns. *Alternative Lifestyles* 3(2): 207–29.

Rapp, S. 1991. *God's country: A case against theocracy*. New York: Harrington Park Press.

Ratner, E. F. 1988. A model for treatment of lesbian and gay alcohol abusers. *Alcoholism Treatment Quarterly* 5(1–2): 25–46.

———. 1993. Treatment issues for chemically dependent lesbians and gay men. In Garnets & Kimmel (Eds.), *Psychological perspectives on lesbian and gay male experiences*, 567–78. New York: Columbia University Press.

Reamer, F. G. 1993a. *AIDS and ethics*. New York: Columbia University Press.

———. 1993b. AIDS and social work: The ethics and civil liberties agenda. *Social Work* 38(4): 412–19.

Reece, R. 1988. Special issues in the etiologies and treatments of sexual problems among gay men. *Journal of Homosexuality* 15(1–2): 43–57.

Reid, J. 1973. *The best little boy in the world*. New York: Putnam (rpt., New York: Ballantine, 1993).

Reid, J. D. 1995. Development in late life: Older lesbian and gay lives. In D'Augelli & Patterson (Eds.), *Gay, lesbian, and bisexual identities over the lifespan*, 215–40. New York: Oxford University Press.

Reiss, J. O. 1994. Recognizing denial among HIV-infected clients. *Focus: A Guide to AIDS Research and Counseling* 8(9): 1–4.

Reiter, L. 1989. Sexual orientation, sexual identity, and the question of choice. *Clinical Social Work Journal* 17(2): 138–50.

———. 1991. Developmental origins of antihomosexual prejudice in heterosexual men and women. *Clinical Social Work Journal* 19(2): 163–75.

Remafedi, G. 1987a. Adolescent homosexuality: Psychosocial and implications. *Pediatrics* 79: 331–37.

———. 1987b. Homosexual youth: A challenge to contemporary society. *Journal of the American Medical Association* 258(2): 222–28.

———. 1987c. Male homosexuality: The adolescent's perspective. *Pediatrics* 79: 326–30.

Remafedi, G. (Ed.). 1994. *Death by denial: Studies of suicide in gay and lesbian teenagers*. Boston: Alyson.

Remafedi, G., J. A. Farrow, & R. W. Deisher. 1991. Risk factors for attempted suicide in gay and bisexual youth. *Pediatrics* 87(6): 869–75.

Renzetti, C. M. 1992. *Violent betrayal: Partner abuse in lesbian relationships*. Newbury Park, Calif.: Sage.

———. 1995. Studying parner abuse in lesbian relationships: A case for the feminist participatory research model. *Journal of Gay and Lesbian Social Services* 3(1): 29–42.

———. 1996. The poverty of services for battered lesbians. *Journal of Gay and Lesbian Social Services* 4(1): 61–68.

Reyes, K. W. & L. F. Farrell (Eds.). 1993. *Lambda gray: A practical, emotional, and spiritual guide for gays and lesbians who are growing older*. North Hollywood, Calif.: Newcastle.

Rich, A. 1980. Compulsory heterosexuality and lesbian existence. *Signs* 5: 631–60.

Richardson, D. 1993. Recent challenges to traditional assumptions about homosexuality: Some implications for practice. In Garnets & Kimmel (Eds.), *Psychological perspectives on lesbian and gay male experiences*, 117–29. New York: Columbia University Press.

Ricketts, W. & R. Achtenberg. 1990. Adoption and foster parenting for lesbians and gay men: Creating new traditions in family. *Homosexuality and Family Relations* 14(3–4): 83–118.

Riggs, M. 1995. Black macho revisited: Reflections of a Snap! Queen. In Creekmur & Doty (Eds.), *Out in culture*, 470–75. Durham, N.C.: Duke University Press.

Riley, J. & R. Greene. 1993. Influence of education on self-perceived attitudes about HIV/AIDS among human services providers. *Social Work* 38(4): 396–401.

Ritzer, G., K. C. W. Kammeyer, & N. Yetman. 1987. *Sociology: Experiencing a changing society*. 3d ed. Boston: Allyn & Bacon.

Roberts, T. L. 1995. African American gay males with HIV/AIDS: Building upon cultural capacities to survive. In Lloyd & M. A. Kuszelewicz (Eds.), *HIV disease*, 75–87. New York: Harrington Park Press.

Robinson, C. S. 1994. Counseling gay males with AIDS: Psychosocial perspectives. *Journal of Gay and Lesbian Social Services* 1(1): 15–32.

Rodriguez, F. I. 1996. Understanding Filipino male homosexuality: Implications for social services. *Journal of Gay and Lesbian Social Services* 5(2–3): 93–114.

Rofes, E. 1996. *Reviving the tribe: Regenerating gay men's sexuality and culture in the ongoing epidemic*. New York: Harrington Park Press.

Rohrbaugh, J. B. 1992. Lesbian families: Clinical issues and theoretical implications. *Professional Psychology: Research and Practice* 23(6): 467–73.

Rosabal, G. S. 1996. Multicultural existence in the workplace: Including how I thrive as a Latina lesbian feminist. *Journal of Gay and Lesbian Social Services* 4(4): 17–28.

Roshenow, D. J., R. Corbett, & D. Devine. 1988. Molested as children: A hidden contribution to substance abuse? *Journal of Substance Abuse Treatment* 5: 13–18.

Ross, M. W. 1990. Married homosexual men: Prevalence and background. In F. W. Bozett & M. B. Sussman (Eds.), *Homosexuality and Family Relations*, 35–58. New York: Harrington Park Press.

Ross, M. W. (Ed.). 1988. The treatment of homosexuals with mental health disorders. New York: Harrington Park Press.

Ross, M. W., J. A. Paulsen, & O. W. Stalstrom. 1988. Homosexuality and mental health: A cross-cultural review. *Journal of Homosexuality* 15(1–2): 131–52.

Rotello, G. 1997. *Sexual ecology: AIDS and the destiny of gay men*. New York: Dutton.

Roth, N. L. & J. Carman. 1993. Risk perception and HIV legal issues in the workplace. In L. Diamant (Ed.), *Homosexual issues in the workplace*, 173–86. Washington, D.C.: Taylor & Francis.

Roth, S. 1985. Psychotherapy with lesbian couples: Individual issues, female socialization, and the social context. *Journal of Marriage and Family Therapy* 11(3): 273–86.

Rothberg, B. & D. L. Weinstein. 1996. A primer on lesbian and gay families. *Journal of Gay and Lesbian Social Services* 4(2): 55–68.

Rothberg, B. P. & D. M. Kidder. 1992. Double trouble: Lesbians emerging from alcoholic families. In Weinstein (Ed.), *Lesbians and gay men*, 77–92. New York: Harrington Park Press.

Rothblum, E. D. 1994. "I only read about myself on bathroom walls": The need for research on the mental health of lesbians and gay men. *Journal of Consulting and Clinical Psychology* 62(2): 213–20.

Rothblum, E. D. & K. A. Brehony. 1991. The Boston marriage today: Romantic but asexual relationships among lesbians. In C. Silverstein (Ed.), *Gays, lesbians, and their therapists*, 210–26. New York: Norton.

Rothblum, E. D. & L. A. Bond (Eds.). 1996. *Preventing heterosexism and homophobia*. Thousand Oaks, Calif.: Sage.

Rotheram-Borus, M. J. & M. I. Fernandez. 1995. Sexual orientation and the developmental challenges experienced by gay and lesbian youths. *Suicide and Life-Threatening Behavior* 25 (Supplement): 26–34.

Rowe, M. & C. Ryan (Eds.). 1987. *AIDS: A public health challenge*. 3 vols. Washington, D.C.: Intergovernmental Health Policy Project, George Washington University.

Rubin, G. G. 1984. Thinking sex: Notes for a radical theory of the politics of sexuality. In C. S.

Vance (Ed.), *Pleasure and danger: Exploring female sexuality*, 267–319. Boston: Routledge & Kegan Paul.

Rudolph, J. 1989a. Effects of a workshop on mental health practitioners' attitudes toward homosexuality and counseling effectiveness. *Journal of Counseling and Development* 68: 81–85.

——. 1989b. The impact of contemporary ideology and AIDS on the counseling of gay clients. *Counseling and Values* 33: 96–134.

Russo, V. 1981. *The celluloid closet: Homosexuality in the movies.* New York: Harper & Row.

Rust, P. C. 1993. "Coming out" in the age of social constructionism: Sexual identity formation among lesbian and bisexual women. *Gender & Society* 7(1): 50–77.

Ryan, C. & R. Bogard. 1994. *What every lesbian and gay American needs to know about health care reform.* Washington, D.C.: HRCF Foundation.

Ryan, R., J. F. Longres, & R. A. Roffman. 1996. Sexual identity, social support and social networks among African-, Latino-, and European-American men in an HIV prevention program. *Journal of Gay and Lesbian Social Services* 5(2–3): 1–24.

Saari, C. 1993. Identity complexity as an indicator of health. *Clinical Social Work Journal* 21(1): 11–24.

Sabar, S. 1995. Shame, gay men, and HIV disease. *Focus: A Guide to AIDS Research and Counseling* 10(5): 1–4.

Saleebey, D. (Ed.). 1997 (original ed., 1992). *The strengths perspective in social work practice.* New York: Longman.

Sang, B. E. 1993. Existential issues of midlife lesbians. In D'Augelli & Patterson (Eds.), *Gay, lesbian, and bisexual identities over the lifespan*, 500–16. New York: Oxford University Press.

Savin-Williams, R. C. 1994. Verbal and physical abuse as stressors in the lives of lesbian, gay male, and bisexual youths: Associations with school problems, running away, substance abuse, prostitution, suicide. *Journal of Consulting and Clinical Psychology* 62(2): 261–69.

——. 1995. Lesbian, gay male, and bisexual adolescents. In D'Augelli & Patterson (Eds), *Lesbian, gay and bisexual identities over the lifespan*, 165–89. New York; Oxford University Press.

Schifter, J. & J. Madrigal-Pana. 1992. *Hombres que aman a hombres.* San José, Costa Rica: Ediciones Ilep-Sida.

Schneider, B. E. 1982. Consciousness about sexual harassment among heterosexual and lesbian wormen workers. *Journal of Social Issues* 38(4): 75–98.

——. 1987. Coming out at work: Bridging the private/public gap. *Work and Occupations* 13(4): 463–87.

Schneider, M. 1988. *Often invisible: Counselling gay and lesbian youth.* Toronto: Toronto Central Youth Services.

——. 1989. Sappho was a right-on adolescent. In G. Herdt (Ed.), *Gay and lesbian youth*, 111–30. New York: Haworth.

Schneider, M. & B. Tremble. 1985. Gay or straight? Working with the confused adolescent. *Journal of Homosexuality* 4(1–2): 71–82.

Schwartz, R. D. 1989. When the therapist is gay: Personal and clinical reflections. *Journal of Gay and Lesbian Psychotherapy* 1(1): 41–51.

Scott, P. R. & E. T. Ortiz. 1996. Marriage and coming out: Four patterns in homosexual males. *Journal of Gay and Lesbian Social Services* 4(3): 67–79.

Seck, E. T., W. A. Finch, M. E. Mor-Barak, & L. M. Poverny. 1993. Managing a diverse workforce. *Administration in Social Work* 17(2): 67–79.

Sell, R. L. & C. Petrulio. 1996. Sampling homosexuals, bisexuals, gays, and lesbians for public health research: A review of the literature from 1990–1992. *Journal of Homosexuality* 30(4): 31–47.

Selwyn, P. A. 1987. Sterile needles and the epidemic of acquired immunodeficiency syndrome: Issues for drug abuse treatment and public health. *Advances in Alcohol and Substance Abuse* 7: 99–105.

Shannon, J. W. & W. J. Woods. 1991. Affirmative psychotherapy for gay men. *Counseling Psychologist.* 19(2): 197–215.

Sharkey, L. 1987. Nurses in the closet: Is nursing open and receptive to gay and lesbian nurses? *Imprint* 34: 38–39.

Shernoff, M. 1995a. Male couples and their relationship styles. *Journal of Gay and Lesbian Social Services* 2(2): 43–58.

———. 1995b. Reflections on living with AIDS. *Journal of Gay and Lesbian Social Services* 3(4): 83–89.

———. 1996. Gay men choosing to be fathers. *Journal of Gay and Lesbian Social Services* 4(2): 41–54.

Shernoff, M. & W. A. Scott. 1988. *The sourcebook on lesbian/gay health care.* 2d ed. Washington, D.C.: National Lesbian and Gay Health Association.

Shidlo, A. 1992. AIDS related health behavior: Psychosocial correlates in gay men. Ph.D. diss., State University of New York, Buffalo.

———. 1994. Internalized homophobia: Conceptual and empirical issues in measurement. In Greene & Herek (Eds.), *Lesbian and gay psychology*, 173–205. Thousand Oaks, Calif.: Sage.

Shilts, R. 1987. *And the band played on: Politics, people, and the AIDS epidemic.* New York: St. Martin's.

———. 1993. *Conduct unbecoming: Gays and lesbians in the military.* New York: St. Martin's.

Shively, M. G. & J. P. DeCecco. 1993. Components of sexual identity. In Garnets & Kimmel (Eds.), *Psychological perspectives on lesbian and gay male experiences*, 80–88. New York: Columbia University Press.

Shon, S. P. & D. Y. Ja. 1982. Asian families. In M. McGoldrick, J. K. Pearse, & J. Giordano (Eds.), *Ethnicity and family therapy*, 208–29. New York: Guilford.

Silven, D. 1993. Behavioral theories and relapse. *Focus: A Guide to AIDS Research and Counseling* 8(2): 1–4.

Silverman, M. & S. Rice. 1995. Ethical dilemmas of working with individuals who have HIV disease. *Journal of Gay and Lesbian Social Services* 3(4): 53–68.

Silverstein, C. 1981. *Man to man: Gay couples in America.* New York: Quill.

Singer, B. L. & D. Deschamps (Eds.). 1994. *Gay and lesbian stats: A pocket guide of facts and figures.* New York: New Press.

Skinner, W. F. 1994. The prevalence and demographic predictors of illicit and licit drug use among lesbians and gay men. *American Journal of Public Health* 84: 1307–10.

Slater, S. 1995. *The lesbian family life cycle.* New York: Free Press.

Slater, S. & J. Mencher. 1991. The lesbian family life cycle: A contextual approach. *American Journal of Orthopsychiatry* 61(3): 372–82.

Sloan, L. & T. Edmond. 1996. Shifting the focus: Recognizing the needs of lesbian and gay survivors of sexual violence. *Journal of Gay and Lesbian Social Services* 5(4): 33–52.

Slusher, M. P., C. J. Mayer, & R. E. Dunkle. 1996. Gays and lesbians older and wiser (GLOW): A support group for older gay people. *The Gerontologist* 36(1): 118–23.

Smith, J. 1988. Psychopathology, homosexuality, and homophobia. *Journal of Homosexuality* 15(1–2): 59–73.

Smith, M. A. H. 1996. AIDS: Black plague. *Advocate* (Los Angeles) (December 10): 12–14.

Snyder, C. R. 1994. *The psychology of hope*. New York: Free Press.

Sohng, S. & L. D. Icard. 1996. A Korean gay man in the United States: Toward a cultural context for social service practice. *Journal of Gay and Lesbian Social Services* 5(2–3): 115–38.

Solomon, B. 1982. The delivery of mental health services to Afro-American individuals and families: Translating theory into practice. In B. Bass, G. Wyatt, & G. Powell (Eds.), *The Afro-American family: Assessment, treatment, and research issues*. New York: Grune & Stratton.

Sontag, S. 1966. *Against interpretation*. New York: Farrar, Straus & Giroux.

Sophie, J. 1986. A critical examination of stage theories of lesbian identity development. *Journal of Homosexuality* 12(2): 39–51.

Spielman, S. & L. Winfeld. 1996. Domestic partner benefits: A bottom line discussion. *Journal of Gay and Lesbian Social Services* 4(4): 53–78.

Spraggs, G. 1994. Coming out in the National Union of Teachers. In D. Epstein (Ed.), *Challenging lesbian and gay inequalities in education*, 179–96. Philadelphia: Open University Press.

Stein, E. 1994. The relevance of scientific research about sexual orientation to lesbian and gay rights. *Journal of Homosexuality* 27(3–4), 269–308.

Stein, T. S. 1988. Theoretical considerations in psychotherapy with gay men and lesbians. *Journal of Homosexuality* 15(1–2): 75–95.

Stein, T. S. & C. J. Cohen. 1984a. Psychotherapy with gay men and lesbians: An examination of homophobia, coming out, and identity. In E. S. Hetrick & T. S. Stein (Eds.), *Innovation in psychotherapy with homosexuals*, 60–73. Washington, D.C.: American Psychiatric Press.

Stein, T. S. & C. J. Cohen (Eds.). 1984b. *Psychotherapy with lesbians and gay men*. New York: Plenum Medical.

Stein, T. S. & C. J. Cohen (Eds.). 1986. *Contemporary perspectives on psychotherapy with lesbians and gay men*. New York: Plenum Medical.

Stevens, P. E. 1993. Lesbians and HIV: Clinical, research, and policy issues. *American Journal of Orthopsychiatry* 63(2): 189–94.

St. Louis Post-Dispatch. 1990 (February 18). Story of boy's torture rocks courtroom (p. 72G).

Straus, M. A. 1983. Ordinary violence, child abuse, and wife-beating: What do they have in common? In D. Finkelhor, R. J. Gelles, G. T. Hotaling, & M. A. Straus (Eds.), *The dark side of families: Current family violence research*. Beverly Hills, Calif: Sage.

Strickland, B. R. 1995. Research on sexual orientation and human development: A commentary. *Developmental Psychology* 31(1): 137–40.

Strommen, E. 1990. Hidden branches and growing pains: Homosexuality and the family tree. In F. W. Bozett & M. B. Sussman (Eds.), *Homosexuality and family relations*, 9–34. New York: Harrington Park Press.

Stulberg, I. & M. Smith. 1988. Psychosocial impact of the AIDS epidemic on the lives of gay men. *Social Work* 33(1): 277–81.

Suchet, M. 1995. "Having it both ways": Rethinking female sexuality. In Glassgold & Iasenza (Eds.), *Lesbians and psychoanalysis*, 39–61. New York: Free Press.

Sullivan, A. 1995. *Virtually normal: An argument about homosexuality*. New York: Knopf (rpt., New York: Vintage, 1996).

Sullivan, G. & Leong, L. W-T. (Eds.). 1995 (Special Edition). Introduction: Gay and lesbians in Asia and the Pacific: Social and human services. *Journal of Gay and Lesbian Social Services* 3(3): 1–10.

Sullivan, T. & M. Schneider. 1987. Development and identity issues in adolescent homosexuality. *Child and Adolescent Social Work* 4(1): 13–24.

Suppe, F. 1994. Explaining homosexuality: Philosophical issues, and who cares anyhow? *Journal of Homosexuality* 27(3–4): 223–67.

Sussal, C. M. 1994. Empowering gays and lesbians in the workplace. *Journal of Gay and Lesbian Social Services* 1(1): 89–103.

Swift, C. & G. Levin. 1987. Empowerment: An antidote for folly. *Prevention in Human Services* 3: xi–xv.

Swigonski, M. E. 1995a. For the white social worker who wants to know how to work with lesbians of color. *Journal of Gay and Lesbian Social Services* 3(2): 7–21.

———. 1995b. The social service needs of lesbians of color. *Journal of Gay and Lesbian Social Services* 3(2): 67–83.

Szasz, T. 1970. *Ideology and insanity*. Garden City, N.Y.: Anchor Books.

Tafoya, T. & D. A. Wirth. 1996. Native American two-spirit men. *Journal of Gay and Lesbian Social Services* 5(2–3): 25–50.

Tajfel, H. (Ed.). 1978. *Differentiation between social groups: Studies in the social psychology of intergroup relations*. London: Academic Press.

Tajfel, H. & J. C. Turner. 1986. The social identity theory of intergroup behavior. In S. Worchel & W. G. Austin (Eds.), *Psychology of intergroup relations*, 7–24. Chicago: Nelson-Hall.

Tallen, B. S. 1990. Twelve-step programs: A lesbian feminist critique. *NWSA Journal* 2(3): 390–407.

Tasker, F. L. & Golombok, S. 1997. *Growing up in a lesbian family: Effects on child development*. New York: Guilford Press.

Tatum, B. D. 1992. Talking about race, learning about racism: The application of racial identity development theory in the classroom. *Harvard Educational Review* 62(1): 1–24.

Taylor, V. & N. C. Raeburn. 1995. Identity politics as high-risk activism: Career consequences for lesbian, gay, and bisexual sociologists. *Social Problems* 42(2): 252–73.

Teague, J. B. 1992. Issues relating to the treatment of adolescent lesbians and homosexuals. *Journal of Mental Health Counseling* 14(4): 422–39.

Temoshok, L., A. O'Leary et al. 1990. Survival time in men with AIDS: Relationships with psychological coping and autonomic arousal. *Sixth International Conference on AIDS*. San Francisco.

Terry, P. 1992. Entitlement not privilege: The right of employment and advancement. In Woodman (Ed.), *Lesbian and gay lifestyles*, 133–44. New York: Irvington.

Thompson, B. J. 1994. Home to die: Therapy with HIV-infected gay men in smaller urban areas. In Cadwell, Burnham, & Forstein (Eds.), *Therapists on the front line*, 275–91. Washington, D.C.: American Psychiatric Press.

Thompson, C. A. 1992. Lesbian grief and loss in the coming out process. *Women and Therapy* 12(1–2): 175–85.

Thompson, C. P. 1991. Homophobia: A comparison study—MSW students and lesbians. Master's thesis, Southern Connecticut State University School of Social Work, New Haven.

Tierney, W. G. & R. A. Rhoads. 1993. Enhancing academic communities for lesbian, gay, and bisexual faculty. *New Directions for Teaching and Learning* 53 (Spring): 43–50.

Tievsky, D. L. 1988. Homosexual clients and homophobic social workers. *Journal of Independent Social Work* 2(3): 51–62.

Torres-Gil, F. M. & M. A. Puccinelle. 1995. Aging: Public policy issues and trends. In R. L. Edwards (Ed.), *Encyclopedia of social work*, 159–64. 19th ed. Washington, D.C.: NASW Press.

Tracy, M. B. & M. Ozawa. 1995. Social security. In R. L. Edwards (Ed.), *Encyclopedia of social work* 2: 2196–2206. 19th ed. Washington, D.C.: NASW Press.

Tremble, B., M. Schneider, & C. Appathurai. 1989. Growing up gay or lesbian in a multicultural context. *Journal of Homosexuality* 17(3–4): 253–67.

Tripp, C. A. 1975. *The homosexual matrix*. New York: McGraw-Hill.

Troiden, R. R. 1979. Becoming homosexual: A model of gay identity acquisition. *Psychiatry* 42: 362–73.

——. 1989. The formation of homosexual identities. *Journal of Homosexuality* 17(1–2): 43–73.

——. 1993. The formation of homosexual identities. In Garnets & Kimmel (Eds.), *Psychological perspectives on lesbian and gay male experiences*, 191–217. New York: Columbia University Press.

Troiden, R. R. 1989. *Gay and lesbian identity: A sociological analysis*. New York: General Hall.

Tully, C. T. 1992. Research on older lesbian woman: What is known, what is not known, and how to learn more. In Woodman (Ed.), *Lesbian and gay lifestyles*, 235–64. New York: Irvington.

——. 1994. To boldly go where no one has gone before: The legalization of lesbian and gay marriages. *Journal of Gay and Lesbian Social Services* 1(1): 73–87.

Turner, P. H., L. Scadden, & M. B. Harris. 1990. Parenting in gay and lesbian families. *Journal of Gay and Lesbian Psychotherapy* 1(3): 55–66.

Ubell, V. & D. Sumberg. 1992. Heterosexual therapists treating homosexual addicted clients. In Weinstein (Ed.), *Lesbians and gay men*, 19–33. New York: Harrington Park Press.

Vaid, U. 1995. *Virtual equality: The mainstreaming of gay and lesbian liberation*. New York: Anchor Books.

Valenzuela, W. 1996. A school where I can be myself. In Kay, Estepa, & Desetta (Eds.), *Out with it*, 45–46. New York: Youth Communications.

Van Den Bergh, N. 1994. From invisibility to voice: Providing EAP assistance to lesbians in the workplace. *Employee Assistance Quarterly* 9(3–4): 161–77.

Van Den Bergh, N. & L. B. Cooper (Eds.). 1986. *Feminist visions for social work*. Silver Spring, Md.: National Association of Social Workers.

Voeller, B. 1986. Nonoxynol-9 and HTLV-III. *Lancet* 1 (May 17): 1153.

Von Schulthess, B. 1992. Violence in the streets: Anti-lesbian assault and harassment in San Francisco. In Herek & Berrill (Eds.), *Hate crimes*, 65–75. Newbury Park, Calif.: Sage Publications.

Van Soest, D. 1996. The influence of competing ideologies about homosexuality on nondiscrimination policy: Implications for social work education. *Journal of Social Work Education* 32(1): 53–64.

Van Soest, D. & A. S. Bryant. 1995. Violence reconceptualized for social work: The urban dilemma. *Social Work* 40(4): 549–57.

Van Wyk, P. H. & C. S. Geist. 1995. Biology of bisexuality: Critique and observations. In deCecco & Parker (Eds.), *Sex, cells, and same-sex desire: The biology of sexual preference*, 357–73. New York: Harrington Park Press.

Vinter, R. D. 1967. Problems and processes in developing social work practice principles. In E. J. Thomas (Ed.), *Behavioral science for social workers*, 425–32. New York: Free Press.

Vlahov, D., A. Munoz, D. D. Celentano et al. 1991. HIV seroconversion and disinfection of injection equipment among intravenous drug users—Baltimore, Maryland. *Epidemiology* 2: 444–46.

Waite, H. 1995. Lesbians leaping out of the intergenerational context: Issues of aging in Australia. *Journal of Gay and Lesbian Social Services* 3(3): 109–27.

Walber, E. 1988. Behind closed doors: Battering and abuse in the lesbian and gay community. In M. Shernoff & W. A. Scott (Eds.), *The sourcebook on lesbian / gay health care*, 250–58. Washington, D.C.: National Lesbian and Gay Health Association.

Waldron, C. M. 1996. Lesbians of color and the domestic violence movement. *Journal of Gay and Lesbian Social Services* 4(1): 43–52.

Walker, E. 1979. *The battered woman*. New York: Harper & Row.

Walker, G. 1995. Family therapy interventions with inner-city families affected by AIDS. In Odets & Shernoff (Eds.), *The second decade of AIDS*, 85–114. New York: Hatherleigh Press.

Wallach, J. J. 1989. AIDS anxiety among health care professionals. *Hospital and Community Psychiatry* 40(5): 507–10.

Waters, M. 1994. *Modern sociological theory*. London: Sage.

Weinberg, G. H. 1972. *Society and the healthy homosexual*. New York: St. Martin's.

Weinberg, M. S. & C. J. Williams. 1974. *Male homosexuals: Their problems and adaptations*. New York: Oxford University Press.

Weinberg, M. S., C. J. Williams, & D. W. Pryor. 1994. *Dual attraction: Understanding bisexuality*. New York: Oxford University Press.

Weinrich, J. D. & W. L. Williams. 1991. Strange customs, familiar lives: Homosexualities in other cultures. In Gonsiorek & Weinrich (Eds.), *Homosexuality: Research implications for public policy*, 32–43. Newbury Park, Calif.: Sage.

Weinstein, D. L. (Ed.). *Lesbians and gay men: Chemical dependency issues*. New York: Harrington Park Press.

Weise, E. R. (Ed.). 1992. *Closer to home: Bisexuality and feminism*. Seattle: Seal Press.

Weston, K. 1991. *Families we choose: Lesbians, gays, kinship*. New York: Columbia University Press.

Whitford, G. S. 1997. Realities and hopes for older gay men. In J. K. Quam (Ed.), *Social services for senior gay men and lesbians*, 79–95. Binghamton, N.Y.: Haworth Press.

Whitford, G. S. & J. K. Quam. 1995. Older gay and lesbian adults. In M. A. Kimble, S. H. McFadden, J. W. Ellor, & J. J. Seeber (Eds.), *Aging, spirituality, and religion*, 374–85. Minneapolis, Minn.: Fortress Press.

Whitlock, K. 1989 (original ed., 1988). *Bridges of respect: Creating support for lesbian and gay youth*. Philadelphia: American Friends Service Committee.

Williams, W. L. 1987. Women, men, and others: Beyond ethnocentrism in gender theory. *American Behavioral Scientist* 31: 135–41.

———. 1993. Persistence and change in the Berdache tradition among contemporary Lakota Indians. In Garnets & Kimmel (Eds.), *Psychological perspectives on lesbian and gay male experiences*, 339–47. New York: Columbia University Press.

Williamson, A. D. 1993. Is this the right time to come out? *Harvard Business Review* (July / August): 26–34.

Wilson, P. A. 1995. AIDS service organizations: Current issues and future challenges. *Journal of Gay and Lesbian Social Services* 2(3–4): 121–44.

Winfeld, L. & S. Spielman. 1995. *Straight talk about gays in the workplace: Creating an inclusive, productive environment for everyone in your organization*. New York: AMACOM.

Wisniewski, J. J. & B. G. Toomey. 1987. Are social workers homophobic? *Social Work* 32: 454–55.

Woodman, N. J. (Ed.). 1992. *Lesbian and gay lifestyles: A guide for counseling and education*. New York: Irvington.

Woodman, N. J., C. T. Tully, & C. Barranti. 1995. Research in lesbian communities: Ethical dilemmas. *Journal of Gay and Lesbian Social Services* 3(1): 57–66.

Woodman, N. J. & H. Lenna. 1980. *Counseling with gay men and women: A guide for facilitating positive life styles*. San Francisco: Jossey-Bass.

Woods, J. D. 1993. *The corporate closet: The professional lives of gay men in America*. New York: Free Press.

Worden, W. J. 1976. *Grief counseling and grief therapy*. Englewood Cliffs, N.J.: Prentice-Hall.

Wrong, D. 1980. *Power: Its forms, bases, and uses*. New York: Harper & Row.

Young-Breuhl, E. 1996. *The anatomy of prejudices*. Cambridge: Harvard University Press.

Zamora-Hernández, C. E. & D. G. Patterson. 1996. Homosexually active Latino men: Issues of social work practice. *Journal of Gay and Lesbian Social Services* 5(2–3): 69–92.

Zimmerman, B. 1984. The politics of transliteration: Lesbian personal narratives. *Signs* 9: 663–82.

Zuckerman, A. J. & G. F. Simons. 1996. *Sexual orientation in the workplace*. Thousand Oaks, Calif.: Sage.

Index